Discover Windows™ 3.1 Multimedia

ROGER JENNINGS

Screen reproductions in this book were created using Collage Plus from Inner Media, Inc., Hollis, NH.

Publisher: Lloyd J. Short

Associate Publisher: Rick Kanucci

Product Development Manager: Thomas H. Bennett

Title Manager: Charles O. Stewart III

Book Designer: Scott Cook

Production Team: Claudia Bell, Julie Brown, Jodie Cantwell, Paula Carroll, Brad Chinn, Michelle Cleary, Brook Farling, Bob LaRoche, Jay Lesandrini, Cindy L. Phipps, Linda Seifert, Sandra Shay, Johnna VanHoose, Phil Worthington

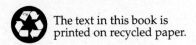

The text in this book is printed on recycled paper.

This book is dedicated to the memory of my mother, Anne Walker Jennings, the daughter of a newspaper publisher, who introduced me to the field of journalism in my early childhood.

CREDITS

Product Director
Steven M. Schafer

Acquisitions Editor
Sarah Browning

Production Editor
Lori A. Lyons

Editors
Sara Kurtz Allaei
Jane Cramer
Kelly Currie
Diana R. Moore
Kathy Simpson
Brad Sullivan

Technical Editors
Tony Schafer
Rob Murtha
Steve Thomas

Composed in *Cheltenham* and *MCPdigital* by Que Corporation.

Roger Jennings is a consultant specializing in Windows database and multi-media applications. He was a member of the Microsoft beta testing teams for Windows 3.1, Microsoft Access, Word for Windows 2.0, Windows for Workgroups, the Microsoft Audio Video Interleaved (AVI) APIs, and the Microsoft Professional Toolkit for Visual Basic. Roger Jennings is the author of *Using Access for Windows*, Special Edition, a contributing author to *Using Visual Basic* and *Killer Windows Utilities*, and was a technical editor for *Using Word for Windows 2*, Special Edition, and *Using Windows 3.1*, Special Edition, all published by Que Corporation.

The author is an amateur musician, composer, arranger, and graphic artist, and was a radio broadcast performer, engineer, and classical music disc jockey while in high school and college. He has more than 25 years of computer-related experience and has presented technical papers on computer hardware and software to the Academy of Sciences of the USSR, the Society of Automotive Engineers, the American Chemical Society, and a wide range of other scientific and technical organizations. You can contact the author via CompuServe [70233,2161].

ACKNOWLEDGMENTS

Discover Windows 3.1 Multimedia could not have been written without the contributions to PC-based multimedia made by Microsoft Corporation. Microsoft's decision to add the audio multimedia extensions to Windows 3.1, late in the beta testing cycle for the product, proves Bill Gates & Co. are masters of software design strategy and marketing tactics.

A particular note of appreciation is due to those firms that provided valuable equipment on extended loan during the course of writing this book: Roland Corporation USA supplied MA-12C monitor speakers and an SCC-1 GS Synthesizer Card; Turtle Beach Systems provided a MultiSound card, despite its substantial backlog at the time; Creative Labs, Inc. supplied Sound Blaster Pro and Video Blaster cards; and Media Vision loaned Pro Audio Spectrum 16 and Plus audio adapter cards, together with a multimedia upgrade kit. A DM-3021 CD-ROM drive provided by Texel Corporation was used to test Trantor SCSI adapters and drivers and the SCSI interfaces of audio adapter cards.

Sony Corporation supplied a CVD-1000 VDeck for evaluation of their VISCA protocol. Most of the television images used in this book were reproduced from Hi8 tapes reproduced by the Vdeck and captured with Truevision Bravado or Creative Labs Video Blaster video-in-a window cards, or a Digital Vision ComputerEyes R/T video capture card. Live video images from broadcast sources were captured with a New Media Graphics TV-Video Windows card that includes a built-in tuner. Permissions from copyright owners to reproduce the video images in this book are gratefully acknowledged.

The review copies of Windows applications supplied by the manufacturers whose products are described in the body of the book and those who provided demonstration CD-ROMs, all of which are listed in Appendix F, are acknowledged with thanks.

The line drawings in this book were prepared with Micrografx Windows Draw! 3.0 with OLE, CorelDRAW! 3.0, and the Microsoft Draw applet. Video and other bit-map images were retouched as necessary for publication with Micrografx Picture Publisher 3.1.

Special thanks are due to Christy Gersiche of Microsoft for her assistance in finding the right person within the rapidly growing Microsoft organization to answer technical questions about Windows multimedia. The assistance of each of the Microsoft employees who provided the answers is gratefully acknowledged.

Thanks to Rick Ranucci, associate publisher of Que Corporation, for believing that Windows multimedia was a viable topic and shepherding this book through the initial acquisitions process. Sarah Browning, acquisitions editor for *Discover Windows 3.1 Multimedia*, made sure that I did not fall too far behind the manuscript submission schedule.

Steve Schafer, product director, provided valuable insight and suggestions for the development of this book's content and organization. Lori Lyons, production editor, and the Production team put in long hours to add last-minute changes and still meet a tight production schedule. Technical editing was done by Tony Schafer, Rob Murtha, and Steve Thomas, each of whom are experts in specific areas of Windows multimedia technology. The responsibility for any errors or omissions, however, rests solely on my shoulders.

Finally, thanks to Ron Person, the author of several best-selling Que books on Microsoft Windows and its applications, who introduced me to the people at Que Corporation. Without Ron, this book would not have been written.

Trademarks

Different typesetting styles have been used in this book to distinguish explanatory text from that used to describe the actions you take and the text you enter in dialog boxes and in programming code editing screens.

Tips, Notes, and Cautions provide important information about a subject and appear in boxes. Marginal icons for common multimedia control buttons—play, record, pause, rewind, and fast forward—are employed where appropriate.

When further details about a subject are available in a different chapter, a "Related Topics" icon is used to refer you to the section title and page number. You might consider these icons to be equivalent to the underlined "hot spots" used in the help files of Windows applications. When you click a help hot-spot, Windows Help takes you to the section of the help file that covers the subject in more detail. This technique is an example of hypertext cross-references that are often used in commercial multimedia titles to link related subjects.

Key combinations you enter to perform Windows operations are indicated by combining the keys with a plus sign, as in Alt+F4. This indicates that you depress and hold the Alt key while pressing the F4 function key. In the rare cases in which you must press and release a control key, then enter another key, they are separated by a comma without an intervening space, as in Alt,F4.

The initial letter of short-cut keys that determine menu choices are set in boldface type, as in **E**dit. The Alt key required to activate the first (main) menu item is assumed and not shown.

CONTENTS AT A GLANCE

TABLE OF CONTENTS

II Using Sound in Windows

III Musical Synthesis and MIDI

IV Digital Audio Techniques

13 Digital Audio Sampling, Reproduction, and Compression 369

14 Editing and Converting Waveform Audio Files 385

V Adding Multimedia Graphics

VI Authoring Multimedia Products

VII Multimedia Programming Techniques

Introduction

When the definitive history of personal computing is finally written, 1992 will undoubtedly be described as "The Year of Multimedia." Multimedia technology, combining computer-generated graphic images with sound, had been implemented on personal computers prior to 1990—first on Commodore Atari and later on Apple Macintosh computers. Microsoft Corporation introduced *Windows 3.0 with Multimedia Extensions* and the *Multimedia PC Specification 1.0* in the fall of 1991. IBM simultaneously unveiled its *Ultimedia* product line. More than 100 firms announced plans to provide hardware and software to support Microsoft's Multimedia PC standard. Microsoft announced in early 1992 that Windows 3.1 would include the audio subset of the Multimedia Extensions, eliminating the requirement for a CD-ROM drive to explore multimedia techniques with the PC. Windows 3.1 was released in April, 1992, and the multimedia market began its upward spiral.

Why a Book on Multimedia

Multimedia is not a product, it's an enabling technology. Multimedia enables you to combine sound and graphic images—still, animated, and video—with your computer. Exploring multimedia techniques is fun, and it's not expensive. You can add basic sound and music capability to your PC with a $100 adapter card. Doubling your investment to $200 or so enables you to record and reproduce stereo sound with audio-CD fidelity. Easy-to-use musical composition and printing applications for Windows cost $100 or less. Never in the history of digital computing has the entry cost of an important new technology been so low.

Another $300 to $400 opens the door to multimedia CD-ROMs (Compact Disc Read-Only Memory) that can hold over 600 megabytes of images and sound on a single 5-inch disc—the equivalent of 100 million words or so. New *titles*, the name given to commercial CD-ROMs, are issued daily. These titles create an electronic library of interactive text, graphics, and sounds pertinent to almost any topic in which you might have an interest. The federal government is one of the largest CD-ROM producers in the world, providing census data, detailed maps of the entire U.S., and Government Printing Office catalogs on CD-ROMs. Book publishers have converted many of their popular encyclopedic products to CD-ROM and are now beginning to issue original works on CDs.

If you own a camcorder, market research shows that you are very likely to have your own PC at home. Video-in-a-Window cards, now available in the $400 range, enable you to watch color television images on your video display. You can capture video frames as still images and save them to disk files with just a few mouse clicks. Add a $250 video output card or plug a video adapter between your VGA adapter card and display, and you have the basic equipment necessary to record your computer-generated images on videotape. The ability to display, edit, and record full-motion video using conventional VCRs and camcorders is creating a new industry—desktop video (DTV), which is the multimedia equivalent of desktop publishing.

One of Microsoft's major contributions to multimedia technology is Windows itself. The Windows graphical environment provides the foundation for displaying still, animated, and video images. The audio multimedia extensions of Windows 3.1 enable you to synchronize sound with images. Microsoft projects that 10 to 15 million copies of Windows 3.1 will be installed by the end of 1993. Every user of Windows 3.1 is a prospective customer for a sound card and a CD-ROM drive. The economics of production scale and suppliers' attempts to capture market share will keep the cost of PC multimedia technology low.

Just a few of the present applications for Windows-based multimedia presentations and CD-ROM titles include the following:

- *Education and curriculum development.* K-12 textbook publishers offer a wide range of interactive instructional material on CD-ROMs. Children tend to learn faster and retain more content with interactive, rather than passive, presentations. IBM's Illuminated Books and Manuscripts series is one of the best examples of this genre. Multimedia techniques are especially suited to adult literacy and English as a Second Language (ESL) courses.

- *Industrial and Commercial Training.* A mini-industry has developed that creates generic multimedia CDs to train workers in safety practices and other industrial operations such as soldering. Interactive training CD-ROMs have been developed for specialized assembly-line operations and even telephone etiquette. American Airlines, for example, plans to provide mechanics with aircraft maintenance manuals on CD-ROMs.

- *Desktop Video Publishing*. Multimedia techniques, combined with videographic adapter cards, enable you to create videotape productions on your computer in the same way conventional desktop publishing applications, such as Aldus PageMaker, enable you to create your own professional-appearing print publications.

- *On-line Help for Windows Applications*. Microsoft's Multimedia Works for Windows and Lotus Development's Multimedia SmartHelp for Lotus 1-2-3 for Windows are harbingers of a new type of entertaining, interactive help system for mainstream applications.

- *Informational kiosks*. Tourist bureaus install booths with touch-screen displays to show animated views of points of interest, together with "how to get there" maps. Advertising firms use similar techniques to create animated mini-billboards with multilingual narration.

- *Point-of-sale product showcases*. Video rental stores use touch-screen displays to let browsers see the trailers of popular new videotape releases. Department stores display products on special sale with illustrations and voice-over narration.

- *Interactive product catalogs*. Office furniture manufacturers use multimedia to provide three-dimensional views of their products in typical settings. Additional files enable interior designers to import scaled images into their own computer-aided designs. Fashion designers issue CD-ROMs with video clips and still images of their new lines so that buyers can review them at their leisure.

- *Product operating manuals*. Microsoft Multimedia Works and Multimedia SmartHelp for Lotus 1-2-3 for Windows use CD-ROMs that expand traditional help files to entertaining explanations of the use of these applications. You can expect other Windows applications to adopt this new approach.

- *Sales presentations*. Real-estate developers and brokers use Kodak's low-cost Photo CDs to provide clients with full-color interior and exterior snapshots of listed properties. Soon, photo finishers will be able to add narration to the presentation.

- *Architectural and engineering proposals*. A&E firms are using Virtual Reality (VR) multimedia techniques to create animated three-dimensional walk-throughs in design proposals. Developers use multimedia productions to entice prospective lessors to acquire space in office buildings and retail malls.

■ *Maps and geographic information systems.* World atlases are published on CD-ROM, together with the national anthems of each country and brief examples of the languages spoken. A complete U.S. atlas with almost every street and address in the country retails for less than $100.00.

■ *Home education.* Titles in CD-ROM formats for those with multi-media-equipped PCs provide children and adults alike an engaging technique to expand their intellectual horizons. Microsoft's *Beethoven* CD-ROM plays the Ninth Symphony in high-fidelity audio and enables you to follow the score during the performance. Software Toolworks' low-cost *Miracle Piano* teaches you how to play by a widely acclaimed multimedia approach to musical instruction.

■ *Personal entertainment.* Computer games with a new level of realism and detail have been created especially for multimedia-equipped PCs. The addition of background music and actors' voices adds to the enjoyment of these products. You can expect a new level of sophistication in computer games, similar to that employed in advanced board games, now that multimedia has arrived.

All of the application categories in this list, except videotape production, share a common characteristic: they require user interaction. An active user role in determining the content and sequence of the presentation of the images and sound distinguishes multimedia from the passive viewing of motion pictures and television. A CD-ROM title that involves no user interaction at all is possible, but such a product would be only a high-cost substitute for a video cassette or a video laserdisc. VCRs and laserdisc players are far less expensive than the PCs required for reproducing multimedia titles. Interaction is what justifies the additional cost of the computer. When you see the word *multimedia*, mentally precede it with *interactive*. Interactive multimedia is what this book is about.

There is no question that multimedia is an effective medium for CD-ROM titles that entertain and enlighten. Multimedia undoubtedly will prove an effective marketing tool for many types of industrial, commercial, and consumer products and services. Whether interactive multimedia productions can be created that will truly enrich the human experience in a manner similar to that of great literary works remains an unsettled question. Authors of fiction, for instance, may not want to relinquish control over the form and sequence of their works to the user. Even if the answer to the enrichment question is ultimately "no," desktop multimedia can and undoubtedly will thrive on its education and amusement values alone.

Hundreds, perhaps thousands, of pages in computer magazines and newsletters have been devoted to explaining what multimedia is about, analyzing whether multimedia is a "real" technology, and reviewing the rash of PC hardware products and software applications that incorpo-rate "multimedia" in their names or descriptions. Multimedia is a "hot topic," and magazine editors need hot topics to break the monotony of those never-ending series of reviews of 80x86 clones, adapter cards, and peripherals. Some writers decry multimedia as nothing but hyper-technology without purpose. Others are enthusiastic proponents. Seldom do two articles share a common definition of the word "multimedia."

Discover Windows 3.1 Multimedia is designed to bring order to the chaos of print and televised material on the subject. A multimedia production on a CD-ROM may be a better method to introduce you to this relatively new technology, but you couldn't realize its content without owning a CD-ROM player. If you purchase a CD-ROM player without understanding the differences between CD-DA and CD-ROM XA, you are very likely to purchase a CD-ROM that will become obsolete quite soon. If you buy a low-cost audio adapter card to go with your CD-ROM player, you may be very disappointed in its fidelity, especially if you are a musician. A bit of study before committing the $200 or thereabouts for a quality MPC sound card and the additional $300 or more for CD-ROM capability will pay handsome dividends.

System Requirements for Multimedia Applications

You can add high-fidelity audio capability to any computer that is ca-pable of running Windows and has one open adapter card slot. Even an 8-MHz 80286 computer can be used. Windows and its applications will run slowly, but sound cards will perform all of their functions—except digital audio recording and reproduction at the higher sampling rates.

Prior to the introduction of Windows 3.1, a CD-ROM drive was required to obtain access to Windows' Multimedia Extensions. This was because Windows with Multimedia (the name later given to Windows 3.0 with Multimedia Extensions 1.0) was supplied only on a CD-ROM. Windows 3.1 now includes the majority of Version 1.0 of the Microsoft Multimedia Extensions (MMEs). Applications that need the MMEs and multimedia applets omitted from Windows 3.1 come with the Microsoft versions or proprietary duplicates on floppy disk.

If you want to take full advantage of PC multimedia, with its capability to combine sound and animated graphics, you need a computer and pe-ripheral hardware that meet at least a minimum set of standards origi-nally established by Microsoft but now maintained by a PC industry organization, known as the Multimedia PC Marketing Council.

The Multimedia PC Marketing Council's Specification 1.0, last modified in December, 1991, requires at least a 16-MHz 80386SX computer with 2M of RAM, a standard VGA display, and a 30M hard disk drive. An audio adapter card and CD-ROM drive completes the minimum package for a Multimedia PC (MPC). This configuration will provide adequate performance with waveform audio and still graphics or simple animation, but not real-time digital video. All requirements of the MPC Specification 1.0 are provided in Appendix A.

The purpose of the MPC Specification is to ensure interoperability of the computer, audio adapter card, and CD-ROM drive. You can purchase an MPC-labeled computer from dealers or by mail order and be assured that it will *probably* meet the MPC basic specifications. These combinations, however, are generally priced somewhat higher than a similar system of equivalent capability purchased from your local PC-clone dealer, and are not necessarily the optimum system for your intended uses. Recommendations for specific computer hardware to meet the needs of multimedia production appear at the end of Chapter 1.

Who Should Read This Book

You do not need to be a computer "expert" or programmer to use this book effectively. *Discover Windows 3.1 Multimedia* is expressly designed for readers who:

- Own a Sound Blaster or Thunder Board card and want to use it with Windows applications.

- Have decided that multimedia may be the reason to make the plunge into personal computing or buy a new and faster PC, and want to know if they should purchase an MPC-labeled product or choose their own components.

- Are considering upgrading their existing PC to add multimedia sound and graphics capabilities and need to know what they should purchase.

- Have already purchased a Multimedia Upgrade Kit, a CD-ROM drive, or an MPC audio adapter card and want to learn to use it more effectively.

- Are thinking of ways to improve the impact of their presentations on management or potential customers for their products.

- Need to consider multimedia as a dynamic new form of product brochure.

- Are photographers seeking new markets for their work through technologies such as Kodak's Photo CD system.

- Want to see what's involved in creating a multimedia training or instructional title and how much it might cost to produce one or more.

- Are musicians or composers who want to learn how MIDI techniques are used in multimedia applications, or choreographers who want to try combining music and animation to design new routines.

- Want to expand their graphic arts consulting practice to include multimedia productions.

- Own a camcorder and would like to use a PC for titling and editing personal or business videotapes.

- Are system integrators or value-added resellers who want to provide their clients with networked multimedia systems based on the MPC standard.

Although multimedia involves computer technology, it also is an art form. Therefore, *Discover Windows 3.1 Multimedia* includes more subjective matter than is common in computer-related books. Readers are encouraged to verify these subjective observations for themselves, especially when they involve the expenditure of funds.

Discover Windows 3.1 Multimedia makes the assumption that you have Windows installed on your computer and that you are familiar with its operations. This book is intended for those who are familiar with Windows and are motivated to learn about multimedia sound and graphics.

Why You Should Use This Book

Discover Windows 3.1 Multimedia is a comprehensive guide to understanding the elements of sound and visual images that comprise multimedia productions within the Windows environment. This book is designed as a tutorial and a reference work to supplement the very limited sound-related content of the *User's Guide* included with Microsoft Windows 3.1. As its title suggests, this book shows you how to use multimedia. This book is written from the viewpoint of a musician and graphic artist, not from that of a programmer.

This book includes a description of the hardware required to create high-fidelity sound with your PC and explains how MPC audio adapter card specifications relate to real-world perception of audio quality. Current and emerging standards for CD-ROM drives are covered in detail.

Discover Windows 3.1 Multimedia explains how to set up the required multimedia drivers for your PC using the Drivers function in Program Manager's Control Panel and how to use the MIDI Mapper applet with your sound card. This book covers the hardware and software you need to view and hear commercial CD-ROMs. You learn how you can make your own Windows-based multimedia presentations and even create multimedia titles for commercial distribution on CD-ROMs.

Musical Instrument Digital Interface (MIDI) techniques, plus MIDI hardware and software, are covered in depth. You learn about recent multimedia technologies, such as real-time, compressed digital video. This book includes a complete glossary of multimedia terminology newly added to "computerese," like CD-ROM XA, CD-I, Red Book audio, and MIDI system-exclusive messages.

This book provides the background you need to use the Windows Media Control Interface (MCI) commands with other programming languages for Windows, such as Visual Basic, Turbo Pascal for Windows, C, or C++. Extensive coverage is given to the Media Control Interface's high-level `mciSendString()` function, together with sample code that uses this function in Visual Basic.

Although *Discover Windows 3.1 Multimedia* is aimed primarily at audio and video hardware and software designed for use under Windows 3.1, other related products are also covered.

How This Book Is Organized

Discover Windows 3.1 Multimedia is divided into seven parts. Each part covers a major element in the development of multimedia productions, whether for your own entertainment or for commercial distribution. This book begins with the basics of the new sound capabilities built into Windows 3.1. You then proceed to the use of still and animated graphics in multimedia. The emerging field of desktop video production is covered with chapters describing the hardware and applications you need to record multimedia productions on videotape. The book concludes with a section on programming multimedia applications and what you can expect from multimedia in the future.

Part I: The Multimedia Functions of Windows 3.1

Part I introduces you to the basic capabilities of the audio extensions of Windows 3.1 that build the foundation for multimedia sound. You learn how to install and use audio adapter cards and CD-ROM drives in the Windows 3.1 environment.

Chapter 1, "What is Windows Multimedia?," introduces the Multimedia Personal Computer (MPC) and explains the significance of the Multimedia PC Specification 1.0 that establishes the minimum standards that a PC must meet to be considered an MPC-compliant system.

Chapter 2, "Understanding Audio Adapter Cards," describes how sound cards record and play back digitally sampled sound and synthesized music, and presents a brief history of pre-MPC sound on the PC. Descriptions of the different types of MPC- and non-MPC compliant audio adapter cards and devices available today are included, together with suggestions for choosing an audio adapter card.

Chapter 3, "Understanding CD-ROM Drives and Adapters," tells how the CD-ROM was developed, describes the basic CD-ROM required by the MPC specification, and then goes on to explain the differences between types of CD-ROM drives as well as other popular CD formats.

Chapter 4, "Preparing Your System for Multimedia," describes how to install a typical audio adapter card and how to avoid problems that arise when audio adapter cards conflict with cards already installed in your computer.

Chapter 5, "Preparing Windows for Multimedia," explains how you set up and use drivers supplied with Windows 3.1 and by audio adapter card manufacturers to link your card to Windows applications.

Part II: Using Sound in Windows

Part II introduces you to the applets supplied with Windows 3.1 to control audio adapter cards and shows you how to add sound to popular Windows applications.

Chapter 6, "Playing and Recording Waveform Audio Files," uses Windows 3.1's Sound Recorder to record and reproduce digitally sampled sound, and explains Media Player's digital sound playback capability.

Chapter 7, "Playing MIDI Files," uses Media Player to demonstrate your audio adapter card's synthesized sound capabilities and demystifies the MIDI Mapper function of Windows' Control Panel.

Chapter 8, "Incorporating Sound in Windows Applications," describes how the object linking and embedding (OLE) features of Windows 3.1 enable you to embed or link sounds to documents created by Windows word processing and spreadsheet applications.

Part III: Musical Synthesis and MIDI

Part III comprises chapters that are devoted to the Musical Instrument Digital Interface (MIDI), an industry standard that predates the MPC by several years.

Chapter 9, "Music Synthesizers," explains how audio adapter cards create synthesized music by digital FM synthesis and by reproducing samples of the actual sounds of musical instruments.

Chapter 10, "The MIDI Standard and Windows 3.1," describes the original MIDI specification that is the backbone of the electronic musical instrument industry today, and the General MIDI (GM) specification incorporated in MPC Specification 1.0.

Chapter 11, "Accessories for MIDI Systems," gives examples of the more common types of MIDI devices, such as piano-style keyboards, that you can connect to the MIDI OUT connection of your audio adapter card.

Chapter 12, "MIDI Applications for Windows," provides examples of the new sequencer applications written for Windows that you can use to record, compose, or edit MIDI music.

Part IV: Digital Audio Techniques

Part IV delves into some of the technical aspects of sampled digital sound and explains how to record professional-quality sound for multimedia presentations.

Chapter 13, "Digital Audio Sampling, Reproduction, and Compression," describes how sound waves are converted to digital data that you can store on a hard disk and then play back through your audio adapter card. Compression techniques to save disk space also are discussed.

Chapter 14, "Editing and Converting Waveform Audio Files," shows you how to use Sound Recorder and commercial sound editing applications to modify your recorded sound files in a variety of ways.

Chapter 15, "Waveform Audio Recording Techniques," aids you in selecting and using the microphones and other audio components you need to record professional-sounding narration and sound effects for multimedia productions.

Part V: Adding Multimedia Graphics

Part V changes the emphasis from sound to vision. Part V covers the hardware and software you need to manipulate still, animated, and video images in the multimedia environment.

Chapter 16, "Graphic Displays and Adapter Cards for Windows," describes how display adapters and video display units work and the VGA and Super-VGA standards that determine your computers graphics capabilities.

Chapter 17, "Image Acquisition, Editing, Interchange, and Compression," covers the use of still graphic images in multimedia applications and discusses the many formats and compression methods used by drawing and image editing applications, including Kodak's new Photo CD technology.

Chapter 18, "Presentation Graphics and Animation Techniques," gives examples of some of the new Windows applications specifically designed for creating multimedia presentations using both still and animated graphics.

Chapter 19, "Incorporating Digital Video," introduces you to the adapter cards you need to view full-motion television in a sizable window and the adapters required to convert your VGA or SVGA adapter card's output to a standard television signal you can record with a VCR.

Part VI: Authoring Multimedia Productions

Part VI covers the techniques used to produce commercial multimedia titles on CD-ROMs and how to create your own multimedia productions on videotape.

Chapter 20, "The Multimedia Production Process," describes how multimedia titles are developed, from the original concept through duplicating the CD-ROM in production quantities. Recommendations for the computer hardware you need to author multimedia productions are included.

Chapter 21, "Advanced MIDI and Waveform Audio Techniques," discusses synchronization of sound and images, including video synchronization with the SMPTE time code. Explanations of how to incorporate digitally sampled sound as a MIDI Meta Event—using MIDI System Exclusive Messages—and the special structures of Windows' multimedia RIFF files are included.

Chapter 22, "Desktop Video Production," introduces you to the new techniques and applications that enable you to create video productions with your PC. The chapter provides detailed information on video recording standards, the video equipment you need, and the new applications for computer-based editing of video productions.

Part VII: Multimedia Programming Techniques

Part VII describes the Windows 3.1 media control interface and how the functions it provides can be used with other applications and programming languages to control the operation of multimedia devices.

Chapter 23, "The High-Level MCI Commands of Windows 3.1," covers the syntax of the media control interface's `mciSendString()` command that you insert in Windows applications, such as MIDI sequencers, or incorporate code you write in programming languages for Windows.

Chapter 24, "Programming with MCI Commands," gives examples of the use of the MCI command strings described in Chapter 23 in Visual Basic programs and with MIDI sequencers.

Chapter 25, "Multimedia in the Future," concludes the book with projections of the new developments you can expect in multimedia hardware and applications in the next two years or so.

Appendixes

A complete glossary includes terms that may be unfamiliar to readers new to multimedia or to the audio and video technologies Windows 3.1 multimedia introduces to the PC.

The appendixes provide multimedia reference material. Appendix A extracts information from the "Multimedia Personal Computer Specification 1.0" and provides additional recommendations for the hardware required to make your PC multimedia-compliant. Appendix B describes the command-line parameters for MSCDEX.EXE, the application that lets DOS and Windows communicate with CD-ROM drives. Appendix C lists the standard melodic and percussive voices for the synthesized sound functions of your MPC-compliant audio adapter card. Appendix D provides tables that list the specific components of MCI command strings for a variety of multimedia devices. Appendix E explains the binary and hexadecimal arithmetic that is used in many MIDI messages. Appendix F consists of a list of suppliers of multimedia hardware and applications, with addresses and telephone numbers. Appendix G describes the CompuServe forums specifically devoted to multimedia or related technologies and how to download multimedia files to your computer. Appendix H describes how to obtain updated multimedia drivers for audio adapter cards and other multimedia-related hardware.

This book includes a music-oriented companion disk. The inside front cover describes the software included on this disk. The last page of this book provides installation instructions for the companion disk.

How To Use This Book

A somewhat unorthodox style is required to accomplish this book's objective of being both a tutorial and a reference for multimedia PC audio and graphics applications. Major topics, such as MPC sound, start with a brief description of the technology involved and the computer hardware and software required to use it within the Windows environment. A description of representative commercial products, available at the time this book was written, follows. Next come step-by-step instructions for installing and using typical hardware products. Complex subtopics, such as CD-ROMs and MIDI systems, are then detailed in entire parts or chapters of their own.

If sound on the PC is a new subject for you, start at the beginning of the book. If you already have a Sound Blaster or another audio adapter card installed and operating under DOS, jump to Chapter 5 and learn how to install the drivers you need to make the card compatible with Windows 3.1. Those readers who are musicians experienced with MIDI applications running under DOS may want to begin with Chapter 7, "Playing MIDI Files," check out the new Windows sequencer applications described in Chapter 12, and then skip to Chapter 21, which explains MIDI synchronization techniques used with Windows multimedia.

The Multimedia Functions of Windows 3.1

PART

I

OUTLINE

What Is Windows Multimedia?

T his chapter introduces you to multimedia in the Microsoft Windows environment, providing an overview of the detailed information contained in the following chapters. This chapter begins with a description of the crucial contribution of quality sound to multimedia technology. You learn about the common denominator of multimedia—audio adapter cards—and learn how these cards are used in multimedia Windows applications to synchronize sound with graphic images.

This chapter also touches on the emerging field of full-motion video technology for multimedia and explains how audio adapter cards relate to video production. If you haven't purchased an audio adapter card for your PC yet, you probably will want one by the time you finish reading Chapter 2, which describes PC audio adapter cards in detail.

The Advent of Sound

When *The Jazz Singer* ushered in the age of talking pictures in October 1927, it revolutionized the entertainment industry. Silent films became obsolete overnight, and the ubiquitous movie-house piano players began to join the ranks of the unemployed. So, too, will the mute PC ultimately become a thing of the past. Windows 3.1 ushers in the age of sound on the PC.

Multimedia technology enables you to combine graphic images and sound in one PC application. Microsoft Windows provides a computing environment that is ideally suited for displaying graphic images. Windows multimedia takes advantage of the existing graphical user interface (GUI) of Microsoft Windows 3.0 and incorporates the newly added sound functions of Windows 3.1 to integrate these two elements.

This simple definition, however, belies the time and effort expended by Microsoft and other firms in adding high-fidelity sound and animated-graphics capability to Windows. The development process was further complicated by Microsoft's primary goal: making PC multimedia affordable and easy to use. The astounding sales growth of PC audio adapter cards since the release of Windows 3.1 attests to the success of Microsoft's multimedia development team.

Almost every computer and software store now has a variety of audio adapter cards on display. As this book was being written, engineers were designing new PCs with built-in stereo speakers. New generations of PC motherboards will include audio components so that users need not purchase separate adapter cards. In the not-too-distant future, CD-ROM drives will be as essential for desktop PCs as hard disk drives are today.

Understanding the Significance of Sound

Until the advent of multimedia sound, most PCs engaged only one human sense: sight, the most subjective of the senses. For example, although a painting by Rembrandt or Klee is capable of evoking an emotional response, your mind first must organize the painting's lines and colors into a mental image. This organization takes a perceptible period of time—sometimes several seconds. Then, if you don't understand the painting's content, or if the painting does not appeal to you, the painting may elicit no emotional response.

On the other hand, sound has an instantaneous, unavoidable emotional effect. You perceive an actor's vocal tone and emphasis long before you ascribe meaning to his or her words. Music without lyrics elicits an almost wholly emotional response, especially when the music evokes an image that occupies your mind.

Through the use of sound, multimedia enables you to add an emotional element to your graphics creations. Multimedia also enables you to avoid visual overload. Substantial amounts of text overwhelm the viewer and detract from his ability to comprehend graphic images. Combining vocal narration with simple graphics that drive home your point is far more effective. Adding background music sets the emotional stage for your presentation and reduces the audience's boredom.

Whether your multimedia creation is a business presentation, a computer-based brochure, a computer game, a television commercial, or an educational program, sound makes it much more interesting. Several studies demonstrate that sound contributes more than half the effect of any graphic image, regardless of the subject matter or the audience.

Adding Sound Capabilities to the PC

The audio adapter card—commonly called a *sound card*—is the basic element involved in adding high-quality sound to PC applications. Like most other PC adapter cards, the audio adapter card adds its specialized functions to those added by more common cards, such as graphics adapter and hard disk adapter cards.

Related Topics
Defining MPC-Compatible Audio Adapter Cards, p. 58
Installing an Audio Adapter Card, p. 125

Figure 1.1 shows the devices you can attach to the card's input and output (I/O) connectors and the types of files you can use.

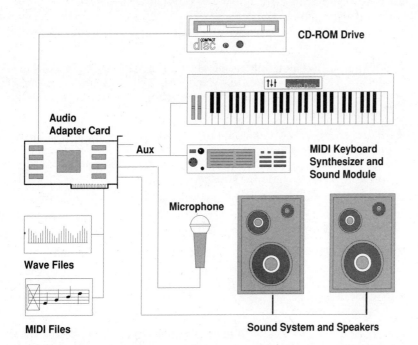

FIG. 1.1

The hardware components of multimedia sound.

The CD-ROM drive, MIDI equipment, and microphone are optional. The only required devices are the audio adapter card and a set of speakers or a sound system. MIDI is an acronym for *Musical Instrument Digital Interface*, an industry standard for interconnecting electronic musical instruments. One of the most important features of audio adapter cards is the ability to control external MIDI devices.

High-fidelity-stereo, digitally sampled audio files (called Wave files in fig. 1.1) occupy about 10M of disk space per minute of playing time. Therefore, you need the high capacity (630M or so) of a CD-ROM drive to store lengthy musical scores in Wave format. MIDI music files are much smaller (typically 10K or less per minute), so you can store MIDI files on hard disk drives with limited free space. If you have an audio adapter card, enjoy music, and don't have a CD-ROM drive, you are likely to make extensive use of MIDI files. The fidelity of music in MIDI files depends on the quality of your audio adapter card.

Audio adapter cards designed for multimedia applications have at least the following capabilities:

- Recording and reproducing digitally sampled (waveform) stereo files, which are similar in format to those contained in compact discs (CDs). Most cards include a monophonic input for consumer-grade microphones.

- Creating electronically synthesized music, using MIDI files as the data source. The techniques by which you synthesize the sounds of various musical instruments depend on the type of card you purchase.

- Hooking up to electronic musical instruments that have MIDI connectors. The most common external MIDI devices are consumer-grade keyboard synthesizers such as those manufactured by Casio and Yamaha.

- Mixing audio CDs, waveform audio, and synthesized music. Most cards also have a general-purpose auxiliary input. You use a graphic-mixer application supplied with the card to control the sound level of each audio source.

- Amplifying the audio output signal so that it is capable of driving small speakers. You also can connect the card's audio output signal to an auxiliary input of a conventional stereo system.

- Controlling CD-ROM drives through a connector for a SCSI ("scuzzy") cable. SCSI is the standard interface for CD-ROM drives, but some cards use special interface connectors for specific brands and models of drives. A few manufacturers offer the CD-ROM interface as an option.

Audio adapter cards come with an assortment of applications designed to enable you to use the card as soon as you install it. Most of the applications are for use with DOS, because Windows 3.1 comes with its own multimedia applications. The multimedia extensions of Windows 3.1 enable you to record, edit, and play waveform audio files and play (but not record) MIDI files.

Because different manufacturers' cards usually have different audio-mixing capabilities, the most common Windows application included with audio adapter cards is an audio mixer control. This control is called an *applet*—a Microsoft-coined term that describes the applications supplied with Windows 3.x. An applet also describes small applications (usually included with other products) that require a mainstream Windows application or special hardware.

All the sound capabilities of Windows 3.1 were included in Windows 3.0 with Multimedia Extensions 1.0 (now called Windows with Multimedia), which Microsoft introduced in the fall of 1991. Windows with Multimedia, however, initially was available only on CD-ROMs from the suppliers of multimedia PCs and upgrade kits. Multimedia PCs and upgrade kits include an audio adapter card and a CD-ROM drive, so this configuration did not constitute a problem.

The cost of the card and drive hovered close to $1,000 through early 1992—definitely out of the impulse-buying category for most PC users. Windows 3.1, however, eliminated the CD-ROM drive requirement, and manufacturers introduced new audio adapter cards with respectable sound quality for street prices in the range of $150 to $200. Sales of audio adapter cards in the United States soared to more than 200,000 cards per month. The mute PC was on its way to "endangered species" status.

Multimedia Icons and Symbols

Windows, with its standard menu structure and extensive use of icons to represent different actions, makes entry-level multimedia applications relatively easy to use. For example, most multimedia applications for Windows use the standard symbols for audiotape and videotape recorders. The buttons shown in the following paragraphs appear in the order (from left to right) in which they appear on many VCRs.

 Stop suspends all action. You must click the Play button to resume playing the file.

 Rewind resets the elapsed time to zero. In some applications, you can click and hold this button to achieve a controllable fast-reverse function. Multimedia applications often enable you to reset the time by double-clicking the Rewind button.

 Back Step moves the action back in time by a specific increment (usually a percentage of the duration of the file). You cannot use this feature with all types of media, and few applications offer Back Step or Forward Step buttons. Some digital video and animated applications provide this feature.

Play starts the application's file or other data source from the beginning if the file is newly loaded or the source is rewound. If you stop play by clicking the Stop or Pause button and then click Play again, playback continues from the point at which you clicked Stop or Pause.

Pause temporarily stops the file. To resume playback, click the Pause button again. This button is a *toggle*—a feature that alternately stops and starts an action.

Forward Step is the opposite of Back Step, moving the action forward in time by a predetermined interval.

Fast Forward is the opposite of Rewind. More applications use the click-hold procedure to fast-forward a file than to fast-reverse a file. In a few applications, Fast Forward moves the action forward to the end of the file.

Record has two symbols: the octagon and a microphone. Unlike VCRs and audiotape recorders, a multimedia application's Record and Play functions are not interlocked; you do not have to click the Play button before you start to record.

Eject Media ejects a videocassette or a CD-ROM (if your player has a remote-controlled eject mechanism). When the file being played is a hard disk file, for example, the symbol on the Eject Media button is gray (indicating inactive status), or the button does not appear on-screen.

Not all multimedia applications display the buttons in this sequence, but the Back Step and Rewind buttons always appear left of or above the Forward Step and Fast Forward buttons.

Multimedia has introduced a new bit of computerese: "playing a file." Playing a file means using an application to process the data contained in a file—not opening the file and loading its data into memory. Most multimedia applications open and load a file or search to a predetermined location on a videocassette, audio CD, or videodisc before the file is played.

Related Topics
Assigning Actions to
Buttons, p. 499

Animated Graphics and Synchronized Sound

Computer games for DOS and Windows have long combined animation and sound to mesmerize their users. Creating a best-selling computer game, however, was one of the most challenging tasks that even experienced programmers could undertake.

Windows multimedia technology, however, enables you to combine entertaining animation and synchronized sound without having intimate knowledge of the workings of the PC. Autodesk Animator, for example, makes the creation of animated images relatively simple; Autodesk Multimedia Explorer for Windows adds synchronized-sound capability.

In the new category of multimedia applications, time, rather than graphic or audio objects, plays the controlling role. In this respect, multimedia applications resemble project-management applications. Still images, animated images, and sound files are both activities and resources, which you can organize so that specific activities occur in a certain pattern or simultaneously. An *activity* is a multimedia verb such as play, stop, step, and so on. *Resources* are nouns that serve as the object of the multimedia verb: pictures, animation, or sound files.

Instead of days, hours, and fractions of hours, the time units of multimedia applications are minutes, seconds, and frames. Many multimedia applications incorporate elements similar to the Timeline window of Macromedia Action!, shown in figure 1.2 with a portion of the image 22.9 seconds into a demonstration.

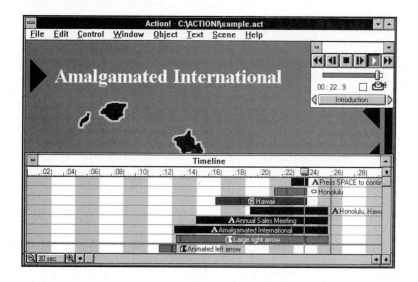

FIG. 1.2

A portion of the image and timing windows of Macromedia Action!

If you use a mainstream Windows application—Microsoft Excel, Word for Windows, WordPerfect for Windows, or any other Windows spreadsheet or word-processing application—you shouldn't have any problem mastering an entry-level multimedia application. If you have experience with project-management or musical-sequencing applications for Windows or DOS, you should feel right at home with time-based multimedia applications. Timing diagrams resemble the Gantt charts associated with project management and the step editors of sequencing applications.

Full-Motion Video in a Window

The ultimate level of PC animation and synchronized sound is *full-motion video*, a technology that Windows 3.1 is bringing into the mainstream (refer to Chapters 19 and 22 for more information). Full-motion video combines television-style images (in a resizable window) with sound. Video images are transmitted at a rate of 30 per second for North American black-and-white TV (and at a slightly slower rate for color).

Video capture cards (often called *frame grabbers*) intercept these television signals and create still images in several standard graphics file formats. These cards, which were introduced well before Windows multimedia, enable you to create images for use with a variety of graphics applications. The cards often have a preview window that helps you select a frame to copy. When you find the frame you want, you save it to a bit-mapped graphics file similar to the files used by Windows Paintbrush. Most video capture cards now include a Windows driver on floppy disk.

Creating full-motion video, however, is much more challenging than simple frame grabbing. If you tried to capture 30 frames of full-screen, full-color video every second, you would fill more than 100M of disk space per second (if your computer could transfer the data that quickly), and you might need to record up to 10M of sound per minute.

A computer can save and replay television images only if the images are quite small and composed of 256 colors or fewer. But even playing small, 256-color television images in real time overtaxes all but the fastest computers. To accommodate slower computers, the full-motion-video process discards duplicated frames during recording or reproduction and compresses the remaining frames. The resulting images may be jerky but otherwise are quite similar to those produced by a TV set.

Figure 1.3 shows the basic elements that combine to provide full-motion video in Windows.

The most common type of full-motion video device for use with Windows is a *video-in-a-window adapter card*. Video-in-a-window cards, such as Creative Lab's Video Blaster, connect to your existing VGA card. These cards convert television signals to a format compatible with your VGA display and provide a sizable window for the display of full-color video images (within the limits of your existing VGA adapter). The source of the signal can be a TV tuner (the video-output terminal of your TV set), a videocassette recorder, a videodisc player, or a video camera (still or motion).

VGA-to-NTSC cards convert the RGB (red-green-blue) analog output of a standard VGA card back to a video signal compatible with the video-input terminal of your television set or VCR. (NTSC is an abbreviation for

National Television Standards Committee, the organization that developed the specifications for video broadcasting signals used in North America.) If you use an advanced type of VGA-to-NTSC adapter called a *genlock card*, you can combine still or animated graphics with the video image and record the composite image on videotape.

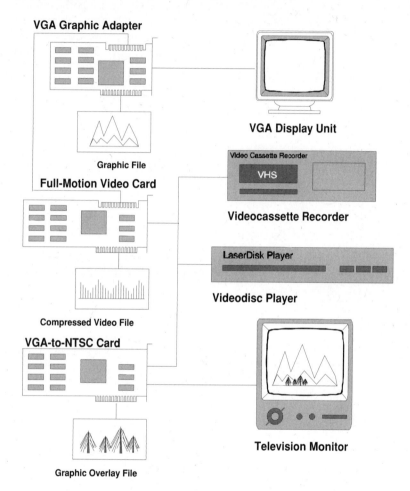

FIG. 1.3

The devices that produce full-motion video.

Neither Windows with Multimedia nor Windows 3.1 includes full-motion video drivers. Windows with Multimedia includes a driver for the Pioneer LD-V4200 videodisc player but none for video-in-a-window adapter cards or videocassette recorders. Standards for compressing video data in the Windows environment were being developed by Microsoft and Intel when Windows 3.1 was released. The Windows drivers to remotely control VCRs and camcorders were being written by the manufacturers of these devices at the time this book was written.

Related Topics
Video Compression, p. 487

Two companies—Intel and Microsoft—currently are the principal developers of full-motion video applications. Intel was first in the market with products that use the digital-video-interactive (DVI) technique. DVI compresses frames through hardware by using special components on Intel's ActionMedia II video adapter cards. The Intel products form the base for full-motion video in IBM's Ultimedia product line. Microsoft has developed a driver for the use of DVI under Windows, but has taken a software-only compression approach with their audio-video interleaved (AVI) driver.

Interactive Applications and CD-ROMs

Most multimedia applications, especially those supplied on CD-ROMs, are interactive. Interactive applications require you to take an active role in determining what information the application presents and how much detail that information provides. You most commonly make choices in interactive applications by clicking command buttons; you also can use conventional Windows menus in some applications.

An example is Composer Quest, a musical-history CD-ROM application produced by Dr. T's Music Software. Composer Quest enables you to select a time period and then listen to the music of the time, view an example of then-current trends in the visual arts, or read simulated newspaper headlines of the day. Figure 1.4 shows Composer Quest's window for topics in the Jazz category. Early Swing is shown in the 1930s and 1940s.

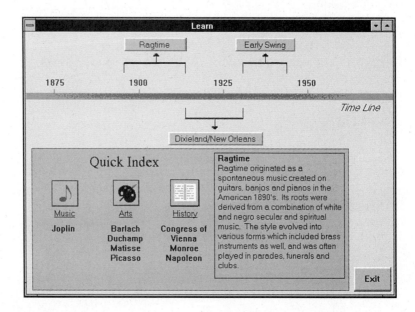

FIG. 1.4

An interactive musical-history multimedia application on CD-ROM.

When you click the Early Swing button, for example, an image of Count Basie appears and a sample of his music plays. You also can click the Music button to hear a sample of a Scott Joplin rag. The capability to jump from an overview to detailed information about a subject and then back to the overview is characteristic of the hypertext techniques provided by most multimedia CD-ROM applications.

Hypertext basically is the linking of related material throughout an application. The Windows Help system, for example, features hypertext links in the form of selections (usually displayed in green) that lead from the Help index to the detailed information you need.

Composer Quest uses waveform audio files and audio CD tracks to produce music and bit-mapped images of paintings and photographs; the application uses conventional Windows text to generate newspaper headlines. Composer Quest also produces animated images, prepared in Autodesk Animator and played back in the Autodesk Animation Player for Windows. Composer Quest is a particularly interesting commercial multimedia product because it uses so many different types of files.

Multimedia PC Specifications

Just a couple of years ago, a PC adapter card that recorded and reproduced CD-quality audio signals, included a built-in sound synthesizer and MIDI control, and sold for less than $200 would have been passed off as "vaporware." But the prospect of 10 million or more copies of Windows 3.1 installed on 80386SX and faster PCs (with the Sound Recorder and Media Player applets waiting for the hardware to bring them to life) has made these cards and prices a reality.

Before the introduction of Windows 3.1, a million or so Sound Blaster, Ad Lib, and similar sound cards were sold in North America. Industry sources predict that millions of additional sound cards will be sold following the introduction of Windows 3.1. The cacophony will be awesome and the prices will drop even further, but the quality of the products is likely to remain high. PC sound cards for Windows must meet a set of basic specifications in order to qualify for Multimedia PC status when the cards are supplied with Multimedia PC computers or with Multimedia PC Upgrade Kits.

What Is the Multimedia PC?

Multimedia PC (MPC), a trademark of the Multimedia PC Marketing Council, refers to IBM-compatible PC computers that meet minimum specifications based on the Multimedia Extensions 1.0 of Windows 3.0.

MPC also refers to upgrade kits that add MPC-compliant audio adapter cards and CD-ROM drives to 80386SX and faster PCs. Windows applications that are compatible with MPC hardware are candidates for MPC-trademark status, as are *multimedia titles*—CD-ROM discs with multimedia content.

Version 1.0 of the MPC specifications includes requirements for audio recording and playback, reading CD-ROM files, and displaying graphic "movies" created by proprietary animation applications. Under the original specifications, the MPC logo could be applied to 10-MHz Intel 80286-based computers; the minimum microprocessor standard now is a 16-MHz 80386SX.

Intel 80x86-series chips and their clones are required. RISC and Motorola 68000-based systems do not apply at present.

Although the current MPC specifications do not include televideo capability, such a specification probably will not be long in coming. Higher-speed processors will be required to implement full-motion video images, and as 33-MHz 80386DX processors become the desktop norm, the minimum specification may be upgraded another notch.

One of PC owners' most frustrating experiences is discovering that the components they just purchased are incompatible and must be returned or exchanged for another (usually more expensive) product. The MPC specification ensures compatibility between the hardware and software used in Windows multimedia. Audio adapter cards and CD-ROM drives must be compatible with Windows' multimedia extensions, for example, and the CD-ROM drive must mate with the sound-card interface. Figure 1.5 shows a complete packaged Multimedia PC.

The Multimedia PC Marketing Council

The Multimedia PC Marketing Council is a subsidiary of the Software Publishers Association. The council's stated purpose is to "educate end users on multimedia personal computing within the business, education, and consumer marketplaces, and to promote the Multimedia PC platform to independent software vendors." The council publishes and maintains MPC specifications and also has the right to test MPC-labeled products periodically. (Product requirements are described in the next section.)

The council is composed principally of vendors of IBM-compatible PCs and manufacturers of upgrade kits for 386- and 486-based PCs. Members pay $100,000 each to join. Manufacturers also pay trademark license fees to the council for each MPC-labeled product they sell (for example, $1.50 per computer and 75 cents per upgrade kit) or pay a substantial one-time fee that covers all their MPC products in perpetuity. The licensing fee for software and CD-ROM titles is a flat $500 per product. Figure 1.6 shows the MPC logo, created by Microsoft Corporation.

FIG. 1.5

A packaged
Multimedia PC.

FIG. 1.6

The MPC logo.

Microsoft transferred ownership of the logo to the MPC Marketing Council in 1991. Microsoft is not even mentioned in the council's glossy, four-color *Bring the World to Your Senses* brochure—and neither is Microsoft Windows—but the Multimedia PC on the cover shows Windows at work. (You can order a copy of *Bring the World to Your Senses* from the MPC Marketing Council at the address listed in Appendix F.)

One of the anomalies of the MPC specification is that although the MPC logo cannot be applied to an audio adapter card sold by itself, multi-media applications designed for audio adapter cards can carry the MPC logo. The reason for this seeming inconsistency is that the specifications require MPC-labeled hardware products to contain CD-ROM drives. Thus, the reassurance offered by the council's trademark is not available to purchasers of sounds cards, which are by far the best-selling multimedia components. If you purchase an audio adapter card that is the same model included in a manufacturer's multimedia upgrade kit, you are not likely to go wrong. If the CD-ROM interface connector is not labeled SCSI, however, you may find that your choice of add-on CD-ROM drives is severely limited.

Hardware Requirements for Multimedia PCs

Not surprisingly, the MPC specification for system software requires conformance to "the APIs, function and performance described in the Microsoft Windows Software Development Kit...and the Microsoft Multimedia Development Kit"—a euphemism for Microsoft Windows 3.0 with Multimedia Extensions 1.0, now called Windows with Multimedia. API stands for *application programming interface*, the term used to describe the functions in Windows that programmers use when creating Windows applications.

MPC Specification 1.0 defines standards for computers used to reproduce, not create, multimedia applications. The hardware required to create multimedia titles and videotapes is substantially higher-performance than the hardware that reproduces applications.

Related Topics
Understanding Multimedia
Hardware Recommenda-
tions, p. 565

When MPC Specification 1.0 was written in mid-1991, the "minimum," or base-level, MPC computer was a 12-MHz 80286 computer with 2M of RAM and 30M of hard disk capacity. After December 1992, the base-level MPC computer will be a 16-MHz 80386SX. The specification was written so that moderately priced computers could qualify for MPC status. Base-level MPCs aren't capable of reproducing full-motion video.

Specifications written by marketers often sacrifice technical adequacy for real or imagined economic "pricing points," such as $1,495, $1,995, and $2,495. MPC Specification 1.0 is no exception. The authors of the MPC specification did not—and probably could not—anticipate the 80386-based-computer price war that erupted in mid-1992. The base specification is likely to be revised upward again in late 1992 or early 1993.

T I P

The most important item missing from the MPC computer specifications is the number of free 8- and 16-bit bus expansion slots that must remain in the Multimedia PC after the adapter cards required to support the specification's audio and CD-ROM requirements have been added. "Standard" 80386 motherboards have six to eight adapter-card slots, but some have as few as four.

One or two open card slots may be satisfactory if you are interested primarily in sound and do not intend to become involved with full-motion video. You probably will want to add a combination fax/modem card and perhaps, a scanner; each item requires a slot. Video-image capturing and recording requires two adapter cards in addition to the VGA card already installed.

Random-Access Memory and Hard Disk Capacity

Memory capacity of 2M RAM barely is enough to run Windows 3.1 itself, let alone applications like Microsoft Word for Windows (with its OLE-server applets), Microsoft Draw, WordArt, and Chart. For most multimedia applications, 4M should be adequate, but you need 8M or more if you plan to view large color images. Like hard disk capacity and money, you never can have too much RAM.

The MPC specification of a 30M hard disk is unrealistic when installation of Windows and a single major Windows application may require more than 20M. Compact-disc-quality 44.1-kHz, 16-bit stereo sound samples alone consume about 10M per minute. Hard disks with capacities of less than 60M are difficult to find, except in inventory clearance sales and in notebook computers. A 120M hard disk is the minimum recommended size. If you plan to display large bit-mapped images or to record digital audio signals, 200M or more is recommended. If you have limited disk space, concentrate on using MIDI music; MIDI files usually are quite small.

If your hard disk is filled with files you aren't willing to live without, you may be able to gain enough free space for multimedia applications by using real-time file-compression software or hardware. Stac Electronics' Stacker compression products, for example, are compatible with Windows 3.1 and are available in software-only and hardware versions. File-compression products can reduce the disk-space requirement of the average file by a factor of about 2.5. Graphic images are compressed even more, but waveform audio files usually are compressed less than the average, if at all.

Related Topics
Disk-Compression Applications, p. 408

The software version of Stacker may slow operation of applications slightly if your disk has an average access time of about 20 milliseconds, but the product can improve the performance of the older 30- to 60-millisecond drives. You probably will not notice any slowdown with the hardware version of Stacker, even with a 15- to 18-millisecond hard disk, but you need a free slot to install the compression/decompression card.

Graphics Adapter Cards and Displays

Related Topics

VGA Displays and Adapter Cards, p. 446

The MPC specifications are vague about the quality of the VGA display required for multimedia applications. Multisynchronous super-VGA (SVGA) displays with a maximum 0.28-mm dot pitch were available from many manufacturers at quite reasonable prices when the specification was written, and the cost has since declined more. Perhaps Version 2.0 of the specification will establish 0.28-mm SVGA with a minimum 256 colors. Such a revision would contribute to improving the ocular health of people who are forced to use a grainy 0.4-mm terminal for any length of time.

A noninterlaced display with a vertical scan rate of 72 Hz or greater is recommended if you plan to use graphics applications extensively. The standard 13- and 14-inch (diagonal) displays are satisfactory for the standard 640-by-480-pixel display mode, and a 17-inch display for SVGA's 600-by-800-pixel mode is adequate. A 19-inch display is the smallest you should purchase if you are planning extensive use of 1,024-by-768-pixel resolution.

VGA adapter cards with 512K of video memory, providing 256 colors in the standard 640-by-480-pixel display mode, were the norm in mid-1991, and 1M of video memory was offered as standard with many 80386DX computers beginning in 1992. Operating speed, not just the number of colors available, will become the principal criterion for these cards when full-motion digital video becomes common. A performance goal is included in the specification, but MPC-labeled products are not required to comply with that goal. You may want to use a Windows graphic accelerator card to speed up animated graphics and full-motion video.

Sampled Digital Audio

Related Topics

Experimenting with Sound Recorder, p. 180
Understanding Sampled Analog Sound, p. 370

One of the reasons that such a large portion of this book is devoted to sound is the low cost of adequate (8-bit) quality and the reasonable price of high-fidelity (16-bit) stereo MPC audio adapter cards. These adapter cards are simple to install in your computer and easy to use. Most of them include a variety of DOS and Windows applications to help you take advantage of all their features.

You can reproduce sounds in standard waveform audio (WAV) format or create and edit your own sounds with Windows' Sound Recorder applet, which is shown playing a waveform audio file in figure 1.7.

FIG. 1.7

Windows' Sound Recorder applet, playing a waveform audio file.

Sound Recorder introduces the other symbol for the Record button—the microphone—shown on the bottom right button in figure 1.7.

You can use Sound Recorder to embed voice notes in Windows applications that support object linking and embedding (OLE). Although OLE was formally introduced with Windows 3.1, the technique was used in Microsoft Excel and PowerPoint, as well as in the applets supplied with Word for Windows 2.0 and Microsoft Publisher (MS Draw, MS Chart, and so on). Chapter 8 explains how to use Sound Recorder as an OLE server to embed sound in applications.

Control Panel's Sound dialog box, shown in figure 1.8, enables you to assign WAV files to events, such as when you launch Windows.

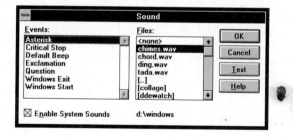

FIG. 1.8

Control Panel's Sound dialog box.

If you have not installed a sound driver for an audio adapter card or the PC's speaker, the items shown in the Files list box will be inactive (grayed). Chapter 6 explains how to use the sound function with an audio adapter card or the PC's speaker.

The specifications related to digital audio recording and reproduction are prefaced by the word "sampling." The technology involved in digitizing audio signals is described in Chapter 13.

The sampling type, called *linear Pulse Code Modulation (PCM)*, is the same as that used for commercial audio CDs. Sampling rate and resolution determine the fidelity of the sound—the higher the numbers, the greater the fidelity. CD audio is recorded in two 44.1-kHz stereo channels with 16-bit resolution. A standard 12-cm (5-inch) audio CD has a capacity corresponding to 630M and holds about 1 hour's worth of digitized sound.

The base-level specification does not require stereo sound recording or reproduction capability. Although the card must "present the output as a stereo, line-level audio signal at the back panel," stereo audio inputs are not required. The decision to allow monaural sound appears to have been made to accommodate Creative Arts' original Sound Blaster 1.0 and 1.5 cards and Media Vision's Thunder Board, for which drivers are included with Windows 3.1. These products were superseded by the 2-channel, MPC-compatible Sound Blaster Pro, Media Vision's Pro AudioSpectrum series, and other stereophonic audio adapter cards.

If you enjoy any form of music, you will want stereophonic capability, but mono is adequate for recording narration or simply for incorporating spoken notes into documents.

MIDI and Synthesized Music

Electronic circuitry to create synthesized music and sound effects is included in all audio adapter cards. The MPC specifications require that the on-board synthesizer be *multi-timbral* and *polyphonic* (see Chapter 10, "The MIDI Standard and Windows 3.1"). Multi-timbral synthesizers are capable of simultaneously playing several different instrument sounds, called *voices* or *patches*. Polyphonic refers to the capability of synthesizers to play more than one note at a time. A synthesizer with 16-voice polyphony can simultaneously play 16 notes chosen from any of the available timbres. For example, you could select 8 piano notes (to accommodate complex chords) and 4 drum notes, and assign the remaining 4 notes of a 16-voice synthesizer to monophonic (one-note-at-a-time) instruments, such as a trumpet, a trombone, a saxophone, and a clarinet. (See Chapter 9 for more information on synthesizers.)

The data used by the sound-synthesis section of modern audio adapter cards is stored in MIDI files, which have the extension MID. The structure of these files is standardized so that a wide variety of musical applications can interchange musical compositions. (See Chapter 7 for more information about playing MIDI files.)

The advantage of MIDI files over the WAV type is that MIDI files usually are about 100 times smaller and yet hold an equivalent amount of sound. Windows' Media Player applet, shown in figure 1.9, is used to play MIDI files; the applet also can play audio CD tracks, waveform files, digital video data stored on CD-ROMs, and animated "movies."

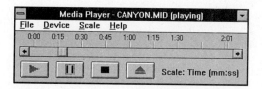

FIG. 1.9

Windows' Media
Player applet.

MIDI provides for 16 individual signal channels, each of which can be assigned to different instrument voices or devices. MIDI Note On messages, which instruct the synthesizer to play a note, start with the channel number to define the type of instrument that will play the note and then continue with pitch and velocity (volume) information. The note continues to sound until the synthesizer receives a MIDI Note Off message for the same channel and note number.

The MPC specifications define two types of musical synthesizers: *base* and *extended*. Base-level synthesizers must be able to play three melodic timbres and two percussive timbres (drums) simultaneously. These synthesizers also must be capable of playing six melodic notes and two percussive notes at the same time. Thus, base-level synthesizers have eight-voice polyphony.

Extended multi-timbral synthesizers are expected to play nine simultaneous melodic timbres assigned to channels 1 through 9 and at least eight simultaneous drum voices on channel 10. The specifications state, however, that the capabilities of extended-level synthesizers need only exceed those of base-level devices. All MPC-labeled audio adapter cards marketed at the time this book was written met or exceeded the nine-eight-voice multi-timbral recommendation.

The International MIDI Association (IMA) and MIDI Manufacturers Association (MMA) have adopted a standardized method of assigning voices to patch numbers, a method developed by Roland Corporation as its General Synthesizer (GS) standard. The IMA/MMA calls this method *General MIDI Mode* (GMM, usually abbreviated GM).

Related Topics
Examining the General
MIDI Mode Standard,
p. 296

In the past, synthesizer manufacturers assigned instrument voices to patch numbers in random fashion. Thus, if you wrote a tune for a Yamaha synthesizer, that tune might sound strange when you played it on a synthesizer made by Ensoniq. General MIDI addressed that problem by establishing a specific type of sound for each of 96 patch numbers.

Manufacturers such as Yamaha and Korg have adopted GM in their new synthesizer product lines. A list of the 96 instruments whose sounds are included in standard MPC audio adapter cards appears in Appendix C.

The MPC specifications define the various musical-instrument sounds that are to be synthesized by the adapter cards but not how the sounds are to be created. The two most common methods of synthesizing instrument sounds—FM synthesis and musical-instrument digital sampling—are described briefly in Chapter 2 and in much more detail in Chapter 9.

Related Topics
Using the Analog Audio
Mixer, p. 418

Audio Mixing and Output Capability

The minimum MPC specification requires a three-channel monaural mixer that can combine sound signals from audio CDs, digitized (sampled) audio, and the card's internal synthesizer. The specification recommends a fourth auxiliary input. Most MPC-labeled audio adapter cards have at least four stereo inputs—digitized audio, synthesizer, CD-audio, and stereo line in—and an additional monaural mixer input assigned to the microphone.

Manufacturers are free to choose their own mixer configurations, so Windows 3.1 does not include a mixer applet to set the volume levels of individual channels. Figure 1.10 shows a typical mixer applet.

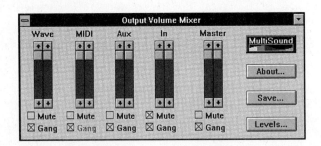

FIG. 1.10

The mixer applet
supplied with Turtle
Beach's MultiSound
audio adapter card.

Vertical scroll-bar sliders, which simulate the faders on an audio mixing console, are used to adjust the relative levels of each input, and left-right balance on each channel may be modified as necessary. The master volume sliders control the combined output of all sound sources.

Most audio cards have 1.5- to 5-watt outputs and can drive small, efficient speakers directly. More commonly, the line outputs are connected to the auxiliary inputs of your stereo sound system or to speakers with self-contained amplifiers. Some audio adapter cards, such as Media Sonic's Sound Commander series, include a pair of small speakers in the package.

CD-ROM Drive and Interface

A common misconception is that you need a CD-ROM drive in order to use an MPC sound adapter card. The rumor may have resulted from magazine articles on MPCs and upgrade kits that usually review CD-ROM drives and audio adapter cards together. The necessity for a CD-ROM drive might be inferred from the MPC specifications, which require MPC-labeled PCs and upgrade kits to include this drive.

Regardless of the source, this rumor is not true. If early-1992 market projections prove correct, one CD-ROM drive will be sold for every four or five audio cards purchased.

You needed a CD-ROM drive to install Windows 3.0 with Multimedia Extensions 1.0 or the Microsoft Multimedia Development Kit (MDK), because these products were supplied only on CD-ROMs. Windows 3.1, however, includes all the audio components of the multimedia extensions. The drivers required for specific sound cards that are not supplied with Windows are included in the software disks that accompany the boards. Windows 3.1 has effectively defeated Microsoft's original objective of making multimedia capability dependent on CD-ROM drives.

Necessary or not, however, a CD-ROM drive added to your computer opens the door to an unprecedented spectrum of new PC applications, ranging from multimedia games to full-text databases of specialized medical journals. CD-ROM drives are available in both internal and external versions, but the internal type that fits in a half-height drive bay is more common.

You must have an MSCDEX.DRV driver, Version 2.2 or later, in order to convert the file-directory information of CD-ROMs to DOS-compatible form. (MSCDEX is an abbreviation for MicroSoft CD EXtensions.) This driver is supplied with MPC PCs and MPC Upgrade Kits. You may have to request a copy from the supplier if you purchase a CD-ROM drive separately, but most dealers supply this driver (although not necessarily the latest version).

Windows 3.1 includes a driver that enables you to play audio CDs in CD-ROM drives that are equipped with internal audio-decoding capability. This driver is called [MCI] CD Audio. You must install this driver before you can play audio CDs in a suitably equipped CD-ROM drive. In the case of CD-ROMs and audio CDs, Media Player 1.0's eject button is enabled (the button is black, not gray, as shown in fig. 1.11).

NOTE There is now a Media Player 2.0.

Related Topics
Using the CD-ROM Drive Interface, p. 75
Understanding How CD-ROMs Store Data, p. 95

Related Topics
Installing MSCDEX and the CD-ROM Device Driver, p. 168
Playing an Audio CD with Media Player, p. 173

FIG. 1.11

Windows' Media Player 1.0 applet playing an audio CD.

```
Media Player - CD Audio (playing)
File  Device  Scale  Help
0:02  5:00  10:00  15:00      25:00       35:00      46:40

[▶]   [II]    [■]    [▲]    Scale: Time (mm:ss)
```

T I P

Many applications, such as Composer Quest, use waveform audio files and audio CD tracks, especially for musical examples. But some CD-ROM drives, especially "bargain" drives, cannot play audio CDs. You usually can tell whether a CD-ROM drive has audio-CD capability by looking for a headphone jack and volume control on the front panel. Look for a six-pin connector at the back of the drive for making an internal audio connection (by a ribbon cable) to your audio adapter card. If the drive does not have one of these connectors, you must connect a shielded miniplug cable between the headphone jack and the auxiliary input of your audio adapter card to hear audio CDs.

The MPC specifications for CD-ROM drives, like those for the MPC itself and for audio adapter cards, should be considered to be the minimum. The performance specifications, especially the allowable seek time (1 second), are not representative of the performance expected of today's CD-ROM drives.

The MPC specifications also failed to standardize the CD-ROM drive interface to be used—a serious shortcoming. This omission appears to have been made in deference to Sound Blaster Pro, which incorporates a proprietary interface that is compatible only with one manufacturer's CD-ROM drive. Most other audio adapter cards include an industry-standard SCSI connector or offer the CD-ROM drive interface as an option on a plug-in accessory board.

Multimedia PC Upgrade Kits

Multimedia PC upgrade kits consist of a CD-ROM drive and a sound adapter card. The adapter card usually incorporates the required joystick and CD-ROM drive ports, conserving scarce expansion slots in your PC.

One of the principal advantages of purchasing an MPC upgrade kit is assurance that the audio adapter card, CD-ROM interface, and drive are compatible. A complete kit, shown in figure 1.12, ensures that you will not be forced to find cables, software drivers, or other missing components to complete an installation.

T I P

The MPC specifications say that "CD-ROM XA audio may be provided." In mid-1992, when this book was written, none of the MPC Upgrade Kits offered CD-ROM XA (extended architecture) capability, even as an option. You will need basic CD-ROM XA capability to view images stored on Eastman Kodak's new Photo CD-ROMs and full XA compatibility to play discs designed for Philips' new CD-Interactive (CD-I) format and for the Sony Multimedia Player, a new portable CD-ROM XA player.

Very few CD-ROM drives provide full XA capability, including interleaved ADPCM-encoded and compressed waveform audio files. If you are interested in these products, you may want to determine what is entailed in upgrading the CD-ROM drive to XA standards before you invest in an MPC upgrade kit. (See Chapter 13 for an explanation of the CD-ROM XA standard and ADPCM audio encoding.)

FIG. 1.12

Typical MPC upgrade kits, including an internal CD-ROM drive.

Most of these products also include Windows 3.1 on a CD-ROM drive and several multimedia CD-ROMs to get your collection started.

CD-ROM drives are available in both internal and external configurations; the external drives include their own power supply. Most MPC adapter kits provide only the internal version, which requires an open half-height drive bay in your PC. Make sure that the upgrade kit you buy includes the plastic slides required to mount the drive in most PCs. If not, you need to purchase a set from your dealer if your PC's case has conventional drive bays with recesses for the slides on each side.

T I P When you are trying to decide which MPC upgrade kit to purchase, carefully consider the CD-ROM titles included (*bundled*) by the supplier. For example, Media Vision includes Macromedia's Action! (an animated presentation application), Compton's Multimedia Encyclopedia for Windows, and a multimedia game. The combined retail price of Action! (described in Chapter 18) and the encyclopedia is greater than the price of the upgrade kit. Other suppliers provide different multimedia title bundles, most of them entertainment-oriented.

Another alternative to the internal drive is a stand-alone package including a CD-ROM drive, audio adapter card, amplifier, and speakers. Figure 1.13 shows Media Vision's CDPC, the first product of this type to be announced.

FIG. 1.13

Media Vision's CDPC, a self-contained MPC adapter kit. (*Courtesy of Media Vision*)

The CDPC is designed to mount on top of your computer (if the kit is not in a tower-type case) or on the desktop. The CDPC has a self-contained 100-watt amplification system, with 20 watts directed to each of two stereo speakers and 60 watts devoted to a proprietary "bass enhancement system" that simulates a woofer. Media Vision also adds a "speaker imaging system" for improved sound quality. You also can attach a set of external speakers to the CDPC.

Chapter Summary

This chapter introduced you to multimedia sound, which is created by audio adapter cards. The Multimedia PC specifications laid a foundation for quality sound and music on the PC, and MPC-compatible audio adapter cards now are available from more than a dozen manufacturers. Multimedia sound is where the action is now, and much of the rest of this book will be devoted to this topic.

Chapters 2 and 3 provide detailed information on audio adapter cards and CD-ROMs, respectively, giving you the background you need to make an informed purchasing decision.

Understanding Audio Adapter Cards

Today's extended-level Multimedia PC audio adapter cards are truly remarkable devices. They combine features on a single card that just a few years ago would have required a rack full of professional audio gear. If you choose a card with professional-quality specifications, you can generate sound of quality and realism that equals or surpasses the sounds of synthesizers and samplers that just a few years ago cost thousands of dollars.

This chapter begins with a brief explanation of the terms and techniques used to describe the capabilities of audio adapter cards, together with diagrams and descriptions of the three basic functions of the cards: sound recording, sound reproduction, and musical sound synthesis. Later chapters provide much more detailed information on each of these topics.

A description of each element of popular types of audio adapter cards is provided, together with an explanation of how the elements are combined to record and reproduce sound on your PC. Descriptions of pre-MPC cards, such as the Sound Blaster, are included because well over a million are presently in use, and they represent the lowest-cost method of adding sound to the PC. Both MPC-compliant and specialty "professional quality" cards are described for those who value sound quality more than price.

At the end of the chapter, specifications are compared for three representative midrange MPC audio adapter cards, each of which takes a different approach to digitally sampled audio, synthesized music, or both, yet meets the extended-level requirements of the MPC specification.

Exploring Digital Sound Generation

Chapter 1 and the MPC specification use the terms "digitally sampled sound" and "FM synthesis" as if they were part of everyone's vocabulary. Unless you are an audio engineer or an electronic musician, you probably need a brief explanation of these terms before you can understand how computers generate sound. Parts III and IV of this book provide a much more detailed discussion of these two techniques of sound generation as they are used in commercial implementations of the MPC specification by audio adapter cards as well as by external MIDI instruments.

Sound waves in the form of electrical signals, such as those created by a phonograph pickup or a microphone, are called *analog* audio because the electrical signal is *analogous* to the properties of the original sound wave. The amplitude (voltage) of the electrical signal's representation of the sound corresponds to its intensity, and the signal's frequency represents the sound's pitch. Until the advent of audio CDs, all consumer sound systems used analog audio techniques. A graphical representation of a short period in the life of two analog sound signals of a simple tone, one with a low frequency (pitch) and a high amplitude (loudness) and the other with a higher frequency and a lower amplitude, is shown in figure 2.1. (In all the waveform diagrams in this chapter, the vertical axis represents amplitude, and the horizontal axis is time.)

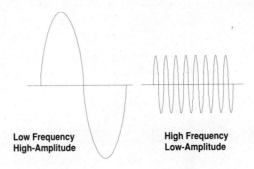

FIG. 2.1

A single cycle of a low-frequency, high-amplitude sound and eight cycles of a high-frequency, lower-amplitude sound.

Low Frequency
High-Amplitude

High Frequency
Low-Amplitude

If you assume that the pitch of the low-frequency sample of figure 2.1 is middle A on the piano (440 Hz in the U.S.), the pitch of the higher-frequency sample would be 3,520 Hz, because eight cycles of the higher-frequency sound wave occur in the same span of time as the single cycle of the low-frequency wave. The second sample is three octaves above middle A, because the frequency doubles for each octave; 440, 880, 1,760, and 3,520 Hz are each A on the musical scale, but one octave apart in pitch.

Analog sound signals are continuous; the waves shown in figure 2.1 repeat, usually diminishing in amplitude, until the source of the sound is extinguished. Computers, on the other hand, store their data in *digital* form: a stream of bits representing 1s and 0s. Digital data is fundamentally discontinuous in nature, because the 1 or 0 value of digital data is valid only at a particular instant in time. Thus, the continuous analog sound signals must be converted into discontinuous digital form so that the computer can store or process the sound. Later, the digital computer data must be translated back to analog form so that you can hear it through a sound system. This two-way conversion between analog and digital signals is the basic function of all MPC-compatible audio adapter cards.

Understanding Digital Audio Sampling and Reproduction

Integrated circuits and low-cost disk drives with high capacities make possible, at a reasonable cost, the conversion of analog audio signals to digital form, the storage of the digital data in disk files, and then the conversion of the digital data in the files back to analog signals (refer to Chapter 13 for more information). Beginning in the early 1980s, single-chip analog-to-digital converters (ADCs), the devices required to convert audio signals to a digital representation, began to appear. Much of the impetus for the development of these integrated circuits came from the telephone industry, because audio sampling techniques support multiple conversations on a single line, using a technique called time-division multiplexing.

An ADC measures the amplitude (intensity or volume) of the audio waveform, shown as a simple sinusoid (a sine wave or pure tone) in figure 2.2, at precisely timed intervals called the *sampling rate*. The speed at which the ADC converts the amplitude to a numeric (digital) sample value is called the *sampling time*.

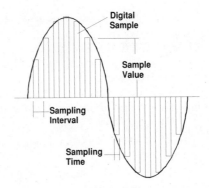

FIG. 2.2

Sampling an analog audio signal to create discrete digital sample values.

Sampling a 440-Hz signal 16 times per cycle, as shown in figure 2.2, requires a sampling rate of 7,040 samples per second (440 * 16). Sampling rate is usually expressed as frequency in kHz, so 7,040 samples/second equals 7.04 kHz. Sampling rates of 44.1, 22.05, 11.025, and 5.0125 kHz are standard in the audio industry. The higher the sampling rate, the better the fidelity, but the disk space consumed for sound storage increases proportionally. Figure 2.3 shows the discrete (discontinuous) numeric values of the samples taken in figure 2.2. Numeric values are shown as decimal integers in figure 2.3, but the actual output of the analog-to-digital converter is a *binary integer*. Binary integers represent numeric values by a pattern of bits. Appendix E includes an explanation of how numbers are represented in binary notation. The sample numbers of figure 2.3 begin with 0, the standard practice when binary notation is used. The individual values are stored in sequence in a file on your hard disk. This type of sampled sound is called *pulse code modulation* (PCM).

The precision of measurement of the amplitude of the analog sound wave is determined, for the most part, by the number of bits (called the *resolution*) of the digital side of the ADC. 8-bit sampling provides only 256 individual amplitude measurement intervals, 12 bits give 4,096, and 16 bits provide 65,536 different levels. The sample values of figure 2.3 represent a signal with about 80 percent of the full-scale range (+127 to –128) of an 8-bit ADC. Increasing the resolution of the measurement also increases the disk space required to store the sample. As mentioned in Chapter 1, recording stereo sound at 44.1 kHz with 16-bit samples consumes about 10M per minute of disk space.

After a digital representation of an audio signal of short length is stored in memory or a longer one is saved to a disk file, you can reconstruct the original signal by sending the digital data to a digital-to-analog converter (DAC) at the same rate at which the sound was sampled. The output of a DAC is a continuous, "staircase" wave that resembles Mayan ceremonial architecture (see the left-hand illustration of fig. 2.4).

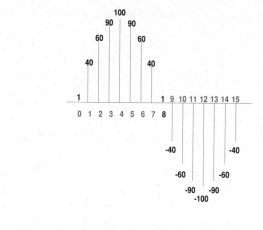

FIG. 2.3

The discrete values obtained by the sampling process of figure 2.2.

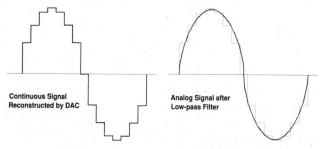

Continuous Signal
Reconstructed by DAC

Analog Signal after
Low-pass Filter

FIG. 2.4

Waveforms reconstructed by a DAC and a low-pass filter.

Analog low-pass filters are used to smooth the output of the DAC to duplicate the original sound waveform. If low-pass filters were not used, the "sharp edges" of the DAC's output would generate undesirable overtones that would give a harsh quality to the sound.

ADCs and DACs are used in pairs to record and reproduce the left and right channels required for stereo sound. When you record stereo sound, the disk space requirement is double that required for monophonic recording.

One of the problems facing today's multimedia producers is selection of the optimum combination of sampling rate and resolution to match the audio adapter cards installed in the purchaser's computer. 8-bit ADCs and DACs at 5.0125 or 11.025 kHz provide telephone-like quality and are adequate for applications such as voice notes attached to documents. 16-bit conversion is the standard for commercial audio CD and Digital Audio Tape (DAT) recordings. Audio CD sound is sampled at 44.1 kHz, and DAT uses 48 kHz. The majority of sound cards in use have 8-bit resolution and a maximum sample rate of 22.05 kHz. You can supply 16-bit sound from an audio CD to an 8-bit converter and obtain a lower-fidelity semblance of the original (the least significant 8 bits are ignored), but you cannot send data at 44.1 kHz to a card with a maximum speed of 22.05 kHz and expect it to output recognizable sound. 8-bit and 16-bit samples at 22.05 kHz are the most common formats for sampled audio on CD-ROMs.

Creating Synthesized Music

Those of you who attended early Beatles concerts or listened to Wendy Carlos's *Switched on Bach* recording for Columbia heard some of the first examples of electronically synthesized music. Robert Moog, the pioneer of synthesized music, combined a keyboard with a maze of electronic circuits and patch cables to create equipment that would produce more complex musical tones than were available from the electronic organs of the day. The Moog Synthesizers used analog techniques—collections of oscillators, filters, and amplifiers—to create their sounds. Performers who employed the early Moog Synthesizers had to combine audio engineering with musical artistry to obtain the effects they wanted. In those days, synthesizers cost upwards of $10,000 and were available only to the wealthiest of musicians. Now, you can buy an audio adapter card with a synthesizer, waveform audio capability, and a multichannel mixer for less than $200.

Related Topics
Yamaha and Digital FM
Synthesis, p. 249

An Introduction to Digital FM Synthesis

John Chowning, a graduate student at Stanford University in the early 1980s, invented a new method of creating sounds that resembled those of conventional musical instruments. He used a digital computer, rather than Bob Moog's analog electronic circuits, to program the creation of sounds by a method called *digital frequency modulation synthesis*. Chowning's technique involved creating digital representations of two or more waveforms and using a digital computer to combine them into complex digital signals. No ADC is involved because the sounds begin life in digital form. The combined digital signals are converted to analog form by the same type of DAC used for the digitally sampled sound reproduction of figure 2.4. Stanford University obtained patents on Dr. Chowning's invention and later licensed the technology to Yamaha Corp. Figure 2.5 is a simplified block diagram that shows the elements of digital FM synthesis of musical sounds.

You can create different types of sounds by changing the digital values of the control inputs listed to the left and right in figure 2.5:

- The fundamental *pitch* of the tone is determined by the *frequency* of the digital carrier waveform, and loudness is controlled by its amplitude.

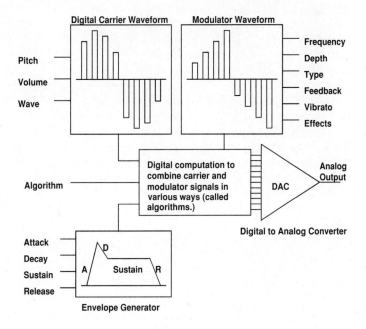

FIG. 2.5

How digital FM synthesis creates sounds with complex overtones.

■ Several different types of waveforms, such as a plain sine wave, half of a sine wave, and other variations, affect the overall "roundness" of the basic tone.

■ *Vibrato*, rapid changes in pitch also called trill, is achieved by making small, fast alterations to the modulator wave's frequency.

■ Increasing the amount of modulation, called modulation *depth*, adds to the brightness of the sound.

■ As the *frequency* of the modulation signal is increased, harmonics farther from the pitch of the carrier are created, altering the sound's timbre.

■ Changing the amount of *feedback* (using the operator to modulate itself) varies the output from its normal tone to a brittle, harsh-sounding tone.

■ The *algorithm* selected determines how the modulator interacts with the carrier to vary the timbre of the sound.

In addition to their characteristic waveforms, musical instruments (including drums) have their own typical sound *envelopes*, shown in figure 2.5 and expanded in figure 2.6.

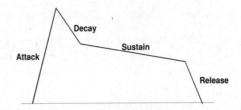

FIG. 2.6

A sound envelope
typical of a note struck
on a piano or plucked
on a guitar.

The sound envelope of figure 2.6 is representative of that for a note
played on a piano or plucked on a guitar or other stringed instrument.
The envelope generator makes adjustments to sound level over time,
a process also called *amplitude modulation*, and serves as a digital
version of a volume control knob. The envelope generator determines
the following:

- *Attack*, the speed at which the sound rises to its initial volume,
  determined by how fast the hammer strikes the piano strings

- *Decay*, the rate of drop-off to a sustained intensity, determined by
  the characteristic of the strings and how they are mounted in the
  piano

- *Sustain*, the normal intensity of the tone, which declines over time
  because of internal friction in the string and the dampening effect
  of the surrounding air

- *Release*, the speed at which the sound level drops to zero when the
  piano key is released, a function of the felt pad of the damper
  mechanism

This type of sound envelope often is referred to as ADSR, the initial letters of each of its components. An effect similar to vibrato, created by
rapid changes in volume rather than pitch and often called tremolo, is an
example of amplitude modulation.

In digital FM synthesis, each of the 14-tone control inputs shown in
figure 2.5 are in the form of individual bytes of digital data stored
in read-only memory (ROM). When you select a type of sound to play,
your computer sends a signal, called a patch change. This signal is converted to a ROM *address*, the location in the ROM where the data for the
sound is stored. You can alter the characteristics of the tones yourself
by sending computer data that overrides a portion of the ROM's data for
the tone. This process is called editing a voice.

Creating and combining digital representations of sound in real time
requires a large number of individual digital circuits operating at high
speed. Fortunately, the developments of digital FM synthesis and Large-
Scale Integrated (LSI) circuit chips occurred at about the same time. The

newly found ability to combine circuitry that previously required thousands of individual components into a few, relatively low-cost LSI chips made FM synthesis an economic as well as a technical success. After a false start or two, Yamaha introduced the DX-7 FM keyboard synthesizer and revolutionized musical synthesis.

The authenticity of digital FM instrument sounds is determined by the number of waveform sources you can use at once (called operators), the number of different ways you can combine them with different algorithms, and the variety of waveform types available. Early audio adapter cards that use the Yamaha YM-3812 chip, such as the original Sound Blaster, offer only two operators. MPC sound cards that use the newer Yamaha OPL-III chips provide four operators and four different waveforms from which to choose, a considerable improvement over the YM-3812.

Instrument Sample-Playback Synthesis

Related Topics
Sample-Playback
Synthesizers, p. 257

Professional musicians constantly strive for perfection in performance—practice and rehearsals consume most of their waking hours. In the early days of synthesized music, bands simply added the unique sounds of Moog and other contemporary synthesizers to those played on members' conventional instruments. After MIDI connections between electronic musical instruments became common, groups began to replace individual performers with synthesized sound modules. This process, of course, required that the electronic stand-in imitate the performance of the now-unemployed member. (For more information on MIDI, see this chapter's subsequent sections on "Using the PC as a MIDI Music Controller" and "Using MIDI Connectors and Breakout Boxes.")

Simulating certain types of instruments by digital FM synthesis, especially those with harmonic content that changes rapidly with time, is difficult. Realistically duplicating the intonation of Baden Powell, a Brazilian acoustic guitarist, for example, is almost impossible with FM synthesis. Digitally recording the sound of a real instrument, played by a live musician, turned out to be the solution.

Creating musical samples is a relatively straightforward process. You have a musician play a set of representative notes and create an audio CD with 16-bit, 44.1-kHz digital samples of the sounds. By altering the rate at which the samples are played back, you can change their pitch and thus create all the notes of the chromatic scale. Halving or doubling the playback rate, for instance, increases or decreases the pitch of a sampled note by one octave.

Unfortunately, a CD-ROM drive isn't fast enough to find and play back specific sounds in real time because of the drive's slow seek time, which is about 20 times slower than a modern hard disk. If you had a hard disk large enough to hold all the samples you needed for a performance, even that disk wouldn't be fast enough to play anything but a dirge. Fortunately, Very-Large-Scale Integrated (VLSI) circuit ROMs came about during the time musical sampling techniques were being developed. The first VLSI ROMs could store the recorded samples in a few chips. Now the four megabytes or so of samples required to synthesize the 128 different sounds of the general MIDI standard, plus several complete sets of drums, can be squeezed onto a single chip. A block diagram of a ROM-based sample-playback synthesizer is shown in figure 2.7.

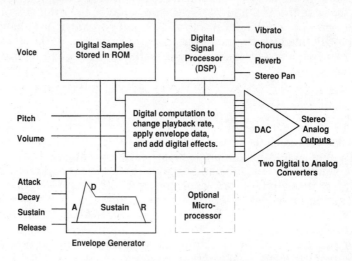

FIG. 2.7

A block diagram depicting musical sample-playback synthesis.

Sample-playback synthesis offers fewer options to control the ultimate composition of the sound waves because many of the choices required for digital FM synthesis are not applicable to sampled sound. Most sample-playback devices enable you to alter the envelope generator. Some, such as the Roland SC-series sound cards and modules, add a limited number of digital effects, including the following:

- *Vibrato,* rapid small variations in the pitch of the sustained tone (sometimes called tremolo), added to any vibrato that may have been included in the original definition of the voices being played

- *Chorus,* the simulation of multiple instruments playing at once, called layering

- *Reverberation,* the duplication of echo effects of various acoustic environments

- *Stereo pan,* the ability to vary the volume of the left and right channels, simulating movement of the sound source from one position to another

A technique called *digital signal processing* (DSP), explained in Chapters 13 and 15, is used to create these effects. Digital effects can add concert-hall realism or weird aberrations to your music. A much wider selection of digital effects is available from MIDI-controlled effects processor modules dedicated to creating effects only.

VLSI ROMs and DSP chips are substantially more expensive than the LSI FM-synthesis chips. Some professional-quality sound cards using 16-bit linear PCM samples, such as the Turtle Beach MultiSound card based on the E-mu Proteus/1 XR, even have their own on-board microprocessors. Thus, this category of sample playback devices is unlikely to approach the lower cost of their FM cousins. Cards using wavetable techniques rather than full PCM synthesis, such as the UltraSound and Audio Master cards, come close to FM board pricing, albeit with somewhat lesser sound quality than PCM products such as the MultiSound. Chapter 9 explains the differences between wavetable and full 16-bit PCM synthesis methods.

All three of the techniques for creating sound by the digital techniques described in this section predate the widespread acceptance of the desktop personal computer. Sampled sound recording and reproduction equipment cost thousands of dollars and was found primarily in recording studios. Quality FM and sampled-instrument synthesizers were priced in the $2,000-and-up category, so their market was limited to professional or serious amateur musicians. The millions of PCs on the desktops of the world, combined with the astounding commercial success of audio CDs, created the economy-of-production scale that allows professional-quality sound to be created by a PC for less than $1,000. If you're willing to sacrifice sound quality, the cost drops to $200 or less.

Looking at Multimedia Sound's Predecessors

Related Topics
Installing and Configuring
Audio Device Drivers,
p. 145

If you have explored the Control Panel's Drivers applet, you may have seen the dialog box shown in figure 2.8 when you clicked the Drivers Add button. The List of Drivers box includes special Windows software required to use several sound cards that predate Windows multimedia extensions. Drivers are used by Windows to accommodate the specific types of peripheral hardware connected to your computer's motherboard. When you originally set up Windows, you selected drivers for the type of keyboard, mouse, and graphic display you use. A special Windows driver is required for the particular type of audio adapter card you install. If your sound card is not on this list, you can find the driver on one of the floppy disks that accompanied the card.

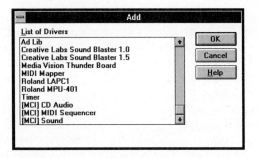

FIG. 2.8

The sound drivers
supplied with
Windows 3.1.

Product names such as Ad Lib, Roland LAPC-1 and MPU-401, and Thunder Board may not be familiar to those of you whose curiosity about PC sound was first aroused by Windows 3.1. Brief descriptions of these early sound cards appear in the following sections. What you may find most surprising is that the PC speaker is not mentioned at all in the list of drivers. Windows 3.1 does not include a multimedia driver for the PC's speaker. Pre-multimedia methods for bringing sound to the PC are described in their chronological order in the sections that follow.

Using the PC's Built-In Speaker

The built-in speaker of the PC was never intended to play music or provide sound effects—it can play only one tone at a time, and you cannot adjust the volume very well. Some speakers are simply glued to the bottom of the PC case, which drastically muffles the sound. Despite these limitations, early hackers discovered that they could write simple computer programs that would send pulses to the speaker to simulate spoken words and create a semblance of music. Producers of game applications for the PC became quite adept at writing code for sound effects and music using the built-in speaker. Jeopardy, a DOS-based game given to the losers and winners alike on the television program of the same name, plays a quite realistic version of the show's familiar theme song on the PC's internal speaker.

Related Topics
Installing Microsoft's PC-
Speaker Driver for Windows
3.1, p. 180

The feeble and sometimes distorted sound heard through your PC's speaker when you're playing computer games has nothing in common with the sound generated by a modern sound adapter card. Even low-cost monaural sound cards, when connected to a speaker of modest size or played through the auxiliary input of a sound system, provide acceptable fidelity. Applications that drive the PC's speaker, other than for an occasional beep, are using the speaker for purposes for which it was not designed. Nevertheless, Microsoft offers a multimedia-compatible driver for the PC's speaker, called SPEAKER.DRV, that can play waveform audio files. Microsoft makes it available only through its on-line Windows technical support services accessible with a modem. The driver's use is discouraged for good reason.

Using the PC as a MIDI Music Controller

Listen carefully to a television commercial. The background music was probably created by a microcomputer connected to a collection of electronic sound synthesizers whose common denominator is MIDI. MIDI is an acronym for the *Musical Instrument Digital Interface*, a standard method of interconnecting electronic keyboards, computers, synthesizers, and effects processors so that they play in unison. Two of the sound drivers included with Windows 3.1—Roland LAPC-1 and Roland MPU-401—are designed for use with MIDI adapter cards. (See Chapter 7 for more information about playing MIDI files.)

Related Topics
Defining the Basic MIDI
Specification, p. 279

The Roland MPU-401 MIDI Adapter Card

Roland Corporation, a manufacturer of professional electronic musical instruments, created a MIDI adapter card for the PC in the mid-1980s, priced it reasonably, and mass-marketed it through the distribution channels for musical products. Music dealers bundled it with DOS music software and a low-cost keyboard synthesizer. Roland's MPU-401, shown in figure 2.9, single-handedly dragged PCs into the musical mainstream. Industry sources estimate that about one million MPU-401s and their counterparts are installed in PCs throughout the world. Windows 3.1 uses the MPU-401 driver for all MPU-401-compatible MIDI controller cards.

Related Topics
The MPU-401/LAPC-1
MIDI Driver (MPU-401.DRV),
p. 195

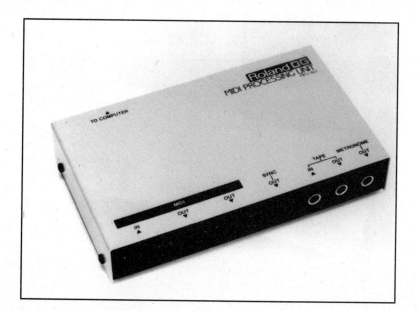

FIG. 2.9

The Roland MPU-401
MIDI adapter card.
(*Courtesy of Roland
Corporation USA*)

Related Topics

Creating a MIDI Map for the MPU-401 or Roland SCC-1, p. 199

Early Synthesizer Adapter Cards

The IBM-Yamaha Music Feature card was the first self-contained audio adapter card for the IBM PC and compatibles. The Music Feature used digital FM synthesis to synthesize a wide range of musical instruments and found a niche market in musical education. Because the Music Feature card was not compatible with the MPU-401 and required special software for programming, it was not accepted by professional musicians and the majority of amateurs. If you have a Music Feature card, you cannot use it with Windows; no Windows drivers have been written for it.

In the mid-1980s, Roland Corp. introduced a sound module called the MT-32 that used a technique called Linear Additive (LA) synthesis. The MT-32 generated sounds that most musicians considered more authentic than those available from the FM synthesizers available at the time. To compete with the Music Feature, Roland took the circuitry of the MT-32 and duplicated it on a PC adapter card to create the LAPC-1 (see fig. 2.10). The LAPC-1 offered an optional set of MIDI connectors so that it could receive MIDI signals from keyboards and control other MIDI-compatible gear. Best of all, the LAPC-1 was MPU-401-compatible, so virtually all PC music software available at the time could control it. An indication of the commercial success of the LAPC-1 is that Windows 3.1 has a standard MIDI patch map (setup) for it. The LAPC-1 uses the MPU-401 driver and is listed as a separate device, possibly to prevent confusion with the MPU-401. Roland's SCC-1 GS Sound Card, described later in the section "The Roland SCC-1 Sound Card," is the successor to the LAPC-1.

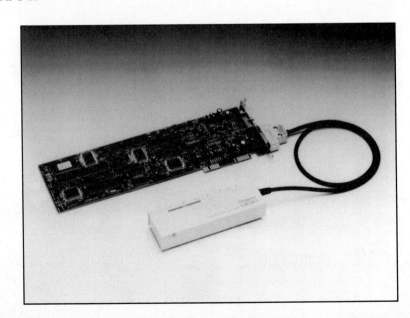

FIG. 2.10

The Roland LAPC-1, an early PC music adapter card. (*Courtesy of Roland Corporation USA*)

Looking at PC Games and Early Sound Cards

Computer games have played a major role in bringing high-quality color displays to the PC. You don't need a color display to use WordPerfect or Lotus 1-2-3 effectively, but Flight Simulator or Dungeons and Dragons is certainly more satisfying in 256 high-resolution colors. Likewise, action and adventure games are much more realistic when accompanied by high-fidelity sound effects and music. Whooping sounds and frantic "pull up, pull up" instructions simulating those of terrain-avoidance systems and radar altimeters add stimulation just before you "buy the farm" in Flight Simulator's Cessna or Lear Jet and can start the adrenaline flowing. PC computer games and the people who play them laid the foundation for today's high-fidelity sound cards.

The First "Blasters"

In 1987 Creative Labs developed the Creative Music System (C/MS), a 12-voice stereo music synthesizer card with an assortment of music software to accompany it. The C/MS board was renamed the Game Blaster in 1989. Tandy Corporation ordered enough Game Blasters to stock its thousands of Radio Shack stores, and Creative Labs was on its way to success.

Spurred by U.S. acceptance of the Game Blaster, Creative's engineers went to work on an upgraded monaural sound card and introduced the first Sound Blaster at the Fall 1989 COMDEX exhibition in Las Vegas. The Sound Blaster combined sampled sound with FM-synthesized music technology from Yamaha and added the option to connect external MIDI music gear. The product's success caused Microsoft to adopt the card's basic specifications as the minimum standard for the Multimedia PC. Creative Labs introduced a stereophonic version, the Sound Blaster Pro, in early 1991 and upgraded the synthesized sound portion of the Sound Blaster Pro in April 1992.

Related Topics
Installing an Audio Adapter
Card, p. 125

The Original Ad Lib Synthesizer Card

Creative Labs was not the only player in the North American market for sound cards. A small company in Quebec City, Ad Lib, Inc., developed a music synthesis card designed to compete with the Game Blaster. The Ad Lib card offered more realistic-sounding synthesized instrumental sounds than the Game Blaster because it used a newly available single-chip FM synthesizer, the YM-3812 from Yamaha Corporation.

Ad Lib, Inc., was successful in convincing many PC game software companies to write applications that used the Ad Lib product. The Ad Lib card became the de facto standard for computer-game synthesized sounds. Creative Labs adopted Ad Lib's digital FM approach to synthesized music for the Sound Blaster, calling it "fully Ad Lib compatible." Proof of the success of the original Ad Lib card is Windows 3.1's inclusion of a driver for it.

The Media Vision Thunder Board

Media Vision was one of the first U.S. competitors of Creative Labs. The firm now produces a complete line of stereo audio adapter cards and multimedia upgrade kits. The Media Vision Thunder Board duplicates the functions of the original Sound Blaster—it even uses the same drivers.

Defining MPC-Compatible Audio Adapter Cards

All MPC audio adapter cards are required by the MPC specification to have five independent sound subsystems:

- *Synthesized sound playback* enables you to choose from 128 different voices that duplicate the timbres of melodic instruments or supply sound effects. In addition, 46 different percussion instruments are available for your rhythm section. FM (frequency modulation) or sampled instrument sounds are used, depending on the card you select.

- *Sampled sound playback* converts sound stored in Pulse-Code Modulation (PCM) form. Two digital-to-analog converters (DACs) change the digital data stored in waveform audio (*.WAV) files to conventional stereo analog sound signals.

- *Sampled sound recording* enables you to record narration or music in the form of PCM-coded *.WAV files. You can choose stereo or mono recording and can control the sampling rate to balance fidelity of the sound against the size of the files created.

- *Audio mixer* functions control the source and level of the audio signals delivered to your speakers or sound system. Some cards include tone controls to boost bass and treble ranges.

- *MIDI input/output* enables you to use your audio card with external MIDI instruments, such as piano keyboards, synthesizers, sound modules, or effects processors.

Each of these subsystems is described briefly in this chapter and then explained in depth in the chapters that follow. Figure 2.11 is a block diagram of a typical MPC sound synthesis adapter card, showing how the subsections are interrelated and the external devices to which the adapter card connects.

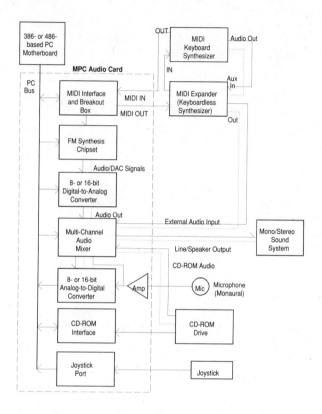

FIG. 2.11

A block diagram of a typical MPC audio card and the devices to which it connects.

In addition to the five audio subsystems, MPC-compliant cards usually include a joystick port, which is also used to provide MIDI connections, and a CD-ROM drive interface. The joystick port is included to assure MPC compatibility, despite the fact that most multifunction input/output boards installed in 80x86 computers include a joystick connector. The CD-ROM interface on some cards is supplied in the form of an optional *daughterboard*. Daughterboards are small cards that plug into a set of multi-pin connectors, called headers, on the main card. Because stereo signal processing is an option under the MPC specification, the second audio channel signals are shown as dotted lines in figure 2.11.

Exploring Types of PC Sound Cards

You do not need an audio adapter card that meets all the MPC specifications in order to enjoy some or all of the sound features included in Windows 3.1. Software drivers are provided by Windows 3.1 and Windows with Multimedia so that you can use adapter cards that predate the MPC standards, such as the early Ad Lib synthesizer, original Sound Blaster, and Thunder Board cards. The Roland MPU-401 MIDI adapter and LAPC-1 synthesizer cards also are supported by drivers included with Windows 3.1 and the Multimedia Extension 1.0 of Windows 3.0. These drivers are discussed in Chapter 5, "Preparing Windows for Multimedia."

Using Pre-MPC and Base-Level Sound Cards

No base-level MPC audio adapter cards were available at the time this book was written, and the appearance of any on the market is unlikely. Extended-level stereo cards are now the de facto standard for MPC audio. The original Sound Blaster, Thunder Board, and Ad Lib audio adapter cards do not fully conform to the MPC requirements because these cards lack a CD-ROM drive interface and an audio mixer. But each does exceed the base-level synthesizer requirements of the specification. The Sound Blaster and Thunder Board include base-level sampled sound recording and playback functions. The original Ad Lib card was designed for FM sound synthesis only and does not incorporate sampled sound capability.

Version 1.5 of the Creative Labs original Sound Blaster card is shown in figure 2.12. It provides basic, 8-bit, monaural, digitally sampled sound recording and reproduction capability and an 11-voice FM music synthesizer that duplicates the instrument sounds of the early Ad Lib card. A joystick port that doubles as a connector to an optional set of MIDI connections is included. MIDI connections are made through what is called a *breakout box*, a separate housing with a cable to the joystick connector. The Sound Blaster's MIDI breakout box option provides one MIDI IN connector and five MIDI OUT connectors and includes two MIDI cables. The joystick port is duplicated in the breakout box and can accommodate two joysticks if you purchase an optional splitter cable.

The Sound Blaster 1.5 provides a connector to adapt the standard 1/8-inch (3.5-mm) stereo audio output minijack to the RCA phono plugs used by most consumer stereo sound systems and some self-contained speakers. You have to buy your own microphone for voice recording. You can buy an optional set of C/MS sound chips from Creative Labs to make the Sound Blaster 1.5 compatible with DOS applications written for the earlier Game Blaster card.

The software supplied by Creative Labs with the Sound Blaster 1.5 consists of drivers and several applications for use directly under DOS, and one application for Windows 3.0. If you want to try the DOS applications supplied, you have to load the necessary DOS drivers for each of them.

These drivers consume valuable memory resources that could otherwise be used by Windows, so removing the entries for them in your CONFIG.SYS and AUTOEXEC.BAT files is wise if you ultimately use the Sound Blaster with Windows applications only. You do not need to use any of the Sound Blaster's software if you have Windows 3.1.

FIG. 2.12

The original Sound Blaster card, Version 1.5. (*Courtesy of Creative Labs*)

Original Sound Blaster cards now have a street price under $100. This price makes them the least expensive route for experimenting with Windows sound functions. If you own MIDI gear but not an MPU-401 or compatible adapter card, a Sound Blaster with a MIDI breakout box is in the same price range as an MPU-401, so you get MIDI capability with digital sound as a bonus. You can combine a Sound Blaster and an MPU-401-compatible sound card like the Roland SCC-1 if you have an extra slot available on your computer's motherboard. Using more than one sound card is explained in Chapter 4. If you already have a MIDI breakout box for your Sound Blaster or you're short on open adapter card slots, consider the Roland SC-55 or Korg 03R/W external sound modules described in Chapter 9.

Using the Media Vision Thunder and Lightning VGA and Audio Card

If you're considering upgrading your VGA capability to 24-bit color and need only limited synthesized sound capabilities or just MIDI IN and OUT ports for outboard sound gear, Media Vision provides a single-board solution. The Thunder and Lightning adapter card is compatible with the original Sound Blaster and Ad Lib cards for computer-game sound reproduction (it uses a single Yamaha YM-3812 synthesis chip to give 11 mono mode voices). 8-bit mono waveform audio recording from a microphone input and *.WAV file reproduction at rates to 22 kHz are supported, as are 2:1 compression and up to 4:1 decompression of waveform audio data. The Thunder and Lightning card can use the PC's internal speaker or a single external speaker (it delivers 2 watts into 4 ohms) to reproduce both types of sound. You control output volume with a thumb wheel mounted on the control plate.

The standard joystick/MIDI connector is provided with the Thunder and Lightning card, and MIDI IN and OUT ports require a MIDI Mate breakout box. The on-board MIDI circuitry duplicates the MPU-401's "dumb UART" mode compatible with the MPU-401 driver supplied with Windows, as well as virtually all DOS and Windows sequencer applications. If you have a consumer-type keyboard synthesizer with MIDI ports (many of the models produced by Casio and Yamaha include them), you can play MIDI files through the synthesizer's speakers and record your performances as MIDI files by using the Passport Trax Windows sequencer application supplied with the MIDI Mate.

The Thunder and Lightning card's VGA circuitry provides simultaneous display of 16.8 million different colors in 640-by-480-pixel resolution, 64,000 colors in 800-by-600 mode, and 256 colors when displaying 1,025-by-768-pixel images. A standard VESA feature connector also is included.

Using External Audio Adapters for Notebook Computers

Notebook and some laptop computers have a problem with audio adapter cards—they don't fit inside the case. Several manufacturers have seized the opportunity and created outboard audio devices that do not require an adapter card slot and do not require you to open your computer to install them. They plug into the bidirectional parallel port (LPT1 or LPT2) of your computer. None of the external audio devices available at the time this book was written were MPC-compliant.

The smallest of the external audio adapters, Media Vision's Audioport, (shown in fig. 2.13), plugs into the parallel port of a laptop (or any other PC) to provide monaural sound through a small, built-in speaker.

The Audioport emulates the original Sound Blaster, with eight-bit monaural sampled audio input and output capabilities, more than adequate for voice notes, and monaural two-operator FM synthesis using the Yamaha YM-3812 chip. You can plug one or two external speakers into the Audioport if you need more volume or higher-quality sound.

FIG. 2.13

Audioport sound
adapter for laptop
computers. (*Courtesy
of Media Vision*)

Using Extended-Level MPC
Stereo Audio Adapters

Four of the major contenders in the MPC audio adapter market are
Media Vision's Pro AudioSpectrum 16 and Pro AudioSpectrum Plus,
Advanced Gravis's UltraSound, and Creative Labs' Sound Blaster Pro.
Each of these cards exceeds the extended-level recommendations of
the MPC specification. These four cards were selected as examples of
extended-level audio adapter cards because they illustrate different
approaches to synthesized sound and have varying sound sampling
capabilities. Differences exist also in their audio mixing specifications.

Media Vision's Pro AudioSpectrum 16 and Pro AudioSpectrum Plus

The Pro AudioSpectrum 16 and Pro AudioSpectrum Plus, manufactured by Media Vision, Inc., are improved versions of the original 8-bit Pro AudioSpectrum introduced in late 1991. The Pro AudioSpectrum 16, shown in figure 2.14, offers a combination of stereo 16-bit digital audio recording and playback at rates up to 44.1 kHz with 4-operator (Yamaha OPL-III) FM sound synthesis—one of the few cards to provide both as standard features. The Pro AudioSpectrum Plus uses 8-bit ADCs and DACs, but its mixer and synthesizer sections are identical to the 16-bit version. Versions of the Pro AudioSpectrum 16 produced after July 1992 include MPU-401 compatibility in "dumb UART" mode.

FIG. 2.14

The Media Vision Pro AudioSpectrum 16. (*Courtesy of Media Vision*)

Both cards include a SCSI CD-ROM interface and a sophisticated stereo audio mixer, but the MIDI breakout box is an extra-cost option. Stereo power output has been increased to four watts per channel, and the cards now include hardware ADPCM compression and decompression for Sound Blaster file compatibility. Each of the cards comes with Media Vision's Pocket Recorder and Pocket Mixer applications for Windows as well as a collection of DOS applications.

The UltraSound from Advanced Gravis

Related Topics
Ensoniq ES-1000 Multimedia
Sound System, p. 262

The UltraSound audio adapter card from Advanced Gravis Computer Technology, Ltd. uses *wavetable* rather than FM techniques for synthesis. Wavetable synthesis employs short digital samples of instrument sounds, one to perhaps ten full cycles, stored in one or more ROM chips. The short samples are repeated for the required duration of the sound, using a process called *looping*, which is described in Chapters 9 and 14. Musical pitch is controlled by the rate at which the stored samples are played back, and an envelope generator determines how the amplitude of the sound varies over time. The UltraSound card uses the DOC II chipset developed by Ensoniq for its sound modules and keyboard synthesizers.

Wavetable sample synthesis is inherently more costly than FM synthesis because of the ROM required to store the samples and the additional circuitry needed to play them back properly. To keep the price competitive with the Sound Blaster Pro and other FM synthesis cards, the SCSI interface for the CD-ROM drive is supplied on an optional plug-in daughterboard. The basic UltraSound card records sampled sound with 8-bit resolution. You can increase the resolution to 16 bits by adding an optional daughterboard.

Wavetable synthesis does not achieve the sound quality of the full 16-bit PCM multi-sampled instrument synthesis used by Turtle Beach's MultiSound card, which is described later in this chapter, in the section on "Exploring Professional-Level and Special-Purpose Cards." The synthesized sounds of the UltraSound card are, however, more than a substantial improvement over those produced by FM methods. Adding the 16-bit sampling option to the UltraSound board provides almost professional-quality sound capability at a moderate price.

The Sound Blaster Pro and Sound Blaster Pro Basic

The Sound Blaster Pro from Creative Labs was one of the first production audio adapter cards to meet the requirements of the MPC specification. In the card's first incarnation in late 1991, Creative Labs added a second Yamaha YM3812 (OPL-II) chip to simulate stereo sound, a second ADC and DAC for stereo sampled sound, an audio mixer, and a proprietary (not SCSI) interface for a Matsushita CD-ROM drive. New drivers were created and a suite of applications were added so that the card could be used with Windows with Multimedia.

The two YM3812 chips were replaced in April 1992 by a single Yamaha YM262 to add true stereo FM synthesis, and a new set of drivers designed for use with Windows 3.1 were added. The 8-bit, 22.05-kHz stereo waveform audio recording and reproduction limits remained unchanged. Look for a chip with the number YM262 printed on it to determine whether it is the new version. When Creative Labs introduced the Sound Blaster Pro, they added a new model, the Sound Blaster Pro Basic, which does not include the MIDI breakout box.

The Sound Blaster Pro is the standard against which all other manufacturers compare their MPC-compliant cards. Boxes for competing audio adapter cards must carry the legend "Sound Blaster and Ad Lib compatible" to achieve widespread distribution. The Sound Blaster Pro was the first MPC-compliant card, so it has the largest number of users, and several major MPC-labeled computer suppliers purchase Sound Blaster Pros to include with their products. Figure 2.15 shows the Sound Blaster Pro card.

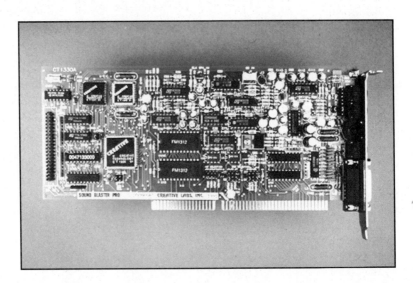

FIG. 2.15

The Sound Blaster Pro card. (*Courtesy of Creative Labs*)

Exploring Professional-Level and Special-Purpose Cards

Musicians who are accustomed to the life-like synthesized sounds of performance-grade sample-playback synthesizers will not be satisfied with the quality of the sound produced by audio cards that use FM synthesis. Although wavetable synthesis offers a substantial improvement in realism, it does not meet the standards of current sample-playback synthesizer technology. Digitally sampled instrument sounds that use longer PCM samples are "brighter" (contain more overtones) than their FM counterparts. They do a better job of duplicating the instrument's sound than wavetable devices during the attack and decay portion of the envelope, because the samples are much longer in duration and precisely follow the initial sound. Only the sustain and decay portion of the envelope is looped. Because the samples are of longer duration and because more samples (usually four to six per octave) of a single instrument are taken over its playable range than for wavetable synthesis, larger ROMs are required to store them.

> **T I P**
>
> Most professional-level sound cards do not provide compatibility with Sound Blaster cards and applications designed specifically for use with the original Sound Blaster. Sound Blaster compatibility is not required for the use of MPC-compliant audio adapter cards under Windows 3.1, either for waveform audio, synthesized sound, or MIDI operations. Sound Blaster compatibility is needed only to enable the audio adapter card to be compatible with the multitude of computer game applications that were written specifically for the Sound Blaster. As more computer games are created to take advantage of the multimedia extensions of Windows 3.1, compatibility with Sound Blaster cards will decline in significance.

The Turtle Beach MultiSound

Turtle Beach Systems's MultiSound adapter card combines high-precision 16-bit stereo sampled sound recording and reproduction capability with 16-bit PCM-encoded sound synthesis derived from E-mu Systems Proteus/1 XR sound module. E-mu's Proteus series, which uses instrumental sounds created with the firm's Emulator III sampler, gained industry acclaim when it was first introduced in 1988. Since then, E-mu has added two more sound modules and a keyboard synthesizer to the Proteus product line. The commercial success of the original Proteus/1 sound module is confirmed by Microsoft's provision of a setup for it in Windows 3.1's MIDI Mapper applet.

Related Topics
E-mu E8801 SoundEngine, p. 263
Using Digital Signal Processors, p. 381

The MultiSound can play 32 simultaneous tones selected from 128 different instruments and can store a total of 384 adjustable presets that you can use to modify the voices to your taste. The general MIDI presets authored by Turtle Beach or those of the Proteus/1 XR can be selected by an applet that Turtle Beach supplies with the MultiSound. The card's sounds are exceptionally *clean*, meaning free from noise, and *dry*, meaning that no special effects are added to them. You can add two digital effects (chorus and stereo pan) by editing individual voices. Most professional users add an outboard digital effects processor to create reverberation and other modifications that affect the sound of all the voices simultaneously.

The MultiSound, shown in figure 2.16, is a full-length card with 4M of ROM to store the PCM instrument samples, a high-speed Motorola 56000 digital signal processor (DSP), and a 68000 microprocessor to control synthesis and DSP operations. A unique feature of the MultiSound is Turtle Beach's "Hurricane Technology," which shares a 32K block of your computer's RAM with the on-card microprocessor. Conventional sound cards use direct memory access (DMA) to transfer waveform audio data from the ADC and to the DAC. Processing 16-bit stereo sound with DMA at 44.1 kHz can consume virtually all your computer's processing time, slowing or halting other operations such as updating the display. The shared memory technique, also used in Turtle Beach's 56-K Digital Recording System, processes waveform audio data approximately 8 times faster than DMA. The 56-K is used by sound studios for audio CD mastering and digital audio tape (DAT) editing.

Related Topics

MIDI Effects Processors, p. 324.

FIG. 2.16

The MultiSound professional adapter card. *(Courtesy of Turtle Beach Systems)*

A simplified block diagram of the MultiSound card appears in figure 2.17. Digital signal paths are shown as solid lines; audio routing uses dotted lines.

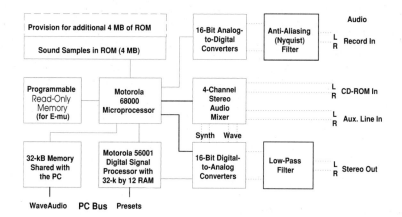

FIG. 2.17

A block diagram of the MultiSound audio adapter card.

The MultiSound's DAC features 18-bit sigma-delta conversion with 64x oversampling and an 8x interpolating filter. The result is frequency response from 0 to 19 kHz with +/– 0.5 dB with a drop-off of –3 dB at 20 kHz at a 44.1-kHz sampling rate. The signal-to-noise ratio is –89 dB (A-weighted) and –86 dB (unweighted), total harmonic distortion (THD) is < 0.01 percent (A-weighted) and < 0.02 percent (unweighted), intermodulation (IM) distortion is < 0.01 percent, and phase distortion is +/– 0.05 percent for 16-bit sampling. The meaning of these terms is explained in Chapter 13. These audio specifications, combined with high-speed digital audio processing, make the MultiSound well suited to authoring commercial CD-ROM titles. A sound engineer in a professional music studio would not hesitate to use the MultiSound's synthesized and waveform audio sound capabilities to create master recordings.

The addition of a digital signal processing chip, together with on-board RAM, provides the MultiSound card with another unique feature that offsets its comparatively high price: software upgradability. Digital audio compression and decompression techniques to reduce the enormous size of the *.WAV files required to store digital sound had not been standardized when the MultiSound was introduced and this book was written. Although the CD-ROM XA type of ADPCM is one candidate, Microsoft and others may settle on new, more efficient methods. Some audio adapter cards may become obsolete when this standardization occurs. The MultiSound's DSP can be programmed through the PC's internal bus to handle future compression/decompression techniques and to add real-time effects such as reverberation (complex echo effects) to digital audio.

The MultiSound does not have a conventional, low-level monaural microphone recording input, which is required by the MPC specification (professionals use a multichannel stereo mixer connected to the line input). On the other hand, none of the other audio cards in production in mid-1992 were capable of the "recommended" 16-bit stereo and "desired" 44.1-kHz sampling rate while consuming the "required" 15 percent or less of the processing capacity available with a 16-MHz 80386SX computer (called "bandwidth" by the specification). The MultiSound achieves this requirement by using its shared memory. The 16-bit analog-to-digital and digital-to-analog converters, together with the mixing circuitry, have the lowest signal-to-noise ratio of any of the audio adapter cards evaluated during the course of writing this book.

You don't find a CD-ROM interface connector on the MultiSound, but if you are serious about waveform audio recording, you probably want a high-performance CD-ROM drive and a fast, high-capacity hard disk drive, both connected to a dedicated SCSI interface board. Finally, no provision has been made for adding a joystick to the MultiSound. This lack is a blessing in disguise, however, because the probability is high that your PC already has a joystick adapter on its multi-I/O card, and you don't have to worry about disabling it to prevent bus address conflicts.

Related Topics
Sample-Playback Voice Editing, p. 265
MIDI Patchbays, p. 327
Editing with Turtle Beach Wave Lite and Wave for Windows, p. 395

Turtle Beach includes Wave Lite, an abbreviated version of the firm's commercial Wave for Windows waveform audio editing application, plus a synthesizer voice editor that duplicates the front panel controls of the Proteus/1 XR sound module, an audio mixer controller, MIDI Patchbay, Sound Prep (an applet for determining peak sound levels prior to recording), and a thorough diagnostic application with the MultiSound. The unique MIDI Patchbay applet enables you to customize the use of the MIDI IN, OUT, and THRU connectors of the optional MIDI breakout cables to suit your outboard MIDI gear's requirement.

If you are an audiophile or a musical purist, you are likely to be concerned less about price than quality. If so, the MultiSound is undoubtedly the audio adapter card for you.

The Roland SCC-1 Sound Card

The Roland SCC-1 GS (General Synthesizer) Sound Card was not designed to be an MPC-compliant device. It does not incorporate digitally sampled audio, an audio mixer, or a CD-ROM interface, but MIDI IN and OUT connectors are provided. If you have a Thunder Board or the original Sound Blaster, use digitally sampled audio only for voice notes or games, and have an open adapter card slot, the SCC-1 is a logical choice to upgrade your synthesized sound radically.

Roland introduced its first successor to the LAPC-1 sound card in early 1992. The sounds of the SCC-1, shown in figure 2.18, are the same as Roland's SC-55 Sound Canvas, a MIDI sound module that was the first device to employ the General Synthesizer (GS) standard for standardizing instrument sounds. Most of Roland's GS standard was incorporated into the MIDI specifications as General MIDI Mode (GMM, usually called GM) and then into the MPC specifications for synthesized sound. If you are not familiar with MIDI instrument voices and patch numbers, they are dealt with briefly in Chapter 7 and covered in detail in Chapters 9 and 10. The 16 categories of GM instrument sounds and the 8 different voices within each category are listed in Appendix C.

FIG. 2.18

The Roland SCC-1 GS Sound Card. (*Courtesy of Roland Corporation USA*)

The SCC-1's sounds have quite good realism, and it includes three programmable digital effects: reverberation, chorus, and stereo pan. One of the card's more interesting applications is as a voice doubler in conjunction with a Turtle Beach MultiSound card, an Advanced Gravis UltraSound card, or even a board with a Yamaha OPL-III. The Multi-Sound's tones, for instance, are pure samples (musicians call them "dry"), and the SCC-1's are rounder and more full-bodied and include default reverberation (they are "wet"). You can combine related sounds from both cards by plugging the output of the SCC-1 into the line input of the MultiSound, UltraSound, or Pro Audio Spectrum Plus to mix ("layer") the outputs of the two cards. The resulting sound rivals that of synthesizers costing more than twice as much as the price of the two cards.

Related Topics
Layering Synthesized Sounds, p. 266

Related Topics
Making MIDI Interconnec-
tions, p. 280

Connecting Other Devices to the Card

Audio adapter cards use a variety of methods to make the connections to external devices—MIDI components and CD-ROM drives—required by the MPC specification. Some cards include the MIDI connectors and the CD-ROM drive interface in the standard version; others offer one or both as options. Specialized cards, such as the SCC-1 and MultiSound, do not offer CD-ROM connections—you must use a separate SCSI interface card to add a CD-ROM drive. The sections that follow explain how connections are made to extend devices from your adapter card.

Using MIDI Connectors and Breakout Boxes

The MPC specification requires that audio cards provide MIDI I/O capability, which means that both MIDI IN and MIDI OUT connectors must be provided. The MIDI IN connector receives signals from instruments, such as MIDI keyboards, guitar pickups, or breath-activated instruments for recording live performances. The MIDI OUT connector sends similar signals to external sound modules, digital effects processors, and drum machines. Some breakout boxes include a MIDI THRU connector that is connected to the MIDI IN port. If you connect a keyboard to the MIDI IN port, you can use an external sound module connected to the MIDI THRU port to create the piano sounds. Computer MIDI THRU connectors are not often used, so the absence of one is not likely to cause you a problem.

Standard MIDI cables have five-pin DIN plugs on both ends, the same connectors used by standard PC keyboards. DIN is an acronym for the Deutches Institut fur Normalization, the German standards organization that established the specification for the connectors. Unfortunately, the diameter of standard MIDI DIN plugs exceeds the width of the adapter card access slots in PCs, so the cables cannot be plugged directly into receptacles mounted directly on audio adapter cards. This situation has led to a variety of methods for making MIDI connections.

The most common MIDI connection method is to provide a connector to the standard 15-pin joystick with three cables: two cables with MIDI IN and MIDI OUT receptacles, and one to connect the joystick. These connectors are called MIDI breakout boxes because early versions were enclosed in a metal box; they are better termed *breakout cables*. Some cards, such as the Roland SCC-1, include adapter cables with mini-DIN connectors to make the transition to the larger standard size. If you plan on using MIDI equipment, bear in mind that the MIDI connectors are an extra-cost option for some boards and not for others. As an example, the Sound Blaster Pro includes a MIDI breakout box, but the Sound Blaster Pro Basic does not.

Industry sources report that as of late 1991, a total of about 10 million MIDI-equipped keyboard synthesizers had been sold in North America. Many of the Casio keyboards sold in chain stores such as Price Club and Wal-Mart have MIDI input and output connectors, as do most consumer-level Yamaha models. Newer electronic organs and pianos include MIDI I/O capability, and some offer exceptional sound quality. If you own any instrument with MIDI connectors, all you need in order to connect it to your sound card is one or two MIDI cables plus, of course, the breakout box or its equivalent. Look for round, 5-pin connectors labeled MIDI IN and MIDI OUT on the keyboard's back panel. Figure 2.19 shows how you connect an external (often called *outboard*) keyboard synthesizer to your audio adapter card.

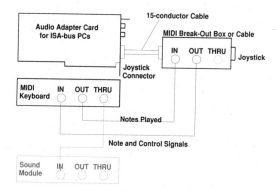

FIG. 2.19

Making MIDI connections to a keyboard synthesizer and sound module.

Your MIDI-equipped keyboard synthesizer can perform two functions: send MIDI messages for the notes you play on the keyboard, and receive MIDI signals from the card to play computer-generated music. If you have only one MIDI device, buy two MIDI cables. All you need to know about MIDI cabling in this case is that MIDI IN is always connected to MIDI OUT, and vice versa.

As mentioned previously, some MIDI breakout boxes and most keyboards and sound modules provide a MIDI THRU connector. MIDI THRU is connected directly to MIDI IN to enable the daisy-chaining of additional MIDI sound modules and accessories. *Daisy-chaining* means that you cable MIDI THRU to the MIDI IN connector of the next module in line, as shown in figure 2.19. The practical limit of the number of modules you can daisy-chain is five or six.

T I P   You need a Windows sequencer application if you want to record your keyboard performances as MIDI files. Media Player, the multimedia applet supplied with Windows 3.1 (and Windows 3.0 with Multimedia) for MIDI can play standard MIDI files (*.MID) but cannot record them. Most MPC audio adapter cards come with a DOS sequencer application, such as a derivative of Voyetra's Sequencer Plus, or provide one with their optional MIDI adapter kits. At the time this book was written, few MPC cards included Windows-compatible sequencer applications, but this situation will change with time. If you are addicted to Windows, you will not be satisfied with a DOS sequencer, and purchasing a Windows-based sequencer may set you back $100 or so. Check the software supplied with the card you intend to purchase to see whether a Windows-compatible sequencer application, such as Passport's Trax, is included. Typical MIDI sequencers for Windows are described in Chapter 12, "MIDI Applications for Windows."

When you use the Media Player 1.0 applet to play one of the MIDI files supplied with Windows through your outboard (external) synthesizer, you will probably hear some strange sounds. The General MIDI Mode (GMM or GM) standard is relatively new, and few keyboard synthesizers supported it when Windows 3.1 was released. Media Player 1.0 expects your synthesizer to adhere to the GM standards for instrument voices or else a MIDI map that converts the GM instrument voice numbers to those used by your synthesizer. Creating the required MIDI map for non-GM synthesizers is covered in Chapter 7.

T I P   Contact the manufacturer of your synthesizer or sound module to see whether a chart is available that translates the names the manufacturer assigned to voices to those used by the General MIDI standard, or to see whether a floppy disk with a MIDI map file for your synthesizer model is offered. Some manufacturers use creative (incomprehensible) voice names—"Scuzzam" for example—that are difficult to translate to those of the standard GM voice list listed in Appendix C. You also may find MIDI map files for popular synthesizer families in CompuServe's WINADV or MIDI forums. Make sure that you save a backup copy of the existing MIDIMAP.CFG file in your \WINDOWS\SYSTEM directory, and better yet on floppy disk, before you copy over it. If you don't, you lose any prior setups you might have created when you installed the new MIDI map file. Chapter 7 explains this procedure in detail.

Using the CD-ROM Drive Interface

Most CD-ROM drives use a Small Computer System Interface (SCSI, pro-nounced "scuzzy"). Some MPC audio adapter cards include a SCSI interface dedicated to the CD-ROM drive; others use a plug-in daughterboard sold as an option. A *dedicated* interface is one to which you cannot connect other SCSI-compatible devices, such as hard disks or scanners. A few cards, in-cluding the Sound Blaster Pro, incorporate a *proprietary* CD-ROM interface, which means that you must use a drive produced by a single manufacturer (and sometimes a limited range of models) or install another adapter card if you add a CD-ROM drive from a different supplier. An in-depth description of CD-ROM interfaces is provided in Chapter 3.

Connections from MPC audio adapter cards to internal CD-ROM drives are made by two sets of cables: one with 50 pins for digital data and control signals, and another with 6 pins for analog signals of audio CDs. Ribbon cables from these connectors, called *headers*, lead to mating connectors on the CD-ROM drive.

Related Topics
Using CD-ROM Adapter
Cards, p. 106

> A 4-pin receptacle attached to wires leading from your computer's power supply provides the +5-volt and +24-volt power required by the drive. If you do not have a spare power supply cable, you need to purchase a Y-connector (one power plug to two receptacles) from your dealer.
>
> **T I P**

Adding a Joystick

Joysticks are used principally in conjunction with computer games. The multimedia extensions supplied with Windows 3.1 do not include the joystick functions provided by Windows with Multimedia, nor was the joystick used as an input device by any multimedia applications for Win-dows at the time this book was written. The joystick interface is of inter-est to you only if you are a computer game enthusiast.

T I P Most input/output boards for the PC include a joystick port in addition to a printer port and two serial I/O ports (COM1 and COM2). The joystick port on audio adapter cards and on multi-I/O cards is located at the same device address. This design is likely to cause both joystick ports to be inoperative. In this case, you need to disable the joystick port of your multi-I/O card by changing the position of or removing a jumper. (Most audio adapter cards do not enable you to disable their joystick port.) Refer to your multi-I/O card documentation to find the correct jumper.

Choosing the Audio Card That Is Right for You

As with most other things in life, you get what you pay for in audio adapter cards. If you're a musician, you want the best synthesized sound you can get and probably are not too concerned with digitally sampled audio quality. On the other hand, if you are into creating your own instrument samples and plan to buy one of the high-performance CD-ROM drives described in Chapter 3 that provide 16-bit stereo digital signals from the audio CDs on which samples are recorded, you want 16-bit, 44.1-kHz stereo from your sound card (and a large disk drive).

If you're a producer of multimedia titles, you want the best sampled audio quality available (16-bit stereo at 44.1 kHz). You don't need to worry about synthesized sound quality for MIDI files, if these are included in the title, because quality is determined by the synthesizer on the board that ultimately reproduces it. If you plan on creating your own MIDI music that will be supplied on CD-ROM in the form of waveform audio files, however, you probably want to choose a Turtle Beach MultiSound and perhaps a Roland SCC-1 to accompany it.

If you have a laptop computer, you probably want or need to use Media Vision's Audioport, which plugs into the printer port and has a small speaker and microphone built in. Finally, if your interest is primarily in sound for games, a Sound Blaster, Sound Blaster Pro Basic, or Media Vision Pro AudioSpectrum Plus card may satisfy your requirement.

The cards whose detailed specifications are compared in the tables that follow—Pro AudioSpectrum 16, UltraSound, and Sound Blaster Pro—were chosen to demonstrate differences among three manufacturers' approaches to meeting the rather vague MPC standards for extended-level audio adapter cards. Technically, any card labeled with the MPC trademark must include MIDI IN and MIDI OUT ports but need not include a CD-ROM drive interface. (The reason is that an MPC upgrade kit might use a separate CD-ROM adapter card, or an MPC computer could have the CD-ROM interface on its motherboard.)

Being able to compare the sounds of several cards through a single set of speakers in one session in a dealer's showroom would be helpful. This comparison may be possible at the computer superstores of the future, but for now, you may have to settle for reading the specs and listening to your candidates for purchase in serial mode. Have the dealer play a MIDI composition that includes piano, guitar, and percussion sounds. You will find the greatest differences between FM and sampled sound with these instruments. Turtle Beach Systems offers an audio CD to show off the sounds of its professional-quality MultiSound card. Perhaps other manufacturers will follow Turtle Beach's lead.

If you don't plan to use MIDI gear, you can save money by purchasing a card without the MIDI breakout box. On the other hand, Media Vision supplies Passport's Trax sequencer for Windows with its MIDI Mate breakout box, which saves you the cost of purchasing a commercial sequencer for use under Windows. Most other cards came only with a DOS-based sequencing application at the time this book was written.

A Caveat for Studying Sound Card Specifications

Multimedia is a dynamic industry. Suppliers of audio adapter cards have contributed to the dynamism by upgrading current models, creating new ones, and discontinuing the old versions at a rapid pace. Major changes occurred in Media Vision's product line while this book was being written, and Creative Labs upgraded its Sound Blaster Pro from the old Yamaha YM3812 to the new YM262 chips in April 1992. New manufacturers of sound cards appear almost monthly, and many manufacturers of MPC-compatible producers plan to add sound to the motherboard, eliminating the necessity for a sound card.

The collection of applications included with audio adapter cards also is a moving target. The majority of the applications supplied with sound cards at the time this book was written were designed for use under DOS. As the number of installed copies of Windows 3.1 increases, manufacturers will add Windows versions of sequencers, text-to-voice converters, and related audio software. The content of the floppy disk may change faster than the artwork on the box, so check the documentation included with the card to determine the type of applications included before you decide on a specific product.

The comparative specifications in the sections that follow were provided to the three manufacturers for review prior to publication and reflect the products in production when this book went to press. To quote their data sheets, however, "Specifications are subject to change without notice." The best approach is to obtain the latest copy of the manufacturer's specifications and then make sure that you purchase a current version of the sound card that reflects them.

Related Topics

Types of Musical Synthesizers, p. 248

Considering Synthesized Music and Sound Effects

Many users will find the synthesized sound portion of the card to be of the most importance. The reason is that the standard MIDI files, in which musical compositions are stored in the form of codes for notes and other events, are much smaller (usually by a factor of 100 or more) than the same tune recorded using digitally sampled audio. The specifications for the synthesized sound section of three typical MPC-compliant sound cards are listed in table 2.1.

Table 2.1. Comparing Synthesized Sound Specifications for Three MPC-Compatible Sound Cards.

Synthesized Sound Specification	Pro Audio-Spectrum 16	UltraSound	Sound Blaster Pro
Sound synthesis type	FM, Yamaha OPL-III	Sampled, wavetable	FM, Yamaha OPL-III
Sound synthesizer chip	1 Stereo, YM262	1 Stereo, Ensoniq DOC II	1 Stereo, YM262
Stereo voices	20	16	20
Mono voices	20	32	20
FM synthesis operators	4	N/A	4
FM synthesis algorithms	4	N/A	4
FM waveform types	8	N/A	8
DAC resolution	16 bits	16 bits	16 bits
Synthesis dynamic range	96 dB	96 dB	96 dB
Signal-to-noise ratio	86 dB	80 dB	86 dB

Synthesized Sound Specification	Pro Audio-Spectrum 16	UltraSound	Sound Blaster Pro
Ad Lib compatibility (for DOS game sounds)	Yes	Yes	Yes
Power-on default mode	Stereo	Stereo	Monoaural

The most important difference in synthesized sound specifications is the method of implementing the sound—digital FM or instrument samples. The UltraSound card provides wavetable samples at moderate cost, and Turtle Beach's MultiSound uses the full 16-bit PCM samples from E-mu's Proteus-series professional-quality sound modules. The Pro AudioSpectrum series and newer Sound Blaster Pro use the Yamaha YM262 4-operator stereo FM synthesis chip, part of the Yamaha OPL-III chipset. The Turtle Beach MultiSound card is not included in the comparison because it is in a totally different league, both in quality and price, than the moderate-cost cards shown in the table. The Roland SCC-1 GS Sound Card is omitted also because it is not MPC-compliant (it lacks waveform audio capabilities and an audio mixer).

> Audio adapter cards that use the Yamaha YM262 stereo synthesizer chip enable individual voices to simulate origin at the left, right, or center. In contrast, YM3812-equipped boards have one synthesis chip devoted to each stereo channel. You must use two voices (one for each channel) at the same sound level to simulate sound emerging from the centerpoint of the two speakers. This approach reduces the effective number of true stereo voices to 11 for the original Sound Blaster Pro card but not for those produced after March 1992. Some MPC computer suppliers continue to use YM38125 because they are lower in cost than the YM262.
>
> **T I P**

Considering Sampled Audio Sound

The principal differences among the sampled audio recording and playback functions of MPC audio adapter cards are sample resolution and maximum sampling rate. For all but professional-quality sound intended for the production of CD-ROM titles or commercial desktop video productions, 8-bit samples at 22.05 kHz are adequate. Many commercial CD-ROM titles, such as Dr. T's Composer Quest, use audio files recorded in this format. 8-bit, 22.05-kHz samples consume one-quarter the disk space of 44.1-kHz, 16-bit audio-CD-quality sound. All MPC-compliant sound cards now offer stereo recording and playback capability, although not a requirement of the MPC specification. Table 2.2 lists the sampled sound recording and playback specifications for the same three cards compared in table 2.1. ADPCM sound compression is discussed in Chapter 13.

Table 2.2. Comparing Digitally Sampled Sound Specifications for Three MPC-Compatible Sound Cards.

Digital (Sampled) Sound Specification	Pro Audio-Spectrum 16	UltraSound	Sound Blaster Pro
Sampling input/output channels	2	2	2
Playback resolution	16 bits	16 bits	8 bits
Record resolution	16 bits	8 bits (16 opt.)	8 bits
Theoretical dynamic range	96 dB	96 dB	48 dB
Sampling data formats	PCM and ADPCM	PCM and ADPCM	PCM and ADPCM
Compatibility with 16-bit PCM files	Yes	Playback only (Record optional)	No
Maximum stereo sampling rate	44.1 kHz	44.1 kHz	22.05 kHz
Hardware ADPCM compression/decompression ratio(s)	2:1, 3:1, 4:1	2:1, 3:1, 4:1	2:1, 3:1, 4:1
Digital audio DMA channel(s)	0, 1, 3, 5, 6, or 7	0, 1, or 3	0, 1, or 3
Selectable interrupts, IRQ	2, 5, 7, 10, 12, and 15	2, 5, 7, 10 12, and 15	2, 5, 7, or 10

Considering Audio Mixer Capabilities

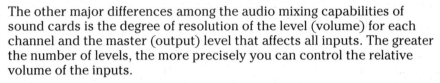

Related Topics
Using the Analog Audio
Mixer, p. 418

The published specifications for the audio mixers of all MPC-compliant audio adapter cards are quite similar. Each includes stereo inputs for an internal CD-ROM drive, synthesized sound, sampled audio, and an auxiliary line input. The line input can be used for the audio output (headphone jack) of external CD-ROM drives, other sound cards, a VCR, a multichannel mixer, or an audio tape recorder. The circuitry employed in the audio mixer and its capability to combine and route analog audio signals, however, varies widely among manufacturers.

The other major differences among the audio mixing capabilities of sound cards is the degree of resolution of the level (volume) for each channel and the master (output) level that affects all inputs. The greater the number of levels, the more precisely you can control the relative volume of the inputs.

Another factor that you should consider is noise and distortion introduced by the mixer section of the board. Noise is determined by component layout and the number of layers used in the manufacture of the board. High-quality boards have an audio ground plane layer that reduces mixer-induced noise by shielding the audio from the digital circuits. This method is similar to the shield (a braided wire or foil conductor wrapped around the signal conductor) used in audio cabling. Only a few firms publish the intermodulation (IM) distortion values for their audio mixers. As with stereo sound system components, the lower the IM distortion, the better the resulting sound.

Audio mixer capabilities for the three selected cards are listed in table 2.3.

Table 2.3. Comparing Audio Mixer and Output Specifications for Three MPC-Compatible Sound Cards.

Analog Audio Mixer Specification	Pro Audio-Spectrum 16	UltraSound	Sound Blaster Pro
Stereo mixer inputs		4	4
Mono mixer inputs		1	2 (mic and speaker)
Sources that can be recorded simultaneously	CD audio, mic, and line in	Not specified	1 input
Volume control resolution on input sources	13 levels	Not specified	8 levels

continues

Table 2.3. Continued

Analog Audio Mixer Specification	Pro Audio-Spectrum 16	UltraSound	Sound Blaster Pro
Programmable output volume control	62 levels	Not specified	8 levels
Programmable output tone control	Yes	No	No
Microphone input gain control	Automatic (AGC)	Automatic (AGC)	Automatic (AGC)
Total harmonic distortion (THD) of mixer	0.14%		0.46%
Stereo output power, watts into ohms (4Ω)	4 (RMS) into 4Ω	2 (RMS)	4 (RMS) into 4Ω

Considering MIDI Specifications

The Musical Instrument Digital Interface specification is an industry standard (refer to Chapter 10). Thus, MIDI implementation is similar for all MPC-compliant audio adapter cards. The basic difference among the cards is whether the MIDI connectors are included with the card or must be purchased as an option. The Sound Blaster Pro, for instance, includes a MIDI breakout cable that also provides a joystick connector, but the Sound Blaster Pro Basic does not. Most MIDI cable sets provide only MIDI IN and MIDI OUT connectors; the MIDI THRU connector is omitted. As mentioned previously, the MIDI THRU connector at the controller end of the MIDI chain is seldom used, so this omission is not likely to be significant. MIDI capabilities for the three cards are listed in table 2.4.

Table 2.4. Comparing MIDI Input/Output Specifications for Three MPC-Compatible Sound Cards.

MIDI Input/Output Specification	Pro Audio-Spectrum 16	UltraSound	Sound Blaster Pro
MIDI IN, OUT, and THRU connectors	MIDI Mate optional, 2 MIDI OUTs	Optional connector	Adapter included (except SB Pro Basic)

MIDI Input/Output Specification	Pro Audio-Spectrum 16	UltraSound	Sound Blaster Pro
Simultaneous MIDI IN and OUT operation	Yes	Not specified	No
MPU-401 compatibility	Yes (after 8/92)	No	Yes (after 9/92)

Considering CD-ROM Interface, Joystick Port, and Optional Modules

Technically, audio adapter cards do not require an on-board CD-ROM drive interface to make them MPC-compliant because a separate SCSI or proprietary interface card can be provided with the CD-ROM drive. This approach is taken by Turtle Beach Systems for its MultiSound card. The advantage of an on-board or daughterboard interface is that it saves a precious adapter card slot. Some audio adapter cards use an optional daughterboard for the CD-ROM drive interface to reduce the manufacturing cost of the basic card. If you purchase a separate internal or external CD-ROM drive, it usually includes its own interface card. The SCSI interface is the industry standard for CD-ROM drives and is used by the majority of their manufacturers. If you purchase a card with a proprietary interface, you are limited in your choice of drives if you don't want to sacrifice an adapter card slot.

Specifications for the CD-ROM interface, joystick port, and other optional modules are listed in table 2.5. If you plan to use a joystick with a fast computer such as a 50-MHz 80486, speed compensation of the joystick port may be important. The Advanced Gravis UltraSound is the only card that offered joystick port speed compensation at the time this book was written.

Table 2.5. Comparing CD-ROM, Joystick Port, and Optional Specifications for Three MPC-Compatible Sound Cards.

CD-ROM Interface, Joystick, and Optional Specifications	Pro Audio-Spectrum 16	UltraSound	Sound Blaster Pro
CD-ROM drive interface type	SCSI included	Optional SCSI	Proprietary, Matsushita

continues

Table 2.5. Continued

CD-ROM Interface, Joystick, and Optional Specifications	Pro Audio-Spectrum 16	UltraSound	Sound Blaster Pro
CD-ROM DMA channel	1 or 3	Not specified	1 or 3
Joystick support	Yes	2 (Y-cable optional)	2 (Y-cable optional)
Joystick speed compensation for fast PCs	No	Yes	No
Additional, optional modules supported	MIDI Mate breakout box	CD-ROM interface, 16-bit recording, additional memory	None

Chapter Summary

The purpose of this chapter was to provide you with the basic information you need in order to choose your first MPC audio adapter card or to select a replacement or an additional card with better sound quality. Although the term MPC was used to describe the new breed of audio adapter cards produced since the release of Windows 3.1, technically a sound card by itself does not qualify for MPC labeling. Only upgrade kits, which consist of a sound card and a CD-ROM drive, computers that include the equivalent of an upgrade kit, and MPC-compliant Windows applications can be labeled with the Multimedia Marketing Committee's logo. Because most manufacturers of audio adapter cards also produce MPC upgrade kits, you can be assured that cards produced by upgrade kit suppliers will meet or exceed the MPC Specification 1.0's audio standards.

After you have acquired a new sound card, you need to know how to install it. The content and the quality of the documentation supplied with audio adapter cards varies widely from manufacturer to manufacturer. Thus, a set of generic steps to install these cards as well as CD-ROM drives follows in Chapter 4. Chapters 6 and 7 explain the basics of using your card with waveform audio and MIDI files.

Understanding CD-ROM Drives and Adapters

Producers of CD-ROM drives have created their own Tower of Babel to describe the various formats accommodated by their equipment. Terms, acronyms, and abbreviations applicable to CD-ROMs abound but are seldom explained when they are used. Red-Book Audio, ISO-9660, CD+Graphics, CD-ROM XA, Karaoke, and CD-DA are just a few of the codes used to describe the various formats in which CD-ROMs are published. This chapter begins by exploring the history of the CD-ROM drive and moves on to explain CD-ROM terminology, standards, and the functions implemented by the various types of drives available today. You also learn about some alternative laserdisc formats.

Unless you decide to purchase one of the professional-quality audio boards, a CD-ROM drive is likely to be the highest-cost element in your multimedia upgrade. You do not need a CD-ROM drive to use any of the sound capabilities of Windows 3.1 with your audio adapter card. But after you have added a sound card to your computer, you probably will want to experience a commercial multimedia title like Microsoft's Multimedia Beethoven-The Ninth Symphony. When you finish reading this chapter, you can make an informed decision before you commit to purchasing a particular type and brand of CD-ROM drive.

Tracking the History of the CD-ROM

A Dutch company, Philips N.V. of Eindhoven, is responsible for the basic technology for storing images, sound, and text in disc form and owns most of the patents covering the technology's implementation. Philips was founded by Gerard Philips, a mechanical engineer, and his father Frederick, a banker, in 1891 to produce carbon-filament lamp bulbs. Today, Philips establishes the standards for CD formats and also licenses the technology to others. With typical Dutch pragmatism, Philips joined with Sony Corporation of Japan in creating many of its standards to make sure that they would enjoy worldwide acceptance. Philips, by the way, also developed the compact cassette that gave birth to the consumer audio tape industry, and the company is the world's largest manufacturer of television sets.

Introducing the Laserdisc

CD-ROMs are members of the laserdisc family, first implemented by Philips in the form of 12-inch LaserVision discs in 1974. All laserdiscs use a semiconductor laser and a photoreceptor to read data in the form of minute pits in the surface of a highly reflective disc, as shown in figure 3.1. The laser, an acronym for *light amplification by the stimulated emission of radiation*, creates a beam of coherent light aimed at a reflective surface located at the top of the disc. *Coherent* means that the light waves are highly organized, not the random jumble of waves emitted, for instance, by a light bulb. The light reflected by the pits interferes with the light reflected by the normal surface of the disc. The interference is detected by a photosensitive component, which converts the light signals into binary bits. The size of the pits is exceedingly small—30 pits equal the diameter of a human hair—and about 2 billion pits are on a typical audio CD. All the dimensions in figure 3.1 are in micrometers (mm). A micrometer is equal to one thousandth of a millimeter. To put things into perspective for you, a human hair has a diameter of about 50mm.

Philips's LaserVision discs, used principally for motion picture and performing arts recordings, provided higher-quality video and audio reproduction than was available at the time on consumer videocassette recorders. LaserVision was the foundation for the more common eight-inch platters used by today's consumer videodisc players. Laserdisc and videodisc players are a significant element of the Multimedia PC picture because Microsoft has provided a driver with the Multimedia Extensions that controls the Pioneer LD-V4000 laserdisc player so that you can view "laserdisc video in a window" if you have the required video adapter card. The laserdisc drives play both LaserVision and audio CDs; videodisc players accommodate only LaserVision CDs. Digital video technology for the MPC is covered in Chapter 19.

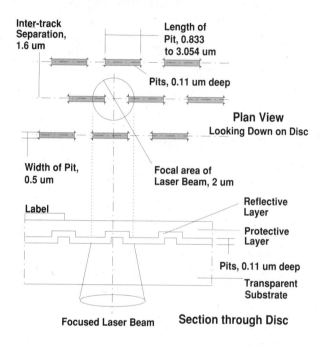

FIG. 3.1

Key elements in a laserdisc reproduction system.

The lens that focuses the laser beam of many CD-ROM and audio CD drives has a tendency to accumulate dirt on its surface over time. "Sealed" drives with "self-cleaning" lenses are becoming more common, but the mechanism that cleans the lens is not necessarily 100 percent effective. Dirt on the lens surface is evidenced by erratic data from the CD-ROM drive and sometimes the incapability to read file-directory entries. Lens-cleaning kits for CD drives are available at a moderate cost from most consumer electronics retailers. You should use a lens-cleaning kit every month or so if you're using a conventional drive and every six months with a self-cleaning drive.

T I P

Achieving Commercial Success with Audio CDs

The next development leading to the CD-ROM was the introduction of the Compact Disc Digital Audio (CD-DA) by Philips and Sony in 1982. CD-DA audio signals are digitally encoded on a 120mm-diameter (about 4 3/4-inch) laser disc. CD-DA discs and players brought a new level of realism to audio reproduction. CD-DA uses the same pulse-code modulation (PCM) sampling and playback techniques employed by audio adapter cards, but the data is stored in a format quite different from WAV files. CD-DA uses a fixed sampling rate of 44.1 kHz and 16-bit stereo samples, while waveform audio offers a choice of sampling rates and resolutions. A standard CD-DA disc plays up to about 1 hour of high-fidelity stereo sound.

Compact Disc Video (CD-V) is a recent and related development, combining laserdisc analog video and CD-DA digital audio on 120mm CD discs (called *singles*). CD-V players handle this new compact format plus longer-playing 8-inch and 12-inch *albums* that use the same encoding methods.

The only serious competition to CD-DA technology is Digital Audio Tape (DAT). DAT offers the highest-fidelity sound you can presently record with a consumer-oriented audio component. DAT uses a helical-scan (rotating) recording-reproducing head similar to that employed in VCRs. Like video and audio cassettes, however, DAT duplication is a major problem because the duplicated tapes must be mounted on a drive and hundreds of feet of tape must pass by the recording head during the tapes creation. This process takes a substantial period of time, even when high-speed duplication techniques are used. CD-DA discs, on the other hand, are "stamped" with specialized equipment, using techniques reminiscent of those employed to create the now almost obsolete vinyl records. Thus, DAT, as a consumer audio distribution medium, cannot compete with the low cost of CD-DA production.

Creating Compact Discs that Store Data

CD-ROMs, based on CD-DA formats and production technology, were introduced by Philips in 1983 and were originally intended as a mass-storage medium for personal computers. Instead of recording 16-bit audio samples on the disc, CD-ROMs record standard 8-bit bytes in file formats similar to those used by floppy and hard data disks. Prior to 1991, virtually all CD-ROMs were devoted to encyclopedic and bibliographic titles such as full-text reproductions of books and periodicals, plus large databases of scientific bibliographies, names and addresses, and the like. The data on early CD-ROMs consisted only of text. As an example, NYNEX, one of the Baby Bells, originally supplied the entire collection of telephone directories in its service area on CD-ROMs; NYNEX is now expanding the coverage to the entire U.S. Other firms produce the equivalent of the *Yellow Pages* in electronic form, and several have created titles consisting of gigantic mailing lists of businesses.

Frost & Sullivan, a major market-research firm, reported that more than 1.4 million copies of CD-ROM database titles were sold in 1991, with a combined retail value of $217 million. A quick calculation shows that the average price of these titles is about $155; some cost as much as $2,000 each. Thus, the majority of purchasers of database titles have been businesses, libraries, and research institutions.

Adding Graphics and Sound to CD-ROMs

Not long after the first CD-ROMs were issued, it became evident that a combination of text and graphic images could be used to create products that would appeal to consumers and thus expand the market for CD-ROM publications. Because the recording format for CDAudio was well established, sound could be added to enhance the presentation. Thus the de facto CD+Graphics format was established, providing still images stored in files on the disc. The first use of CD+Graphics was with Commodore Amiga and Apple Macintosh computers, the early leaders in computer-based multimedia applications.

Not to be outdone by Commodore and Apple, Microsoft Corporation launched the first worldwide CD-ROM conference in 1984, emphasizing that DOS-based personal computers could participate in this emerging technology for sound and graphics on CD-ROMs, too. Until the advent of Windows 3.0 in May 1990, however, PCs were used primarily with text-based CD-ROMs. Macs and Amigas, with a multitude of graphics and sound applications written for them, continued to dominate the fledgling CD-ROM multimedia industry. The tide is expected to turn to the PC, now that Windows 3.1 includes multimedia capabilities.

One problem with the CD+Graphics format was that separate tracks were required for audio and graphics or text. CD-DA is a data-intensive process—that is, a great deal of computer-processing time is required to create sound from waveform audio files. CD-ROM drives are not known for their speed; most of them take 20 or more times the interval required by today's hard disks to access a file or track randomly. Thus, techniques such as temporarily uploading graphic images to the hard disk were required to back an image with the appropriate sounds. In 1989, Microsoft, Sony, and Philips combined their technical teams to create the CD-ROM XA standard that enables audio, text, and graphic images to

be interleaved within a single file and thus synchronized in their reproduction. At the same time, the companies adopted the adaptive differential pulse-code modulation (ADPCM) technique to encode waveform
audio signals. ADPCM requires much less storage space than PCM to
achieve equivalent fidelity.

New and different techniques for using CD-ROMs in multimedia applications appear frequently. Kodak's Photo CD product line enables
photofinishers to develop 35mm snapshots as slides, prints, and discs.
Intel's Digital Video Interleaved (DVI) technology promises full-screen,
full-motion video and high-fidelity audio, stored in a proprietary, compressed file format on CD-ROMs. Philips CD-Interactive (CD-I) players,
designed principally for the consumer market, extend CD-ROM XA technology to the mass markets. The balance of this chapter is devoted to
explaining the similarities and differences among these formats and
describing the drives required to play discs of each format.

Examining the Types of CD-ROM Drives and How They Work

CD-ROM drives and the specifications for the media with which they are
compatible are "color-coded" by the hue of the covers of the Philips
publications that delineate their formats. Some of these publications are
more than a foot thick. The four industry-standard Philips-Sony formats
that apply to consumer and computer-based CD-ROM players are described briefly in the following paragraphs:

- *Red-Book* Audio is the standard specification for consumer
  CD-Digital Audio (CD-DA or CDAudio) and is the basis for all
  subsequent CD encoding techniques. It has been adopted as an
  international standard, IEC 908, maintained by the International
  Electrotechnical Commission. The MPC specification requires that
  CD-ROM drives have CD-DA outputs and be capable of mode 1
  operation on subchannel Q. Mode 2 and forms 1 and 2 are optional,
  as is subchannel P and R through W capability. These terms are
  explained in this chapter's subsequent section on "Defining the
  CD-ROM Modes, Forms, and Subchannels."

- *Yellow-Book* CD-ROMs are capable of storing data in the form of
  files that can be translated to conventional DOS, Macintosh, or
  Amiga file structures. The translation is accomplished by a driver,
  such as Microsoft's MSCDEX.EXE for DOS-based computers. ISO
  9660, another international standard maintained by the United
  Nations International Standards Organization, is based on the

recommendations of the "High Sierra" group and provides a uniform set of table of content and directory structures. ISO 10149 defines the characteristics of CD-ROM data, such as the format of the data tracks, error-detection codes (EDC), and error-correction codes (ECC). Most Yellow-Book drives have stereo audio outputs, are capable of playing CD-DA discs, and are equipped with headphone jacks.

■ *Green-Book* CD-Interactive (CD-I) devices use an extended version of the CD-ROM XA format that does not have its own color. Chartreuse might be appropriate, however, because CD-ROM XA combines most of the Green-Book with the Yellow-Book specifications. Green-Book drives can read CD-DA, CD-ROM, CD-ROM XA, CD-I, and Kodak Photo CD discs.

■ *Orange-Book* drives are capable of being written by suitable drives. Orange-Book 1 drives are erasable and rewritable. These drives use magneto-optic technology and are designated CD-MO. Orange-Book 2 drives use CD-ROMs that have a specific type of surface designed for write-once operations—thus the abbreviation CD-WO or WORM for Write Once, Read Many. The Rock Ridge extensions propose an updatable directory structure to supplement the ISO 9660 standard. Kodak Photo CD-ROMs are a variant of Orange-Book 2; Photo CDs enable more than one write operation (called *multiple sessions*), but data can be added only to an unfilled disc. CD-ROM XA drives must support mode 2 format to be able to read Photo CD multiple-session files. You cannot reuse CD-WO or Photo CD ROMs by writing over their prior content.

In the following sections, you learn more about these various types of CD-ROM drives.

Consumer Audio CD Drives

Audio compact disc players were introduced by Philips in 1982 and have enjoyed phenomenal market acceptance. By the end of 1991, more than 100 million consumer CD audio players were estimated to be in use worldwide. You can purchase a simple CD-DA player for about $100, or you can spend over $1,000 on the more stylish variety. Unless you have very good hearing, discerning the difference between these players is difficult when they're playing through the same sound system.

Unfortunately, you cannot use your home CD-DA player, or any other audio CD or consumer CD-I player on the market as of mid-1992, to play multimedia CD-ROMs. The CD-DA digital interface (a connector to your computer) is missing. On the other hand, most CD-ROM drives have standard stereo audio output jacks, as well as a headphone jack and volume control, so you can listen to your audio CDs when you are not playing multimedia titles. You can, however, connect the audio output of an audio CD player to the line input of the analog audio mixer and record the sound in a waveform audio file.

A characteristic common to consumer audio CD players and CD-ROM drives is the use of *Constant Linear Velocity* (CLV) recording techniques. CLV means that the point on the CD media passes the read head assembly (which contains the laser and photoreceptor) at a constant rate. The rotational speed (rpm) of the spindle drive motor therefore must be varied at a rate inversely proportional to the distance of the point being read from the centerline of the spindle. For CDs, the spindle speed is automatically varied from 200 rpm when reading at the outside to 530 rpm at the inside of the disc to give a reading rate of 75 sectors per second.

Standard audio CDs have a maximum playing time of 74 minutes, 33 seconds—about the length of Beethoven's Ninth Symphony. Most CD-DA players now enable you to play 3-inch "single" audio CDs as well as the standard 5-inch size labeled "albums." Sony uses the 3-inch variety (CD-3) as the media for its portable Data Discman CD-ROM drive.

Using Standard CD-ROM Drives

Virtually all CD-ROM drives included in the MPC upgrade kits available at the time this book was written are "plain-vanilla" products capable of reading-only standard Yellow-Book files and playing only Red-Book CD-DA audio. CD-ROM XA-compatible drives, the subject of the subsequent section on "Using Photo CD and CD-ROM XA Extended Architecture Drives," began to appear in quantity in late 1992. Some manufacturers have labeled their MPC products "XA-ready" but have failed to define just how ready they really are, and when whatever might be required to add extended architecture to these products will be available. Some may require a trip to a local service center to have new printed circuit boards installed or old ones replaced. Extended architecture capability is a *requirement* if you want to be able to view Kodak Photo CDs or play CD-I discs with your computer.

Another characteristic that differentiates Yellow-Book CD-ROM from Red-Book CD-DA drives is the error-detection and error-correction methods employed. An error in audio data may, at worst, result in a slight crackle or pop in the sound, much less audible than a scratch on a vinyl recording. Errors in digital data, however, are almost intolerable, especially if they occur in data involving money, medical research results, or other critical information. Thus, when developing the Yellow-Book specifications, Philips and Sony concentrated on creating "bullet-proof" error-detection and error-correction codes (EDC/ECC). These codes not only detect errors but also attempt to reconstruct any erroneous data. Unrecoverable error rates—that is, those that cannot be fixed by EDC/ECC—for most CD-ROMs are in the range of 1 in 10^{12}, or 1 in a quadrillion. To make this number more meaningful, a CD-ROM contains about 630M or 2.5×10^9 (2.5 billion) bits. Thus, you can expect to get no more than a single uncorrectable error in 400 ($10^{12}/[2.5 \times 10^9]$) beginning-to-end reads of a CD-ROM.

CD-ROM drives come in both external and internal versions. The external drives include a wall-mount power supply. Most MPC upgrade kits (Media Vision's self-contained CDPC is a notable exception) provide internal drives that in most instances use a set of plastic slides to mount in a standard half-height drive bay and require a single adapter card slot for the interface. The various types of CD-ROM drive interfaces used by MPC upgrade kits are discussed in Chapter 4.

Examining CD-ROM Carriers and Juke Boxes

Unlike audio CD players, the majority of CD-ROM drives utilize a carrier (called a *caddy*) to protect the CD-ROM during insertion into the drive. The caddy is approximately the size of the "jewel box" case in which commercial CDs are housed. A few manufacturers produce "caddyless" drives, similar to front-loading audio CD players, in which the entire drive mechanism slides out to expose the spindle that clamps and rotates the CD-ROM. Most caddies are manufactured to dimensions established by Sony and are interchangeable but are not yet easy to find at the average computer store. A few extra caddies purchased for frequently used CD-ROMs saves you from constantly having to juggle CD-ROMs from case to caddy and prevents the possible damage that can occur if you drop CD-ROMS in the process.

Low-cost CD-ROM changers with multiple-CD cartridges were just emerging on the market when this book was written. Six-CD cartridges were the first to appear, because these are employed in consumer audio CD players, but 10- and 12-CD cartridge players will undoubtedly follow. Cartridge-loading CD-ROM drives are often called *juke boxes*.

Defining Basic CD-ROM Specifications

CD-ROM drives are characterized by four basic specifications: access (also called *seek*) time, data-transfer rate, data-block size, and the size of the internal data buffer. MPC Specification 1.0 establishes requirements for these specifications as listed in the following paragraphs:

■ *Access time* is defined as the average time in milliseconds (ms) required to locate and load the first data block to the internal data buffer—that is, make a minimum amount of data available to your PC. MPC Specification 1.0 requires an average access time of 1,000 ms (1 second or less), but most drives now offer seek times well below 500 ms. Access time of about 340 to 380 ms is the most common. Access time does not include spin-up time, the period the drive takes to reach the minimum operating speed of 200 rpm (usually about 1 second). Because the majority of hard disk drives now have access times in the 18-ms range, industry-standard CD-ROM drives access data at about 1/20 the rate of a hard disk. You would find the 1-second seek time allowed by the MPC specification to be intolerably slow for interactive multimedia applications.

■ *Data-transfer rate* is determined by the speed at which the disc spins combined with the density of the data on the disc. The density is the number of bits (or pits) per inch (or mm) of circumference. These two factors—disc speed and data density—must combine to meet the CD-DA audio requirement of stereo 44.1 kHz of 16-bit samples, which results in a calculated bit rate of 1.4 Mbits/s (megabits per second). Dividing by 8 bits/byte gives 176,400 bytes/second, the fundamental rate at which a CD-ROM must be able to transfer data. The basic MPC specification is a bit more lenient at a *sustained* rate of 150,000 bytes/second but adds the requirement that maintaining this transfer rate must not require more than 40 percent of your computer's capacity. All CD-ROM drives for personal computer use appear to meet or exceed this requirement. Processing compressed video data, such as that from AVI files, may consume *all* your computer's capacity.

■ *Data-block size* is the minimum number of bytes that can be transferred to your computer at one time through the interface card. Data blocks are similar to the clusters associated with hard disk drives (2K). The minimum data-block size specified for MPC upgrade kits is 16K. Because files on CD-ROMs have a tendency to be large, the *slack* (empty space in a data block) resulting from a larger data block size is inconsequential.

■ *Data-buffer size* is the size in kilobytes of the data buffer, which enables the drive to read CD-ROM data into local memory at the sustained data rate and then transfer the data from the memory to your PC at a much higher speed. The MPC specifications recommend but do not require an on-board data buffer (also called *cache memory*) of 64K, corresponding to about 0.4 seconds of 44.1 kHz, 16-bit stereo audio. Most CD-ROMs used in MPC upgrade kits have at least a 64K buffer.

The MPC specifications require a minimum of 10,000 hours MTBF (Mean Time Before Failure), a statistical quality-control method designed to predict how long the average drive can be expected to play before it breaks (1.4 years at 24 hours per day). The MPC number corresponds to the MTBF of the ball bearings used in the spindle drive assembly. MTBF values of 20,000 and 30,000 hours are commonly given by drive manufacturers, although their use of even multiples of 10,000 may cause you to wonder about the accuracy of the computation and the methods used to determine MTBF.

Using High-Performance CD-ROM Drives

Several CD-ROM drive manufacturers announced high-performance versions in mid-1992. These drives spin the CD-ROM at twice the standard speed of audio CD players and provide a data-transfer rate of about 300K per second. The Sony CDU-561, shown in figure 3.2, the Texel DM3024, and the NEC InterSect CDR-74 and 84 are typical of these faster drives. All the double-speed drives have larger buffers than the standard 64K of earlier versions, and both the Sony and NEC models can read Kodak Photo CD discs.

FIG. 3.2

The Sony CDU-561 double-speed internal CD-ROM with Photo CD compatibility. (*Courtesy of Sony Corporation*)

Understanding How CD-ROMs Store Data

Data on audio CDs and CD-ROMs is organized into tracks that contain 24-byte frames played at a rate of 75 frames per second. Data can include sound, text, still and animated graphic images, and video frames. Conventional CD-ROM drives store each type of data in separate tracks. CD-ROM XA enables you to store different types of data interleaved in one track.

A sector of data, similar to a sector on your hard disk, consists of 98 frames and is equal to 2,352 bytes. In the standard (mode 1) CD-ROM format, 16 bytes are used for synchronization and header information, and 288 bytes for error detection and correction, leaving 2,048 bytes per sector for user data. The theoretical maximum number of sectors on a CD-ROM is 330,000, with a maximum capacity of 660M. This number is reduced to about 630M by the error-correction code included with the data in form 1 for all modes. Form 2, available in mode 2 only, is a less common format that eliminates the 288 bytes of error detection and correction, leaving 2,336 bytes per sector for user data. The following paragraphs give you more details about the modes, forms, subchannels, and directory structures.

Defining the CD-ROM Modes, Forms, and Subchannels

MPC Specification 1.0 requires that CD-ROM drives operate in mode 1 and provide access to subchannel Q. The specification also recommends adding the capability to read mode 2 data (in forms 1 and 2) and subchannels P and R through W. Nowhere in the specification are these terms explained. *Subchannels* are special blocks of data, in addition to music or CD-ROM data, that are used for the purposes shown in table 3.1. *Modes* specify what type of data is contained in each of the 8 subchannels. Subchannel Q, table of content and track number data, for instance, is used by high-end consumer audio CD players to display the name of the track being played, the time into the track, and the time remaining on the track. *Forms* 1 and 2 determine whether the 288 bytes per sector of error detection/correction is provided for the data (form 1) or whether all 2,336 bytes of data per sector are available to store user information (form 2).

Each frame includes one bit for each subchannel. The subchannel bits are collected by circuitry in the drive and arranged into blocks stored in memory. If you multiply the 6 bits comprising subchannels R through W by 75 frames per second and then by a playing time of about 1 hour, or 3600 seconds (6 * 75 * 60 * 60), the result is 1,620,000 bits or 202,500 bytes. Thus, the R through W subchannels can contain an appreciable amount of text or MIDI data—especially if it is compressed—but not many graphic images. Text contained in R through W subchannels is intended to be displayed on TV monitors and may include simple text-type menus to select tracks. R to W subchannels are used in the CD+Graphics and CD+MIDI formats discussed in sections that follow.

Table 3.1. Audio CD and CD-ROM Subchannels and Modes.

Subchannel	Mode	Content
P	All	One bit used to mark the beginning, end, and pauses between tracks and to identify the lead-out area at the end of the CD. Most drives do not need this information.
Q	1	Table of content, track numbers, time within a track, and absolute time from the start of recording. Also contains all error-detection and error-correction codes.
Q	2	CD catalog number in Universal Product Code (UPC) numeric, not bar-code, format.
Q	3	International Standard Recording Code (ISRC), country code, owner code, year recorded, and serial number.
R through W	1	192-by-288-pixel, 16-color graphic images (originally proposed).
R through W	2	Compressed graphics and text, using CD-I standards.

Adding High-Sierra and ISO-9660 Directory Structures

When Philips and Sony collaborated on creating the Yellow-Book CD-ROM standard in 1983, they neglected one key element: how to organize and place individual files on the CD-ROM and provide a directory to list and access the files individually. Apparently, the assumption was made that a CD-ROM would contain only a single, large file and that the application software used with CD-ROMs would sort through it to find the required data. This assumption turned out not to be the case for the majority of titles produced. The omission resulted in a race by CD-ROM pioneers to establish their favorite directory format as an *ad hoc* standard, and another Tower of CD-Babel was constructed.

By 1985, all CD-ROM producers understood clearly that none of the proprietary solutions to the file location and directory structures proposed would be acceptable to all as a standard. An industry group was formed to create an agreed-upon, industry-wide specification for directory structures. The specification came to be known as *High Sierra*, named for the resort at which the group met. You may see the abbreviation HSG, which stands for High Sierra Group, used to identify the CD-ROM type.

High Sierra directories are structured similarly to DOS or UNIX directories; a hierarchical or tree structure is used with the familiar root directory and subdirectories. The High Sierra structure was adopted, with minor changes, by the International Standards Organization (a branch of the United Nations) as the ISO-9660 standard. Substantially more information, however, is contained in the CD-ROM's directory entry, and file size information is provided in both Intel (PC) and Motorola (Macintosh) formats so that a CD-ROM theoretically can be used by either type of computer. In practice, however, CD-ROMs often contain built-in applications or special file formats that require the directories to be authored separately for the two computer types. An additional field is provided in the file record for the long file names used by Macintosh computers. All MPC-compliant CD-ROM drives are capable of reading High Sierra and ISO-9660 directories. The only difference between the two directory types is the length of one of the directory parameters.

A DOS device driver written by Microsoft Corporation, MSCDEX.EXE, is required to translate the ISO-9660 or High Sierra directory structure so that DOS can treat a CD-ROM as if it were a read-only floppy disk. MSCDEX.EXE requires another device driver, supplied by the manufacturer of the drive, for the specific model of drive installed. MSCDEX and CD-ROM hardware device drivers are described in Chapter 5. The complete syntax for MSCDEX.EXE is provided in Appendix B.

Using Photo CD and CD-ROM XA Extended Architecture Drives

Related Topics
Kodak Photo CD Images,
p. 474

Very few drives that support the CD-ROM XA standard were available when this book was written. Eastman Kodak's announcement of its Photo CD process, which requires an extended architecture drive, breathed new life into the XA-compatible drive market. Several CD-ROM drive manufacturers announced new models with full Photo CD compatibility for availability in mid- to late-1992. Some drives are fully CD-ROM XA-compatible; others are not. The latter drives often are referred to as Photo CD-capable. You must read CD-ROM specifications carefully, or test the drives at the dealer's store with the CD-ROM media you plan to use, before you buy one. If you do not, you may find that you need to spend another $300 or so for a special interface card, and a free adapter card slot to hold it, to obtain full extended architecture capability in the future.

Kodak's new Photo CD process enables amateur and professional photographers to have images transferred from 35mm film to CD-ROMs by photofinishing outlets at a cost of about $20 per disc (for 24 pictures). Although Kodak has targeted the consumer market with its Photo CD players to display images on TV sets, many computer-based applications exist for which the Photo CD-ROM is by far the best medium. Photo CDs hold up to 100 images—more if you don't need almost-photographic quality—and you can have new images added to an unfilled disc by the photofinisher. CD-ROM XA drives, however, must have multiple-session capability to display the added images, and few offered this feature in mid-1992. The technology of the Photo CD and a few of the applications that use the Photo CD format are described in Chapter 17.

Consumer Photo CD players have audio playback capability that enables them also to play conventional audio CDs, but the initial Photo CD-ROMs will not have soundtracks. By mid-1993, photofinishers are scheduled to be able to add narration (called *Sound Captions* by Kodak) and text to the discs to create interactive Photo CDs. These future Photo CDs will use the standard Red-Book (PCM) audio of consumer audio CDs, not the ADPCM encoding of the digital audio data required by the XA standard. Thus, you find CD-ROM drives, such as the Sony CDU-561, that offer multi-session Photo CD compatibility but do not offer ADPCM for CD-ROM XA audio compatibility.

Exploring the Advantages of CD-ROM XA and ADPCM Audio Encoding

CD-ROM XA provides two advantages over conventional CD-ROM waveform audio and graphic file organization:

- The audio data is *interleaved* with the graphic images.

- The digital audio data is *compressed* to reduce storage requirements.

Interleaving means that audio and image data are stored in alternating blocks within a single track rather than in the separate tracks required when Red-Book audio is used. Compression calculates the differences between sound samples rather than their absolute value, which reduces the number of bits needed to express the value of successive samples.

The original Yellow-Book standard for CD-ROMs did not anticipate that this medium would be used to store waveform audio information associated with graphic images, especially images that move. To display animated images with synchronized sound by using conventional Red-Book audio, you must store the data for the animated graphics in memory and then process the audio data from the CD. Handling stereo audio sampled at 44.1 kHz consumes the entire capacity of conventional CD-ROM drives to transfer the sound at 150K per second, which is specified as the minimum data-transfer rate for an MPC-compliant drive. A quick calculation shows that 2 channels of 16-bit (2-byte) audio require 2 times 2 times 44.1 or 176.4K per second. Another problem is created by the relatively slow movement of the drive mechanism, compared with hard disk drives, when seeking files stored on different tracks. Double-speed drives help, but they don't solve the problem.

Related Topics
Using ADPCM Compression
Techniques, p. 382

Adaptive pulse-code modulation uses compression-decompression schemes that vary the compression ratio depending on the content of the sound. ADPCM is not a single standard but simply describes a technique; many varieties of ADPCM are described in Chapter 13. Sophisticated ADPCM techniques do not reduce sound quality significantly when compared with conventional PCM, despite the substantial data compression. The CD-ROM Interactive (CD-I) and Intel Digital Video Interactive (DVI) CD-ROM standards both use ADPCM and require CD-ROM XA drives, but DVI and CD-I use different encoding methods. The CD-ROM XA and CD-I standards provide for several levels of compression and fidelity, in both mono and stereo modes, as listed in table 3.2.

Table 3.2. Comparing Differences among Audio CD, Conventional PCM, and ADPCM Audio Encoding.

Class	Sampling Rate	Resolution	Range and S/N Ratio	Use
Audio CD	44.1 kHz	16-bit PCM	20 Hz to 20 kHz bandwidth, > 100 dB	High-fidelity stereo music
Waveform audio (WAV files)	11.025, 22.05, and 44.1 kHz	8-bit or 16-bit PCM	Varies with sampling rate and resolution	Narration at less audio CD sampling rates and resolutions
Hi-Fi XA	37.8 kHz	8-bit ADPCM	20 Hz to 17 kHz bandwidth, 90 dB	Music and high-quality sound, close to audio CD quality
Mid-Fi XA	37.8 kHz	4-bit ADPCM	20 Hz to 17 kHz bandwidth, 60 dB	Narration and background music; better than 8-bit waveform audio at 44.1 kHz

Class	Sampling Rate	Resolution	Range and S/N Ratio	Use
Speech XA	18.9 kHz	4-bit ADPCM	20 Hz to 8.5 kHz bandwidth, 60 dB	Narration and other sound; better than 8-bit waveform audio at 22.05 kHz

The CD-ROM XA and waveform audio classes of audio data can be recorded in mono or stereo modes, but CD audio is always stereophonic. Using monaural speech-quality CD-ROM XA compression, storing more than 19 hours of sound on a CD-ROM is possible. Speech-only CD-ROMs using ADPCM are ideal media for "talking books."

You need a special interface card to convert the ADPCM-encoded sound to Red-Book audio for digital processing as a WAV file. Some adapter cards are expected to convert ADPCM to analog stereo sound for listening. At the time this book was written, the issue of compatibility with ADPCM audio was not of great significance because no CD-ROM titles using ADPCM were available. Philips's consumer CD-I (compact disc-interactive) player, discussed in more detail in this chapter's subsequent section, entitled "Examining CD-Interactive Consumer Drives," was the only device that promised to use ADPCM audio. As of mid-1992, CD-I had not sparked serious interest in consumer markets.

Looking at the Sony Multimedia Player Portable CD-ROM XA Player

Sony Corporation of America announced its then-unnamed portable player to the U.S. market at the March 1992 CD-ROM and Multimedia exposition. This new Sony consumer product, later named the Multimedia Player, is unique in several respects:

- Incorporates CD-ROM extended architecture functions with a single integrated-circuit chip developed by Sony. This design reduces the cost of adding XA functions to conventional CD-ROMs; most of the components presently required to implement ADPCM and other XA features are replaced by one chip.

- Includes a standard QWERTY keyboard, cursor keys, and a numeric keypad, plus keys for Yes and No answers. The keyboard uses buttons rather than keys and is not designed for touch-typing significant amounts of text.

■ Has a 4.5-inch (diagonal) 320-by-200-pixel backlighted LCD display capable of displaying 7 shades of gray. A full-color version, perhaps with a "future version of Windows" stored in ROM, may be available in future models if the black-and-white model is successful.

■ Uses a 16-bit V-20 microprocessor, similar in operation to the Intel 80286, and Microsoft DOS 3.21 is stored in a read-only memory chip. Thus, CD-ROMs don't need to include the operating system— it's already there when you turn on the power.

■ Unlike most Sony CD-ROMs, the player does not require a caddy. You place the CD-ROM in the player by lifting the keyboard and dropping the disc on the spindle underneath.

■ You can obtain two hours of continuous playback with a single charge on the nickel-cadmium battery pack—the same battery used by Sony's 8-mm camcorders.

■ A video output port is provided so that you can show full-color CD-ROM presentations on a conventional television set or through a TV projector. Thus, you don't need a computer to give multimedia presentations to large or small audiences.

In addition to these features, the Sony Multimedia Player, shown in figure 3.3, enables you to listen to conventional audio CDs through headphones or a set of self-amplified speakers.

FIG. 3.3

The Sony Multimedia Player, a portable CD-ROM XA player. (*Courtesy of Sony Corporation*)

If the Sony Multimedia Player achieves commercial success in the U.S., titles created for the Multimedia Player will increase the demand for CD-ROM XA-capable drives for the PC. This event, together with the proliferation of Kodak Photo CD processing centers, should increase CD-ROM XA drive production rates and thus reduce the price differential between conventional and XA drives.

Storing Video Data on CD-ROMs

Recording video images in a digital form results in extremely large file sizes. A single frame of NTSC video at 640-by-400-pixel resolution with 16-bit color would require 512K of data per frame. At 30 frames per second, a data transfer rate of over 15M per second would be necessary. This speed is far beyond the capability of CD-ROM drives, now or in the foreseeable future. A CD-ROM with 630M capacity could hold only 42 seconds of digital video, with no space left for audio. Thus, image compression must be used if CD-ROMs are to contain what is called full-motion video. Several standards for compressed storage of video signals are in use or in various stages of development. Most of the techniques require special driver software or computer hardware, and some require drives with CD-ROM XA capabilities. The most important of these standards are described in the following paragraphs:

■ *Intel Digital Video Interleaved (DVI)* format provides storage of both full-motion video and high-fidelity audio data in compressed form on CD-ROMs. IBM has adopted DVI as the standard for displaying video for its Ultimedia product line. DVI is based on a specific Intel chipset and is thus called a proprietary format. Whether DVI becomes a true industry standard depends heavily on IBM's success in the multimedia market. DVI will be supported through the Media Control Interface (MCI) for Windows; the required DVMCI driver was being jointly developed by Intel and Microsoft at the time this book was written. DVI is discussed at length in Chapter 20, and the Windows MCI is covered in Chapters 23 and 24.

■ *Microsoft Audio Video Interleaved (AVI)* is a special compressed file structure designed to enable video images and synchronized sound stored on CD-ROMs to be played on PCs with standard VGA displays and audio adapter cards. AVI emulates the interleaved file structure of the CD-ROM XA standard on conventional CD-ROM drives. The audio and video information is interleaved (alternated in blocks) in the CD-ROM file to minimize delays that would result from using separate tracks for video and audio information. The slow data-transfer rate of conventional CD-ROM drives limits the size of the video image that can be displayed; 160-by-120-pixel images are the largest images supported in the current AVI version.

■ *MPEG compression* is a set of methods (called an *algorithm*) for compression of video images so that full-screen, full-motion images can be displayed without increasing the basic 150K-per-second data transmission rate of standard CD-ROM drives. MPEG is an abbreviation for the *Moving Pictures Experts Group*, which is in charge of developing a standard that, like DVI, requires specialized hardware for high-speed compression and decompression but can use software methods if cost, not speed, is of primary concern. MPEG is an *open* standard; hardware manufacturers and software publishers are free to implement MPEG techniques any way they choose.

■ *JPEG compression* is another open standard for compressing images to save hard disk or CD-ROM space. JPEG was designed for still images rather than video, but several manufacturers supply JPEG compression adapter cards for video applications. The Joint Photographic Experts Group is in charge of maintaining this standard that can be implemented solely by software. Specialized hardware simply increases the speed at which compression and decompression occur.

■ *Apple QuickTime* format is slated to become available for use under Microsoft Windows on the PC in late 1992. The QuickTime format, like AVI, uses software compression and decompression techniques but also can employ hardware devices, similar to those employed by DVI, to speed processing. QuickTime is the official Apple method for displaying animation and video on Macintosh computers, so it has become a *de facto* multimedia standard. Apple's QuickTime and Microsoft's AVI take a parallel approach to the presentation of video stored on CD-ROMs, and the performance of the two systems is similar.

■ *Commodore CDTV* formatted CD-ROMs use a proprietary version of the CD+Graphics and CD-MIDI formats and can be read only by the company's CD-1000 CDTV player, which is based on Amiga computer hardware. CDTV drives also can play CD-DA discs.

Full-motion video implies that video images shown on your computer's screen simulate those of a television set with identical (30-per-second) frame rates, and that these images are accompanied by high-quality stereo sound. Two approaches to the use of CD-ROM for video applications—DVI and AVI—are described briefly in the following paragraphs. Additional details on the compression techniques used by both storage formats can be found in Chapter 17, "Image Acquisition, Editing, Interchange, and Compression." (CDTV is designed specifically for the Amiga computer, and QuickTime was restricted to Macs at the time this book was written; thus these two formats are beyond the scope of this book.)

Using Intel's Digital Video Interactive Format

Intel Corporation manufactures integrated circuits and, in the hope of selling more of them, created a specialized set of ICs for processing video and audio data stored in a special compressed format on CD-ROMs. Intel joined with IBM to create the Digital Video Interactive (DVI) storage format, which is the video-playback standard for IBM's Ultimedia product line. Displaying DVI presently requires one of Intel's Action-Media cards, although other manufacturers are likely to incorporate Intel's i750 chips on DVI adapter cards if the format achieves commercial success. Several firms have announced plans to introduce lower-cost DVI adapter cards. At the time this book was written, DVI cards were selling for $2,000 and up.

DVI can compress a frame of video to an average of about 5K through a technique similar to ADPCM, in which only the differences between successive frames are stored. At the beginning of each new scene, a full frame (requiring about 15K) is saved so that specific images can be reconstructed without having to start from the beginning of the file. The compression process for high-quality, full-screen images is complex and requires a specialized minicomputer to create DVI files frame by frame from videotape at a cost in the range of $200 per minute. DVI cards are capable only of decompressing large, high-quality images; thus the compression method is called *asymmetric*. Asymmetric compression-decompression implies that compression is off-line and not done in real-time, but decompression is a real-time (30-frames-per-second) process. Asymmetric compression usually results in greater compression ratios than can be achieved by symmetric techniques that compress and decompress in real time. DVI cards can symmetrically compress small, lower-quality video images.

Using the 5K-per-frame average, a simple calculation shows that a 630M CD-ROM can hold about 126,000 frames, roughly 70 minutes of video at 30 frames per second. The playing time is reduced by the number of 15K full images stored and the storage requirement of the audio sound track, which uses ADPCM compression. In mid-1992, the cost of an Intel DVI ActionMedia II video adapter card with a video image capture daughterboard was about $3,000. DVI in Windows is supported by Microsoft's DVMCI driver for the media-control interface, which was in the beta-testing stage when this book was written.

Using Microsoft's Audio Video Interleaved Technique

In early 1992, Microsoft began demonstrating its Audio Video Interleaved (AVI) technology, which enables video images stored on CD-ROM drives to be displayed on PCs without the costly video adapter cards required by DVI. AVI uses symmetrical software compression-decompression techniques, which means that you can create AVI files yourself by recording video images and sound in AVI format from a VCR or television broadcast in real time, if you have enough free hard disk space.

AVI is limited in the size of the video image displayed (80×60 to 160×120 pixels), the number of custom-defined colors (238), and the rate at which frames are displayed (usually 15 frames per second or less). The frame rate is determined by the data-transfer rate of your CD-ROM drive (normally 150K per second) or your computer's capability to process video and audio data, whichever is the bottleneck. With 8-bit monaural audio encoding at 22.05 kHz, the beta version of Microsoft's MCIAVI driver delivered about 5 frames per second with a standard (150K-per-second) CD-ROM drive in a 33-MHz 80386DX computer. Use of a high-speed drive approximately doubles the number of frames per second.

Like DVI, AVI compression stores the differences between successive frames. You can set the rate at which full frames are captured to minimize the time required to re-create a specific frame. The relatively small image size compensates, to some degree, for the slower frame rates of AVI. Images of persons speaking exhibit somewhat "jerky" movement, but the small window, combined with sound, tends to minimize the perceived degradation of the animation.

Using CD-ROM Adapter Cards

You need an adapter card that provides a connector for (called an *interface to*) the CD-ROM drive to be able to use it with your PC. The majority of MPC-compliant audio adapter cards include a CD-ROM drive interface, but a few manufacturers implement the connector for an internal CD-ROM drive on an optional, extra-cost daughterboard. Audio adapter cards can be labeled with the MPC trademark only when sold with a CD-ROM in an MPC adapter kit, so manufacturers are free to implement the CD-ROM drive interface any way they choose. The following sections describe the most common implementations.

Using the Small Computer System Interface (SCSI)

The industry standard for connecting CD-ROM drives to computers is the *Small Computer System Interface* (SCSI). The advantage of the SCSI interface is that you can connect up to seven devices to a single SCSI adapter card through a *daisy-chain* of cables, as illustrated by figure 3.4. A daisy-chain is a method of cabling in which devices can be connected by cables that have double-ended connectors. You plug the cable from the computer into the SCSI device and then plug the cable to the next SCSI device into an extra connector provided on the cable. A special connector without a cable, called a *terminator*, is attached to the extra connector at the end of the daisy-chain to prevent interference by reflected signals.

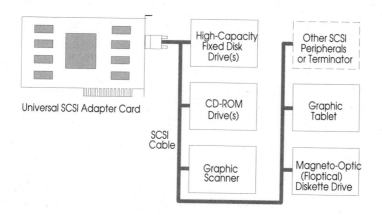

FIG. 3.4

Connecting SCSI peripherals to a universal SCSI adapter card.

SCSI cards designed to attach to a wide variety of devices are called universal SCSI adapters. Each device attached to the SCSI adapter is assigned its own special code, called a *device address*. Small switches on the device, usually located near the miniature 25-pin, D-type SCSI connectors, similar to those used to connect a printer to your PC, are used to set the device address. The adapter card communicates with a specific device in the daisy-chain by sending it the assigned device address. Each SCSI card also has its own device address so that you can add more than one SCSI adapter to your PC.

The most common devices that use the SCSI standard are hard disk drives; tape drives for backing up hard disks; CD-ROM, CD-WO, and rewritable CD drives; scanners; and specialized graphic drawing tablets. The new high-capacity "floptical" disk drives, discussed at the end of this chapter, also use SCSI connections. Special-purpose SCSI adapters are used to connect high-speed, large-capacity hard disk drives used as file servers in PC networks. Much of the popularity of SCSI is attributable to Apple's adoption of SCSI as the standard method of connecting peripheral components to its Macintosh products.

Many early SCSI adapter cards and hardware devices with SCSI interfaces did not work together properly. The initial SCSI standard allowed too much variation in the type and timing of the signals used to communicate between the adapter card and the devices. This problem, for the most part, has been overcome by the SCSI-2 standard that is the basis for the majority of SCSI adapter cards and devices used in multimedia applications today. A typical universal SCSI adapter card, Trantor Systems T128, is shown in figure 3.5.

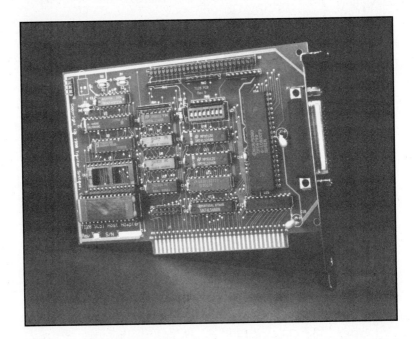

FIG. 3.5

The Trantor T128, a universal SCSI adapter for CD-ROM drives, hard disk drives, and other SCSI devices. (*Courtesy of Trantor Systems, Ltd.*)

SCSI adapter cards often include a separate 50-connector designed to connect to internal CD-ROM drives by a ribbon cable. All SCSI cards supplied with internal CD-ROM drives include this connector. In this case, the CD-ROM drive is assigned the first address in the chain by default, although you can usually change the CD-ROM drive's address by using a set of switches on the adapter card. Connecting internal CD-ROM drives to SCSI adapters, either on a card by themselves or as an element of an MPC audio adapter card, is described in the next chapter.

Using Parallel-Port-to-SCSI Converters

If you use a laptop or notebook computer, it is not likely to contain enough room to mount a SCSI adapter card that enables you to connect an external CD-ROM. Trantor Systems solved this problem by creating an outboard SCSI adapter, the T348 MiniSCSI Plus, shown in figure 3.6. The MiniSCSI Plus plugs into the parallel printer port of your computer. The adapter is powered by the computer and thus does not require a separate wall-mounted power supply. Driver software is included to support most popular external CD-ROM drives.

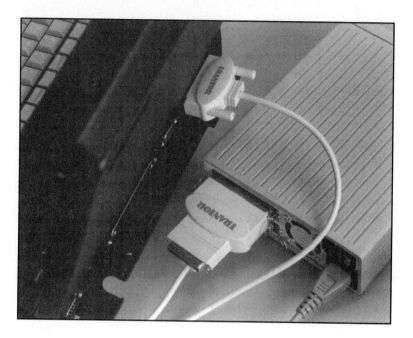

FIG. 3.6

The Trantor MiniSCSI Plus, a parallel-port-to-SCSI adapter for laptop and notebook computers. (*Courtesy of Trantor Systems, Ltd.*)

A parallel-port-to-SCSI adapter enables you to use a notebook or laptop computer to make presentations that include text, images, and sound stored on CD-ROMs. You can "piggy-back" Media Vision's AudioPort external sound adapter behind the Trantor SCSI adapter. Projection panels, RGB display projectors, or even TV projectors can be used to display full-color images. If you use large-screen or projection television, you need another outboard adapter that converts the RGB analog signals used for conventional VGA monitors to standard NTSC composite color (RS-170A) television signals. The collection of adapters, together with their wall-mount power supplies, often exceeds the weight and bulk of a laptop computer.

Using Proprietary CD-ROM Interfaces

Some manufacturers of CD-ROM drives use proprietary interfaces that require a special dedicated adapter card or a nonstandard connector on audio adapter cards. Implementing a SCSI interface in a CD-ROM drive is more costly than simply bringing internal signals to a connector at the rear of the drive. CD-ROM drives included in MPC adapter kits, such as those produced by Matsushita, Mitsumi, and Sony, often employ proprietary interfaces to reduce the production cost of the kit.

If you purchase an MPC upgrade kit, the CD-ROM interface supplied need not be a consideration. If you buy an audio adapter card and plan to add a CD-ROM drive later, however, a proprietary CD-ROM drive interface on the card means that you are forced to purchase a particular make and model of drive. CD-ROM drives with proprietary interfaces are rarely available in retail computer stores. The only alternative is to purchase a SCSI-interface drive and add the required SCSI adapter card, if you have an available slot for it.

T I P When you buy an audio adapter card and plan to add a CD-ROM drive later, make certain that you purchase a card with a SCSI interface. When you add the CD-ROM drive, you probably also have to obtain the device driver for the SCSI adapter on the audio card directly from its manufacturer, because driver software is seldom included with audio adapter cards sold by themselves. Due to licensing restrictions, these device drivers usually are available only on floppy disk, not by downloading from the manufacturers' bulletin boards. A good time to request the driver disk is when you send in your warranty registration card.

Exploring Other Laserdisc Formats

Most of this chapter has been devoted to CD-ROMs because of their suitability for use with Windows multimedia applications. A number of other laserdisc formats are available, most of which are designed for playback through television sets. The two formats that have the greatest potential for integration with Windows multimedia applications are described in the following sections.

Examining LaserVision and CD-V Drives

LaserVision discs come in 8-inch and 12-inch versions and use analog techniques for storing both video and audio information. LaserVision (LV) discs are the equivalent of videotapes converted to optical platters.

LV discs deliver composite video and FM audio signals essentially identical to those from a VCR, but LV offers stereo audio as a standard feature, and most LV drives provide a somewhat higher-quality image than conventional VHS tapes. LaserVision drives that also can play audio CDs are called *laserdisc drives*. Some laserdisc drives, such as the Pioneer LD-V4400, can be remotely controlled by PCs through a cable connected to an RS-232-C serial (COM) port. Microsoft included a driver for the Pioneer LD-V4400 (MCIPIONR.DRV) with Windows 3.0 with Multimedia Extensions 1.0, but this driver is not included with Windows 3.1. You will find it in the MDK for Windows 3.0 and 3.1.

Compact Disc Video (CD-V) adds digital audio sound to the analog video and sound capabilities of LaserVision discs. CD-V players can play conventional LV discs, LV discs with digital audio, as well as CD-size discs called "singles," which store about 6 minutes of combined video and digital audio plus 20 more minutes of digital audio only. You thus can play the audio portion of the disc on a conventional audio CD or CD-ROM drive with audio CD capability. CD-V singles appear to have been designed specifically for the pop-rock and MTV markets.

CD-V has the greatest potential for Windows multimedia applications because CD-V discs fit the standard mechanism used for audio CD and CD-ROM drives. The additional components required to make CD-V signals compatible with computers are integrated-circuit chips. If CD-V players gain even a fraction of the popularity of audio CD devices, CD-V will be an ideal medium for mass distribution of short presentations created by desktop video techniques.

Examining CD-Interactive Consumer Drives

Philips's CD-Interactive (CD-I) products are based on the CD-ROM mode 2 format with interleaved audio, video, and text information. Audio data is stored in PCM or one of the three ADPCM formats described in the section on CD-ROM XA drives. CD-I stores video and other graphics information in several levels of pixel and color resolution, as shown in table 3.3. CLUT is an abbreviation for *color look-up table*; the Windows 256-color palette, for example, is an 8-bit CLUT. Other graphics terms used in table 3.3 are explained in Chapter 16, "Graphic Displays and Adapter Cards for Windows." YUV digital encoding of analog television signals, also used by PC video adapter cards, is discussed in Chapter 19, "Incorporating Digital Video."

Table 3.3. Video and Graphic Formats of CD-I Systems.

Picture type	Pixel resolution	Encoding	Color Range
Video	Normal, 360 by 240 Double, 720 by 240 High, 720 by 480	Delta YUV	4:2:2 (4-bit)
RGB graphics	Same as Video	Compressed	15 bits/pixel
CLUT graphics	Same as Video	Compressed	8 bits (256 colors) 7 bits (128 colors) 4 bits (16 colors)
Animation	Same as Video	Run-length (RLE)	7 bits (128 colors) 3 bits (8 colors)

CD-I discs are CD-ROMs designed to be played through special-purpose consumer drives connected to television sets. The first consumer CD-I player introduced by Philips appears in figure 3.7. The principal difference between CD-I and CD-ROM XA discs designed for use by computers is the method of storing graphic data. The aspect ratio of the normal and high-resolution images, 1.5:1, is designed for television sets, not for computers. The video encoding technique is intended to create conventional and super-video (S-video) analog television signals, not digital video data or the RGB analog signals used by computer monitors.

FIG. 3.7

The Philips CDI910 Compact Disc-Interactive player for consumer markets. (Courtesy of Philips Interactive Media Systems)

You will be able to play consumer CD-I discs on future XA-compatible CD-ROM drives that have ADPCM capability, using CD-ROM XA/CD-I "bridge" drivers and software to be supplied by Philips and publishers of CD-I authoring applications. Philips is investing heavily in creating new CD-I titles, some of which have considerable artistic and educational merit. The success of CD-I as a consumer product remains open to question, but its widespread use for interactive product and service training applications appears assured.

Examining CD-WO Write-Once CD-ROM Drives

You can create Red-Book–, Yellow-Book–, and Green-Book–compatible CD-ROMs, including CD-ROM XA discs, with the Sony CDW-900E write-once (CD-WO) drive shown in figure 3.8. The CDW-900E can create a prototype or limited-distribution CD-ROM in about 30 minutes. The advantage of having a CD-WO drive with multimedia capability is the fact that you can preview a commercial CD-ROM title before you send it to a CD-ROM production firm to have it mastered and stamped in production quantities.

Single-purpose CD-WO drives that create only standard Yellow-Book CD-ROMs are used for archiving and hard disk backup applications, especially with computer-based document-imaging systems designed to replace microfilm and microfiche systems. All CD-WO drives are priced in the $5,000-and-up range, so relatively few PC users can afford to own one. CD-ROM service bureaus can produce a CD-WO test CD-ROM for you at a moderate price. You supply the files to be included in tape backup form, using one of the standard formats described in Chapter 20, "The Multimedia Production Process." The service bureau returns a finished CD-ROM, usually in a day or two.

Examining CD-MO Rewritable Magneto-Optical Drives

Magneto-optical CD-ROMs and related products combine the magnetic read-write technology associated with conventional floppy disk and hard disk drives and the laser-optic systems used by CD-ROM drives. Optical techniques provide the high data densities (bits per square millimeter) required to store 600M on a 5-inch-diameter disc. Magnetic methods provide the capability to erase and re-record data, but the techniques employed are quite different from those for conventional disk drives. High-speed CD-MO drives that rival the performance of high-performance hard disk drives for PCs began to make their appearance in mid-1992. Because of their cost, CD-MO drives usually are employed as graphic image servers to networked PC clients.

Sony's CDW-900E CD-WO drive for creating CD-ROMs and CD-I discs. *(Courtesy of Sony Corporation)*

Examining Floptical Disk Drives

A device that uses magneto-optic technology and is priced in the range that most PC users can afford is the *floptical* disk drive. A floptical is a floppy disk, in a conventional 3.5-inch disk housing, that can hold 20M or more of data. Floptical drives, such as the GrassRoots model 2020i, sell for less than $500, but the disks cost about $25 each.

The GrassRoots 2020i also can read and write conventional low- and high-density 3.5-inch floppy disks and uses a standard SCSI interface. Average access time is 128 milliseconds, about 8 times slower than common hard disk drives but much faster than run-of-the-mill floppy drives. Floptical disks are an ideal medium for storing large numbers of waveform audio files and graphic images, as well as compressed video data in AVI or DVI formats. Floptical drives have a higher data-transfer rate than most CD-ROM drives, so performance when using Microsoft's AVI files improves substantially.

Chapter Summary

Chapter 2 introduced you to the inner workings of audio adapter cards, and this chapter provided most of what you need to know about CD-ROM drives so that you can make an informed decision on which MPC upgrade kit to purchase or whether to buy components and create your own upgrade. Chapters 2 and 3 give you the background you need to analyze suppliers' specifications for the various MPC-labeled computers offered through retail and mail-order channels. With this knowledge, you can determine whether one or more computers can meet your particular set of multimedia requirements.

Chapter 4 shows you how to install an audio adapter card, a CD-ROM drive, or both in your PC. The process is easier than you may imagine, but some of the manuals supplied with audio adapter cards and CD-ROM drives are sketchy regarding installation techniques. Installing the necessary software drivers to make audio adapter cards and CD-ROM drives play under Windows is the subject of Chapter 5. Parts II and III of this book concentrate on showing you how to use your audio adapter card and CD-ROM drive to best advantage.

Preparing Your System for Multimedia

Y ou don't need to be a member of the Audio Engineering Society or an electronic technician to take full advantage of the advanced features of an audio adapter card or a Multimedia PC Upgrade Kit. Windows 3.1 has made the installation and testing process simple and straightforward. This chapter gives you instructions for installing typical audio adapter cards and connecting them to speakers or sound systems. Because audio adapter cards and CD-ROM drives often are purchased together in the form of MPC Upgrade Kits, instructions for installing a typical internal CD-ROM drive are provided near the end of this chapter in the section, "Adding a CD-ROM Drive."

 NOTE If you have an early Sound Blaster, Thunder Board, or Ad Lib card installed in your computer, and you are a newcomer to Windows, skip to Chapter 5. Chapter 5 leads you through the driver installation process for Windows 3.1. The drivers for pre-MPC audio cards are included with Windows 3.1.

Sound Blaster or Thunder Board owners have the opportunity to add a Roland SCC-1 GS Sound Card and obtain sampled digital audio capability and the rich musical voices of Roland's Sound Canvas module. This chapter also explains how you choose device address and interrupt settings that allow multiple audio adapter cards, or sound cards, to be installed in your computer.

This chapter is meant to complement, not replace, the instructions provided with your audio adapter card, CD-ROM drive, or MPC Upgrade Kit. This chapter also is designed to give you an idea of what is involved in the installation of these components before you purchase an audio adapter card, CD-ROM drive, or MPC Upgrade Kit.

Preparing for Installation

The mechanics of installing an MPC audio adapter card in your computer are no more difficult than those involved in adding any other adapter card. If you're installing an MPC Adapter Kit, complete with a CD-ROM drive, the process is similar to adding a new hard disk drive; you also need to install the ribbon-type cables that interconnect the card and the drive.

This chapter describes the installation process in general, and is applicable to most MPC-compatible cards. If the instructions given here conflict with those in the instruction manual that came with the card, take the manual's advice. You should read the entire content of the manual devoted to the installation process before you start. Not all manuals are written with topics in the sequence in which the steps should be performed.

Installing an audio adapter card or a CD-ROM drive requires a few basic tools: a medium-size Phillips (cross-head) screwdriver is a requirement. A pair of needle-nose pliers is handy if you need to change jumpers on a card to select a nonstandard device address or interrupt level. The most important tool, however, is an understanding of each step in the process. Most installation manuals use terms like device address, I/O port, and DMA channels as if everyone should know what they mean. This chapter begins by explaining these terms and their significance to the installation process.

T   I   P   Always check the disk that accompanies any adapter card for a file that provides the latest information on the product, plus last-minute changes that didn't make it into the printed manual. These files are usually named READ.ME, README.TXT, README.1ST, WHATSNEW.DOC, or something similar. These are ASCII text files you can read with Windows Notepad. Sometimes the information they contain is *critical* to the successful installation of the adapter card or the accompanying software.

Using Device Addresses, Interrupts, and DMA Channels

Before you take the audio adapter card out of its protective envelope, find the section of the manual that discusses device or I/O addresses, interrupt (also called IRQ) levels, and DMA channels. You need to know what these terms mean and the default values the manufacturer has assigned to each of them to properly configure your system and ensure that your new audio card does not conflict with another type of card already installed.

Some adapter cards come with software that enables you to determine if address or interrupt conflicts will occur with other cards—before you open your computer and plug in the card. Other manufacturers require you to plug the card in and then run the installation and diagnostic software. If a conflict occurs, you may need to turn off the power, remove the card, make the necessary changes, and then plug the card in again. Changes in settings for some cards—for example the Pro AudioSpectrum series—are made by the installation software, so you don't need to worry about jumpers.

> It is very important that you discharge the static electricity your body may have accumulated before you remove the adapter card from its static-protection envelope. The best way to do this is to touch a piece of bare metal near or attached to your computer's enclosure. A plated screw head is a good spot to ground yourself (provided that you are using a proper three-wire grounding receptacle for the power cord) but not the key lock. Key lock mechanisms seldom are connected by a wire to the enclosure.

T I P

If you are installing a second audio adapter card, you probably are familiar with the process described in the following paragraphs. Suggestions and precautions on how to avoid device address and interrupt conflicts when installing a second audio adapter card are given later in this chapter, in the section titled "Installing Multiple Audio Adapter Cards."

Selecting Device Addresses

Your PC chooses the adapter card to which specific microprocessor unit (MPU) or central processing unit (CPU) instructions and data are to be sent by its device address. A device address is a special code the microprocessor sends on the bus that electrically interconnects all of the adapter card connectors on your PC's motherboard. Each adapter card has one or more unique device address codes assigned to it. Some cards, such as conventional graphic display adapters and serial/parallel I/O adapters, have permanent device addresses. Others, including audio adapter cards, have selectable addresses. Device addresses also are called I/O (Input/Output) addresses, locations, or ports.

Each function performed by an adapter card is considered to be a separate device. When an adapter card receives a device address code that it recognizes as one of its own, the card "turns on" and accepts data from or sends data to the microprocessor. Adapter cards that can perform more than one function, such as the multi-I/O boards common in 80x86 computers, have several different device addresses; printer (LPT), serial (COM1 and COM2), and joystick ports are the usual combination.

Device addresses are expressed in hexadecimal numbers. Hexadecimal numbers are based on 16 digits, instead of the 10 used by the common Arabic system. Hexadecimal numbering begins with 0 instead of 1, and the extra digits, 10 through 15, are expressed as the letters A through F. MIDI signals also use the hexadecimal system, so an understanding of simple hexadecimal (also called hex) arithmetic is also helpful to musicians. An explanation of binary arithmetic, upon which the hexadecimal system is founded, and hex notation is found in Appendix E.

Device addresses consist of a sequence of three hex digits, such as 2AB; and sometimes with an H suffix (2ABH or 2ABh) to identify the number as hexadecimal; and occasionally with a leading zero (02AB), 0x (0x02AB), or dollar sign ($2AB) that you may disregard. You don't need to convert device addresses to their decimal equivalents to use them in the context of installing adapter boards. Some types of devices, audio adapter cards included, require a group of addresses (also called address space or range) because each device performs a number of functions or sends and receives different types of data. In this case, each different function or type of data is identified by a specific address code.

Addresses for common devices, such as disk drives, printers, COM ports, and joysticks are fixed by the PC's basic input-output system (BIOS) and its disk operating system (DOS). The remaining group of device addresses are up for grabs among manufacturers of specialty adapter cards. Some device addresses become *de facto* standards for specific card types. 330, for instance, is the standard for MPU-401 and other MIDI adapter cards; early versions of the cards were hard-wired to this location. You could not install two of these cards to obtain additional MIDI channels because their addresses would conflict; two adapter cards cannot share the same device address. Most adapter cards now enable you to choose a device address by changing jumpers on the card, if the address chosen by the manufacturer conflicts with a preexisting device. The device addresses commonly employed by audio adapter cards are shown in table 4.1.

Table 4.1. PC Device Addresses Used by Representative Audio Cards.

Address	Function	Comment
200-207	Analog joystick	Fixed address (also used by multi-function I/O cards)
210-260	Sound Blaster and compatibles	Default is 220 (210, 240, 250 or 260 selectable on Sound Blaster, 240 on Blaster Pro)
290	MultiSound	Default is 290 (210-3E0 are selectable by jumper)
300-320	MPU-401	Allocated by Windows but seldom used with MPU-401s
330, 331	MPU-401, SCC-1	Default address for MPU-401 and compatible cards
332-337	MPU-401, SCC-1	Allocated alternate addresses for SCC-1 and MIDI cards
388-389	Sound Blaster and compatibles	Alternate FM data/status/register ports

Unless you know that another card has been assigned to the device address used by the manufacturer of the card as the default value, you do not need to change the address jumper to start. The installation or diagnostic applications supplied with the card usually is able to detect conflicts. If you do change the address jumper, write down the new address you selected. You will need the new address later when you configure Windows drivers for the card. Cards that have programmable device addresses assigned by the installation software, rather than by jumpers, store the address (assigned by a parameter of the driver software) in memory on the card. You can change the address later, if conflicts arise with additional cards, by running the installation software again.

T I P

The most common device address problem is two joystick ports at the same address—one on your multi-I/O card and one on the audio adapter. If your joystick doesn't work, disable the joystick port on the sound adapter (usually accomplished by removing a designated jumper) and use the multi-I/O card's port instead. If you cannot disable the sound card's joystick port, disable the one on your multi-I/O card.

Choosing an Interrupt Level

Interrupts are an electrical "wake-up call" sent by a device such as an adapter card to the microprocessor to indicate that the card or a device to which the card is connected needs attention. When the MPU receives an interrupt, it stops what it is presently doing and checks to see why the interrupting device called it. The MPU processes the request from the device, and then returns to what it was doing before the interrupt occurred. Interrupts are used most often to process incoming signals, such as keystrokes on the PC's keyboard, MIDI note messages from a piano keyboard, or data received via a modem.

Standard 80x86-based computers have 16 interrupts, numbered from 0 to 15 in decimal, not hex notation. Interrupt numbers are often called interrupt levels because interrupts that occur simultaneously are processed by their priority, with the lowest number first. IRQ, an abbreviation for Interrupt ReQuest, is commonly used as a prefix to the interrupt number. Standard PCs that use the ISA (Industry Standard Architecture) bus require that each device needing an interrupt use a separate IRQ number. Devices can share interrupts on EISA (Extended Industry-Standard Architecture) and MCA (Micro Channel Architecture) computers.

You need an interrupt free (not in use by other devices) to install an audio adapter card. Only four interrupts on 8088 computers (the original PC) are not already assigned to specific functions. You can use a few of those assigned, however, because they are not commonly required for the assigned device. Table 4.2 lists the 16 interrupts available on 80x86 computers; the original PC had only eight. You are much more likely to have to change the default interrupt level of your card than the device address because far fewer interrupt levels are available.

Table 4.2. Interrupt Assignments and Options for 80x86-Based PCs.

IRQ	Function	Comment
0	Internal timer	Dedicated, not accessible
1	Keyboard	Dedicated, not accessible
2	Tied to IRQ9	Enhanced mode problem solved by Windows 3.0a and 3.1
3	Second serial port	COM2 and COM4, usually assigned to a modem
4	First serial port	COM1 and COM3, usually for a serial mouse
5	Second parallel printer	Often used for bus mice and scanner cards

IRQ	Function	Comment
6	Floppy disk drives	Dedicated, do not use
7	First parallel printer	Used by some scanner cards, otherwise available
8	Time-of-day clock	Dedicated, not accessible
9	IRQ2 on 80x86 computers	IRQ2 is rerouted to IRQ9, often shown as IRQ2/9
10	Unassigned	Good choice for the first audio card if offered
11	Unassigned	Not a common option, use if 10 assigned
12	Unassigned	Not a common option, use if 11 assigned
13	80x87 coprocessor	Dedicated, do not use even if 80x87 not installed
14	Hard disk drive	Dedicated, do not use
15	Unassigned	Not a common option, use if 12 assigned

The default interrupt for the original Sound Blaster and MPC-compatible audio adapter cards is IRQ7. Although IRQ7 is assigned to the first parallel printer (LPT1), few printers require an interrupt and therefore IRQ7 usually is free. Some hardware key devices that plug into the printer port to prevent use of more than one copy of the application at a time, often called a *dongle*, may use IRQ7. If you have an internal laser printer card, such as the QMS JetScript, it probably uses IRQ7 as the default, as do several brands of scanners.

The majority of audio adapter cards come with installation or diagnostic software that detects interrupt as well as device address conflicts. If you have a number of specialty adapter cards installed, IRQ7 and IRQ5 probably have been used by them.

IRQ2/9 is the default interrupt for the MPU-401 MIDI adapter and its clones and is best left free for their use under Windows 3.0a or 3.1. If you are using the original release of Windows 3.0 and your MPU-401 or compatible card has interrupt options, IRQ7 is a good choice. If IRQ7 is occupied, IRQ10 is a good choice if your card has a jumper for it. Relatively few pre-MPC adapter cards offer IRQ levels above 7 because they are not available on the original 8088-based PCs.

T I P

IRQ2 (cascaded to IRQ9 on 80x86 computers and often called IRQ2/9) should be avoided if you are running the original version of Windows 3.0. This version of Windows had a problem with IRQ2/9 when running in Enhanced mode. The problem was solved in a later maintenance release, 3.0a, which was placed in retail distribution during late 1990. You can determine which version you have by choosing **Help**, and then **About Program Manager** from Program Manager's menu. The dialog box tells you that you are running Version 3.00 or 3.00a. If you do not have Windows 3.00a and have an early MPU-401 adapter card hard-wired to IRQ2/9 (has no interrupt jumper pins), start Windows in Standard mode by using the WIN /S command, instead of the usual WIN command.

As with device addresses, interrupt levels are chosen by jumpers on many cards. Use needle-nose pliers, not your fingers, to remove and reinsert the jumper; you are much less likely to drop it. Jumpers are very small and hard to find under a desk or computer table. A few cards use small switches to set IRQ or device addresses. The trend is to set the IRQ level and device address with a DOS or Windows driver when you boot your computer or start Windows.

Using DMA (Direct Memory Access) Channels

You probably will not need to change the DMA (direct memory access) channel of your audio card. Some cards don't even provide the option to change the channel. DMA is a process used by devices that must transfer data at high speeds—sampled audio data and information from your hard disk or a CD-ROM are examples. DMA transfers data directly from the adapter card to the main memory (RAM) of your computer. DMA does not require intervention by the MPU in the process, so the MPU can perform other duties while the data is being transferred.

The original 8088-based PC had only one DMA channel, but AT-class and higher PCs have several. DMA channels 0 and 2 are assigned to internal uses. Channel 1 is the normal (default) DMA channel for audio adapter cards, as well as most other adapters. Modern adapter cards allow DMA channels to be shared, so using channel 1 seldom causes problems. Most adapter cards give you the option of using DMA channel 3, and some offer several additional choices.

Network adapters, SCSI adapter cards, and cards designed to defeat software copy-protection schemes sometimes require exclusive use of DMA channel 1. If this is the case, and you have a card that does not provide a DMA channel choice (the original Sound Blaster is one of these cards), you must change the DMA channel of the conflicting card if it has jumpers or switches. If you make a change, you may have to make substantial alterations to the software switches (command line parameters) for the driver software required for these cards. If you have any of these types of cards installed, make sure that you buy an audio adapter card with a selectable DMA channel.

Installing an Audio Adapter Card

The first step in installing an audio adapter card is opening the case. Many PC users never have opened the enclosure, a testimony to the reliability of that product. Before the advent of tower cases and IBM's PS/2 PCs, instructions for removing the case of your PC were simple, as in the following steps:

1. Turn off the power to the computer, monitor, and other powered peripherals.

2. Relocate the monitor and keyboard, unplugging them if necessary.

3. Remove the five or six screws around the periphery of the back of the PC.

4. Slide the cover forward.

If you have a PS/1 or PS/2 (which requires a special adapter assembly to accept standard AT-type ISA bus cards), or a tower or minitower case, you probably need to refer to the instructions that came with your PC to expose the computer's components. Remove the cover plate corresponding to an unoccupied adapter-card connector. The preferred location for an audio adapter card is the bus connector closest to the edge of the case, separated from other adapter cards (especially the VGA adapter card) as far as possible.

Related Topics
Audio Noise, Hum, and
Grounding, p. 414

If you are installing an internal CD-ROM drive, follow these steps:

1. Choose the open slot closest to the drive bay in which you plan to install the drive.

2. If the CD-ROM interface is provided on a separate daughterboard, connect the daughterboard to the adapter card by plugging the rectangular connector on the daughterboard into the multipin header on the adapter card. Make sure that the connector is aligned and no header pins are visible on either end of the connector.

3. Refer to the topic on installing a CD-ROM drive near the end of this chapter for details. You may want to review the CD-ROM installation process before installing the adapter card.

Most MPC-compliant sound cards require a 16-bit adapter card slot, even though the lower priced cards are basically 8-bit devices. 16-bit slots are the longer of the two types of connectors found on PC motherboards. Some motherboards have a slot reserved for memory expansion not available for use with adapter cards. Memory expansion slots have connectors even longer than the 16-bit type and usually are identified with a silk-screened legend that includes the word *memory* or *expansion*.

After you have selected the slot to use, follow these steps:

1. Touch an exposed metal component of the case to discharge any static electricity that may have accumulated on your body.

2. Insert the printed-circuit fingers into the connector.

3. Press down firmly on the top edge of the card so that it becomes fully seated in the connector.

4. Check that the card is fully inserted by verifying that the top of the card is parallel with the other cards installed.

5. If the card includes a speaker connection, remove the small connector (attached to the wires leading to the speaker) from the motherboard, and plug it into the pins on the header (a name used to describe a series of connector pins) on the adapter card.

6. Complete the installation of the internal CD-ROM drive, if you have purchased an MPC Upgrade Kit. Installation suggestions are provided at the end of this chapter. Return to this point when you finish installing the CD-ROM drive. If you are installing an external CD-ROM drive, finish the audio adapter card installation before adding the drive.

7. Replace the cover and relocate the monitor and keyboard to their usual places. You may not want to replace all the screws that restrain the cover until you have determined that your choices of device address and interrupt level are OK.

8. Don't turn on the power yet because you still have the audio output connections to make.

Installing Multiple Audio Adapter Cards

If you already have a Sound Blaster or Thunder Board installed, you may want to install an MPU-compatible board such as Roland's SCC-1 or an additional MPU-401 MIDI adapter card or one of its clones to add 16 or more MIDI channels. Conversely, you may have an LAPC-1, MPU-401, or SCC-1 installed and would like to use the digitally sampled audio of an MPC-compatible adapter card. If you have an available slot and a free interrupt, this is as easy as following the preceding instructions. All of the widely available MPC-compatible cards, as well as the Sound Blaster and Thunder Board, coexist with MPU-compatible cards. Just make sure that each uses a separate device address and interrupt level. You need one of the Windows sequencer applications described in Chapter 12 that enables you to assign MIDI tracks to either of the two MIDI devices installed.

CAUTION: Early MPU-401 MIDI adapter cards do not have selectable interrupts. They are assigned permanently ("hard-wired") to device address 330 and 331, and interrupt level IRQ2/9. If you have an MPU-401 installed and have reassigned the device address or interrupt level of the audio adapter card you installed (because of a conflict with other adapter cards in your system) and chose either IRQ2 or device addresses 330 or 331, a conflict occurs. Select a different interrupt level or device address to eliminate the conflict. You can install two MPU-401 MIDI adapter cards in your computer to obtain 32 MIDI channels with Windows 3.1, but one of MPU-401s must have selectable interrupts and device addresses.

Making Audio Output Connections

If you want to hear the output of your audio adapter card, you need at least a set of small speakers. Self-amplifying speakers or stereo systems provide substantially better sound quality.

Related Topics
Audio Cables, p. 412

Figure 4.1 depicts the connectors used for audio cabling between audio adapter cards and external components such as speakers, microphones, and the auxiliary inputs of your stereo set. Stereo 1/8-inch mini-plugs are used to make audio connections to and from most audio adapter cards. RCA phono plugs and jacks are most commonly employed for self-amplifying speakers and the individual left and right stereo inputs of hi-fi components. MIDI equipment and professional self-amplifying speakers use 1/4-inch phone plugs and jacks (double the size of the 1/8-inch variety).

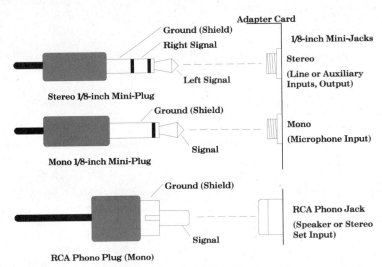

FIG. 4.1

Audio cable connectors used with audio adapter cards.

Most audio adapter cards and multimedia upgrade kits, except Media Vision's CDPC, don't include speakers, and few provide a microphone for recording. You need one of the following sound components, and possibly an adapter cable or two, to hear the output of an audio adapter card:

- A stereo sound system with an auxiliary or tape input
- Small unpowered speakers, 4 inches in diameter or smaller
- Stereo headphones
- Self-amplifying speakers (sometimes called monitors)

Using a Stereo Sound System

Most stereo sound systems have at least one set of auxiliary inputs, usually with the standard RCA phono jack (RS-170) input jacks. Almost all MPC audio adapter cards have a stereo 1/8-inch (3.5-mm) mini-jack as the audio output jack. If the adapter card you buy doesn't come with the appropriate connector with a stereo mini-plug on one end and two RCA phono plugs on the other, you need to buy a Radio Shack 42-2475A adapter cable, or its equivalent, to make the connection. This adapter cable is about three feet in length, so if your computer is farther away from the stereo system, you need a pair of shielded audio extender cables with RCA phono plugs on one end and jacks on the other. These come in an assortment of standard lengths up to about 15 feet.

The Roland SCC-1 GS Sound Card uses RCA phono jacks as its audio output connectors, so all you need for this card are a set of standard shielded audio patch cables (RCA phono plugs on both ends) of adequate length to reach your amplifier, pre-amp, or tuner.

Using Speakers and Headphones

If your computer and sound equipment are not in the same room, or you use your audio card in an office environment in which stereo systems are rare, you can take your choice of three approaches. A self-contained speaker-amplifier system, such as the Roland CS-10 Stereo Micro Monitor, is the simplest approach (see fig. 4.2). This system sits on top of your computer or desk, and the monitor is placed on its top. The Roland CS-10 contains two small stereo speakers, plus a six-inch "woofer," and has front-panel volume and tone controls. This system uses RCA phono jacks for stereo, line-level audio inputs.

FIG. 4.2

The Roland CS-10 Stereo Micro Monitor. (Courtesy of Roland Corporation USA)

Any set of stereo headphones with the standard 1/8-inch (3.5mm) stereo mini-plug can be used with audio adapter cards. Radio Shack offers a pair of tiny speakers equipped with a mini-plug, but they offer much lower fidelity than the least costly headphones and provide negligible stereo separation.

Connecting Unpowered Speakers to Amplified Cards

You need very efficient speakers to obtain satisfactory dynamic range from the meager 1- to 4-watt audio outputs common for audio adapter cards. Small speakers designed to be driven by high-powered stereo systems usually sacrifice efficiency for the ability to produce bass notes with a small-diameter cone. Some speakers require close to 5 watts just to deliver audible sound.

T I P   Be sure to observe proper polarity when connecting stereo speaker pairs. If you get the connections backwards to one of the speakers, you will observe some very strange sound patterns caused by out-of-phase interference between the two channels. Most cables are color coded or consist of a central wire and a braided or foil shield. Connect the black wire or shield to the negative (–) or black terminal of the speaker and the red or central wire to the positive (+) or red terminal. If the terminals are unmarked, make sure that the red or central wire goes either to the left or right terminal (it is not critical which) of both speakers.

Using Self-Amplifying Speakers

A more costly approach, but one that delivers higher-quality sound in adequate volume for a room full of people, is to use individual self-amplifying speakers for each stereo output channel. A pair of Roland MA-12C Micro Monitors, designed expressly for use with computer audio cards, provide sound quality you normally might associate with studio monitors. Self-amplifying speakers that flank your PC are called *near-field* monitors, meaning that they are designed for close-up listening rather than filling a room with sound. The advantage of near-field monitors is that they are relatively immune from acoustic effects, such as excessive reverberation (echoes), contributed by the room in which the speakers are located.

If you are an audio purist, you may want to use the studio reference near-field monitors available from firms that traditionally serve audio professionals. For auditioning 16-bit waveform audio files, your choice might be a pair of 75-watt JBL 4208s, with 8-inch woofers and 1-inch titanium-domed tweeters. Acoustic Research, Tannoy, and Yamaha produce similar monitors. Smaller studio reference monitors are priced in the $350 to $600 range (per pair). Investment in audio components of this quality is warranted only if you use an audio adapter card with 16-bit waveform audio and sampled sound capability.

CAUTION: Some speakers have very powerful permanent magnets that can radiate a magnetic field beyond their enclosures. Magnetic fields can have disastrous effects on floppy disks (erasure of their data content and format) and can cause distortion in the image of your monitor. The majority of speakers designed specifically for computer applications incorporate special magnetic shielding; these are recommended. To be on the safe side, keep all speakers at least a foot from your color monitor. If your monitor begins displaying strange colors or the edges of your image become scalloped, the tube's aperture mask has become magnetized and needs to be *degaussed* (residual magnetism removed.) More expensive displays have built-in degaussing capability. You can buy a degaussing wand from Radio Shack and other electronic supply firms to solve the problem.

Using Microphones for Recording

The MPC specification requires that audio adapter cards include a microphone input but does not specify the type of microphone to be accommodated. Consumers interpret "microphone" to mean one similar to those supplied with portable tape recorders. Audio engineers and professional musicians expect 600-ohm balanced outputs with XLR connectors. The differences are explained briefly in the following two sections.

Related Topics
Choosing Microphones,
p. 425

Consumer Microphones

The microphone inputs of all but one of the MPC-compliant audio adapter cards available at the time this book was written were monaural, used mono 1/8-inch (3.5-mm) mini-jacks as connectors, and were compatible with consumer-level microphones. Low-cost microphones, such as the Realistic 33-1067 from Radio Shack, are adequate for monophonic voice recording with 8-bit resolution at 5.0125 kHz or 11.025 kHz. One of the better grades of microphone is recommended if you are recording music with 16-bit resolution or higher sampling rates.

Professional Microphones

Professional sound systems use microphones with *balanced* output signals. Balanced means that two separate electrical signals, identical except that they are 180 degrees out of phase with one another, are transmitted over the microphone cable. Using the sine wave example, when one of the signals is at its peak positive voltage, the other is at the corresponding negative voltage. The signals then are recombined at the input to the sound system, with the phase of one signal shifted by 180 degrees. The advantage of this approach is that any noise induced through the cable imparts a similar voltage on both wires. Because one of the signals is phase-shifted 180 degrees at the receiving end, the noise signals on the two wires cancel one another, but the original voltages are unaffected. The three-wire connectors used for balanced signals are called XLR, the model designation assigned to them by Cannon Electric Co., which originated the connector's design.

Creating professional-quality 16-bit recordings at 44.1 kHz requires a multi-channel stereo microphone mixer or at least a microphone preamplifier. The mixer's or preamp's line output is connected to one of the stereo line inputs or stereo auxiliary inputs of the audio adapter card, rather than the microphone input. The reasons are explained in Chapter 15, "Waveform Audio Recording Techniques."

Adding a CD-ROM Drive

Installing an internal CD-ROM drive is a process almost identical to that for a hard disk drive. You must have an open, half-height drive bay and a spare disk drive power connector cable leading from your computer's power supply.

The standard drive bays of most conventional and tower cases for PCs have recesses that accommodate plastic mounting rails fastened to the side of the drives or, for 3.5-inch drives, their 5.25-inch wide mounting kit. Most CD-ROM drives come with these rails, but some do not. Check the content of the shipping carton before you leave the store or verify that the rails are included if you purchase a mail-order drive.

T I P

One of the major incentives for purchasing a sound card and internal CD-ROM together as a multimedia upgrade kit is the assurance that the proper cables to connect the two devices are included. If you purchase an audio adapter card first and later add an internal CD-ROM drive, you need two cables to connect them. 50-pin ribbon cables are now the standard for drives and cards with SCSI interfaces and usually are available from the manufacturer of the card. No standard exists, however, for internal audio connector cables. Most audio adapter cards have 5- or 6-pin headers for internal audio connections, but rear-panel audio connections on CD-ROM drives range from 3- to 6-pin headers. If you cannot obtain an audio ribbon cable compatible with the combination, you need to make the audio connection between the front-panel headphone jack of the CD-ROM drive and the line (auxiliary) input of your audio adapter card. This consumes the only external stereo input available on most audio adapter cards that you might want to use for audio input from, as an example, a VCR.

The instructions in this section apply to the installation of a CD-ROM drive that uses a dedicated SCSI interface on your audio adapter card. The control cable connections between the internal, 50-pin connector of a dedicated SCSI card and the CD-ROM drive are similar to those shown in figure 4.3. If your CD-ROM drive uses a proprietary interface, the control ribbon cable may have fewer than 50 pins on its connectors.

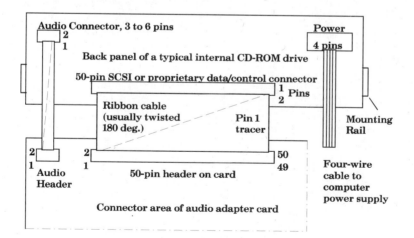

FIG. 4.3

Installing an internal CD-ROM drive in a half-height drive bay.

If you are installing an external CD-ROM drive, the manufacturer usually includes an interface adapter card with the drive. In some cases, you must purchase a SCSI adapter card separately. The instructions for installing an audio adapter card (refer to the earlier section, "Installing an Audio Adapter Card") also apply to CD-ROM interface cards—either SCSI or proprietary types. Most SCSI adapter cards use 25-pin miniature D-type connectors, similar to the PC's printer connector, to connect external drives. This connector mates with a cable leading from the case of the external drive.

T   I   P

SCSI adapters, whether a component of an MPC-compliant audio adapter card or installed as a dedicated adapter, require a device address (but not a special interrupt assignment.) A common default device address used for SCSI adapters is CC00. If you have installed a graphics accelerator card or another type of specialty graphics card, you may find a device address conflict with the SCSI card. Most SCSI cards provide a set of device address jumpers, similar to those on audio adapter cards, that can be used to change the SCSI adapter to an unoccupied device address. If you change the device address, you may need to change a parameter of the driver for the SCSI adapter. Device drivers for CD-ROM drives are discussed in Chapter 5.

To install a CD-ROM drive, do the following:

1. Turn off the power to your computer, monitor, and any other powered peripheral equipment. Refer to the earlier section, "Installing an Audio Adapter Card," for instructions on removing the case of the computer, if necessary.

2. Before removing the drive from the plastic protective envelope, ground yourself to the computer frame to discharge any residual static electricity that has accumulated on your body. If the drive electronics are exposed, avoid touching the printed wiring board or its components.

3. Attach the mounting rails, if required, to the sides of your drive with the screws provided. The tapered ends of the rails point to the back of the drive and the bottom of the rails should be about 1/4-inch above the bottom of the drive.

4. Remove the screws that hold the small sheet-metal keepers adjacent to the rail recesses in the case, if your case includes them.

5. Plug one end of the 50-conductor ribbon cable to the connector on the back of the drive before you slip it into the drive bay. Observe the precaution in the following tip regarding the location of the colored tracer of the ribbon cables.

Most ribbon cable connectors are not *polarized*; in other words, you cannot plug them in two ways. Murphy's Law assures that you always will choose the wrong cable unless you follow the instructions exactly. All ribbon cables have a colored *tracer* that identifies the wire corresponding to pin 1 of the connector. A tracer is an inked line, usually blue or red, applied to one side of the ribbon cable during its manufacture. Silk-screened legends on the printed wiring board, adjacent to its CD-ROM drive connector, indicate the pin numbers. Usually you see 1 or 2 at one end of the connector and 49 or 50 at the other (for the 50-conductor cable, 5 or 6 for the audio cable.) The same legends are usually silk-screened on the rear panel of the CD-ROM drive. Make sure that the side of the cable with the colored tracer is plugged into the 1/2 end of the headers.

T I P

6. If your sound card has a multi-pin audio connector, plug one end of the multi-conductor audio ribbon cable into the audio connector at the back of the drive, observing cable polarity.

7. Route the cable(s) through the drive bay and place the free ends where they will not be damaged.

8. If the power supply cable is sufficiently long, plug it into the mating receptacle on the back panel of the drive. If the cable is not long enough, remember the location of the receptacle and the position of the polarizing key (a 45-degree bevel at one side of the plastic housing of the receptacle) because you may have to insert the power supply plug "by feel."

9. Gently slide the drive into the drive bay until its front panel is flush with the other drives of your computer.

10. If you were unable to insert the power plug into the receptacle in step 6, do so now.

11. Connect the 50-conductor cable connector to the corresponding header on the audio adapter card or the dedicated interface card. Plug the multi-pin audio ribbon cable into your audio adapter card's audio header. Again, observe the proper polarity of the cables as noted in the following caution.

12. Replace the sheetmetal keepers you removed in step 4.

13. Do a double-check of the location of the colored tracers of both ribbon cables.

14. Inspect the interior of the CD-ROM drive's insertion slot or drive drawer for protective shipping material, and remove any found.

CAUTION: Connecting the audio adapter card and CD-ROM audio outputs in parallel by using Y-connectors (two RCA phono jacks connected to one RCA phono plug) is not a recommended practice. Connecting two speaker outputs together can damage the output amplifiers on one or both cards. Audio output signals from most audio adapter cards are low-impedence; in other words, they are designed to drive speakers and headphones. If you connect the two output signals in parallel and do not blow out the card's output amplifier, the output level of the CD-ROM will be very low or not audible at all. If your self-amplifying speakers do not have two inputs or your stereo set does not have an extra auxiliary input, you may be able to use a mixing Y-connector that adds a resistor in series with each output. Your local Radio Shack store may have these, or your can cobble one together by soldering a 2,200-ohm resistor between a phono jack and a phono plug. You may have to experiment with resistor values to obtain the proper output levels.

15. If your audio adapter card does not have an auxiliary audio input, you need a 1/8-inch stereo mini-plug to dual RCA phono plug cable (Radio Shack 42-2475A). The phono plugs are connected to the second input of your self-amplifying speakers (if they have a second input) or an additional stereo input of your sound system. The headphone outputs of CD-ROMs seldom have sufficient power to drive unamplified speakers directly.

16. Replace the cover on your computer and reapply power to the computer and its peripheral equipment.

17. Place a CD-ROM in the caddy and insert it in the drive, if you have a drive that uses caddies (most do). Otherwise, follow the instructions in the manual for CD-ROM installation.

Always handle CD-ROMs by their edges, the same way you handle audio CDs and vinyl LP records, to prevent fingerprints on their surfaces. Fingerprints cause dust to adhere to the surface of the media and may interfere with the ability of the CD-ROM player to read a smudged CD-ROM's data. The dust and other particles that adhere to fingerprints or other foreign materials on a CD-ROM's surface may become dislodged and interfere with the internal light path in the drive. Remember that the active side of a CD-ROM is the underside, opposite the label side, so be particularly careful not to mar that surface. Keep CD-ROMs in their protective jewel cases or plastic envelopes when they are not in the caddy. This minimizes the amount of dust that accumulates on their surfaces.

T I P

Chapter Summary

This chapter explained the basic steps involved in installing an audio adapter card, a CD-ROM drive, or the two together in an MPC Upgrade Kit. If you are like most PC owners, this will be the first time you have opened the case of your computer. The instructions given in this chapter for installing audio adapter cards and dedicated SCSI or proprietary CD-ROM adapters apply when you install a graphic accelerator card or one of the video-in-a-window cards described in Part V of this book.

After you have completed the mechanical installation of a audio adapter card, a CD-ROM drive, or both, you need to install the device drivers required by Windows to use them. The CD-ROM drive requires a DOS driver because the drive acts as if it were a read-only floppy disk drive. Windows drivers for audio adapter cards and DOS drivers for CD-ROM drives are the subject of the next chapter, "Preparing Windows for Multimedia."

Preparing Windows for Multimedia

Microsoft Windows provides a wide range of standard "services" to its applications. Services simplify the programming of Windows applications by supplying built-in capabilities to perform basic operations. One service enables Windows to display an image of a specified size in a window at a particular location. Without the service, a programmer would spend hours writing code to do this. The individual elements that comprise Windows services are called *functions*. Each function performs a specific operation when requested to do so by an application—referred to by programmers as "calling a function."

Before the introduction of the Multimedia Extensions for Windows 3.0, Windows services basically managed the keyboard, display, printer, COM ports, and disk files. The Multimedia Extensions 1.0—added to Windows 3.0 in late 1991 to create Windows with Multimedia—is the foundation for all multimedia services within the Windows environment. When introduced in April 1992, Windows 3.1 included most of the functions of Windows with Multimedia. Emphasizing sound, Windows 3.1 supplies a complete set of audio functions for playing and recording waveform audio files, plus the playing of MIDI files and audio CDs.

This chapter begins by describing the multimedia services of Windows 3.1. You progress to the subject of device drivers and how they are used to adapt specific hardware devices to the standards enforced by Windows multimedia services. The major portion of this chapter discusses the techniques you use to install and set up device drivers for sound cards.

Examining Windows Drivers for Multimedia

Before you install the drivers for your audio adapter card under Windows 3.1, take time to learn a bit about how Windows uses the multimedia-related files in your \WINDOWS\SYSTEM directory to integrate sound with Windows applications. This knowledge is especially helpful if you have problems getting your sound card to work properly with your applications. This knowledge also is useful if you are installing the software required for newer types of media, such as digital video or for animation applications. (Animation applications were included in Windows 3.0 with Multimedia, but not in Windows 3.1.)

Drivers for CD-ROM drives operate directly under DOS, not Windows, so they are described in a section of their own at the end of this chapter, "Installing CD-ROM Device Drivers and Applications." The CD-ROM driver must be a DOS driver because a CD-ROM drive is equivalent to a read-only floppy disk drive. You read CD-ROM data through DOS, even when you are running Windows.

The foundation layer of Windows multimedia is contained in a file called MMSYSTEM.DLL, a *dynamic link library*, which comprises the multimedia system. Dynamic link libraries (DLLs) contain groups of related functions that Windows applications use to perform many of their tasks. The individual functions contained in DLLs can be used simultaneously by any applications that need them. This saves memory and disk space that would be consumed if each application had to have its own set of basic service functions. All requests for multimedia services are made through MMSYSTEM.DLL.

Gaining Hardware Independence with Device Drivers

Another benefit of Windows to programmers and users is *hardware-independence* of applications. Each application designed for use under DOS must have its own set of *device drivers* for peripheral hardware, such as displays and printers. Device drivers receive instructions from the application and translate them into the commands required by specific types of printers (dot-matrix or laser), displays (monochrome or VGA), keyboards, and mice. Therefore, if you are using the DOS versions of Lotus 1-2-3 and WordPerfect, each requires an individual set of drivers for your computer hardware configuration.

Although Windows requires device drivers for each peripheral component, all applications can share one driver for each type of device. Applications programmers do not need to write driver code. This shared use of device drivers also saves hard disk space.

Windows includes a set of drivers for popular displays, printers, keyboards, and mice. When manufacturers develop new or improved products, the supplier (not the application programmer) is responsible for creating and supplying a Windows device driver to accompany the products.

Figure 5.1 shows the relationships between Windows applications, the DLLs that provide Windows services, and the device drivers required to implement these services.

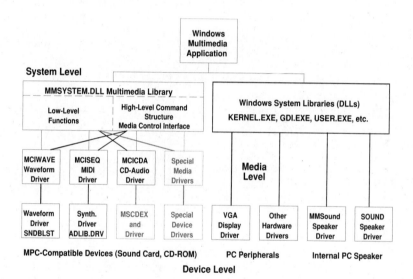

FIG. 5.1

The relationship of Windows dynamic link libraries and device drivers to applications.

The addition of multimedia audio capabilities to Windows 3.1 requires an intermediate level of specialized media drivers, shown at the media level in figure 5.1. Media drivers not included in Windows 3.1 are shown in gray. These specialized media drivers are used for the following applications:

■ *Waveform audio.* MCIWAVE.DRV provides media level services for recording and playing waveform audio files through a device driver—such as SNDBLST2.DRV—that controls the mixer of your audio adapter card and analog-to-digital and digital-to-analog converters.

■ *Playing synthesized sound and music in MIDI files.* MCISEQ.DRV opens and closes MIDI files and controls the operation of the sound synthesis functions of audio adapter cards with a device driver, such as ADLIB.DRV. Some firms combine the waveform audio, mixer, and synthesized sound functions for their adapter cards in a single driver. Another driver, MIDIMAP.DRV, is supplied by Windows.

■ *CD-audio.* MCICDA.DRV controls the operation of CD-ROM drives when playing audio CDs. MCICDA.DRV requires that MSCDEX.EXE, the general-purpose CD-ROM driver, and a device driver for the CD-ROM drive be installed. These drivers are not supplied with Windows 3.1; they are supplied on floppy disk with the CD-ROM drive by the manufacturer.

■ *Special-purpose drivers.* These drivers at the media and device levels are supplied by third parties. Media Vision, for instance, supplies MMMIXER.DLL for audio mixer control at the media level. MMMIXER.DLL instructs MVMIXER.DRV to send commands to the audio mixer on their Pro AudioSpectrum adapter cards.

These intermediaries are not real device drivers; they would more appropriately be called media-specific DLLs. Many third party media drivers use the DLL extension rather than DRV to distinguish special-purpose DLLs that apply to a type of media instead of a specific piece of hardware.

The structure shown in figure 5.1 is called an *application programming interface* or API. Microsoft designed the Windows multimedia API so that it can accommodate new types of standard multimedia devices—such as digital video—to be added as the technology for required hardware evolves. This chapter covers functions provided by MCIWAVE.DRV, the media driver used for waveform audio, and by MCICDA.DRV, used to control your CD-ROM drive when you use it to listen to audio CDs. Chapter 7 covers the more complex subject of MIDI media and device drivers.

Integrating Sound with Windows Applications

Related Topics
Multimedia Programming
Interface and Data
Specification, p. 632
Embedding or Linking
Source Documents,
p. 223

Requests to play or record sound are passed by the Windows application—such as Sound Recorder or Media Player—through MMSYSTEM.DLL and then through the appropriate media driver. The application passes the request finally to the hardware device driver that translates it to instructions recognized by the manufacturer's audio adapter card.

MMSYSTEM.DLL has two elements: *low-level* and *high-level*. Programmers of commercial Windows applications use low-level commands to perform specific functions, such as send a MIDI message telling a synthesizer to play a specific note. The high-level commands, called the *Media Control Interface* (MCI), enable even nonprogrammers to control multimedia hardware with simple commands expressed in common English—**play** and **stop**, for example. You are introduced to a few of these commands in Chapter 8, "Incorporating Sound in Windows Applications," and to all of them in Chapter 23, "The High-Level MCI Commands of Windows."

Windows is a pseudomultitasking environment. Most PCs have only one microprocessor, but the microprocessor can be shared by two (or more) applications under the guidance of Windows. This means that more than one task can appear to be processed simultaneously—you can edit a Word for Windows document and download (receive) a file from CompuServe with your modem at the same time. In addition, you can play a sound file with Media Player or listen to an audio CD while you create an Excel worksheet. The data for the file being downloaded from CompuServe is processed during the intervals when Windows is waiting for keystrokes in Excel and when Windows is not sending control messages to the CD-ROM drive.

One more distinction should be made before you proceed to install drivers for your audio card—simple versus compound devices. *Simple devices* are audio and video devices, such as CD-ROM drives, that do not (and cannot) use files when they are playing audio CDs and CD-I (Compact Disc-Interactive) discs, videodisc, and videotape devices. (Audio CDs have tracks, not files.) Simple device types are supported by the high-level MCI commands only. *Compound devices* require their data (images, sound, and text) to be in the form of files, whether on a hard disk, floppy disk, CD-ROM, or images of a file (called a *buffer*) in your computer's memory.

Examining Windows' Waveform Audio Drivers

About one million Sound Blaster cards and their clones had been installed in PCs when Windows 3.1 was introduced to the retail market; so Microsoft supplied the waveform (sampled) audio device drivers for both early (Version 1.0, SNDBLST.DRV) and later (Version 1.5, SNDBLST2.DRV) versions. These drivers were provided for the convenience of Windows users so that they didn't need to request drivers from the card's manufacturer. All MPC-compatible adapter cards come with the required Windows hardware drivers on their installation disk.

Figure 5.2 shows how Windows applications use the collection of functions in MMSYSTEM.DLL, MCIWAVE.DRV, and hardware-dependent device drivers to record and reproduce digitally sampled sound. Those elements involved directly in multimedia audio are shown in thicker-bordered boxes. MMSOUND.DRV is used to substitute sound effects stored in WAV files for Windows familiar beep. MMSOUND.DRV is used by Windows itself and applications written for Windows 3.1 to accompany pop-up message boxes or other events with dings, chimes, Bronx cheers, or vocal admonitions.

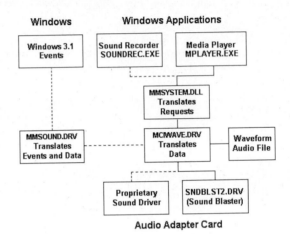

FIG. 5.2

The multimedia services of Windows 3.1 involved in playing waveform audio.

When your application requires sampled sound to be played, the following steps are involved:

1. The application—for example, a Media Player—sends a request to MMSYSTEM.DLL. The request includes the name of the file in which the digitized sound is stored and the location within the file where the action is to begin. The default starting position is the beginning of the file.

2. MMSYSTEM.DLL is loaded into your computer's memory, if this is the first time it is to be used by an application. MMSYSTEM.DLL remains in memory until all the applications that use it are shut down and another application needs the memory it appropriates.

3. The MMSYSTEM.DLL function called by the application determines what type of sound has been requested—in this case waveform audio—and opens the specified file. The type of sound can be determined by a specific instruction, or MMSYSTEM.DLL can infer the type of sound by the extension of the file—for example, WAV for waveform audio files.

4. The function translates the request to one or more instructions recognizable by the media driver, in this case MCIWAVE.DRV. Like MMSYSTEM.DLL, MCIWAVE.DRV is loaded into memory.

5. Assuming that playback has been selected, MCIWAVE.DRV translates the information in the file to the standard data format for waveform audio device drivers and stores it in a reserved memory location, called a *buffer*.

6. The waveform audio device driver, in this case SNDBLST2.DRV, translates the data in the buffer to the specific instructions required by Sound Blaster Version 1.5 and sends them via the selected DMA channel to the device address specified.

7. The digital-to-analog converter of the Sound Blaster card receives the stream of instructions and translates the individual bytes in the stream to a continuous (analog) sound signal reproduced by external speakers.

Despite the number of steps involved, the transmission of instructions through the chain described is very rapid. A 16-MHz 80386SX computer can reproduce 16-bit stereo digital audio at 44.1 kHz, which is 88,200 samples per second—about the maximum rate at which data can be transmitted from most current CD-ROM drives.

Installing and Configuring Audio Device Drivers

All multimedia drivers are added to Windows through the Drivers dialog box from the Control Panel. Note that the Drivers icon, shown in figure 5.3, includes images of a video (or perhaps digital audio) tape cassette, a CD-ROM, and a keyboard synthesizer. The MIDI Mapper driver is installed by Windows, but you will not see its icon until you install a driver for a card that supports MIDI operations. Similarly, the list boxes of the Sound dialog in figure 5.3 are disabled (their entries are gray) until you install the driver for an audio adapter card that has waveform audio capability.

Whenever you add a new multimedia component to your system, you need to install the drivers required for Windows to use it. If you add a CD-ROM drive, for example, most installation applications copy MSCDEX.EXE, the DOS CD-ROM driver, and a device driver to your \WINDOWS or another directory. The installation applications then make the necessary modifications in your CONFIG.SYS file to load the device driver and to the AUTOEXEC.BAT file to load MSCDEX.EXE when you start your computer.

FIG. 5.3

Windows 3.1
Control Panel with
the audio multimedia
functions.

Installing Drivers for Pre-MPC Adapter Cards

Windows 3.1 supplies a set of standard drivers, shown in the List of Drivers list box in figure 5.4, for pre-MPC adapter cards so that you do not have to request them from the manufacturer. The original Ad Lib, Sound Blaster 1.0 and 1.5, Thunder Board, and MPU-401-compatible cards are supported—the LAPC-1 and MPU-401 use the same Microsoft driver.

The procedure for adding the required drivers for newer MPC-compliant sound cards differs for those that predate the MPC standards. If you are installing an MPC-compliant card that includes Windows drivers on its accompanying floppy disk, skip to the next section, "Installing Drivers Supplied by the Manufacturer."

Windows 3.1's Control Panel provides the Drivers function for installing drivers. To add a sound driver for pre-MPC adapter cards, follow these steps:

1. Run the Control Panel by double-clicking its icon.

2. Click the Drivers icon to bring up the dialog box that displays the drivers installed by Windows during the setup process or that had been added previously.

3. If your card is not on the list of installed drivers or you upgraded Windows 3.0 with Multimedia to Windows 3.1, choose Add. The Add dialog box appears (see fig. 5.4).

4. Choose the driver for your particular sound card from the list by double-clicking on its name (or single-click the name and then click OK). The Sound Blaster 1.5 and the Thunder Board use the same device drivers. The MPU-401 driver is used for all MPU-401-compatible cards, including the Roland LAPC-1 and SCC-1.

5. The driver you select is added to the list of Installed Drivers, shown in figure 5.5. If you are installing a Thunder Board or an original Sound Blaster, the Ad Lib driver also is installed to handle the synthesized sound functions of the card.

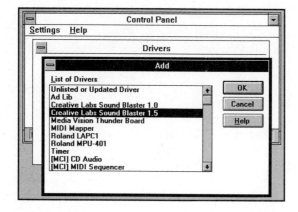

FIG. 5.4

Control Panel's Driver's Add dialog box for multimedia device drivers.

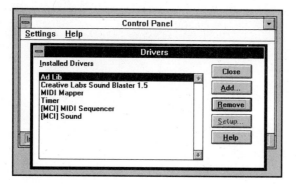

FIG. 5.5

Control Panel's list of Installed Drivers.

Now that you've added sound drivers for pre-MPC adapter cards, skip the next section and proceed to "Setting Up the Audio Driver."

Installing Drivers Supplied by the Manufacturer

MPC-compliant audio adapter cards are supplied with drivers created especially for each model by the manufacturer and supplied on the installation floppy disk. These are called *OEM* drivers—the abbreviation stands for original equipment manufacturer. The SETUP or INSTALL application supplied with most cards installs the required driver for you. You may need to install the driver yourself, however, or update the driver for your card.

Related Topics
Exploring Device Drivers for MIDI Adapter Cards, p. 195
Setting Up MIDI Mapper, p. 196

T I P
Make a backup copy of MIDIMAP.CFG, the configuration file for the MIDI Mapper applet, before you install the device driver for your sound card. Most manufacturers supply their own version of MIDIMAP.CFG, which contains information related to their product only. On installation, the original copy of MIDIMAP.CFG supplied with Windows 3.1 is overwritten by the new one. Although you may never need the original, you should keep it around in case you do—for example, to test an original Sound Blaster or Ad Lib card. To make a backup copy, follow these steps:

1. Open File Manager.

2. Click the SYSTEM subdirectory of WINDOWS.

3. Locate MIDIMAP.CFG in the right file list. Click it to highlight it.

4. Choose **F**ile, then **C**opy from File Manager's menu.

5. Enter **MIDIMAP.W31** in the **T**o: text box of the Copy dialog box.

6. Click OK.

7. Close File Manager.

To install the driver yourself, use the following procedure:

1. Run Control Panel by double-clicking its icon.

2. Click the Drivers icon to bring up the dialog box that displays the drivers installed by Windows during the setup process or that have been added previously.

3. If your card is not on the list of installed drivers or you upgraded Windows 3.0 with Multimedia to Windows 3.1, choose **A**dd.

4. Choose Unlisted Or Updated Driver by double-clicking it (or single-click and then click OK). The Install Driver dialog box appears (see fig. 5.6).

5. Insert the disk with the required driver in disk drive A or B. If you choose drive B, enter **B:** in the dialog box and click OK.

6. If you are installing an updated driver, you receive a message box informing you that a driver for the product already has been installed.

7. The driver is copied to your \WINDOWS\SYSTEM directory. When you reboot your computer, the driver is added to the list of installed drivers shown in figure 5.5.

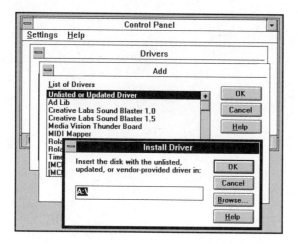

FIG. 5.6

Installing an OEM
multimedia device
driver supplied by the
manufacturer.

When Windows attempts to install a device driver from a floppy disk, it first searches for a file called OEMSETUP.INF. OEMSETUP.INF provides the name of the driver(s) required and the name that appears in the list of installed drivers when the process is completed. If you copy the driver but not the OEMSETUP.INF file, the Install Driver dialog box reappears. You do not receive a message that the required file was not found.

If you remove from the Install Drivers dialog box a driver that was not supplied with Windows, you may not be able to reinstall it from the \WINDOWS\SYSTEM directory where the driver file is located. The driver floppy disk may not have installed the OEMSETUP.INF on the hard disk. You must have the floppy disk, supplied by the manufacturer, that includes the driver and OEMSETUP.INF. This is not a problem with the drivers supplied with Windows, because the equivalent of the information in OEMSETUP.INF for these drivers is included in the \WINDOWS\SYSTEM\SETUP.INF file. The content of OEMSETUP.INF is covered in "Understanding the OEMSETUP.INF File," later in this chapter.

Setting Up the Audio Driver

You're almost finished when you install the driver. You still need to set up the selected driver to suit the device address and interrupt level the manufacturer or you chose for the card. Figure 5.7 shows the setup dialog box for Sound Blaster cards with the default device address (port) and interrupt level—the dialog box for other cards is similar.

To set up the driver you installed, follow these steps:

1. Click the **S**etup command button in the Drivers dialog box. A setup dialog box similar to that shown in figure 5.7 for MPC-compliant cards appears. The name in the title box depends on the driver you selected.

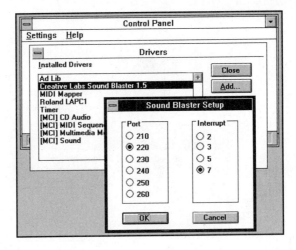

FIG. 5.7

The Sound Blaster
Setup dialog box.

2. Click the Port option button corresponding to the default device address or the alternate address you selected.

3. Click the Interrupt option button for the default IRQ level or the chosen alternative.

4. Click the OK button or press Enter to close the dialog box.

5. The Driver function is quite intelligent. It checks to see whether you made the correct settings. If not, the message box shown in figure 5.8 appears, and you need to correct your settings.

FIG. 5.8

The message box
indicating incorrect
device address or
interrupt settings.

6. Click the Close button of the Drivers dialog box. An information message box similar to figure 5.9 appears.

7. Because the driver must be installed before Windows is launched, you must restart Windows. Select Reset, and Windows closes— after offering you the opportunity to save any work in progress— and then automatically restarts.

After you restart Windows, inspect the installed drivers by starting Control Panel, then double-clicking the Drivers icon. The MIDI Mapper driver has been installed. If you installed a Sound Blaster or compatible card, the Ad Lib driver for synthesized sound also has been installed for you.

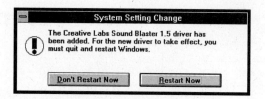

FIG. 5.9

The message box indicating completion of the device driver installation.

The process for setting up the required MIDI map for your adapter card using Control Panel's MIDI Mapper function is described in Chapter 7, "Playing MIDI Files." If you have installed the MPU-401 driver, skip to Chapter 7. Otherwise, the next step is to use a waveform audio file to test your installation.

Testing Your Installation with the Sound Function

You can test the waveform functions of your sound card, the waveform audio driver, and the connections to your stereo or speaker system with Control Panel's Sound function. Sound is used to assign the four waveform audio files (WAV) supplied with Windows 3.1—DING.WAV, CHORD.WAV, CHIMES.WAV, and TADA.WAV—to the occurrence of a group of selected Windows events. Windows with Multimedia provides some additional interesting sounds.

Related Topics
Experimenting with Sound Recorder, p. 180

If you used the Custom setup option when you installed Windows 3.1 and did not choose to install the WAV sound files, you need to install them now. To install these files into your \WINDOWS directory—the only directory from which Sound can play these files—follow these steps:

1. Run Windows **S**etup.

2. Choose **O**ptions from Setup's main menu, then choose **A**dd/ Remove Windows Components.

3. Click the **F**iles button for **W**allpapers, Misc.

4. Highlight each file in the right list box with Sound in its name. If you did not install the Canyon MIDI song file during initial installation, click it now.

5. Choose OK.

6. Insert the distribution floppy disk that includes the selected files. They are expanded from their compressed form and copied into your \WINDOWS directory.

Related Topics

Obtaining Other Waveform Audio Files, p. 189

Assigning Sounds to Windows Events

Windows 3.1 adds an audio feature long enjoyed by users of Apple Macintosh computers—sound effects for events. The four standard WAV files supplied by Microsoft and listed in the Files list box of figure 5.10 are designed to add musical accompaniment to the seven events shown in the Events list box. The sounds you assign to events are processed by MMSOUND.DRV, which loads the proper WAV file into memory. MMSOUND.DRV then sends the data to the device driver for your audio adapter card, which reproduces the data through your sound system.

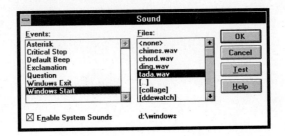

FIG. 5.10

The Sound dialog box for assigning waveform audio files to events.

Default Beep, Windows Exit, and Windows Start are events generated by Windows. The other events are associated with message boxes that include the listed icons. These icons are used by Windows applications for the following purposes:

Asterisk/Information indicates that the message box contains information to assist the user. In most applications, a white lowercase i in a circular blue field substitutes for the asterisk.

Critical Stop, a replica of the conventional red stop sign, warns the user that the action requested may lead to serious consequences. These message boxes usually request that the user confirm the action with a "go ahead anyway" button and offer the opportunity to cancel the request.

Exclamation, a black exclamation point in a yellow field, is used as a warning less severe than that for a critical stop.

Question, a white question mark on a green field, usually requests a selection between two options or confirmation of an action, such as overwriting an existing file with a new version.

You assign sounds to the seven events with the following steps:

1. Run Control Panel from the Main group by double-clicking its icon.

2. Display the Sound dialog box in figure 5.10 by double-clicking the Sound icon in Control Panel's window.

3. The **F**iles list box displays all files with the WAV extension in your \WINDOWS directory. All sounds associated with events must be located in this directory.

4. The **E**vents list box shows the seven different occurrences to which sounds may be attached.

5. The default sound for each event is <none>. Before you assign the sounds, only the default beep, played through your PC's speaker to signal a Windows complaint, can be heard.

6. Click the event to which you want to assign a sound to highlight it. Windows Start is a good point to begin.

7. Click the name of the sound file you want to associate with the event. For Windows Start, tada.wav is the obvious choice, and it is highlighted. You can preview the sound by clicking the Test button.

8. Repeat steps 6 and 7 for each remaining event. ding.wav is a good choice for Default Beep and Critical Stop. You might choose chord.wav for the remaining events.

9. Make sure that an X appears in the E**n**able System Sounds check box. If the check box is empty, click the interior of the box to turn sound on.

10. Click OK to save your choices. As you can see, you can easily substitute other waveform audio files for your initial choices.

11. Close the Control Panel by double-clicking the Control bar in the upper left corner.

If you assign sound other than those supplied with Windows to events, you may receive the error message, Unable to Play Sound or hear no sound when the event is known to have occurred. The problem may lie with either of the following:

T I P

The sampling frequency of the WAV file you are attempting to play. Although Sound Recorder can play files recorded at 11.025, 22.05, and 44.1 kHz, Sound accepts files recorded at a 22.05 kHz sampling rate only. Substitute one of the files supplied with Windows to see if this is the problem.

Sound code missing from the application. If the event is the appearance of a message box, your application has not been updated to Windows 3.1, or the programmer who created it did not add the code required to play sounds. Many of the Microsoft applets supplied with Windows 3.1 do not include this code.

Testing Message Box Sounds with Soundex

Windows itself issues the beep, exit, and start messages that cause the files you assign to them to be played. Applications that have not been updated for use with Windows 3.1 do not include the code necessary to add sound to signal the appearance of message boxes. Strangely, the dialogs used by Windows 3.1 itself do not incorporate the sound code.

Mike Mezaros of CheckBox Software has created a freeware application written in Microsoft Visual Basic to demonstrate these message boxes and the sound that accompanies them. His Soundex application (short for Sound Examples, not the soundex coding system used for phonetic searches of proper names) creates sample message boxes to exercise your choice of sounds. The opening (and only) window of Soundex, which you can download from CompuServe's WINADV forum, Library 12 as SOUNDX.ZIP, is shown in figure 5.11.

FIG. 5.11

CheckBox Software's application to demonstrate association of sounds with message box icons.

To run Soundex, you need a copy of VBRUN100.DLL installed in your \WINDOWS or \WINDOWS\SYSTEM directory. VBRUN100.DLL is the run-time library for Visual Basic, the language in which Soundex was written; it is required to run all Visual Basic applications supplied in the form of executable (EXE) files. You can download VBRUN100.DLL from CompuServe's Microsoft Basic forum (GO MSBASIC), Library 6, Visual Basic.

When you click the command bars of Soundex, the message box with the appropriate icon appears, accompanied by the sound you selected.

Troubleshooting Your Adapter Card Installation

If you do not hear the selected sound when you click the **Test** button, use the following troubleshooting guide.

Most problems with sound adapter cards are related to the audio output cabling and settings on the consumer sound systems most often used to drive speakers.

1. Some cards with multiple miniphone jacks do not label the jacks. Make sure that your audio output cable is plugged into the output, not an input connector. You may have to refer to the instructions to verify the position of the output connector.

2. If you are using your sound system as the output device, check that the audio output cable is plugged into the Aux(iliary) inputs. If you have more than one Aux channel, make sure that your source selection switch is set to the proper one.

3. Some sound systems do not have an auxiliary input, but most have a tape monitor input. If you are using the tape monitor input, make sure that the input selector is set to tape or that the tape monitor button is depressed.

4. If you are using self-powered speakers, make sure that the power is on to both speakers.

5. Remove the miniplug from the output of the audio adapter card and place the tip of your finger on the tip end. Turn up the volume control, and you should hear 60-Hz induced hum (from surrounding power lines) through the speakers. If you don't, you have a problem in your sound system, not the card.

6. When all else has failed, plug a set of stereo headphones into the audio output jack of the adapter card. Click **Test** again to see if the card itself is working. If you hear sounds, again your sound system is at fault.

Setup applications for audio adapter cards usually include an audio mixer applet. These applets have a variety of names, but usually include *mix* in them. Launch the mixer application and verify that the sliders or knobs for all inputs and outputs are set to their 100% or maximum position. One or more of the sliders or knobs could be set to zero or a low value due to an error during installation. Using audio mixer applications is covered in Chapter 15.

T I P

If the above steps do not break the silence, you have a problem with the drivers or the card itself. Try these steps:

1. Exit Windows to the DOS prompt. Do not use the MS-DOS Window for these steps because some diagnostic programs may install a terminate-and-stay resident (TSR) application. TSR applications loaded from within Windows can cause Windows or your applications to crash.

2. From the DOS prompt, run the diagnostic software supplied with the card—TEST-SBC.EXE for the Sound Blaster, TBTEST.EXE with Thunder Boards. Most other sound cards come with DOS diagnostics having similar names.

3. If the diagnostic program shows an error, check to make sure that the adapter card is fully seated in its connector. Follow the manual's instructions for further tests or return the card for a replacement. Some computers have problems with specific audio adapter cards, so check with the supplier's technical service department before you give up and return the card for replacement.

4. Reboot (Ctrl+Alt+Del) your computer after running these tests to remove from memory any TSR applications that may have been installed during the diagnostic process.

5. Start Windows. If the problem is with the drivers you installed, you should receive a message describing the problem when Windows boots. If such a message occurs, try reinstalling the driver. If this doesn't work, get a new copy of the driver software from the manufacturer of the card or download one from a source listed in Appendix H.

If none of the above suggestions solves your problem, have a friend check your work. Sometimes a fresh look at the problem by a less-frustrated person results in an immediate solution.

T I P Users of sound cards have reported problems with noise (a high-frequency hiss) on audio inputs as well as erratic behavior of FM-synthesized sound with audio adapter cards using the Yamaha OPL-3 chipset. These problems may be related to the chipset used on your motherboard. If you experience such a problem, note the manufacturer's name printed on the larger, square chips on your motherboard and contact the technical service department of the audio adapter card's manufacturer. Updated drivers with fixes for specific motherboards may be available.

Removing Unneeded Device Drivers

When you change audio adapter cards or if you have added a driver not required by your card, you should remove the unneeded driver. This frees the memory assigned to the driver when starting Windows. To remove drivers, follow these steps:

1. Start the Control Panel application from the Main group.

2. Choose the Drivers icon. The Installed Drivers list box appears.

3. In the Installed Drivers list box, click the name of the driver to be removed to highlight it.

4. If you are removing the driver in conjunction with installation of an updated driver, click Setup to display its settings. Make a note of the Port and IRQ numbers, along with any other settings in the dialog box. Click Cancel when you are finished.

5. Click the Remove button. The confirmation box in figure 5.12 appears.

6. Click the **Yes** button to confirm that you want to remove the driver.

7. You are asked if you want to exit and restart Windows now. If you are removing more than one driver, click **D**on't Restart Now.

8. Repeat steps 3 through 7 for each driver you want to remove. Do not attempt to remove drivers preceded by [mci] or the Timer driver. These are not device drivers; they are required by the multimedia system.

9. Click **R**estart Now to exit and restart Windows to make the deletion(s) effective.

Installing Updated Device Drivers

Suppliers of audio adapter cards periodically issue new sets of drivers for their products to improve performance or solve compatibility problems. Many of these suppliers operate electronic bulletin boards from which you can download updated drivers. Most technical service departments also will mail you a floppy disk upon request. Microsoft provides a driver-updating service directly and on CompuServe. Instructions for downloading updated drivers are given in Appendix H.

Before you install an updated set of device drivers, you should remove the existing device driver entry, using the method described in the preceding section. After you remove the existing driver and restart Windows, follow these steps:

1. Start Control Panel from the Main group.

2. Double-click the Drivers icon to display the **Installed Drivers** list box.

3. Click the **Add** button.

4. Double-click the Unlisted or Updated Drivers item in the **List of Drivers** list box. The Install Driver dialog box appears (see fig. 5.13).

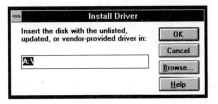

5. Enter the disk drive designator where the floppy disk with the updated device drivers has been inserted. The device driver set does not have to be installed from a floppy disk, but this is the standard method employed by the Install Driver dialog box. If you downloaded an updated driver set and placed it in its own subdirectory on your hard disk, enter the drive and path to those files.

6. The driver installation application reads the OEMSETUP.INF file on the floppy disk and copies the required drivers to your hard disk. The application then makes the required changes in SYSTEM.INI (and sometimes in WIN.INI) to accommodate the new drivers.

7. You may see the Driver Exists dialog during installation (see fig. 5.14). If this box appears, click the **New** button to use the updated driver, not the driver currently in your \WINDOWS\SYSTEM directory.

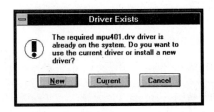

8. You are asked for setup information for the driver. Set the device address (Port) and interrupt level (IRQ) to those of the prior version of the driver.

9. Click **R**estart Now to exit and restart Windows to use the new drivers.

If you receive a message that a required file is missing or the Install Driver dialog box of figure 5.13 repeatedly reappears after you click OK, read the following section on the OEMSETUP.INF file to determine the source of the problem.

Understanding the OEMSETUP.INF File

All drivers not part of the standard complement of Windows 3.1 require an OEMSETUP.INF file to guide the installation process so that the drivers are loaded during Windows start-up. OEMSETUP.INF contains the name of the driver set to be added to your **I**nstalled Drivers list box, the names of the files to be added to your \WINDOWS\SYSTEM.INI directory, and the entries to be added to or modified in SYSTEM.INI.

The OEMSETUP.INF file for an updated Sound Blaster Pro driver for Windows 3.1, obtained in mid-1992 from the Microsoft Windows Driver Library (WDL), has the following content:

```
[disks]
1=.\,"Microsoft Windows Driver Library - Audio Disk 1"

[Installable.Drivers]
SBPWaveMidi = 1:sbpsnd.drv, "Wave,MIDI", "Creative Sound Blaster Pro
    Wave and MIDI", 1:vsbd.386,,
SBProFM     = 1:sbpfm.drv,  "MIDI",      "Creative Sound Blaster Pro
    MIDI Synthesizer",,
SBProAux    = 1:sbpaux.drv, "AUX",       "Creative Sound Blaster Pro
    Auxiliary Audio",,

[SBPWaveMidi]
1:sbpmixer.cpl

[SBProFM]
1:midimap.cfg
```

The purpose of each section of OEMSETUP.INF, identified by headings enclosed in square brackets, is discussed in the following paragraphs.

[disks] supplies the name of the disk when errors are reported in the installation process.

[Installable.Drivers] lists the following information:

The name assigned to the driver by the manufacturer (SBPWaveMIDI)

The file name of the device driver to be copied to the
\WINDOWS\SYSTEM directory (sbpsnd.drv)
Its function (for waveform audio or MIDI files, AUX for mixers)
The name that appears in the list box of the drivers to install
Other drivers required by the device driver (vsbd.386).

If more than one installable driver is listed, the list box in figure 5.15 appears. You must install each device driver individually.

FIG. 5.15

The list of installable
drivers that appears
when more than one
driver is included on a
floppy disk.

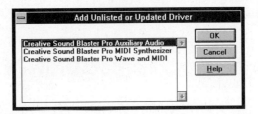

[SBPWaveMIDI] installs an additional file, sbpmixer.cpl, when you
choose installation of the Creative Sound Blaster Pro Wave and
MIDI driver. It adds an icon for the Sound Blaster Pro's mixer applet
to Control Panel's window.

[SBProFM] installs a new version of midimap.cfg, the MIDI Mapper
configuration file when you choose installation of the Creative
Sound Blaster Pro MIDI Synthesizer. You are given a choice of
using the new configuration file or keeping your old file.

OEMSETUP.INF files provided by other manufacturers have similar
content, but different driver and file names.

If a file required by the installation is missing or defective, you see an
Install Driver dialog similar to that of figure 5.16. You can tell that an
error has occurred because the name appearing in the [disks] section
of OEMSETUP.INF now appears in the text of the dialog, replacing the
message Insert the disk with the unlisted, updated, or
vendor-provided driver in:

FIG. 5.16

The dialog that
appears when a
component of the
driver is missing.

Unfortunately, the dialog box does not tell you which file is missing or defective. You need to compare the names of the files appearing in OEMSETUP.INF with the directory of your device driver floppy disk to determine if a file is missing. Use Windows Notepad to print the content of the file. If all file names listed in OEMSETUP.INF are present, a file probably is defective. In either case, you need to obtain another set of drivers on floppy disk from the manufacturer of the card.

Examining SYSTEM.INI and WIN.INI Entries for Audio Adapter Cards

Windows uses two initialization files, WIN.INI and SYSTEM.INI, which it reads during the start-up procedure. The information in WIN.INI is used primarily to determine Windows environment. This file contains separate sections that, as an example, control the appearance of the desktop and list the typefaces available for your printer. Applications can add sections to WIN.INI to save the information they need to operate correctly in your Windows environment.

SYSTEM.INI stores information about your computer's capabilities and peripheral equipment and instructs Windows to use a specific set of operating files when it starts. SYSTEM.INI includes information about the sound cards and other multimedia peripheral equipment you have installed so that the proper drivers for them are loaded when you run Windows.

An explanation of all of the entries in WIN.INI and SYSTEM.INI is beyond the scope of this book. Microsoft publishes the *Windows Resource Kit for Operating System 3.1*, which explains most of the content of both files in detail. The *Resource Kit*, however, touches only briefly on the content of the sections devoted to the multimedia extensions provided with Windows 3.1 and makes no reference to entries for audio adapter cards or other multimedia devices. The entries in the multimedia-related sections of SYSTEM.INI and WIN.INI are described in the following topics.

Installing and Using the System Editor Applet

Windows includes the System Editor applet designed to simplify display and editing of the four files that contain information Windows uses when it starts: CONFIG.SYS, AUTOEXEC.BAT, WIN.INI, and SYSTEM.INI. When you installed Windows, SYSEDIT.EXE, the System Editor's file, was copied to your \WINDOWS directory, but no icon was added for it to Program Manager's groups.

No instructions for the use of System Editor are available in the *User's Guide* that accompanies Windows 3.1. Microsoft states in the introduction to the *User's Guide* that the content of WIN.INI and SYSTEM.INI is of interest to "advanced users only." This may explain why System Editor, whose windows are shown in figure 5.17, is hidden in your \WINDOWS directory.

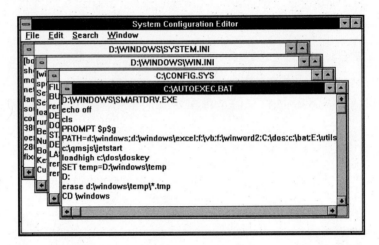

FIG. 5.17

The SysEdit applet.

The contents of WIN.INI and SYSTEM.INI are of interest to all users of Windows because sooner or later, you will need to make changes in one or both of these files.

System Editor is a very useful application. You may want to add its icon to your Control Panel's Accessories group. To install System Editor, follow these steps:

1. Display the Accessories group. If you use tiled group windows, click its title bar to select it.

2. Choose **F**ile from Program Manager's menu, then choose **N**ew. The option button for New Program **I**tem of the New Program Object dialog box that appears is highlighted. Click the OK button. The Program Item Properties dialog box is displayed.

3. Enter **SysEdit** in the **D**escription text box, press Tab, and then enter **sysedit.exe** in the **C**ommand Line text box. Click the OK button or press Enter.

4. The SysEdit icon appears in the Accessories group. If the icon is initially outside the bounds of the Accessories group window, move the scroll bars until you find it. Drag the icon with the mouse to the desired position.

5. Double-click the SysEdit icon to launch System Editor. The windows shown in figure 5.17 appear.

Select the file you want to view by clicking the appropriate title bar of the overlapping windows to bring it to the foreground. Click the maximize button for a full-screen display of the selected file's content. System Editor uses the same procedures as Windows Notepad for viewing and editing the four files.

Adding to SYSTEM.INI for Multimedia Devices

Using Control Panel's Drivers dialog box to install multimedia sound drivers adds entries to your SYSTEM.INI file so that Windows loads them into memory during the boot process. The SYSTEM.INI entries that follow are only a few of the entries that appear under the section name enclosed in square brackets.

```
[boot]
drivers=mmsystem.dll
sound.drv=mmsound.drv
```

Multimedia drivers in the [boot] section are available, regardless of the operating mode of Windows 3.1—standard or enhanced. Real-mode operation of prior Windows versions no longer is available in Windows 3.1. The MMSYSTEM.DLL driver is required for all Windows 3.1 multimedia applications. If you did not use Control Panel's Sound function to select WAV files that play when specified Windows events occur, the sound.drv=mmsound.drv line reads sound.drv=sound.drv.

```
[386enh]
device=vsbd.386
device=vadlibd.386
```

The [386enh] section lists supplemental drivers required for sound cards when Windows is run in enhanced mode. The entries appear only if you install an audio adapter card. Installing drivers for cards other than the original Sound Blaster or Ad Lib may result in substitution of different file names or additional entries in this section. For the Sound Blaster, vsbd.386 processes digital and synthesized sound, and vadlibd.386 is used for synthesized sound of the original Ad Lib board in enhanced mode.

```
[mci]
Sequencer=mciseq.drv
WaveAudio=mciwave.drv
CDAudio=mcicda.drv
MMMovie=mcimmp.drv
```

The [mci] section lists the Media Control Interface (MCI) drivers used to play MIDI files (Sequencer), play and record digitally sampled audio files (WaveAudio), play audio CDs (CDAudio), and display animated graphic sequences (MMMovie). The CDAudio entry appears only if you install the CD Audio driver for a CD-ROM drive. The MMMovie driver, MCIMMP.DRV, is not a component of Windows 3.1; it is installed by Windows with Multimedia or the Professional Toolkit for Visual Basic.

When new MCI drivers become available from Microsoft and other suppliers of multimedia applications, they are added to the [mci] section during their installation process.

```
[drivers]
midimapper=midimap.drv
timer=timer.drv
Wave=sndblst2.drv
MIDI=sndblst2.drv
MIDI1=msadlib.drv
MIDI2=mpu401.drv
```

Installable multimedia device drivers are listed in the [drivers] section. If more than one driver for a particular type of device is installed, sequentially numbered suffixes are assigned to successive entries.

If you install a driver supplied with your audio adapter card, the Wave= and MIDI= entries reflect the company or product name, such as MIDI=mvfm for the synthesized sound and MIDI driver of the Media Vision Pro AudioSpectrum products. The preceding example is for Sound Blaster Version 1.5 plus an MPU-401 adapter or MPU-compatible card, such as the Roland SCC-1.

```
[mciseq.drv]
disablewarning=true
```

The MIDI sequencer driver can display a warning message if a DOS application running in a window attempts to access the sequencer while a Windows application is using it. This message does not appear if disablewarning=true (the default).

```
[sndblst.drv]
port=220
int=7

[mpu401.drv]
port=330
int=9
```

The device address and interrupt level set during installation for each device are listed in a separate section. These entries would appear if you install both a Sound Blaster and an MPU-401 adapter card or a sound card that emulates it.

Most of the device drivers listed in the [drivers] section create their own section header in SYSTEM.INI, followed by the parameters required for proper operation.

T I P

When attempting to install a driver, if you receive an error message indicating that a device address or interrupt conflict has occurred and you don't know which card is using the conflicting entry, check SYSTEM.INI first. If you installed the conflicting device for use under Windows, there is probably an entry in an INI file with the entry. Use SysEdit or Notebook and search for port, int, or the number. Don't include = in your search because some applications enclose the = with spaces. Some applications have private INI files located in the \WINDOWS or their designated directory. Check those if you cannot find the conflict in SYSTEM.INI.

Including Multimedia File Information in WIN.INI

When you install it, Windows 3.1 adds a new multimedia-related section to your WIN.INI file and another section that assigns the WAV files you associated with Windows events using the Sounds function of Control Panel.

```
[mci extensions]
rmi=sequencer
mid=sequencer
wav=waveaudio
```

The [mci extensions] section provides file extension information for sound drivers. Files with the extension RMI and MID use the sequencer application, MCISEQ.DRV; WAV files use MCIWAVE.DRV, the waveaudio driver.

```
[sounds]
SystemAsterisk=D:\WINDOWS\CHIMES.WAV,Asterisk
SystemHand=D:\WINDOWS\DING.WAV,Critical Stop
SystemDefault=D:\WINDOWS\DING.WAV,Default Beep
SystemExclamation=D:\WINDOWS\CHIMES.WAV,Exclamation
SystemQuestion=D:\WINDOWS\DING.WAV,Question
SystemExit=D:\WINDOWS\DING.WAV,Windows Exit
SystemStart=D:\WINDOWS\TADA.WAV,Windows Start
```

When you substitute waveform files for Windows defaults with the Sounds dialog, the preceding entries are created in a new [sounds] section. The actual drive and directory that appear reflect the one chosen when you first installed Windows 3.1.

You can edit your WIN.INI file with SysEdit or Notepad to use any other WAV file you choose for the events listed, so long as it was recorded in 8-bit, 22.05-kHz monaural format. Using Control Panel's Sounds dialog to change files is safer. You can test the new WAV file before an application calls it.

Related Topics
Registration of OLE
Applications, p. 221

Examining the Registration Database and File Manager

The registration database (REG.DAT) file is a new feature of Windows 3.1. It provides information needed by File Manager and Print Manager to implement the new drag-and-drop feature that enables you to open and print files by dragging their icons. The registration database also is used to support Object Linking and Embedding (OLE) operations. Using OLE to link or embed sounds in documents is the subject of Chapter 8.

Control Panel's Accessories group includes an icon for the registration database editor, REGEDIT.EXE. When you launch RegEdit, a window similar to that of figure 5.18 appears. The applications listed are those contained in the original REG.DAT file when you installed Windows 3.1, plus any applications specifically designed for use under Windows 3.1 that you added to your system after you installed Windows 3.1. The entries for Media Player and Sound (Recorder) enable File manager to associate MIDI and WAV files with these applications.

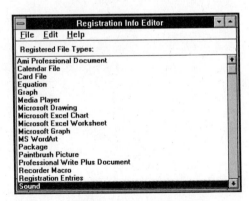

FIG. 5.18

The opening window of the Registration Database File Editor applet, RegEdit, in normal display mode.

When you double-click Sound, the Modify File Type dialog box appears (see fig. 5.19), with the following items:

Identifier contains the name of the application—Sound Rec(order) in this case.

File Type: Sound consists of files with the WAV extension.

SoundRec = Sound and .wav = SoundRec, two presently invisible entries in REG.DAT, associate File Type: Sound with Sound Rec(order).

File Manager's Action in this case is to Open a file and to run SoundRec.exe with the file name you choose. File Manager substitutes the name of the file for the replaceable parameter, %1, which is used in the same way that DOS uses it in batch files.

You should never have to modify REG.DAT with the Modify File Type dialog box unless your REG.DAT file becomes corrupted.

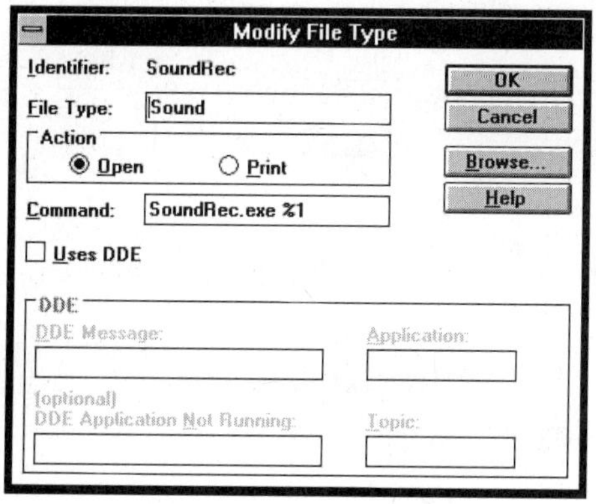

FIG. 5.19

The editing dialog box of the Registration Database File Editor for modifying entries in REG.DAT.

You can use File Manager to demonstrate how data in REG.DAT is used by Windows 3.1 to associate file types with applications:

1. Start File Manager from the Main group.

2. If it is not currently displayed, click the file folder icon for your \WINDOWS directory. The content of your \WINDOWS directory appears in the right file list box.

3. Scroll down the file list box, if necessary, until a WAV file appears.

4. Double-click the file folder icon for the WAV file you want to play. Sound Recorder's window appears (see fig. 5.20).

5. Click the Play button (the single, right-pointing arrow) to hear the selected sound through your sound system. If you play the sound without stopping it, clicking Play again plays the file from the beginning.

6. You can adjust the position in the file at which Play begins by dragging the scroll bar slider with the mouse. The position, expressed in seconds corresponding to the location of the scroll bar button, changes as you move the button.

7. Close Sound Recorder when you are through by double-clicking its Control Bar at the upper left.

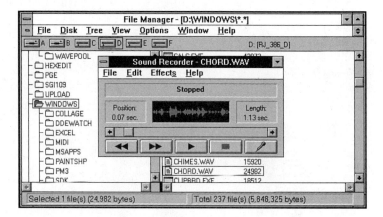

FIG. 5.20

The Sound Recorder dialog box.

Installing CD-ROM Device Drivers and Applications

Most MPC Upgrade Kits and stand-alone CD-ROM drives come with a floppy disk containing an installation application requiring that you run the installation application from the DOS command line. The installation application makes the necessary entries in your CONFIG.SYS and AUTOEXEC.BAT files to load the required drivers during your computer's start-up (boot) operation. Both MSCDEX.EXE and a device driver are copied to your hard disk. Although the process is automatic, knowing something about the drivers being used and how to read the new entries in your start-up files can be useful.

Related Topics
Adding ISO-9660 and High Sierra Directory Structures, p. 97

Installing MSCDEX and the CD-ROM Device Driver

CD-ROMs do not have the file allocation table (FAT) used by floppy and hard disks to indicate the physical location of files, but they do have a file directory. MSCDEX.EXE is a terminate-and-stay-resident (TSR) application that translates the special file directory information of CD-ROMs to the standard 12-character format required by DOS (including the period separator for the extension). MSCDEX.EXE must be loaded in your computer's memory before starting Windows.

In addition to a DOS application—MSCDEX.EXE—CD-ROM drives need a DOS device driver so that DOS recognizes them as drives. This device driver controls the SCSI or proprietary interface to the drive. Each manufacturer is likely to have a device driver with a different name. For the examples that follow, TSLCDR.SYS, the Trantor Systems Ltd. driver for their SCSI host adapter card, is used. The name of the device driver supplied with your MPC Upgrade Kit or CD-ROM drive may be different, but the syntax for the entries shown below is similar for all. A full explanation of the syntax of MSCDEX.EXE is provided in Appendix B. Those portions of the examples that differ between drivers are shown in *monospace italic* type in this subtopic.

When you run the CD-ROM drive installation application from the floppy disk, the application creates its own directory on the drive you specify, in this case C:\TSCSI, and copies the device drivers TSLCDR.SYS and MSCDEX.EXE into that directory. A diagnostic application and some additional files may be copied. If you have not added the line

```
lastdrive = x
```

to your CONFIG.SYS file, the application may add it for you, preferably as the first line in the file. The *x* in this line is normally the next letter of the alphabet following the last letter of the drives installed on your computer and any network drives that you may use. For safety, some applications substitute the letter *z*, which allocates enough space for DOS to hold records for all 26 possible drives.

Next, the application adds a line similar to the following to your CONFIG.SYS file:

```
device=c:\tscsi\tslcdr.sys d:\TSLCDR
```

This line causes the device driver to be loaded into memory before AUTOEXEC.BAT is run during your computer's start-up (boot) cycle. An additional line is added to your AUTOEXEC.BAT file to run the MSCDEX.EXE application that uses the device driver installed previously by CONFIG.SYS. This line is similar to the following:

```
c:\tscsi\mscdex d:/TSLCDR
```

When the installation application completes, you must warm-boot your computer with Ctrl+Alt+Del to load the device driver and MSCDEX.EXE.

After your computer restarts, you see a message from the driver indicating that it has been loaded and has found the CD-ROM driver, ordinarily assigned drive 0 (the first and only drive), connected to the SCSI host adapter card. The message is similar to the following example:

```
SCSI host adapter detected at address cc00h
Device 0, Read-Only Optical Device (Removable media)
1 CD ROM Drive found
```

Another message created by MSCDEX.EXE shows the assignment of the next drive letter after the last valid hard disk drive letter on your computer to the CD-ROM drive. For users of DOS 4.0 and above, the CD-ROM drive probably is assigned drive designator D: unless you are using network drives starting with designator D.

```
Drive D: = Driver TSLCD unit 0
```

The first drive connected to a SCSI adapter always is identified as unit 0.

T I P

If you are using a network, the line containing the command to load MSCDEX in your AUTOEXEC.BAT file should come after any lines that contain commands to load networking applications. MSCDEX acts as a CD-ROM "redirector" and tricks MS-DOS into believing the CD-ROM is a network drive. If the network redirector is installed after MSCDEX, the network application intercepts requests for CD-ROM access instead of MSCDEX. Have your network administrator make the fix or use DOS 5.0's EDIT application to check the position of the MSCDEX line and move it, if necessary.

Test your installation with a CD-ROM installed in the drive by typing **DIR D:** (or the higher drive letter assigned by MSCDEX) at the DOS prompt or selecting the CD-ROM drive from File Manager. Figure 5.21 shows the appearance of File Manager when viewing the directories of a CD-ROM assigned as drive G. (That is not a tongue in the icon for drive G, it is half of a CD-ROM.) Both the DOS and File Manager directories resemble those of hard disks and floppy disks. You can copy files from the CD-ROM to your hard disk, but not vice-versa.

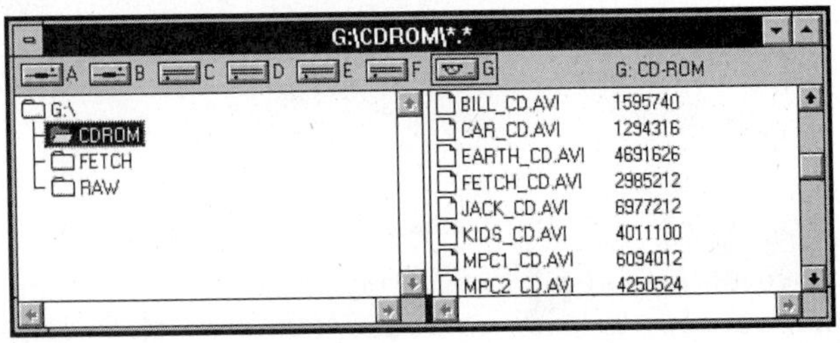

FIG. 5.21

File Manager's display of the directories and files on a typical CD-ROM.

T   I   P

The device driver and MSCCDEX.EXE together occupy 60K to 70K of conventional memory. This would appear to make them logical candidates for DOS 5.0's `devicehigh` and `loadhigh` instructions that attempt to place them in high memory if sufficient room is available. Memory managers compatible with Windows 3.1 may attempt to load one or both files into high memory with memory optimizing applications.

MSCDEX.EXE Version 2.21 cannot be loaded high with DOS 5.0 (see *CD-ROM Programmer's Guide for MS-DOS CD-ROM Extensions Version 2.21*, Microsoft Corp., January 1992, p. 12-8). If you have allocated *expanded* memory, you can save about 16K of low memory by loading MSCDEX with the /E command line switch.

Do not attempt to load MSCDEX or the device driver for your CD-ROM drive high or into expanded memory until you have thoroughly tested your CD-ROM with the files loaded into conventional (low) memory. You may find that either file loaded high locks your computer when you attempt to read the directory of the CD-ROM from DOS or Windows, sometimes requiring a cold (reset-button or power off-on cycle), not a warm (Ctrl+Alt+Del) boot.

When experimenting with loading the files into high memory, place a pause instruction immediately before the line in AUTOEXEC.BAT that executes MSCDEX.EXE so that you can use Ctrl+Break to halt subsequent executions of AUTOEXEC.BAT before a lockup occurs. This enables you to edit AUTOEXEC.BAT and CONFIG.SYS to remove the experimental commands if they fail.

Version 2.20 of MSCDEX causes an error when used with DOS 5.0. If your CD-ROM drive did not come with MSCDEX.EXE Version 2.21 or higher (with a file date of 2/4/92 or later), you are using DOS 5.0, and you receive a DOS version error, take the following steps:

1. Add the following line as the first line of your CONFIG.SYS file:

   device=setver.exe

   This sets up the version table for applications that do not recognize DOS 5.0.

2. Add the following line to your AUTOEXEC.BAT file:

   setver c:\tscsi\mscdex.exe 4.01

   This line must precede the line that loads MSCDEX. The path name preceding `mscdex.exe` must, of course, point to the drive and directory in which MSCDEX.EXE is located on your hard disk. This line adds MSCDEX.EXE to the version table created by SETVER.EXE when installed as a driver. The easiest way to make these changes is with SysEdit.

3. Reboot your computer. You must start from ground zero with Ctrl+Alt+Del to install the driver and run AUTOEXEC.BAT again.

The latest version of MSCDEX.EXE (2.21 when this book was written) can be downloaded from the Microsoft Windows Drivers Library (WDL). This version also is available in the Microsoft Software Library on CompuServe (GO MSL) or directly from the Microsoft Download Service (MSDL). Appendix H provides instructions for downloading from both sources. Version 2.21 of MSCDEX.EXE eliminates the need to use SETVER with DOS 5.0 and corrects a couple of minor bugs in Version 2.20 related to use of CD-ROM drives on networks. You can expect MSCDEX.EXE to be updated periodically to add new features, such as the capability to load it into high memory with DOS 5.0.

> **CAUTION:** Make sure that you have a copy of your current version of MSCDEX.EXE on floppy disk before installing an updated version. Your CD-ROM device driver may not be compatible with the new version. If incompatibilities exist, you may be unceremoniously dumped out of Windows to the DOS prompt when you attempt to read your CD-ROM drive. This may occur without any error messages when the driver and MSCDEX.EXE are loaded by your CONFIG.SYS and AUTOEXEC.BAT files. If you encounter problems with a new version of MSCDEX.EXE, reinstall the prior version and contact the manufacturer of the CD-ROM drive or SCSI adapter card for an updated device driver.

Installing MCICDA.DRV for Windows

You need to install the audio CD device driver to control your CD-ROM remotely if you want to be able to play audio CDs. Windows 3.1 copies MCICDA.DRV to your \WINDOWS\SYSTEM directory during installation, but it does not install the driver for you. MCICDA.DRV is installed in the same way as any other Windows-supplied driver:

1. Run Control Panel by double-clicking its icon in the Main group.

2. Double-click the Drivers icon in Control Panel's window to display the Installed Drivers dialog box.

3. Click the **A**dd button to display the List of Drivers list box.

4. Double-click the entry for [MCI] CD Audio to install the driver. The message box shown in figure 5.22 confirms that MCICDA.DRV has been installed.

5. Click OK.

FIG. 5.22

The message box indicating successful installation of MCICDA.DRV.

6. Contrary to other device drivers you have added, you do not need to restart Windows to make MCICDA.DRV active. The required device drivers have been loaded already by DOS before Windows loaded into memory.

7. Close Control Panel.

If you receive a message box indicating that a CD-ROM drive was not found, use the diagnostic applications supplied with your CD-ROM drive or MPC Upgrade Kit to find the source of the problem. One application usually tests the SCSI interface, and another is used to verify proper installation of the CD-ROM. In most cases, the problems are related to cabling errors or an incorrect parameter of the device driver or MSCDEX.EXE.

Playing an Audio CD with Media Player

You now have a new device to choose in the Media Player's Device menu. Choose this device by following these steps:

1. Remove the CD-ROM and insert an audio CD in your CD-ROM drive.

2. Start Media Player by double-clicking on its icon in the Accessories group.

3. Turn the volume control on your drive to about mid-range.

4. Choose **D**evice on Media Player's menu, then choose **C**D Audio. Media player displays markers and numbers for each track on your audio CD, as illustrated in figure 5.23.

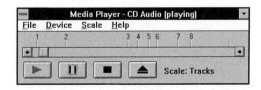

FIG. 5.23

Media Player playing an audio CD.

5. Click Play, the leftmost button, to start the sound. The scroll bar slider button follows the progress of the laser across the active surface of the CD-ROM—much, much more slowly than when playing a waveform audio or MIDI file.

6. You can play any track or portion of a track by moving the slider button to the desired position while the CD is playing or when it is stopped.

Notice that the Eject (rightmost) button of Media Player's window now is active. You can click this button to eject the CD-ROM from drives that have a remotely controllable media eject feature.

Troubleshooting CD Audio

If you hear no sound at all and the slider button is moving, check the following in the order specified:

1. The volume control of the drive. It should be at midpoint.

2. The ribbon cable leading from the audio output connector at the back of the CD-ROM drive to the audio adapter card's connector, if it is connected to your audio adapter card. Make sure that the cable's polarity is correct—the colored tracer conductor should be at the pin 1 end of each connector.

3. The mixer application installed from the floppy disk accompanying your audio adapter card, sometimes added to Control Panel. The slider for the CD Audio channel may be set to 0 or a very low value. Double-click the mixer application's icon and increase the volume of the channel. You can leave the mixer application open while you are running Media Player to adjust the sound level.

4. The audio cabling to the inputs to your speaker or sound system.

If the above steps fail to solve the problem, plug headphones into the CD-ROM to see if its audio subsection is functioning. If you don't hear your audio CD playing, your only option at this point is to refer to the drive documentation for further troubleshooting instructions.

Chapter Summary

The services provided to applications by MMSYSTEM.DLL and the media-specific DLLs for sound applications constitute the core of Windows 3.1's multimedia extensions. Device drivers called by the media-specific DLLs translate requests to play and record sound into instructions understood by your audio adapter card or CD-ROM drive. Most applications use the high-level MCI commands included in MCIWAVE.DRV, MCISEQ.DRV, and MCICDA.DRV to perform multimedia-related hardware tasks. Use of the high-level MCI commands is explained in Chapters 23 and 24.

Now that you have your audio adapter card and CD-ROM drive installed and operating, you probably want to experiment with sound. Chapter 6 gives you the details on using the digitally sampled sound functions of your audio adapter card with waveform audio (WAV) files. Chapter 7 explains how to play standard MIDI files (with the MID extension) using the Media Player applet and simple sequencing applications.

Using Sound in Windows

Playing and Recording Waveform Audio Files

W*aveform audio* is the simplest type of sound reproduction—and the only built-in method for recording sounds—offered by Windows multimedia. Also referred to as *digitally sampled sound, PCM sound, WAVE, waveaudio,* and *WaveAudio,* waveform audio achieves very high fidelity by duplicating the recording methods used for audio CDs. Unfortunately, this excellent sound reproduction comes at the expense of hard disk space; the resulting WAV files often occupy many megabytes.

If you want to play waveform audio files with your PC's speaker, instructions for obtaining and installing Microsoft's SPEAKER.DRV are included in this chapter. Because this driver was not fully qualified when Windows 3.1 was released, you must download it from CompuServe or Microsoft's driver bulletin board.

If you followed the steps provided in Chapter 5, you already have used the Control Panel Sound function to test your audio card installation. Windows 3.1 includes two applets—Sound Recorder and Media Player—for use with waveform audio files. Sound Recorder enables you to play and record WAV files; Media Player can only play them. This chapter shows you how to use these two applets with WAV files and how to obtain a wide range of entertaining (but disk-filling) sound files from CompuServe.

Experimenting with Sound Recorder

The Sound Recorder and Media Player applets supplied with Windows can play waveform audio files, but only Sound Recorder enables you to create or edit these files. Most audio adapter cards include a Windows application that duplicates Sound Recorder's functions and provides additional features (such as more sophisticated editing capabilities). This chapter discusses Sound Recorder because it is the common denominator for all operations with waveform audio files; it includes the basic functions upon which other applications improve. If you have installed an audio adapter card that has waveform audio capability, you may want to skip the next section that explains the use of a special Windows 3.1 speaker driver to play waveform audio files.

Related Topics
Installing and Configuring
Audio Device Drivers,
p.145
Using Device Addresses,
Interrupts, and DMA
Channels, p.119

Installing Microsoft's PC-Speaker Driver for Windows 3.1

Microsoft offers a special driver called SPEAKER.DRV for those who do not have an audio adapter card. SPEAKER.DRV plays Windows' digitally sampled audio (WAV) files through the PC's speaker. This driver was included in the beta test version but not in the final distribution version of Windows 3.1. A copy of SPEAKER.DRV is included on the floppy disk that accompanies this book. You also can download the file via modem from the Microsoft Software Library on CompuServe (GO MSL) or directly from the Microsoft Download Service (MSDL) as SPEAK.EXE. Appendix H explains the downloading process in detail.

SPEAKER.DRV must have total control of your computer to play sounds not excessively distorted. When SPEAKER.DRV plays sounds, it disables your keyboard, mouse, and any other devices that use your computer's interrupts. (See Chapter 4 for a description of interrupts and how they are used.) Using the PC-speaker driver to replace the standard warning beep with the sounds contained in a WAV file (as discussed in Chapter 4) might interfere with the operation of modem communications applications, which make extensive use of interrupts. In order to help you avoid this problem, the new version of SPEAKER.DRV helps you decide whether to enable or disable interrupts during sound playback.

To install the PC-speaker driver, follow these steps:

1. Place the floppy disk containing SPEAKER.DRV and OEMSETUP.INF in drive A or B. The driver and its information file are required for successful installation.

2. Start Control Panel and double-click its Drivers icon. The **I**nstalled Drivers list box appears.

3. Click the **A**dd button. The **L**ist of Drivers box appears with its Unlisted Or Updated Driver selection highlighted.

4. Double-click Unlisted Or Updated Driver, or click the OK button. The Install Driver dialog box appears (see fig. 6.1).

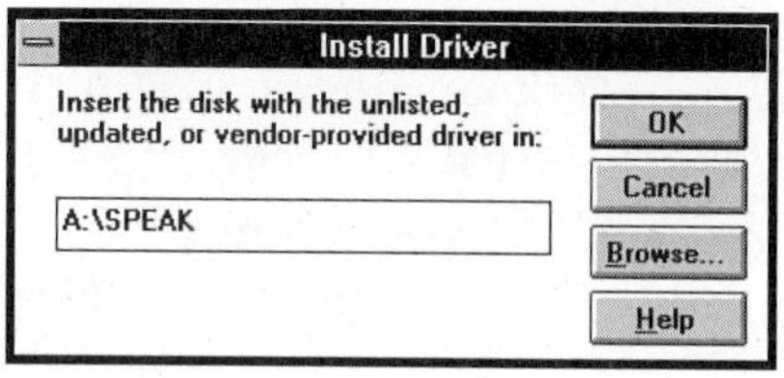

FIG. 6.1

The Install Driver dialog box when installing SPEAKER.DRV.

5. Type the correct drive and directory location for the speaker driver—**A:\SPEAK**, for example—and press Enter or click OK.

6. The PC-Speaker Setup dialog box appears (see fig. 6.2). You use this box to adjust playback speed and volume. Click the **T**est button a couple of times to check its operation.

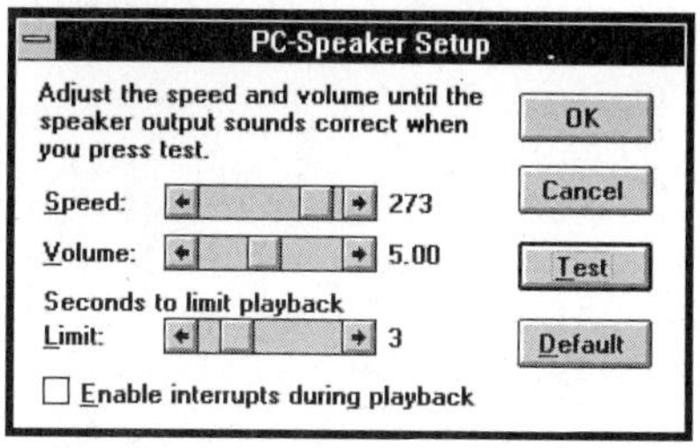

FIG. 6.2

The PC-Speaker Setup dialog box.

7. If the **T**est button is disabled (the word Test appears in gray rather than black), the driver cannot find any WAV files to play in your \WINDOWS directory. Chapter 2 provides instructions for installing such files, using the Windows Setup application. Even without WAV files, you can check the operation of the PC-speaker driver by clicking **D**efault. This option plays four simple tones in sequence.

8. The dialog box instructs you to adjust the speed and volume until it "sounds correct." This can be a difficult step unless you already have heard the sounds through an audio adapter card and can recognize what is "correct." The default sound played by Test is DING.WAV, which should sound like the "dinging" Autocall signals formerly heard in department stores or the sonar pings in submarines.

9. Adjust the volume and speed scroll bars to suit your taste. You can set the sound duration to any value between one and ten seconds. Three seconds of sound—the default maximum duration—is sufficient for most purposes. Increasing the maximum duration of a sound reserves a larger sound buffer, reducing the memory available for your other applications.

10. Test the effect of enabling your computer's interrupts during playback by clicking the appropriate check box, then clicking **T**est. You can hear any distortion added to the sound by periodic tests for interrupt messages. Disable interrupt testing by clicking the check box again to remove the mark.

11. Click OK to close the PC-Speaker Setup dialog box. The message shown in figure 6.3 appears. Windows installs drivers during its start-up process, so you must exit and restart Windows in order to activate the new driver. If you do not have an audio adapter card and its driver installed, click **R**estart Now and skip to step 16 below.

FIG. 6.3

The System Setting Change message box.

12. If you have installed an audio adapter card and driver that have digital audio capability, you must remove that driver (such as the one used by the Sound Blaster) before the restart procedure. In this case, click **D**on't Restart Now. The **I**nstalled Drivers list box reappears with a new entry for Sound Driver for PC-Speaker.

13. Double-click the name of the audio adapter card driver or click it and then click **S**etup to display the driver's Setup dialog box. Make a note of the Port and Interrupt numbers the card uses and click OK.

T I P   Confirm that the floppy disk containing the sound card driver is available before you remove it by using the following procedure. In the event that a problem comes up and Windows cannot find the driver file, you will not be able to reinstall the file without a floppy disk that contains its OEMSETUP.INF and DRV files.

14. Click the **R**emove button, and then click OK when the Remove confirmation dialog box appears.

15. Click **R**estart Now when the System Setting Change dialog box appears. Windows closes and then restarts.

16. When you start Control Panel and double-click the Drivers icon, you see that a Sound Driver For PC-Speaker option has been added to the list of drivers (see fig. 6.4). The other drivers shown in figure 6.4 are unlikely to correspond to those in your list box—some are installed automatically by Windows and others must be added manually by the procedures described in Chapter 5.

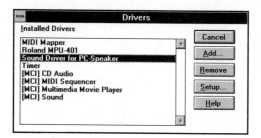

FIG. 6.4

The list of installed drivers after adding SPEAKER.DRV.

17. Click Cancel, then close Control Panel. If you removed the driver for your sound card, you can reinstall it later by following the procedure outlined above or the more detailed procedure covered in Chapter 5.

You can assign any of the four standard sound files installed by Windows 3.1 to chosen events by using the Control Panel Sounds function. Refer to "Assigning Sounds to Windows Events" in Chapter 5 for helpful instructions. Now MMSOUND.DRV uses SPEAKER.DRV to play the assigned sounds.

Listening to Waveform Audio Files

Sound Recorder can play WAV files recorded at 5.0125, 11.025, 22.05, and 44.1 kHz sampling rates with 8-bit or 16-bit resolution in mono or stereo format. Each file has a *header* (discussed later in this chapter) that indicates its specifications; Sound Recorder passes these specifications to MCIWAV.DRV via MMSYSTEM.DLL. MCIWAV.DRV opens the file and translates its data to a standard format accessible to all sampled-sound device drivers. Your card's device driver then sends this translated data to the audio adapter card.

To play waveform audio files with Sound Recorder, follow these steps:

1. Start Sound Recorder from the Accessories group by double-clicking its icon.

2. Choose **F**ile, then **O**pen. The Open dialog box appears (see fig. 6.5).

   The Open dialog box shows only WAV files located in the \WIN-DOWS directory by default, but you can choose any other directory that contains WAV files. You might choose, for example, a \SAMPLES subdirectory created when you installed your sound card software.

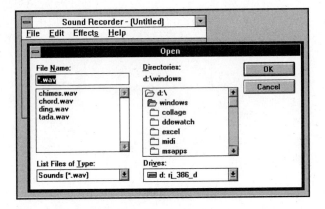

FIG. 6.5

Opening a waveform audio file to play with the Sound Recorder applet.

3. Double-click one of the WAV files. Sound Recorder loads its contents into a sound file buffer—a reserved portion of your computer's memory. With exceptionally large waveform audio files, Sound Recorder loads only a portion of the contents initially and then transfers successive blocks of data from the file to the buffer as required.

4. Sound Recorder displays buttons that correspond to those found on an audio or video cassette recorder. From left to right, the buttons are Rewind (to beginning of file), Fast Forward (to end of file), Play, Stop, and Record.

5. Click the Play button to listen to the sound. The simulated oscilloscope display (see fig. 6.6) shows the amplitude (intensity) of the sound in the vertical direction (Y-axis) and time in the horizontal direction (X-axis).

6. You can play the sound starting from any position in the file by moving the slider button of the horizontal scroll bar to the desired position (determined by the position indicator), then clicking on the Play button. Current position and complete file length are displayed in seconds.

7. If you want to make your first recording (covered in the next section of this chapter), remain in Sound Recorder. Otherwise, click the Application Control Bar, then choose E**x**it to close Sound Recorder.

FIG. 6.6

Sound Recorder's window showing the simulated oscilloscope display.

You can mix sound files with one another and add effects to sound files with the Edit and Effects menu choices of Sound Recorder. Chapter 14, "Editing and Converting Waveform Files," explains the editing functions available with Sound Recorder and commercial waveform audio editing applications for Windows.

Recording Sampled Audio

Sound Recorder is capable of recording only one type of waveform audio file—monaural sound with a 22.05 kHz sampling rate. This is the standard sound file specification used by MMSOUND.DRV when associating sounds with Windows events (refer to Chapter 5). Sound Recorder uses 8-bit resolution by default unless your card supports 16-bit resolution. If you want to create sounds with other specifications, you must use the waveform audio application supplied with your sound card or a commercial application such as Turtle Beach's Wave for Windows or Voyetra's AudioView.

The principal use of Sound Recorder is to create voice notes that embellish your word processing documents or spreadsheets. Recording your voice with a microphone is a simple task with Sound Recorder; just follow these steps:

1. If you have not already done so, plug your microphone into your sound card's microphone connector (usually labeled Mic).

2. Begin Sound Recorder by double-clicking on its icon in the Accessories group.

3. Choose File from Sound Recorder's main menu, then New to create a memory buffer for your sampled-sound data.

4. Most audio cards with low-level microphone inputs compatible with consumer-grade microphones have automatic gain control (AGC). AGC automatically adjusts the amplification of the sound from the microphone for the optimum recording level. If your sound card does not have AGC, use the mixer application to set the proper level before you start recording.

5. Click the Record button (the button with the microphone symbol). A period of intense hard disk activity occurs in preparation for the recording process.

6. When the Recording announcement appears, start speaking into the microphone. As you speak, you see a representation of your words on the simulated oscilloscope display. Adjust the distance of the microphone from your lips to keep the average sound level at about half the overall height of the display, as shown in figure 6.7.

   Keep your comments brief, because WAV files consume a substantial amount of disk space. Your recording uses 44K per second at 16-bit resolution and 22K per second at 8-bit resolution.

FIG. 6.7

Sound Recorder's display while recording with a microphone.

7. When you finish recording, click the Stop button (the button with the square symbol).

8. Click the Rewind button (the leftmost button) to start from the beginning of the file.

9. Click the Play button to hear your performance as an announcer.

10. To save the result of your audition, choose **F**ile from Sound Recorder's menu, then choose Save **A**s. The Save As dialog box appears (see fig. 6.8). Enter a suitable name—such as **test.wav**— and press Enter or click OK. Don't forget that all waveform audio files must include the extension WAV.

T   I   P   Unlike most other Windows applications, the Windows 3.1 Sound Recorder applet does not automatically add the correct default file extension when you save a file. If you do not add the WAV extension yourself, the Sound Recorder file is saved without an extension. Without the extension, your file does not appear in the file box list when you attempt to open a file with Sound Recorder. As far as your software is concerned, extensionless files have no association with Sound Recorder. Therefore, be sure to add the WAV extension to your file name when you save a newly recorded sound.

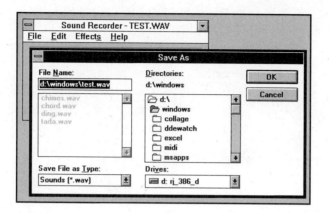

FIG. 6.8

Saving a waveform
audio file created with
Sound Recorder.

Sound Recorder also enables you to trim the beginning or end of your file and to *overdub*, or record over previously recorded material. Chapter 15, "Waveform Audio Recording Techniques," covers these advanced procedures.

Using Media Player with Waveform Audio Files

You can use the Windows 3.1 Media Player applet to play waveform audio files, MIDI files, and audio CD tracks. Media Player also can display animated graphics in the form of MultiMediaMovie (MMM) files, but the required MCIMMP.DRV driver is available only if you are using Windows with Multimedia (or you upgraded Windows with Multimedia to Windows 3.1) or if you purchase an application that includes MCIMMP.DRV. MCIMMP.DRV and a sample animation file in MMM format are provided with the Microsoft Professional Toolkit for Visual Basic.

To play WAV files with Media Player, follow these steps:

1. Load Media Player by double-clicking on its icon in the Accessories group.

2. Choose File from Media Player's main menu, then choose Open. An Open dialog box similar to the one used by Sound Recorder appears (see fig. 6.9).

3. Media Player does not use a default file type, so you must choose WAV files manually. Click the down arrow of the List Files of Type drop-down box to display the list of file types and extensions.

4. Click Sound (*.wav) in the List Files of Type box and the available files appear in the Files list box above it. Double-click your choice to load the file.

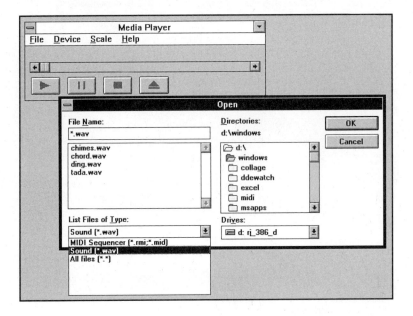

FIG. 6.9

Opening a waveform audio file for Media Player.

5. The control buttons of Media Player—listed from left to right—are Play, Pause, Stop, and Eject (see fig. 6.10). The Eject button is enabled only for devices such as CD-ROM drives and remote-control VCRs that can eject their media.

FIG. 6.10

The Media Player window while playing a WAV file.

6. Click the Play button to play the file. If you're quick, you can click the Pause button to stop the sound, then click the Pause button again to start from the current position. As with Sound Recorder, you can position the horizontal scroll bar slider to start play from any position in the file.

Media Player's **D**evice menu option is used to select files with nonstandard extensions not associated with Media Player in REG.DAT. **S**cale enables you to choose between measurement of time in seconds or tracks when playing audio CDs. You seldom need to use the **S**cale menu choice.

Obtaining Other Waveform Audio Files

As Windows 3.1 gains momentum and more audio adapter cards are sold, you can expect a vast proliferation of pre-recorded WAV files to appear on on-line services such as CompuServe, America OnLine, GEnie, and private electronic bulletin board systems. When Windows 3.1 was introduced, the vast majority of digitally sampled audio files for use with the PC were in the form of VOC files for the original Sound Blaster card. Sound aficionados are busy converting these files (as well as sound files for the Apple Macintosh and Atari Amiga computers) to WAV format. If you have a collection of VOC files and can't wait for others to convert them for you, refer to the conversion instructions in Chapter 14.

The software supplied with MPC audio adapter cards usually includes at least a few short WAV files for testing and demonstration purposes. Some cards come with CD-ROMs containing longer samples, but you need a CD-ROM player to make use of them. Your best source for the largest variety of WAV files is CompuServe. Most of the WAV files are located in the Windows Advanced forum (GO WINADV), Library 12, Multimedia. Browse Library 12 using the keyword *wave* to find files with subjects that interest you.

Chapter Summary

This chapter introduced you to the methods used and the applets supplied by Windows 3.1 to play and record waveform audio files. Part IV of this book, "Digital Audio Techniques," delves deeper into waveform audio technology, methods of editing and converting WAV files, and the special techniques you can employ to obtain professional-quality waveform audio recordings.

Chapter 7 introduces you to playing MIDI files with Media Player and then with two commercial sequencing applications designed for MIDI neophytes. Like this chapter, Chapter 7 provides you with tips for obtaining additional files that enable you to expand your musical horizons beyond CANYON.MID, the sole MIDI file supplied with Windows 3.1. Part III of this book, "Musical Synthesis and MIDI," explains the use of the MIDI connectors in your breakout cable or box with external MIDI devices.

Playing MIDI Files

Many purchasers of audio adapter cards plan to use them for playing or creating music. Waveform audio files are easy to use, but they consume too much disk space to be practical for storing musical compositions on hard disks of affordable capacity. The Musical Instrument Digital Interface (*MIDI*) and the synthesized sound capabilities of audio adapter cards provide a more effective method of storing and playing musical compositions. They enable you to store the notes, not the sounds, on disk and to create the sounds during play rather than simply reproducing them.

This chapter acquaints you with the basics of playing MIDI files through the synthesizer components of your audio adapter card. Most of the examples in this chapter use the Media Player applet of Windows 3.1 because it represents MIDI file operations at the most basic level (like Sound Recorder for waveform audio files). If you want to create, edit, or record MIDI files, you will need a sequencer application. This chapter introduces you to *Passport Trax*, a popular piano-roll sequencer for Windows that is delivered with several MPC-compliant sound cards and MIDI breakout devices, and *MusicTime*, a commercial Passport application that uses conventional musical notation and can print your scores. Brief looks at Dan McKee's *WinJammer*, a shareware sequencer, and Howling Dog's *Power Chords*, a musical construction application, complete the chapter.

Using Media Player with MIDI Files

Windows 3.1 provides one standard MIDI file—CANYON.MID—that you can use with Media Player to demonstrate your audio adapter card's synthesized sound capabilities. If you are using an MPU-401, one of its clones, or a LAPC-1, skip to the section of this chapter called "Setting Up MIDI Mapper." Otherwise, you can play CANYON.MID now by following these steps:

1. Start Media Player from the Accessories group by double-clicking its icon.

2. Choose File, then choose Open. The Open dialog box appears (see fig. 7.1).

3. Click the down arrow beside the List Files of Type combo box, and then click the MIDI Sequencer type. The list that appears contains CANYON.MID, the MIDI file supplied with Windows 3.1, and any other MID files in your \WINDOWS directory.

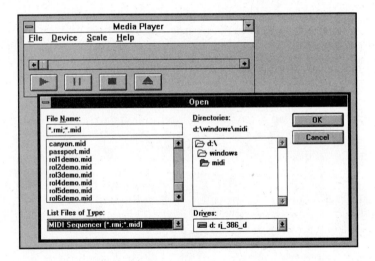

FIG. 7.1

The Media Player Open dialog box displaying *.MID files.

4. Double-click CANYON.MID to load the file.

5. Click the Play button (the leftmost button) and you hear CANYON.MID. The slider on the horizontal scroll bar moves as the tune is played. If you were expecting Ferde Grofe's *Grand Canyon Suite*, you will be disappointed.

To stop play temporarily at any point, click the Pause button; click it again to resume playing from that point.

To repeat a phrase, click Stop, move the slider to the desired starting point, then click Play.

6. When you're done, double-click the Control Bar.

If CANYON.MID sounds strange, or you don't hear anything at all, the correct MIDI map for your audio adapter card probably is not installed. Skip to the section of this chapter called "Setting Up MIDI Mapper" to install the correct setup for your card, then try steps 1 through 6 again.

Using Windows Synthesized Sound Drivers

Related Topics
Working with MIDI Channels and the Multimedia Extensions, p. 300
Synchronization Systems for Sequencers, p. 576

Media Player uses Windows multimedia services provided by MMSYSTEM.DLL to send instructions to MCISEQ.DRV, the media driver for synthesized sound. When you instruct Media Player to open a MIDI file, it first verifies that the file contains MIDI information by checking for a MID or RMI file extension. The RMI extension is quite rare; it indicates that the file is in *Resource Interchange File Format* (RIFF), rather than standard MIDI file format. After verifying the extension, Media Player sends the file name to MMSYSTEM.DLL, which then calls MCISEQ.DRV— because the file is in MIDI format and Media Player uses the high-level Media Control Interface (MCI) commands that MCISEQ.DRV processes. If you skipped Chapter 5, you may want to review its "Examining Windows Drivers for Multimedia" section at this point. It describes the relationship between applications, MMSYSTEM.DLL, media drivers, and device drivers in greater detail. Figure 7.2 shows a diagram of the Windows components involved in playing MIDI files.

MCISEQ.DRV opens the file and creates a buffer in your computer's memory to hold the file's contents. The driver then translates the *.MID file information in the buffer to MIDI instructions and uses the tempo specified by the composer to determine the rate that the data in the buffer should be sent to the MIDI device. MCISEQ.DRV also provides timing and other services necessary to synchronize MIDI music with visual displays generated by other applications (animated graphics software, for example). Tempo and MIDI synchronization functions use the Timer driver that appears in the Installed Drivers list box. Synchronization techniques are described briefly in Chapter 12 and in much greater detail in Chapter 21.

MCISEQ.DRV next passes the modified data to MIDI Mapper— MIDIMAP.DRV—which uses a *MIDI setup*, also called a *channel map*, to select the device driver to which the MIDI messages are to be sent. MIDI has 16 channels that can be assigned to different MIDI instruments, including the synthesizer section of your audio adapter card. If the file was not composed using general MIDI standards, a *patch map* determines how the MIDI messages are to be translated into the instrument sounds available with the selected adapter card. Sequencer applications, discussed at the end of this chapter, can bypass the MIDI Mapper and send their MIDI instructions directly from MMSYSTEM.DLL or MCISEQ.DRV to the device driver you select in the sequencer's setup window.

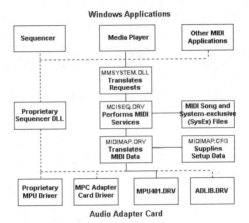

FIG. 7.2

Windows services diagram for synthesized music and MIDI applications.

The MIDI device drivers supplied by Microsoft and supplied with most audio adapter cards cannot be used for more than one application at a time. You cannot use a sequencer application, for example, when you already have selected a MIDI file and opened a Media Player window. If you attempt to use multiple applications at once with a MIDI driver, a message box like the one shown in figure 7.3 appears. This limitation probably was implemented to prevent you from sending two sets of MIDI data to the same device simultaneously (definitely not a recommended practice!). Unfortunately, you also cannot send MIDI messages to two MIDI devices installed on the same computer (using a multiple MIDI card such as those supplied by Music Quest, for example, or a combination of a sound card and an MPU-401 card). This problem, along with MIDI Mapper's inability to accommodate different configuration files (MIDI maps), will be corrected in a future version of Windows. In the meantime, some sequencer applications (such as Passport's MusicTime) enable you to direct their output to two or more MIDI devices by supplying proprietary device drivers.

FIG. 7.3

Message box that appears when you attempt to use MIDI Mapper or the same device driver with two applications simultaneously.

Exploring Device Drivers for Synthesized Sound and MIDI Adapter Cards

The device drivers for MPC-compliant audio adapter cards usually combine drivers for waveform audio and synthesized sound in a single file (SBPSOUND.DRV for the Sound Blaster Pro, for example). Pre-MPC cards like the Thunder Board and original Sound Blaster use two files—SNDBLST2.DRV for waveform audio and the Ad Lib driver for FM-synthesized sound. The following three sections describe drivers included with Windows or supplied by other manufacturers for synthesized sound and MIDI applications.

The Ad Lib Driver (MSADLIB.DRV)

MSADLIB.DRV is a MIDI device driver written by Microsoft for the original Ad Lib FM-synthesis card. If you have an original Ad Lib card, MSADLIB.DRV is the only driver you need to install to use it. The MIDI Map created by Microsoft for the Ad Lib card is used with the Ad Lib card to shift the MIDI channel for percussion sounds from 10 to 16. The MIDI Map is used with all audio adapter cards compatible with the original Sound Blaster. MIDI Maps are the subject of the next section of this chapter. The Ad Lib driver is not required for most MPC-compatible sound cards because its functions are built into a single device driver that can process waveform audio and synthesized sound.

The MPU-401/LAPC-1 MIDI Driver (MPU401.DRV)

Roland's MPU-401 MIDI adapter and compatible audio cards (such as the Roland LAPC-1 and SCC-1) use the MPU401.DRV driver supplied with Windows 3.1 and Windows with Multimedia. The MPU-401 provides a means for you to connect external piano keyboards, keyboard synthesizers, sound modules, and other MIDI gear to your PC. Audio adapter cards with MIDI breakout boxes serve the same purpose, but the MPU-401 provides special features that include a clicking metronome that

Related Topics
Working with MIDI Channels and the Multimedia Extensions, p. 300
FSK Synchronization for Audiotape Recorders, p. 579

enables you to synchronize your playing with a sequencer application. The MPU-401 also had a synchronization input and output for use with tape recorders.

Microsoft created a MIDI map for the LAPC-1 sound card, but neglected to create one for the MPU-401 itself. This omission offers you an opportunity to create your own; refer to "Setting Up MIDI Mapper" later in this chapter for instructions.

Creative Labs' SNDBLST.DLL and JUKEBOX.EXE for Windows 3.0

If you have not yet upgraded to Windows 3.1, you can sample *.MID files with a simple Windows 3.0 application provided by Creative Labs. This application plays MIDI files without requiring the multimedia extensions of Windows 3.1 or Windows with Multimedia; it uses JUKEBOX.EXE to perform Media Player's functions and SNDBLST.DLL to perform the functions of MMSYSTEM.DLL and MCISEQ.DRV. If you are still using Windows 3.0, give it a try. (Then upgrade to Version 3.1 so that you can gain all of the benefits that Windows offers when using your Sound Blaster.)

T I P Do not try to use Creative Labs' JUKEBOX.EXE, which was supplied with early versions of the Sound Blaster 1.5 with Windows 3.1 or Windows with Multimedia. JUKEBOX.EXE calls functions in Creative Labs' SNDBLST.DLL that conflict with the Microsoft Ad Lib driver (ADLIB.DRV). When such a conflict takes place, you might see a message box that states The Sound Blaster cannot be installed. Please check your WIN.INI settings. You can obtain another version of the same program—MMJBOX.EXE—which is compatible with Windows 3.1 and uses the multimedia extensions. Simply contact the technical support department at Creative Labs.

Related Topics
MIDI Mapper
Revisited, p. 300
Understanding the Dual
Composition Version
Requirement for MPC
Compliance, p. 312

Setting Up MIDI Mapper

Control Panel's MIDI Mapper is designed to convert internal MIDI messages to meet the requirements of various audio and MIDI adapter card setups. A *setup* consists of a table that assigns each of the 16 individual MIDI channels available to a specific device driver. If you have a single Ad Lib (not Gold), Sound Blaster (not Pro or Basic), or Thunder Board card, or an audio adapter card that is 100 percent compatible with one of these cards, you can use one of the MIDI maps provided with Windows 3.1.

Most MPC-compliant audio adapter cards install their own MIDIMAP.CFG file, which MIDI Mapper then uses as a default. You can skip this section if your adapter card sounded right when you tried it out at the beginning of this chapter, but you may want to review the section "Third-Party MIDI Maps" if you encounter difficulty (such as silence) when attempting to play MIDI files you have obtained from other sources.

Windows 3.1 provides eight standard setups for popular pre-MPC sound cards and the Roland MT-32 and E-mu Proteus/1 external sound modules (see fig. 7.4).

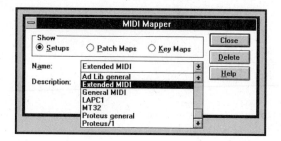

FIG. 7.4

The MIDI Mapper dialog box showing 7 of the 8 standard setups provided by Windows 3.1.

Ad Lib assigns MIDI channels 13 through 16 to the original Ad Lib synthesizer card to provide MPC base-level synthesizer operation (three simultaneous melodic voices and one percussion channel).

Ad Lib general assigns all 16 MIDI channels to the original Ad Lib synthesizer card and assigns source channel 10 to destination channel 16, the only percussion channel of the Ad Lib card. Source channel 16 is assigned to destination channel 10. This procedure is necessary because the standard percussion instrument channel
is 10, but the Ad Lib card uses channel 16 for its percussion sounds.

Extended MIDI assigns channels 1 through 10, the extended level synthesizer channel group, to the Media Vision Thunder Board or original Sound Blaster card. You then can use the MIDI OUT connector of these boards to control General MIDI (GM) sound modules such as the Roland SCC-1 Sound Canvas, the Korg 03R/W, and the Yamaha TG-100. You are likely to hear very strange sounds if you use a non-GM product like the Yamaha DX7 synthesizer or a TX81Z sound module with this setup.

General MIDI assigns all 16 MIDI channels to the original Sound Blaster; otherwise it is the same as Extended MIDI.

LAPC1 assigns channels 1 through 8 and channel 10 to the Roland LAPC-1 card. LAPC1 is designed to play *.MID files that meet the General MIDI standard on the LAPC-1 with the MPU-401 driver. Because the LAPC-1 card can play only eight simultaneous melodic voices (instead of nine), LAPC1 assigns MIDI only channels 1 through 8 to the corresponding channels of the card. The MT-32 patch map is used with each melodic channel. Channel 10 is assigned to percussion instruments and requires the MT32 perc(ussion) patch map so that the correct set of drums is played. The Roland MT-32 is an external sound module and is the predecessor of the LAPC-1; the LAPC-1 is an MT-32 built on an adapter card.

MT32 assigns channels 1 through 8 and channel 10 to the Sound Blaster's MIDI system. MT32 plays standard *.MID files with a Roland MT-32 sound module connected to the MIDI OUT connector of the original Sound Blaster's MIDI breakout box. Because the sounds of the LAPC-1 and the MT-32 are identical, MT32 uses the same patch maps as LAPC1.

Proteus/1 plays channels 1 through 10 of GM *.MID files with E-mu Systems' Proteus/1 (rock/pop) sound module connected to the MIDI OUT connector of the Sound Blaster. This setting does not work with the Proteus/2 (orchestral) or Proteus/3 (world sounds) modules.

Proteus General is the same as Proteus/1, except that all 16 channels are assigned to the MIDI OUT port.

If you are installing an MPU-401 card, or another card that is 100 percent compatible with the MPU-401, skip to the next section of this chapter. If you are installing a Sound Blaster, Thunder Board, or LAPC-1 audio card, install the appropriate Microsoft-supplied MIDI map, using the following steps:

1. Start Control Panel and double-click the MIDI Mapper icon.

2. Click the down arrow of the **Name** drop-down box to display the list of setups.

3. Click the appropriate setup for your adapter card (and sound module, if you are using one). If you are using an Ad Lib card, choose the Ad Lib option. Otherwise, use one of the Extended choices to assign the first 10 channels to your card. The box closes with your choice in its text box.

4. Click the Close button.

   If a message box like the one shown in figure 7.5 appears, you have selected a setup that contains a device driver you have not installed. This choice will not work for you; click **No** and review your choice using the information contained in the list above.

5. Close the Control Panel.

Now try playing CANYON.MID again with Media Player.

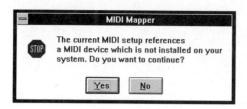

FIG. 7.5

The message box that appears when you select a MIDI setup that specifies a driver you haven't installed.

Creating a MIDI Map for the MPU-401 or Roland SCC-1

Microsoft omitted one of the most important setups for pre-MPC devices—a setting that might be called *MPU-401 Vanilla*. If you are using an MPU-401, one of its clones, or a Roland SCC-1 GS sound card, you need to create this setup; otherwise you can skip this section. MIDI maps are explained in detail in Chapter 10, "The MIDI Standard and Windows 3.1."

You can create an MPU-401 Vanilla setup (it is called Vanilla because it sends all 16 MIDI channels to the corresponding channels of your MPU-401 without making any changes en route) by following these steps:

1. Start Control Panel from the Main group.

2. If you already have installed the MPU-401 driver, skip to step 6. Otherwise, double-click the Drivers icon to open its dialog box.

3. Click the **Add** button, then double-click Roland MPU-401 to install the driver. The MPU-401 Compatible Setup dialog box appears (see fig. 7.6).

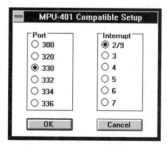

FIG. 7.6

The MPU-401 Compatible Setup dialog box for selecting the device address and interrupt level.

4. The default Port (device address) for the MPU-401 and the SCC-1 is 330 and Interrupt level is 2/9. Unless you know that your MPU-401 uses other settings, choose these by clicking the corresponding option buttons.

5. Click OK. If you receive a message box advising that these settings are incorrect, check the jumpers on your MPU-401 or SCC-1 to determine its current device address and interrupt (IRQ) level. Chapter 4 provides suggestions for choosing device addresses and interrupts.

6. Double-click the MIDI Mapper icon in Control Panel's window. The dialog box shown in figure 7.7 appears.

FIG. 7.7

MIDI Mapper's opening dialog box.

7. If the **S**etups option button in the Show box is not highlighted, click it to create a new setup.

8. Click **N**ew, then enter the name—**MPU-401 Vanilla**—and description—**Channels 1-16 direct to MPU-401**—in the New MIDI Setup dialog box (see fig. 7.8).

FIG. 7.8

Adding the name and description for the Plain Vanilla MPU-401 MIDI setup.

9. Click OK. A blank MIDI map form similar to the one shown in figure 7.9 (but with all 16 channel entries indicating [None]) appears.

10. Click the down arrow of the **P**ort Name drop-down box to display the drivers that can be assigned to each MIDI channel. If you have not installed any other drivers, your only options are Roland MPU-401 and [None]. You do not need to assign a patch map, so [None] should appear for all sixteen channels in the Patch **M**ap Name column.

11. Click Roland MPU-401 to select it and the box progresses to the next channel.

12. Repeat steps 10 and 11 until you have assigned all 16 channels to the MPU-401 driver.

13. Click OK and confirm that you want to save the setup when the dialog box shown in figure 7.10 appears.

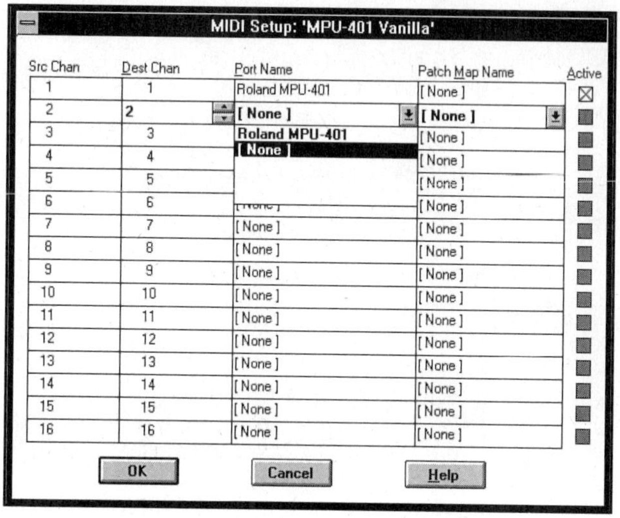

Src Chan	Dest Chan	Port Name	Patch Map Name	Active
1	1	Roland MPU-401	[None]	☒
2	2	[None]	[None]	■
3	3	Roland MPU-401	[None]	■
4	4	[None]	[None]	■
5	5		[None]	■
6	6	[None]	[None]	■
7	7	[None]	[None]	■
8	8	[None]	[None]	■
9	9	[None]	[None]	■
10	10	[None]	[None]	■
11	11	[None]	[None]	■
12	12	[None]	[None]	■
13	13	[None]	[None]	■
14	14	[None]	[None]	■
15	15	[None]	[None]	■
16	16	[None]	[None]	■

OK   Cancel   Help

FIG. 7.9

Creating the MIDI setup (channel map) for the MPU-401 and Roland SCC-1 cards.

Save Changes...

The Setup 'MPU-401 Vanilla' has changed. Do you want to save the changes?

Yes   No   Cancel

FIG. 7.10

The Save Changes message box.

The MPU-401 Vanilla map should be used to play any standard MIDI file that is not composed specifically for MPC-compliant sound cards. If you have installed an SCC-1, play one of the demonstration files on the accompanying floppy disk. If you are setting up an MPU-401 for use with an outboard synthesizer, start with this file and then create one with the necessary patches for your synthesizer. See Chapter 10 for patching instructions.

Creating MIDI Maps for the MPC Authoring Standards

You need a special MIDI map for compositions like CANYON.MID that have not been created to conform with the MPC specification's dual-authoring standard. The dual authoring standard requires that two

Related Topics
Understanding the Dual Composition Version Requirement for MPC Compliance, p.312

versions of each MIDI composition be included in a MIDI file: one for
base-level (Ad Lib-type) synthesizers that use channels 13 through 16,
and another for extended-level (GM) synthesizers that use channels 1
through 10.

Repeat steps 8 through 13 above, but this time name your map **MPU-401
Extend** and describe it as **MPC, Channels 1-10 only**. This time assign
only channels 1 through 10 to the Roland MPU-401 driver; leave channels 11 through 16 set to [None]. Now go back to the beginning of this
chapter and try playing CANYON.MID. All you hear is silence, because
CANYON.MID is authored only to the base-level MPC standard that uses
only MIDI Channels 13 through 16.

If you would like to verify that CANYON.MID is authored to the base-level
specification, create a third MIDI map. Name it **MPU-401 Base** and describe it as **MPC, Channels 13-16 only**. Assign the Roland MPU-401
driver to channels 13 through 16 only; leave the remaining channels set
to [None]. Try out CANYON.MID again; this time it works! You may never
need MPU-401 Base again; if you want to delete it, follow the instructions
given in the "Deleting Unneeded MIDI Maps" section of this chapter.

CAUTION: When you create custom setups, patch maps, or key
maps for your synthesizer or drum machine, take the time to create
a backup of your MIDIMAP.CFG file as soon as you are satisfied with
your creation. This step is especially important if you are using
Windows with Multimedia and plan to upgrade to Windows 3.1.
When you install Windows 3.1, the MIDIMAP.CFG file supplied on
the distribution disks overwrites your existing MIDIMAP.CFG file
without warning; if you do not have a backup, all of your work is
lost. The same disaster might occur when you install the drivers for
a new audio adapter card. When you have a backup file of your
custom configurations, you can copy it over MIDIMAP.CFG after
installation.

Using Third-Party MIDI Maps

Many MPC audio adapter cards install their own MIDIMAP.CFG file
to replace the version supplied with Windows 3.1. These configuration
files usually include one or more maps designed specifically for the
manufacturer's product in addition to the standard MIDI maps supplied
by Microsoft. The product-specific MIDI maps may not be adequate to
the task of playing MIDI files not composed to meet base-level MPC standards. Figure 7.11 shows an example of a third-party MIDI map—a map
provided by Media Vision with its early Pro AudioSpectrum cards.

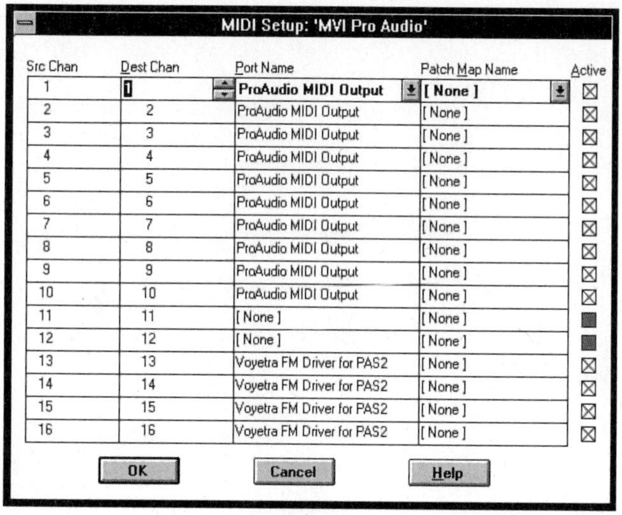

FIG. 7.11

The MIDI map provided by Media Vision, Inc. for its Pro AudioSpectrum audio adapter cards.

Instead of sending MIDI note messages on the first ten channels to the FM synthesizer circuitry of your Pro AudioSpectrum card, the MIDI map of figure 7.11 sends them to the MIDI OUT port of your MIDI breakout box. Only messages in tracks programmed for MIDI channels 13 through 16 are routed to the FM synthesizer. You need to edit this type of MIDI map, or create a new one, if you want to play files composed at MPC extended-level or General MIDI standards. To complicate matters further, the Voyetra Driver for PAS2 does not follow the General MIDI requirement that Channel 10 be reserved for percussion instruments; it uses the Ad Lib's Channel 16 assignment.

In order to add a MIDI map for use with extended-level and GM MIDI files, follow these steps:

1. Start Control Panel from the Main group.

2. Double-click the MIDI Mapper icon.

3. Click the **New** button to create a new MIDI map.

4. Enter **MVI Extended** as the map name and **Channels 1-10 to PAS FM** as the description in the two text boxes of the New MIDI Setup dialog box, then click OK.

5. Click the down arrow for the Channel 1 Port to view a list box containing the names of available drivers. Choose Voyetra Driver for PAS2.

6. Repeat step 5 for Channels 2 to 10.

7. When you complete step 5 for Channel 10, click the up arrow (called a spin button) in the Destination Channel column six times to change the Destination Channel from 10 to 16. This re-routes General MIDI percussion parts sent on Channel 10 to the drum kit that the Voyetra driver assigns to Channel 16. Your MVI Extended MIDI map now should look like the map shown in figure 7.12.

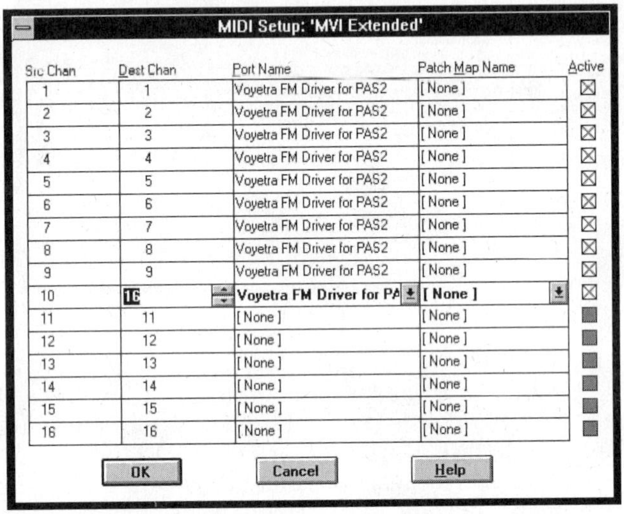

MIDI Setup: 'MVI Extended'

Src Chan	Dest Chan	Port Name	Patch Map Name	Active
1	1	Voyetra FM Driver for PAS2	[None]	☒
2	2	Voyetra FM Driver for PAS2	[None]	☒
3	3	Voyetra FM Driver for PAS2	[None]	☒
4	4	Voyetra FM Driver for PAS2	[None]	☒
5	5	Voyetra FM Driver for PAS2	[None]	☒
6	6	Voyetra FM Driver for PAS2	[None]	☒
7	7	Voyetra FM Driver for PAS2	[None]	☒
8	8	Voyetra FM Driver for PAS2	[None]	☒
9	9	Voyetra FM Driver for PAS2	[None]	☒
10	16	Voyetra FM Driver for PA	[None]	☒
11	11	[None]	[None]	■
12	12	[None]	[None]	■
13	13	[None]	[None]	■
14	14	[None]	[None]	■
15	15	[None]	[None]	■
16	16	[None]	[None]	■

OK   Cancel   Help

FIG. 7.12

An extended-level MIDI map for Pro AudioSpectrum audio adapter cards.

8. Click OK, then choose **Yes** when prompted to save your changes.

9. Click the Close button in MIDI Mapper's opening dialog box. MVI Extended is now the default MIDI map used by Media Player.

10. Close Control Panel.

11. Start Media Player from the Accessories group by double-clicking its icon.

12. Choose **F**ile, then **O**pen. Load an extended-level or GM MIDI file.

13. Click Play to verify that your MIDI map is operating properly. If the percussion continues to play as a melodic voice (a piano, for instance) you probably forgot to set Source Channel 10 to Destination Channel 16 in step 7.

In this example, the driver for Source Channel 10 is assigned to Destination Channel 16. You might expect that it would also be necessary to reassign the driver in the row for Channel 16 when making your MIDI map. But this step is unnecessary because Microsoft chose to associate the driver selection with the source channel rather than the destination channel, despite the fact that the source of the data is a MIDI file (or a sequencer application) and the destination is the selected driver.

You also can accomplish the reassignment of the percussion channel from 16 to 10 by adding an instruction to the driver in your SYSTEM.INI file. If you are using the Voyetra OPL-III drivers for Pro AudioSpectrum cards, for example, you can add the following lines at the bottom of your SYSTEM.INI file:

```
[opl3.drv]
drumchannel=10
```

You should add this line only if you use primarily MIDI files composed at General MIDI, rather than base-level synthesizer (AdLib-compatible) standards. If you do add this line, you also need to patch Source Channel 16 of your base-level MIDI map to Destination Channel 10.

Deleting Unneeded MIDI Maps

MIDI Maps that are no longer needed do not consume significant amounts of disk space, but they clutter the selection box. You can delete a MIDI map by following these simple steps:

1. Start Control Panel.

2. Double-click the MIDI Mapper icon.

3. Click the down arrow of the Name drop-down box.

4. Select the name of the MIDI map you want to delete. The list box closes.

5. Click Delete.

6. If you attempt to delete a MIDI map while it is being used by Media Player or another application, the message box shown in figure 7.13 appears. In this case, close Media Player or the application using the MIDI map and try the deletion again.

7. Click OK in the message box that confirms the deletion.

FIG. 7.13

Message box indicating that an application is using the MIDI map to be deleted.

Exploring Sources of MIDI Song Files

Personal computers have been used to create and edit MIDI music since the early 1980s. Musicians tend to share their creations and arrangements with others, so thousands of musical files have found their way to information services like CompuServe and to private electronic bulletin boards. Although most music files from these sources are now in Standard MIDI Format (SMF—indicated by the MID extension) adopted by the International MIDI Association in the late 1980s, some are in proprietary formats and must be converted to SMF before you can play them with Media Player. Chapter 12, "MIDI Applications for Windows," covers methods for converting proprietary sequencer file formats to SMF.

After you have the synthesizer portion of your sound card up and running or you have installed the drivers for your MPU-401, you may want to test your card with a wider range of MIDI compositions than the one provided by CANYON.MID and the sample files on your sound card's floppy disk. CompuServe's MIDI forum (GO MIDI) has one of the best collections of *.MID files available—over 1,000 to choose from at the time of this writing. The electronic bulletin boards listed in Appendix F of this book are also good sources of *.MID files, helpful information, and utilities for synthesized sound.

Many of the *.MID files that can be downloaded from CompuServe are composed to meet the General MIDI standard. But some files assign voices to MIDI channels that reflect the composer's synthesizer and drum machine setup rather than the GM arrangement of melodic voices and percussion sounds. A sequencer application is a virtual necessity for reassigning voices to the correct GM channels. If the author includes a text file that describes the channel assignments made, you can create a MIDI Map to make the required changes. Chapter 10 describes this process. Make sure that you assign the percussion track(s) to channel 10, and then hope for the best.

You also can purchase pre-recorded MIDI compositions from a wide range of sources. Some of these sources offer current pop and rock tunes that are copyrighted—like sheet music—and have restrictions on their use. Others, like Prosonus' MusicBytes CD-ROMs, were commissioned specifically for multimedia presentations and may be distributed with them subject to the provisions of the license agreement. MusicBytes' MIDI files are authored to the dual composition standard. MusicWriter's NoteStation kiosk, shown in figure 7.14 and found in many music stores, uses Passport's Encore scoring application to print popular and classical sheet music in your choice of key signature. NoteStation also copies Passport's Pro-MIDI sequences onto floppy disks at the press of a button. Some sources of commercially pre-recorded MIDI and wave-form audio music are listed in Appendix F.

FIG. 7.14

MusicWriter's NoteStation music publishing and MIDI file-dispensing kiosk.

If you plan to purchase pre-recorded, orchestrated MIDI sound sequences on floppy disks, make sure that their patches comply with the General MIDI standards for voicing. If your favorite MIDI tune supplier hasn't converted them yet, ask for an MPC- or General MIDI-compatible MIDI map so that you don't have to create one of your own.

T I P

Using MIDI Sequencer Applications

Creating or modifying MIDI music files requires a music *sequencer* application. A sequencer does what its name implies; it sends MIDI messages to audio adapter cards or external sound modules to play a series of notes in sequence. Although Windows refers to MCISEQ.DRV as a sequencer, this driver is only capable of transferring MIDI messages between *.MID files and applications. You need a sequencer application to do any serious work with MIDI music.

A brief description of entry-level MIDI sequencers for Windows is included in this chapter because all pre-MPC and many MPC-compliant sound cards do not include sequencers on their accompanying floppy disks. Most audio adapter cards come with DOS sequencers of varying capabilities, but the graphic environment of Windows is far better than that of character-based DOS for displaying and editing musical notation. For this reason, virtually all development work on new and improved sequencer applications for PCs is devoted to Windows-based versions.

The sequencers for Windows described in this section provide a number of useful functions that you don't find in Media Player:

- *Recording* MIDI data from external piano-style keyboards or MIDI instrument pickups used with guitars and other string instruments. You also can purchase electronic woodwinds that send MIDI signals in response to breath velocity and key fingering.

- *Editing* the recorded data to remove or change sour notes or to tighten up the music by making sure that all notes start on the beat or fraction of the beat (quantizing).

- *Re-arranging* *.MID files to play individual parts with different instruments, to change the tempo of the song, or to adjust the relative volume of the voices.

- *Composing* new tunes on the computer by adding representations of notes of the desired pitch and duration to a graphic display.

- *Transposing* individual parts (instrument voices) by a specified interval.

- *Translating* song files from formats native to the sequencer to standard *.MID format and back again.

- *Synchronizing* recording or playing of music with an external device such as a tape recorder or drum machine.

Professional-level sequencers, described in Chapter 12, combine these abilities with additional features necessary to create music for television productions, commercials, and live performers. The recording industry makes extensive use of MIDI-sequenced synthesized sound in pop and rock releases.

MIDI music composed with one type of audio adapter card may sound quite different when reproduced with audio adapter cards using different synthesizer techniques and FM-synthesis chipsets. If you sequence Mozart's *Eine Kline Nachtmusik* with a Turtle Beach MultiSound or Roland SCC-1 and play it back on an original Sound Blaster, for example, the music is recognizable but lacks the realism of the original. If you plan to create presentations that incorporate MIDI music, make sure that you evaluate your accompaniment on one of the most common adapter cards—a Thunder Board or Sound Blaster—before you release it.

T I P

The DOS Sequencer Supplied with Your Audio Adapter Card

The most common sequencer application that accompanies audio adapter cards is a version of Voyetra's Sequencer Plus for DOS customized for the card you purchased. Media Vision calls the version supplied with its Pro AudioSpectrum cards *SP Spectrum*. Creative Labs refers to its version as *SP Pro*. You can enter or edit notes with a keyboard or mouse, record tracks from your keyboard, and save files in SP Spectrum's or SP Pro's native *.SNG or standard *.MID formats. Both versions of Sequencer Plus include a set of drivers for the audio adapter card and a window for controlling the mixer functions of the card. These applications are for DOS use only; they should not be run in Windows.

Don't attempt to run any version of Sequencer Plus from the Windows DOS command line or from a DOS Window. Sequencer Plus uses drivers for the sound card that are loaded into memory as terminate-and-stay-resident (TSR) applications. TSRs loaded after you launch Windows often cause problems with Windows' operation. Because the device address and interrupt levels of the Sequencer Plus TAPI and VAPI drivers must be the same as those you assigned when installing the Windows drivers, a conflict occurs when the second driver loads. To run a Voyetra DOS sequencer, exit Windows and then run SP from the command line using **SEQ**. SEQ.BAT is a batch file that loads the required drivers, then runs SP itself. When you exit Sequencer Plus, the last command of SEQ.BAT removes the drivers from memory (eliminating the TSR problem).

T I P

Trax from Passport Designs

Trax is an entry-level MIDI sequencing application for Windows that comes with Media Vision's MIDI Mate breakout box for Pro AudioSpectrum cards. The inclusion of a Windows-based sequencer such as Trax with an audio adapter card can be an important consideration in your purchasing plans; buying one separately can add $100 or more to your investment.

Trax uses buttons like the ones used by tape recorders (and Sound Recorder) to control the playing and recording of music. The symbols on the buttons are exactly the same (see fig. 7.15). Your current position in the file being played is shown in measures and beats as well as hours, minutes, and seconds. A slider bar in the Conductor window enables you to change the tempo of the music while you are playing it.

Sequencers use the term *track* to refer to a single musical part—a saxophone or an entire section of saxophones, for example—in a composition. The most common Type 1 MIDI files usually assign each instrument type to a single track. Figure 7.15 shows the Track Sheet window for GTRBLUES.MTS, a demonstration file included with Trax. Track 1 contains the organ part; the guitar, bass, and drum parts are added in tracks 2 through 5. Each track is assigned one of the 128 or more instrument voices available with General MIDI audio adapter cards.

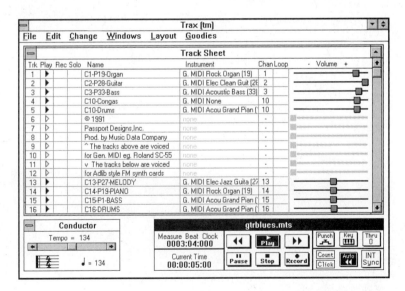

FIG. 7.15

Passport's Trax sequencer.

Because the Track Sheet assigns voices to channels, most sequencers can bypass MIDI Mapper and send instructions via MMSYSTEM.DLL directly to the device driver. Trax, like most other sequencers, enables you to choose whether to send and receive MIDI messages through MIDI Mapper or to bypass MIDI Mapper and go directly to the device driver for your adapter card. The MIDI Setup dialog box for Trax is shown in figure 7.16.

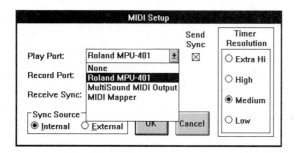

FIG. 7.16

The MIDI Setup dialog box for Passport's Trax sequencer.

You can assign more than one track to a channel with the Track Sheet. With piano parts, for example, the notes played by the right hand are often assigned to track 1 while the bass line notes played by the left hand are assigned to track 2. Trax enables you to use up to 64 tracks in a single sequence (MIDI composition)—more than you will ever need when working with only a sound card.

Notice the additional entries for MIDI channels 13 through 16 in the Track Sheet shown in figure 7.16. The demonstration files supplied with Trax meet the MPC requirement that MIDI files be created in two versions—one for base-level synthesizers (channels 13 through 16) and another for extended-level synthesizers (channels 1 through 10). The arrangements for these two sets of tracks are often different. In this example, the Acoustic Grand Piano (GM voice number 1 on track 15) substitutes for the Acoustic Bass (voice 33 on track 3) and both drums (tracks 4 and 5) are combined on track 16, which is the percussion channel for base-level devices.

T I P

If the MIDI files you play with MIDI Mapper or your sequencer sound somewhat strange, you may be playing the base-level and extended-level versions of the music simultaneously. To avoid this problem, change to a MIDI Mapper setup that uses only the first 10 channels, edit your current MIDI map to replace the driver name with [None] for channels 11 through 16, or mute channels 13 through 16 (if you are using a sequencer). With Trax, you can mute a channel by clicking the triangle to the left of the corresponding track number. Other sequencers use similar muting techniques.

Trax uses the piano-roll format for adding and editing MIDI note data in its Step Editor window (see fig. 7.17). The pitch, corresponding to keys on the simulated piano keyboard on the left, is shown in a window—*G#5* corresponds to G-sharp of the fifth MIDI octave. *A 440* (440 Hz in the U.S.), the standard pitch used to determine all other pitches in the chromatic scale, is represented in MIDI terminology as *A5*. Figure 7.17 displays six measures of Track 1, which are divided into four beats each because the file was created in 4/4 time (meter). The duration of each note is determined by the length of its corresponding line. The first series of notes shown are quarter notes with a length of 1 beat in 4/4 time.

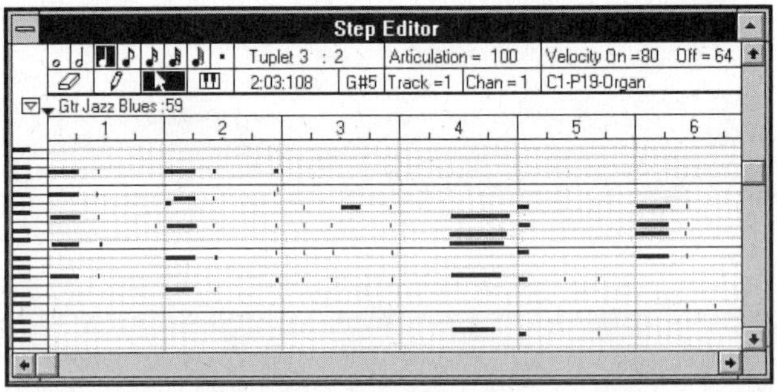

FIG. 7.17

Trax's piano-roll
Step Editor.

You can enter notes in the Step Editor window by playing them on a MIDI keyboard in Step Edit mode or by using a mouse. After a note is entered, you can adjust its duration or move it to another pitch by using the mouse. You also can delete a note with the Backspace key. Trax offers a wide range of other editing functions including Copy, Paste, and Delete operations that use the Windows Clipboard.

Passport's MusicTime Sequencer

MusicTime is unique among entry-level sequencers because of its use of conventional musical notation (rather than a piano-roll display) and its capability to print musical compositions on laser or dot-matrix printers. MusicTime's composing and scoring features are easy to learn; it is an excellent tool for musical instruction. The application is based on Passport's original version of Encore, a professional application for printing musical compositions. Figure 7.18 shows MusicTime's note entry and editing window.

Each MusicTime track has its own staff, and MusicTime allows up to six staves in a composition. Although this scheme seems to limit you to six voices, that isn't the case. Each staff can hold up to four individual voices, making MusicTime the equivalent of a 24-track sequencer.

MusicTime also offers the capability of assigning each track to one of two audio adapter cards. If you are using a Pro AudioSpectrum 16 in combination with a MIDI drum machine connected to an MPU-401, for example, you can play the melodic parts on the Pro AudioSpectrum and assign the percussion parts to your drum machine.

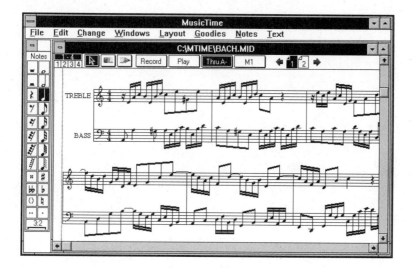

FIG. 7.18

The Staff Sheet window of Passport Design's MusicTime sequencer.

MusicTime comes with Adobe Type Manager's Sonata musical font, which is the industry standard for professional scoring applications. Helvetica, GillSans, Courier, and two versions of Times Roman typefaces are included. You can add titles and lyrics to your works. A 24-pin dot-matrix printer gives quite presentable results. Scores from 9-pin printers are readable.

Midisoft's Music Mentor and Recording Session

Midisoft's Recording Session sequencer, shown in figure 7.19, is included with the firm's Music Mentor music education application. Recording Session, derived from Midisoft's Studio for Windows (described in Chapter 12), provides notation-based sequencing and score printing capability. This sequencer takes full advantage of Roland's General Synthesizer standard (more on this topic in Chapter 9) and provides a graphic control panel with small dials that enable you to adjust the chorus, reverberation, and stereo pan effects of each channel. Overall and individual channel volume levels are set with sliders.

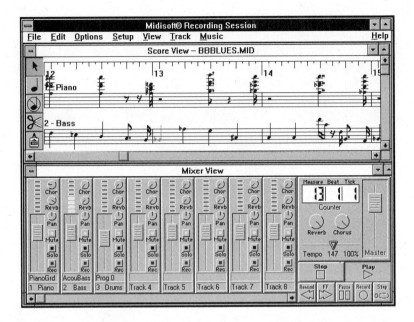

FIG. 7.19

Midisoft Recording
Session's Score and
Mixer windows.

Because it controls their digital effects, Recording Session is an excellent
choice for the Roland SCC-1 GS Sound Card or the SC-55 or SC-155 Sound
Canvas modules. The product is easy to use and is a handy tool for editing pre-recorded MIDI sequences to create MIDI or waveform audio files
to back commercial presentations.

WinJammer, a Shareware
Windows Sequencer

Dan McKee's WinJammer is an easy to learn Windows sequencer distributed as a shareware product. You get to test WinJammer without charge,
but if you use it, you are expected to pay the author a registration fee.
WinJammer's track sheet and piano-roll note entry and editing windows
are similar to those used by Trax and other commercial sequencers (see
fig. 7.20). WinJammer provides full System Exclusive (SysEx) send and
record capabilities using the MIDIEX file format. MIDIEX is an informal
standard used by musicians to exchange instrument voice patches for
synthesizers and sound modules. Chapter 9 describes MIDI System Exclusive messages; Chapter 12 covers the use of voice patches and
MIDIEX files.

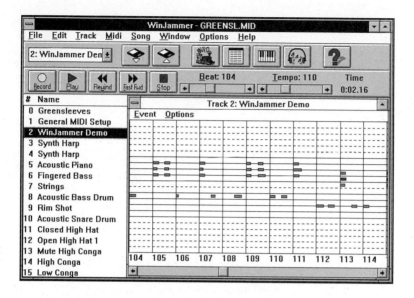

FIG. 7.20

WinJammer's track sheet and piano-roll step editing windows.

Power Chords—a Musical Erector Set

Power Chords, by Howling Dog Software, is a musical construction application that enables you to compose tunes by combining melodies, chords, bass lines, and drum patterns. You create each component within its own window, then drag an icon representing the component—a chord, for instance—to the Song window shown in figure 7.21. Power Chords is an excellent tool for classroom or individual musical instruction. You can learn how to use it in about half an hour with its interactive demonstration and tutorial modes. After creating a song, you can save it as a standard MIDI file and then tweak it to perfection with a sequencer application.

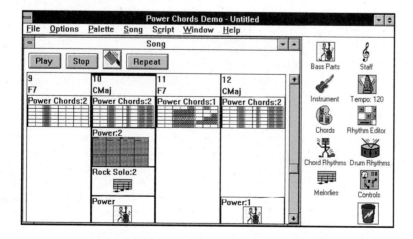

FIG. 7.21

The song construction window of Power Chords.

Power Chords uses a guitar fretboard, rather than a piano keyboard, to create chords. You can finger the chords with the right mouse button, or choose them by clicking option buttons in the Chord Request window shown in figure 7.22. Power Chords enables you to create a guitar with nonstandard numbers of strings and frets, if you like; you can even emulate a sitar or a koto.

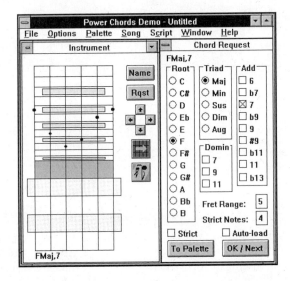

FIG. 7.22

Power Chords'
Instrument window and
Chord Request dialog
box.

Chapter Summary

This chapter has served as an introduction to the reproduction of synthesized music by your audio adapter card, using standard MIDI files. MIDI's advantage is that its files are much smaller—often by a factor of 1,000—than those required to make music sounds of the same quality and duration with waveform audio. MIDI's major disadvantage is that the type and quality of the synthesizer section of the card used to reproduce your music may have drastic effects on how your music sounds.

Part III of this book, "Musical Synthesis and MIDI," provides more detailed coverage of the use of MIDI with your audio adapter card, whether it is an MPC-compliant version, a pre-MPC Sound Blaster or Thunder Board, or an MPU-401 compatible device. Chapter 10 describes MIDI standards and how they are implemented by the multimedia extensions of Windows. Chapter 12 extends the discussion of MIDI sequencers to their professional versions, dealing with subjects such as MIDI System Exclusive (SysEx) messages, patch librarians, and voice editors. Chapter 21, "Advanced MIDI and Waveform Audio Techniques," deals with more technical aspects of MIDI including MIDI synchronization techniques for multimedia graphics, television images, and sound recording.

Incorporating Sound in Windows Applications

O bject linking and embedding (OLE), which makes its formal debut in Windows 3.1, is destined to make a fundamental change in the way you use Windows applications. OLE (pronounced like the Spanish word *¡Olé!*) achieves Windows' original objective of seamlessly integrating multiple applications and their data into a composite structure called a *compound document*. With this capability, you can, for example, create a Word for Windows 2 report and insert (*embed*) voice notes created with Sound Recorder to produce a compound document that contains the text of the report and a copy of your vocal annotations.

OLE embeds in your report instructions that tell Sound Recorder where to find the embedded waveform audio data that comprises the voice notes. The result is as though Word for Windows 2 had sound recording and playback functions included within it—thus the term *seamless*. Just double-click the Sound Recorder icon, which indicates the presence of a voice note, and Sound Recorder plays the embedded data. You can edit the voice data or even re-record it with the Sound Recorder applet.

OLE is an advanced form of Windows' dynamic data exchange (DDE), which has been present since Windows 2.03 was introduced in 1987. With DDE, you can copy data from another application to Windows' Clipboard and then paste the data into your application. You can choose to have the pasted data remain static (a *cold* DDE link) or be updated whenever the source data changes (a *hot* link). OLE retains this dual capability. *Embedding* is similar to a cold DDE link because the embedded data becomes a part of the compound document with no connection to the original source file; *linking*, on the other hand, creates a reference to the file and uses the file as the source data. Later, this chapter explains the differences.

The use of OLE in Windows applications predates Windows 3.1 by more than a year. Microsoft Excel 3.0 and PowerPoint 1.0 made extensive use of OLE but didn't advertise they were doing so. Word for Windows 2, introduced in late 1991, incorporated the OLE services now provided by Windows 3.1 for its accompanying applets, Microsoft Draw, Chart, Equation Editor, and Word Art. OLE is incorporated in Apple Computer's System 7.0 for its Macintosh product line. All Microsoft and most other major Windows applications introduced after April 1992 are expected to be OLE-compliant.

Although OLE is much simpler and more straightforward in its use than DDE, OLE provides a challenge for programmers to implement properly within applications. Not all mainstream Windows applications support OLE yet; however, OLE eventually will become a part of every Windows application.

Understanding Objects

OLE introduced object-oriented programming (OOP) techniques to Windows users. Although OLE is designed so that you don't need to be a programmer to use it, you still need a basic understanding of *objects*—as the term is used by programmers—so that you can understand how OLE works.

Objects are entities that contain information (data, or *properties*) and a set of instructions that manipulate the information (programming code, or *methods*). The properties and methods are said to be *encapsulated* into the object, and all the methods applicable to the properties constitute the object's *behavior*. You can think of a Windows application such as Paintbrush as a large, complex object. The data is the bit-mapped image you create or edit. You alter the properties of the data using methods you choose from Paintbrush's menus or by using a mouse.

Paintbrush works in much the same way as other Windows paint applications that manipulate bit-mapped images; it may be considered a member of the "paint" class of objects. Programmers pigeon-hole the objects they create into classes with subclasses and sub-subclasses, all which share common characteristics with the base class. You can liken this hierarchy to Windows' menus: the File choice is the base class for file operations in general and Open is one of its subclasses. This chapter deals solely with the Sound class of OLE objects.

Before OOP, data and the programming code that serves to manipulate it were considered two distinct entities. OOP requires programmers to leave the traditional method of creating applications and to retrain themselves to think in a new way about their craft. The benefit of this effort is the capability of creating libraries of self-contained, reusable objects that you can combine with one another in different ways to create new applications. OOP makes programming a more efficient and organized process.

Understanding Compound Documents

A *document*, in Windows' terminology, is any data that you can display and manipulate with conventional input devices such as keyboard, mouse, and graphic tablet or pen. The data is the document's *content*. Different categories of applications (such as word processing programs, spreadsheets, and databases) use different file structures. Each application within a category usually has its own internal data format, and the applications cannot use each other's files without conversion because of these different structures. Some applications cannot interchange data through DDE because their data formats cannot be converted to a type recognized by Windows' Clipboard or other applications that use the Clipboard. The documents discussed in this chapter are limited to those used by OLE-compliant applications.

OLE is designed to enable a single *destination document* to be built with contributions, called *source documents*, from foreign applications. The destination document may be of any type—a proposal created in Word for Windows, an Excel spreadsheet, or a PowerPoint presentation visual. More than one application contributing to the content of a document is called a *compound document*. A compound document may contain "chunks" of data in the formats of the destination and source documents. The application that creates the compound destination document is called the OLE client, and the foreign applications that contribute source documents to it are called OLE *servers*.

Dynamic data exchange enables you to transfer data and any of its related properties between applications, as long as the client and the server support the Clipboard format that accommodates the properties. The code you write in your client application, however—not the client supplying the data—determines the methods applied to DDE data. When you use DDE to paste the data from a range in an Excel spreadsheet into a Word for Windows table, for example, the data loses all the behavior it previously exhibited within Excel. You must write a WordBASIC macro if you want to manipulate the data in the table with code.

An OLE server, on the other hand, encapsulates all its methods—and the properties of the data it creates—within the OLE object. It then embeds the OLE object within your client's destination document, which acts as a *container* for each source document object contributed by OLE servers, plus any data contained in the client application. Obviously, the code to perform the server's methods isn't incorporated in the destination document; think of the size of a document containing a copy or two of EXCEL.EXE. Instead, the server's methods are incorporated by *reference*, to use legal terminology, in the source document. Figure 8.1, itself an OLE diagram object created by the Microsoft Draw applet, shows the difference between OLE and DDE techniques.

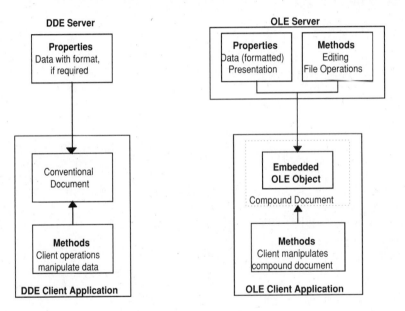

FIG. 8.1

Differences between DDE and OLE.

Presentation of OLE Objects

OLE objects have an additional characteristic, *presentation*, which is a cross between a property and a method. Presentation defines how the object appears on-screen or printed. The class of the embedded object defines the method of presentation, but the client controls some of its properties. The margins you set in Word for Windows, for example, constrain an Excel chart to fit within these margins if the chart's dimensions exceed the current line width. Your client can specify that the object be invisible and use a marker or icon to indicate its presence.

Sound Recorder indicates its presence in a document with its icon because waveform audio data has no visual content to display. If you copy a sound object to the Clipboard and then use Clipboard Viewer to display it, you see only its presentation icon, as shown in figure 8.2. The paragraph mark is an artifact from the client application—in this case, Word for Windows 2, which was used to write this book.

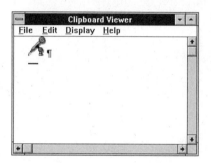

FIG. 8.2

The presentation icon for Sound Recorder.

Registration of OLE Applications

Chapter 5 introduces Windows 3.1's registration database and shows how File Manager uses REG.DAT to associate file extensions with applications. The registration database also serves as a central source of information about the OLE clients and servers installed on your computer. Each application that participates in the creation of a compound document must be located on your hard disk—not, for example, on a network server. The source and destination documents can be held on a server, however, and a source document for embedding even may be located on a CD-ROM.

The entries for an OLE server in REG.DAT inform OLE-client applications of the capabilities of the server. The registration editor application, RegEdit, enables you to view and edit the content of the registration database in two different forms—a list of applications, as shown in Chapter 5, or all its content in a graphic format, which Microsoft calls the *Advanced Interface* (shown in fig. 8.3). To display REG.DAT information in the Advanced Interface format, you need to add the *verbose* command line switch, /V, to the Command Line entry in the Program Item Properties dialog box for the RegEdit application.

To add the verbose command-line switch, follow these steps:

1. Click the Registration Database icon in Program Manager's Accessories group.

2. Choose **File**, **Properties** from the Program Manager menu. The Program Item Properties dialog box appears.

3. Press Tab to move to the Command Line text box and add a space; then type **/V** after `regedit.exe`.

4. Click OK to close the dialog box.

5. Double-click RegEdit's Program Manager icon. The Registration Info Editor window shown in figure 8.3 appears.

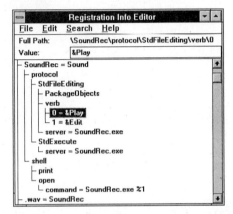

FIG. 8.3

RegEdit's Advanced Interface format.

RegEdit displays registration database information in a form similar to that used by File Manager to display directories. The root, to the extreme left, includes the registered names of OLE-compliant applications, prefixed by protocol, as well as other applications that have associated file extensions, indicated by the shell prefix. The file extensions and the registered names of applications that use them also are located at the root level: `.wav = SoundRec` is an example.

OLE has a set of predefined protocols that determine how the client and server applications interact with each other. Sound Recorder uses two protocols: *standard file editing* (StdFileEditing), which displays Sound Recorder's window so that you can edit the sound, and *standard execution* (StdExecute), which plays the embedded or linked sound. `StdFileEditing` and `StdExecute` are shown at the next level under `protocol` in figure 8.3. The `PackageObjects` entry under the `StdFileEditing` entry tells you that an OLE package created with Object Packager uses StdFileEditing. (Packaged sound objects are discussed later in this chapter.) The standard file editing protocol enables the command buttons and menus of Sound Recorder's window when the sound object is linked or embedded. As you add new OLE-compliant applications created after the advent of Windows 3.1, information about their capabilities is added to REG.DAT.

T I P

Periodically backing up your WIN.INI and SYSTEM.INI files on floppy disks always has been recommended in case a hardware failure corrupts these files. Adding REG.DAT to your backup list and creating a new backup each time you add a new OLE-compliant application is also a good idea. Corruption of your REG.DAT file can cause strange behavior when you use File Manager or attempt OLE operations and may even cause unrecoverable application errors (UAEs).

OLE is an emerging technology; the present version is only 1.0. Microsoft and suppliers of major Windows applications are working together on the development of OLE 2.0, which will greatly expand OLE capabilities and its entries in REG.DAT.

Embedding or Linking Source Documents

The client application can deal with a source document in two ways: embedding it or linking it. When embedding a source document, Windows creates a copy of the source document information and inserts the copy as a block of data in the destination document. The client retains no connection to the embedded source document. When you link a source document, you embed only its file name and the path to the file, not the data in the file.

Embedding is your only choice if you do not or cannot save the source document as a file. The Microsoft Draw, Graph, WordArt, and Equation Editor applets, for example, enable you only to embed a file; they have no **S**ave or Save **A**s options on the **F**ile menu. When you choose **F**ile, E**x**it after making changes to the source document, these applets cause a message box to appear, asking whether you want to update the destination document with the edited source document. Thus, you can embed the source document you create with these applets only in your destination document.

Embedding Sound in a Word Processing Document

You can embed a waveform file in any destination document created by an OLE-compliant word processing application. This example uses

Microsoft Word for Windows 2.0a, but you also can use Windows 3.1's Write applet or Lotus Development's Ami Pro. At this writing, WordPerfect for Windows doesn't support OLE.

To embed a voice note or incorporate one of your favorite *.WAV files in a Word for Windows 2 or Windows Write document, follow these steps:

1. If Sound Recorder is active or minimized, close it so that no file association exists for this example. Press Ctrl+Esc to view the Task Manager's list to see whether instances of Sound Recorder are hidden under other windows. Click Task Manager's End Task button with Sound Recorder selected to close them.

2. Position the insertion point in your word processing document at the location where you want to place the embedded annotation.

3. Choose **I**nsert, **O**bject from Word for Windows' menu; or choose **E**dit, **I**nsert Object from the Write menu. A dialog box similar to Word's Object dialog box appears (see fig. 8.4). The appearance and name of the dialog box depend on the source application.

4. Use the scroll bar or down arrow to show the Sound option. Double-click Sound to insert a waveform audio file. Sound Recorder's window appears, as shown in figure 8.5.

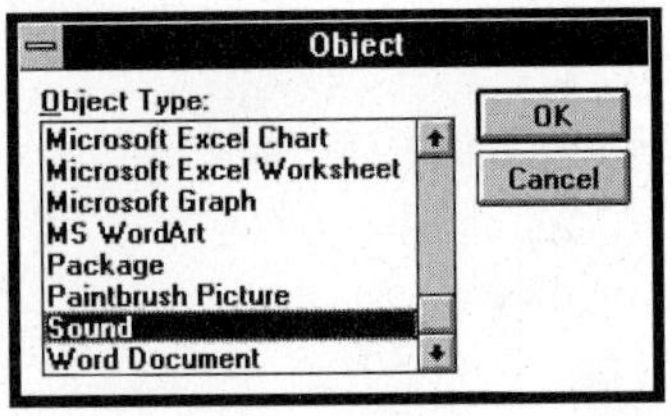

FIG. 8.4

An Object dialog box.

T   I   P   Don't click the mouse when the mouse pointer is outside the surface of Sound Recorder's window. If you do, Sound Recorder's window disappears behind that of Word for Windows. To restore the window, press Ctrl-Esc to bring up the Windows task manager's Task List window (see fig. 8.6). You should see an entry for Sound Recorder. Double-click this entry to bring Sound Recorder back to the foreground.

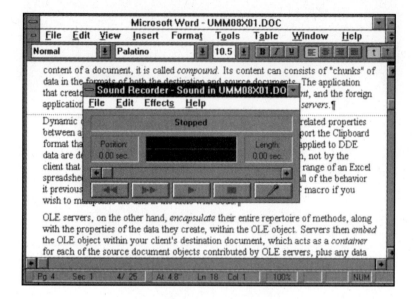

FIG. 8.5

Selecting a file
to insert.

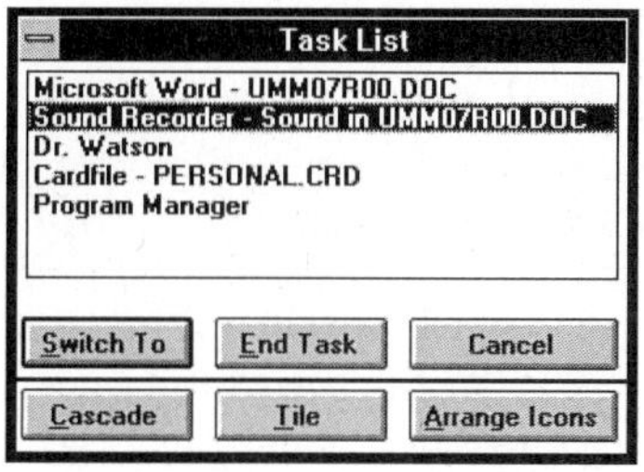

FIG. 8.6

Windows' Task List
dialog box with a
hidden copy of Sound
Recorder.

5. To use an existing file for your annotation, choose **E**dit, **I**nsert File
    from Sound Recorder's menu. The Insert File dialog box shown in
    figure 8.7 appears.

    If you want to record a voice note, skip step 6 and go to step 7.

    If you have used other OLE servers, note that Sound Recorder
    doesn't use the **F**ile, **O**pen choices to load a waveform audio file
    when its current instance doesn't have a file associated with it. The
    File menu choices are reserved for operations with files. In this
    case, you are embedding the waveform audio data within your com-
    pound document.

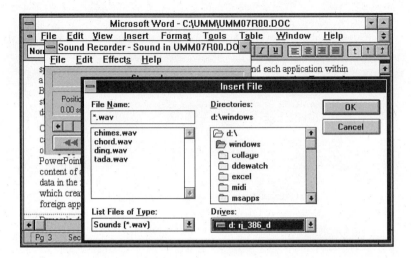

FIG. 8.7

The Insert File
dialog box.

6. Use the **Drive** and **Directories** boxes to locate the wave files from which to choose. Double-click the *.WAV file you want to embed. Click Sound Recorder's Play button to audition the file. Now go to step 9.

7. Click Sound Recorder's Record button. Start talking after the word `Record` replaces `Stopped` in the label under the title bar. Adjust the distance of the microphone from your lips, if necessary, to keep the sound peaks, as shown on the simulated oscilloscope display, at about three-quarters of the height of the window. Click Stop after you finish.

T I P   Before recording a voice note, make sure that you know what you want to say. Keep the annotation as short as possible to conserve disk space.

8. Click Play to audition your file. If you like what you hear, skip to step 12. Otherwise, click Rewind to return the position to 0.00 seconds.

9. Choose **E**dit to display Sound Recorder's editing options (see fig. 8.8).

10. Choose Delete After Current Position. You are asked to confirm your deletion by a message box similar to the one in figure 8.9.

FIG. 8.8

Sound Recorder's
Edit menu.

NOTE If Delete **A**fter Current Position isn't active (is dimmed), or Delete **B**efore Current Position and Delete **A**fter Current Position are active, you didn't click Rewind to reset the position to 0.00. Click the Rewind button; then click **E**dit again.

Chapter 14 covers the other editing functions and how to use the Effects menu.

FIG. 8.9

Confirming a deletion.

11. Repeat steps 7 and 8.

12. Double-click the Control bar at the upper left corner of Sound Recorder's window to close the server. A message box similar to the one shown in figure 8.10 appears unless you have edited data or chosen **F**ile, E**x**it to close Sound Recorder. In the latter case, a different message box appears (see fig. 8.11). Click Cancel or press Esc, and use the Control menu to close Sound Recorder unless you want to save your annotation in its own file.

    The presentation symbol for Sound Recorder now appears at the insertion point in your Word for Windows or Windows Write document (see fig. 8.12).

Although the message bar at the bottom of the document window in figure 8.12 states `Double-click to Edit Sound`, the message doesn't mean what it says. You double-click the icon to hear the sound. Editing the sound requires a different process, which is described in "Editing an Embedded or Linked Object" later in this chapter.

FIG. 8.10

Closing Sound
Recorder using the
Control menu's
Close option.

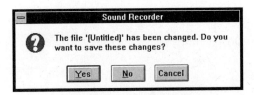

FIG. 8.11

Closing Sound
Recorder by choosing
File, Exit.

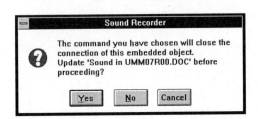

FIG. 8.12

Sound Recorder's
active presentation
icon (selected) in a
document.

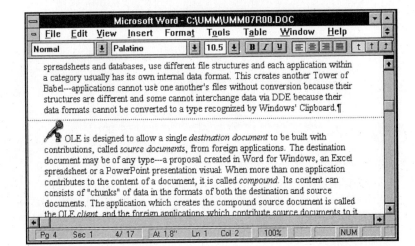

T I P   Embedding waveform audio files of substantial length consumes large amounts of memory. During the process, multiple copies of the sound file are created in memory or in virtual memory temporary disk files. If a problem with memory or disk space availability occurs (indicated by the message Insufficient memory to complete this operation), close any other applications that may be open and try the operation again. If you cannot complete the operation with all other applications closed, try using the linking process.

Microsoft Excel has been used as the application for demonstrating object linking because Word for Windows 2.0a doesn't support links to Sound Recorder files. If you choose Edit, Paste Special from Word for Windows' menu, the Paste Special dialog box appears (see fig. 8.13).

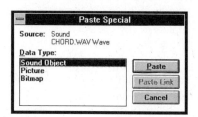

FIG. 8.13

The Paste Special
dialog box.

Notice that the Paste Link button is inactivate (dimmed). The statement on page 683 of the *Microsoft Word User's Guide* for version 2.0 states that the Paste Link button is dimmed when "the application from which you copied the information doesn't support linking or embedding." In this case, the statement is incorrect. Word for Windows uses fields for creating links to objects and has no field data type for waveform audio files. Excel, on the other hand, supports linked sound files.

Linking a Sound File to an Excel Spreadsheet

When linking an object, you don't incorporate a copy of the source information in the destination document; instead, you create a reference, or *link*, to the path and file name of the source document. If you edit a linked object, you are performing an edit on the source document's data. When you return to the destination document, it contains a link to the object's source document, not the document itself. If you want to link to an object, you first open the OLE server and load the file that contains the data to incorporate; then you create the link in your destination document.

To link a waveform audio file into an Excel 3 or later spreadsheet, follow these steps:

1. Start Sound Recorder and choose File, Open to load the waveform audio file of your choice.

2. Choose Edit, Copy from Sound Recorder's menu to place a copy of the file in the Clipboard. (You may close Sound Recorder now or after you complete this example.)

3. Start Excel and open any spreadsheet file, or use default Sheet 1.

4. Position the insertion point at the location where you want to insert the link. An empty cell is recommended because the link replaces the contents of a cell.

5. Choose **E**dit, Paste **L**ink from Excel's menu. #N/A (not applicable) appears in the cell, and the Excel formula for a linked object appears in the formula bar, as shown in figure 8.14.

   SoundRec, the name of Sound Recorder as registered in REG.DAT, identifies the application. The exclamation point acts as a separator for Wave, indicating that the file name preceding it contains waveform audio data. Chapter 23 describes this standard format for the high-level Media Control Interface commands.

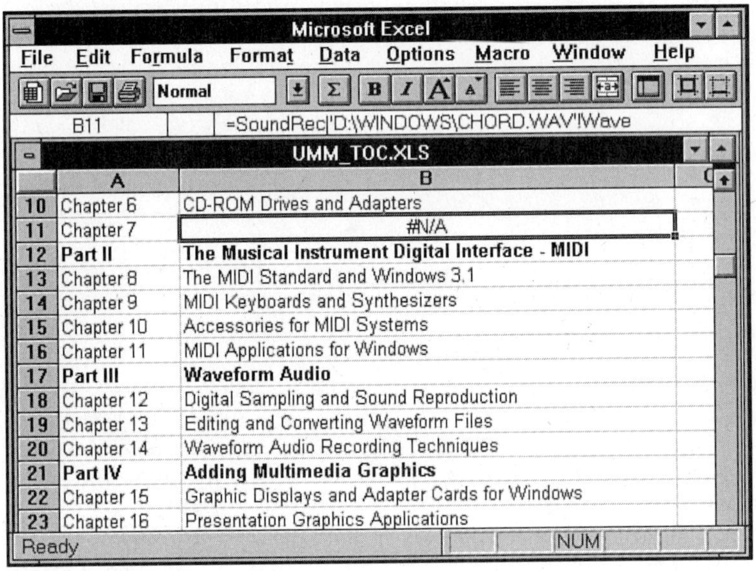

FIG. 8.14

An Excel spreadsheet with the entry for a linked waveform audio file.

6. Double-click the cell containing the link (#N/A). Sound Recorder plays the file.

   When linking is used, Sound Recorder's window appears, as shown in figure 8.15. If you embed the file using **P**aste, Sound Recorder's icon displays in the cell and the formula bar reads =EMBED("SoundRec","Wave"), the Excel formula for embedding an OLE object. If the Clipboard contains an OLE object, most client applications can embed it with the **P**aste option from the **E**dit menu.

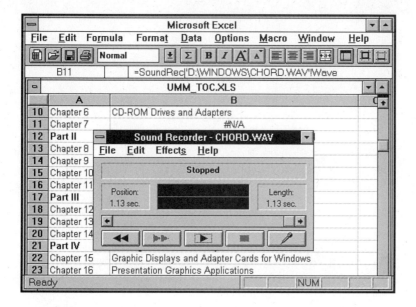

FIG. 8.15

Playing a waveform audio file linked into an Excel spreadsheet.

 You can edit, re-record, or add effects to your waveform audio file when you link it. Keep in mind that the file—not an embedded copy of its data—is altered.

7. You can choose to have your linked object updated automatically when another application updates it (a *hot link*), or perform the operation manually (a *cold link*, the default).

   Excel and most other applications that accommodate OLE and DDE links provide an option to choose between these two methods. In the case of Excel, choose **Files**, **Links**. Click the SoundRec link in the Links list box to highlight it, and then choose the Options button. The DDE/OLE Options dialog box appears (see fig 8.16). If you want to have the link updated automatically, click the **A**utomatic check box to activate a hot link. If the link is hot (an X is in the box), you can revert to manual updating by clicking the check box. Choose OK to close the dialog box. Choose **U**pdate to update the link with new file data if you have chosen a cold link.

8. Close Sound Recorder by double-clicking the Control Bar or by choosing **F**ile, E**x**it from Sound Recorder's menu. In the case of linking, both operations exhibit the same behavior—they close the file.

9. Close the original copy of Sound Recorder you used to create the link.

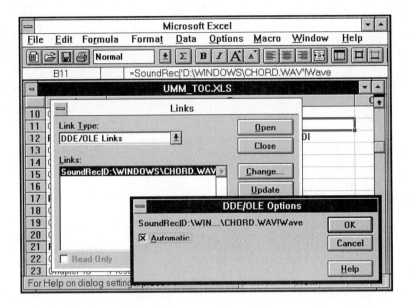

FIG. 8.16

The DDE/OLE Options dialog box for an object linked into Excel.

T   I   P   Linked OLE objects require that the file associated with the object be available to the recipient of the destination document. Although OLE requires that the client and server application reside on a local disk drive, you can access the destination document and its linked files from a network server, but only if the source and destination documents are in the same subdirectory or in subdirectories with identical paths (including the drive designator letter) on your computer and that of the recipient.

If you distribute your source document on floppy disk, don't forget to include the linked files with it, in the same subdirectory as for your destination document. You may have to edit formulas for the linked file in the distribution version of an Excel spreadsheet file to remove the drive letter and path if the linked file isn't copied into an identically named directory on the same logical drive.

You can apply this example of the linking process for OLE objects to most other OLE clients. The menu choices may have somewhat different wording or may be located under a different main menu. The Common User Access terminology doesn't appear to be standardized for linking objects, even within Microsoft applications.

Packaging a Sound Object for Embedding or Linking

The Object Packager applet in File Manager's Accessories group is designed for two purposes:

- To create OLE objects to embed or link using applications that aren't OLE servers. You can package Media Player and a MIDI file or audio CD track in a destination document, for example, because Media Player isn't an OLE server. File Manager uses this method to create OLE objects that it then uses in drag-and-drop operations, file editing, and printing.

- To enable you to embed selected portions of source documents created by OLE servers rather than the entire document. You can use this technique to insert only a portion of a waveform audio file into a document.

Object Packager always places an icon representation of the object, not the object itself, into the destination document. This representation is called a *package*, an apt demonstration of encapsulation. The packaged application contains the methods; the associated file contains the properties. Packages may contain linked or embedded objects, but the packages themselves are always embedded, not linked. You can embed packaged OLE objects only in documents created by an application that has OLE-client capabilities.

A package has all the properties and methods of an embedded object. When you click a package icon, the object it contains "appears" in the presentation of the application used to create it. You can package Media Player, which isn't an OLE server, with a *.MID file and then embed the package in a document. Its icon appears at the insertion point. Click the icon and Media Player's window appears, enabling you to play the tune.

Packaging a MIDI Object

To package an embedded MIDI file with Media Player that you then can embed as a MIDI object in your destination document, follow these steps:

1. Start Object Packager from Program Manager's Accessories group.

2. Choose **File, Import** from Object Packager's menu. The Import dialog box shown in figure 8.17 appears.

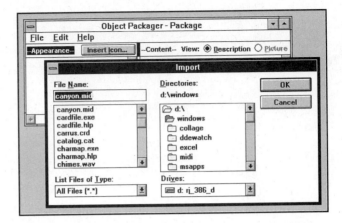

FIG. 8.17

Selecting a file to
import into an
OLE package.

3. In the **Directories** list box, select a directory containing *.MID
files and then select the MIDI file you want to package. Object
Packager's window becomes the active window (see fig. 8.18). Object Packager always includes the name of the imported file under
the icon.

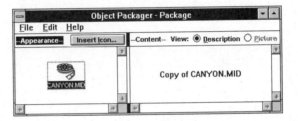

FIG. 8.18

Object Packager's
window.

4. Choose **E**dit, Copy **P**ackage. A copy of the packaged file as an OLE
object is placed in the Clipboard.

5. Close Object Packager by double-clicking the Control Bar. You can
choose **F**ile, **E**xit from the menu if you want.

6. Start the application in which to insert the packaged object, if it
isn't already in use, and open a file.

7. Position the insertion point where the package is to be embedded.

8. Choose **E**dit, **P**aste. The icon and the file name are embedded at the
insertion point (see fig. 8.19).

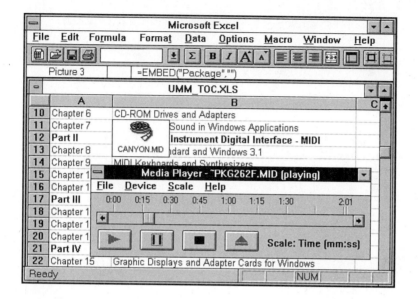

FIG. 8.19

A packaged
MIDI object,
CANYON.MID,
and Media Player.

NOTE If you are using Excel 4.0, you cannot link a packaged object; the Paste **L**ink option is deactivated (dimmed). The Paste Special option enables you to create a package within your application, as explained in the next section.

9. Click Media Player's start button; the MIDI file plays.

10. If you want, play another file with Media Player. Choose **F**ile, **O**pen and select the other file to play.

11. Close Media Player by double-clicking the Control Bar. If you don't close Media Player before you choose another file in your client application or exit the client application, Media Player remains open. If you don't close Media Player each time it appears, you end up with several instances of Media Player that consume your Windows resources. You can find open instances of Media Player or Sound Recorder by pressing Ctrl-Esc and checking the Task List. Delete the ones you don't need.

12. If you played another file in step 10, try playing the MIDI object you created again. It's the same file you originally specified. Media Player didn't edit the object when you selected the other file.

You are limited to embedding linked MIDI files until Microsoft releases Media Player 2.0, the OLE-compliant version of Media Player 1.0 included with Windows 3.1. When Media Player 2.0 becomes available, you then can link a MIDI file, or perhaps a portion of a MIDI file, directly or with Object Packager.

Creating a Package with Partial File Content

You can use OLE servers that can copy their data to the Clipboard (in a format corresponding to a recognized protocol) to embed data in a package rather than link it. Data embedded in a packaged object is useful primarily to embed only part of a file whose data is inherently divisible. Graphics examples are bit-mapped images created by Windows Paintbrush and Windows meta file data generated by Microsoft Draw, in which a portion of the image may be selected by drawing a frame around it and copying the content of the interior of the frame to the Clipboard.

Sound Recorder doesn't offer a simple, mouse-based method of framing a portion of a waveform audio file or recorded data. You can delete beginning and ending portions of a file, however, by setting the position and using the Edit commands.

To package a staccato version of CHORD.WAV into Word for Windows or Window Write, follow these steps:

1. Start Sound Recorder from the Accessories group.

2. Choose File, Open and double-click the entry for CHORD.WAV to load it.

3. Position the slider button of the scroll bar at 0.03 seconds, the time at which the sound is beginning to rise to its maximum intensity (see fig. 8.20).

FIG. 8.20

Deleting a beginning portion of waveform audio data.

4. Choose Edit, Delete Before Current Position. Choose OK when the message box requests confirmation.

5. Position the slider button at 0.19 seconds, the time at which the sound begins to reduce greatly in amplitude, as shown in figure 8.21.

FIG. 8.21

Deleting an ending portion of waveform audio data.

6. Choose **E**dit, Delete **A**fter Current Position. Choose OK to confirm the deletion.

7. Click the rewind button; then play the abbreviated data held in a memory buffer.

8. Press Ctrl+C to copy the edited waveform audio data to the Clipboard. Then close Sound Recorder.

9. Start Object Packager from the Accessories group. Object Packager's empty window appears.

10. Click the Content (right) panel to select it. Choose **E**dit, **P**aste from Object Packager's menu. You place the content of the Clipboard, an anonymous copy of Sound, in the Content panel and add Sound Recorder's icon with the title Sound to the Appearance panel (see fig. 8.22).

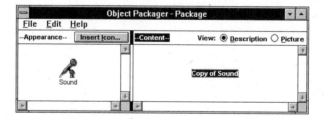

FIG. 8.22

Embedding waveform audio data in a packaged object.

11. Choose **E**dit, Copy Pack**a**ge from Object Packager's menu to place a copy of the package in the Clipboard. If you want to verify, start Clipboard Viewer from the Main group to view a magnified version of the icon in the Appearance panel.

12. Activate your client application and position the insertion point where you want the package inserted.

13. Choose **E**dit, **P**aste from the client application's menu. The Sound Recorder icon with the Sound caption appears at the insertion point, as shown for Windows Write in figure 8.23.

FIG. 8.23

An abbreviated
version of
CHORD.WAV
embedded in a
Windows Write
document.

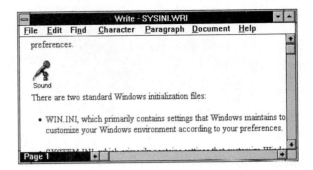

14. Double-click the icon to hear the abbreviated chord.

15. Close the client application. (You probably don't want to save the file.)

16. Close Sound Recorder. Make sure that you don't save the file, or you will destroy CHORD.WAV.

Sound Recorder has only primitive editing capabilities, but when this book was written, it was the only commonly available waveform audio tool that had OLE server capabilities.

Creating a Packaged Object from within an Application

OLE-compliant applications that offer the Paste **S**pecial command as an Edit menu choice enable you to run Object Packager as an OLE server from within your application. To try this approach, follow these steps:

1. Move the insertion point to a new location within your compound document and choose **E**dit, Paste **S**pecial. The Insert Object dialog box appears (see fig. 8.24).

2. Double-click the Package object. A blank Object Packager window appears, and a blank frame to receive the icon you select is added at the insertion point.

3. Choose **F**ile, **I**mport from Object Packager's menu, and import the MIDI file you want to play, as in the example in "Packaging a MIDI Object."

4. Close Object Packager by double-clicking the Control Bar. Your screen resembles figure 8.25. Note that the formula bar displays an empty package name (the " " following "Package").

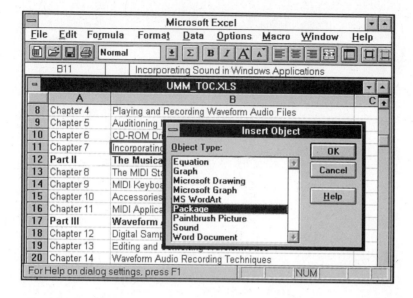

FIG. 8.24

The Insert Object dialog box.

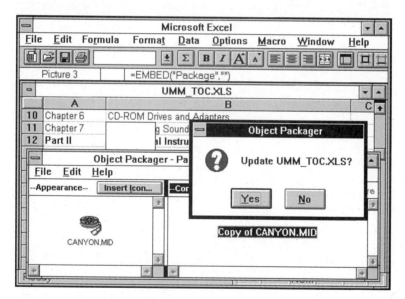

FIG. 8.25

Inserting a packaged MIDI object into an Excel spreadsheet.

5. Click OK; the package's icon is added to your source document. Double-click the icon, and the MIDI file is ready to play.

6. Click Media Player's Play button to hear the MIDI file.

Editing an Embedded or Linked Object

OLE clients enable you to edit embedded objects, usually by double-clicking the icon, as suggested by the prompt that appears at the bottom of their window. In the case of embedded waveform audio data, however, double-clicking the icon causes the sound data to play through your audio adapter card. Thus, applications that anticipated such an occurrence provide a menu choice for editing objects.

To edit a waveform audio object embedded in Word for Windows 2, follow these steps:

1. Select Sound Recorder's icon by clicking it or using the cursor and shift keys.

2. Choose **Edit**. Notice that Sound **Ob**ject has been added to the **Edit** menu choices, as shown in figure 8.26.

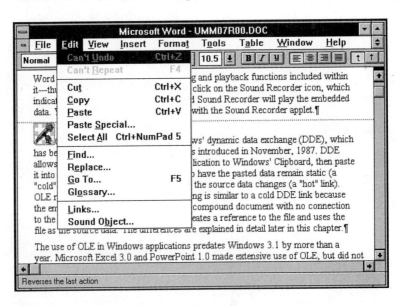

FIG. 8.26

Word for Windows'
Edit menu with an
embedded waveform
audio object selected.

3. Choose Sound Object. Sound Recorder's window appears.

4. You now may use any Sound Recorder commands to edit the sound, including replacing the current content with data from a file, re-recording a voice note, adding effects, and so forth.

5. If you decide to replace the contents with a file or re-record the note, choose **F**ile, **N**ew to erase the previous data in the buffer.

6. After you finish, close Sound Recorder's window.

7. Audition the change by double-clicking the Sound Recorder icon in your document.

The editing process for linked objects is similar. Excel, for example, uses the same submenu to edit the link as to change from a hot link to a cold link, or vice versa. The only edit you can make on a linked object is on the file name and the path of the linked file. The capability to change the path to a linked file is useful when distributing spreadsheets with linked files.

To edit a linked object in Microsoft Excel, follow these steps:

1. Choose **F**ile, **L**inks from Excel's menu. The Links dialog box shown in figure 8.27 appears. Notice that you can prevent changes to the link by using File Manager or DOS to set the read-only attribute of the file. If you do so, the Read Only check box is marked and the **C**hange button is inactive.

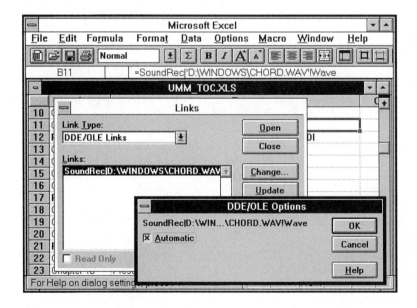

FIG. 8.27

Editing a linked OLE object in Microsoft Excel.

2. Choose Change to bring up the Change Links dialog box.

3. Edit the path or file name; then choose OK, **C**lose to close the Change Links and Links dialog boxes.

4. Double-click the cell with the #N/A entry, which symbolizes a linked object to test your editing.

5. If you enter an invalid file name or path, you receive the message box shown in figure 8.28.

NOTE   The message shown in figure 8.28 is ambiguous because the source application was activated, but Excel couldn't find the file it was instructed to open. Further, the object is linked, not embedded. An `Unable to find file` message would be more appropriate in this circumstance.

FIG. 8.28

Warning message indicating an error in editing an object's link in Excel.

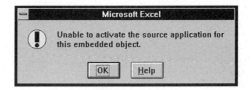

The examples of editing embedded and linked objects in the preceding examples are typical of those used with most OLE-client applications. When editing, embedding, and linking, the names of menu choices may differ, but the methodology remains the same.

Third-Party OLE Sound Servers

Media Vision's Pocket Mixer and Pocket Recorder applets, included with the Pro AudioSpectrum Plus and Pro AudioSpectrum 16 audio adapter cards, are OLE servers. Thus, you can embed both applications in a compound document. Pocket Recorder, like Sound Recorder, enables you to play and record voice notes or other waveform audio data. Pocket Mixer enables you to adjust the level of the sound from each audio source it supports.

Figure 8.29 shows an example of embedding Pocket Recorder in a Word for Windows document. You need to embed only Pocket Recorder because you can click the button in the lower right corner of Pocket Recorder's window to cause Pocket Mixer to appear beside Pocket Recorder.

Pocket Recorder behaves differently from Sound Recorder when you double-click its icon. Sound Recorder, as discussed earlier in this chapter, simply plays the sound. Pocket Recorder, however, appears on-screen, and you must click the Play button to hear the sound.

Related Topics
MediaOrganizer,
p. 626

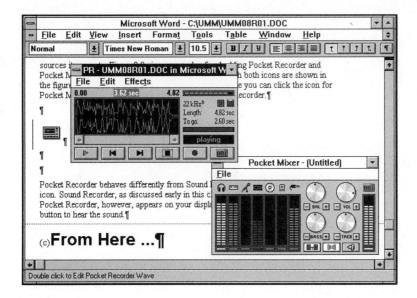

FIG. 8.29

Media Vision's Pocket Recorder and Pocket Mixer applets.

Lenel Systems' MediaOrganizer is a multimedia OLE server that enables you to link combinations of sound and graphic images into compound documents. MediaOrganizer is an object-oriented database application for cataloging and presenting multimedia sound and images. You can use MediaOrganizer to embed waveform audio and MIDI files in a document, but the application's strength lies in its capability to create OLE objects consisting of full-motion video clips from video cassette and laser disc sources. You link the objects created by MediaOrganizer into compound documents, such as the OLE fields of the new generation of database managers for Windows. When you double-click the object's presentation (usually an icon), the video image appears in a small window (as shown in fig. 8.30), and you hear the clip's soundtrack.

The example shown in figure 8.30 is a Sony Hi8 demonstration tape played by the firm's VDeck remotely controllable VCR through a Truevision Bravado video-in-a-window adapter card. Multimedia authoring and presentation applications with OLE-client capability were in the development stage when this book was written. OLE is an ideal technique encapsulating the presentation method (video-in-a-window) with the data (analog video and sound) in a simple, easy-to-use package. Thus, you can expect an increasing number of multimedia applications to include OLE compliance as a principal feature.

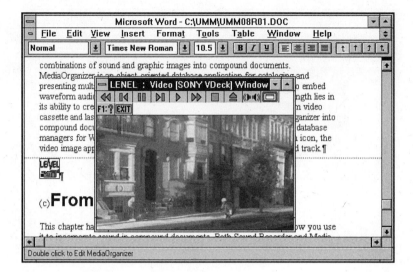

FIG. 8.30

A video clip linked to a compound document with Lenel's MediaOrganizer.

Chapter Summary

This chapter introduced you to object linking and embedding and explained how you use these capabilities to incorporate sound in compound documents. Sound Recorder and Media Player are effective applets for adding voice notes and musical accompaniment to your memos and spreadsheets. Of course, the recipient must have an audio adapter card to hear your embedded embellishments as well as a copy of the files you used, if you chose to link them.

A MIDI file is just another type of document. The authors of the specification for Standard MIDI Files provided for compound MIDI files by permitting the inclusion of "meta events" that can contain any type of data you want.

This chapter completes your introduction to Windows 3.1's multimedia extensions and the hardware used to implement them. Part III delves into the MIDI Specification 1.0 and how Windows deals with it using MCISEQ.DLL and MIDI Mapper. You also learn about external MIDI instruments such as keyboards, synthesizers, and a wide range of accessories that use the MIDI communication protocol.

PART III

Musical Synthesis and MIDI

OUTLINE

Music Synthesizers

S ynthesized music is all around you, but you may not recognize it as "synthetic." Professionals use musical synthesizers to create much of the theme music for television productions and most of the background music for radio and TV commercials. Performers ranging from rock stars to church choirs use "synth" pianos and organs. You may never hear actual guitar sounds from a guitar equipped with a MIDI pickup; plucking a string can play a prerecorded sample of another instrument, such as a flute. Plastic saxophones use electronic breath and bite detectors instead of reeds, and fingering the keys sends MIDI note messages instead of closing holes with pads.

Most audio adapter cards use an integrated circuit (IC) to create synthesized music. With two notable exceptions—the Roland SCC-1 and the Turtle Beach MultiSound—MPC audio adapter cards do not create music that meets production-music standards. *Production music* is a term used to describe music incorporated into a multimedia presentation, television program, or radio commercial rather than presented as a product in itself, such as a track on an audio CD release.

If you are a musician and have a keyboard synthesizer, you may want to use it (perhaps in conjunction with sounds from your audio adapter card) to create and play MIDI files. This chapter explains how to connect external synthesizers to your audio adapter card's MIDI OUT and MIDI IN ports—and how to avoid some of the pitfalls in the process.

When you create musical compositions for full-scale multimedia productions, you (or the musician you employ) undoubtedly will use at least one external, MIDI-controlled sound module. To take full advantage of the synthesized sounds of an audio adapter card, program a MIDI-equipped instrument, or modify the factory-supplied sounds of the card or the instrument to suit your requirements, you need to learn how synthesizers work and how you use them to create music.

Types of Musical Synthesizers

The first musical synthesizers consisted of one or more voltage-controlled oscillators (VCOs) whose output frequency was controlled by a keyboard. Each key sent a precise voltage to the input of the VCO, which caused the oscillator to produce a sine (pure sound) wave at the frequency corresponding to the note being struck. These early synthesizers produced thin tones lacking the harmonics and overtones that give conventional instruments their characteristic richness and timbre.

The rapid pace of development in the electronics industry caused a myriad of new synthesizers to appear on the market, each synthesizer having its own audio spectral characteristics and, thus, its own distinctive sound. A variety of electronic organs and pianos developed during the 1960s and 1970s gained a following among amateur and professional musicians. Most of these instruments were very expensive, however, and few could be considered truly portable. Musicians got plenty of body-building exercise lugging Hammond B-3 organs (affectionately called "Beasts") to gigs.

Robert Moog developed the first musical synthesizer that was practical for use in professional performances. Moog synthesizers were designed to imitate a wide range of instruments, rather than just an organ or piano. Moog developed the electronic *envelope generator*, which controlled the amplitude of the VCO over time with the following individually adjustable parameters:

- *Attack* determines how fast the sound rises in intensity when a note is struck.

- *Decay* is the rate at which the sound intensity drops after the initial impact of the key on a string.

- *Sustain* determines how long the sound is audible while the musician holds the key down.

- *Release* determines the rate at which the sound intensity decreases to zero after the musician releases the key.

This four-element envelope—usually called ADSR (an abbreviation for attack, decay, sustain, and release)—remains the standard for today's synthesizers (see fig. 9.1). Although a piano is used in the example, the ADSR envelope is applicable to almost every conventional musical instrument.

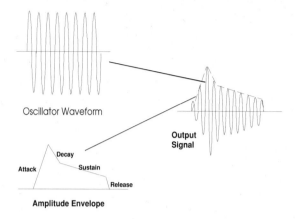

Oscillator Waveform

Output Signal

Decay

Attack · Sustain

Release

Amplitude Envelope

FIG. 9.1

An amplitude envelope
applied to the output of
an oscillator.

Moog's early synthesizers were a maze of knobs, switches, and patch cords that configured the devices to play more than one voice (sound) at once, thus increasing the richness of the music the synthesizers produced. Moog synthesizers were used in many commercial recordings, perhaps the most popular of which was Wendy Carlos' *Switched-On Bach*, released by Columbia Records in the early 1980s. Carlos was preparing a new release of *Switched-On Bach* on CD-ROM when this book was written.

The availability of low-cost hybrid operational amplifiers that could be adapted for use as oscillators, envelope generators, and filters resulted in sharply lower prices for simple analog keyboard synthesizers and electronic organs. In the mid-1980s, the analog sound circuits were replaced by digital integrated circuits that created and manipulated the sounds much as a computer manipulates text and graphic images. The step up to digital sound processing in synthesizers can be likened to the advance from analog vinyl recordings to digital audio CDs.

The creation of the MIDI specification in 1983 expanded the market for synthesizers among professional musicians and recording studios. As MIDI became more widely implemented, amateur musicians began to create their own low-cost MIDI setups. Industry representatives estimate that more than 15 million MIDI keyboard synthesizers had been sold in the United States by the end of 1991.

Yamaha and Digital FM Synthesis

A substantial number of synthesizers and most MPC audio adapter cards use *digital frequency-modulation* (FM) music synthesis. Digital FM synthesis was developed in the early 1970s by John Chowning, now the director of Stanford University's Center for Computer Research and Musical Acoustics. Yamaha Corporation, then known primarily for its pianos and other conventional musical instruments, licensed the technology from Stanford and introduced digital FM sounds to professional musicians in 1982 with the famous DX7 synthesizer. The DX7 revolutionized synthesized music.

The MPC specification does not define a particular synthesis method. Digital FM synthesis can be implemented with the fewest components of any sound-synthesis technique, making digital FM the lowest-cost method of generating synthesized sound. As a result, most sound synthesis cards use Yamaha's patented digital FM synthesis technique. FM synthesis by itself no longer is used in MIDI sound modules because sampled waveforms provide more realistic instrument sounds. Many current sample-playback synths, however, provide samples of the unique sounds of early analog and DX7 synthesizers.

As Chapter 1 briefly explained, FM synthesis adds the *modulator* waveform (which creates overtones) to the *carrier* waveform (which determines the basic pitch), creating a complex waveform that usually includes controlled amounts of harmonics and often includes nonharmonic overtones. Figure 9.2 illustrates the FM-synthesis process.

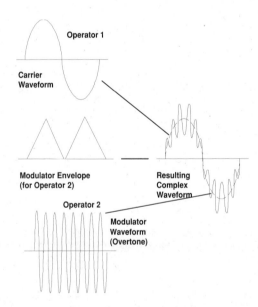

FIG. 9.2

A carrier and modulator combined in a complex sound wave.

Harmonics are frequencies that are even multiples of the *fundamental* (basic pitch) determined by the carrier oscillator. Harmonics are numbered by the multiple, or octave. For example, the second harmonic of A5 (440 Hz) is A6 (880 Hz); the third harmonic is A7 (1,320 Hz).

Overtones can be any frequency higher than the basic pitch. You also can generate *subharmonics*, which are specific fractions (one-half, one-quarter, one-eighth, and so on) of the fundamental pitch, and *subtones*, which can be any fraction of the pitch.

You can set each waveform, or *operator*, to operate as a carrier or as a modulator. You can hear a carrier by itself, but you cannot hear a modulator without adding it to a carrier. You add *brightness* (color) to the resulting tone by increasing the *amount* (depth) of the modulation.

Operators and Waveforms

Operators are created by oscillators. An *oscillator* is an electronic circuit that causes a waveform to repeat indefinitely until you turn it off. Basic FM synthesis requires only two operators, but the richness of the sound improves as more operators are added. Additional operators add to the complexity of the resulting sound wave by adding more harmonics or overtones.

Early audio adapter cards used two-operator FM synthesis, but most MPC audio adapter cards now use Yamaha's four-operator FM chips. These chips derive from those developed for Yamaha keyboard synthesizers and sound modules. The most popular digital FM sound module was the Yamaha TX81Z, a rack-mounted four-operator, eight-waveform device (see fig. 9.3).

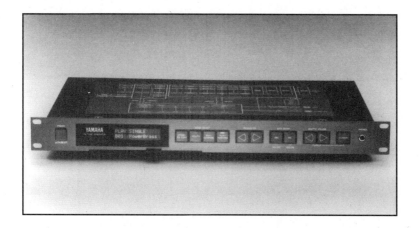

FIG. 9.3

The Yamaha TX81Z. *(Courtesy of Yamaha Corporation of America)*

Until Yamaha introduced the TX81Z, most synthesizers (including the DX-7) used sine waves to generate sounds. (Sine waves are similar to those shown for the oscillator and modulator in figure 9.2.) *Sine waves are pure tones*—in other words, a sine wave has no overtones or harmonics. The TX81Z and the DX11 keyboard synthesizer, which combined the circuitry of the TX81Z with a keyboard, offered eight different oscillator waveforms, ranging from sine to triangular to square waves. Each of the TX81Z's four operators could use eight waveforms, further increasing the capability of FM synthesis to replicate the complex timbre of traditional musical instruments.

The TX81Z is no longer in production, having been replaced by new Yamaha products that use sampled sounds. The TX81Z is discussed here, however, because it laid the foundation for the Yamaha integrated-circuit chipsets that most audio adapter cards use today. Musicians still use TX81Zs and DX11s, but now primarily in conjunction with sample-playback synthesizers. Most users of FM synthesizers modify the built-in sounds to their liking or create new ones.

Figure 9.4 shows the waveforms and other sound-adjustment characteristics of the TX81Z and of the Yamaha OPL-III chipset (described briefly in Chapter 2).

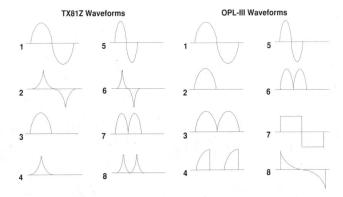

FIG. 9.4

The waveforms available in the Yamaha TX81Z and OPL-III.

Four of the eight waveforms of the TX81Z (1, 3, 5, and 7, in figure 9.4) are incorporated into the new Yamaha OPL-III digital FM synthesis chipset, which uses the waveforms illustrated in the two right columns of the figure. Waveforms with "sharp corners" (OPL-III waveforms 4, 7, and 8, in the figure) incorporate more harmonics. A square wave (OPL-III waveform 7, in the figure) incorporates the most harmonics of all waveform types and has a "hollow" sound resembling that of an oboe or English horn. If you start with a waveform with more built-in harmonics, you can create greater sonic complexity with the same number of operators.

FM Algorithms

You combine operators in a variety of ways by choosing an *algorithm*. Algorithms define which operators are used as carriers, which are used as modulators, and how the resulting sounds of the modulated carriers are combined.

The TX81Z offers eight algorithms, shown diagramatically in figure 9.5 (1-8), whereas the OPL-III chipset provides four (1, 2, 9, and 10).

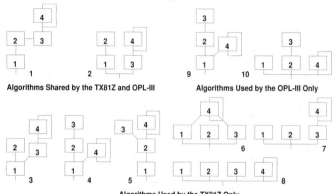

Algorithms Shared by the TX81Z and OPL-III

Algorithms Used by the OPL-III Only

Algorithms Used by the TX81Z Only

FIG. 9.5

The algorithms of the TX81Z and the OPL-III.

The operator(s) at the lowest level of each diagram are carriers, and those above the lowest level are modulators. Algorithm 1 has one carrier and three modulators, whereas Algorithm 8 has four carriers and no modulators. The following list describes the combinations that comprise the 10 algorithms shown in figure 9.5.

- Algorithms 1, 3, 4, and 5 create only a single sound, with varying types of modulation.

- Algorithm 2 combines the sounds of two modulated carriers.

- Algorithms 6, 7, and 10 combine three carriers, two of which are modulated in 6 and one of which is modulated in 7 and 10.

- Algorithm 8 combines four carriers without modulation, except for operator 4.

Operator 4 is a special-purpose operator that has adjustable feedback. *Feedback* means that an adjustable portion of the operator's output is routed back into its input. The most common example of feedback is the screeching you hear when a public-address system's microphone picks up some of the sound generated by the speakers. Operator 4 combines a carrier and a modulator; the feedback signal modulates its own carrier. As the amount of feedback increases, the resulting tone becomes brighter, then more brittle, and finally harsh.

Each of the operators shown in figure 9.5 has controls that determine its contribution to the final composite sound. Each operator can use any available waveform. You can vary the amplitude of the carrier or the depth of the modulation, depending on how the operator is to be used. You also can adjust the envelope generators for each operator independently. Another set of controls adjusts the overall properties of the composite sound, such as overall volume and left-right channel balance.

The versatility of digital FM enables you to create almost any sound you can imagine. Duplicating instrument sounds electronically is not always necessary, however, so musicians continue to use DX7s and TX11Zs to produce special-purpose sounds. Unfortunately, Yamaha did not incorporate all the capabilities of the TX81Z into the OPL-III, so you cannot use TX81Z voice patches with audio adapter cards. Many of the OPL-III's standard sounds, such as the acoustic piano, are inferior to the factory-set voices of the TX81Z and DX11.

Yamaha FM-Synthesis Chipsets and the Gold Sound Standard

The OPL-III can emulate the OPL-II's two-operator sounds to provide backward compatibility with music written for the earlier version. Figure 9.6 shows how current audio adapter cards use the Yamaha OPL-II and OPL-III chipsets.

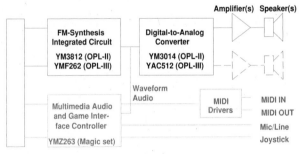

Block diagram of the Yamaha OPL-II and OPL-III chipsets.

The basic FM synthesis chipset consists of an integrated circuit that provides the FM synthesis functions and sends a digital representation of the sounds created to a digital-to-analog converter (DAC). The analog output of the DAC is amplified and sent to speakers or to an auxiliary input of a sound system. The YM263 chip adds 12-bit waveform audio recording and playback capability plus joystick functions to the OPL-III set.

The OPL-II is a monophonic combination, so simulation of stereo sound requires two YM3812 synthesis chips and two YM3014 DACs. The OPL-III has built-in stereo-sound-simulation capability, so only one YMF262 and one YAC512 are required. The added audio channel is shown in dashed lines in figure 9.6.

The YM3812 and the YMF262 include a noise generator to simulate percussion sounds. A *noise generator* is an oscillator that generates a wide range of waves at different frequencies, much like the sound you hear when you tune a television set to an unused channel. The YMF262's stereo sounds are much richer than those of the monaural YM3812, but even a four-operator FM chip cannot compare with the realism of reproduced digital recordings of the instrument itself.

Yamaha produces another integrated circuit—a Multimedia Audio and Game Interface Controller (MAGIC). Manufacturers can combine this circuit with the OPL-III, audio mixer and amplifier components, and the optically isolated drivers required for MIDI connectors to provide all the basic functions of an MPC-compatible audio adapter card. The YMZ263 integrated circuit reduces the number of chips required to implement these functions. Thus, sound and joystick circuits require less space on a printed wiring (circuit) board. The reduction in what engineers call "real estate" enables manufacturers of MPC-compliant computers to easily add the circuitry and connectors to their motherboards.

Yamaha calls the combination of the OPL-III and the YMZ263 the MAGIC chipset and has developed a standard specification for this chipset called the Yamaha Gold Sound Standard. Yamaha recommends that one Windows driver be used with any Gold Sound Standard product, whether implemented on an audio adapter card or the motherboard.

Table 9.1 compares Yamaha's OPL-II and OPL-III chipsets and the MAGIC chipset.

Table 9.1. Comparing the Yamaha OPL-II, OPL-III, and MAGIC Chipsets.

Yamaha product	OPL-II	OPL-III	MAGIC
Synthesis chip code	YM3812	YMF262	YMF262
Operators (oscillators)	2	4	4
Waveform types	4	8	8
Algorithms available	2	4	4
Output	mono	stereo	mono
Waveform audio resolution			12 bits
ADPCM compression			3:1

continues

Table 9.1. Continued

Yamaha product	OPL-II	OPL-III	MAGIC
Audio sampling rates (kHz)			5.5125, 7.35, 11.025, 22.05, 44.1
Used by MPC cards (typical)	Sound Blaster (1, mono), early Sound Blaster Pro (2, stereo), Tandy Audio Card	Pro Audio Spectrum Plus and 16, new Sound Blaster Pro (after April 1992)	MediaSonic

You can expect many new computer models to incorporate digital FM sound as a standard feature, eliminating the requirement for an adapter card. This feature will allow microphone and headphone connectors to be placed on the front panel, where they belong. MIDI and audio line connectors, like the keyboard connector, will be made accessible through slots in the back panel.

Related Topics
Windows Editors and
Librarians, p. 361

FM Voice Parameters

The FM synthesis settings that affect the sound of a single voice are called the *parameters* of a voice. Parameters include waveform, envelope, overall volume, and balance.

Creating a new voice for a four-operator FM synth can be a daunting project. The TX81Z, for example, has 87 individual editing parameters for each voice, each parameter having data values ranging from 0 to 1 (on/off) up to 0 to 99. The various synthesizer parameters are stored in memory in the form of groups of data called *patches*. The term *patch* derives from the rat's nest of audio patch cords required by early synthesizers and is related to (but not the same as) the *program patches* of MIDI Mapper's patch map.

Program patches select the voice to be assigned to a MIDI channel. This book uses *voice patch* for changes to voice parameters so as to distinguish the two usages of the term *patch*.

To create a voice patch, you usually start with a factory-supplied sound that is close to what you want and then modify that sound to suit your requirement. You can modify the sound by pressing combinations of front-panel buttons on a TX81Z, DX7, or DX11 by sending complex MIDI SysEx messages or by using a computer-based application called an *editor*. Because audio adapter cards don't have push buttons, you are left with the choice of writing your own SysEx messages or using an editor. A graphic voice patch editor can save you many hours of frustration in attempting to write SysEx messages that work.

Voyetra's PatchView FM, an editor application for Windows, enables you to view and modify the FM voice parameters of audio adapter cards so that you can adjust or create new FM sounds. The Voyetra product supports the OPL-II chipset with a two-operator editor and provides a four-operator version for the OPL-III. Figure 9.7 shows the primary screen of the OPL-III version.

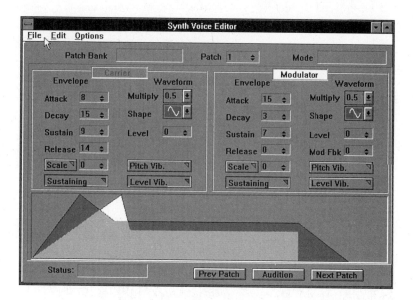

FIG. 9.7

Voyetra's
PatchView FM.

Because of the complexity of the sound-editing process, you can purchase groups of special sounds, called *voice banks*, for synthesizers. Voice banks are supplied on floppy disks and are loaded into a synthesizer's RAM memory by an application called a *librarian*.

CompuServe's MIDI forum enables you to download a wide range of patch banks for popular synthesizers. Universal editor/librarian applications for Windows, which combine these two functions and which can be used with a wide range of different synthesizers, are described in Chapter 12.

Sample-Playback Synthesizers

Synthesizers that store actual sound samples from musical instruments are called *sampling synthesizers* or *samplers*. Instrument sound samples are created by a method essentially identical to that used for creating waveform audio files. You play a note on an instrument and record its sound for a predetermined period. Because the characteristic timbre of instruments changes with pitch, many samples are recorded over the instrument's playable range. Using more than one sample of an instrument to regenerate the sound in different pitch ranges is called *multisampling*.

After the instrument sound samples are recorded, a portion of the sample is selected by a sample editor. The editing may be done by a computer application or a special sampling synthesizer; in either case, the basic steps are the same.

Figure 9.8 shows how an instrument sample is edited for synthesized playback.

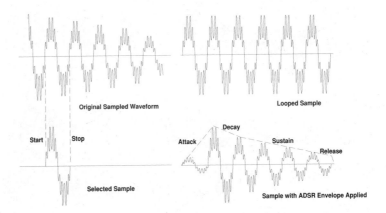

FIG. 9.8

Editing an instrument sample for synthesized playback.

To edit an instrument sound sample, follow these steps:

1. One or more cycles of the recorded waveform are selected as the sample.

2. Starting and stopping points (called *loop points*) for the selected sample are established, and the digital representation of the sample is stored in RAM memory.

3. The sample is tested at constant amplitude (the looped sample shown in figure 9.8) to determine whether the selected loop points produce a clean, consistent sound.

4. The amplitude of the looped sample is modulated by a conventional ADSR envelope to simulate the instrument's dynamics.

5. Other editing parameters are added. These parameters may include time-variant filters, which increase or decrease the apparent harmonic content of the waveform over time.

6. The resulting sample and its looping and editing parameter values
    are stored in disk files for later incorporation into the ROM memory
    of a sampling synthesizer as a factory-standard voice.

The preceding steps are repeated for each instrument voice to be included in the synthesizer's repertoire and then stored in on-board ROM
chips in what are called *lookup tables*. Each waveform and its parameters
are organized in the form of a table that begins at a specific position
in the ROM memory, called an *address*. When you play a note, the
synthesizer's microprocessor reads the tabular data at the ROM address
for the chosen voice and adjusts the rate at which looping is performed
to correspond to the note's pitch. Therefore, sample-playback synthesis
also is called*wavetable synthesis*.

Creating looped samples that faithfully reproduce the sound of an instrument with complex harmonics is both an art and a science. Recordings
of orchestral, jazz, and rock instruments are available on audio CDs from
several companies and at least one university (McGill University in
Montreal). Synthesizer manufacturers often commission their own
sample-recording sessions and employ independent firms or consultants
to create the sounds that contribute uniqueness to their synthesizer
products.

The first sampling synthesizers with recording and playback capabilities
were so expensive that only professional recording studios and the most
successful musicians could afford them. The development of microprocessors and the availability of relatively low-cost memory IC chips,
however, has reduced the price of some 16-bit playback-only models,
complete with keyboards, to less than $1,000.

The Roland SCC-155 Sound Canvas module, introduced in early 1992,
is a typical moderate-cost, General MIDI sample-playback module (see
fig. 9.9). Eight built-in sliders, which can be used to adjust the level of
individual MIDI channels or to adjust the level of effects, distinguish the
SCC-155 from other recent entrants in the General MIDI market.

When you send a MIDI message to a sampler, the sampler performs
many preset operations (stored as voice patches or as banks of voice
patches) on the designated sample. If you were to store samples for all
88 piano notes, for example, these samples might occupy about 1M of
ROM memory. Samplers, however, store perhaps 8 to 12 individual piano
samples, adjusting the pitch and envelope of each within a limited range.
This procedure saves the memory that you otherwise would need to
store samples for each possible pitch and waveform modification, and
still maintains acceptable fidelity to the original sound.

Samplers are far better than FM synthesizers at duplicating the timbre of
conventional acoustic instruments. Samplers particularly excel at imitat-
ing percussion and string instruments, including pianos, harpsichords,

guitars, and drums. Using FM techniques to synthesize a natural-sounding nylon- or steel-string acoustic guitar, for example, over a wide range of pitches is virtually impossible, so all General MIDI sound modules employ sample-playback synthesis.

FIG. 9.9

The Roland SC-155 Sound Canvas GM sound module. (Courtesy of Roland Corporation, USA)

Korg USA, a major supplier of performance-grade keyboard synthesizers, has entered the General MIDI sound-module market with the Korg 03R/W. The technology and samples for the 03R/W are derived from the firm's 01/W Wavestation, a self-contained musical "workstation" used by professional musicians and composers.

The Korg 03R/W is the first commercially available General MIDI sound module that incorporates many of the special features musicians and sound engineers have come to expect in professional-level synthesizers. Those features include the following:

- 255 different editable PCM voices (Korg calls them "multisounds") stored in ROM, of which the first 128 conform to the General MIDI voice list.

- 100 programmable "combinations" of up to eight different voices and effects that are stored in memory. These combinations are equivalent to what Yamaha calls "performances."

- 119 editable drum sounds, of which 46 correspond to the General MIDI percussion voices.

- 20 digital effects (of which you can select four simultaneously) including reverb, delay, chorus, flanger, phase shifter, distortion, rotary speaker, and exciter.

- 4 independent audio outputs that you can configure as a pair of stereo outputs with and without selected effects.

- 2 front-panel slots that accept plug-in ROM memory cards containing additional PCM voices or combinations. RAM cards are available for storing combinations, but you ordinarily would use your computer for this purpose.

The 03R/W exemplifies a growing trend toward incorporation of digital signal processors (DSPs) into sound modules. The Yamaha TG-500 General MIDI sound module, for example, includes all the effects offered by the firm's top-of-the-line SY99 keyboard synthesizer. DSPs add many of the effects that previously required a separate effects-processor module to implement.

Related Topics
Using Digital Signal Processors, p. 381

Korg offers a remote editing controller for the 03R/W that includes a large LCD display panel and eight sliders (similar to those included with the Roland SC-155) that adjust the various editable voice parameters. Sliders are particularly useful for fine-tuning effects parameters while you listen to the sound.

T I P

Audio adapter cards currently offer few of the features that are routinely incorporated into today's outboard sound modules. The Roland SCC-1 GS Sound Card, for example, provides reverb, chorus, and stereo pan effects, but you must use rather complex SysEx messages to tune reverb and chorus effects. If music plays more than a background role in your multimedia presentations or titles, you should consider acquiring a professional-grade sound module to substitute for or to complement the synthesized sounds of your audio adapter card. Make sure that your selection conforms to the General MIDI or General Synthesizer standard.

Sample-Playback Subsystems for Audio Adapter Cards

Sound modules that use PCM sample playback have all but displaced FM synthesis in the professional market. Yamaha no longer produces synthesizers based on FM synthesis alone but combines the two technologies in some of its advanced products. Yamaha, with its exclusive license of the Stanford FM synthesis patents, however, currently dominates the market for audio adapter cards because of the low parts cost of FM synthesis chipsets, including the OPL-III chipset.

As the demand for more realistic synthesized sound increases, additional manufacturers will introduce cards based on wavetable synthesis, and the prices of sample-playback products will become increasingly competitive. An indication of this trend is the introduction of the Advanced Gravis UltraSound card, which uses a modified version of the Ensoniq ES5506 wavetable chip, at a price competitive with products based on the OPL-III. Two of the first sample-playback subsystems designed specifically for audio adapter cards are described in the following sections.

Ensoniq ES-1000 Multimedia Sound System

Ensoniq Corporation, a manufacturer of professional sample-playback synthesizers since 1986, introduced the ES-1000 Multimedia Sound System (also known as the DOC II chipset) in 1991. Figure 9.10 shows a block diagram of a fully implemented ES-1000 system with an on-board microprocessor.

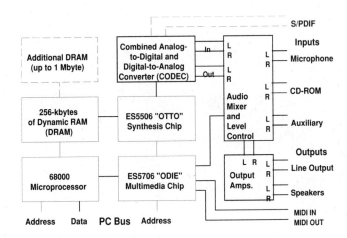

FIG. 9.10

Block diagram of the Ensoniq ES1000 sound subsystem.

The ES5506 chip contains the circuitry necessary to process the wavetable samples stored in 256K or more of dynamic RAM. Sample patches are loaded from a hard disk into the on-board RAM during start-up. The standard ES-1000 configuration provides 32 voices (16 voices when stereo output is used), but two ES5506 chips can be combined to double the number of voices.

The ES5706 chip provides additional functions required to implement the MPC specification, including MIDI IN and OUT signals, joystick port, control of a CD-ROM SCSI controller, and level controls for the mixer. One interesting feature of the ES5706 is its serial digital stereo input channel, which can be connected to the S/PDIF outputs of audio CD players and DAT drives. Analog-to-digital and digital-to-analog conversion is handled by a single-chip CODEC (coder-decoder), described in Chapter 13. CODECs, which use a serial conversion technique, are called "1-bit" converters in consumer-oriented advertising for audio CD drives.

Ensoniq's module produces sound approaching the quality of modules that store samples in large banks of ROM. At least 2M of sample ROM is required to create what musicians would accept as professional audio quality for the 128 General MIDI voices. The basic ES1000 system stores its samples and the microprocessor's program code in 256K. The advantage of RAM storage of both the operating system and samples is that you can reprogram the entire synthesis section of the card simply by loading a new set of data into the RAM from a floppy disk or a hard disk.

Manufacturers that use the Ensoniq ES5506 may modify the chip to add special features or incorporate additional circuitry. Advanced Gravis, for example, uses a customized version of this chip to perform most of the basic functions of the firm's UltraSound audio adapter card. The card includes 256K of RAM but can store more complex patches if you increase the memory to 1M by adding six 256K-by-4 bit (44,256) RAM chips. These chips cost about five dollars each, so the investment is not substantial. The chips also eliminate the need for both the microprocessor and the ES5706, thus reducing the manufacturing cost.

Related Topics
The UltraSound from Advanced Gravis, p. 65

The AudioMaster card, manufactured by Omni Labs, Ltd., uses circuitry closer to Ensoniq's ES1000 standard. The card includes an MC68008 microprocessor and 384K of on-board RAM. You can expand the RAM to 1.5M by plugging in an optional daughterboard.

Card suppliers often commission firms that specialize in creating voice patches for professional synthesizers to create the GM and supplemental voices for their cards. As more wavetable cards reach the market, you can expect to find a proliferation of third-party voice patches on the market.

E-mu E8801 SoundEngine

When E-mu Systems, Inc. introduced the Proteus/1 sound module in 1989, the module was an instant success. The Proteus/1 combined a wide selection of high-quality 16-bit sampled PCM sounds and provided advanced programming capabilities at a list price of less than $1,000. The fact that Windows 3.1's MIDI Mapper includes a standard MIDI patch map for the Proteus/1 attests to that module's market share.

E-mu's SoundEngine daughterboard is an example of a professional 16-bit sampling MIDI expander on a small printed circuit card (see fig. 9.11). This daughterboard includes 4M of sampled sound data derived from the Proteus 1/XR sound module as General MIDI voices stored in ROM memory. The SoundEngine can modify sampled waves with two envelope generators and two low-frequency oscillators per voice channel, enabling you to alter the General MIDI sounds to your liking. The SoundEngine can provide up to 32 multi-timbral voices pannable across a stereo output signal, so you don't sacrifice timbres for stereo operation.

E-mu Systems licensed its E8801 SoundEngine technology to Creative Labs in July 1992 on an exclusive basis. When this book was written, the two firms were in the process of developing a new digital signal processing (DSP) chip to implement the SoundEngine technology with fewer parts. The agreement between E-mu and Creative Labs will accelerate competing manufacturers' adoption of sampled-sound technology.

FIG. 9.11

The E-mu E8801 circuitry in the SoundEngine daughterboard. (Courtesy of E-mu Systems, Inc.)

Turtle Beach Systems uses the E-mu E8801 components in its MultiSound Board, but this board adds a digital signal processor chip and a substantial amount of additional circuitry to achieve professional-level performance in both the synthesis and waveform audio sections. Although the basic voices of the General MIDI and the Proteus/1 XR are stored in ROM memory, you can upload new voice patches from disk files to the Turtle Beach card. These patches may be modifications of the samples in ROM or new samples from other sources, such as third-party "patch factories."

Related Topics
The Turtle Beach MultiSound,
p. 67

Sample-Playback Voice Editing

All sample-playback synths can modify a sound by changing its pitch, attach, decay, and sustain, and by otherwise changing its pattern so as to achieve the desired timbre. The Roland SCC-1 sound card and the SCC-55 and SCC-155 sound modules, for example, enable you to adjust their Time Variant Filter (TVF) and Amplifier (TVA) to alter cutoff frequency, resonance, vibrato, and the sound's envelope through the special MIDI System Exclusive (SysEx) messages described in Chapter 21.

Turtle Beach Systems' MultiSound audio adapter card includes an applet for editing its standard set of General MIDI and Proteus/1 XR voices. The window, shown in figure 9.12, is designed to duplicate the front-panel controls of Proteus sound modules.

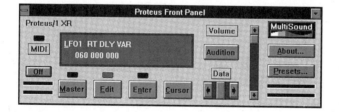

FIG. 9.12

Turtle Beach's voice editor for the E-mu Sound Engine chipset.

LF01 indicates that the first low-frequency oscillator (LFO) is being edited. The remaining symbols and data are the default values assigned to editable parameters of the LFO for the selected voice.

> If you plan to purchase or have acquired a MultiSound card, you may want to purchase the operating manual for the Proteus/1 XR from E-mu Systems (see Appendix F). This manual provides details on programming and remote-control techniques that are not included in the documentation that accompanies the MultiSound card.
>
> **T I P**

Third-party universal editor/librarians such as Dr. T's Xor graphic application (described in Chapter 12) can be used with a variety of wavetable and FM synthesizers. Graphic editors enable you to adjust the amplitude and pitch envelopes of the sound by dragging the end points of the line segments that define the ADSR envelope. This process usually is much simpler than entering individual values with a Windows scroll bar or a front-panel slider.

Layering Synthesized Sounds

Combining two or more timbres that respond simultaneously to MIDI note messages on one channel is called *layering* of voices. If you have two synthesized sound sources and cannot obtain the particular quality of sound you are seeking, you often can solve the problem by combining a voice from one source with a related voice from the other. Layering, which adds body to sound, can be used to simulate distinctive instrumental playing styles. If you have a Media Vision Pro AudioSpectrum Plus or 16 and a Roland SCC-1 or an outboard General MIDI sound module, for example, you can combine the audio outputs of the two devices with the Pro AudioSpectrum's mixer. Figure 9.13 shows the required connections.

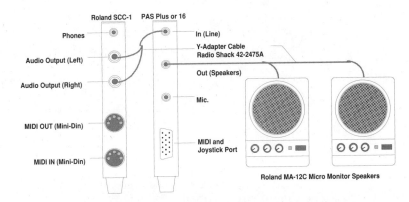

FIG. 9.13

Connections for layering sampled sounds from a Roland SCC-1 and FM voices from a Pro AudioSpectrum Plus or 16.

You also need a sequencer application that provides for multiple MIDI synthesizer output devices. Passport Designs' Trax sequencer, supplied with Media Visions' MIDIMate adapter kit and by some other audio-card manufacturers, does not include this capability. Passport's MusicTime and Master Tracks Pro, Twelve Tone Systems' Cakewalk for Windows, and Big Noise Software's Cadenza for Windows provide multiple MIDI input and output sources.

You can simulate layering with the chorus effect available in Roland Sound Canvas products (including the SCC-1), the Korg 03R/W, the E-mu SoundEngine adapter card, and the Turtle Beach MultiSound.

The SoundEngine enables you to patch voices to layer other timbres, but layering reduces the polyphonic capability. Because the SoundEngine can simultaneously produce 32 timbres, however, polyphony usually is not a problem.

Keyboard Synthesizers

If you play or want to learn to play the piano, and you don't have access to an acoustic piano, you need a keyboard to provide the MIDI IN signals to your audio adapter card's MIDI breakout box or cable. Although you can purchase MIDI keyboards without built-in synthesizers, the price of a keyboard that includes a moderate-quality, sample-playback synthesizer is close to that of a MIDI keyboard alone.

The advantage of a keyboard synthesizer is that you or your family can play this type of synthesizer without tying up a computer. At the time this book was written, only one General MIDI keyboard synthesizer was available, but several manufacturers had announced plans to introduce GM-compliant models.

Related Topics
MIDI Keyboards, p. 317

Miracle Piano

Software Toolworks' Miracle keyboard synthesizer (see fig. 9.14) is not an MPC-compliant device, and its application software is strictly for DOS. But several computer-related periodicals, including *MPC World*, have given this device very high marks.

FIG. 9.14

Software Toolworks'
Miracle piano
keyboard synthesizer.
*(Courtesy of Software
Toolworks, Inc.)*

Although several keyboard synthesizers in the same price range have MIDI inputs and outputs, the Miracle stands out from better-known brands such as Casio and Yamaha because of its PC-based Piano Teaching System. According to the manual, an "average student" who has no musical training can complete the course in 6 to 12 months.

The Miracle's application software teaches you how to read musical notation and trains you in two-handed playing using common chords and rhythms. The software writes your mistakes on a "chalkboard" and suggests specific exercises that help you correct the errors you make. The Miracle's Piano Teaching System differs greatly from the rote techniques used in traditional piano training. The result is the same, but the Miracle makes learning fun.

The principal reason for including the DOS-oriented Miracle in a book on Windows 3.1 multimedia is that you need a keyboard to really enjoy using the synthesizer section of your audio adapter card. The Miracle piano has 49 full-size keys (a standard piano has 88) and covers MIDI note numbers ranging from 36 to 84—the four octaves between C3 and C7. The Miracle may not be the instrument on which you would choose to play Charles Ives' *Concord Sonata*, but you can use it to record MIDI files, transposing any notes that are out of the keyboard's range. Because the Miracle is self-contained (it has two speakers and a headphone jack), your children can learn to read music and play the piano when you're not using it.

The synthesizer is distributed widely at discounted prices; most music stores and large computer and electronics stores carry it. The Miracle is one of the very few low-priced keyboard synthesizers made in the United States.

You don't need MIDI ports to use the Miracle because it comes with a cable that connects directly to your computer's nine-pin serial (COM) port, although the Miracle also provides both MIDI IN and OUT connectors. As a result, your children can run the Miracle's teaching software on their own computer (even an 8086 PC with a mono graphics display) and don't need a sound or MIDI adapter card.

Related Topics
Trax from Passport Designs, p. 210
Professional MIDI Sequencers, p. 342

At the time this book was written, the only Windows sequencer applications with drivers for the Miracle were Passport Designs' Trax and Master Tracks Pro. If you don't have one of the Passport products, you need two standard MIDI cables to connect the Miracle keyboard to the MIDI breakout box or the connectors of your audio adapter card.

T I P The Miracle keyboard will not work with both the serial port and MIDI IN/OUT ports simultaneously connected to computers. When changing between serial and MIDI operation, you must disconnect the cables you are not using and then turn the Miracle's power off and on to reset its mode of operation. If you do not turn the power off, the Miracle does not respond to the new signal source.

GM Keyboard Synthesizers

Roland's General MIDI keyboard synthesizer, the JV-30 (see fig. 9.15), combines a 49-key or four-octave keyboard with Sound Canvas samples to create an entry-level product.

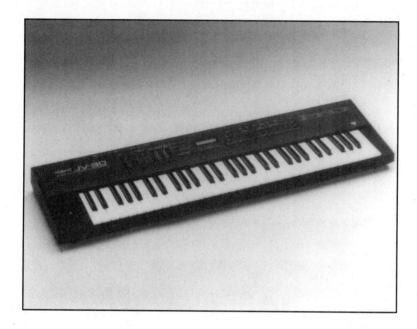

FIG. 9.15

The Roland JV-30
General MIDI
keyboard synthesizer.
(Courtesy of Roland
Corporation, USA)

The list price of the JV-30, however, is about $350 higher than the combined list prices of the PC-200 MIDI keyboard and the SCC-1. If you choose to combine a PC-200 and an SCC-1 instead of purchasing a JV-30, you need a MIDI adapter for your computer. If you decide on a JV-30, you must purchase either an MPU-401-compatible device or a MIDI breakout cable or box for your audio adapter card.

All the GM voices are included in virtually every synthesizer manufactured today; these voices simply have different names assigned by different manufacturers. Every GM sound card and module tested during the course of writing this book has different-sounding instrument voices. Korg's 03R/W is a step in the right direction—toward professional GM gear—to make General MIDI a true industry standard.

Professional Keyboard Synthesizers and Workstations

Professional-quality keyboard synthesizers usually have 76- or 88-note "weighted" keyboards covering 6 to 7 octaves (plus 3 notes). By comparison, most moderately priced synthesizers are limited to 4 or 5 octaves with 49 or 61 keys. A weighted keyboard has a "touch" similar to that of an acoustic piano.

Professional synthesizers, used for composing and performance, start at about $2,000. Most of these synthesizers offer a wide range of programmable digital effects and provide features such as polyphonic aftertouch, which sends continuous MIDI signals representing the pressure applied to each key after the notes are struck (and which is a major source of MIDI choke in slower systems). Some professional synthesizers also respond to MIDI Note Off velocity signals.

Figure 9.16 shows a professional keyboard synthesizer, the Yamaha SY-99.

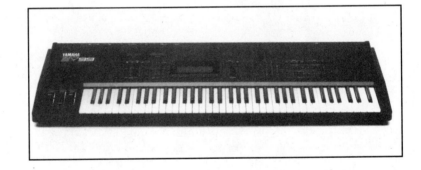

FIG. 9.16

The Yamaha SY-99 professional keyboard synthesizer. *(Courtesy of Yamaha Corporation of America)*

Add a built-in sequencer to a professional keyboard synthesizer, and you have a workstation. Workstations are self-contained systems that enable you to create special-purpose voices and write musical compositions, using the keyboard as the input source. A built-in sequencer offers two advantages: the workstation is completely self-contained, and you don't need a computer and a sequencer application to record or play back performances.

Built-in sequencers are more convenient for recording individual parts of a composition and enable you to leave your computer at home when you play a gig. Most professional musicians, however, now use computers to edit the individual parts of a composition and combine those parts into an arrangement. You can transmit the computer's MIDI data back to the built-in sequencer for self-contained playback.

Special-Purpose Synthesizers

Related Topics
MIDI Instruments and Pickups,
p. 319

Many special-purpose MIDI synthesizers now are available to vocalists
and to musicians who play nonkeyboard instruments. The most common
devices are for percussion, guitar, and woodwind instruments, but specialized pickups and processors for violins and other string instruments
also are available. (Pickups for creating MIDI signals from nonkeyboard
instruments are described in Chapter 11.)

No General MIDI-compliant, special-purpose synthesizers are available;
General MIDI implies a single synthesizer playing all the parts of a composition (with the drum parts assigned to MIDI Channel 10), rather than
a collection of devices serving specific purposes.

Percussion Synthesis

Emulating the sounds of percussion instruments is very difficult for
FM synthesizers. Thus, *drum machines*—the name applied to special-
purpose percussion expanders—were among the first moderately priced
MIDI instruments to incorporate digitally sampled sounds.

Drum machines have several features that ordinarily are not incorporated into sound modules. Those features include the following:

- Small rubber-covered switches, called *pads*, that you can assign to
  a set of drums. You tap the pads to play a percussion track for your
  composition. Most rack-mounted drum modules omit the pads and
  use remote input devices.

- A built-in sequencer that stores a pattern in memory. A *pattern* is
  one or two measures of a group of drum sounds repeated for a
  number of measures (*verse*), followed by a transition pattern (*fill* or
  break), followed by a repetition of another pattern for several more
  measures (*chorus*). The combination of patterns is called a *song*,
  which is stored in the drum machine's memory.

- A built-in clock that establishes the tempo for the rhythm part. You
  can play each pattern of a song at a different tempo, if you want.

- The capability to send MIDI clock signals to establish the rate at
  which the sequencer plays back the melodic tracks. You must set
  the sequencer to External Sync in order to use the drum machine's
  clock as the timing reference.

- Input connectors for remote drum pads or instrumented drum kits,
  which duplicate the action of the built-in pads. These connectors
  usually appear only on rack-mounted drum modules. *Remote drum*

pads are switches (called *triggers*) mounted on larger rubber pads that you play with conventional drumsticks. *Instrumented drum kits* are conventional percussion instruments equipped with acoustic pickups that act as switches.

Figure 9.17 shows a typical professional drum machine, the Alesis SR-16.

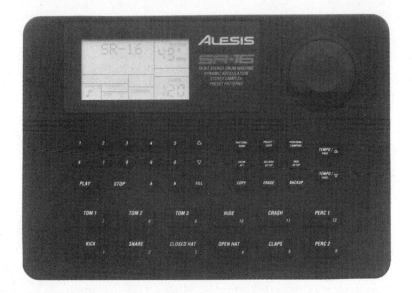

FIG. 9.17

The Alesis SR-16 stereo MIDI drum machine. *(Courtesy of Alesis Corporation)*

The SR-16 has 233 percussion-instrument samples, many of which are in stereo. Thus, a drum machine provides a much wider range of percussion sounds than the 60 included in the General MIDI standard.

Adapter cards that use FM synthesis have very unrealistic percussion voices. If you aren't satisfied with the percussion sounds that your MPC audio adapter card produces, you can add a MIDI drum machine at moderate cost. Many older models, such as the Yamaha RX-17, are available in the used-equipment market for as little as $100. These drum machines don't have as many drum kits as the SR-16 and don't offer stereo samples, but most include 50 or more factory patterns and a few standard songs to help you learn how to play rhythm tracks.

One advantage of a drum machine is that you can create patterns and then combine the patterns into rhythm-section tracks more easily than you can with a sequencer application. You then play the patterns or songs into the percussion track of your compositions.

To use a drum machine for percussion parts, you need a sequencer (such as Cakewalk for Windows or MusicTime) that enables you to choose between two or more output devices so that you can assign the sound card's percussion track to the drum machine. You also need an MPC-compatible audio adapter card with a driver that assigns the FM sounds and MIDI ports to separate devices. The Thunder Board and the original Sound Blaster drivers provided by Microsoft with Windows 3.1 do not provide separate synthesis and MIDI ports, so you cannot use these non-MPC boards with a drum machine.

All MPC-compliant sound cards described in this book provide the required dual drivers. For example, Media Vision provides drivers called Voyetra FM Driver for PAS2 and ProAudio MIDI Output with its Pro AudioSpectrum products.

To use a drum machine with an MPC-compatible audio adapter card, follow these steps:

1. Connect the drum machine's MIDI OUT connector to the MIDI IN port of your audio adapter card, and use a second cable to connect the MIDI IN connector of the drum machine to the adapter card's MIDI OUT port. Figure 9.18 shows the connections.

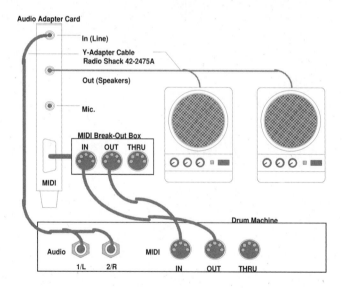

FIG. 9.18

Connections between a drum machine and an audio adapter card.

2. Connect the audio output(s) of your drum machine to the auxiliary line input of your audio adapter card. You need a 1/8-inch stereo miniplug to two RCA phono plugs (Y-adapter) cable and two 1/4-inch phono plugs to RCA phono jack cable to make this connection.

3. Using the MIDI function of your drum machine, set the MIDI note number of each sound of the drum kit to the corresponding General MIDI note number between 35 and 81. (Your drum machine may not

have a sound for each of the GM percussion instruments, so you may have to modify compositions that use unavailable drum sounds.)

4. Set the drum machine to send and receive all drum sounds on MIDI Channel 10. Depending on your make and model, you may have to set the channel number of each instrument in the kit individually.

5. Set the drum machine's synchronization to Internal, if necessary. Internal sync usually is the default mode.

6. Select one of the factory-preset songs by pressing the appropriate combination of buttons on your drum machine.

7. Press the drum machine's Start button, adjust the tempo so that the drum part sounds right, and then press Stop. Notice the tempo you chose. Depending on the internal programming of your drum machine, the part may sound peculiar because the drum voices were reprogrammed to new note numbers in step 3.

8. Set the synchronization to MIDI (sometimes called External) so that the drum machine responds to MIDI Start and Clock messages from your sequencer.

9. Launch your sequencer application, set its MIDI input source to your audio adapter card's MIDI input, and choose Internal synchronization (the default).

10. Choose an empty track and set its MIDI channel number to 10 (the standard General MIDI percussion track). Click the Rewind symbol to make sure that you are at the first beat of the first bar to start. Set the sequencer's tempo to the number of beats per minute you chose in step 7.

11. Click the Record symbol on your sequencer's control panel to send first a MIDI Start message and then MIDI Clock messages to the drum machine's MIDI IN port.

12. After a few bars, stop recording and examine the result in the piano-roll (step edit) window of your sequencer.

13. Set your drum machine back to the normal Internal synchronization.

14. Play back the percussion track you recorded through the drum machine.

You must modify the MIDI files of compositions in which you want to use a drum machine for percussion parts. After you load the MIDI file, change the Device or Port parameter of the Channel 10 percussion track from the standard (FM Synthesis) driver to the MIDI driver for the card.

You can make this change on most sequencers by double-clicking the Device or Port entry cell for the track in the sequencer's Track/Measure window.

Figure 9.19 shows an example of the proper Track/Measure setup for Cakewalk Professional for Windows used with a Pro AudioSpectrum Plus audio adapter card (see Chapter 10 for more information about Cakewalk Professional). Other Windows sequencer applications have similar Track/Measure displays.

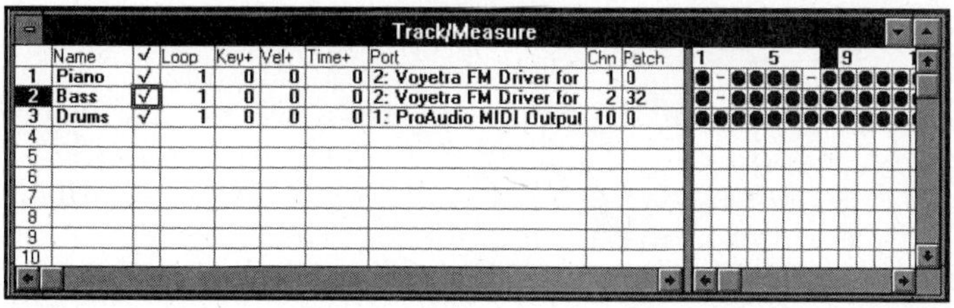

	Name	√	Loop	Key+	Vel+	Time+	Port	Chn	Patch	1	5	9	1
1	Piano	√	1	0	0	0	2: Voyetra FM Driver for	1	0				
2	Bass	√	1	0	0	0	2: Voyetra FM Driver for	2	32				
3	Drums	√	1	0	0	0	1: ProAudio MIDI Output	10	0				
4													
5													
6													
7													
8													
9													
10													

FIG. 9.19

The Track/Measure window of Cakewalk for Windows.

If you have a MIDI keyboard capable of transmitting MIDI data on Channel 10, you can play the GM drum sounds from the keyboard by connecting the MIDI OUT connector of the keyboard or keyboard synthesizer to the drum machine's MIDI IN port. Associating the keys with individual drum sounds may take practice, but many keyboard players also become proficient percussionists.

T I P

If you decide to acquire a drum machine, purchase one that can assign each drum sound to a different MIDI note number (corresponding to the GM percussion list) than the standard factory assignment. MIDI Mapper is an output-only device; you cannot use MIDI Mapper's key maps to reassign the MIDI note numbers received in your audio adapter card's MIDI IN port. Fortunately, almost all drum machines have this capability.

Instrument Expanders

Special-purpose MIDI sound modules that duplicate specific instruments or groups of instruments are called *expanders* or *expander modules*. These devices often use multisampling capability at closer pitch intervals with longer-duration samples to improve the realism of their sampled sounds. A piano expander, for example, might have 1M to

2M of ROM devoted exclusively to a Bosendorfer grand. Guitar expanders offer samples of various manufacturers' acoustic guitars and even provide special samples of strings of varying thickness and composition.

With the exception of drum machines and the moderately priced piano expanders designed to duplicate the distinctive sounds of Baldwin, Steinway, and Yamaha pianos for amateur players, expander modules usually are found only in recording studios.

Chapter Summary

This chapter provided a brief history of electronic music synthesizers and Yamaha Corporation's domination of digital FM synthesis. Although digital FM synthesis is used in most of the audio adapter cards produced today, sample-playback synthesis is the wave of the MPC's future. Roland's SCC-1 and Turtle Beach's MultiSound are the pioneers; you can expect all the major sound-card suppliers to introduce sampled-sound adapter cards by the end of 1993.

Chapter 10 describes the wide range of accessory products that you can connect to the MIDI IN and OUT ports of your MIDI breakout box. If you make extensive use of MIDI in your multimedia presentations, you will find many of these accessories to be indispensable.

The best sources of up-to-date information on trends in electronic musical synthesis and the capabilities of synthesizers are *Electronic Musician* and *Keyboard* magazines, both of which usually are available at newsstands. The names and addresses of the magazines' publishers appear in Appendix F.

The MIDI Standard and Windows 3.1

T he Windows multimedia extensions enable you to choose from two methods of adding music to your presentations or titles: wave form audio and MIDI (Musical Instrument Digital Interface). Waveform audio, the subject of Chapters 13 through 15, offers the advantage of simplicity but exacts a high price in the space required to store the *.WAV files that contain digitally sampled music, especially if you want reasonable fidelity in reproduction. As an example, 53 minutes of waveform audio recorded with 16-bit resolution at 44.1 kHz occupies an entire CD-ROM. Music reproduced by MIDI techniques requires less disk space and offers you the opportunity to modify prerecorded music to suit specific timing requirements and your taste. Several hours of complex music in the form of standard MIDI files can fit comfortably on a CD-ROM, and at least a half-hour's worth of contemporary music can be stored on a high-density floppy disk.

This chapter provides an overview of the Musical Instrument Digital Interface and the industry specifications that define its implementation and also explains how the multimedia extensions implement these MIDI standards. MIDI synchronization methods and system exclusive messages are explored in Chapter 21.

NOTE Multimedia titles distributed on CD-ROM use waveform audio rather than MIDI for music. The reason is that the various sound cards used to reproduce the music have digitally sampled sound capabilities that differ less than the voices available from their synthesis components. Vocals and narration, of course, require sample audio techniques. Even if your plans are to use only waveform audio in a title, you will undoubtedly employ MIDI to generate some, if not all, of your musical background material. Whether you create the MIDI music yourself or employ others to do it, an understanding of MIDI is an essential ingredient to obtaining the musical background for a multimedia production distributed on CD-ROM or floppy disks.

What Is MIDI?

As musicians attempted to improve the realism of synthesized music, they realized that they would have to connect a number of synthesizers to create polyphonic and multi-timbral sound. Although these terms are described in Chapter 1, they bear repeating here because the two are often confused. *Polyphonic* means the capability to play a number of notes simultaneously, as can be done with a piano or guitar but not by an oboe or French horn. *Multi-timbral* means the capability to play the sounds of different instruments simultaneously. Polyphony and multi-timbral capability was difficult to achieve in the early days of synthesizers because no established standards existed for the signals that would turn on and off the sound-creating oscillators and determine their frequency.

Musicians were forced to become electronic technicians and cobble together the circuitry required to interconnect their synthesizers so that they would play predetermined notes at the same time. This action ultimately led to the original development of the Universal Synthesizer Interface in 1982 by Dave Smith, then president of Sequential Circuits, Inc., a California manufacturer of synthesizers. American and Japanese synthesizer manufacturers took Smith's proposed standard, renamed it the Musical Instrument Digital Interface, and produced the first specification for MIDI in 1983. MIDI Specification 1.0 revolutionized the electronic musical instrument industry.

Defining the Basic MIDI Specification

MIDI Specification 1.0 is the bible of the electronic music industry. The specification, which has been supplemented but not significantly revised since its inception, defines the following items:

- The cabling method for interconnecting MIDI devices

- Electronic signal input and output circuitry

- Basic types of MIDI messages

- The format and general content of each type of MIDI message

A *MIDI device* is any electronic element that incorporates at least two MIDI connectors. Devices include adapter cards, synthesizers, keyboards, various types of instrument pickups, and MIDI accessories, such as digital signal processors and MIDI-controlled audio mixers. Synthesizers include those with and without keyboards—the latter are referred to here as *sound modules*. MIDI percussion synthesizers, called *drum machines*, are classed as keyboard synthesizers because they usually include small pads (rubber push buttons) to play the individual percussion instruments. Synthesizers are commonly called *synths* by musicians, and MIDI devices without keyboards are often referred to collectively as *boxes*.

Several supplements to MIDI Specification 1.0 have been designed to standardize new elements of MIDI technology. These new elements include the following:

- Standard MIDI files that enable you to use the same file with different sequencer applications

- MIDI Time Code (MTC) to synchronize MIDI music with television and motion picture productions

- MIDI Machine Control (MMC) designed to control tape recorders and other MIDI accessories

- MIDI Show Control (MSC) to control stage lighting by MIDI messages

These supplemental MIDI specifications are covered in separate sections throughout this chapter. MIDI Show Control is omitted from the discussion because it does not apply to multimedia applications.

The International MIDI Association (IMA) maintains and updates the MIDI specification. When manufacturers like Roland, Yamaha, and Casio adopted MIDI as the standard method of interfacing their electronic musical products, they formed the MIDI Manufacturers Association (MMA). The MMA, in conjunction with the Japan MIDI Standards Committee (JMSC), carries most of the weight in the approval of supplements to the basic specification and coordinates manufacturer-specific additions, such as supplier identification numbers.

Making MIDI Interconnections

MIDI Specification 1.0 defines the hardware requirements to accommodate cabling between electronic musical instruments and also defines the basis for the software used to send and respond to the messages carried over the cables. Three types of MIDI connections are specified:

- MIDI IN receives MIDI messages from devices, such as keyboards and MIDI adapter cards installed in computers.

- MIDI OUT sends MIDI messages to sound-generating and accessory devices, such as sound modules and digital effects processors.

- MIDI THRU retransmits messages received at the MIDI IN connector without adding to or changing them. Most but not all MIDI devices have a MIDI THRU connector.

All MIDI devices have receptacles (jacks) for standard MIDI cables, which terminate on both ends in five-pin DIN circular plugs, the same connectors used by most PC keyboards. The cables are two-conductor and are shielded to minimize noise pickup from surrounding electrical fields. You have to follow only one, simple rule for connecting MIDI cables: MIDI OUT or MIDI THRU are *always* connected to MIDI IN. MIDI cabling was designed for musicians, not engineers.

The MIDI THRU connection is used for *daisy-chaining* MIDI devices. Daisy-chaining means connecting cables and devices in series—MIDI OUT of device 1 to MIDI IN of device 2, MIDI THRU of device 2 to MIDI IN of device 3, and so on through a theoretically unlimited chain of devices. The MIDI specification limits the total length of all cables in a *setup*—the name musicians apply to a group of connected devices, to 50 feet (15 meters). Longer lengths, however, seldom cause problems if you use high-quality cable. A typical daisy-chained MIDI setup is shown in figure 10.1.

Figure 10.1 depicts a MIDI setup that uses external devices and is typical of the kind used by independent musical composers and small commercial studios to produce custom scores for multimedia productions. The cost of this combination, less the computer, ranges from about $2,500 to $7,500, depending on the sound quality and versatility of the devices. These figures do not include the cost of a multi-track audio tape recorder that easily can double the investment.

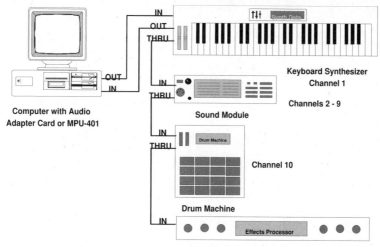

Computer with Audio
Adapter Card or MPU-401

Keyboard Synthesizer
Channel 1

Channels 2 - 9

Sound Module

Channel 10

Drum Machine

Digital Effects Processor - Channel 11

FIG. 10.1

A simple MIDI daisy-chained setup using outboard synthesizers and MIDI accessories.

Each device in the daisy-chain is assigned its own channel number or group of numbers. When you play MIDI songs with Media Player or a sequencer application in the setup shown in figure 10.1, your computer's adapter card sends all MIDI messages to the keyboard synthesizer. Assuming that the synthesizer has been set to play a piano part on MIDI channel 1, the synthesizer responds only to MIDI messages that include the channel 1 address code. All the MIDI messages, including the channel 1 messages, are passed on to the sound module through the MIDI OUT port of the keyboard synth.

The sound module in figure 10.1 has been adjusted to play other melodic parts on channels 2, 3, and 4; it does not respond to messages sent on other MIDI channels. The drum machine is assigned to channel 10; all the rhythm parts are sent on that channel, and it ignores messages on all other channels. Finally, effects (reverberation, chorus, and so on) applied to the audio outputs of the three synthesizers can be adjusted by messages sent to the digital effects processor on channel 11. The logic behind the assignment of channel numbers is explained in the sections that follow.

Transmitting MIDI Signals

MIDI signals are transmitted in *serial* form so that only two conductors are required to carry them (the cable shield does not carry MIDI information). MIDI serial transmission is similar to that used by telex machines, FAXes, and modems that send and receive digital information over telephone lines, which also are two-conductor (twisted-pair, unshielded) cables. Like the COM ports of your computer, MIDI devices use *universal asynchronous receiver-transmitters* (UARTs) to send and receive the serial data and convert it into the *byte* format required by MIDI.

The representation of a data byte corresponding to the decimal number 76 in serial format is shown in figure 10.2. (Binary arithmetic and hexadecimal representation of numbers are explained in Appendix E.) Ten serial *bits*, an abbreviation for *bi*nary dig*its*, are necessary to send one data byte, which consists of eight bits. The extra two bits, marked with x's in the figure, are called start and stop bits. They frame the data bits and are used for synchronization purposes. The clock pulses shown are not the MIDI Clock messages described in the next section but are used internally to send the serial data at the rate established by the MIDI specification.

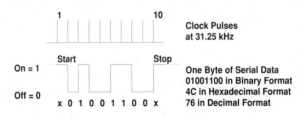

FIG. 10.2

The serial data communication signal format used by MIDI.

MIDI transmits serial data at 31.25 bits per second (bps or kHz, sometimes called baud), so a MIDI port can send 3,125 MIDI bytes per second. Because MIDI Note messages use 3 bytes, and each message to turn on a note must be followed by one to turn it off, you thus could send, theoretically, about 500 complete Note messages per second to devices connected to a MIDI adapter card. MIDI Clock messages are being transmitted along with the Note messages, however, so the actual maximum is reduced to between 300 and 400 notes per second.

If your computer tries to send messages faster than the maximum allowable rate, you run into a problem called *MIDI choke*, where some of the messages "get lost"—that is, are not transmitted. Modern computers are capable of sending serial data at much higher rates than 31.25 bps, and new sequencers could receive them, but millions of MIDI instruments in the world have their UARTs tuned to 31.25 kHz. Thus, you can expect to live with this data rate in the foreseeable future. Some day, perhaps, you will see a set of FAST MIDI connectors on your synths, running at 4 or 8 times the current rate.

Transmitting MIDI Messages

MIDI uses precisely spaced clock pulse messages for external synchronization. These messages are transmitted at 24 pulses per quarter note (24 ppqn), so they are dependent on the tempo you set. At 120 beats per minute (bpm) in 4/4 time, 120 quarter notes are played per minute, or 2 per second. This tempo results in a MIDI clock rate of 48 Hz. All instruments in the chain respond to the Clock messages, so the instruments play notes synchronized with the originating clock pulses. Only one device in the chain can supply the MIDI Clock messages: your MIDI adapter card, a drum machine, or a sequencer built into a keyboard synthesizer.

Interspersed with the clock pulse messages are other messages, much like those used by Windows and its applications to communicate with one another. The basic types of MIDI messages described by the specification include the following:

■ *Note* messages instruct a synthesizer to begin playing a note of a particular pitch (Note On message) and to stop playing it (Note Off). All MIDI messages except system messages are prefixed with the MIDI channel number (1 to 16). Note messages are followed by the MIDI note number (0 to 127) that specifies the pitch (middle C is 60) and key down velocity (loudness, Note On) or key up velocity (release rate, Note Off), both in the range of 0 to 127. Few synthesizers respond to release rate information, even if the keyboard should send it.

■ *Polyphonic (individual) or Channel (collective) Aftertouch* messages transmit continuous information on key pressure while one or more keys are depressed. Keyboards that transmit aftertouch information send a great quantity of MIDI messages—hundreds or thousands more than simple Note On and Note Off messages.

■ *Control Change* messages affect controllers, which usually are implemented on external devices by pedals, sliders, wheels, or dials. Controllers typically include sustain, vibrato, tremolo, and pitch bend (frequency change) information and are classified as the "on-off" type (like a pedal) or "continuous" (from a wheel or slider). When you send a Control Change message for one of these controllers, you simulate movement of, for example, the modulation wheel. Control Change messages are used for other purposes such as Bank Select, which enables you to choose among different sets of timbres for a specific Program Change message.

■ *Program Change* messages are device-specific. In other words, the way an individual synthesizer or accessory responds to them is determined by its manufacturer. Synthesizers use Program Change messages to change timbres assigned to channel numbers. General

MIDI mode (GM or GMM) and the MPC specification assign a standard set of voices (timbres) to Program Change messages 1 through 128. The 128 standard GM voices are listed in Appendix C. Windows' MIDI Mapper calls program changes *patches*.

■ *Pitch Bend Change* messages alter the pitch of all notes on a particular channel by an amount determined by the data in the message, combined with the pitch bend range set in the synthesizer.

■ *Mode* messages set the Omni On, Omni Off, Poly, and Mono modes described in "Using MIDI Mode Messages," later in this chapter. Mono Mode messages include the capability to determine the number of channels to which individual Note messages will be assigned. The Local Control Off message disconnects the keyboard from the synthesizer, enabling the sound portion of a keyboard synth to be controlled by an external device. Local Control On restores the internal connection.

■ *System Common* messages include the MIDI song position pointer (SPP) that corresponds to the position (measured in beats) in a sequenced composition at which playing will commence when a System Real-Time Start message is received. Song Select determines which song or sequence is to be played and is often used by drum machines to play a prerecorded pattern stored in memory. Another System Common message, Tune, instructs analog synthesizers to tune their oscillators to a standard pitch. All System Common messages are received by all devices in the chain, regardless of the channel numbers to which the devices are assigned.

■ *System Real-Time* messages are used to synchronize all MIDI devices in the chain. Real-Time messages include MIDI Timing Clock, Start, Continue, Stop, Active Sensing, and System Reset. Start, Continue, and Stop correspond to the Start, Pause, and Stop buttons of Media Player. Active Sensing messages are optional and are sent every 0.3 seconds or so by the controller (when no other MIDI messages are being sent) to inform devices that it is still alive. When an Active Sensing message is sent to the devices, and they do not receive a message within 300 milliseconds, the devices turn off any voices still playing. Like System Common messages, all devices respond to System Real-Time messages.

■ *System Exclusive (SysEx)* messages are prefixed with a manufacturer's identification number, usually followed by an arbitrary code designating the manufacturer's device type and model number. SysEx messages do not include a MIDI channel address code. Each device capable of responding to System Exclusive messages is expected to respond only to messages intended for it and then act in accordance with the instructions that follow.

The values of the individual bytes that determine the type of message being sent, the number and range of data bytes applicable to different types of messages, and the subject of status bytes are discussed in Chapter 12, "MIDI Applications for Windows." The purpose of this chapter is to acquaint you with the various types of messages you will use with your sound card or synthesizer, not to delve into the technicalities of MIDI message bytes and hexadecimal arithmetic.

Using MIDI Note Messages

MIDI Note messages consist of Note On messages, which cause the synthesizer to play a sound, followed by Note Off messages, which turn the sound off. Each message has four components:

- The code that indicates the type of message (9 for Note On or 8 for Note Off)

- The channel number on which the messages are sent (1 through 16)

- The pitch to be played, indicated by a MIDI note number ranging from 0 to 127

- The volume (velocity) at which the note is to be played for Note On messages or the rate at which the key was released with Note Off messages

Few synthesizers respond to release velocity codes. Sending a second Note On message with a velocity code of 0 turns a note off just as a Note Off message does, but this method violates the rule of the MIDI specification stating that Note On and Note Off messages shall always occur in pairs.

MIDI note numbers correspond to notes on a staff, with 12 semitones per octave. The staff positions corresponding to MIDI note numbers are shown in figure 10.3, created with Cakewalk Professional for the Windows Staff window display. The range of MIDI note numbers is from 0 (C0) through 127 (G10), but the C1 through C8 shown in the figure can cover the majority of music you are likely to play. The range of the piano (88 keys) is A2 to C9.

Using MIDI Mode Messages

The MIDI specification defines two messages that control how a device responds to messages with channel numbers assigned:

- *Omni On.* The device responds to messages on all 16 MIDI channels.

■ *Omni Off.* The device responds only to the channels it is set to receive, usually by a sequence of push-button operations. Some early sound modules have a fixed channel assignment, which is also called an address. Most synthesizers normally operate in Omni Off mode.

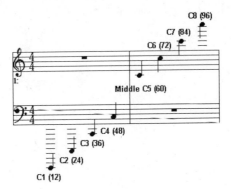

FIG. 10.3

Eight octaves of MIDI note numbers shown in staff notation.

The following two modes are available in Omni On or Omni Off mode:

■ *Poly(phonic)* mode is for synthesizers that can play more than one note at a time.

■ *Mono(phonic)* mode causes the device to play only one note at a time on each channel to which it is set to respond, regardless of how many simultaneous notes might be sent on that channel.

(Mono and Poly modes are mutually exclusive. A more consistent term for Mono mode might be Poly Off.)

The two messages and the two modes are combined to create a total of four operating modes, described in the following paragraphs for synthesizers:

■ *Mode 1, Omni On/Poly.* The device responds to MIDI messages sent on any channel and plays all Note messages sent by the controller, up to the number of voices it can produce simultaneously (the polyphonic voice limit, typically 8, 16, 24, or 32). Voice assignments to specific MIDI channels are made internally by the synthesizer, not by the controller. Use of mode 1 is uncommon.

■ *Mode 2, Omni On/Mono.* The device plays a single voice, regardless of the channel on which it is received. Mode 2 is even less common than mode 1.

■ *Mode 3, Omni Off/Poly.* The device responds to MIDI messages on any channels it is set to receive and plays as many simultaneous notes on each channel as it is sent, up to the total of its polyphonic limit. This mode is the default for MPC-compliant audio adapter cards and almost all synthesizers and keyboards. Although MPC cards need not respond to channels 11 and 12, all those tested do.

■ *Mode 4, Omni Off/Mono.* The device responds with only one note at a time on each channel it is set to receive. Mode 4 is uncommon in a receiving device but is useful for recording music played on stringed instruments equipped with MIDI pickups. MIDI pickups convert the sound generated by each string into a series of MIDI Note messages sent on the channel assigned to the string. MIDI instrument pickups are described in Chapter 11.

Nearly all of today's synthesizers are both polyphonic and multi-timbral. Synthesizers with 16-, 24-, and 32-note polyphony are common. Most offer a wide variety of timbres; you can select from a few hundred different voices even in moderately priced synths. You may want to assign all 24 or 32 polyphonic notes of a keyboard synthesizer to the piano part. Even though you have only 10 fingers, you need all the notes you can get to maintain the decaying sound of previous chords, especially when holding the sustain pedal down. If you are synthesizing an acoustic guitar with a sound module, however, you need assign only one note per string (or pair of strings for a 12-string guitar). As a general rule, all the notes for a particular instrument are sent on a single channel, so the basic limit of a single MIDI chain is 15 different melodic timbres plus the percussion parts.

Using Program Change Messages and Synthesizer Voice Channel Mapping

A MIDI setup using an MPU-401-type MIDI adapter card and the equipment shown in figure 10.4 is common among computer-equipped musicians. Figure 10.4 is a diagram of the assignment of MIDI channels that you might make to simulate a group consisting of a pianist, two guitarists, and a drummer. Both the keyboard synthesizer and the sound module shown are multi-timbral and are assumed to have 16-channel polyphony. Drum machines are multi-timbral by definition and require only a single channel because the pitch data contained in the MIDI Note messages sent to the drum machine select the percussive voice to be played.

The process of setting up keyboard synthesizers and sound modules to play specific instrument timbres when notes are received on particular MIDI channels is called *configuring*. Configuring a synthesizer ordinarily involves pressing a particular combination of push buttons to specify the voice to be played and the number of notes assigned to the instrument. The result is a *program*, also called a *voice channel map*, which is stored in the synthesizer's memory. The instruments in figure 10.4 are set up with the following programs:

- MIDI Note messages assigned to channel 1 play up to 16 simultaneous piano notes on the keyboard synthesizer.

- Note messages for channel 2 sound a maximum of six notes of the sound module's acoustic guitar voice.

- Channel 3 notes are played by the sound module's second guitar voice, also assigned six notes.

- Channel 4 is programmed to play up to four string bass notes on the sound module.

- The drum machine plays all percussion notes transmitted on MIDI channel 10. Channel 10 is becoming the standard channel assignment for percussion instruments because it is assigned to drum parts by the general MIDI specification (see this chapter's subsequent section, "Examining the General MIDI Mode Standard").

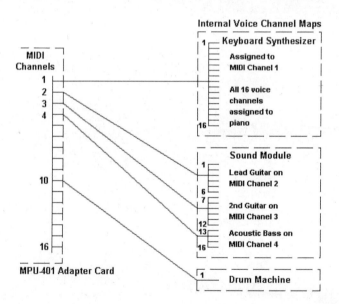

FIG. 10.4

Synthesizer voice assignments required to simulate a group of musicians.

You instruct the synthesizer to use the program you have created by issuing a *program change* command. You can initiate program changes by pressing the appropriate buttons on the synthesizer or by having your sequencer application transmit MIDI Program Change messages before the first notes are played. You set the initial program changes in the Track List window of the sequencer. Program changes are often called *patches* by the MIDI Mapper applet, but this term also is used by musicians to mean a modification to an instrument's timbre to adjust the sound to their liking. In this book, MIDI Mapper's usage is referred to as *program change patches*, and timbre modifications are referred to as *voice editing patches*.

Yamaha Corporation uses the term *performance* to refer to a specific group of program change patches. If you were using a Yamaha TX81Z sound module, for example, all three of the program change patches would be stored in a single performance. You load a performance into Yamaha synths as you would load a program change. Korg calls a group of program change patches *combinations*. The MIDI specification contains no standard for the terminology involved.

Using Voice Banks and Control Change Messages

The MIDI specification provides for only 128 different Program Change messages, but today's synthesizers may offer up to several hundred different voices from which you can choose. Yamaha's approach solves this problem by using performance changes, but another method had to be devised for conventional program change patches. Most synthesizers use a *bank select* technique, consisting of a MIDI Control Change message to select a specific group of up to 128 different timbres, followed by a Program Change message to assign one member of the group to a MIDI channel. A specific implementation of this technique employed by Roland Corporation for its General Synthesizer (GS) product line is described in "Examining Roland's General Synthesizer Standard" later in this chapter.

Exceeding the Synthesizer's Limits and Prioritizing Channels

If you send a device, such as a synthesizer, more messages to play notes than its polyphonic capability can handle, some method must be employed to decide what to do with those messages that exceed the limit. *Note stealing* is the most common approach and is the method recommended by the MPC specification. Note stealing means that when a new message to play a note is received, and the synthesizer is playing at its polyphonic limit, the new note takes the place of the oldest note of the highest channel number in use, by a process called *prioritizing*.

The general MIDI standard, the subject of a later section in this chapter ("Examining the General MIDI Mode Standard"), provides for prioritizing the sounds assigned to MIDI channels in accordance with the channel number, with the exception of percussion instruments (channel 10).

Percussion sounds are assigned the highest priority (1). The remainder of the channels are assigned lower priorities in sequence—channel 1 is priority 2, channel 2 equals priority 3, and so on. For this reason, you should assign solo and melody parts to the lower channel numbers.

Some synthesizers, such as the Roland SCC-1 GS Sound Card and the SC-55 Sound Canvas, amend the prioritizing process just described by adding a *voice reserve* feature. If you attempt to exceed the polyphonic limit, voice reserve guarantees that specified channels receive a minimum number of voices. The Roland products reserve six voices for percussion parts and two voices each for MIDI channels. Channels 11 through 16 do not reserve voices.

If more voices are attempted than the synthesizer's multi-timbral limit can handle, usually the 16 available MIDI channels, the MPC specification recommends *timbre stealing*. Most synthesizers have more timbres available than MIDI channels, so you should seldom, if ever, encounter this situation.

Using More Than 16 MIDI Channels

If you decide to transcribe Igor Stravinsky's *Rite of Spring* with a sequencer application, you are out of luck with only 16 MIDI channels. Mr. Stravinsky specified one of the largest orchestral complements ever assembled to play this work. You need either a special 32-channel MIDI card, such as Music Quest's MQX-32, or two (or more) MIDI adapter cards, each assigned different device addresses and interrupt levels, to use more than 16 MIDI channels. The MQX-32 requires a special driver when used with the multimedia extensions—the driver is supplied by Music Quest and is included with many Windows sequencer applications. Passport's MusicTime and most professional sequencer applications for Windows enable you to send MIDI signals to more than one adapter card.

Sequencing *Rite of Spring* is a task not to be taken lightly and requires several sound modules to play all the parts. More than 32 channels are required if each voice is assigned a separate channel. You can use a single channel for more than one timbre, however, if the individual instruments do not have to be played simultaneously. To do so, send a MIDI Program Change message to the module to tell the synthesizer to change the timbre played on a specified channel at a particular measure in the composition. Piccolos and timpani are not often played together, so you might use a single channel to play their parts. You can send program change patches to MPC audio adapter cards as well as to outboard synths. Program change patch techniques are discussed in the later section, "Creating a MIDI Mapper Patch Map."

Making Control Change Assignments

MIDI Specification 1.0 assigned Control Change messages 0 through 63 to continuous controllers, such as wheels and sliders, assigned 64 through 95 to switch type (on-off) controllers, and reserved channels 122 through 127 for Channel Mode messages. The specification assigned only one continuous controller, the modulation wheel (which acts as a pitch adjustment device), to channel 1. The MIDI Manufacturers Association (MMA) and the Japan MIDI Standards Committee (JMSC) have jointly allocated eight additional controllers commonly found on keyboard synthesizers and MIDI wind instruments to specific Control Change message numbers. The definition of Control Change messages 64 through 95 has been changed from only the switch type to include continuous controllers that require values only within the range of 0 to 127.

Manufacturers are free to use unassigned or undefined controllers for their own purposes. Table 10.1 lists the Control Change message numbers that correspond to or can be implemented by physical controllers on MIDI device panels. The table also shows the use made of assigned and a few unassigned controllers by the Roland SC-55 and SC-155 GS sound modules and the SCC-1 Sound Card. All Control Change messages apply to individual MIDI channels only.

Notice that the first controller in table 10.1 begins with the value 0 rather than 1. All MIDI messages are based on the hexadecimal counting system used by modern computers, which begins with 0, rather than the decimal counting system, which starts with 1. Traditionally, voice (program change) numbers and MIDI channels start with 1 and are offset from their hexadecimal representation in a MIDI message by 1. But controller numbering begins with 0, and the controllers have a one-to-one correspondence with the MIDI hexadecimal values. Perhaps the reason is that controller 0 is unassigned in the MIDI specification.

Table 10.1. Standard Control Change Assignments for Physical Controllers and Their Use by Roland GS Devices.

CC#	IMA or MMA/JMSC assignment	Use by Roland GS synthesizers
0	Unassigned	Bank Select
1	Modulation Controller (varies pitch)	Modulation
2	Breath Controller (MIDI woodwinds)	Not Used
4	Foot Controller (not piano pedals)	Not Used
5	Portamento Time (to slide to a new note)	Same
6	Data Entry Slider (adjusts values)	Specified by RPN/NRPN
7	Main Volume (channel volume)	Volume
8	Balance	Not Used
10	Stereo Pan (left/right balance)	Panpot
11	Expression (ganged volume control)	Expression
16	General Purpose Controller 1	Not Used
17	General Purpose Controller 2	Not Used
18	General Purpose Controller 3	Not Used
19	General Purpose Controller 4	Not Used
20	Unassigned	Bank Select (not implemented)
64	Sustain Pedal On/Off	Hold 1
65	Portamento On/Off	Portamento
66	Sostenuto Pedal On/Off	Sostenuto
67	Soft Pedal On/Off	Soft
68	Unassigned	Legato Control
69	Hold 2 On/Off	Not Used
80	General Purpose Controller 5	Not Used
81	General Purpose Controller 6	Not Used
82	General Purpose Controller 7	Not Used
83	General Purpose Controller 8	Not Used
91	External Effects Depth	Reverb(eration) Send Depth
92	Tremolo Depth	Not Used
93	Chorus Depth	Chorus Send Depth
94	Detune (celeste) Depth	Not Used
95	Phaser (phase change) Depth	Not Used
96	Data Increment (push button)	Not Used
97	Data Decrement (push button)	Not Used

In addition to controllers that may be implemented physically, the Control Change messages shown in table 10.2 are reserved for special uses. Control Changes 121 through 127 are called Channel Mode messages.

Table 10.2. Control Change Assignments for Parameters and Channel Mode Messages.

CC#	IMA or MMA/JMSC assignment	Use by Roland GS synthesizers
98	Nonregistered Parameter Number	Nonregistered Parameter Number
99	Nonregistered Parameter Number	Nonregistered Parameter Number
100	Registered Parameter Number	Registered Parameter Number
101	Registered Parameter Number	Registered Parameter Number
121	Reset All Controllers	Reset All Controllers
122	Local Control On/Off	Not Used (separates keyboard)
123	All Notes Off	All Notes Off
124	Omni Mode Off	Not Recognized (Omni always off)
125	Omni Mode On	Not Recognized
126	Mono Mode On (Poly Mode Off)	Mono Mode On (Poly Mode Off)
127	Poly Mode On (Mono Mode Off)	Poly Mode On (Mono Mode Off)

Using Registered and Nonregistered Parameters

MIDI parameters are used to expand the availability of controller numbers by combining 2 controller numbers to add 128 additional potential controllers to the list. These additions were made despite the substantial number of unassigned controllers already available. The problem was that device manufacturers had appropriated the unassigned values for their own purposes; thus assigning official uses for them could obsolete existing equipment.

Registered Parameter Numbers (RPNs) are assigned jointly by the MMA and JMSC. Only four of these parameters, listed in table 10.3, were assigned as of the end of 1991.

Nonregistered parameters are another monument to musical anarchism and appear destined to repeat the problem with arbitrary assignment of controller numbers. Nonregistered parameters are manufacturer- and often device-specific to the model number. The nonregistered parameters used by Roland Corp. for their GS synthesizers are listed in table 10.4 and are specific to Roland's equipment. The purpose of the NRPMs is to enable you to modify the voice parameters by means of control changes rather than SysEx messages (which are more difficult for users of sequencer applications to implement). In this case, the hexadecimal numbering system is used, because the decimal equivalents are somewhat confusing.

Table 10.3. Registered Parameter Numbers Assigned by the MMA/JMSC.

RPN#	MMA/JMSC assignment	Purpose
0	Pitch Bend Sensitivity (range)	Sets the number of semitones corresponding to full-scale adjustment of the pitch bend (modulation) controller. The default is two semitones, and the maximum is two octaves.
1	Master Fine Tuning (by 0.01 semitone)	Tunes or detunes synthesizers.
2	Master Coarse Tuning (by 1 semitone)	Can be used to shift the pitch of all notes by up to two octaves.
127	Registered Parameter Reset	Returns all registered parameters to their power-on (default) values.

Table 10.4. Nonregistered Parameter Numbers for the Melodic Voices of Roland GS Synthesizers.

NRPN#	Roland GS description	Purpose
01H 08H	Vibrato Rate	Determines the frequency of the vibrato effect applied to the sound
01H 09H	Vibrato Depth	Determines the extent to which vibrato changes the pitch of the sound
01H 0AH	Vibrato Delay	Determines the time after the start of the sound when vibrato is applied
01H 20H	TVF Cut-off Frequency	Determines the frequency spectrum of the sound that the filter passes (affects sound brightness)

NRPN#	Roland GS description	Purpose
01H 21H	TVF Resonance	Determines the shape of the amplitude-frequency curve (makes sound more or less metallic)
01H 63H	TVF and TVA Envelope Attack	Determines the attack rate of the sound in a conventional attack-decay-sustain-release (ADSR) envelope
01H 64H	TVF and TVA Envelope Decay	Determines how fast the sound decays after the initial attack to the sustain level
01H 66H	TVF and TVA Envelope Release	Determines how fast the sound decays to zero amplitude when a MIDI Note Off message is received

The sound-generation technique in Roland's GS synthesizers uses *time-variant amplifiers* (TVAs), which vary the attack-decay-sustain-release amplitude envelope of the sound described in Chapter 3. *Time-variant filters* (TVFs) control the frequency spectrum of the sound during the ADSR interval. TVAs and TVFs manipulate the sampled sounds stored in ROM and can be adjusted to change the volume, shape, and brightness of the sound. You may vary the factory-preset values for each sound by up to +/– 50 percent. The effect of changes in NRPN values can be duplicated with SysEx messages, which are the subject of the next section.

Five Roland NRPNs exist for individual drum voices, but these NRPNs are seldom used and are not included in table 10.4. Persons who are particular about the quality of their percussion sounds usually employ dedicated drum machines to create them.

Using System Exclusive Messages and Voice Bank Data

Early synthesizers could save and restore banks of voice parameters and programs only in reliable but expensive plug-in memory cards or by recording them on low-cost but risk-prone audio tape. This process is known as a voice or patch "dump," whereby parameters for individual voices or programs are saved or read singly or as a group. With the advent of the Roland MPU-401 adapter card, saving SysEx data on a computer disk, using MIDI System Exclusive messages, became possible.

System exclusive data is transmitted to and received by all MIDI devices in the chain, regardless of the MIDI channel numbers to which they are set. Each manufacturer is assigned a specific two-digit code by the MMA/JMSC coalition. MIDI Specification 1.0 specifies only the beginning and ending portions of a SysEx message stream; each manufacturer specifies the format of its own system exclusive data. The format of the data varies for types and models made by the same manufacturer.

SysEx messages are ordinarily used for purposes similar to those of non-registered parameters: creating new sounds from those supplied by the manufacturer with the synthesizer (called factory presets). More advanced sample-playback synthesizers include random-access memory (RAM) in which you can store new samples you create yourself or purchase on floppy disk. Audio adapter cards with 16-bit, 44.1-kHz sampling capacity, combined with professional waveform editing tools such as Turtle Beach's Wave for Windows (not the Lite variety) and a high-quality microphone, enable you to create and edit samples to your liking. You also can purchase high-quality recorded sounds of various instruments on CD-ROMs and edit them as necessary for use in a sample-playback synthesizer. A MIDI sample dump standard specifies the format of sample files so that you can load the same sample into synthesizers with MIDI. MIDI SysEx messages are described in detail in Chapter 21.

Commercial applications called *editors* are used to modify and store FM and sampled sounds, and *librarians* are used to catalog and load them into your synthesizer. Universal editor/librarian applications combine both functions for a multiplicity of different synthesizers. Two universal editor/librarian applications for Windows are described in Chapter 12.

Examining the General MIDI Mode Standard

MIDI Specification 1.0 determines how synthesizers should behave in response to MIDI messages, but not what instruments they simulate for specific Program Change messages or, in the case of drum machines, a particular note. Thus, if you play a MIDI sequence written for a combination of a Kawai K-1 keyboard synthesizer, an E-mu Proteus/1 XR sound module, and a Yamaha RX-7 drum machine, the sequence sounds quite differently when played on a Yamaha SY-77 synth and a Turtle Beach MultiSound card. Although the MultiSound shares the same voices as the

Proteus/1 XR, the voices are assigned to different program change numbers. Matching the sound used in the composer's setup with those available with your equipment can be an arduous task.

David Kusek, president of Passport Designs, first proposed a standardization scheme for synthesizer voice assignments in 1989. The International MIDI Association formed a working committee to develop a "general" MIDI specification based on his proposal. The first specification for general MIDI mode operation of synthesizers was approved by the IMA in early 1991. Roland Corp., who had ideas in a similar vein, developed their own General Synthesizer (GS) standard while the general MIDI specification was still "in committee." Roland introduced their first GS product, the SC-55 Sound Canvas designed to the emerging general MIDI standard, at the National Association of Music Merchants exposition in January 1991. This product has become the *de facto* standard for general MIDI synthesizers, despite some technical controversy regarding whether the Sound Canvas is capable of playing all its sounds with true 24-voice polyphony.

The current general MIDI specification requires, at the minimum:

- Automatic assignment of MIDI channels 1 through 16 to the synthesizer operating in Omni Off/Poly mode.

- A standard set of melodic instrument voices and sound effects of adjustable pitch assigned to MIDI channels 1 through 9 and 11 through 16, selected by Program Change messages 1 through 128. The sounds are organized in 16 basic classifications, from Piano to Sound Effects, each with 8 different instruments of the class. The program change number and name of each general MIDI sound is provided in Appendix C.

- A standard set of 46 percussion instruments assigned to MIDI channel 10 and MIDI note numbers 35 (B2) through 81 (A6).

- A minimum of 24-voice polyphony and 24-voice multi-timbral capability. The voices may be dynamically allocated or permanently assigned (16 to melodic and 8 to percussion instruments).

The general MIDI mode specification is a minimum standard, and most GM synths exceed its basic requirements. The selection of the 128 standard sounds has created controversy in the musical industry, accompanied by accusations that standardized voices "stifle creativity." Similar objections were voiced when the original MIDI standard was proposed. Because 255 bank changes are possible with just 2 different MIDI Control Change messages, a total of 32,640 additional sounds can be made available in a single synthesizer. The Roland SCC-1 Sound Card and the SC-55 and SC-155 Sound Canvas modules, for instance, have 315 built-in melodic tones, 9 different drum sets, plus a special sound-effects set.

The general MIDI specification makes no attempt to determine what method is used to create the individual voices, nor exactly how they should sound. A Polysynth Pad 3 or Voice Oohs on one manufacturer's GM keyboard synth may sound quite different from those played on another supplier's GM sound card.

Examining Roland's General Synthesizer Standard

Roland Corporation's General Synthesizer standard is an extension to the general MIDI specification and defines how additional banks of voices relate (or don't relate) to the 128 capital voices of general MIDI. The term *capital* in this context means the top of a column, as shown in figure 10.5, which defines how the capital voices, variations on capital voices, subcapital voices, and variations on the subcapitals are organized in banks. Bank numbers begin with 1, and the corresponding Control Change message numbers start with 0. The column designated SFX is reserved for the 16 adjustable-pitch sound effects specified by the GM standard, plus 7 additional subcapital sound effects banks. A total of 128 GS voices are reserved for adjustable-pitch sound effects.

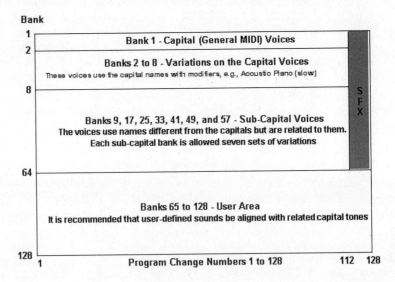

FIG. 10.5

Voice bank assignments for Roland Corp.'s General Synthesizer standard.

The advantage of the GS standard becomes apparent when you understand the "fall-back" technique implemented electronically in GS devices. The purpose of voice fall-back is to attempt to duplicate as closely as possible the sounds the composer used to create a MIDI composition when it is played back with synthesizers having fewer voice selections.

The composer's GS synth might have had a Fiddle timbre, for instance, but yours may not. All GS synthesizers have a Violin voice, so you can have the violin substitute for the nonexistent sound of the fiddle. GS voice fall-back does this substitution automatically—you don't have to modify the composition.

Voice fall-back is applicable to sounds stored in banks 2 through 64, corresponding to MIDI Control Change values 1 through 63. If you request a GS synthesizer to assign a variant of a capital voice that does not exist, the capital voice is played instead. If you try for a variant of a subcapital voice not present, the subcapital voice is checked. When no subcapital voice exists, the choice cascades to the capital voice. Examples of some of the subcapital voices included in the Roland SC-55, SC-155, and SCC-1 are listed in table 10.5.

Table 10.5. Some Subcapital Voices of the Roland Sound Canvas Family of Synthesizers.

Voice	Capital name, Bank 1	CC#	Substantial voice name
5	Electric Piano 1	8	De-tuned Electric Piano 1
6	Electric Piano 2	8	De-tuned Electric Piano 2
7	Harpsichord	8	Coupled Harpsichord
15	Tubular Bell	8	Church Bell
26	Steel-stringed Guitar	8	12-string Guitar
		16	Mandolin
27	Jazz Guitar	8	Hawaiian Guitar
28	Clean Guitar	8	Chorused Guitar
125	Telephone 1	1	Telephone 2
		2	Door Creaking
		3	Door
		4	Scratch
		5	Windchime

If you have sequenced a tune with mandolins on a Roland Sound Canvas product and then play it on a Korg 03R/W general MIDI sound module that does not have a mandolin sound, you get Korg's rendition of a steel-stringed guitar. Fathoming how a door creaking is a variant of a ringing telephone is difficult, but apparently the rules regarding naming variants of capital tones are not so rigidly applied to sound effects.

In addition to a collection of subcapital and variant voices, the Roland products also include imitations of the sounds of prior Roland products located in the user area. You obtain the voices of the CM-32P PCM Sound Module by issuing Control Change message number 126, and can duplicate the MT-32's and LAPC-1's sounds by using Control Change 127. These user banks are included so that files sequenced for these products can be played without modification on the Sound Canvas series.

You select drum sets named Room, Power, Electronic, TR-808, Brush, and Orchestra by issuing Control Change message numbers 9, 17, 25, 26, 41, and 49 on MIDI channel 10. With the exception of the Brush and Orchestra sets, each complies with the general MIDI percussion key (pitch) assignments to play individual percussion instruments. The Orchestra set is useful because it includes 13 semitones of timpani sounds, 2 (large) concert cymbals, and applause.

The GS standard includes a number of recommendations for authoring compositions. Some of its recommendations have been incorporated in the authoring standards included in the MPC specification, the subject of the following section.

Working with MIDI Channels and the Multimedia Extensions

The Multimedia PC specification, like the General Synthesizer standard, extends the general MIDI mode specification by imposing restrictions on channel assignments. Fortunately for Windows multimedia users, the MPC specification and GS standards are quite similar and do not conflict with one another.

Neither MIDI Specification 1.0, the general MIDI mode specification, nor the GS standard specify what channels, other than channel 10, are to be used for what purposes, but the MPC specification does. The MPC specification reserves MIDI channels 1 through 9 for the 9 simultaneous multi-timbral melodic voices of extended-level audio adapter cards. Channel 10 is defined as a percussion track, both by the GM and the MPC standards. Channels 11 and 12 are defined as unused by MPC, but if your synthesizer has more than 9-note polyphony, you have no reason not to use these channels for your own purposes. You should not, however, use channels 11 and 12 for authoring MIDI files for distribution, because MPC audio adapter cards are allowed to disregard MIDI messages on MIDI channels 11 and 12. Channels 13 through 15 are used for the 3 simultaneous multi-timbral voices of base-level synthesizers, such as the original Ad Lib card, and channel 16 is for base-level percussion sounds.

MIDI Mapper Revisited

MIDI Mapper, which you probably used in Chapter 7 to help set up your sound card, enables you to specify source and destination data for any number of setups you choose. MIDI Mapper can be used with MIDI files not authored to the GM standards and MIDI devices not GM-compliant. Its purpose, however, is to map non-GM-compliant MIDI devices to the Windows implementation of the GM standard, accomplishing this through *setups*. A setup consists of the following components:

■ One *channel map* having up to 16 source entries corresponding to the 16 MIDI channels defined by the MIDI specification. These entries are mapped (assigned) to one of the 14 destination channels allocated to standard MPC adapter cards or the 16 channels of external MIDI instruments. If you have more than one board installed in your computer with MIDI capability, you can map source channels to each. The setup also designates the patch map to be used by each channel. The MIDI setup supplied with Windows 3.1 for the Roland LAPC-1, the predecessor of the SCC-1 GS Sound Card, appears in figure 10.6.

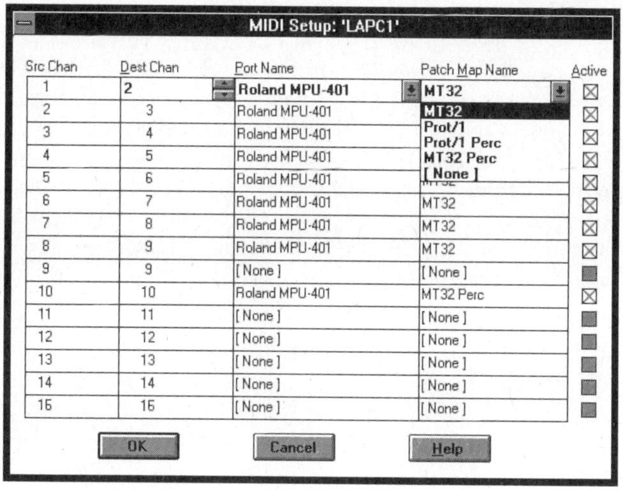

Src Chan	Dest Chan	Port Name	Patch Map Name	Active
1	2	Roland MPU-401	MT32	☒
2	3	Roland MPU-401	MT32	☒
3	4	Roland MPU-401	Prot/1 / Prot/1 Perc	☒
4	5	Roland MPU-401	MT32 Perc	☒
5	6	Roland MPU-401	[None]	☒
6	7	Roland MPU-401	MT32	☒
7	8	Roland MPU-401	MT32	☒
8	9	Roland MPU-401	MT32	☒
9	9	[None]	[None]	■
10	10	Roland MPU-401	MT32 Perc	☒
11	11	[None]	[None]	■
12	12	[None]	[None]	■
13	13	[None]	[None]	■
14	14	[None]	[None]	■
15	15	[None]	[None]	■

MIDI Setup: 'LAPC1'

OK   Cancel   Help

FIG. 10.6

MIDI Mapper's setup for the Roland LAPC-1 Sound Card.

■ Up to 16 *program change patch maps* (one for each channel) with a maximum of 128 individual program change patch entries per map. Figure 10.6 shows a patch map that processes MIDI Program Change and Volume Control messages for the Roland MT-32, which the LAPC-1 emulates.

■ Up to 2,048 *key maps* that provide note number mapping for each of 128 patch entries for the 16 allowable patch maps. These key maps are used for mapping standard percussion instruments' note numbers to those used by sound modules and drum machines that do not adhere to the general MIDI standards (most do not). You also can use key maps to shift the pitch of synthesizers that do not play middle C when you send them MIDI note number 60. Figure 10.6 displays a few of the entries applicable to the percussion voices of the MT-32 and LAPC-1. Key maps are optimal elements of program change patch maps.

Each of these maps is described in separate sections that follow.

Using the MIDI Channel Map

MIDI Mapper's channel maps serve two purposes: to assign the appropriate driver to the MIDI channels in use and to assign patch maps to each channel that requires one. Suppose, for instance, that you are using a Roland LAPC-1 synthesizer card or an MT-32 sound module connected to an MPU-401 adapter card and want to play standard MIDI files authored to the general MIDI standard. In this case, you must send the appropriate program changes to each voice to cause it to play the voice that most closely duplicates a standard general MIDI voice. (Creation of the program change patch maps to accomplish this task is discussed in the subsequent section, "Creating a MIDI Mapper Patch Map.")

You need to assign a separate program change patch map in the channel map for each non-GM synthesizer in use. If you have both an MT-32 and a Proteus/1 sound module, you might assign channels 11 through 16 to the Proteus/1. Then you would add the Proteus/1 patch map to channels 11 through 15 and the Proteus/1 percussion patch map to channel 16. If you are creating a patch map for a synthesizer for which Microsoft has not provided patch maps and key maps for percussion instruments, you have to create them in the reverse order: a key map first, then the melodic and percussive patch maps, then the setup.

The source and destination channel numbers of the LAPC-1 are offset by 1 so that the first channel of the LAPC-1, which reserves extra voices, is not used. You can choose to accept the default map as provided by Microsoft or reassign the first eight channel numbers without the offset by changing the destination channel numbers to equal the source channel numbers.

Using MIDI Map Setups with External Devices

The simplest method of connecting external MIDI devices, even if you have an audio adapter card with MIDI connectors, is to use a separate MPU-401-compatible MIDI adapter card. Most owners of computers and MIDI equipment have one of these cards installed. Unless you do not have an available adapter card slot to install a sound card, don't throw away your MPU-401.

You encounter a problem with most sound cards if you want to use their on-board synthesizer capabilities in conjunction with their MIDI outputs. You may want to create a setup similar to that shown in figure 10.7 in which your audio adapter card replaces the sound module of figure 10.1 at the beginning of this chapter.

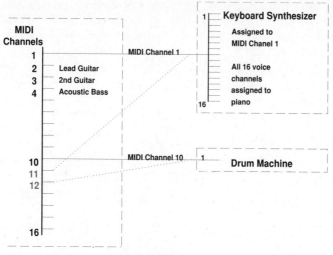

FIG. 10.7

Using the MIDI OUT connector of an audio adapter card with external MIDI synthesizers.

Suppose that you plan to use the audio adapter card to control your keyboard synth and drum machine. You also want to play standard MIDI files that were authored for figure 10.1's setup. Following are statements of the problems you face:

1. Your audio adapter card creates sounds on channels 1 through 16 when MIDI signals addressed to these channels, not just the extended channels 1 through 10, are received. Thus, it reproduces sounds in parallel with your outboard synth and drum machine, no matter what channels you assign to these devices. Because you want the card's audio output for the guitars and bass, you cannot just unplug its audio output cable from your amplifier or mixer.

2. If MPC-compatible sound cards truly adhered to MPC Specification 1.0, they would not play sounds addressed to MIDI channels 11 and 12. Such cards *might* pass MIDI signals for channels 11 and 12 to the MIDI OUT port. In this case, you could use these two channels for external devices, as shown by the dotted lines in figure 10.7. All the sound cards tested during the course of writing this book played sounds on all 16 channels.

3. You are in luck if your external devices enable you to program the Control Change messages to which the devices will respond. If your synthesizers can turn off their response (or not respond) to the Expression Control (Control Change 11) messages, for instance, you can set your sound card's Expression Control (if it recognizes this controller) to 0, turning the audio off on all channels but those

you want from the card. You then can control the relative volume of the external devices by their Main Volume Control (Control Change 7), the conventional control change used for setting channel volume.

4. If step 3 doesn't work for your setup, you must use a System Exclusive message to turn off the channels 1 and 10 of the synthesizer, but not the MIDI OUT signals. This step assumes that your card is capable of turning off its voices' response to Note On messages by a SysEx message and that your Windows sequencer can send SysEx messages. At the time this book was written, neither Passport Trax nor MusicTime possessed SysEx capability. All professional-level sequencers are capable of sending SysEx messages.

The procedure for accomplishing step 4 is discussed in Chapter 12 because the method for sending SysEx messages depends on the sequencer application you use. Commercial and shareware Windows applications that you can use to send the required SysEx messages to specific types of audio adapter cards also are described in that chapter. If one of these applications is available for your sound card, you may want to use it instead of writing your own SysEx messages.

The problem with the use of external MIDI devices could have been eliminated if the manufacturers of audio adapter cards had assigned the MIDI port to one device address and the internal synthesizer function to another, adjacent address. Because only one card is involved, and all messages to it are synchronized by the sequencer, the same interrupt level could be used for both the sequencer and the MIDI ports, but this design is not a necessity for 80x86 computers. Perhaps audio adapter card manufacturers will incorporate this feature in future designs so that sequencers can treat the synthesizer section as port 1 and the MIDI connections as port 2.

Creating a MIDI Mapper Patch Map

The Multimedia Extensions of Windows assign 128 standard melodic instrument patches, classified within 16 different instrument type groups. A total of 47 MIDI note numbers are assigned individually to particular types of drums. Both assignments are made in accordance with the MIDI Manufacturers Association's General MIDI mode specification and are listed in Appendix C.

You need to patch only those voices used by the files you want to play. Biting the bullet and patching all 128 general MIDI voices, however, is a good idea. Then you are not surprised when you play a file containing embedded program changes to an unpatched voice. A violin playing an electric guitar lead makes strange music.

Figure 10.8 shows an example of the patch map for the Roland MT-32.

Src Patch	Src Patch Name	Dest Patch	Volume %	Key Map Name
			MIDI Patch Map: 'MT32'	
		0 based patches		
1	Acoustic Grand Piano	1	100	[None]
2	Bright Acoustic Piano	2	100	[None]
3	Electric Grand Piano	4	100	[None]
4	Honky-tonk Piano	8	100	[None]
5	Rhodes Piano	6	100	[None]
6	Chorused Piano	7	100	[None]
7	Harpsichord	18	100	[None]
8	Clavinet	22	100	[None]
9	Celesta	23	100	[None]
10	Glockenspiel	102	100	[None]
11	Music Box	102	100	[None]
12	Vibraphone	99	100	[None]
13	Marimba	105	100	[None]
14	Xylophone	104	100	[None]
15	Tubular Bells	103	100	[None]
16	Dulcimer	106	100	[None]

OK   Cancel   Help

FIG. 10.8

The MIDI Mapper patch map for the Roland MT-32's melodic timbres.

The source patch is always the general MIDI voice number, but in the case of MIDI Mapper, numbering starts with 0 rather than 1 by default. Click the 1 Based Patches button to change the display to start with 1 if you prefer, to make the numbers correspond to those used by the GM voice assignment table of Appendix C. The documentation for the Roland LAPC-1 also uses 1-based patch numbers. The button's caption does not display what you are seeing. If you choose the button, the patch data does not change; only the display is altered. The destination patch is the voice number of your synthesizer to which the source patch voice number will be converted (mapped).

Notice that only the GM Acoustic Grand Piano shares the same voice number with the MT-32 or LAPC-1; the rest differ. The first group of voices on almost all modern synthesizers consists of pianos. The MT-32 and LAPC-1, which share the same set of voices, do not have all the sounds specified by the GM standard. Thus GM's Glockenspiel (10) and Music Box (11) are mapped to the MT-32/LAPC-1's Glockenspiel voice (102). If you scan through the remaining 118 voices with the vertical scroll bar button, you can see several instances of multi-mapped sounds.

To create a program change patch map for your outboard synthesizer, follow these steps:

1. Start the Control Panel from the Main group.

2. Load the MIDI Mapper applet from the Control Panel.

3. Choose the **P**atch Map option button; then choose **N**ew. The New MIDI Patch Map dialog box appears in which you can enter the name of the patch map and its description (see fig. 10.9).

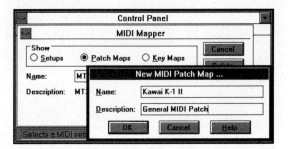

4. Give the patch map a name and description and then choose OK. Both names must fit in the text box, or they will be truncated.

   A patch map similar to that shown in figure 10.8 appears.

5. Refer to your synth's manual for the voice names and destination patch numbers. If the first voice is number 1, choose the 1 Based Patches button.

6. You can patch only those voices in the first voice bank (voices 0 to 127) of your synthesizer because MIDI Mapper does not provide a bank change option. Click the first destination patch window in the **D**est Patch window.

7. Two spin buttons appear in the destination patch area, as shown in figure 10.8. With these buttons, you can change the destination patch number from 0 to 127 or 1 to 128, depending on the setting of your patch base number. Choose the appropriate voice number for your synthesizer by clicking the "up" spin button.

8. Click the next destination patch window and repeat step 7 until you have assigned all the patches. You may have to guess at what your synthesizer might use for GM's "Fantasia" voice and other abstract voice names. The supplier of your synth may have created a list of voices that more or less correspond to GM voice names. Check with the supplier's technical-support department.

9. Repeat step 8 until you have assigned some destination patch, no matter how far off the mark, to each of the source patches.

10. Choose OK and then choose Yes to save your changes when you are asked whether you want to save the new patch map (see fig. 10.10).

FIG. 10.10

Deciding whether
to save your new
patch map.

Understanding Percussion Notes and MIDI Mapper Key Maps

Percussion sounds have been treated differently than melodic voices since the development of the first MIDI drum machine. Using individual MIDI channels to play different percussive voices would consume several of the 16 channels available. Because most drums, other than toms, bongos, congas, timbales, and timpani, do not have multiple pitches, the individual drum voices were assigned to different notes on the scale rather than to MIDI channels. Timpani, which can be tuned to various pitches, is assigned a range of notes, usually those corresponding to their actual pitch. Examples of notes corresponding to various types of drums are shown in figure 10.11. Conventional notation for rhythm parts would substitute appropriate symbols (crosses and so on) for the standard note heads shown.

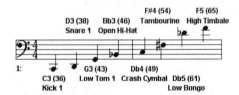

FIG. 10.11

Examples of general MIDI percussive voice note assignments.

Prior to the general MIDI standard, no convention existed for assigning percussive voices to particular notes. Synthesizer and drum machine manufacturers adopted whatever random patterns appealed to them. As with melodic voices, a drum part written for one drum machine or synthesizer would play differently, or perhaps not at all, through a device from a different manufacturer. MIDI Mapper provides a key map, shown in figure 10.12, to take care of this problem. The key map transposes individual notes corresponding to MIDI note numbers 27 through 88, the standard group of 46 percussive voices (Src Key), to the note numbers used by the drum machine or synthesizer (Dest Key) to play the same or related instruments.

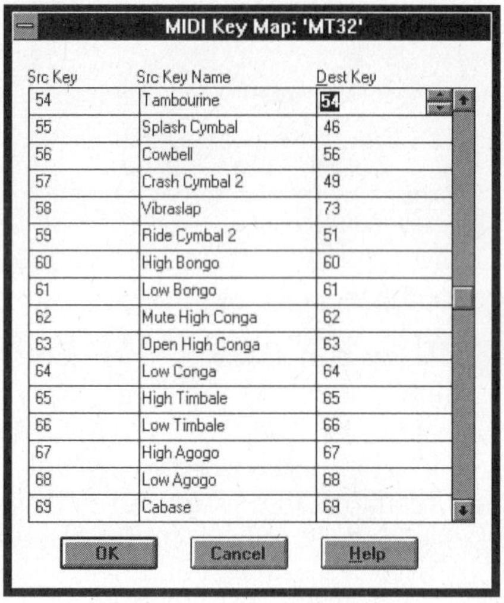

MIDI Key Map: 'MT32'		
Src Key	Src Key Name	Dest Key
54	Tambourine	54
55	Splash Cymbal	46
56	Cowbell	56
57	Crash Cymbal 2	49
58	Vibraslap	73
59	Ride Cymbal 2	51
60	High Bongo	60
61	Low Bongo	61
62	Mute High Conga	62
63	Open High Conga	63
64	Low Conga	64
65	High Timbale	65
66	Low Timbale	66
67	High Agogo	67
68	Low Agogo	68
69	Cabase	69

OK   Cancel   Help

FIG. 10.12

MIDI Mapper's key map for the percussion sounds of the Roland MT-32 and LAPC-1.

Notice that a closer correspondence exists between the source and destination patches for drum sounds than for melodic voices. The reason is that the note numbers adopted by the general MIDI specification were derived from those used by Roland in their percussion synthesizers.

The process of creating a key map is identical to that for creating a patch map, but you also must create a patch map to reference your key map. To do so, follow these steps:

1. Choose the **K**ey Map option button in MIDI Mapper's opening window, and then choose **N**ew.

2. Give your key map a name and description, and then choose OK.

3. For each source key not described as Reserved, assign the note number of your drum machine voice that corresponds to the source key name. You can choose note numbers between 0 and 127 with the spin buttons.

NOTE You are unlikely to have to guess at the correct patch for percussion instruments, but you may have to make substitutes for GM instruments not available from your drum machine.

4. Choose OK when you are finished, and choose to save your key map patch.

5. Create a percussion patch map, following the process outlined in the preceding section. Give the patch map a name and description that identifies it as a percussion patch.

6. In this case, you need to make only one patch entry for your key map. Choose the first Key **M**ap Name box and choose your key map name from the drop-down list box that appears.

7. Choose OK to close the Patch Map window.

The fact that suppliers of major sequencer applications have not provided an equivalent to MIDI Mapper's key map transposition capability is surprising. In the days before the multimedia extensions, you had to transpose manually each drum note number (fortunately, not each of the individual notes) to another within each sequence. A version of a key map built into the sequencer, with the capability to select key map files, would have been a boon to users of song files created by others.

Using Key Maps To Change Pitch

Key maps are useful if you have a synthesizer that does not play middle C when you send it MIDI note 60. Relatively few synthesizers fall into this category, because modern ones are reasonably well standardized as to MIDI note number versus pitch. If you have a synth or module that is an octave off, you can use one of the octave-shift key maps, such as +1 octave, shown in figure 10.13, to adjust the pitch. The Dest Key number is 12 greater than the Svc Key number because each octave contains 12 half tones.

Creating the New Setup

After you have created your melodic program change patch map and a key map and patch map for your drum machine or the percussion voices of your keyboard synthesizer, you have one more task to complete: creating the setup. To create the setup, follow these steps:

1. Choose the **S**etup option button in MIDI Mapper's main window.

2. Choose **N**ew to create a new setup.

3. Enter a short name for your setup, such as **K-1/RX-7**, and give the setup a description, such as **K-1 II Synth and RX-7 Drums**. Then choose OK.

4. Unless you have a compelling reason to map source channels to different destination channels, accept the default 1:1 channel mapping.

5. Choose the Port Name box and choose the driver for your MIDI adapter card from the installed drivers list.

6. Choose the Destination Patch Name box and choose the name of your synthesizer patch.

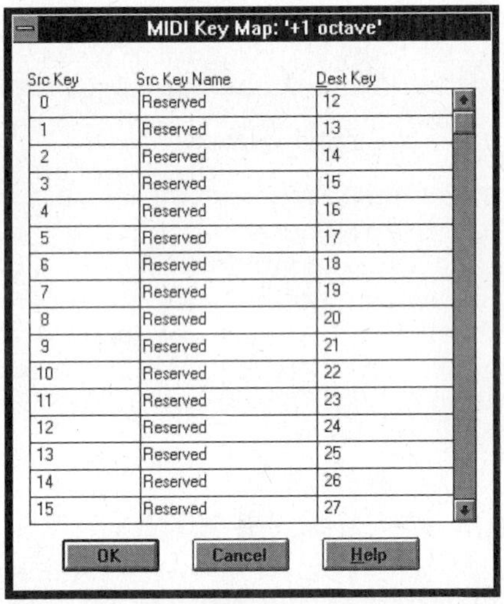

Src Key	Src Key Name	Dest Key
0	Reserved	12
1	Reserved	13
2	Reserved	14
3	Reserved	15
4	Reserved	16
5	Reserved	17
6	Reserved	18
7	Reserved	19
8	Reserved	20
9	Reserved	21
10	Reserved	22
11	Reserved	23
12	Reserved	24
13	Reserved	25
14	Reserved	26
15	Reserved	27

MIDI Key Map: '+1 octave'

OK   Cancel   Help

FIG. 10.13

A key map designed to increase the pitch of a synthesizer's voices by one octave.

7. Repeat steps 4 and 5 for channels 1 through 9.

8. If you want to create a non-MPC-standard patch, you can repeat steps 4 and 5 for channels 11 through 16. If you play files authored to the MPC standard, however, you probably will not like the result of doubling voices on channels 13 through 15 and percussion parts played on the melodic instrument assigned to channel 16.

9. Repeat step 4 for channel 10.

10. Choose the Patch Name box for channel 10 and choose the name of your percussion patch.

11. When you are finished, choose OK. The setup you just created is used by MIDI Mapper until you make a change.

T I P MIDI Mapper, in its present incarnation, is not a multitasking driver. You can use it with only one adapter card at a time. Most sequencers enable you to select MIDI Mapper as a MIDI input or output device or the driver for the sound card itself. In the latter case, you bypass MIDI Mapper. If you are using a sequencer application that enables you to use two or more MIDI ports, you cannot use MIDI Mapper for both ports. When you have Media Player in use, either maximized or minimized to an icon, with a MIDI file loaded, Media Player is using MIDI Mapper. Your sequencer cannot open it. Attempts to open multiple instances of MIDI Mapper are met with a Device in Use message box. You must close the conflicting application before MIDI Mapper can be available to your sequencer.

Looking at Standard MIDI Files

In the early days of MIDI, each sequencer application used its own proprietary format to store MIDI data as disk files. The only way you could transfer a sequence between two different sequencing applications was by using two computers. You had to cable the MIDI OUT connector of the computer with the originating application to the MIDI IN port of the computer with the receiving sequencer. Then you transferred the data by playing the sequence with the first computer and recording it with the second. As you might guess, this process was not very satisfactory.

The Standard MIDI File (SMF) specification was developed by David Oppenheim of Opcode Systems, a firm that specializes in musical applications for the Apple Macintosh. The specification was adopted in late 1988 by the MMA and is now supported by all commercial sequencer applications. Standard MIDI files, which almost always carry the extension *.MID, are now the standard for exchanging MIDI compositions between different sequencer file formats, as well as for distributing orchestrated music as commercial compositions. Most shareware and freeware compositions on electronic bulletin boards are available in *.MID format.

Standard MIDI files consist of "chunks" of data. Two types of chunks are presently in use: a *header* chunk at the beginning of the file that tells the sequencer what type of file it is, followed by one or more *track* chunks that incorporate the MIDI data. Each chunk has its own header that identifies the type of chunk and its length.

The Windows multimedia extensions enable you to read, create, edit, and save standard MIDI song files in two different formats, which are described in the following section. Most sequencers have retained their own proprietary file formats optimized for use with the routines incorporated in the application. When you load a MIDI file, the sequencer converts the file into data in its specific format. You then can save the file in the sequencer's format for quicker loading or as an SMF for interchangeability.

Examining Type 0 and Type 1 MIDI Song Files

Three standard MIDI song file types exist: 0, 1, and 2. The type 0 and 1 files are the most common, however, and are the only formats supported by the Multimedia Extensions. Type 0 files contain the MIDI data for all tracks in a single track chunk, and type 1 files use a separate chunk for each track. The tempo information in a type 1 file is always contained in the first track, which must be equal to or greater than the length of any other track.

The Multimedia Extensions documentation recommends that MIDI files for multimedia titles be stored as type 0 to conserve memory and minimize delays caused by CD-ROM seek operations. If you anticipate that the users of your MIDI files will want to look at them or modify them in any way, distribute them as type 1 files. The appearance of a portion of CANYON.MID in figure 10.14 shows what a musical mess a type 0 file can be when viewed in a Cakewalk Professional for Windows notation window.

T I P Save your compositions in type 1 format; then consider carefully whether you want to use type 0 files for distribution. Type 1 files can be converted to format 0 by some but not many Windows sequencer applications. Midisoft Studio for Windows is one of the few Windows sequencers that enable you to save files in type 0 format. The reverse process, conversion from type 0 to type 1, requires a great deal of work with your sequencer application. Files that you distribute with the intention that others should be able to view and modify them should always be supplied in type 1 format.

Cakewalk's MIDI Event List window in figure 10.15 shows only a portion of the note messages destined for five different MIDI channels during the first beat of measure 39 of CANYON.MID. The only method you can use to sort out what notes of figure 10.14 are played by a specific instrument is to refer to the MIDI event list.

FIG. 10.14

Two bars of the Windows MIDI type 0 file, CANYON.MID.

Understanding the Dual Composition Version Requirement for MPC Compliance

When you create or edit MIDI compositions for your own entertainment, you can assign voices to any channel you want by using an appropriate patch. If you plan to distribute a multimedia title or presentation, you must adhere to the MME authoring standards. This step assures that your composition will play the sounds you specify on any MPC-compatible computer.

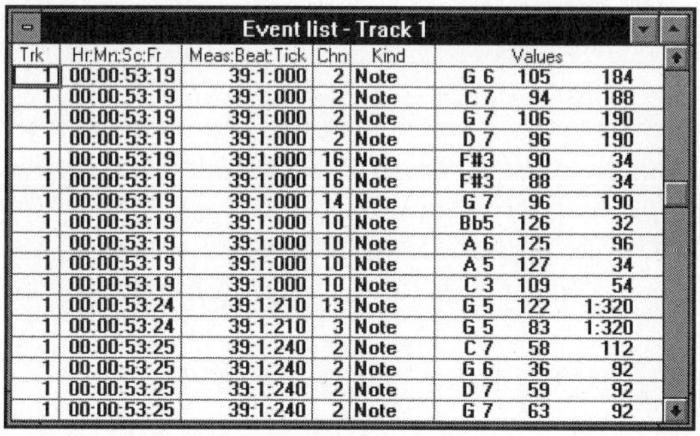

Trk	Hr:Mn:Sc:Fr	Meas:Beat:Tick	Chn	Kind	Values		
1	00:00:53:19	39:1:000	2	Note	G 6	105	184
1	00:00:53:19	39:1:000	2	Note	C 7	94	188
1	00:00:53:19	39:1:000	2	Note	G 7	106	190
1	00:00:53:19	39:1:000	2	Note	D 7	96	190
1	00:00:53:19	39:1:000	16	Note	F#3	90	34
1	00:00:53:19	39:1:000	16	Note	F#3	88	34
1	00:00:53:19	39:1:000	14	Note	G 7	96	190
1	00:00:53:19	39:1:000	10	Note	Bb5	126	32
1	00:00:53:19	39:1:000	10	Note	A 6	125	96
1	00:00:53:19	39:1:000	10	Note	A 5	127	34
1	00:00:53:19	39:1:000	10	Note	C 3	109	54
1	00:00:53:24	39:1:210	13	Note	G 5	122	1:320
1	00:00:53:24	39:1:210	3	Note	G 5	83	1:320
1	00:00:53:25	39:1:240	2	Note	C 7	58	112
1	00:00:53:25	39:1:240	2	Note	G 6	36	92
1	00:00:53:25	39:1:240	2	Note	D 7	59	92
1	00:00:53:25	39:1:240	2	Note	G 7	63	92

Event list - Track 1

FIG. 10.15

A portion of the MIDI messages occurring in the track chunk of CANYON.MID at beat 1 of measure 39.

The Windows Multimedia Extensions standards require that MIDI files created for use with MPCs be authored in two versions within a single file—one for the base synthesizer type (MIDI channels 13 through 16) and another for extended synthesizers (MIDI channels 1 through 10). This requirement is designed to assure compatibility with adapter cards that provide only minimum-standard MIDI capabilities. The MPC specification does not require that audio adapter cards play channels 11 and 12, so some may mute these channels.

MIDI musical compositions for distribution should be thoroughly auditioned on a minimum-standard MPC card prior to mastering, especially if you have created them by using a sophisticated MPC card or your own MIDI setup. You may need to change the balance among voices when playing a composition on a single-channel (monaural) MPC card, compared with one having 16-voice or 32-voice multi-timbral capabilities. You also may find that minimum-standard boards are not capable of playing complex piano or guitar chords, so your music will have to be rewritten to reduce the number of simultaneous notes on channels 13 through 16.

Understanding Standard MIDI File Meta Events

Standard MIDI files provide for non-MIDI information stored in a type of chunk called a *meta event*. The standard MIDI file specification defines a number of specific types of meta events as containing text information, such as lyrics, copyright notices, and the like. Most sequencers recognize some meta events, such as the Sequence/Track Name event and the End of Track event (which is required), but few handle them all.

The SMF specification provides for sequencer-specific meta events in which any type of data can be inserted. Cakewalk Professional for Windows, for instance, enables you to embed waveform audio data from the Clipboard or from prerecorded files in a Sequencer-Specific event. You also can embed Windows's Media Control Interface (MCI) instructions to load and play waveform audio files or even audio CD tracks in conjunction with your MIDI music. Other professional-grade sequencer suppliers are likely to follow Twelve-Tone Systems's lead and add these and other multimedia-specific meta event capabilities to their products.

Learning about Additional MIDI File Authoring Recommendations

Roland Corporation has issued a set of recommendations for authoring files compatible with its General Synthesizer standard. Many of these recommendations, such as backing a presentation distributed on floppy disk with MIDI rather than waveform audio files, are also applicable to files created for MPC audio card playback. Some of the recommendations contain amplifications related to the MPC specification not included in the Roland document from which they were derived. The following paragraphs describe these authoring recommendations.

1. Avoid program change patches in the body of the music. If you include them, users who want to try new voices will find their choices overridden. Using the Rewind and Fast Forward controls may cause such patches to behave erratically.

2. Adjust the dynamic volume (crescendo and diminuendo) of tracks assigned to channels 1 through 10 with the Expression Control change, not Main Volume. Users then can adjust the main volume to control relative volume. Main volume is used with tracks 13 through 15 because most base-level synthesizers do not support the Expression Control.

3. Use 96 ticks per quarter note as the timing resolution. This value should not overtax slower computers and provides adequate timing for most compositions. Remember that some users may play your compositions with Thunder Boards or original Sound Blasters on 4.77-Mhz 8088-based PCs.

4. Minimize the number of events in pitch bends (continuous changes of pitch for the instrument on a single track) to a number that provides an acceptable slide effect. Continuous bends generate hundreds of MIDI messages. Pitch bend techniques are described in Chapter 12.

5. Assign only one track to a channel, if practical for the composition. If you have enough MIDI channels available, keep the left- and right-hand parts on separate channels, each assigned to the piano voice.

6. When creating type 1 files, make sure that your first track is as long as or longer than (preferably by one measure) any other track in your sequence.

7. Avoid the use of System Exclusive messages for significant elements of your composition because these messages are device-specific.

Examining the MIDI Machine Control Specification

The MIDI Machine Control (MMC) specification, adopted in early 1992, further defines the MTC cuing messages and determines how devices should respond to them. In this respect, it is quite similar to the Media Control Interface commands of Windows' multimedia extensions. The MCI commands now provide for the control of audio mixers built into MPC-compatible audio adapter cards and for selecting tracks when playing audio CDs video laserdiscs. A typical setup using an MMC-compatible mixer and multi-track tape recorder appears in figure 10.16. MIDI cables are shown as solid lines, and audio cabling is depicted by dashed lines.

When MMC is fully implemented by suppliers of MIDI accessory hardware, your MIDI adapter card may be able to take the place of devices such as Sony's VBox controller for video equipment. The VBox, described in Chapter 22, is similar in function to a MIDI adapter card except that the VBox connects to one of your computer's serial ports instead of plugging into the computer's bus. The appearance of MMC equivalents of breakout boxes in the near future would not be surprising. These would have MMC-compatible MIDI IN ports and would issue commands based on MMC messages to remotely controllable outboard mixers, multi-track audio tape recorders, DATs, VCRs, camcorders, and other audio-visual equipment.

 NOTE A related specification, MIDI Show Control (MSC), provides control of stage lighting and other special effects by MIDI messages. Because MSC is predominantly oriented to rock concert light-show productions, it is not covered in this book.

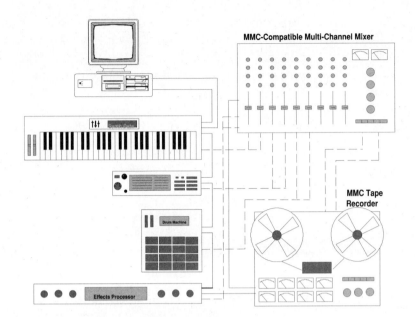

FIG. 10.16

MIDI Machine Control applied to a multi-channel mixer and reel-to-reel tape recorder.

Chapter Summary

You will find that your foundation in the principles of the Musical Instrument Digital Interface presented in this chapter will be useful, whether you intend to write your own MIDI compositions, use prerecorded MIDI tracks, or have a professional musician prepare them for your presentations or titles. A working knowledge of the MIDI specification and how it is implemented by sound cards and outboard devices alike is critical to implementing MIDI sequences properly in your multimedia projects.

The remaining chapters of Part III of this book take up commercial implementations of the MIDI standard in both hardware and software. The basic MIDI components, keyboard synthesizers, and sound modules are covered in detail in Chapter 9. If you are musically inclined and don't have a keyboard synthesizer now, you may want to go to your local music store and try out a few different ones. Street prices start below $300 for consumer-oriented types with MIDI capability.

Other MIDI devices, such as master keyboards, digital effects processors, patch bays, mixers, and tape recorders are described in Chapter 11. Chapter 12 completes the section on basic MIDI operations with a description of the professional-level Windows sequencer applications that came into the market as new or improved products after Windows 3.1 was released. MIDI and video synchronization techniques are covered in Chapter 21.

Accessories for MIDI Systems

A wide range of specialty and accessory products is available to aid in creating MIDI-based compositions. You may never require anything but your audio adapter card to add background music to presentations. For more sophisticated multimedia productions, however, you may hire a professional musician to compose your background music or use a sound studio to produce your audio tracks. In this situation, you probably will use one or more of the MIDI accessory components described in this chapter.

The overwhelming acceptance of the MIDI standard has created a significant market for almost any type of MIDI-compatible accessory you can imagine. This chapter provides an overview of some common MIDI accessory products and what these products can add to your multimedia production or to your enjoyment of a MIDI-based musical performance. A brief description of the MIDI hardware required to synchronize the operation of sequencer applications with audio and video tape recorders is included. Sequencer applications are described in the next chapter.

MIDI Keyboards

Whether you are an accomplished pianist or keyboard beginner, the first MIDI accessory you need to accompany your audio adapter card is a MIDI-equipped keyboard. MIDI keyboards range from the bare minimum

49 keys offered by Software Toolwork's Miracle synthesizer and the Roland PC-200 to fully weighted 88-key professional keyboards. If you have a consumer-level keyboard synthesizer that has a MIDI OUT connector, you can use its keyboard to send MIDI signals to your sound card's MIDI IN port and record your performances. The MPU-401 has a built-in metronome to help you keep the beat while recording. Most new Windows sequencer applications can synthesize a metronome's clicks on one channel of your audio adapter card.

Roland's PC-200, shown in figure 11.1, is an example of a moderately priced, consumer-grade, 49-key keyboard-only device. The PC-200 is designed to complement the firm's Sound Canvas product line, which includes the SCC-1 GS sound card. The PC-200 provides some of the capabilities of professional-level devices, such as the ability to split the keyboard so that you can play one instrument voice with the left hand and another with the right. Like all other MIDI keyboards, the PC-200 can send MIDI Program Change messages to your adapter card to choose the desired voice. The price of the PC-200 is about $300 at most music stores. A lower-cost, battery-operated version is available as the PC-100 MIDI Data Keyboard.

FIG. 11.1

The Roland PC-200 49-key MIDI keyboard. *(Courtesy of Roland Corporation US)*

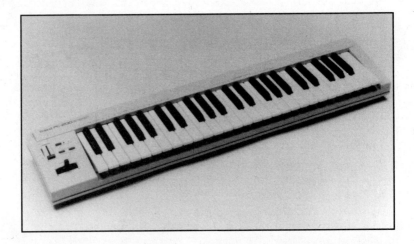

Professional 88-key MIDI keyboards range in price from about $1,000 to more than $3,000, depending on the quality of their action and the additional features offered. If you're willing to settle for fewer than 88 keys, 61-key synthesizers that cover a five-octave range are available for about the same price as a keyboard-only device with similar range. If you have a piano whose action suits you perfectly, you can add a Gulbransen sensor strip under the keyboard. Upright and grand pianos with MIDI are available in the Yamaha Disklavier product line. Prices range from about $7,500 for an upright version to more than $40,000 for a Disklavier grand.

Connecting the keyboard to your audio adapter card is as simple as connecting a MIDI cable from the keyboard's MIDI OUT connector to the card's MIDI IN connector. If you're using an external sound module, some sequencers can echo MIDI IN messages to the MIDI OUT port. Turtle Beach's MIDI Patch Bay application for the MultiSound card, discussed later in this chapter, enables you to connect MIDI IN or your sequencer output to MIDI THRU, an even more versatile arrangement. Either approach eliminates changing MIDI cabling when using an external sound module with a MIDI keyboard.

MIDI Instruments and Pickups

The keyboard is the primary MIDI input device for live performances and recording musical input. A wide range of other instruments also can generate MIDI signals for recording performances or driving special sound modules. The more popular types of commercial instruments are described in this section. You also can get MIDI versions of violins and banjos, as well as "MIDI-ized" exotica—such as sitars, kotos, and samisens.

Guitar Pickups and Synthesizers

The popularity of acoustic and electric guitars has created a market for MIDI synthesizers that respond to plucked strings rather than pressed keys on a piano-style keyboard. Guitar synthesizers have two basic elements: a MIDI pickup that mounts under the strings and a conversion box. The box contains the electronic circuitry necessary to convert the MIDI pickup's electrical signals to conventional MIDI Note On and Note Off signals that your adapter card can understand.

The MIDI pickup is similar to the conventional variable-reluctance pickups used with electric guitars. If you connect an E-mu Proteus/3 World sound module to the box's MIDI OUT, your guitar can imitate an Indonesian gamelan or the didjeridu—an Australian aboriginal instrument with a unique drone.

A typical pickup/synthesizer package, the Roland GK-2/GR-50, is shown in figure 11.2. The GK-2 Driver is a combination pickup and control device that you mount behind the existing pickups, next to the whammy (tremolo) bar. The GK-2 senses string movement and sends its signals— along with the output of the conventional pickups—to the GR-50 Synthesizer. To provide fast response, special circuitry in the GR-50 measures the wavelength, rather than the frequency, of the sound from each string.

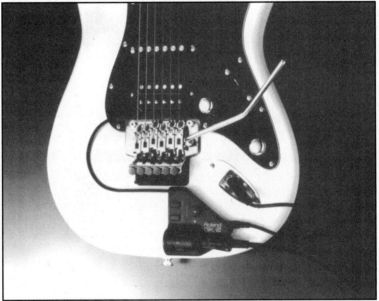

FIG. 11.2

The Roland GK-2
Driver and GR-50
Guitar Synthesizer.
(Courtesy of Roland
Corporation US)

MIDI Note On and Note Off signals are created for abrupt changes in pitch; pitch modulation signals are generated to follow complex bends. The intensity of the sound of each string determines the Note On velocity. You can assign each of the six strings to an individual MIDI channel in Mono mode or combine all six on a single channel using Poly mode. The GR-50 provides up to two tones per string for 12-voice polyphony.

In addition to giving guitarists the ability to play a flute on the first string and timpani on the sixth, MIDI guitar pickups enable you to record your licks with a sequencer. Rock guitar compositions are difficult to transcribe by analyzing taped sessions and then entering notes in a sequencer's step editor. A guitar pickup usually is the answer if you want to save that particularly good lick for later analysis or incorporation in another tune.

Breath-Actuated Instruments

Woodwind players have not been forgotten in the MIDI instrument market, despite the emphasis on stringed instruments. Yamaha's WX11 Wind MIDI Controller and WT11 Wind Tone Generator (fig. 11.3) combine to produce digital FM simulations of many brasses and strings and all single- and double-reed instruments.

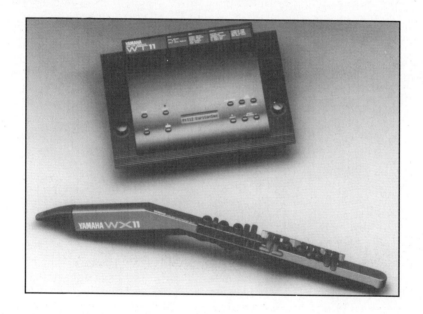

FIG. 11.3

The Yamaha WX11/
WT11 Wind MIDI
System. (Courtesy of
Yamaha Corporation
of America)

The fingering of the WX11 is based on the clarinet. Additional key combinations enable you to cover a seven-octave range. Loudness and timbre are determined by how hard you blow into the single-reed mouthpiece. Lip pressure on the mouthpiece adds pitch changes and vibrato—the same method used when playing an acoustic clarinet or saxophone. Unlike the real instruments, you can play more than one note at a time—the WT11 offers eight-note polyphony. Automatic trill keys make playing half- and full-step trills easier. The WT11 includes a variety of digital effects, including reverb, echo, delay, and distortion.

During the early days of MIDI, a variety of breath-actuated instruments—classed as MIDI wind controllers—were produced by several suppliers. Akai Professional's EVI1000, which used a three-valve mechanism of a trumpet, is an example. You bite the EVI1000's mouthpiece to simulate the slide of a trombone. The EWI1000 electronic woodwind is fingered like a saxophone, rather than a clarinet. MIDI wind controllers never achieved the popularity of their keyboard counterparts; today you seldom see a wind controller at your local music store.

Pitch-to-MIDI Converters

Pitch-to-MIDI converters have been around almost as long as MIDI itself. These devices are similar to guitar pickups but are limited to translating only one note at a time in Mono mode. A contact-type sensor and a microphone are provided with Roland's CP-40, a consumer-grade pitch-to-MIDI converter shown in figure 11.4. The CP-40 converter enables your voice to control a synthesizer or record performances from brass, woodwind, or string instruments (including guitars) with a sequencer application. A pitch-to-MIDI converter is an excellent training device because you can see immediately if you're singing or playing on key.

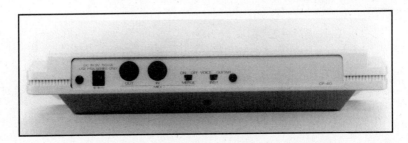

FIG. 11.4

The Roland CP-40 Pitch-to-MIDI Controller. (Courtesy of Roland Corporation US)

The SynchroVoice MIDIVox is a more sophisticated pitch-to-MIDI converter designed for vocals only. With the MIDIVox, the singer wears a collar that positions extremely sensitive pressure transducers in strategic locations to detect vocal cord movement in the throat. Data from the pressure sensors is sent to a small box that outputs a stream of MIDI signals to drive a synthesizer that simulates a harmonizing backup group. The DigiTech Vocalist is an example of this synthesizer.

Harmony Processor

DigiTech has created a voice synthesizer called the Vocalist, which is designed to add backup harmonies to vocals (see fig. 11.5). You can sing into a microphone connected to the Vocalist's input and have the Beach

Boys back you up with 1960s surfing sounds. The collection of preset harmonic types ranges from the Beach Boys to Four Freshmen, Henry Mancini, gospel music, and even barbershop quartets.

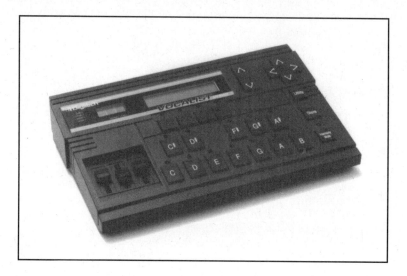

FIG. 11.5

DigiTech's Vocalist, a MIDI harmony processor. *(Courtesy of DigiTech)*

A principal feature of the Vocalist is its ability to compensate for significantly off-key voices. On the other hand, very few human vocalists can sing exactly on key. So the Vocalist also includes a pitch randomize function and provides a chorus effect by slightly shifting the pitch of the harmonized notes. It also controls vibrato and portamento timing—the rate at which the harmony glides (slurs) from one note to another. MIDI signals control the type of harmony produced, along with a wide range of other adjustments to create different harmonic effects.

MIDI Drum Controller

The MIDI drum machines described in Chapter 10—especially those with "humanizing" capabilities—can provide a basic rhythmic background for your music. You can either use their internal song patterns or sequence drum parts yourself. If you want your music to sound like a live performance, however, you need a live drummer. MIDI drum kits consist of a set of pressure-sensitive pads you play with standard drumsticks and foot pedals. These kits create MIDI Note On and Note Off signals that you can send to a drum machine to simulate any drum kit you choose. A typical MIDI drum controller is KAT, Inc.'s drumKAT.

The drumKAT has 10 rubber pads, each with a sensor that measures the impact with which the pad is struck. You can combine the drumKAT controller with foot switches that simulate those used with acoustic hi-hats and bass drums. In the normal operating mode, each pad transmits a MIDI Note On signal corresponding to the MIDI Note Number of the percussion instrument to which the pad is assigned. Each pad has an adjustable time period before the Note Off signal is sent, so you can simulate an open hi-hat or cymbal. The sounds from these instruments may be audible for a few seconds after striking them. You also can assign the left and right halves of the controller to separate MIDI OUT ports.

MIDI Effects Processors

Low-cost sound modules and audio adapter cards—such as the Roland Sound Canvas and SCC-1—also provide digital effects to improve the realism of the sound they create. The digital effects included in the Korg 03R/W General MIDI synthesizer described in the preceding chapter are quite impressive. All sound studios and most serious MIDI musicians, however, use a dedicated, MIDI-controlled effects processor to add or subtract realism in the finished product. Studio effects processors cost several thousand dollars. Stereo effects processors with adequate frequency response and distortion specifications, however, are available with list prices under $500.

Effects processors use digital signal processor (DSP) chips, combined with 16-bit ADCs, to convert analog audio to digital form and DACs to convert the digital data back to analog signals for recording. Except for the DSP, the components are similar to those used by 16-bit MPC-compliant audio adapter cards for waveform audio processing. The Alesis QuadraVerb is a popular MIDI-programmable effects processor (see fig. 11.6). This processor handles signals ranging from 16 Hz to 20 kHz with a total harmonic distortion of about 0.1 percent or less and a dynamic range of 85 dB.

The digital effects available from the QuadraVerb and other moderately priced effects processors fall into the following classes:

- *Reverberation* adds a controlled echo effect to the sound that simulates the acoustic reflections in different environments, called *rooms*. Reverb effects that simulate those once produced by various combinations of mechanical plates and springs also are provided.

- *Delay* uses internal memory to store a sliding sample of the sound in a first-in-first-out (FIFO) buffer memory. The maximum delay is a function of the sampling rate and the memory available. The QuadraVerb provides a maximum delay of 1.5 seconds.

FIG. 11.6

The Alesis QuadraVerb, a MIDI-programmable digital effects processor. (Courtesy of Alesis Corporation)

■ *Chorus* is similar to reverberation in that it adds copies of the sound, usually shifted slightly in pitch by detuning. Chorus effects can take the sound of a violin and make it sound like an entire string section is playing.

■ *Flanging* is similar to chorus, except that a delay is introduced in the process.

■ *Stereo pan* causes monaural sound to appear to move from left to right, or vice versa, when played through a stereo sound system.

■ *Rotating speaker* effect is similar to stereo pan, but occurs at a much faster rate. This replaces speakers, mounted on motor-driven turntables, that adorned older electronic organs.

■ *Phasing* changes the phase relationship of stereo signals by delaying one channel with respect to the other. Changes of less than 180 degrees in the phase of stereo signals can be used to cause the apparent source of the sound to change position without changing its volume.

■ *Pitch detuning* adjusts the frequency of the incoming sound by a specific percentage of a whole-tone step.

■ *Equalization* is used to emphasize or de-emphasize a particular band of frequencies in the source signal. *Parametric equalization* and *resonators* are special types of equalization; resonators emphasize heavily a specific frequency in the sound.

■ *Distortion* effects modulate the incoming sound to create the sometimes bizarre sounds created by rock guitarists. Distortion also can be introduced by clipping the tops of the sound signals to create trapezoidal-shaped or almost-square waves.

Like most digital effects processors, the QuadraVerb enables you to combine the basic effects in series with one another to generate multiple effects. You can combine stereo pan with chorus or flanging, reverberation, delay, and equalization for a total of five effects in series.

Digital effects processors can be used to add effects to the mixed audio signal. Usually, however, you use one effects processor per instrument or section, recorded on one track of a multi-track tape. Adding effects in the mixing process is discussed in "Multichannel Audio Mixers," later in this chapter.

MIDI Signals

The concept of daisy-chaining MIDI instruments is simple in theory. But you can rapidly run out of the right combination of MIDI IN and OUT ports when you begin to connect multiple keyboard synthesizers, sound modules, a few effects processors, a drum machine, and MIDI-controlled mixer and tape recorder. Theoretically, the number of instruments in a MIDI daisy chain has no limit.

Timing delays caused by the optical isolators between the MIDI IN and MIDI THRU ports of devices can become significant, however. Changing cabling configurations from recording to playback mode can take a substantial amount of time when many devices are involved. Therefore, a group of devices classified as *MIDI signal managers* has come into common usage, especially in MIDI sound studios.

MIDI THRU Boxes and Mergers

MIDI THRU boxes are the simplest MIDI accessories you can buy. A MIDI THRU box simply takes one MIDI IN signal and duplicates it at multiple MIDI THRU connectors. The signal may come from the MIDI OUT connector of your audio adapter card's MIDI breakout cable, for example. The MIDI THRU box also electrically isolates the signal to eliminate ground loops and other noise. A 1:4 MIDI THRU box is diagrammed on the left in figure 11.7. Without exceeding the generally accepted limit of four MIDI devices per MIDI-IN-to-MIDI-THRU chain, the four MIDI THRUs in the box enable you to connect the following:

> Eight sound modules
> Five effects processors
> A drum machine
> A MIDI-controlled mixer
> A tape recorder

The opposite of a MIDI THRU box is a MIDI merger, represented by the right diagram of figure 11.7. The MIDI merger has multiple MIDI IN ports and combines (*merges*) the signals into one MIDI OUT port. In this case, however, you need some electronic circuitry in addition to the isolators in the box. You have no guarantee that two MIDI signals will not arrive at the same time.

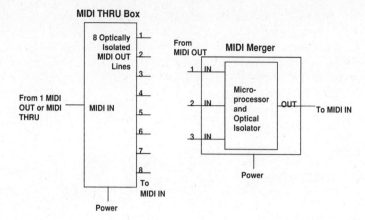

FIG. 11.7

Block diagrams of a
MIDI THRU box and
a MIDI merger.

MIDI mergers are used when you are recording MIDI signals originating from members of a group, perhaps consisting of a keyboard synth, MIDI guitar, MIDI bass, and MIDI drum controller. If the group was playing exactly on the beat, you would receive MIDI Note On messages from every member's instrument at once. MIDI mergers delay MIDI messages that appear simultaneously until a pause in the message stream occurs. MIDI mergers often include small microprocessors. The process is more efficient if the merger is smart enough to collect an entire MIDI message and pass it as a single group when no other messages are being sent.

MIDI Patchbays

The process of disconnecting and reconnecting MIDI cables to create different combinations of keyboards, sound modules, effects processors, and other MIDI devices takes valuable studio time and is prone to setup errors. In addition, you ultimately wear out your devices' MIDI connectors if you repeat the process often enough.

MIDI patchbays enable you to connect the MIDI OUT or MIDI THRU port of any device to any other device's MIDI IN port. Large patchbays, combined with a sufficiently large MIDI merger, enable all equipment in a studio to be connected permanently to the patchbay. MIDI signals control the connections by devices, usually by sending a control change message to the patchbay that selects one of 64 or more different connection patterns. A typical MIDI patchbay is diagrammed in figure 11.8.

Turtle Beach Systems implemented a small-scale version of a MIDI patchbay in the application software provided with the MultiSound audio adapter card. The MultiSound patchbay enables you to connect the MIDI input connector of the card to the synthesizer section of the card, directly to the input of your sequencer, to the MIDI THRU port, or to all three. You select from the check box shown in the External Connector frame at the upper left of figure 11.9. You can connect similarly the MIDI OUT port to the synthesizer output or to your sequencer's output. This enables you to bypass the Proteus/1 sounds when you don't need them.

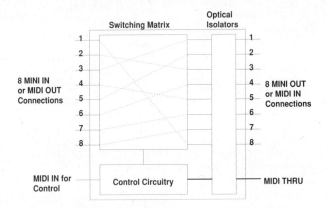

FIG. 11.8

A block diagram of a typical MIDI patchbay.

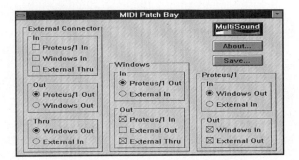

FIG. 11.9

Turtle Beach Systems' MIDI Patch Bay dialog box.

The Audio Side of MIDI

Up to this point, the discussion of MIDI accessory devices has focused on digital MIDI signals. Ultimately, however, you must create the final product: a digital or analog sound recording. The equipment used on the audio side of the MIDI equation becomes involved when you work with a MIDI production studio or establish a semi-professional music production facility. This audio side includes multi-channel mixers, multi-track tape recorders (both controlled by MIDI), and the synchronization of the MIDI signals with the sound on the tapes you create. If you plan to use only the mixer included on your audio adapter card and to record MIDI music directly to *.WAV files on your hard disk drive, you may want to skip this section.

Multi-Channel Audio Mixers

Multi-channel audio mixers control the relative volume of sound originating from a variety of sources, ranging from multi-track audio tape recorders to microphones and instrument pickups at live performances. Studio-grade mixers may have 64 or more individual mixing input channels; those designed for industrial and home studio use usually provide 8 to 16 inputs. Mixers are designed to combine groups of individual audio inputs into blended output signals. The input groups are organized in pairs for stereo recording. The number of outputs—called *stereo busses*—usually corresponds to the number of tracks of the multi-track audio tape recorder.

If the two basic stereo input channels of your audio adapter card's mixer—line (or aux) and microphone—don't meet your audio requirements, you need a multi-channel audio mixer. The Mackie 1604 (see fig. 11.10) is a popular, moderately priced mixer with 16 inputs and three pairs of mixed stereo outputs—main left/right, alternate left/right, and solo left/right. Six of the input channels have microphone preamplifiers with balanced XLR connections; the remaining 10 channels have line-level inputs. Phantom power for condenser microphones is provided. Each channel has a fader, solo, and mute switch, three-band equalizer, and a complete set of controls for six auxiliary output lines (called *aux sends*).

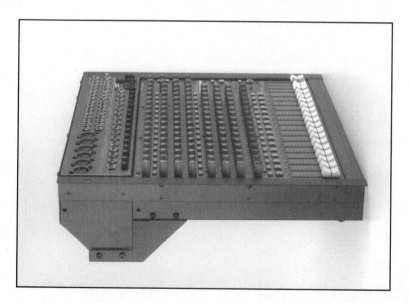

FIG. 11.10

The Mackie 1604, a 16-channel stereo audio mixer. (Courtesy of Mackie Designs, Inc.)

The Mackie 1604 provides a frequency response of 20 Hz to 20 kHz +/– 1 dB, has less than 0.025% total distortion over this frequency range, and has a 90 dB signal-to-noise ratio. The dynamic range of 108 dB provides increased *headroom* to accommodate the occasional peaks that exceed the rated level of the inputs. A block diagram of a typical multi-channel audio mixer, based on the Mackie 1604, appears in figure 11.11.

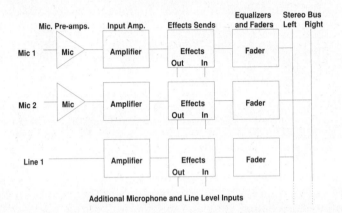

FIG. 11.11

Block diagram of a typical multi-channel audio mixer.

Mackie supplies an add-on board that provides MIDI control of the 16 input faders, two master faders, and the four stereo aux returns. MIDI control enables you to program levels and fades with your sequencer. Depending on the Windows sequencer application used, you can store a variety of mixer settings and call them with a single command. The Mackie model 1202, a smaller 12-channel mixer with a single stereo output and two aux sends, has a list price of less than $400.

T I P   A second MIDI output port should be used when you are controlling mixers with MIDI signals. Fades may consist of a very long series of MIDI Control Change messages that must be precisely spaced in time to assure a smooth transition between the two volume levels. Intermixing MIDI Note On and Note Off or pitch bend messages with the fader messages causes delays that can be audible in the final mix.

Multi-Track Analog Audio Tape Recorders

The final product of a recording session at a MIDI studio is a reel of multi-track audio tape on which the final mix is recorded. The final mix for an audio CD or a videotape consists of the left and right sound tracks, plus one track with SMPTE timing (synchronization or sync) signals recorded on it. The synchronization signals are required so that you can find a particular spot in the sound track quickly if your tape player has sync search capability. Tape synchronization with MIDI signals is discussed at the end of this chapter.

When combining narration and music, record them on a separate pair of tracks. Then you can control the relative volume level of music and voice when you create the final waveform audio file for a CD-ROM. One-inch 24-track and 1/2-inch 16-track recorders are the most common. The remaining tracks hold the original components of the mix—you can re-create a different final mix if necessary. Open-reel multi-track recorders using Dolby Laboratories S or SR (Spectral Recording) circuitry achieve noise and frequency response similar to or better than that provided by digital audio tape (DAT) and audio CDs.

Multi-Track Audio Cassette Tape Decks

Professional-grade open-reel (also called reel-to-reel) multi-track audio tape recorders cost in the $10,000-and-up range. Therefore, they are not commonly found in home recording studios or alongside PCs used to create multimedia presentations or CD-ROM titles.

Fortunately, multi-channel tape recorders that use high-quality compact audio cassettes as the recording medium are available at prices well below $1,000. Most of these recorders have self-contained mixers that provide a total of six or eight inputs. Half of those outputs can accept low-level inputs from professional-quality microphones equipped with XLR connectors. Tape speed is usually 3-3/4 inches per second, twice the standard compact cassette tape speed of 1-7/8 inches per second. MIDI control by Program Change or SysEx messages is an extra-cost option for most products.

The Fostex 280 Multitracker is typical of moderately priced audio cassette recorders that offer optional MIDI control of the transport functions (play, record, stop, fast forward, and rewind). Multi-track audio cassette recorders in the lower price ranges use a tape position counter, rather than a fifth (synchronization) track, to position the tape at a predetermined location.

Because tape has a tendency to stretch, position counters based on tape footage are not accurate enough for synchronization purposes. If you need to synchronize the recorder to your MIDI sequencer application, you must assign one of the four audio channels to record the sync signals. In addition, you need one of the synchronization devices described at the end of this chapter to record the sync signal on the track and play it back to your sequencer.

Three audio tracks and a synchronization track are an effective combination to use as background music for a desktop video production. For example, you can record a live acoustic guitar and percussion session to be mixed with MIDI piano and bass tracks, as follows:

- The guitar is a point sound source, so it requires only one microphone and track.

- Two microphones and tracks are used for percussion to maintain stereo separation of components of the drum kit.

- The performers wear headphones to hear the piano and bass parts played by the sequencer through your audio adapter card.

- The sequencer is locked to the tape recorder through a prerecorded sync track by a process called *striping*.

- After recording the session, the MIDI sequencer application uses the synchronization signals on the tape to adjust its playback speed. This ensures that the piano and bass parts are timed properly with the live tracks.

Related Topics
Choosing Audio Tape
Recorders and Outboard
Mixers, p. 433

Dolby Laboratories' C-type noise reduction circuitry, discussed in Chapter 15, is incorporated in all multi-track cassette recorders. It reduces high-frequency tape noise, called *hiss*, without losing the higher frequency components of the sound.

The Fostex 280 has a frequency response of 40 Hz to 14 kHz, a dynamic range of 70 dB, and total harmonic distortion of less than 1.5 percent. These specifications are adequate for creating 8-bit mono or stereo waveform audio files at a 22.05-kHz sampling rate, the most common format used for commercial CD-ROM titles. Even the best multi-track cassette recorders, however, cannot be used to create 16-bit, 44.1-kHz WAV files of audio CD quality.

T I P   Many recording studios are equipped to provide waveform audio files on tape cartridges in formats commonly used for backing up hard disks. The files are created from the final mix tracks on the analog audio tape. Backup tape drives that hold 300M to 600M of data are available at moderate cost. If you have the hard disk capacity to hold the data on the tape, this approach avoids the requirement for a multi-track tape recorder to create the waveform audio files. Make sure that the studio can provide standard WAV files—also called IBM-Microsoft RIFF WAVE format. Most Windows waveform editing applications are not capable of converting proprietary formats, such as that used by DigiDesign equipment or the AIFF format used by Apple Macintosh computers, to WAV files.

Punch-In Recording

Obtaining a perfectly performed recording with live musicians seldom is possible, especially in sessions that involve playing times of five minutes or more. Both open-reel and cassette recorders provide the capability of recording over sour notes or mispronounced lyrics without re-recording the entire session. In the early days of audio recording, when only reel-to-reel recorders were available, mistakes were fixed by re-recording the badly performed segment. The re-recorded version then was cut and spliced into the old tape with a razor blade and adhesive splicing tape.

Cutting and splicing tape enclosed in a compact cassette is inconvenient at best. Multi-track cassette recorders, as well as modern open-reel recorders, use a process called *punch-in recording* to achieve the same effect. Punch-in recording involves the following steps:

1. You determine the beginning (punch-in) and end (punch-out) of the badly played sequence by the tape counter or time-code value readout on the recorder. Recorders with *auto punch* capability, such as the Fostex 280, save these values in an internal memory.

2. You rewind the tape to a position a few measures before the bad spot.

3. The performers synchronize their playing with the preceding measures by listening to the tape with headphones.

4. When the tape reaches the punch-in point in auto-punch mode, the recorder switches to record mode and records the new performance over the old. You use the record button or a foot-switch if auto-punch mode is not used or not available.

5. When the punch-out position is reached, recording automatically stops, or you switch the deck back to play mode.

Punch-in recording requires practice on the part of the musicians and the operator of the recorder. The punch-in and punch-out transitions are inaudible under the following conditions:

- The record and playback head are located very close to one another.

- The tape speed is high enough.

- The position settings are accurate.

- Your reaction times are quick.

Digital Audio Tape Recorders

The commercial success of audio CDs created a burgeoning market for professional-quality, multi-track tape recorders that record sound in digital, rather than analog, format. Open-reel, multi-track digital tape recorders are in the $50,000-and-up price range. Alesis Corporation began shipping the ADAT, an eight-track digital audio tape recorder with a list price of $3,995, in early 1992. The ADAT provides audio-CD quality performance at about one-fifth the cost of open-reel recorders with similar performance specifications (see fig. 11.12).

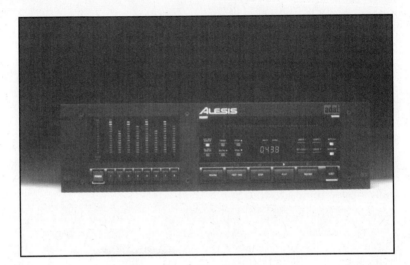

FIG. 11.12

The Alesis ADAT, an 8-channel digital tape recorder using S-VHS tape cassettes as the recording medium. (Courtesy of Alesis Corporation)

The ADAT may revolutionize the audio recording industry. It records eight channels plus a SMPTE synchronization track on conventional S-VHS (super-VHS) videotape cassettes with up to 40 minutes of recording time. If you need more than 8 channels, you can add up to 15 additional ADATs for a maximum of 128 perfectly synchronized tracks. The standard sampling rate of the ADAT is 48 kHz (the standard used for DAT recording), but you can adjust the sampling rate to 44.1 kHz to match that for audio CDs. An optional remote control unit generates SMPTE time code from Alesis' proprietary time code used to synchronize multiple ADATs. The unit then creates MIDI Time Code (MTC) and MIDI clock messages to synchronize with sequencer applications.

Although you can use the standard line-level analog outputs, digital inputs and outputs are provided. Another optional device adds the capability to record digital data from audio CDs and DAT players via AES/EBU and S/PDIF connections. This destines the ADAT as a major player in the all-digital multimedia audio systems of the future. Chapter 25 gives a glimpse of the equipment expected to comprise the multimedia authoring computers of the mid-1990s.

Digital audio tape (DAT) recorders are available at about half or less the cost of the ADAT. Most multimedia applications that involve recording live sound, however, require multi-track capability and SMPTE or MTC synchronization. Other manufacturers of analog tape recorders designed for use in MIDI-oriented environments are planning products similar to the ADAT but using the 8-mm tapes used by Hi8 camcorders. At the time this book was written, the ADAT was the multi-track recorder of choice for creating audio-CD quality sound.

MIDI Tape Recorder Synchronization

Most purchasers of MPC computers, upgrade kits, and compliant audio adapter cards intend to use a MIDI breakout cable or box to make their MIDI connections. If you already have an MPU-401, you probably want to continue to use it. If you need the MIDI synchronization capabilities discussed in Chapter 21, however, you need a more sophisticated MIDI adapter card or a separate synchronization device, usually called a *sync box*. Figure 11.13 shows the connections between a multi-track audio tape recorder and a MIDI synchronization device, whether built into the MIDI adapter card or in the form of an external sync box.

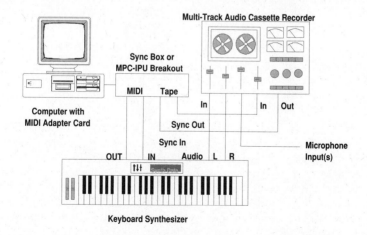

FIG. 11.13

Connections between tape recorders and MIDI devices for synchronization purposes.

FSK Synchronization with the Roland MPU-401

The Roland MPU-401, introduced in Chapter 2, was designed in the mid-1980s when frequency-shift keying (FSK) was the primary method of synchronizing tape recorders with MIDI sequencer applications. FSK sync translates timing pulses to a frequency-modulated signal, with one frequency representing the off (0) state of the pulse and another frequency corresponding to the on (1) state. FSK enables you to synchronize the rate at which your sequencer application runs to follow the speed of the tape.

The problem with FSK sync is that it is a relative time code; FSK cannot tell you the absolute position of the tape in hours:minutes:seconds since recording started. Your sequencer has to count the FSK pulses from the starting point of recording on the tape to determine a specific location. Therefore, FSK sync gave way to other methods—first to MIDI Song Position Pointer (SPP) synchronization measured in measures:beats and later to SMPTE and its shorthand version, MIDI Time Code.

Digital Synchronization with a MIDI Adapter Card

Related Topics
Using More Than 16 MIDI Channels, p. 290
MIDI Synchronization, p. 578

To score complex MIDI production numbers or synchronize your music with modern analog audio, DAT, digital audio, or television tape recorders, you need a more sophisticated PC-MIDI interface than a MPU-401 or the MIDI breakout cable supplied with your audio adapter card. Music Quest's MQX-32M is a professional-level MIDI adapter card that adds functions not provided by the MPU-401 (see fig. 11.14):

■ Two independently controllable MIDI OUT ports enable you to access up to 32 MIDI channels simultaneously.

■ Two merged MIDI IN ports enable you to merge, rather than simply mixing MIDI IN signals. The necessity for merging is discussed in "MIDI THRU Boxes and Mergers," earlier in this chapter.

■ Chase lock synchronization (CLS) matches the measure and beat of your MIDI sequence to any point on a tape. When you start the tape at a given position, the sequencer automatically positions itself to the corresponding measure and beat. From that point, it continues at the same rate as the tape.

■ 24, 25, 30 drop-frame and 30 non-drop SMPTE synchronization is provided for motion-picture and television applications. SMPTE is the universal standard for synchronizing audio and video sources. SMPTE 30 frame-per-second synchronization is the most common, with drop-frame for synchronization with video signals and non-drop used for audio-only applications. SMPTE 30 drop-frame sync skips 108 frames per hour to approximate the 29.97-per-second frame rate of NTSC color television.

■ MIDI Time Code (MTC) generation and synchronization is used. MIDI time code is an abbreviated version of the SMPTE standard.

■ Real-time tape error correction provides immunity to tape synchronization data dropout. If portions of the time-code track on your tape become unreadable, error-correction (called *jam sync*) prevents your system from locking up or losing synchronization.

■ Selectable port address (200 to 350) and interrupt levels through IRQ15 avoid conflicts with other adapter cards.

FIG. 11.14

The Music Quest MQX-32M 32-channel MIDI adapter card. *(Courtesy of Music Quest, Inc.)*

Most added features of the MQX-32M are related to synchronization. A detailed description of MIDI and SMPTE synchronization systems is included in Chapter 21. The MQX-16S provides most of the features of the MQX-32M—except the 32-channel capability—at lower cost. The firm's newly announced Array interface provides 128 MIDI IN and 128 MIDI OUT channels—the equivalent of 8 individual MIDI devices. The Array can replace both a MIDI merger and a MIDI THRU box. Roland Corporation produces an updated version of the MPU-401, similar to the MQX-32M, called the Super MPU/AT that provides 32 MIDI channels and includes SMPTE synchronization capability.

The Windows 3.1 driver for all Music Quest MIDI adapter boards is available directly from Music Quest or by downloading MQXDRV.ZIP from the

Music Quest library in the MIDI Vendors forum of CompuServe (GO MIDIVEN). Version 1.02 enables you to install two MQX-32M boards to get a total of up to 64 MIDI channels. The driver supports up to eight individual MIDI applications running simultaneously. The setup dialog for the Music Quest Windows 3.1 driver is shown in figure 11.15.

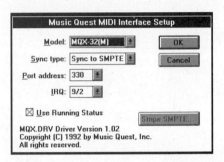

FIG. 11.15

The Windows 3.1 driver setup dialog for the MQX-32M.

T I P

To take advantage of the MQX-32M or other MIDI adapter cards that provide more than 16 MIDI channels, you need a Windows sequencer application with the ability to select between at least two MIDI ports. Using MIDI Mapper in conjunction with these boards is not recommended because it can be used with only one MIDI device (16 MIDI channels) at a time and introduces delays into the MIDI message stream.

After you install the Music Quest driver, you can stripe SMPTE time code on your tapes from driver setup dialog by clicking the Stripe SMPTE button shown in figure 11.15. *Striping* a time code means recording the time code track before you record any audio signals on the tape.

T I P

Stripe the entire length of your tapes before using them to record a session. Although you can add the time code as you record, striping the entire tape before recording anything on it is a better practice. Striping assures you that you can stop the session and then use punch-in techniques to continue it later without having to overwrite the old time code data with new data. Overwriting time code data is the major source of sync data drop-out problems.

External MIDI Synchronization Devices

A wide range of external MIDI synchronization devices for audio recording applications is available. Most provide basic SMPTE read and write capability and can convert SMPTE to MIDI time code. MidiMan's SYNCMAN Pro, a rack-mounted sync box shown in figure 11.16, has additional features that make syncing to audio and video tape easier:

■ SMPTE to MIDI Song-Position Pointer (SPP) conversion is available for use with sequencers that do not have MTC/SMPTE sync capability or if you are using an MPU-401 or your audio adapter card as the MIDI master controller.

■ Spot-Lock video sync is provided for synchronizing audio with the video images on videocassettes. A single SMPTE time code is pre-recorded on the audio track of the videocassette prior to the appearance of the first image on the tape. When the single time code is encountered, the SYNCMAN Pro locks to the frame rate of the VCR. This enables you to add synchronized audio to the tape without using a track for synchronization purposes only.

■ Settable SMPTE and display offset enable you to start the SMPTE time at any combination of HH:MM:SS or automatically subtract a preset time from the SMPTE time display.

■ You can read and write the 32 extra bits of the SMPTE time code reserved for user information with MIDI messages. A maximum of 8 digits (0 through 9) can be used.

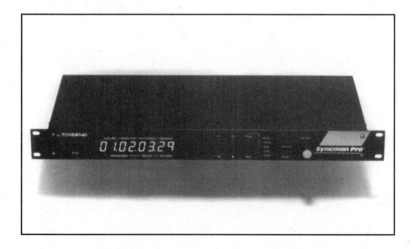

FIG. 11.16

The MidiMan SYNCMAN Pro SMPTE/MTC external synchronization device. (Courtesy of MidiMan)

One advantage of using an external sync box is the SMPTE time code value display window that shows the position of the tape in HH:MM:SS:FF format whenever the deck is in use. If you use a MIDI adapter card with built-in SMPTE synchronization capabilities, however, you do not need an external sync box unless one of the special features it offers—such as the Spot-Lock video sync capability of the SYNCMAN Pro—is not available from your card.

Chapter Summary

This chapter gave you a glimpse of the many accessory products that you can connect to the MIDI OUT connector of your audio adapter card. A complete description of each type of MIDI accessory devices available today would require a book in itself. The devices described in this chapter are those most commonly used in MIDI systems by both professional and amateur musicians.

Common accessory devices available for MIDI-based systems are intimately associated with specific functions of the professional-level Windows sequencer applications described in the next chapter.

Technical details of the synchronization process are discussed in Chapter 21, "Advanced MIDI and Waveform Audio Techniques."

MIDI Applications for Windows

M IDI Specification 1.0 and the IBM Personal Computer appeared on the market about the same time. Manufacturers of electronic musical instruments added MIDI circuitry to their products. PC producers supplied IBM-compatible computers with faster operating speeds and enhanced features at lower prices. In the mid-1980s, Roland Corporation introduced the MPU-401, which enables PCs to connect to MIDI devices. Software developers immediately began writing for DOS-based PC applications that used the MPU-401 as the master controller for MIDI gear. A new musical industry—computer-controlled composition— emerged.

Passport Designs' Master Tracks Pro, transported to the PC from its origin on the Apple Macintosh, was the first Windows-based sequencer application. Midisoft Studio was born in the days of Windows 3.0.

The advent of Windows 3.1 with its multimedia extensions created a flurry of activity among the publishers of PC-sequencing applications. Big Noise Software moved their Cadenza sequencer from Digital Research's ill-fated GEM graphical environment to Windows 3.1. Twelve Tone Systems adapted their successful DOS sequencer, Cakewalk Professional, to Windows. Master Tracks Pro added compatibility with Windows 3.1's multimedia extensions. Voyetra Technologies, whose Sequencer Plus application dominated the DOS sequencer market for many years, had not introduced a Windows version when this book was written.

This chapter explains how sequencing applications work and describes the characteristics that distinguish the four leading professional-level sequencers for Windows. It includes representative applications for transcribing your compositions to printed scores—usually called *scoring programs*. Universal patch editors and librarians for popular MIDI synthesizers enable you to modify the factory-supplied voices or create new voices from scratch. This chapter also describes two special-purpose Windows voice editors: one for the Roland Sound Canvas products and one for audio adapter cards using Yamaha OPL-II and OPL-III chipsets.

Professional MIDI Sequencers

Music is an art, but its foundation is the science of mathematics. The frequencies used to determine the pitch of the twelve tones of the tempered chromatic scale and the notes in chords have a precise mathematical relationship to one another. Rhythmic patterns are determined by division of measures into beats. Note lengths are expressed as arithmetic fractions. A musical composition thus can be reduced to a series of numbers representing the pitch, loudness, and occurrence in time of each note. *Intonation*—the characteristic that enables you to distinguish one musician's performance of the same composition from another's—is the only element of music that defies mathematical quantification.

The early analog musical synthesizers, described in Chapter 9, were keyboard instruments and had very limited capability to store the settings that determined the timbre of their sounds. Early synthesizers, such as the Fairlight CMI of the mid-1970s, used microprocessors that stored sampled sounds in memory. Fairlight's next step was to store in memory a series of commands that could substitute for the keyboard signals and play a series of sampled sounds. The Page R, developed in the mid-1970s for the $25,000 CMI synthesizer, was one of the first computer programs that qualified as an interactive musical sequencer. Today, even moderately priced keyboard synthesizers include dedicated, self-contained microprocessor-based systems that can record, edit, and play sequences of notes.

Personal computers and sequencing applications, rather than dedicated sequencers, predominate today because computer video displays can convey much more information than the small liquid-crystal displays (LCDs) used by synthesizers. Both dedicated and computer-based sequencers perform four basic functions:

- *Recording* MIDI Note On, Note Off, and other types of MIDI messages that arrive at the MIDI IN port of your audio or MIDI adapter card. The application time-stamps each message as it is stored in your computer's memory. This preserves the time relationship of the incoming message to messages recorded previously.

■ *Editing* the numeric values of the MIDI messages as necessary to produce a musical composition. Editing includes the ability to copy and delete phrases, adjust all notes so that they begin and end on the beat (called *quantizing*), change the pitch of notes, and add new notes to create chords or more complex melodic lines.

■ *Playback* of the recorded or edited sequences in memory through either the MIDI OUT port of your audio or MIDI adapter card. Playback includes the ability to reproduce the MIDI messages in the files at a rate determined by an internal or external clock, equivalent to a metronome. Using an external clock, usually derived from signals on a tape recorder track, enables you to synchronize playback with live or previously recorded MIDI music.

■ *Saving* recorded and edited sequences of MIDI messages in the form of disk files and loading sequences stored in files into memory for editing or playback. All present-day computer-based sequencers and many dedicated sequencers use the standard MIDI file (SMF) format.

Present-day, computer-based sequencer applications offer a wide range of functions in addition to the basic operations listed. The principal improvements have been in the form of the user interface, making the recording—particularly the editing process—simpler and more intuitive.

Examining Commercial MIDI Sequencers for Windows

The four leading sequencing applications for Windows—Cadenza for Windows, Cakewalk Professional for Windows, Master Tracks Pro, and Midisoft Studio for Windows—share many common characteristics.

■ Each is a full-featured, professional-level product designed for use with Windows 3.x.

■ All except Midisoft Studio for Windows use the piano-roll method described in Chapter 7 for note entry and editing.

■ All take full advantage of the Windows graphical user interface for note entry and editing. Two applications provide conventional musical staff notation. Cakewalk offers it as an option, and Midisoft Studio uses staff notation exclusively. Midisoft Studio also can print your score. Windows GUI enabled this new capability to be added to sequencing applications.

■ Each has its own proprietary file format for storing MIDI sequences and is compatible with standard MIDI .MID files—the common denominator of the sequencer industry and of Windows multimedia extensions.

■ Except for Midisoft Studio, each uses graphical techniques to create continuous MIDI controller messages—such as modulation wheel position, main volume, and pan—plus continuous pitch bend data that affects a single voice. This is the single most significant advance in sequencers made possible by Windows graphical environment.

■ Drivers for the MPU-401 and Music Quest MQX-32 are provided. If you substitute the MPU-401 driver included with Cakewalk Professional for Windows for the driver supplied with Windows, multiple applications can use the MPU-401 port simultaneously.

When the applications have so much in common, choosing the sequencer that best suits your needs is difficult. Your choice may be dictated by a special feature offered by one of the applications, such as Midisoft Studio's score printing capability or Cakcwalk's built-in method of playing *.WAV files or its access to the MCI commands of Windows 3.1.

If you prefer to enter notes on a musical staff, rather than by the tradition piano-roll technique, your choices of full-feature sequencers are limited to Cakewalk and Midisoft Studio. Passport Designs' MusicTime, an entry-level sequencer described in Chapter 7, and Encore, the firm's musical scoring application described near the end of this chapter, use staff notation entry.

Screen displays from each of the four Windows sequencer applications are used in the examples that follow.

T   I   P   Comparing the features of the four commercial sequencing applications for Windows in a single chapter is impossible. The manual for each application ranges from 1/2 to 1 inch thick. Music stores that specialize in MIDI applications are likely to carry at least two of these applications in stock and can demonstrate them for you. Bring your favorite Type 1 MIDI file to use as an example. (Don't try to use CANYON.MID, a Type 0 File.) The greatest difference between these applications is the user interface, especially in the note-editing window where you are likely to spend most of your time with a sequencer. Select the application whose note-editing protocol seems most natural to you.

Using a Windows Sequencing Application

When you launch a MIDI sequencing application, the first window that most sequencers display is the track editor. MIDI compositions are divided into tracks that represent the part played by a particular instrument. The bass (left hand) and treble (right hand) elements of piano parts often are divided into two tracks. Occasionally, individual percussion instruments are assigned to separate tracks. Early sequencers were limited to 16, 32, or 64 tracks; most Windows sequencers offer 256 or more.

Playing a Sequencer File

Your first use of a sequencing application likely is to play a MIDI file to see if the program works properly.

The Track Editor window of Master Tracks Pro 4, after loading a sample file in Master Tracks format (GTRBLUES.MTS), is shown in figure 12.1. All sequencer applications include a few sample files to demonstrate their prowess. To load a sequencer file—whether in standard MIDI or a proprietary format—use the conventional **File**, **O**pen menu command. If you load a MID file, the application converts the data in the file to its proprietary format during the loading process.

The Tk column indicates the track number, starting with track 1. Solid arrows in the P(lay) column show that the track is to be played, and open arrows indicate the track is muted (silent). The next column, R(ecord), is discussed in "Recording Live Performances" later in this chapter. S(olo) causes only the selected track to play. L(oop) causes the track to play repeatedly.

Track names usually include the name of the part and may incorporate a reference to a particular MIDI instrument or patch that identifies the source of the sound. In figure 12.1, the first set of characters identifies the MIDI Channel Number (C1 for track 1) and the second set shows the Program Change number (P19 for track 1) that determines the voice to be used for the track. The actual name of the voice is shown in the Program Name column.

The Chnl column determines the MIDI Channel Number, 1 to 16, to which the note data in the track is sent. Master Tracks Pro, as well as the other Windows sequencers described in this chapter, can send and receive MIDI data from more than one MIDI device. The letter preceding the channel number indicates the MIDI device—A in this case.

You select the MIDI device to use with Master Tracks Pro by choosing MIDI **S**etup from the **G**oodies menu. The MIDI Setup dialog appears (see fig. 12.2). The setup dialog boxes of other sequences are similar, except that the synchronization settings may be made from another menu choice.

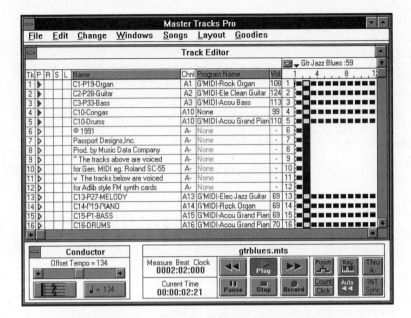

FIG. 12.1

The opening window
of Master Tracks Pro 4
after loading a
demonstration file.

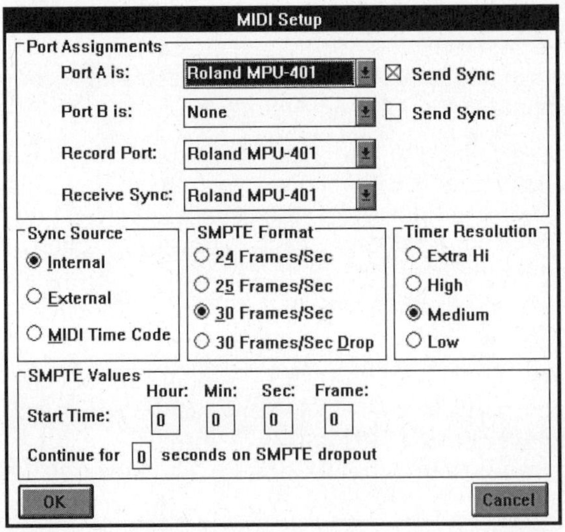

FIG. 12.2

The MIDI Setup
window of Master
Tracks Pro.

The default setting for the Synch Source is the Internal clock of your
computer, which is divided down to create a timer for the sequencer.
Timer resolution usually is expressed in pulses per quarter-note
(PPQN)—48, 96, and 192 PPQN are commonly used. The PPQN determines the degree of exactitude to which you can offset the timing of MIDI

Note On and Note Off messages from the beat. Master Tracks Pro's resolutions are chosen with Low (48), Medium (96), High (192), and Extra Hi (384 ppqn) option buttons. External synchronization uses MIDI Clock messages from another MIDI device, such as a drum machine, to control playback speed. MIDI Time Code (MTC) and SMPTE synchronization are covered in Chapter 21, "Advanced MIDI and Waveform Audio Techniques."

Referring back to figure 12.1, GTRBLUES.MTS was composed to be played by extended-level (General MIDI) audio adapter cards, synthesizers using channels 1 through 10, or base-level FM synthesizers. The original Ad Lib card that uses channels 13 through 16 is a base-level FM synthesizer. A General MIDI card (the Roland SCC-1) is used in this example, so channels 13 through 16 for the Ad Lib card are muted. Any time you see a set of tracks on channels 13 through 16 with names related to those for channels 1 through 10, you can assume that the sequence was authored for both extended- and base-level synthesizers.

The last column in the header of the Track Editor window, Vol, controls the overall volume of the track. Each MIDI Note On signal is accompanied by a velocity value that determines that note's relative volume. The overall volume adjusts each velocity value by the percentage shown in the column. Therefore Channel 2, the guitar part, is played at a value of 124 (127 is the maximum), about 98 percent of the normal volume.

All Windows sequencers have adopted the tape recorder metaphor to control recording and playback functions. Rewind, play, fast forward, pause, stop, and record are controlled by the buttons in Master Tracks Pro's Transport window (see fig. 12.3).

FIG. 12.3

Recording and playback functions controlled by the Transport window.

The Transport window also shows the current measure and beat. If the sequence is playing, the window also shows current time in hours:minutes:seconds:frames. The remaining buttons control the following:

- Punch-in and punch-out for rerecording parts of a sequence

- An audible count and click that duplicates a metronome

- Automatic return to beat 1 of measure 1 when playing stops

■ Operation of the MIDI THRU port

■ The synchronization mode

When you click the Play button in the Transport window, the sequencer begins playing the data from the file. An expanded view of the track editor shows the vertical reverse video bar that follows the progress of the playback (see fig. 12.4). A block represents each measure in which MIDI data appears, corresponding to the measure numbers at the top of the window. The blocks in the first measure of channels 6 through 12 represent the text in the Name column, which the application treats as silent MIDI data.

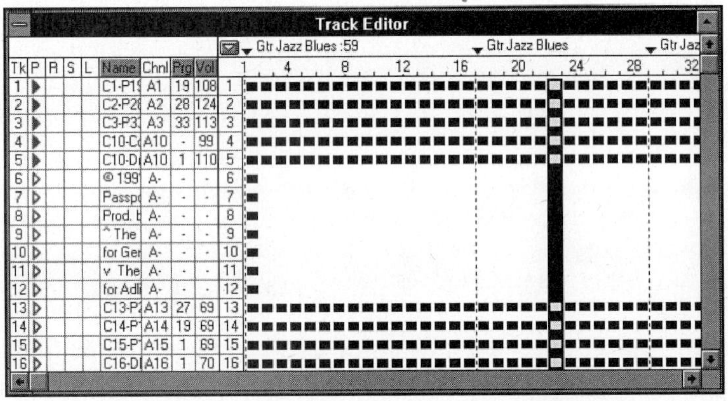

FIG. 12.4

The Track Editor window of Master Tracks Pro playing a file.

When you click the Stop button and then the Play button in the Transport window, playback starts over from beat 1 of measure 1 when the auto-rewind feature is turned on. You can click the Pause button to stop playing and then click it again to resume from the stop point.

You can adjust the tempo of the playback by adjusting the slider of the horizontal scroll bar in the Conductor window, shown in figure 12.5. Tempo is measured in beats per minute.

FIG. 12.5

The Conductor window used to control the playback tempo.

Midisoft Studio for Windows takes a unique approach when it starts, as shown in figure 12.6. Tracks are displayed in the form of conventional musical staves in the top Score View window. Track and voice assignments are made in the middle Studio Panel View window. The bottom Tape Deck window controls the recording and playback functions.

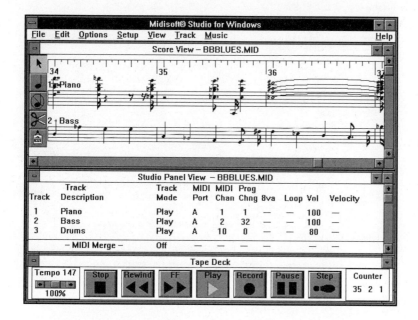

FIG. 12.6

Midisoft Studio for Windows playing a standard MIDI file.

Each staff in the Score View window represents a track. You can maximize and scroll the Score View window to display additional tracks.

In the Studio Panel View window, you assign track names and control modes (Play, Record, Mute, Punch-in, and so on). You also use this window to select MIDI devices (A, B, or C), MIDI Channel Numbers, and Program Changes and to adjust overall volume levels. You transpose tracks up and down by the number of octaves entered in the 8va column.

Cadenza for Windows takes a similar approach to Master Tracks Pro and Cakewalk, except that the track assignment and editing are done in separate windows (see fig. 12.7). Cadenza enables you to select a patch bank with the patch number for those synthesizers that provide multiple banks of patches.

Cadenza uses separate applications (EXE files) for MIDI device driver selection, driver setup, and synchronization control (see fig. 12.8). Cadenza's MIDI Director sets up the metronome, which can play a drum or produce clicks with the PC's internal speaker, sync, and other system parameters. One Options menu choice of MIDI Director is Output Port Mapping, which duplicates the functions of Windows MIDI Mapper. Both

Keyboard maps—primarily for mapping percussion instruments—and
Program Change maps for voice assignments are provided. Cadenza's
MIDI mapping utility can be used with multiple ports, unlike Windows
MIDI Mapper, which is restricted to a single instance.

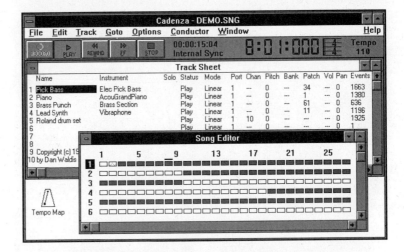

FIG. 12.7

Cadenza Track Sheet
and Song Editor
windows.

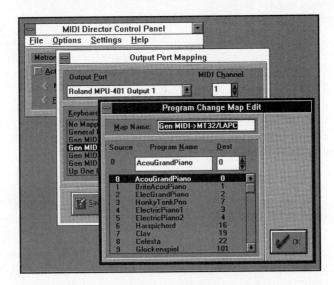

FIG. 12.8

Cadenza's equivalent
to MIDI Mapper
included with the
MIDI Director
application.

Entering and Editing Notes in Sequences

Piano-roll note editors are used to edit existing sequences and create
new compositions. The note editors of Cakewalk, Master Tracks Pro, and
Cadenza have similar displays and user interfaces. Because Cakewalk's
editor provides several unique features, Cakewalk Professional for Windows is used for the editing examples (see fig. 12.9). The musical
phrases are from the solo violin part of the first movement, *Primavera*, of
Antonio Vivaldi's *Il Quattro Stagioni*, *The Four Seasons*.

> Do not attempt to edit Type 0 files, such as CANYON.MID supplied
> with Windows 3.1. All MIDI events from the tracks that originally made
> up the file are combined into a single track in Type 1 MIDI files. Type 0
> files are used when the author of a composition wishes to discourage
> or effectively prevent editing of the file's contents.

T I P

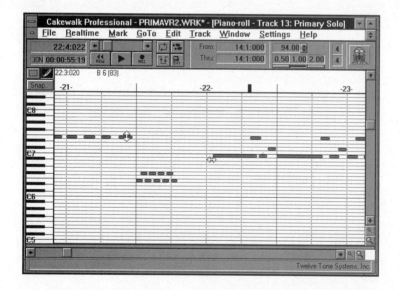

FIG. 12.9

Cakewalk Professional
for Windows piano-
roll note editing
window.

With conventional piano-roll editors, you edit one track at a time, but
you can use cascaded or tiled windows to switch quickly between
tracks. Cakewalk uses the following techniques for adding notes and
changing note values:

■ To add a note, hold Ctrl and click the mouse with the pointer at the position where you want to add the note.

■ To copy a note and drag the copy to a new location, click the note with Ctrl held down, then release Ctrl. Hold the left mouse button down to move the copy where you want it, then release the mouse button.

■ To change the pitch, click the middle third of one of the bars that represents a note. The mouse pointer changes to the vertical, double-headed arrow shown in measure 21 of figure 12.9. Drag the bar up or down to adjust the pitch in half-tone steps. The sound of the new pitch accompanies each change.

■ To change the starting position of the note without changing its length, click the head (beginning third) of the bar. The mouse pointer changes to a horizontal double-arrow, shown in measure 22. You drag the head of the bar to the new starting position.

■ To change the duration of a note, click the tail (ending third) of the bar. The mouse pointer again changes to a double-arrow that you can drag without changing the note's beginning position.

■ To delete a note, point to the note with the mouse, hold down the left mouse button, and press the Delete key.

You can make the beginning and end of the notes you enter or edit align on beat or fractional beat boundaries. Just click the Snap button shown in figure 12.10 and set the desired value in the Snap-to dialog that appears.

Snap-to values are measured in clock ticks. In this case, the clock resolution is set to 120 pulses per quarter note, so choosing 30 clock ticks results in notes snapping to the nearest sixteenth note (one-quarter of a quarter-note). If you are creating triplets or more strangely tupled notes (such as 11 sixteenth notes played in two beats), turn off the Snap-to feature.

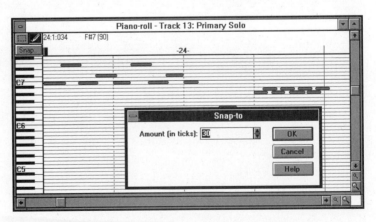

FIG. 12.10

A magnified view of a single measure and the Snap-to adjustment window.

Figure 12.10 illustrates another feature of Cakewalk's editor: the ability to expand either the time base or the pitch distance (width of the piano keys) of the display, or both. In figure 12.10, one measure occupies about 80% of the width of the display, about a three-fold expansion compared with figure 12.09. This provides increased resolution when you are entering notes with Snap-to disabled.

If you are oriented to staff notation, you can use the Cakewalk Staff window to edit your sequences (see fig. 12.11). When you expand the time base of the piano-roll editor to the maximum, it corresponds approximately to the fixed time base of the Staff window.

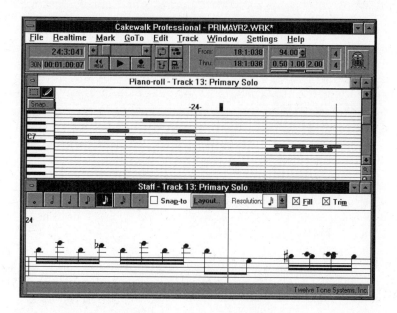

FIG. 12.11

The staff view corresponding to a piano-roll view of a measure.

> **T I P**
>
> If you are entering a sequence from a printed score, rather than editing a performance, staff view usually is the easiest method of transcription. One advantage of staff view in Cakewalk is that you can enter notes in more than one track at a time. Multi-track entry is helpful when entering piano parts with the treble clef on one track and the bass clef on another. If you need to create tuples—not available in staff view—you can switch to piano-roll editing and change the note positions and durations to suit.

Major alterations to the structure of a performance are made in the track editing window. All operations in the track editing window are restricted to entire measures. You can delete, copy, and insert new measures anywhere in the performance. Just select the measures with the mouse and then use standard Windows Clipboard Cut, Copy, and Paste operations from the Edit menu or the Ctrl-X, Ctrl-C, and Ctrl-V key combinations.

Quantizing Recorded Performances

All note editors have the capability to quantize the performances you record. When you record a keyboard performance, some notes are slightly ahead of the beat and some behind. Note durations are not likely to be exactly whole-, half-, quarter-, or eighth-beats. *Quantizing* is the process of adjusting the timing of MIDI Note On messages so that they occur exactly on the beat or an allowable fraction of a beat. The effect of quantizing is identical to the application of a Snap-to value during note entry or editing; quantizing applies Snap-to to an entire track or a selected portion of a track.

An example of Cakewalk's quantizing capabilities is shown in figure 12.12. The phrase that begins on B6 has notes that lead and lag the beat, shown by solid and dashed vertical lines. You can quantize to a variety of note lengths. Sixteenth-note quantizing for both note start and note duration was used to create the quantized phrase shown an octave below the original (B5). Each quantized note begins and ends on exact multiples of one-quarter of a beat, and in this case, each note became exactly a sixteenth-note in duration.

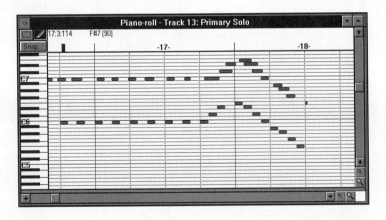

FIG. 12.12

Quantizing a phrase to sixteenth-notes in Cakewalk.

Two principal problems are associated with quantizing musical performances:

■ Quantizing converts triplets and other tuples to the next shorter even-fraction note. Tripleted eighth-notes (three notes played in one beat in 4/4 time) are converted to 16th notes. An example of triplet conversion to sixteenth notes is shown in fourth beat of measure 17 in figure 12.12.

■ Music played exactly on the beat acquires a mechanical effect, as if it were played by a robot. For this reason, sequencers enable you to quantize by percentage, bringing the notes closer to their ideal positions but allowing a bit of the random element to remain.

T I P

If you intend to record a blues piece that involves many sets of triplets in 4/4 time and plan to quantize the performance to "tighten it up," consider selecting 6/8 or 12/8 time instead of 4/4. In 6/8 time, your triplets become eighth notes, and even-fraction notes receive a dot. The quantizing process can handle dotted notes, but not triplets, so using 6/8 or 12/8 time can save a substantial amount of editing of the quantized version.

Humanizing, offered by Master Tracks Pro and Cadenza, and called Randomizing by Cakewalk, is the opposite of quantizing; it introduces an adjustable degree randomness into note start and note duration timing. You can achieve a similar effect by making minor variations in the tempo with the graphic tempo maps provided by Cakewalk, Cadenza, and Master Tracks.

Cakewalk's Randomize operation is implemented by its built-in programming language, CAL (Cakewalk Application Language). CAL is similar to LISP, a list processing language also used to write programs for AutoCAD, with a bit of C added. Programming in CAL is not for the faint of heart because its syntax is arcane, at best. Despite its shortcomings, CAL is a powerful language for automating note entry. As an example, Cakewalk supplies CAL programs that automatically create chords (major and the major, minor, and dominant 7th) using selected notes as the root.

Programming Pitch Bends and Continuous Controllers

Programming pitch bends that, for example, duplicate the effect of the whammy bar on an electric guitar is a tedious process with DOS sequencer applications. The same is true for continuous controller messages, such as fades created with the Main Volume controller or simulated movement with the Pan controller. Using character-based sequencers, you manually enter numerous MIDI pitch change or controller numbers from the keyboard. Windows enables you to trace these changes on a grid with the mouse, resulting in a series of individual MIDI messages. An example of pitch bend applied to an electric guitar track is shown in figure 12.13.

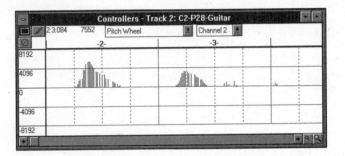

FIG. 12.13

MIDI pitch bend events created by drawing a controller profile with a mouse.

Using MIDI Event Lists

When strange sounds emerge from your audio adapter card or synthesizer and you don't know why, it's time to check the MIDI event list. MIDI event lists are displayed as a series of entries for a single channel, displayed in Windows text boxes in time sequence. A portion of a MIDI event list for the second measure of track 2 is shown in figure 12.14. When you double-click an entry, you can either edit the time at which the event occurs or select an event and then click the Del key to remove it. You can insert an event that duplicates a selected event by pressing the Ins key. Then you edit the duplicate as necessary to achieve the desired result.

Trk	Hr:Mn:Sc:Fr	Meas:Beat:Tick	Chn	Kind	Values		
2	00:00:01:24	2:1:011	2	Note	C 6	107	56
2	00:00:01:29	2:1:088	2	Note	Bb5	109	28
2	00:00:02:03	2:1:169	2	Note	C 6	117	1:050
2	00:00:02:06	2:1:213	2	Wheel	32		
2	00:00:02:07	2:1:232	2	Wheel	75		
2	00:00:02:08	2:2:015	2	Wheel	162		
2	00:00:02:09	2:2:035	2	Wheel	216		
2	00:00:02:10	2:2:055	2	Wheel	281		
2	00:00:02:11	2:2:073	2	Wheel	400		
2	00:00:02:12	2:2:091	2	Wheel	444		
2	00:00:02:13	2:2:108	2	Wheel	465		
2	00:00:02:14	2:2:126	2	Wheel	487		
2	00:00:02:16	2:2:159	2	Wheel	498		
2	00:00:02:18	2:2:190	2	Wheel	563		
2	00:00:02:19	2:2:211	2	Wheel	628		
2	00:00:02:21	2:3:016	2	Wheel	238		
2	00:00:02:22	2:3:022	2	Note	C 6	113	119

Event list - Track 2: C2-P28-Guitar

FIG. 12.14

A portion of Cakewalk's MIDI Event list for Channel 2.

The values for MIDI Note events consist of pitch, note-on velocity (0 to 127), and note duration, expressed in beats and clock ticks. Pitch wheel values consist of the numeric value representing wheel position, –8192 to +8192. The list does not display program changes based on settings in the Patch column of Track/Measure view transmitted immediately prior to playing.

Cakewalk enables you to choose one of the six different types of standard MIDI events shown in figure 12.15 when you edit entries in the event list. In addition, you can choose among four special MIDI meta events:

System Exclusive meta events send designated sets of SysEx messages (in called banks) to your audio adapter card or synthesizer to change its operating characteristics or to alter a voice. Real-time SysEx messages interrupt the flow of MIDI Note On and Note Off messages, so they should be kept short to avoid glitches in the music. SysEx banks are stored as files in the standard MIDIEX format with SYX extensions. Cakewalk includes a SysEx editor to edit or create SysEx bank files. Chapter 21 describes MIDI SysEx operations.

Text meta events, consisting of strings up to 80 characters long, are used for storing comments or lyrics in a MIDI file.

MCI command meta events enable you to execute any command string valid for the media control interface drivers and MCI-compatible hardware installed. Using the MCI commands with Cakewalk Professional for Windows is described in Chapter 25.

Wave audio meta events embed waveform audio files in your MIDI file so that they can be played in synchronization with your synthesized sounds. You can embed sound effects or lyrics in waveform audio format and play the sounds at the designated time. This feature is covered in Chapter 23.

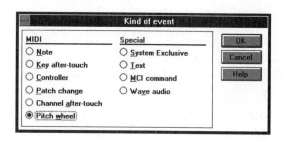

FIG. 12.15

Cakewalk's MIDI event type selection dialog for editing event lists.

If you use the MCI command meta event, Play WAVEFILE.WAV, to play a waveform audio file, MCIWAVE.DRV opens WAVEFILE.WAV and sends the data it contains to your audio adapter card. The Wave audio meta event requires that you paste the waveform audio data from the clipboard to the meta event so it can be embedded in the MIDI file. The difference between the two techniques is similar to the difference between linking and embedding OLE objects in a compound document.

Recording Live Performances

The four sequencer applications described in this chapter use a similar process for recording MIDI data from keyboards, drum pads, instrument pickups, and drum machines. The basic steps to recording a live performance are the following:

1. Set your keyboard or synthesizer to send MIDI data on Channel 1. This is the default MIDI transmit channel for most keyboards and keyboard synths.

2. If you have a keyboard synthesizer and it has a Local Control option, set Local Control to On (the default) so that the synthesizer plays the notes. If you are using a MIDI keyboard, such as the Roland PC-200, your audio adapter card produces the piano sounds.

3. Check to make sure that the MIDI OUT connector of your keyboard or synth is cabled to the MIDI IN connector of your audio or MIDI adapter card.

4. Launch your sequencer application and set it up so that the track editing window is displayed.

5. Enable the metronome to provide the timing reference for your performance. The MPU-401 has a built-in metronome, but most Windows sequencers default the PC's speaker to play one tone for the first beat of the bar and another for the remaining beats. If you are using a sound card, you can select two percussion instruments on Channel 10 for the metronome (see fig. 12.16). If you are using a synthesizer, set it to receive MIDI messages on Channel 10 and use a percussive voice to act as the metronome.

6. Set the time signature (meter) for your tune. All sequencers default to standard 4/4 time.

7. Set the tempo in beats per minute. 120 beats per minute is the usual default.

8. Set the mode of track 1 to record. Most sequencers automatically set track 1 to record mode when a file is not loaded.

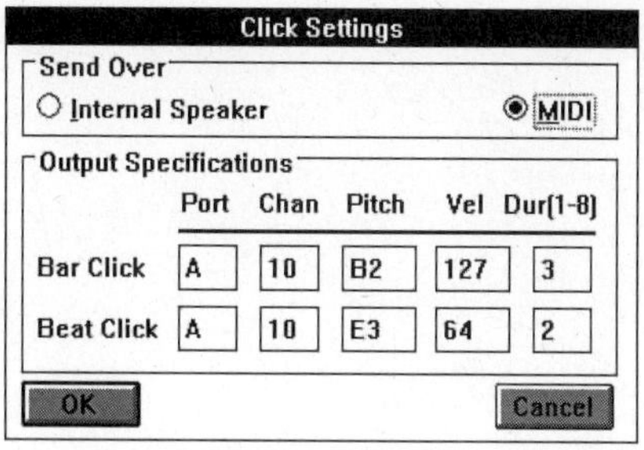

FIG. 12.16

Master Tracks Pro's
Click Settings dialog
that assigns percussion
instruments to the
metronome.

9. Check the metronome and your MIDI setup by clicking the Record button. Most sequencers provide a measure or two of lead-in beats before recording starts.

10. Play a few measures and adjust the volume of the piano sound and the metronome so that the beat is clearly audible. If you are using Midisoft Studio, the notes appear in the Score View window; otherwise, the measure you are playing is shown by a progress indicator in the track editing window. Master Tracks Pro uses a vertical black bar to indicate the measure (see fig. 12.17).

11. Click the Stop button, or click the Record button again if your sequencer does not have a Stop button; then change the mode of track 1 to Play and click Rewind.

12. Use the note editor to verify that what you played was recorded; then return to the Track Editor window.

13. Change the mode of track 1 back to Record and click Rewind to record over your test track.

14. Click Record and play your performance.

15. To audition your performance, stop recording and change the mode of track 1 to Play, click Rewind, then click the Play button.

16. Save your performance by choosing Save **As** from the **F**ile menu and giving your file a descriptive name. Use the native file format of your sequencer until you have completed editing operations. This saves time because the application does not have to convert the file to and from Standard MIDI format each time you save or load it.

Staying on or close to the beat is the most important aspect of recording performances. If you lose the tempo while recording, the notes become offset from their proper position in the measure by increasing numbers of beats. Editing an off-tempo performance ranges from difficult to next-to-impossible.

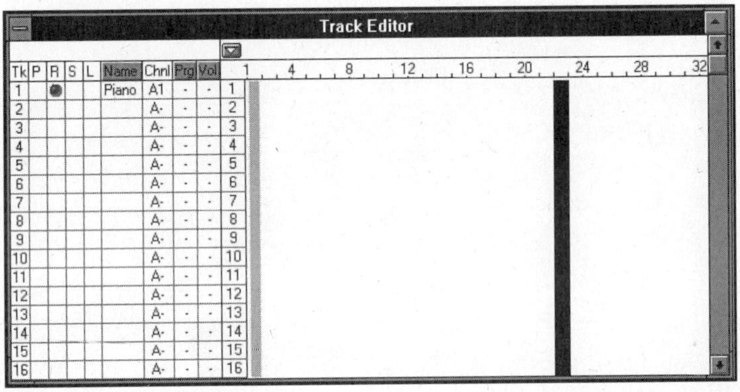

FIG. 12.17

The Track Editor window of Master Tracks Pro while recording.

T I P   Save the original version of recorded performances twice. Some operations, like quantizing, can make drastic changes to your recorded data. If you make a serious error while editing one of the files and accidentally save it, you can recover by using the copy of the original version.

Music Publishing Applications

Passport Designs MusicTime sequencer, described in Chapter 7, includes score printing capabilities. Midisoft Studio for Windows enables you to print a draft-quality version of your composition. Both applications are designed for printing relatively simple scores and can use any printer supported by Windows. If you have a laser printer and are really serious about publishing your works, you need an application designed specifically for music publishing. These applications produce sheet music that rivals the quality achieved by the expert engravers of the nineteenth and early twentieth centuries.

Passport Design's Encore is an example of a professional-level musical scoring application for Windows. Encore uses a proprietary file format, ENC, but you import files in MID and MTS formats. A simplified sequencer application is included with Encore so that you can record and play back compositions through an audio or MIDI adapter card. The metronome, quantizing, and external MIDI clock synchronization capabilities of Master Tracks Pro are included. You use the mouse and the Notes toolbox, shown in figure 12.18, to enter notes on multiple staves when you are writing, rather than recording, a composition.

FIG. 12.18

The main note entry window of Passport Encore.

Musical scoring applications—such as Encore and Coda Music Software's Finale—are used for publishing sheet music and printing individual parts for band members, studio musicians, and students. Encore uses Adobe Type Manager and Adobe's Sonata font to achieve high-quality printed output. Encore is the publishing application used by the MusicWriter NoteStation sheet music and MIDI file vending machine described in Chapter 7. If you are preparing scores with high-valued tuples (quintuplets or more) or other complex rhythmic patterns, or orchestrating a tune, you will find writing music in a scoring application to be considerably simpler than entering notes in single-track piano-roll editors.

Windows Editors and Librarians

Most professional musicians using MIDI synthesizers and sound modules are seldom satisfied with the collections of factory-supplied voices built into the product. Chapter 9 gave you an introduction to the creation of patches that alter the voices of audio adapter cards based on the Yamaha OPL-II and OPL-III digital FM synthesis chips. Dedicated voice editors are satisfactory if you need to edit the voices of only a single synthesizer. (Voyetra's PatchView FM is described in Chapter 9, and WinCanvas is the subject of the last topic of this chapter.) If you have several synthesizers or sound modules, a universal editor/librarian is a more economical choice.

Using Universal Editor/Librarians for Windows

Using the pushbuttons and sliders provided on keyboard synthesizers and sound modules to modify voices can be a laborious task. Most synthesizers have more than 100 different voice-editing parameters from which to choose and a limited amount of memory to hold custom-designed voice patches. Some devices can store patch data on special RAM cards that plug into a slot on the front or back of the instrument. Compared with a hard disk, RAM is an expensive form of data storage.

Universal editor/librarian applications are designed to serve four basic purposes:

- Changing the editable parameters of voices of a variety of popular synthesizers to create new patches with sounds more to your liking. Windows provides a graphic interface ideal for adjusting the shape of ASDR envelopes and altering parameters by using sliders. Editors include simple sequencers that enable you to play a scale or selected notes to test your changes.

- Storing SysEx messages that control MIDI accessories—such as effects processors, MIDI-controlled mixers, and patch bays—so that you can re-create a particular setup quickly. This feature is especially useful in MIDI studios where inter-connections to equipment must be changed frequently.

- Storing the patches in the form of disk files that can be transmitted to the synthesizer when the particular custom-programmed voice is required.

- Cataloging bank files of patches you create and patches supplied by the factory to make a library of sounds in database form. You assign the individual patches descriptive names and search for particular types of sounds by entering key words.

Voice editing requires that the editor portion of the application be able to send and receive data from your synthesizer by MIDI System Exclusive messages. The structure of SysEx messages is not a part of the MIDI specification, so manufacturers use widely differing SysEx protocols for their instruments. The individual bytes that make up a SysEx voice message vary substantially between individual models from the same firm. To be categorized a *universal* editor, the product must include a device driver—similar to the device drivers used by Windows—for each make and model. The device driver, also called a *template*, contains information about the voice parameters that may be edited, including limitations in the range of values you may enter for each parameter.

A small portion of the voice editing window of X-oR, a Windows universal editor/librarian published by Dr. T's Music Software, is shown in figure 12.19. You use the vertical and horizontal scroll bars to obtain access to controls for all voice parameters. At the time this book was written, Dr. T's did not offer a device driver for audio adapter cards using the Yamaha OPL-II or OPL-III chipsets, nor for the Roland Sound Canvas product line (although the Roland MT-32 is supported). These drivers (Dr. T's calls them *profiles*) are likely to be available for X-oR in the future.

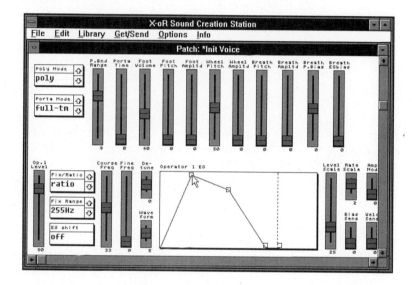

FIG. 12.19

A portion of the voice editing window of Dr. T's X-oR universal editor.

In addition to its editing and cataloging functions, X-oR provides the capability to create performances that store the current patch data for all of the equipment in a single file. You can re-create a particular MIDI setup that you used for a composition when you need to make changes to it several months afterward. You can save comments with the performance to remind you of settings that cannot be controlled remotely.

WinCanvas, a Voice Editor for the Sound Canvas

Roy Terry's WinCanvas is a shareware application dedicated to editing the voice parameters of the Roland Sound Canvas product line, which presently includes the SCC-1 GS Sound Card and the SC-55 and SC-155 sound modules. Each product uses the same basic circuitry, so the SysEx instructions for altering voice characteristics are the same. WinCanvas, shown with its Filter window open in figure 12.20, can edit every adjustable parameter of these very flexible instruments.

FIG. 12.20

The Filter editing window of Roy Terry's WinCanvas editor for the Roland Sound Canvas.

You can make a remarkable number of adjustments to the Sound Canvas products. The Filter window, shown in figure 12.20 and at the right in figure 12.21, sets the attack, decay, sustain, and release characteristics of the group of the 24 partial tones (oscillators) that may combine to create a single voice. Figure 12.21 shows all but two of the other adjustments you can make, including the following:

- The Master controls affect all voices in the patch.

- Reverb and Chorus, the two digital effects available, enable you to choose the type of reverberation and chorus techniques (called *macros*) used.

- Controls change the range of continuous controllers for each partial comprising the voice.

- Tone, shown minimized to an icon in figure 12.21, defines the amount of Reverb and Chorus effect for each of the 16 parts comprising the patch.

You can copy selected patch data to the Windows Clipboard, then paste it into the SysEx editing window of a sequencer application, such as Cakewalk Professional for Windows. You also can save the data to a text file for use with WinCanvas or in the standard MIDIEX format, discussed earlier in the chapter.

A full explanation of all modifications you can make to the voices of the Sound Canvas products is beyond the scope of this book. You can download the shareware version of WinCanvas from the MIDI Forum on CompuServe. Browse with CANVAS as the keyword to find the library in which it is located.

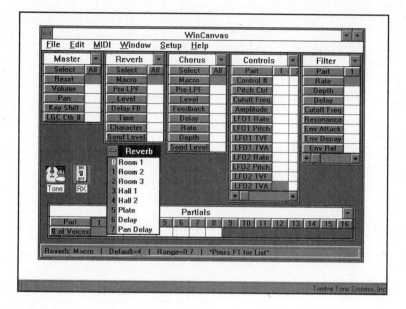

FIG. 12.21

All but two of the
editable voice
parameter windows
of WinCanvas.

Chapter Summary

Until the advent of Version 3.1, few MIDI applications were designed for
use with Windows. As a result of Microsoft's decision to include the
multimedia extensions for sound with Windows 3.1, the use of PCs for
musical applications has increased at a remarkable rate, resulting in the
introduction of Windows versions of DOS-based sequencers and upgraded versions of those created for Windows 3.0. The sequencer applications described in this chapter prove that you don't need a Mac or an
Amiga computer for composing or editing MIDI performances.

New features will be added to the sequencing applications described
in this chapter to expand their usefulness in creating sound tracks for
multimedia presentations. Publishers of DOS sequencing and related
MIDI applications are reported to be in the process of programming Windows versions of their products so as not to be excluded from Windows
multimedia market.

The more technical aspects of MIDI—such as embedding waveform au-
dio files as meta events in MID files and the MCI commands applicable to
MIDI applications—are covered in Chapter 21, "Advanced MIDI and
Waveform Audio Techniques," and Chapter 23, "The High-Level MCI
Commands of Windows 3.1."

Digital Audio Techniques

PART

IV

OUTLINE

Digital Audio Sampling, Reproduction, and Compression

The success of the first consumer product that used digital rather than analog audio, the audio compact disk, caused an upheaval in a field that had been dominated by professional recording studios equipped with digital recording equipment priced in the $100,000-and-up range. The mass market generated for high-quality digital audio components by sales of CD-ROM players brought the cost of the chips that reproduce the sound on audio CDs, digital-to-analog converters (DACs), to under $10 each. Digital-to-analog conversion is the heart of the reverse process, analog-to-digital conversion, that is used to sample the sound. Thus, the cost of analog-to-digital converters (ADCs) has dropped, too.

After ADCs and DACs with the 16-bit or better resolution required to achieve CD quality became affordable, they were employed by manufacturers of specialty adapter cards for Apple Macintosh computers and IBM-compatible PCs to create a new market called direct-to-disk recording. Firms like DigiDesign sold combinations of multichannel cards and digital audio editing software for the Macintosh, and Digital Audio Labs provided the CarD and the EdDitor to perform similar functions for PCs at a cost less than that of the high-quality, multichannel analog tape recorders they replaced.

By the end of the 1980s, the cost of 8-bit ADCs and DACs, implemented as integrated circuit chips, became low enough to enable firms such as Creative Labs to create audio adapter cards for PCs at a price almost anyone could afford. The market for MPC-compatible audio adapter cards created by Windows's multimedia extensions drove the street prices of the original 8-bit monophonic variety below $100. By mid-1992, a trend toward improving the quality of the sound of MPC-compatible cards began, and low-cost 16-bit boards became available from virtually all the adapter card manufacturers.

With 16-bit ADCs and DACs aboard, digital signal processing (DSP) chips will be needed to compress and expand the 10M-per-minute files created by stereo 16-bit recording at 44.1 kHz. By the mid-1990s, the majority of audio adapter cards will use DSPs not only for real-time file compression and expansion, but also to generate the synthesized sounds that now originate from the Yamaha OPL-III digital FM synthesis chips.

This chapter introduces you to the techniques used to convert conventional analog sound signals to digital form and then convert the stored digital data back to analog form so that you can hear it.

Understanding Sampled Analog Sound

The heart of the waveform audio functions of Windows 3.1 multimedia is *sampled sound*. The audio sampling and reproduction process for digitally sampled sound consists of the following steps:

1. Create an analog electrical signal with an acoustic transducer.

2. Amplify the analog output of the microphone to create electrical signals (waves) with a greater amplitude.

3. Measure the amplitude (loudness) of the electrical analog signal sound at predetermined intervals with an analog-to-digital converter.

4. Store the measured values in digital form (numbers) in memory or on a disk drive.

5. Manipulate the digital sound data by numerical techniques to change pitch, timbre, or amplitude as necessary to create a certain ambiance or effect.

6. Recall the digital signals from memory or the disk drive at the same rate at which they were measured.

7. Reproduce the digital signals as analog electrical sound waves, using a digital-to-analog converter.

8. Amplify the analog sound waves as necessary.

9. Make the electrical waves audible through acoustical transducers such as speakers or headphones.

Sampling is technically a measurement or recording process only. The term generally is used in the context of the waveform audio functions, as well as with musical synthesizers, to include all the elements of the sampled sound recording, storage, and reproduction process in the preceding list. Sampled sound is often referred to as PCM (pulse-code modulated) sound because the measurement process treats the wave as if it were made up of a series of pulses whose individual heights (amplitudes) are measured and then encoded at the sampling intervals.

The analog-to-digital conversion process is described in the following sections.

Examining Analog Sound Waves

Physical sound pressure waves are converted to corresponding electrical signals by an acoustic transducer, such as a microphone or phonograph cartridge. The electrical output of the transducer is called an *analog* signal because the electrical signal is analogous to (representative of) the pressure patterns of the sound wave that created it. Sound signals are most often represented in the form of two-dimensional wave patterns whose Y-axis is the intensity or amplitude of the signal and whose X-axis represents the passage of time. Figure 13.1 shows an analog waveform of a series of sound waves from a chime, changed into an analog voltage by a microphone and amplified to a maximum level (amplitude) of +/– 0.5 volt, also called an amplitude of 1 Volt peak-to-peak, abbreviated V(pp) or Vpp.

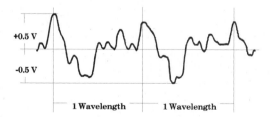

FIG. 13.1

A 1-Volt peak-to-peak analog sound signal of a chime.

The frequency of a wave is determined by the time that elapses between repetitions, called the *wavelength*. Most sound waves do not repeat precisely, but you can observe a pattern in the waveforms created by most musical instruments. The wavelength of electrical sound signals is expressed in milliseconds (one thousandth of a second) or microseconds (one millionth of a second); that of sound pressure waves in feet or meters, abbreviated Λ (Greek lambda). The frequency, measured in Hz (cycles per second), is defined as the reciprocal of l, $1/\Lambda$. If the wavelength is measured in milliseconds, the frequency in Hz is 1000/l. The wavelength of middle A is about 2.273 milliseconds, resulting in a frequency of 1000/2.273 or 440 Hz.

The additional waves superimposed on the basic wave are called *overtones*. Overtones are higher-frequency waves, with frequencies that are multiples of the basic wave (called harmonics) giving sounds their characteristic timbre. The harmonics interact with one another to create the complex waveforms of the human voice and acoustic musical instruments. Overtones play an important part in the determination of the fidelity with which sounds are reproduced by digital processes.

Using Analog-to-Digital Conversion for Sampling

Analog-to-digital converters or ADCs, as their name implies, are used to measure the analog signal and express instantaneous values of the signal's amplitude in digital form. The digital representation of the analog signal then can be stored in memory or on a disk drive as a series of binary numbers, one for each measurement.

NOTE The examples throughout this chapter are for the typical 8-bit converters found in MPC-compatible audio adapter cards. But the principles of analog-to-digital and digital-to-analog conversion described here are equally applicable to digital audio tape (DAT) and CD-ROM sound recording and reproduction technology.

The accuracy with which the signal may be measured is determined in part by the number of bits in the ADC's output, called its *resolution*. 8-bit ADCs are limited to 255 different sound levels, excluding 0 (no sound). 12-bit ADCs give 4,095 levels, and 16-bit versions provide 32,767. Low-cost 16-bit ADCs are seldom capable of measuring the signal with an accuracy of one part in 32,767, but the better ones come close. Higher resolution ADCs have *quantizing error*, which is the difference in sound level corresponding to a 1-bit change in the ADC's output. High-quality 16-bit ADCs have 1/255 (0.4%) of the quantizing error of 8-bit ADCs. Regardless of accuracy issues, 12- and 16-bit ADCs produce much higher-fidelity sound than 8-bit ADCs.

Representing Analog Sound Signals as Binary Numbers

ADCs convert the analog signal to a binary number scaled to a percentage of its maximum allowable range of amplitude. (An explanation of binary numbers and hexadecimal arithmetic is provided in Appendix E.) An 8-bit converter that divides a 10-Volt peak-to-peak signal into 256 linear steps is used in the examples that follow. Each step represents an increment or a decrement in signal level equal to 10/256, resulting in a value of 0.039 volts or 39 millivolts (mv) per step. In the examples of analog-to-digital conversion shown in figure 13.2, the minimum allowable amplitude of the analog signal, –5 volts or 0 percent of the range, corresponds to 00H or binary 0000 0000 (0). The maximum value, +5 volts or 100 percent of the range, is represented by FFH, binary 1111 1111 (255). 0 volts is represented by 80H, binary 1000 0000 (128). Hexadecimal (byte) values are indicated here by the suffix H.

Figure 13.2 illustrates the analog-to-digital conversion process for a portion of a single cycle of the wave of figure 13.1. An input signal of +0.39 volts is equivalent to 10 of the 256 steps available to encode the analog signal into digital form. Thus, +0.39 volts corresponds to 8AH, binary 1000 1010, or 138. Similarly, a level of –0.45 volts translates to 12 steps below 80H, resulting in 74H, 0111 0100 binary, or 116 decimal.

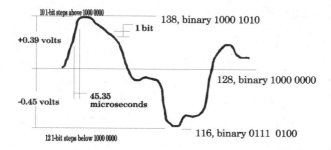

FIG. 13.2

Analog-to-digital conversion of a portion of the waveform of figure 13.1.

The digital data from 8-bit ADCs used in MPC-compliant audio adapter cards is called *unsigned 8-bit binary*, although the first (most significant or sign) bit can be used to the polarity of the analog signal. Data from 16-bit ADCs is stored in WAV files as a conventional, signed integer. Linear conversion is used for clarity in the examples, but the ADCs in audio adapter cards use a logarithmic scale for conversion. The reason is that the human ear perceives sound intensity, expressed in *decibels* or dB of sound pressure level, logarithmically.

Sampling Rates and Aliasing

The time between the measurements, 45.35 microseconds in figure 13.2, is called the *sampling interval* or *sampling period*. The sampling interval is the rate at which the ADC measures the analog voltage and converts it to binary digital data. Audio equipment manufacturers have established standard sampling rates of 11.025, 22.05, and 44.1 kHz, corresponding to 90.7, 45.35, and 22.67 microsecond (ms) sampling intervals. These sampling rates were adopted for the WAV files of the multimedia extensions. The waveform in figure 13.2 is sampled at a rate of 22.05 kHz. 48 kHz is the standard sampling rate for digital audio tape (DAT) recorders.

The audio quality (fidelity) of the sound conversion process is roughly proportional to the sampling rate—the faster the better. The maximum frequency that can be reproduced (without distortion) by digital sampling techniques is exactly half the sampling rate. Therefore, sampling at 11.025 kHz gives a maximum reproducible frequency of 5,512 Hz. Because the maximum fundamental frequency of most instruments is below 5,512 Hz, 11.025 kHz would appear to be adequate for recording music. 11.025 kHz is not sufficient, however, because the harmonics above 5,512 Hz that give the sound much of its characteristic timbre would be lost. Half the sampling frequency is called the Nyquist frequency, the upper frequency response limit of sample audio, named for the scientist who discovered this phenomenon.

A more serious problem, called *aliasing*, occurs when you sample sounds that contain harmonics or overtones with frequencies substantially higher than the Nyquist frequency. Aliasing causes the harmonics to be shifted in frequency, resulting in distortion when the sound is reproduced. As an example, if a harmonic with a frequency of 15.05 kHz is sampled at 22.05 kHz, the harmonic frequency you hear when the signal is reproduced is 22.05 kHz minus 15.05 kHz, or 7 kHz.

To prevent aliasing, audio adapter cards employ certain circuitry, called *low-pass filters*, to remove frequencies greater than the Nyquist frequency before they reach the ADC. The cut-off frequency of the low-pass filter is automatically adjusted to slightly below the Nyquist frequency when you change recording parameters. Multi-pole, active low-pass filters give the best sound quality because their cut-off characteristics are sharp. In other words, all frequencies below Nyquist frequency pass through the filter with little or no reduction in amplitude, and those frequencies immediately above the Nyquist frequency are almost completely eliminated.

Storing Sampled Sound in *.WAV Files

Microsoft has established a standard format for the storage of waveform audio Resource Interchange File Format (RIFF) WAVE files that have the extension WAV. This type of file includes a header with information about the sampling process used to create the file, followed by a stream of digital sound data. The header of the file includes information about the following elements:

- The format of the data, such as 8-bit mono, 8-bit stereo, 16-bit mono, or 16-bit stereo pulse code modulation (PCM).

- The number of channels—1 for stereo, 2 for mono.

- The playback sampling rate for each channel in Hz—11,025, 22,050, and 44,100.

- The playback rate in average number of bytes per second. This rate is the same as the sampling rate for 8-bit samples, and twice the sampling rate for 16-bit samples.

- The block alignment of the data, which is a function of the format and the number of channels.

- Other optional (undefined) parameters for the selected format.

Monophonic samples are stored in a continuous stream of data, and stereo samples are interleaved in blocks to avoid delays between left- and right-channel data transmission. Block alignment data is required to keep the data for the right stereo channels aligned. Additional details about the structure of WAVE files is explained in Chapter 21, "Advanced MIDI and Waveform Audio Techniques."

When you record sampled sound, Windows creates a temporary WAV file with the header information based on the recording parameters you set with the recording application. The digital audio data from your adapter card is stored in your computer's memory before being added to the temporary file. When the data fills one block of memory, called a *buffer*, that block of data is written to the temporary file while another buffer receives the next block of data. This structure is an example of multitasking with Windows; the recording and disk-writing processes occur simultaneously and share the resources of your computer's CPU.

The duration of recording is limited by the amount of memory or disk space available to hold the temporary file. Sound Recorder stores the data you record in memory. Commercial waveform audio recording applications periodically append the data in the buffer to a disk file. To determine the approximate storage requirement of the WAV file of a recording session in bytes, follow these steps:

1. Multiply the estimated recording time in seconds by the sampling rate in Hz.

2. Multiply the value obtained in step 1 by 2 if you are using 16-bit samples. Otherwise, 1 byte per sample per channel is consumed.

3. Multiply the value of step 2 by 2 if you are using stereo sampling.

If you are recording audio CD-quality stereo sound at 44.1 kHz, for example, the calculation is 44,100 * 2 * 2, which equals 176,400 bytes per second or 10,584,000 bytes per minute.

The temporary file that holds the data appended from the buffer is created on the drive designated by the SET TEMP= d:\directory line in your AUTOEXEC.BAT file. If the SET TEMP= line is missing, the temporary file is created in your \WINDOWS directory.

T I P   Add or edit the SET TEMP= line in your AUTOEXEC.BAT file to specify the drive and directory in which you want to store the sound files you record. If you save the recording to a logical drive or directory other than that specified in the SET TEMP= line, Windows makes a copy of the temporary file in the new location and then erases the temporary file. If you do not have enough disk space to hold two copies of the file, a Cannot write to... error results. If the temporary file and the final file are in the same directory, Windows simply renames the temporary file to the file name you choose.

Reproducing Sampled Sound

After you have stored the sound signal in a file, you ultimately must convert the signal back to analog form so that it can be reproduced by a speaker or headphones. You accomplish this conversion by reading the file and transferring the data to a digital-to-analog converter, a DAC. DACs perform the inverse of analog-to-digital conversion. Like ADCs, the resolution of DACs is expressed in bits. You have little advantage in having more resolution in the output than in the input, unless oversampling, discussed in this chapter's section on "Looking at Oversampling Techniques and Digital Filtering," is used in the digital-to-analog conversion process. On conventional audio output cards, analog input signals processed by an 8-bit ADC are usually reconstructed to analog output signals by an 8-bit DAC. The staircase voltage output of a DAC and the resulting analog output signal of an 8-bit DAC are shown in figure 13.3.

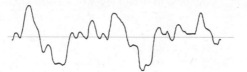

The output of the DAC is a series of square waves superimposed on one another to create a rough approximation of the analog signal. If you could listen directly to the output of a DAC, the sound might resemble that of an oboe rather than a stringed instrument because of the large number of overtones produced by square-shaped waves. Low-pass filtering, the subject of the next section, is required to re-create realistic sound, especially of musical instruments.

Low-Pass Filtering and Amplification

The DAC's output is smoothed to the reconstructed sound waveform, shown as the curved line in figure 13.1, by a low-pass filter circuit similar to the anti-aliasing filter employed by ADCs. Low-pass filtering is handled by the speaker itself. Because its cone cannot precisely duplicate the movement corresponding to the square-shaped waves, the speaker smooths (filters) the output signal physically. The larger the diameter of the speaker, the more filtering that occurs. This principle is employed by the PC to create warning beeps. The signal applied to the PC's small speaker is a series of simple square-wave pulses, but the sound waves you hear are similar to the one in figure 13.3 and include many overtones because of the small diameter of the speaker.

The filtered sound signals from the DAC are converted back to audible sound waves amplified to a level, usually 1 to 2 watts, which is adequate to drive headphones and small speakers. The *fidelity* of the entire sampling and reproduction process is related to the quality of the transducers, amplifiers, and filters involved as well as to the performance of the ADC and DAC. Fidelity is defined as the degree to which the sound pressure waves produced by the speaker are perceived by the listener to resemble those originally received by the microphone during recording.

Looking at Oversampling Techniques and Digital Filtering

A common term used in the advertising copy for audio CD players is "4x oversampling." *Oversampling* is a technique with which you can improve the apparent quality of the sound by using a faster rate of digital-to-analog conversion than that originally used to sample the sound. The term "4x oversampling" means that the digital-to-analog conversion process runs at 176.4 kHz rather than 44.1 kHz. This feat may appear to be impossible, because you cannot reproduce more samples than were originally present in the file. In fact, oversampling does work, but DACs with oversampling capabilities are presently found only in higher-quality audio adapter cards that sell at premium prices.

Oversampling involves adding samples with 0 values (no amplitude) to the original samples. In the case of 4x oversampling, three 0-value samples are inserted between each pair of original samples. A circuit called a digital filter calculates appropriate values for the 0-value samples by a process referred to as *interpolation* and substitutes these values for the 0s. Thus, digital filters are often referred to as *interpolating filters*. Oversampling and digital filtering improves reproduction fidelity and reduces noise in the output signal. The more times by which you oversample, the better the result. 8x and 16x oversampling have become common in high-performance audio CD players.

If oversampling techniques were applied to the 8-bit samples most commonly used with audio adapter cards, achieving apparent sound quality about halfway between 8- and 16-bit resolutions, roughly 12 bits, would be possible. Only PC users with oversampling audio adapter cards, however, would reap the benefits.

Considering Monophonic and Stereophonic Sound

The previous examples given in this chapter apply to monophonic audio sampling or to one channel of a stereo system. To create a stereo system, you simply add a duplicate set of the electronic components required for monophonic processing. If you sample stereo sound data at the same rate you do for mono, however, the storage requirements double. Stereo sound is seldom encountered with audio samples stored on CD-ROMs because of the additional storage space it requires.

In the majority of multimedia presentations and CD-ROM titles, 16-bit stereo sound is not a requirement. If your presentation is designed to be distributed on video tape, relatively few VCRs offer stereo sound reproduction capability. More than 90 percent of all sound cards installed in PCs as of mid-1992 have 8-bit DACs. At the time this book was written, about 75 percent of the audio cards provided monophonic reproduction only and could not reproduce 44.1-kHz samples. The percentage of stereo audio adapter cards with 44.1-kHz reproduction capability is expected to increase substantially in the future, but whether 16-bit ADCs and DACs will become the standard is open to question. The most common recording format for commercial CD-ROM titles produced in 1991 and early 1992 was mono 8-bit samples at 22.05 kHz.

> **T I P**
>
> If you need stereo sound reproduction to simulate movement of the sound source or to provide left-right separation of instruments in a musical composition, and you are using 16-bit samples, you may be able to use 8-bit resolution to compensate for the increased storage requirements of the additional channel. The additional quantizing error resulting from the lower resolution of the 8-bit samples is approximately halved when the two sounds are combined. You perceive the two samples as blended when you listen to both channels.

Using Audio Compression

You can compress disk files that contain repeating groups of digital data by searching for identical groups of data and assigning each member of the repeating group a special code, called a *token*. You need to save only one copy of the repeated data; then you can use the token to represent the remainder. This type of compression is used by the disk file compression utilities discussed in Chapter 4, "Preparing Your System for Multimedia." Audio signals seldom have repeating groups, so tokenized compression and decompression does not save significant amounts of disk space, unless the data includes periods of silence.

Reducing the amount of data needed to transmit and store digitally sampled audio requires that the compression be done by modifying the encoding process during analog-to-digital conversion. Similarly, decompression must be accomplished during the digital-to-analog conversion step. Audio compression and decompression can be accomplished by various types of algorithms (calculations) incorporated in software applications or programmed into special-purpose integrated-circuit chips. Simply processing 16-bit stereo samples at 44.1 kHz requires a substantial share of most PC's CPU resources, so hardware implementations of compression and decompression are the most common.

No final standards have been established for compressing and expanding the waveform audio files used in Windows multimedia applications. Intel's Digital Video Interleaved (DVI), Microsoft's Audio Video Interleaved (AVI), and CD-ROM XA use different compression and decompression techniques, but the basic approach is similar. AVI uses software to compress and decompress audio data, and the other methods require you to add special chips to the audio adapter card. When a Windows standard is established, it undoubtedly will be based on adaptive differential pulse code modulation (ADPCM), the subject of the following sections. ADPCM or closely related compression methods offer the greatest compression ratios that can be achieved on a real-time basis.

Using Differential Pulse Code Modulation

Digital audio samples follow one another in patterns that increase or decrease in value by small amounts compared with the full-scale range of the ADC. If the sampling rate is fast enough, the maximum change between the values of any 2 successive samples might be no more than 1 or 2 bits of the 8-bit or 16-bit range of the converter. If you store only the difference between successive samples, you can substantially reduce the amount of data that needs to be transmitted or stored without losing sound quality.

Differential pulse code modulation, also called *delta modulation*, requires that a prediction of the value of the next sample be made before the time the next sample is to be measured. Predicted values are established by storing the average value of a specific number of preceding samples. The difference between the measured value of the sample and the predicted value is stored as a single bit, set to 1 for a higher value and to 0 for a lower value. If the sampling rate is fast enough so that only a one-bit change can occur during the sampling interval, no sound quality is lost by storing only one bit. In this case, a high sampling rate is required, and thus the savings in the number of bits is offset by the requirement for more samples. Delta modulation is used in digital transmission of telephone signals where high fidelity is not a requirement, but not for recording music.

Using ADPCM Compression Techniques

Adaptive pulse code modulation (ADPCM) is an extension of differential pulse code modulation that uses more than one bit to describe the difference in value between two successive samples. ADPCM uses either 4-bit or 8-bit values to encode the difference between signals, depending on the sound quality required. The additional difference-value bits contribute greatly to sound quality; 4-bit ADPCM can provide the equivalent of about 12-bit PCM, and 8-bit ADPCM rivals 16-bit PCM in frequency response.

The term "adaptive" in ADPCM means that the 4 or 8 bits that comprise the difference in value between the measured and predicted values of samples can be scaled to suit the waveform being processed. In addition to the next value being predicted from preceding values, the expected change in the next value is also predicted. A dynamic scale factor is assigned to the bits that comprise the ADPCM data, depending on how fast the amplitude of sound is changing. Using 4-bit ADPCM, for instance, 0000 might represent a change of –1 volt, and 1111 a change of 1 volt when the amplitude of the signal is changing slowly, but then be scaled to –5 and +5 volts when higher-frequency sounds occur.

Creative Labs was the first to use ADPCM on a PC audio adapter card in the company's original Sound Blaster product. Sound Blaster VOC files offer 2:1, 3:1, and 4:1 compression, with 4-bit, 2.6-bit, and 2-bit ADPCM encoding, respectively. The hardware ADPCM algorithm used by Creative is adequate for recording sound effects and musical accompaniment for games but not for high-fidelity music applications. Windows does not support ADPCM files as a standard RIFF file type, so you need to convert compressed VOC files to WAV files prior to using them with Windows applications.

Philips uses 4- and 8-bit ADPCM for encoding audio on CD-I interactive CD-ROMs, and both 4- and 8-bit ADPCM are supported in the CD-ROM XA standard employed by the Sony Bookman. After the final standard for Windows ADPCM audio in RIFF files is established, you can expect ADPCM to be added to the Multimedia PC Specification as a "recommended" capability.

Special-purpose PC adapter cards that implement ADPCM have been available for several years, and IBM provides an M-Audio Adapter that employs ADPCM. The principal use of these special audio cards is in education applications in which lessons are distributed on CD-ROMs or stored on hard disks. Using 4-bit compressed ADPCM audio increases the number of lessons that fit on a CD-ROM, minimizing the exchange of CD-ROMs by students. ADPCM can be implemented by specially designed integrated circuit chips or by general-purpose devices called digital signal processors.

Using Digital Signal Processors

A *digital signal processor* (DSP) is a microprocessor designed specifically for processing sampled audio data. Using a DSP instead of your computer's CPU to process audio data frees the computer's resources so that it can display animated graphic or video images and play high-fidelity sound simultaneously. The architecture of the DSP's microprocessor is optimized for sequential sample processing, so DSPs make the predictions and other calculations required for ADPCM more quickly than a general-purpose 80386 or 80486 of the same speed.

DSPs have on-board memory and their own I/O bus structure to add RAM and ROM in various combinations. The newer DSPs have floating-point numeric processors, similar to the 80287 and 80387 math coprocessor chips used in PCs, to speed calculations that return precise values. Your computer sends data and simple control instructions over its I/O bus to the DSP adapter card, which handles all the complex operations necessary to process the audio data.

Using ADPCM with Digital Signal Processors

Because audio compression standards for Windows multimedia have not been established, commercial MPC-compliant audio adapter cards that support other compression standards such as CD-ROM XA have not appeared on the market. Ultimately, ADPCM must be implemented together with the SCSI CD-ROM interface if these cards are to be capable of playing CD-ROM XA or CD-I audio. Antex Corporation, for instance, has developed a high-end MPC-compatible audio adapter card that provides ADPCM capabilities for CD-ROM XA, CD-I, DVI, and AVI audio and also implements Dolby Laboratories' AC-2 compression system for broadcast-quality sound.

One of the principal incentives for adding DSPs to MPC-compliant adapter cards is reprogrammability, either by substituting different read-only memory (ROM) chips or sending special programming instructions to the card from a Windows application. In contrast to a dedicated hardware implementation of one basic type of ADPCM, such as used by the Sound Blaster cards, the reprogrammability of DSP chips prevents obsolescence. When a new audio compression standard, such as MPEG, appears, you simply add another ROM chip to implement it. If optional RAM chips are added to the card, you can load a program into the card when you boot your computer, or Windows, to perform special signal processing operations.

The DSP can eliminate much of the circuitry otherwise required to implement analog-to-digital and digital-to-analog conversion. This capability compensates in part for the additional cost of the DSP chip, plus the additional memory chips it requires, compared with the dedicated ICs found on today's high-volume sound cards.

You also can use the DSP for musical synthesis and can add digital effects, the subjects of the following two subsections.

Using DSPs for Musical Synthesis

Turtle Beach Systems was the first firm to add a DSP to a commercial MPC-compatible audio adapter card—the MultiSound described in Chapter 2. The synthesis circuitry was designed by E-mu Systems for its

SoundEngine daughterboard, which implements the sounds of the Proteus 1/XR. Creative Labs licensed the E-mu technology in mid-1992, so you can expect to see a new "Blaster" with a DSP chip on board and greatly improved synthesized sound quality.

Another candidate for musical synthesis with DSPs is the WaveGuide technology developed at Stanford University's Center for Computer Research in Music and Acoustics. WaveGuide is a computer model of the physics of acoustical musical instruments and the human singing voice. WaveGuide technology is related to digital FM synthesis because it creates the waveforms representing a clarinet, for example, instead of using samples of actual sounds made by the clarinet. Digital FM provides you with oscillators and modulators that you combine in an attempt to simulate the timbre of an acoustical instrument. With WaveGuide, you combine individual physical models of the components of an instrument on a computer. Component models for a clarinet include a single reed, a bore representing the body of the clarinet, tone holes for specific notes, and the bell at the end of the instrument. When your model is complete, the elements are implemented by digital filters, and the instrument's timbre is duplicated.

The advantage of WaveGuide synthesis is the capability to add expression to the playing of synthesized music. Although attempts have been made to add expression to MIDI instruments, such as the MIDI wind instrument described in Chapter 11, these efforts have met with limited success. With WaveGuide, breath pressure, lip pressure (embouchure), and fingering or valving techniques used by an individual artist can be duplicated. With the proper models, you can re-create the styles of Louis Armstrong or Miles Davis on a WaveGuide trumpet.

An additional feature of WaveGuide techniques is that you can record the output of a MIDI sequence directly as digital data, without going through the additional digital-to-analog and analog-to-digital conversion steps imposed by current synthesis-to-waveform recording.

Media Vision is developing a special, dedicated DSP to implement both real-time WaveGuide and conventional wavetable synthesis on an MPC-compliant audio adapter card. This new product is expected to be in commercial distribution in 1993. Although the initial version of the product is expected to be a professional-level card and to be priced accordingly, lower-cost versions for the consumer market are sure to follow.

Using DSPs for Digital Effects

The digital effects processors described in Chapter 11 utilize DSP chips to perform a variety of digital manipulation of sound. MIDI-controlled effects processors take an analog signal, sample it, perform operations on the samples, and then convert the sound back to analog form. This process introduces two additional conversions in the chain that can contribute to reduced bandwidth and increased noise.

Algorithms for DSP chips on audio adapter cards can add effects, such as reverberation or chorus, to the sound by superimposing duplicates of the sampled data, delayed in time, on the original data. You can imitate any electric guitar "effects processor" functions by using the appropriate (and usually complex) program code for the DSP. Depending on the speed of your computer and the efficiency of the DSP code, you can create the effects in real time, processing the audio data on the fly. Without a high-speed DSP, you are relegated to off-line processing that manipulates data stored in files. An off-line application can read a block of data from a file, modify the content of the block, write the modified data to the disk, and then proceed to process the next block in sequence.

Chapter Summary

This chapter explained how waveform audio technology works so that you can take full advantage of all its features. Improved digital audio compression techniques, such as full-fidelity ADPCM and advanced DSP hardware, will appear on an increasing number of audio adapter cards as users demand higher-quality sound. Future audio adapter cards will use DSPs for waveform audio recording and reproduction, as well as synthesized music and sound effects.

The balance of Part IV of this book delves into applications you can use to edit the waveform audio files you create, explains how to convert files in other formats to the WAV variety required by Windows multimedia, and tells you how to make your waveform audio files have broadcast-quality sound. Advanced topics, including synchronizing waveform audio files with other material such as MIDI music or video tape productions, are covered in Chapter 21, "Advanced MIDI and Waveform Audio Techniques."

Editing and Converting Waveform Audio Files

Audio recording techniques have made great strides since the days of 78-rpm records and radio transcription disks. In those times, "cutting" a record meant just that—you used a "lathe" to inscribe the sound-containing grooves in a master record. The performance had to be right on, or you had to start over, because you had no way to edit grooves in a shellac-surfaced master.

Wax cylinder dictation machines were on the market before World War II, and versions using thin plastic records came out in the postwar era; none of these devices were adequate, however, for musical reproduction. Then Webster Electric Corporation introduced the first consumer sound recorder, the Webcor Wire Recorder, in the late 1940s. You could edit its recordings by clipping and tying sections together with square knots, but the knots made annoying clicks when they passed the recording head. In the mid-1950s, Ampex Corporation revolutionized the recording industry, first with its studio-quality audio tape recorders and later with the first video tape systems.

The advantage of tape recorders, second only to their sound quality, was the capability they gave you to make noiseless edits. You could cut out the sour notes and splice in sweet ones. This task required a splicing block, special adhesive tape, and a great deal of patience on the part of the audio engineer who created the final master tape. The ability to "punch in a new take" automatically that was added to modern tape recorders saved much time and effort for the performers, but the discipline enforced by the unforgiving cutting lathe was lost forever.

Now, direct-to-disk recording techniques eliminate the need for tape recorders. If you have a fast disk drive with a large capacity, you can record 16-bit stereo signals with audio CD quality on your hard disk. Duplicating an 8-track tape recorder, however, consumes about 40M per minute of disk space, so you can store only 15 minutes of 8-track data on a 600M disk drive. Fortunately, disk drives in the gigabyte (1,000M) range are now beginning to appear.

This chapter deals with the methods you use to edit the waveform audio files you record and how to convert waveform audio files stored in other formats to WAV files compatible with Windows 3.1.

Editing waveform audio files is an art that is almost a science. The examples of editing in this chapter use Sound Recorder's limited capabilities; the results are unlikely to be artful or scientific. Serious editing requires a commercial waveform editing application for Windows. Two of the first waveform audio editing applications for Windows are described in this chapter.

Converting waveform audio files created on other computers or by pre-Windows applications on the PC is a more cut-and-dried process. Most audio adapter card suppliers provide DOS file-conversion utilities for popular sound-file formats, and many shareware utilities are available for the same purpose. This chapter describes Makin' Waves, a Windows utility that converts most sound files to WAV files that work.

Exploring Digital Audio Editing Techniques

When you edit from a tape recorder, an oscilloscope enables you to view the audio output of the recorder, but you need to crank the recorder's reels manually to find the clicks or other noise to cut from the tape. With the advent of the personal computer and digital sampling, you can see as well as hear sound in real time. Digital audio stored in disk files, transferred to your computer's memory, and then shown on your display makes editing sound files a comparative snap. Step-by-step instructions for using Windows Sound Recorder applet to perform a few of the basic edits of sound files are given in the next section. Later sections show you how selected Windows applications, supplied with audio adapter cards or available as commercial products, provide an arsenal of more sophisticated editing techniques.

Mixing Sound Files with Sound Recorder

Mixing sounds from more than one source remains primarily an analog process, but digital mixers are beginning to appear on the market at prices that professional musicians, not just sound studios, can afford. You can simulate the digital mixing process by combining as many sound files as you want with Sound Recorder, up to the point where you create a random jumble called noise. Try mixing some of the files supplied with Windows 3.1 by following these steps:

1. Make backup copies of the WAV files supplied with Windows so that you don't lose the originals if you accidentally overwrite them in the steps that follow. The easiest way to make backups is to start MS-DOS from the Main group, type **copy *.wav *.wak** at the DOS prompt while in your \WINDOWS directory (the default directory for the MS-DOS function of Windows), and then press Enter. Do not use BAK as the extension, because other files in that directory may have that extension. After the copies are made, type **exit** and press Enter to return to ProgMan.

2. Start Sound Recorder from the Accessories group by double-clicking its icon.

3. Choose **F**ile, **O**pen and double-click TADA.WAV in the file list box of the Open dialog box to load the file into memory. TADA.WAV is long enough, 1.25 seconds, to enable you to add several sounds and hear them individually.

4. Click the Play button, the one with the single, right-pointing arrow, to remind yourself of TADA's original sound.

5. You can control the point at which you mix the second file with the sample in memory by using the scroll-bar slider, now positioned under the right edge of the simulated oscilloscope display. Place the mouse pointer on the scroll-bar slider and, holding down the left mouse button, adjust the slider to the left until `1.00 secs.` appears in the Position window, as shown in figure 14.1.

FIG. 14.1

Adjusting the mixing position of TADA.WAV to 1.00 seconds.

6. From Sound Recorder's menu, choose **Edit**. The drop-down menu shown in figure 14.2 appears.

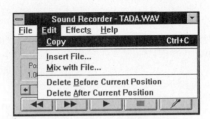

FIG. 14.2

The waveform editing options of Sound Recorder.

7. Choose **Mix** with File and double-click CHORD.WAV to mix it at the 1.00-second point in TADA. Notice that the length of the file is now 2.13 seconds, because CHORD.WAV is 1.13 seconds in length and was inserted 1.00 second into the TADA sample (see fig. 14.3).

FIG. 14.3

CHORD.WAV mixed with TADA.WAV.

8. Click the Rewind button (the double left-pointing arrows) and then click Play. You hear CHORD.WAV mixed into the TADA sample.

9. Position the slider to 2.00 seconds, choose **Edit**, choose **Mix** with File, and double-click CHIMES.WAV. Click the Rewind button and then choose Play again.

   You can mix as many files as many times as you want into the sample in memory.

10. Choose **File** and then choose Save **As** when you want to save your sample as a file. The Save As dialog box shown in figure 14.4 appears.

11. In the File Name text box, enter a new name for the file, such as **new_tada.wav**, and click OK. (Make sure that you add the WAV extension because Sound Recorder will not do it for you. This lack is an oversight in the first release of Windows 3.1's Sound Recorder applet.)

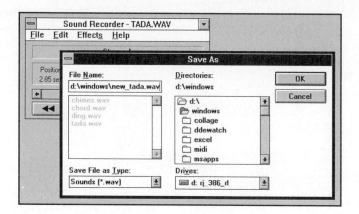

FIG. 14.4

Saving an edited
waveform file with
Sound Recorder.

Adding Echo, Reverberation, and Chorus Effects

Most of the pop and rock CDs you hear today are laden with digitally generated effects created by inventive sound engineers who are directed by zealous record producers. Digital chorusing makes a single "do wah" singer sound like a group, and distortion (intentional) gives electric guitars their characteristic rock sound. You seldom hear a "clean" (meaning no effects, sometimes called "dry") guitar on any but a classical track. Reverb makes tunes recorded in 8-by-12-foot studios sound as if they came live from Carnegie Hall. Many newer (and higher-priced) audio CD players offer various reverberation effects. Judicious use of digital effects can make even the Concertgebouw or the Berlin Philharmonic sound better in your living room.

Sound Recorder offers one automatic effect: the echo. Echo effects are created by mixing a copy of the sound, delayed and attenuated (at lower volume), with the original. Reverb effects comprise multiple echoes with very short delays and very attenuated levels. Unfortunately, Sound Recorder does not enable you to adjust either the delay or the level of the echoes it adds. The following practice procedure illustrates this limited effect:

1. If you haven't already done so, make a backup copy of your sound files, as suggested in the preceding section on sound mixing.

2. Choose **F**ile, **O**pen and load DING.WAV. Click the Play button so that you remember the sound of DING.WAV. (DING.WAV is the best choice for adding echoes because it has an ASDR envelope with fast attack and decay followed by a sustain portion of reasonable length.) Examine the oscilloscopic trace of the file with the scroll bar slider. Notice that the maximum intensity, represented by the

vertical or Y-axis of the display of figure 14.5 at about 0.05 second (50 milliseconds), is roughly 33 percent of the total height of the window. This intensity is about the level that you should attempt to maintain when you use Sound Recorder. Now move the slider to about 0.18 second.

3. Choose **Effects**, choose **Echo**, and then play the sample. Repeat this process three times. The echo, which you can see in the oscilloscope trace of figure 14.6, begins at about 0.18 second into the file.

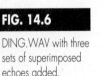

4. You can add multiple echoes to the file. Each is added after the other if you simply choose **Effects**, then **Echo** several times in succession. Notice, however, that the file does not grow in duration; it remains at the original 0.52 second. Here is where adding an echo differs from mixing multiple copies of the file.

You can reinforce the sound of a single echo by playing the file between successive additions of echoes. This act resets the internal echo position counter back to 0. If you repeat this procedure several times, you can see the increase in the amplitude of the first echo at 0.19 second, as shown in figure 14.7. Because the time at which the echo is inserted is controlled by Sound Recorder, repetitions are timed precisely, and the echoes reinforce one another.

You can more or less duplicate reverberation and chorusing effects by mixing multiple copies of the file offset by small intervals, but you cannot control the amplitude of the added copies. For this reason, the sounds you create resemble chorusing more than reverb. Try this example:

FIG. 14.7

DING.WAV with echoes reinforced with Sound Recorder.

1. Start another instance of Sound Recorder by double-clicking its icon in the Accessories group. You can run as many instances of Sound Recorder as can fit on your display.

2. Load TADA.WAV into both instances of Sound Recorder. TADA.WAV is the best of the four standard WAV files for this example because, unlike DING, the attack and decay levels of TADA's envelope are similar to the sustain level. The first instance is used so that you can quickly compare the original with the modified copy.

3. Set the position of the second Sound Recorder instance at 0.10 second with the scroll-bar slider and mix in another copy of TADA.WAV.

4. Choose Mix with File from the Edit menu.

5. Select TADA.WAV in the File Name list box.

6. Click the OK button to close the dialog box.

7. Rewind and play the example; then play the first instance of Sound Recorder to compare the two sounds.

8. Repeat steps 3 through 7 four times with the position set at 0.02, 0.03, 0.04, and 0.05 seconds.

   You may want to choose Effects and then Decrease Volume to maintain the amplitude of the two sounds at a similar level. Each time you choose Decrease Volume, the amplitude of the sound as a whole (not just the additions you made) is reduced by 25 percent. Compare the original and modified sounds after each addition of TADA.WAV.

If you examine the oscilloscope trace at 0.10 second, you see the result of the mixing process. Figure 14.8 was produced without reducing the amplitude of the sound. The top window in the figure is the first instance of Sound Recorder with only one TADA.WAV added; the bottom window is the second instance with the multiple copies of TADA.WAV added to produce the chorus effects.

FIG. 14.8

Chorus effects created
by mixing files with
Sound Recorder.

You can create slightly different chorus effects by reducing the amplitude of the sound in the buffer before you mix in the delayed copies. Progressively increasing the delay between additions—for example using 0.01, 0.02, 0.04, 0.08, and 0.16 seconds—yields a slightly different sound. With TADA, these differences are quite subtle.

Sound Recorder will not destroy the market for the digital effects processors described in Chapter 11, but you can gain insight into how effects are generated by experimenting with the examples presented.

Related Topics
MIDI Effects Processors,
p. 324

Looping To Extend Duration

Digital representations of the sounds of musical instruments used in sample-playback modules must provide for different note durations. When writing a dirge, you may want to have a trumpet sound for one or two entire measures—perhaps four or five seconds. If samples of instruments capable of sustained tones had to be stored for the longest duration anyone might want to use, the memory required to hold them would be excessively large. Engineers developed a technique called *looping* to overcome this problem and provide sustained sound capability without consuming megabytes of ROM.

The sound created by most musical instruments is characterized by an initial period during which rapid changes in pitch and amplitude occur, followed by a sustained period of relatively consistent sound. Players of string and wind instruments use vibrato—rapid small changes in pitch also called tremolo—to add character to their parts. A looped sample of a clarinet might consist of the initial period, attack and decay, plus a single sample of the period of perhaps one vibrato cycle. The controller for the sound module, usually a microprocessor, plays the attack and decay portion and then repeats the vibrato cycle sample as many times as necessary to create the desired duration.

You can create a crude simulation of looping with Sound Recorder to extend the duration of TADA.WAV as long as you want. Follow these steps to see how it works:

1. Load TADA.WAV into both instances of Sound Recorder.

2. Using the second instance of Sound Recorder, set the position to 1.14 seconds. Choose **E**dit and then choose Delete **B**efore Current Position. Click OK to confirm the deletion in the dialog box that appears.

3. Set the position to 0.07 second. Again, choose **E**dit, but then use Delete **A**fter Current Position to remove the silence that follows. You now have a 0.07-second loop sample.

4. Choose File, choose Save **A**s, name your loop file **tadaloop.wav**, and click OK to save it.

5. Choose File, choose **O**pen, and reload TADA.WAV. Set the position to 1.14 seconds.

6. Choose **E**dit, choose Insert File, and double-click TADALOOP.WAV to insert it at the 1.14-second position.

7. Repeat step 6 about 10 times. Notice that the length of your sound grows by 0.07 second each time you repeat the step, but the position remains at 1.14 seconds.

8. Play the sound. You hear TADA.WAV plus a stuttering sound created by the inserted loop file. This sound is the result of a short initial silence in each sample, a good example of a bad loop. Finding the proper starting and ending points for the loop file is difficult with the oscilloscope display. Commercial waveform sound editors, to be described shortly in this chapter's section "Using Commercial Waveform Editing Applications," solve this problem.

Related Topics
Embedding or Linking Source
Documents, p. 223

Using **C**opy and **P**aste commands to add copies of the loop sample to create an extended sound, as you would expect to be able to do with the Clipboard, would be much simpler. Sound Recorder has a Copy choice in its **E**dit menu, but no **P**aste option. The help file for Sound Recorder states that the sound is copied to the Clipboard, but what is actually copied is an OLE sound object you can insert into documents created with OLE-compliant applications. This use is described in Chapter 8. Unfortunately, you cannot use the **C**opy choice in conjunction with Sound Recorder's editing functions.

T I P

Restoring Accidentally Overwritten WAV Files

If you made the backup copies of your WAV files as recommended in the section on "Mixing Sound Files with Sound Recorder," you can restore WAV files that you accidentally have overwritten by following this simple procedure:

1. At the DOS prompt, type **copy *.wak *.wav**, and press Enter.

2. If you want to conserve disk space, erase the WAK files by typing **del *.wak** and then pressing Enter.

3. Type **exit** and press Enter to return to ProgMan.

If you didn't heed the advice regarding backup WAV file copies, you need to restore the files from the Windows 3.1 distribution disks by following these steps:

1. At the DOS prompt, erase the WAV files you overwrote, or use File Manager to delete them. You must delete the overwritten files to be able to install the original versions.

2. Start the Setup application from the Main group.

3. Choose **O**ptions from the main menu and then choose **A**dd/Remove Windows Components.

4. Click the Files button for Wallpapers, Misc.

5. Locate the files to reinstall and click each one to highlight them.

6. Click the Add button and then click the OK button in the Windows Setup dialog box. You are instructed to insert the Windows distribution disk on which the files are located.

7. Insert the proper floppy disk, enter the appropriate drive letter, and click OK. The files are reinstalled.

8. Exit Setup by clicking the Control Panel bar (upper left corner) and then choosing **C**lose.

After you have performed a few experiments and observed the restricted editing capabilities of Sound Recorder, you probably will consider acquiring one of the waveform editing applications for Windows described in the following section.

Using Commercial Waveform Editing Applications

Sound Recorder has limited waveform file editing capabilities, as you have seen, but it comes at no charge with Windows 3.1. As with sound cards, you get what you pay for in sound editors. Most sound cards come with waveform sound editors of varying capabilities, and several firms have created quite sophisticated commercial sound editing applications. Media Vision, for instance, supplies Sound Forge, a Windows waveform file editing and conversion application, with its Thunder and Lightning adapter card. If you plan to use waveform audio files in presentations, you need a commercial waveform editing application. Brief descriptions of the first of these applications for Windows are provided in the following sections.

Editing with Turtle Beach Wave Lite and Wave for Windows

Turtle Beach created its Wave for Windows sound editor based on the technology employed in the firm's 56K Digital Recording System, a DOS application used by professional sound engineers to create CD audio and digital audio tape (DAT) masters. A truncated version of Wave for Windows, Wave Lite for Windows, is included with Turtle Beach's MultiSound card, described in Chapter 2. Wave Lite, whose main editing screen is shown in figure 14.9, has most of the functions audio enthusiasts need in order to edit files.

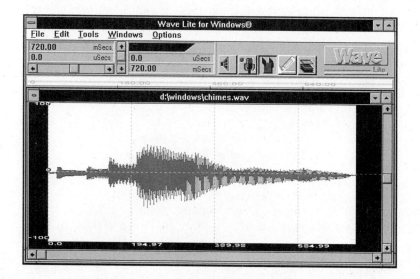

FIG. 14.9

The main waveform audio editing screen of Wave Lite for Windows.

Wave Lite enables you to manipulate up to four individual windows containing waveform audio data stored in separate memory buffers. You create a new sound by combining portions of three other files into a new sound buffer and then saving it to a file. You can perform accurate copy and paste operations by expanding the time base and amplitude scales with the horizontal and vertical scroll bars shown in the upper left corner of figure 14.9. Figure 14.10 shows a 275-microsecond portion of TADA.WAV in a window that displays approximately 3.5 milliseconds of the sound. The amplitude axis in figure 14.10 has been expanded by a factor of 4.

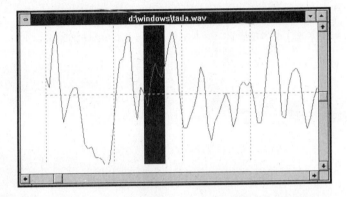

d:\windows\tada.wav

FIG. 14.10

A 275-microsecond portion of a waveform audio file selected for Clipboard operations.

The benefit of using commercial editing applications such as Wave Lite for Windows is their capability to select portions of sound files precisely. Unlike Sound Recorder, these applications use the Windows Clipboard to copy the selected sound clip to a buffer where you can edit the clip as necessary. After you have adjusted the amplitude of the sound clip to the proper value and deleted any extraneous sound, you can insert the sound data in the buffer at any location in another buffer.

Wave for Windows, designed for use by audio professionals, adds an assortment of sophisticated editing features, including audio *transform* operations, to the Lite version. Transforms manipulate all or a portion of the file, providing automated fades, amplitude changes, and pitch conversion, to name a few of the features.

Editing with Voyetra's AudioView

Voyetra Technologies is the author of Sequencer Plus, a leading MIDI sequencer application for DOS, and manufactures MIDI adapter cards. Voyetra supplies Windows drivers to manufacturers of MPC audio adapter cards, and several card producers include a version of

Sequencer Plus and Voyetra's FM Edit, a DOS voice editor for the Yamaha OPL-II and OPL-III chipsets, with their products. Voyetra's AudioView, whose main editing window is shown in figure 14.11, is a full-featured waveform audio file-editing application.

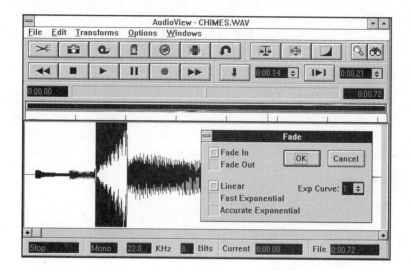

When you expand the time base with the magnifying glass button in the upper right corner of AudioView's editing window, a display similar to that in figure 14.12 results. When the time base is expanded, AudioView displays the amplitude of each discrete sample. Turtle Beach's Wave Lite displays a series of curved lines that connect the individual samples, and the display represents a signal that has been passed through a high-pass filter.

Like Wave Lite for Windows, AudioView can cut, copy, paste, and insert selected portions of a file with the Windows Clipboard. AudioView provides a number of transforms, such as fades, cross-fades, and noise gating, which eliminates samples whose amplitudes are below a specified threshold. AudioView is oriented toward working with the content of a single file, but Wave Lite is designed for multiple file or buffer applications. To create new files from sound clips copied from other files, you use multiple instances of AudioView. You paste the copied clip into an instance of AudioView that has no file loaded.

Editing with Microsoft's WaveEdit Application

Microsoft includes in the Multimedia Development Kit (MDK) a simple waveform audio editing application called WaveEdit, whose editing screen is shown in figure 14.13. The MDK version accommodates both WAV files and the AIFF (audio-independent file format) used by the Apple Macintosh computers. A supplemental release of WaveEdit supports the audio portion of the Microsoft Audio Video Interleaved (AVI) format. You can open a file in one format and then save it in another.

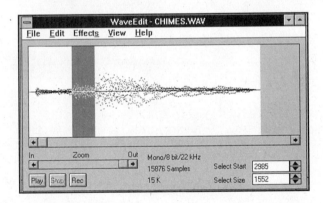

WaveEdit provides a limited range of audio transforms accessed from its **E**dit menu. You can insert periods of silence, perform up- and down-fades, and change the amplitude of a selected portion of the audio file. In addition, you can convert files from one sampling rate to another, change the resolution, and combine both channels of a stereo file into a mono sample.

Creating WAV Files from Other Formats

Users of Sound Blaster cards are known to accumulate large libraries of VOC digital sound files. Apple Macintosh users have been able to associate sounds with events for several years. The Amiga has been a favorite of both audio and graphics enthusiasts since its introduction, so a wealth of sound files are available for it. Because of these products and their sound capabilities, a wide range of sound files in Sound Blaster, Macintosh, and Amiga formats are available from a variety of sources. CompuServe, for example, has several forums that offer an eclectic assortment of prerecorded sound files.

Fortunately, Macintosh and Amiga computers, as well as Sound Blaster cards, store sampled sound in formats similar to those used by Windows 3.1. Windows' only requirement is a special *header* at the beginning of the file to identify what follows as waveform audio (WAVE) data. The header serves as a short prefix to the data and must include the letters *RIFF*, to signal Windows that this file is a Resource Interchange Format File, and *WAVE*, to identify the type of RIFF file. Other required information, such as the sampling rate, the number of bits, and whether the file is stereo or mono, follows. After you convert a Macintosh or Amiga sound file to a format compatible with DOS, you can use one of several applications to add the required RIFF WAVE header so that the header is compatible with Windows. Shareware applications described in the following sections make the header addition and conversions for you.

Using To Wave, a Digital Audio File Converter for Windows

Most applications that convert digitally sampled audio files to the WAV format required by Windows run under DOS. To Wave, a freeware application from Bells and Whistles Software of Fort Worth, Texas, is a Windows application written in Microsoft Visual Basic. You can download To Wave as 2WV10A.ZIP from Library 12, Multimedia/Sounds, of the WINADV forum on CompuServe. In addition to the ZIP file, you need a copy of VBRUN100.EXE, the run-time version of Visual Basic, which is available in the Visual Basic library of CompuServe's MSBASIC forum.

To Wave is truly a generic converter—it converts *any* file, regardless of its content (even a graphic file), to waveform audio format by adding a standard RIFF WAVE header to the beginning of the file. (Playing a 256-color bit-mapped graphic file with Sound Recorder produces strange noises.)

To convert files with To Wave, you must know the parameters used to record the original file so that you can create the required header for WAV files. The Sound Parameters dialog box of To Wave, shown in figure 14.14, enables you to select the header data that will be added to the file chosen for conversion. The default values—22.050-kHz sampling rate,

8-bit resolution, and monophonic channels—comprise the most common format for sound files created by the Macintosh and Amiga computers. Unfortunately, you cannot assume that the recording parameters for all sound files with a common extension are the same; SND and SOU, for instance, are used to identify many different types of sampled audio files. When in doubt about how the sample was recorded, try the default format first. If the sound is excessively high-pitched, change the sample rate to 11.025 kHz and try the conversion again.

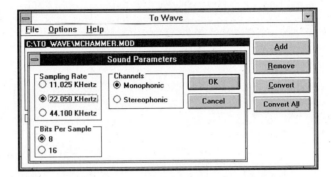

FIG. 14.14

To Wave in the process of converting a file in Amiga MOD format to a WAV file.

After you have added the header, you may need to delete the first few milliseconds of the file with a sound file editing application to eliminate the clicks and pops that result from your sound card's attempt to create sound from the original file's header data.

You cannot convert Sound Blaster VOC files to playable WAV files with To Wave because the audio data contained in VOC files is compressed. Files created by Sun's Sparc workstations and NeXT computers come in a wide variety of formats, but the most common are 16-bit linear PCM and u-law, a type of compression used in the telephone industry. You can convert linear files, which are usually recorded at 22.050 kHz, but not the compressed types.

Makin' Waves for VOC, SND, and SOU Files

Geoff Faulkner's Makin' Waves is a Windows shareware application written in Visual Basic to convert specific types of sound files—Sound Blaster VOC, Sounder and Sound Tool SND, and Macintosh SOU files (in DOS file format)—to WAV format. Makin' Waves uses a DOS application, WaveIt, written by Media Vision and described in the next section, to perform the file conversions.

As with To Wave, you can download Makin' Waves from Library 12 of the WINADV forum as MKWV12.ZIP; the program requires you to have

VBRUN100.EXE in your \WINDOWS or \WINDOWS\SYSTEM directory or on your DOS path. Because Makin' Waves is a shareware application, the author requests a registration fee if you decide to use the application.

The Makin' Waves window, after the program attempts to convert two VOC files supplied with the Sound Blaster Pro to WAV files, is shown in figure 14.15. Makin' Waves indicates that both files were converted properly (the WAV versions of the VOC files appear in the Files list box). Conversion of BBCNEWS.VOC was successful, but that of CONGA.VOC was not; CONGA.VOC causes Sound Recorder to display a `not a valid WAVE file` message. Sound Blaster VOC files can contain programmed loops and other artifacts that cause the conversion process to fail.

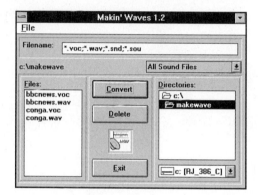

FIG. 14.15

Makin' Waves after attempting to convert two VOC files to their WAV counterparts.

Using Sound File Conversion Applications for DOS

The majority of applications capable of converting sound files from one format to another run from the DOS command line. A large collection of DOS sound file conversion applications is contained in Library 4 of the IBM New User forum (GO IBMNEW) on CompuServe. Most of these applications convert other formats to VOC files for the Sound Blaster, which you need in order to convert to WAV format with another application. In the following sections, you learn about a couple of these sound file conversion applications: WaveIt and VOC2WAV.

Using Media Vision's WaveIt File Converter

WaveIt converts VOC and other 8-bit file formats that include headers with data on the recording parameters. You can download WAVEIT.EXE, the same version used by Makin' Waves, from Library 17, Games/Fun, of

CompuServe's WINADV forum. The basic command-line syntax for converting files with WaveIt, which may be run from Windows DOS prompt, is

WAVEIT *OLDFILE.EXT NEWFILE.WAV*

OLDFILE.EXT is the name of the file to be converted (with a VOC, SND, or SOU extension), and *NEWFILE.WAV* is the name of the WAV file to be created. Type the WAVEIT command without the file names to see an on-screen explanation of the optional command-line switches you can use to change the sample rate or create a stereo version. WaveIt indicates that the *NEWFILE.WAV* parameter is optional by enclosing it in square brackets, but you must enter the WAV file name for WaveIt to function.

If WaveIt detects a component of the header that it cannot process, such as a REPEAT in a VOC file (the cause of the failure of Makin' Waves to convert CONGA.VOC, as discussed in the preceding section), WaveIt creates a WAV file with an invalid format, usually with 0 length. You are warned that the header contains a parameter not presently supported.

Converting VOC Files with Creative Lab's VOC2WAV

VOC2WAV.EXE is included on the floppy disks accompanying both the Sound Blaster and Sound Blaster Pro audio adapter cards. VOC2WAV is similar in function to WaveIt, but it successfully converts the compressed CONGA.VOC, which includes repeats (loops), to a readable CONGA.WAV file; WaveIt does not make this conversion. The basic DOS command-line syntax of VOC2WAV is

VOC2WAV *OLDFILE*[.VOC] [*NEWFILE.WAV*] [*/switch*]

You do not need to enter the items enclosed in brackets in the example—the VOC extension. VOC2WAV adds the extensions for you, giving the new file the same name as the old file but adding a WAV extension. VOC2WAV offers the following four optional command-line switches that enable you to control the conversion process. You can use as many of these switches as you need.

- /C1 and /C2 enable you to create a mono (/C1) or stereo (/C2) WAV file. VOC files are monophonic only.

- /R11, /R22, and /R44 specify the sampling rate parameter of the WAV file at 11.025 kHz (/R11), 22.05 kHz (/R22), or 44.1 kHz (/R44). If you want to use a VOC file for one of Windows' system sounds assigned by the sound driver, you must use the /R22 switch.

- /LON and /LOFF determine whether REPEATs in the file header are used to create the WAV file. If you add the switch /LON when expanding CONGA.VOC, the WAV file is about 110K rather than 22K in length and plays five times longer. /LOFF is the default.

■ /SON and /SOFF control the expansion of the SILENCE header entry that inserts periods of silence into the sound; the default is /SOFF.

Creative Labs also includes another DOS utility application, WAV2VOC.EXE, that performs the reverse conversion from WAV to VOC format.

Converting Amiga MOD Files

A variety of shareware and public domain applications are available for converting sound files having the MOD extension, which are created by the Amiga computer in SoundTracker format. CompuServe's Library 4 of the IBM New User forum, for example, has several utility applications to convert MOD files to VOC files. The most popular of these are PROMOD1.ZIP and PROMOD.ZIP, both designed for use with the Sound Blaster Pro. After you have converted the MOD files to VOC format, you need WaveIt or VOC2WAV to convert them to WAV files.

Converting Sound Files on the Macintosh

A popular Apple Macintosh application, Soundedit, supports the conversion of sound files between all the formats commonly used for playing sound on the Mac. If you have a Mac, a SuperDrive, Soundedit, and Microsoft's Multimedia Development Kit, you can use Microsoft's "official" method of converting these files, described in document Q81985 from the Microsoft Knowledge Base. To convert sound files, follow these steps:

1. Load the Mac sound file into Soundedit.
2. Save the sound file in AIFF format.
3. Convert the Macintosh AIFF file to DOS format.
4. With your PC, convert the DOS AIFF file to WAVE format, using the CONVERT.EXE or WaveEdit applications supplied with the MDK.

In addition to the Macintosh and Soundedit, you also need a copy of the Multimedia Development Kit, so the capital investment is quite high for this approach.

Chapter Summary

Only two third-party products were available at the time this book was written, and beta-test versions of Wave Lite for Windows and AudioView were used to create the examples in this chapter. As the PC multimedia market matures, a variety of editing applications for WAV files is sure to appear on the market. The file-conversion utilities described in this chapter are satisfactory for simple file formats but cannot handle the ADPCM formats used by CD-ROM XA and CD-I disks. Commercial file-conversion applications are expected to be necessary to adapt WAV files to their CD-ROM ADPCM counterparts.

Chapter 15, "Waveform Audio Recording Techniques," gives you the background you need to create waveform audio files that have the sound quality necessary to create a professional presentation. Chapter 21, "Advanced MIDI and Waveform Audio Techniques," explains the structure of Windows' RIFF files.

Waveform Audio Recording Techniques

C hapter 4 introduced you to the basic element of recording multimedia sound: the microphone. This chapter details the entire sound-recording process, from choosing the proper microphone for specific audio duties to choosing audio tape recorders. This chapter also explains waveform audio files and some of the problems associated with sampled sound techniques.

If you are interested in sound only for recording voice notes or playing MIDI files, you can skip this chapter; you don't even need to use the audio card's mixer for those two activities. If you're producing a presentation for an audience or creating a multimedia title, however, you should read this chapter because sound can contribute more than half the overall effect of your presentation. The fidelity of your narration and background music, recorded as waveform audio files, determines whether sound adds or detracts from the effect. A low-fidelity, badly mixed soundtrack turns off audiences much faster than muddy graphics or pixelated videos.

Reading this chapter does not qualify you to be a full-fledged audio engineer. If you follow this chapter's suggestions and take the time to test, choose, and install your audio components carefully, you can use your PC to create waveform audio soundtracks that rival those produced in professional recording studios.

Understanding the Audio Chain

Today's MPC-compatible audio adapter cards provide more flexibility in audio sources than was available in professional recording studios 10 or 20 years ago. An investment of as little as $200 in a sound card turns your computer into a desktop audio (DTA) device that enables you to blend the following elements:

- Synthesized sound stored in MIDI files

- Digitally sampled sound stored in waveform audio files on your hard disk

- Waveform audio files stored on CD-ROMs

- Stereo inputs from audio CDs

- Monaural and sometimes stereo microphone inputs

- Auxiliary inputs from mixers or audio tape recorders

Add a moderate-cost multichannel tape recorder/mixer combination (which you might consider to be the DTA equivalent of desktop publishing's laser printer), and you can create high-quality soundtracks for animated presentations, videotapes, or multimedia titles.

Figure 15.1 illustrates the basic components of a desktop audio system.

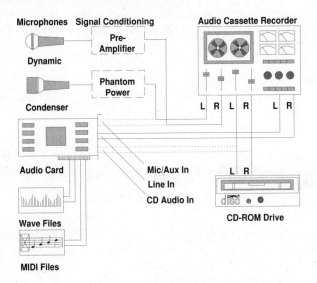

FIG. 15.1

Components of the desktop audio chain.

The solid lines in figure 15.1 denote the proper connections when a cassette recorder is used as an intermediate storage point for audio data. The connections used for direct-to-disk recording are dotted.

The connections among the audio components shown in the figure are those used to record multisource stereo audio as waveform audio files on your hard disk. You can, of course, reverse these connections and record the mixed output from your sound card onto a cassette tape. The cassette need not be an audio tape; if you have a videocassette recorder with high-quality audio-dubbing capability, you can use your audio adapter card to add sound to the audio tracks of videotapes without worrying about the video images. (Audio tape recorders are discussed in the last section of this chapter.)

> The recommendations against using many typefaces in a DTP publication also apply to sounds in desktop audio tracks. Combining waveform audio and MIDI background music often is distracting because of the differences in timbre between the two media. If you record the audio output of your MIDI sequences on tape rather than on your hard disk, consider doing the same with narration so that the sound quality of the two recordings does not differ.
>
> **T I P**

NOTE Pronounced stereo effects and "ping-pong" sounds may irritate your audience. You should avoid intrusive sound effects, using them only to illustrate a point or to enhance animation, not for entertainment purposes.

Setting Up To Record Waveform Audio

The length of the waveform audio recordings that you can make with Windows' Sound Recorder applet is limited by the amount of RAM available at the time you start recording. Typically, 45 seconds to a minute or two of recording time is available.

Sound Recorder is limited to 8-bit recording at a fixed 22.05-kHz sampling rate. To record longer sessions or to use a different format, you must use a commercial Windows recording application. All audio adapter cards come with Windows recording applications, some of which enable you to edit waveform audio recordings.

You may encounter problems in freeing sufficient disk space to store long waveform audio files, in finding the correct cables for your audio connections, and in minimizing hum and noise in your recording setup. The following sections discuss these subjects.

Disk Space and Performance Requirements

The first problem you are likely to encounter in recording long waveform audio files is insufficient hard-disk space to hold them. The following table lists the amount of disk space required to hold a one-minute conventional PCM waveform audio file recorded at varying sampling rates and resolutions.

Sampling rate	8-Bit mono	8-Bit stereo	16-Bit mono	16-Bit stereo
11.025 kHz	0.6615M	1.323M	1.323M	2.626M
22.05 kHz	1.323M	2.626M	2.626M	5.292M
44.1 kHz	2.626M	5.292M	5.292M	10.584M

The term "hold" rather than "record" is used because most waveform recording applications (typified by Microsoft's WaveEdit) store the waveform data in a temporary file during recording. When you complete the recording, the temporary file is copied to a file under the file name that you designate. Therefore, twice the theoretical hard-disk space shown in the preceding table may be required.

The same disk-space requirements apply to editing waveform files. You create a temporary file in which to perform all the editing so that an unsatisfactory edit does not destroy the original file.

Depending on the application, you may not be able to control the location of the temporary file. Some applications use your \WINDOWS directory for the temporary file; others use the drive and directory in which the application is located or that are specified by the SET TEMP entry in your AUTOEXEC.BAT file. A few applications, such as WaveEdit, enable you to specify the location of the temporary file through a line in the application's private INI or your WIN.INI file. Read the application's documentation to find how the program handles temporary files.

Disk-Compression Applications

You can use real-time file-compression applications (such as Stac Electronics Stacker) to gain additional hard-disk space for storing waveform audio files. These applications compress the existing conventional files in the drive rather than the waveform audio files themselves.

The following table shows the compression ratios displayed by Stacker's SDIR application for waveform audio files created by Turtle Beach's MultiSound card, with differing sample rates and resolutions. SDIR.EXE is a variation of DOS' DIR command that displays the compression ratio of each file in a directory of a Stacker-compressed volume. The two Silence columns were recorded with no input signal; the 100 percent column was recorded with the input signal level at maximum (+6 db), and the 0 percent column was recorded with the input signal muted.

Input type: Sampling rate	Music 8-bit	Silence 16-bit	(100%) 8-bit	Silence 16-bit	(0%) 8-bit	16-bit
11.025 kHz	1.1	1.0	16.0	2.3	16.0	2.7
22.05 kHz	1.3	1.0	16.0	2.6	16.0	3.1
44.01 kHz	1.3	1.0	16.0	2.6	16.0	3.5

The use of this data to provide an indication of the signal-to-noise ratio of an audio adapter card and your input sources and cabling is discussed later in this chapter, in the section "Audio Noise, Hum, and Grounding."

Stacker does not compress most waveform audio files at or near its reported average compression ratio of 2.5, because these files do not contain the substantial percentages of repeating byte patterns typically found in text and even in executable files. Stacker's proprietary LZS compression-decompression algorithm relies on the creation of abbreviations, called *tokens*, for repeating byte patterns. Only one copy of the repeating pattern is stored, and the tokens insert the copy into the file as many times as the copy is needed. On decompression, these tokens are expanded back to their original content. This type of compression is called *lossless compression*; no difference exists between the information in the original file that you compressed and the decompressed data that your computer uses.

T I P

If you have a digital effects processor with a gate function, you may want to use this processor in recording narration. Gating shuts off the output signal when the input level is below an adjustable threshold point, reducing or eliminating background noise during periods of silence in the narration and enabling Stacker to compress your files to a greater degree (providing that your audio adapter card itself is not noisy).

Compacting WAV files held in Stacker partitions with PKWare's PKZIP application provides an additional 25 percent compression, on average. PKZIP uses more-complex algorithms to compress files, imploding TIF graphic files, for example, by a ratio as high as 40:1. More-complex algorithms, however, take longer to execute and thus are not suitable for real-time compression-decompression methods executed by software.

Stacker also effectively compresses graphics files, compressing a typical 16-bit color .TGA file created from a video image by a factor of 1.7. Thus, you gain hard-disk space for storing waveform audio files when you use Stacker volumes to store graphic images and animation files for multimedia presentations. (For additional examples of Stacker's compression of graphics files, see Chapter 17.)

Hardware Compression and Decompression

The most effective way to increase the amount of waveform audio data that your hard disk can hold is to use a digital audio adapter card that performs real-time ADPCM compression and decompression, using the digital-signal-processing (DSP) techniques described in Chapter 13. Professional-quality digital audio and MPC adapter cards with fast floating-point DSP chips are priced in the same range as fast high-capacity disk drives.

The advantages of purchasing an adapter card with DSP compression over increasing hard-disk capacity are as follows:

- Real-time audio decompression enables your sound card to process compressed audio files through hardware rather than software. This capability is especially important in full-motion video applications; these applications use most of your computer's capacity to process graphics information.

- The compression capabilities of DSP hardware minimize the amount of computer processing and DMA (direct-memory address) transfer time required to send audio data accompanying video information to your hard disk. For example, real-time hardware audio compression enables you to increase the number of frames per second of video information you can send to your hard disk.

- DSP chips can be programmed by software to perform real-time manipulation of digital audio data. This manipulation includes adding digital effects such as reverberation, phase adjustment, and pitch shifting to your sound files.

Although DSP currently is used primarily for audio compression and decompression, the DSP chips used by professional-quality digital audio cards are programmable. You need only load a different set of operating instructions into a DSP chip's RAM memory to make it perform functions other than compression and decompression.

Writing the software to program DSP chips is difficult, however, and manufacturers' priorities have been directed to compression-decompression. As the use of adapter cards with DSP in Windows applications becomes more common, chip and card manufacturers (and also third-party authors) will meet the demand for other uses of DSP with new Windows drivers and applications.

Disk- and Computer-Speed Considerations

Recording waveform audio files requires that you periodically store on disk the digital data from your audio adapter card; otherwise, you would be limited to the 45 seconds or so of recording time available with Sound Recorder.

Most recording applications transfer data in 16K blocks (or multiples of 16K blocks). As you increase the sampling rate, use 16-bit rather than 8-bit resolution, or switch from mono to stereo recording, the demands on your computer and the disk drive increase. You can demonstrate this increase by making sample recordings with different parameters and observing the frequency and duration of the flashes of your hard disk's activity light. The faster the flashing and the longer the light is on, the longer the file.

Make sure that the drive in which you intend to store your temporary audio file has been defragmented by a disk-organizer application (such as Symantec's Norton SpeedDisk, Stac's SDEFRAG utility, or Allan Morris' DOG application) before you begin a serious recording operation. Excessive disk fragmentation causes the recording head to move great distances during the recording process.

Fragmentation can become a major problem in large hard disks with a single partition (for example, logical drive C:). You should use a separate partition for recording waveform audio files, because you can defragment a portion of a disk much more rapidly than you can the entire disk. Unfortunately, in order to create a new partition, you have to back up all your files, run the FDISK DOS utility, reformat your disk, and reinstall all your files.

Making 16-bit stereo audio recordings at 44.1 kHz requires most of the resources of a 33-MHz 80386DX computer. If you are using a 16- or 20-MHz 80386SX computer and a relatively slow hard disk drive (average access time of 30 milliseconds or more), you may be limited to 8-bit recording at a 22.05-kHz sampling rate. You should make test recordings to determine the capabilities of your computer and disk drive before attempting a major recording project. Listen carefully for *dropouts* (missing vocal syllables or musical notes) caused by hardware limitations.

T I P   If you intend to record MIDI background music mixed with narration in the form of WAV files, copy the MIDI file to the logical drive and directory in which the temporary waveform audio file is stored. If the hard-disk head must make long-distance moves to read the MIDI file during recording the WAV file, you may hear strange musical effects— for example, brief pauses in the MIDI music or notes of extra-long duration caused by missed MIDI Note Off messages. Before you mix the narration, make a test recording of the MIDI music to check for disk choke, the PC equivalent of MIDI choke (described in Chapter 10's "Transmitting MIDI Signals" section).

Tests conducted while this chapter was being written compared recording with the software version of Stacker with the use of conventional disk files. The tests were performed on a 33-MHz 80386DX PC with a hard disk drive rated at 18-millisecond average access time. Stacker appeared to begin to affect the recording of 16-bit mono recordings at 44.1 MHz. If you plan to record CD-quality 16-bit stereo sound at 44.1 kHz, you should use an 80486DX computer or the hardware version of Stacker.

Audio Cables

Chapter 4 briefly described audio cabling in conjunction with installation of audio adapter cards. When you get serious about mixing and recording various audio sources, you need a variety of cables, the most common of which are shown in figure 15.2.

Most of these plugs and adapters are available from Radio Shack stores in 1-, 3-, and 6-foot lengths. Use the shortest cable you can find that is capable of making the required connections; the shorter the cable, the less opportunity for noise pickup.

The cables and adapters shown in figure 15.2 are used for the following purposes:

- 1/8-inch stereo miniplug to 1/8-inch stereo miniplug (mini stereo patch) cables primarily are used to connect the output of one audio adapter card to the input of another.

- 1/8-inch stereo miniplug to two 1/8-inch mono miniplug (Y) cables connect the output of your audio adapter card to small speakers. A version with 1/8-inch stereo miniplug to two 1/8-inch stereo miniplugs or minijacks (called an *input splitter*) also is available.

- 1/8-inch stereo miniplug to two RCA phono-jack Y-cables are the standard method of connecting the output of your audio adapter card to self-amplifying speakers and stereo sound systems.

- A pair of RCA gender changers is handy, especially if you already have a collection of standard audio patch cables.

- 1/4-inch phono plug to RCA phono-jack adapters converts the 1/4-inch mono audio connections of outboard MIDI devices to RCA phono jacks for compatibility with the preceding cable or standard audio patch or with extension cables.

- Audio patch cables with RCA phono plugs on both ends are the most common type of cable used to interconnect stereo and video components. Make sure that you purchase shielded cables, not the kind designed for connecting speakers. Speaker cables use two parallel conductors instead of a round cable with a single signal conductor inside a foil or braided shield (ground) conductor.

- Audio extension cables have RCA plugs on one end and jacks on the other, enabling you to extend standard audio cables in increments of 6 feet or more. You can use an RCA gender changer to convert a patch cable to an extension cable.

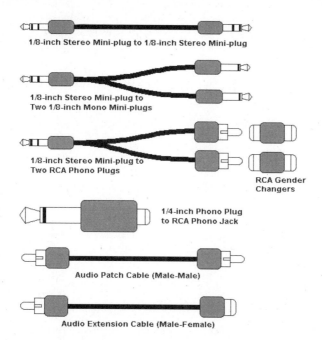

1/8-inch Stereo Mini-plug to 1/8-inch Stereo Mini-plug

1/8-inch Stereo Mini-plug to Two 1/8-inch Mono Mini-plugs

1/8-inch Stereo Mini-plug to Two RCA Phono Plugs

RCA Gender Changers

1/4-inch Phono Plug to RCA Phono Jack

Audio Patch Cable (Male-Male)

Audio Extension Cable (Male-Female)

FIG. 15.2

Components of the desktop audio chain.

T I P

Several manufacturers produce "audiophile" cables with extra-heavy conductors and gold-plated connectors, selling them at prices much higher than those of standard audio cables. The added cost of these cables usually is not warranted with audio adapter cards unless you find no other way to eliminate objectionable noise or hum.

Audio Noise, Hum, and Grounding

Audio noise and hum are the bugaboos of audio engineering. Engineers and technicians dedicate much of their lives to reducing the level of these two undesirable audio effects.

Noise consists of signals (usually in the form of clicks or pops) that occur at random intervals. Noise events that occur at a rapid rate produce a hissing sound. *Hum* is a low-frequency sound with a pitch equal to the frequency of power lines (60 Hz, in the United States.) Noise and hum are spurious voltages induced in conductors by rapidly changing electromagnetic and electrostatic fields.

Noise most often is the result of coupling high-frequency signals from your computer's bus and components on audio adapter cards into the inputs of analog-to-digital converters. Hum ordinarily is the result of improper grounding of external audio components or the use of unshielded audio input cables.

Figure 15.3 shows how noise appears in Turtle Beach's Wave for Windows and Wave Lite for Windows applications (described in Chapter 14) when the amplitude (vertical, Y-axis) and time base (horizontal, X-axis) are expanded greatly.

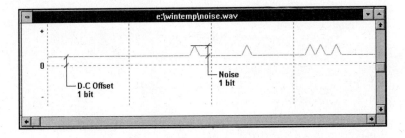

FIG. 15.3

One bit each of DC offset and noise in an 8-bit waveform file.

The small triangles shown in the figure as noise represent 1 bit in height; their width corresponds to the sampling interval, 90.7 microseconds. A microsecond (μs) is a millionth of a second; 90.7 is the reciprocal of the sampling frequency, 1/11025, times 1 million. The noise shown in figure 15.3 is the result of interference by the clock frequency of the PC with the signals between the components on the audio adapter card.

Computers are small but sometimes powerful transmitters. Federal Communications Commission certification of computers for interference with consumer electronic devices deals with electromagnetic radiation outside the case and into the power lines, not with internal noise levels. You cannot rely on an FCC Class B rating to ensure a low internal noise level. You can identify noise created by the computer bus or adjacent adapter cards by removing all input cables, using the mixer application to set all input levels to zero, recording a file with no input, and then listening to the induced noise with the monitor level turned up.

The following suggestions may reduce induced noise:

- Use the mixer application to set the levels of all unused audio inputs to zero. A microphone input with no microphone connected often is the culprit. If your mixer application has a mute check box, mute all the unused inputs.

- Move the adapter card to the last slot on the bus, adjacent to the computer case.

- Move any video cards you have installed as far as possible from the audio adapter card.

- Maintain as many open slots as possible between the audio adapter card and other adapter cards on the bus.

- Use the closure plates that came with your computer to cover any open adapter-card slots. Use sheet-metal plates to cover any other slots or holes greater than a quarter-inch in diameter.

- Route audio input and output cables as far as possible from video and VGA display cables and from the computer's power cord.

- Install a power-line isolation filter between the computer's power plug and the power outlet strip. Power-line isolation filters are available at industrial electrical supply stores for less than $100.

- If the noise is confined to the microphone input, use an external microphone preamplifier or mixer with its output connected to the auxiliary line input. The low-level signals associated with dynamic microphones require high-gain amplifiers that do not belong in close proximity to digital circuits.

- Purchase a higher-quality audio adapter card. Cards with 16-bit recording and playback capability usually are better-designed (and, thus, quieter) than 8-bit cards.

Figure 15.4 shows a signal in Turtle Beach's Wave for Windows application that combines a severe case of hum with substantial noise.

This waveform audio file was created by connecting a cable to the microphone input of a standard 8-bit audio adapter card and placing a finger on the tip of the connector at the other end. The hum component of the sound is represented by the dark patterns that resemble a 60-Hz sine wave viewed with an oscilloscope. The spikes represent noise induced by the computer's clock (in this instance, by removing the computer's case).

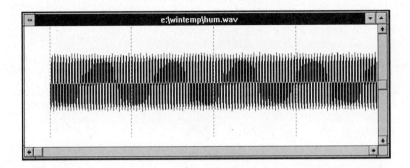

FIG. 15.4

Severe hum almost buried in noise in a waveform audio file.

The periodic nature of hum is more evident in figure 15.5, which shows the wave from figure 15.4 displayed in Microsoft's WaveEdit application.

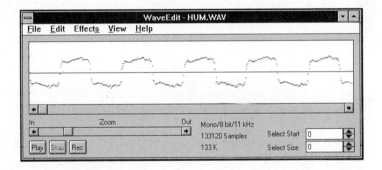

FIG. 15.5

Noise and hum displayed in Microsoft's WaveEdit application.

Notice, however, that the figure shows only the end-points of the samples rather than the line displayed by Wave for Windows. Seeing the sharp noise spikes in the WaveEdit file is difficult (because the spikes are represented by single pixel dots) unless you use the Zoom slider to further expand the time base.

The following suggestions may minimize hum and reduce externally induced noise:

- Make sure that all the external audio components are plugged into the same power strip as your computer, each with a three-pronged grounding power plug.

- If you run out of power outlets, connect a separate power strip and plug your monitor and other peripherals (but not your self-amplifying speakers) into the power strip. Do not use extension cords or separate power outlets with external audio devices.

- Verify that the cables you are using are shielded and are not speaker extension cables.

■ Route all cables away from your computer's cabinet and your VGA display. Do not lay cables on the computer case, and keep the audio cables as far from the video cables as possible.

■ Make sure that the RCA phono plugs are fully inserted into their jacks and that the outer shell of each plug makes a tight connection with the corresponding grounding surface of the jack. Squeeze each plug's shell slightly with pliers to improve grounding.

■ If the hum is on the microphone channel, purchase an outboard microphone preamplifier or, better yet, use a professional microphone with XLR connections and an audio mixer with a microphone preamplifier.

■ If you are using two-conductor shielded cables with XLR connectors, make sure that the shield is grounded only at one end of the cable (preferably at the microphone-preamplifier input).

■ If hum persists, connect a heavy (14 AWG or larger) wire between the chassis of each external audio device and a single grounding point on your computer. Using a connecting lug under a screw head is the best method of connection, and the best place to attach the grounds is under the hold-down screw head that restrains your audio adapter card. The next-best place is under one of the screw heads that hold down the computer's power supply.

■ If hum still is a problem, connect a heavy wire between a grounding point on your computer and a galvanized steel or (better) copper water pipe. Before you make this connection, measure the voltage between the water pipe and the ground cable with an AC voltmeter to make sure that no significant ground current exists. If you don't have a voltmeter, try brushing the exposed end of the wire against the pipe to see whether sparks appear. If more than a few volts appear on the voltmeter or you see sparks when you brush the wire against the pipe, you have a grounding fault in your power lines. Have an electrician correct the problem before you proceed.

You also can use Stacker's compression-ratio data (obtain this data by running the SDIR application) to determine whether your audio adapter card's analog-to-digital converter and its associated circuitry are contributing noise to your recordings. Stacker's maximum compression ratio is 16.0 for a waveform audio file of total silence (data is all zero-valued: 80H for 8-bit cards and 8000H for 16-bit cards). A completely clean file of moderate size (more than 100K) produces a compression ratio of 16.0 when you run SDIR on the directory of a Stacker volume that contains it.

Noise and hum result in bit patterns in the file, reducing the compression ratio, but the compression ratio itself is not necessarily an indication of how much noise or hum is occurring. Using SDIR check to examine a waveform audio file for noise is much faster than using an editing application. You need to use a waveform audio editor, however, to determine the amplitude and frequency of the noise or hum.

Using the Analog Audio Mixer

The MPC specifications require only three monaural audio inputs: microphone, CD-ROM, and waveform audio. A fourth line input and stereo capabilities for all components except the microphone are recommended but not required.

The specifications do not define the type of audio mixer to be used to combine these signals. All MPC-compliant audio adapter cards now include multichannel stereo mixers, but mixers vary substantially in their implementation methods and in the applications that control them. The signal-to-noise ratio of audio adapter cards' mixer components varies substantially among manufacturers.

The following sections describe the audio mixers of three typical audio adapter cards and the manufacturer-supplied applications that control those mixers.

Pro AudioSpectrum Mixers

The mixers used in Media Vision's Pro AudioSpectrum Plus and 16 audio adapter cards are the most flexible of all the products evaluated during the course of writing this book. Like most audio adapter cards, the Pro AudioSpectrum cards accommodate stereo inputs from the CD-ROM drive (by an internal connector), an auxiliary signal source (audio tape or VCR), waveform audio files, and an FM synthesizer; the cards also accommodate a monaural (left-channel) microphone input. The Media Vision products, like most other audio adapter cards, enable you to mix any or all these signals into a single stereo output with a master level (volume) control on the mixer's output signal.

The Pro AudioSpectrum cards provide a separate level control for the speaker output signal (monitor), as shown in figure 15.6.

You can record waveform audio files at a relatively high level (to maximize the signal-to-noise ratio) but monitor the output signal at a moderate level. Independent control of the monitor level also enables you to turn off the monitors to prevent feedback when you are recording voice notes.

Media Vision supplies three mixer applets and one recording application for Windows with its Pro AudioSpectrum cards. You can use Pocket Mixer and Pocket Recorder in combination to record waveform audio files (see fig. 15.7).

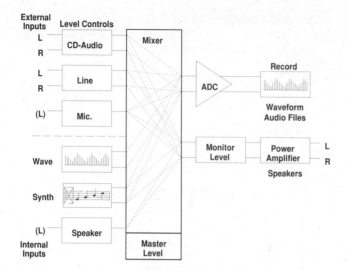

FIG. 15.6

The audio mixer functions of the Pro AudioSpectrum series.

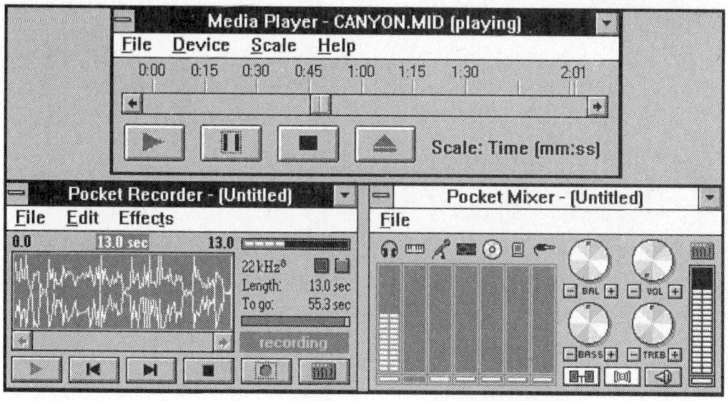

FIG. 15.7

Recording a waveform audio file from a MIDI tune.

You set the level of the inputs you want to mix in the recording by dragging the LED symbols (pairs of rectangular bars in vertical frames under the inputs' symbols). You can combine inputs from the FM synthesizer (piano symbol), microphone, waveform audio, CD-ROM, PC speaker, and external input (miniplug symbol). Master gain is displayed in the window at the right, and monitor level (headphone symbol) is displayed in the window at the left. Knobs for tone controls (bass and treble boost/cut) and stereo enhancement (a sound-phase adjustment) are provided.

The Pocket-series applets use small windows, enabling you to keep those windows on-screen while you use other applications without overlapping the primary application's critical controls.

Related Topics
Third-Party OLE Sound
Servers, p. 242

The Pocket Recorder uses the standard push-button symbols for controlling the recording process. LED symbols display the recording level, and a synthetic oscilloscope displays the sound envelope. Mono or stereo recording at 11.025, 22.05, and 44.1 kHz is provided at 8-bit resolution for the Pro AudioSpectrum Plus and at 8- or 16-bit resolution for the Pro AudioSpectrum 16. Both Pocket Recorder and Pocket Mixer are OLE applications and can be embedded in compound documents.

Media Vision also supplies a simple Multimedia Mixer applet (see fig. 15.8) with four adjustable input levels—FM music, line input, CD-ROM, and microphone—and an easy-to-use master-level control.

FIG. 15.8

The Multimedia
Mixer applet.

Media Vision's Pro Mixer application is described in detail in Chapter 23, "The High-Level MCI Commands of Windows 3.1."

Sound Blaster Pro Mixer

Creative Labs' Windows mixer application for the Sound Blaster Pro is similar in concept to Media Vision's Multimedia Mixer applet. Figure 15.9 shows the circuitry of the Sound Blaster Pro's audio mixer.

The Sound Blaster Pro's output volume control is mounted at the rear of the printed wiring board and can be adjusted through a slot in the rear mounting plate.

Figure 15.10 shows the single window of the Sound Blaster Pro Mixer Control (SBMIXER.EXE), the Windows 3.1 version of which uses the Sound Blaster Pro Auxiliary Audio Driver (SBPAUX.DRV). This window is identical to an earlier version designed for use in Windows 3.0 with SNDBLST.DLL.

The Sound Blaster Pro Mixer Control provides a test function that enables you to check the level of CD audio, microphone, or stereo line (auxiliary) inputs by connecting the selected input directly to the input of the output amplifier connected to your speakers or sound system. Creative Labs substitutes low- and high-frequency cutoff filters for the continuously variable tone controls found on Pro AudioSpectrum audio adapter cards.

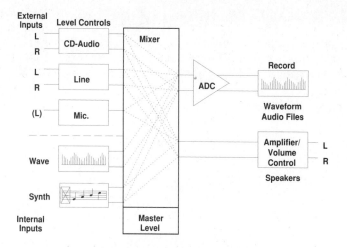

FIG. 15.9

Diagram of the audio mixer of the Sound Blaster Pro.

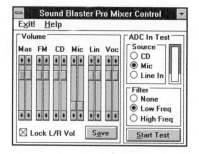

FIG. 15.10

Creative Labs' SBMIXER application for the Sound Blaster Pro.

 Early versions of the Sound Blaster Pro's Windows application included the mixer-control application SBMIXER.EXE, which is known to cause computers to behave erratically or freeze. Creative Labs' technical-service department provides an updated version that also adds the mixer icon to Windows' control panel. If you are using Windows 3.0 and your copy of SBMIXER.EXE is 25,792 bytes long or SNDBLST.DLL is 23,776 bytes long, you should contact Creative Labs to obtain the new version of both files.

If you are using Windows 3.1 and have not installed the Windows 3.1 drivers for the Sound Blaster Pro (including the version of SBMIXER.EXE designed for use with the multimedia extensions), see the "Installing Drivers Supplied by the Manufacturer" section in Chapter 5 for information on obtaining and installing the updated drivers.

Turtle Beach's MultiSound Mixer

The mixer for the Turtle Beach MultiSound audio adapter card is simpler than that of most other MPC-compliant audio adapter cards. Figure 15.11 shows a diagram of the mixer application supplied with the MultiSound.

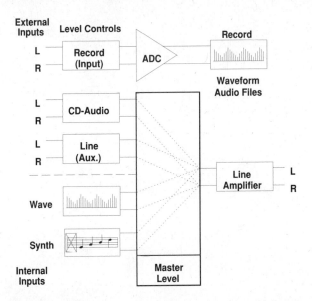

FIG. 15.11

Simplified diagram of the MultiSound card's mixer application.

The high-level record-input signal is routed directly to the analog-to-digital converter through a buffer amplifier equipped with a level control. As Chapter 2 mentioned, the MultiSound does not include a microphone preamplifier.

Befitting the professional level of the MultiSound audio adapter card, the card comes with sophisticated mixing applications. The Record Prep application enables you to preview your audio material, determining the maximum output level so that you can preset mixer gain accordingly. The Record Prep window displays the equivalent of two peak-reading VU (volume unit) meters with needles that remain at a position representing the maximum amplitude of any sound on the track. You play the track and then check the Record Prep window to determine the maximum sound level from each stereo channel (see fig. 15.12).

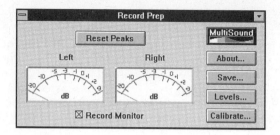

FIG. 15.12

The recording-level-indicator window of the MultiSound mixer application.

The MultiSound mixer control panel resembles the control panels of other mixer applications, with individual input level controls for each channel of stereo waveform audio, synthesized sound, auxiliary line (audio CD), and recording input (In). Turtle Beach goes one step further by providing the calibration dialog box shown in figure 15.13.

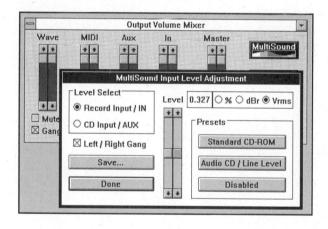

FIG. 15.13

The MultiSound Mixer application with the input-recording-level window open.

This dialog box enables you to set the level precisely to correspond with the manufacturer's specified output level (usually 0.327 volts, –7.5 db) or to the level you observe with Sound Prep. You can choose among voltage, percent of full scale, and Vrms—volts, root-mean-square, which is the usual method of measuring an audio signal's voltage.

The MultiSound's mixer does not provide an internal signal path between the mixer output and the recording input. Because the MultiSound is considered to be a professional device, Turtle Beach expects you to have a multichannel audio mixer to handle input mixing. If you don't have such a mixer, you need a stereo input splitter cable (described in the "Audio Cables" section of this chapter). Connect one of the stereo plugs to the input and another to the output. The third plug goes to another splitter cable (a 1/8-inch stereo minijack to two mono RCA plugs) to your self-amplifying speakers so that you can monitor the sound. If you use headphones, their low impedance may attenuate the signal level to the input.

Related Topics
Using Audio and Video
Cables, p. 543

Audio Mixers on Video Adapter Cards

If you have installed a video-in-a-window (VIW) card with audio mixing capabilities, you can use the VIW card's mixer to add another pair of stereo or three mono inputs to the line input of your audio adapter card. Truevision's Bravado and Creative Labs' Video Blaster card provide for two stereo inputs (with adjustable level controls) and a stereo output signal designed to drive speakers or headphones.

Figure 15.14 shows a diagram of the typical audio portion of a VIW card.

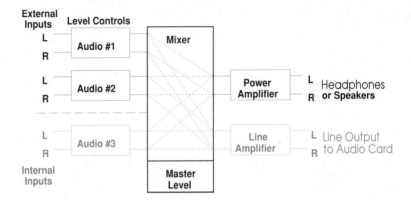

FIG. 15.14

A typical audio mixer provided with VIW adapter cards.

The Bravado 16 has an additional internal audio input, and both the basic Bravado and the 16 have a separate output amplifier for speaker/headphone monitor and line outputs. The additional inputs and outputs appear in gray in figure 15.14 because these features are not available on all VIW cards.

Audio input and output connections usually are made through the breakout cable. Input connections, for the most part, are RCA phono plugs; the oxutputs are stereo minijacks that accommodate headphone plugs. For many cards (Bravado-series cards included), you must purchase a special cable assembly to obtain more than one set of audio inputs and outputs. If your VIW card has a speaker/headphone output only, you should use an attenuating connector (pad) between the audio output connector and the input of your audio adapter card to prevent overloading and possible damage to the card's line-input circuitry.

Figure 15.15 shows the audio control windows of the application supplied with Truevision Bravado cards.

The Audio Control Panel window sets the volume, balance, and treble and bass tone controls. Stereo or mono selection and control of the type of output when only one audio output connection is used is determined by the option buttons and check boxes in the Audio Setup window. You make a **C**ontrol menu selection to determine the input to which the settings of these windows apply. The internal input of the Bravado 16 card ordinarily is connected to the audio output from an audio digital-to-analog converter daughterboard.

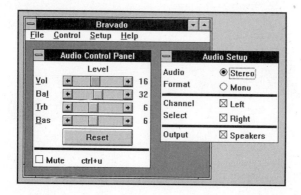

FIG. 15.15

The audio control and setup windows of Truevision's Bravado application.

The applications supplied with most other VIW cards are similar. Some manufacturers supply a separate application for controlling audio setup and mixing.

Choosing Microphones

Selecting and positioning microphones, especially for recording musical performances, is an art, not a science. Audio engineers spend long apprenticeships learning the idiosyncrasies of thousand-dollar studio and stage mics, how the mics should be used with specific instruments, and how to entice vocalists to use the mics properly.

The first maxim of audio recording is "Use the best microphone you can afford." Mics and their placement determine the quality of recorded sound to as great an extent as the sound card itself does. A low-quality microphone can make a 44.1-kHz 16-bit stereo sample sound like it was recorded at 8 bits and 11.025 kHz or even less.

Selecting a microphone to plug into the Mic input of your audio adapter card for recording voice notes is easy. As Chapter 4 discussed, all you have to do is make sure that the microphone has a 1/8-inch mono miniplug on the cable and doesn't cost more than $15.

Many sound cards have relatively low-quality microphone preamplifiers and include automatic gain control (AGC) on the Mic input. AGC is designed to accommodate a wide range of consumer microphones and to prevent overloading of the waveform audio signal circuitry. AGC, however, prevents you from effectively controlling the input level of the recorded sound. You gain no advantage by plugging a professional-quality microphone directly into a sound card's Mic input.

The same principle applies to waveform audio recordings made at 11.025 kHz with an upper-frequency limit of less than 5 kHz. Microphone selection becomes increasingly important for 22.05-kHz and 44.1-kHz sampling rates, especially with 16-bit resolution.

T I P   The microphone amplifiers of most video camcorders employ automatic gain control. AGC can cause severe difficulties when you use a camcorder to record synchronized sound for multimedia productions, especially under noisy conditions. If you plan to purchase a camcorder, make sure that microphone AGC can be turned off or that an audio line input is provided so that you can use an external microphone amplifier or mixer to record the audio track.

Choosing a microphone that creates crisp, clear audio tracks requires basic knowledge of how professional-quality microphones change sound waves into electrical signals. You also need an audio mixer (or at least a microphone preamplifier) to raise the signal level of dynamic microphones to the level that the line input of your audio adapter card requires. (For more information on these microphones, see the "Dynamic Microphones" section later in this chapter.)

Professional-quality microphones use the basic sound-reception patterns shown in figure 15.16. In all four diagrams, the front of the microphone faces zero degrees.

The following list describes the four sound-pattern types:

- *Omnidirectional.* The microphone responds equally to sound waves converging on it from all directions. Most omnidirectional mics are cylindrical or spherical.

- *Unidirectional.* The microphone's response is limited primarily to sounds originating in a relatively narrow area. The ultimate unidirectional microphone is the *parabolic* microphone, the device that sportscasters use to eavesdrop on the quarterback in a football huddle. Another unidirectional mic is the *shotgun* microphone often used with camcorders; these microphones are so named because they resemble the barrel of a 12-gauge shotgun. The microphones supplied with most portable consumer tape recorders also are unidirectional.

■ *Bidirectional.* These microphones respond to sounds coming from two opposite sides. Bidirectional microphones, which no longer are widely used, once were standard in radio broadcasting.

■ *Cardioid.* These microphones have a heart-shape response pattern, with maximum sensitivity to sounds originating within a 180-degree angle and some response to sounds beyond this angle. Cardioid microphones now are the most commonly used professional mics. A cardioid mic is a good choice if you plan to use one microphone for many different purposes.

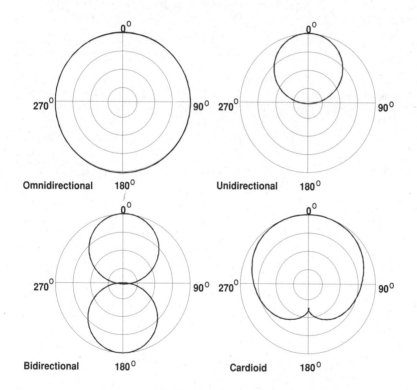

FIG. 15.16

The sound fields of the four basic types of professional microphones.

You can purchase wireless versions of most types of microphones to eliminate the traditional cable. Wireless mics have a small, battery-operated FM transmitter and a separate receiver. The receiver usually includes a preamplifier that raises the signal level to that of a conventional microphone or standard line level.

Balanced versus Unbalanced Outputs

Consumer-grade microphones use 1/8-inch monaural miniplugs and provide an unbalanced output. An *unbalanced output* consists of two electrical conductors, a signal wire, and a ground (earth or return). The ground conductor normally is a braided wire or metallic foil wrapped around a plastic-insulated signal conductor. Unbalanced outputs sometimes are called *high-impedance* or *single-ended* outputs.

Professional microphones, as Chapter 4 mentioned, use balanced outputs that end in a standard three-pin plug called an XLR connector. The outputs are carried by a three-conductor cable with two signal wires and one ground (earth or return) conductor. The signal conductors carry voltages 180 degrees out of phase with each other. Because of the differing voltages, the signals are recombined at the receiving end of the cable, a process that cancels most of the noise that might have been added to the signal during the cable run.

Most balanced microphones have low-impedance outputs (600 ohm or less). Balanced signals often are called double-ended outputs.

You cannot connect a microphone with a balanced output to the microphone input of your audio adapter card, even if you wire a mating XLR connector to a mini phone plug (a combination called a *kludge*). The output impedance does not match that of consumer microphones, and the result is little or no sound. You must use a impedance converter in order to make the transition.

Microphone impedance converters change balanced outputs to the unbalanced type compatible with the Mic input of audio adapter cards and the external Mic inputs of consumer camcorders. Similar devices perform the same function in reverse, but usually with unsatisfactory results. Consumer versions of these converters, which are available at Radio Shack stores, consist of a small transformer housed in a case with an XLR connector on one end and a 1/4-inch phone plug on the other. You need an adapter to convert the 1/4-inch connection to a 1/8-inch miniplug. These converters are satisfactory for narration, but the transformers do not have the frequency response required to record music with adequate fidelity.

Figure 15.17 shows how impedance converters are connected to a microphone.

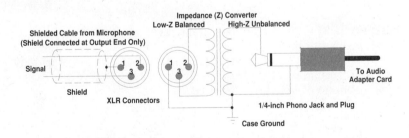

FIG. 15.17

Connectors and impedance converters for balanced microphones.

Dynamic Microphones

Dynamic microphones are the least costly type of professional-quality microphone and have a wide dynamic range. These microphones are sturdy and withstand substantial overloading without damage to their acoustic mechanisms.

A dynamic microphone basically consists of a metallic diaphragm that vibrates in response to sound waves. A small coil of wire, wound around a magnet located near the diaphragm, generates a minute electrical current in response to the diaphragm's movement.

Dynamic mics are good choices for general-purpose recording, especially of narration by male voices. These microphones range in cost from about $5 (for the types used with portable dictation machines and low-quality audio tape recorders) to several hundred dollars (for professional models). A unidirectional dynamic microphone in the $100-to-$150 price range provides adequate quality for narration.

Figure 15.18 shows the Shure SM-57, a moderately priced dynamic mic that is widely used for recording vocals and a wide range of jazz and rock instruments.

FIG. 15.18

The Shure SM-57 microphone.

Dynamic mics are considered to contribute "warmth" to recordings, probably due to their emphasis of the middle ranges of the audio spectrum. Specialized dynamic mics with thin diaphragms made of special alloying compounds such as neodymium extend the high-frequency range close to that of condenser microphones. When in doubt about which type of mic to use, start with a general-purpose dynamic type such as the SM-57 and then experiment. Most firms that rent audiovisual equipment offer a wide variety of microphones for short-term needs.

T   I   P   When you are videotaping or audiotaping an interview, you may want to use two dynamic microphones—one for the interviewer and one for the person being interviewed—and record the outputs on separate stereo channels. (For videotaping, you need a camcorder with stereo microphone input jacks.) In this case, you may want to violate the $15 rule on single-ended consumer mics and try the varieties that sell in the range of $30 to $50. Lapel-type dynamic microphones, which clip onto clothing, are especially useful for videotaped interviews.

Condenser Microphones

Condenser microphones use a "capsule" consisting of a thin metal plate located close to a fixed plate. The two plates are electrically isolated and create the equivalent of a variable electrical condenser (capacitor), similar to the variable condensers used to tune radio receivers before the advent of solid-state tuning devices. Sound pressure on the thin diaphragm changes the electrostatic charge (similar to static electricity) between the two plates. A built-in amplifier converts the charge variations to an electrical current similar to that of a dynamic microphone, to a line-level signal, or both.

The metal plate that picks up sound-pressure variations can be much thinner than the diaphragm of a dynamic microphone. Condenser microphones then have a wider frequency-response range (especially at the high-frequency end of the audio spectrum) because of the low mass of the plate. The price you pay for higher-frequency response, however, is fragility. You can damage a condenser microphone's capsule easily by dropping the mic or by using it to record extra-loud sounds.

Figure 15.19 shows a typical mid-range professional-grade condenser microphone, priced at about $400.

Condenser microphones are recommended for recording female narrators and vocalists because women's voices carry higher-frequency overtones than men's voices do. Microphone placement is critical with condenser microphones because some narrators and vocalists have problems with sibilants; a hiss accompanies words containing the letters *s* and (sometimes) *z*. These microphones also are subject to broadcast popping noises, created by the impact of the narrator's breath on the thin diaphragm. You can prevent most of these problems by constructing a "pop screen": a piece of nylon mounted in a small frame between the performer and the microphone. If you're videotaping the recording process, you can tie the nylon around the microphone.

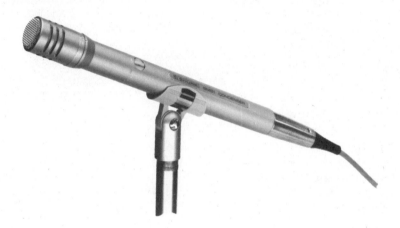

FIG. 15.19

A professional-level condenser microphone.

Condenser microphones require a source of power for their internal amplifiers. This power, called *phantom power*, often is supplied by an internal battery or by the audio mixer to which the mic is connected. If the mic does not have a battery or the mixer does not provide this power source, you need a separate phantom-power supply.

T I P

If you are purchasing a condenser microphone, choose one that includes a line-level output (in addition to the standard XLR 600-ohm balanced output), if you can find one. A line-level output enables you to connect the microphone's output directly to the auxiliary input of your audio adapter card for making direct-to-disk recordings. Because the direct-to-disk technique eliminates potential sources of sound-quality degradation (such as audiotape recording and reproduction), it offers the highest possible level of fidelity.

The Acoustic Environment and Microphone Placement

The acoustic properties of the room in which you record narration substantially affect the overall sound quality of the narration. Large rooms with many hard surfaces (especially uncovered windows) are called *live* acoustic environments, which can create distracting reverberation effects. A small, thickly carpeted room in which cloth draperies cover the windows is the best place to record narration.

To determine whether the acoustic environment of a room is too live, record a short sample of the script and listen to the playback carefully through headphones and again through a good set of speakers. If you hear reverberation, you may need to cover the walls with blankets in order to deaden the audio reflections.

Another factor to consider is the distance between the speaker's lips and the microphone. "Crowding" the mic adds a measure of intimacy to the sound, but at the risk of recording sibilants and pops, even if you use a pop screen. If the microphone is placed close to the sound source, you may notice an increase in bass response (a proximity effect). Excessive distance creates a stentorian tone, as the narrator must project his or her voice to the mic.

Professional narrators have their own preferred mouth-to-mic distances for specific types of microphones. If you are using amateur narrators, start with a distance of about six to eight inches. Make multiple recordings of the same paragraph or two of the script, at equal peak recording levels but at different mouth-to-mic distances, and listen to the playback through both headphones and speakers.

T I P A good set of fully padded stereo headphones is essential for a narration session. Assuming that you do not have a soundproof engineering booth, padded headphones (through which you can listen to the recording results without hearing the narrator's voice in the background) are essential. If you are creating a soundtrack for a production to be reproduced by the user's sound card, audition the track by playing it over a pair of small, high-quality monitor speakers set about 24 inches apart to simulate the normal location of the user's speakers (on either side of a PC). Stereo effects that sound fine on speakers set ten feet apart in a large room may sound quite different through a pair of small speakers only two feet apart.

Choosing Audio Tape Recorders and Outboard Mixers

Miniaturized magnetic recording heads enable manufacturers to produce palm-size video camcorders and 3.5-inch hard disk drives that hold 300M or more of data. Similar technology has been applied to recording heads for audio cassette recorders. Special electronic circuitry developed by Dolby Laboratories improves the signal-to-noise ratio of cassette tapes and reduces the high-frequency hiss that was associated with early audio cassette drives. The result is moderately priced cassette decks (decks and drives describe any tape-recording device) that rival the quality of consumer-grade digital audio tape (DAT) and reel-to-reel broadcast-quality recorders. Demonstrations conducted by one manufacturer at the 1992 National Association of Broadcasters convention proved that the vast majority of listeners were unable to distinguish between high-quality analog (conventional) audio cassette tapes and digitally recorded (DAT and CD-ROM) sound.

The combination mixer/cassette recorders described in Chapter 10 (used for recording MIDI music on audiotape) are equally well suited for recording voices. Most mixer/recorders are designed to add vocal tracks to cassette recordings and provide at least two XLR microphone inputs with preamplifiers. Some units also include phantom power for condenser mics.

> **T I P**
>
> Beware of using consumer-grade mixers intended for blending sounds from television sets, VCRs, audio CD players, and similar devices. Battery-operated versions in particular have a low tolerance for high-level signals and introduce a significant amount of distortion. Four-channel stereo "prosumer" mixers are available at musical-instrument discount stores at prices ranging from $200 to $400. Because a four-channel cassette recorder is not likely to cost much more than a mixer/recorder, the combination device is recommended, if for no other reason than to back up a DAT system in case of emergency.

Unless you have a laptop or lunchbox computer with a high-capacity disk drive and a high-quality audio adapter card, you are likely to record location audio on tape. *Location audio* (also called remote audio) is any material recorded away from the studio or the room where you record narration, usually consisting of interviews and sound effects. If you are fortunate enough to have a Hi8 camcorder that provides high-fidelity (preferably stereo) audio recording capability and has at least one external microphone connector, you can use it for recording location audio. The stereo microphones provided with the camcorder are designed to record at a distance, so you should plan to use a pair of properly positioned professional microphones to obtain the sound quality of the Hi8 medium.

If you are even more fortunate and have a DAT recorder (a Sony D3 WalkDAT is satisfactory for field use), you can record location audio that rivals a recording made in a professional studio. The sound quality of DAT recordings compares with that of audio CDs, a fact that has generated controversy about making DAT technology available to consumers.

DAT recorders basically are two-track (stereo right and left) devices. Most of these recorders do not include mixers, as do most of the cassette decks commonly used in home studios. Therefore, you need a multichannel mixer if you plan to use more than one pair of microphones for recording sessions.

T I P   You need a quiet microphone/mixer combination for DAT recording because digital audio is extremely sensitive over a wide dynamic range. Some microphones are noisy when used with the microphone preamplifiers in one mixer and acceptably noise-free when used with another manufacturer's mixer. Although the Shure SM-57 (shown earlier in figure 15.18) does not have a reputation for being quiet enough for DAT recording, it reportedly performs well when used with the Mackie Designs 1604 mixer described in Chapter 11.

Conducting a Typical Waveform Audio Recording Session

A typical recording session might consist of narration and background music from a MIDI file or audio CD combined into a waveform audio file. Windows and mixer applications enable your computer to simulate a four-channel stereo digital tape recorder.

Media Vision's Pro Mixer and Pocket Recorder are used as examples in this section. The mixer applications supplied by most manufacturers of audio adapter card manufacturers use a similar procedure but do not provide timed-fade capability for the music.

To mix two sound sources into a waveform audio file, follow these steps:

1. Start Media Player by double-clicking its icon in the Program Manager's Accessories group.

2. Open the MIDI file you want to use as background music. (A MIDI file is used in this example because setting the correct starting track position on an audio CD can be difficult.)

3. Start Pro Mixer from Media Vision's Multimedia Tools group.

4. Pro Mixer's menu appears when you click its icon; you don't make a choice from a convention menu bar in a window. Click the icon, and the Pro Mixer menu shown in figure 15.20 appears.

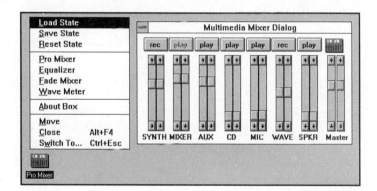

FIG. 15.20

The Pro Mixer menu.

> **T I P**
>
> Pro Mixer is designed to be included in the Windows 3.1 Startup group. To have Pro Mixer load automatically when you start a Windows session, drag its icon from the Multimedia Tools group to the Startup group, choose **P**roperties from the Program Managers **F**ile menu, and check the Run Minimized check box.

5. Choose **W**ave Meter from the Pro Mixer menu to display the recording-level indicators, called *VU* (volume-unit) *meters*. The VU meters appear in the lower right corner of your display.

6. Start Pocket Recorder from the Multimedia Tools group.

7. Minimize the Program Manager window, and arrange the windows for the three applications into a recording-control console configuration. If you are using a standard VGA display, the Pocket Recorder and Pro Mixer windows overlap slightly (see fig. 15.21).

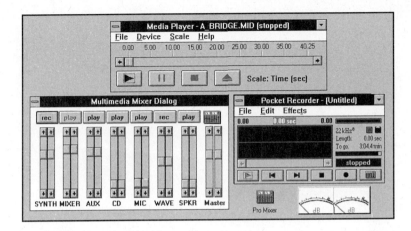

Creating a simulated recording console.

8. Set the initial levels of the SYNTH, MIXER, WAVE, and Master inputs to about 66 percent of maximum by dragging each of their vertical scroll-bar sliders two-thirds of the distance to the top. Sources that you are not using at this point, including the microphone, should be set to zero (the bottom of the range).

9. Make a test recording to set the level of the background music. Choose **F**ile from Pocket Recorder's menu, and then choose **N**ew to display the Record Parameters dialog box shown in figure 15.22.

   Because you are making a test recording, a mono file with 8-bit resolution at a sample rate of 11.025 kHz or 22.05 kHz is sufficient. Choose OK when you complete your selections.

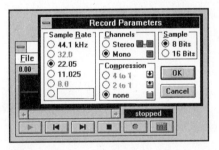

The Record Parameters dialog box of Pocket Recorder.

10. Click the Play button above Pro Mixer's SYNTH fader. This action sets the FM synthesizer to Record mode. Each click of the Play/Record buttons alternates (toggles) between Play and Record modes for the source. If any other buttons indicate Record mode (rec), click them to activate Play mode.

11. Click Pocket Recorder's Record button and then immediately click Media Player's Play button. Pro Mixer's Wave button automatically changes to Record mode.

    Reduce the level of the background music source (SYNTH or CD) by moving its slider until the peaks of the background music just reach the first scale mark on the VU meter—about 30 percent of the slider's travel for normal recording levels. Then use the Master slider to adjust the volume level of your monitor speakers (this slider does not affect the recording level).

12. Click Pocket Recorder's Stop button after 30 or 40 seconds. A delay occurs while the sound data in the memory buffer is written to a temporary disk file.

13. Click Pocket Recorder's Rewind button to reset the cursor to the beginning of the file, and then click the Play button to listen to your test recording. The VU meter displays the level of your recording during playback. Use the WAVE sliders, if necessary, to adjust the playback volume.

14. Repeat steps 8, 10, and 11 if you want to make another test recording. Otherwise, double-click the window's control bar to close Pocket Recorder.

15. Choose No in the dialog box that asks whether you want to save your untitled recording.

For a real recording session, you probably would have your narration sequences on audiotape, and the tape recorder's output would be connected to the auxiliary input of your audio adapter card. For this exercise, however, you record a short segment of narration live.

To experiment with Pro Mixer's Timed Fade option, follow these steps:

1. Click Pro Mixer's icon and then choose **F**ade Mixer from the Pro Mixer menu. The Timed Fade dialog box appears (see fig. 15.23).

2. Set the time you want the fade to start and the duration of the fade. This example uses a MIDI file about 40.25 seconds long, starts the fade at 30 seconds, and sets the duration of the fade to 10.2 seconds, approximating the total playing length of the file. Use the Delay and Duration sliders to set the approximate times for your MIDI file or CD track, and click the up- and down-arrow buttons of the Delay and Duration scroll bars to trim the times 0.1 second per click.

3. The initial levels of the Fade Mixer are those that you set in Pro Mixer's Multimedia Mixer window. The level to which the sound is to fade is set in the Fade Mixer window. Because you want to fade the music to zero level in this exercise, use the Fade Mixer slider to set the SYNTH level to zero.

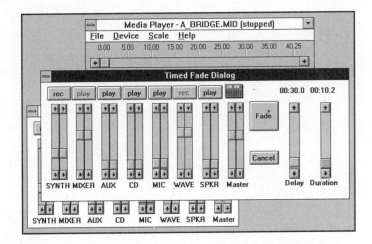

FIG. 15.23

Pro Mixer's automatic
Timed Fade dialog
box.

4. Click the Fade button to test the fade. After the delay you specified
   in your Delay setting, you see the SYNTH slider move toward zero
   level at the rate established by your Duration setting.

T I P   A simpler way to implement a timed fade is to set Delay to 0 and Duration to the desired rate of fade. Click the Fade button in the Timed
Fade window when you want the fade to begin. You can perform
stereo pans (crossfades) that make the sound seem to be moving
from the left to right channel, or vice versa. You can fade sound in or
out, but you can use only one fader setting at a time in Pro Mixer.

5. After the fade is completed, click Pro Mixer's icon, and then choose
   Reset State to return your level settings to their original values.

6. You can save the mixer state with default mixer settings by clicking
   Pro Mixer's icon and then choosing **S**ave State. The Select a Mixer
   State File dialog box appears (see fig. 15.24).

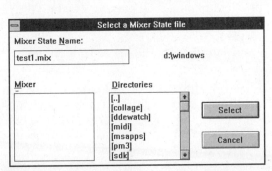

FIG. 15.24

Pro Mixer's Select
a Mixer State File
dialog box.

7. Type a file name (such as FADE1.MIX) in the text box and then click the Select button to save the file. You can load the saved settings later by choosing **L**oad State choice from the Pro Mixer menu.

8. Prepare to record your narration. Use the sliders to set the microphone level in both the Multimedia Mixer and Timed Fade windows to about 66 percent so that your voice does not fade to zero along with the music. Reset the Delay and Duration sliders, if necessary.

9. Click the Play buttons above MIC in the Multimedia Mixer and Time Fade windows to add the microphone as a record input. If you hear a high-pitched squeal, reduce the Master volume level to eliminate the feedback.

10. Click Pocket Recorder's icon and then choose **S**ave State to include the microphone settings in your mixer-settings file.

11. Chose **N**ew from Pocket Recorder's **F**ile menu, and then click No when the message box asks whether you want to save your earlier untitled recording.

12. Change the Record Parameters settings, if you want, and then choose OK.

13. Click Pocket Record's Record button, Media Player's Play button, and the Fade button in Pro Mixer's Timed Fade window in rapid succession. When you hear the music begin, start your narration. Adjust the level of your voice or the position of the microphone so that the VU-meter needle does not enter the red area. As the music begins to fade, stop talking into the microphone.

14. Upon completion of the timed fade, click Pocket Recorder's Stop button. A delay occurs as the sound data in the buffer is written to the temporary file.

15. Click Pocket Recorder's Rewind and Play buttons to listen to your performance.

16. If you are satisfied with the recording, choose Save **A**s from Pocket Recorder's **F**ile menu. The Select a Mixer State File dialog box appears.

17. Type a file name with the default WAV extension. The temporary file is copied to this new file, and the temporary file is erased.

18. Pro Mixer includes a set of tone controls: the Bass and Treble sliders. To access these controls, click Pro Mixer's icon and then choose Equalizer from the Pro Mixer menu. The Equalizer dialog box appears (see fig. 15.25).

19. To adjust the low-frequency components of the sound, move the Bass slider up or down; to adjust the level of the high-frequency components, move the Treble slider.

When the Loudness check box is checked, bass boost is provided at lower listening levels. Stereo Enhance introduces a slight phase shift between the left and right channels to simulate additional stereo separation. Equalizer settings affect playback through your monitor speakers and have no effect on recording levels.

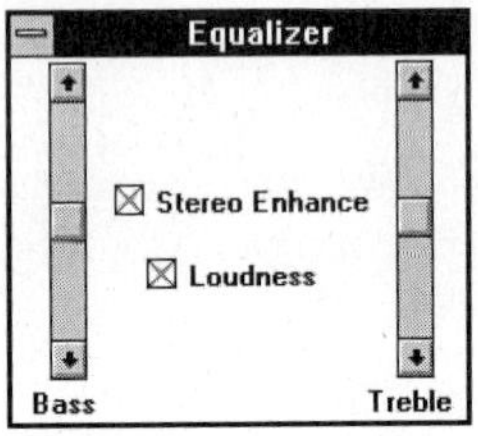

FIG. 15.25

Pro Mixer's Equalizer dialog box.

Narration usually is associated with a predetermined sequence of graphic images, still or video, that comprise the portion of a presentation that does not use video images with synchronized sound. When you transfer narration from audiotape to waveform audio, or if you are using direct-to-disk recording techniques, record the portion of the script for each image or video segment as a separate waveform audio file. You then can change the sequence of the images and the accompanying narration as necessary, without having to cut and paste segments from a large audio file.

You can recombine the sounds, if you want, by adding one file to the other during the final edit; then you can mix in (digitally dub) your background-music file. Even the Sound Recorder applet can perform these functions, but only for 22.05-kHz 8-bit monaural files. For serious audio work, you need one of the commercial waveform editing applications described in Chapter 13.

Chapter Summary

This chapter served only as an introduction to the audio techniques employed in digital recording. The chapter discussed some basic techniques for setting up, recording, and mixing waveform audio files, using applications supplied with audio adapter cards. The chapter also discussed how to choose the right microphone and how to eliminate sources of noise and hum.

Hundreds of books have been written to guide audio enthusiasts, technicians, and engineers toward the ephemeral goal of perfect sound recording and reproduction. If you want to explore the subject more thoroughly and cannot find the books you need, try Mix Bookshelf (listed in Appendix F). This firm, a subsidiary of the firm that publishes *Mix* and *Electronic Musician* magazines, carries a wide range of books on digital and analog audio techniques and publishes a catalog of its titles.

Chapter 21 provides examples of playing waveform audio and MIDI files in synchronization with video sources, as well as using a Windows sequencer application, Cakewalk for Windows, instead of a dedicated mixer applet to control your audio adapter card's mixer. Chapters 23 and 24 describe the Windows media control interface (MCI) and how you use MCI commands in conjunction with audio devices.

Adding Multimedia Graphics

P A R T

V

O U T L I N E

Graphic Displays and Adapter
Cards for Windows

Image Acquisitions, Editing, Interchange, and Compression

Presentation Graphics and Animation Techniques

Incorporating Digital Video

Graphic Displays and Adapter Cards for Windows

M ultimedia combines graphic images and sounds on your computer to provide information in an entertaining and often captivating manner. Up to this point, this book has concentrated on sound, because sound is new to most users of multimedia-compliant PCs. Multimedia Specification 1.0 devotes several pages to audio specifications but makes only one reference to the VGA graphic display necessary to meet the base-level requirement.

Almost all Windows users have VGA (video graphics array) adapter cards and color video display units (VDUs), but Microsoft Corporation estimates that only 25 percent to 30 percent of all PCs in the United States are VGA-equipped. The remaining 70 percent to 75 percent have monochrome displays, the grainy CGA (computer graphics array) displays, and the somewhat better EGA (extended graphics array) displays. The VGA display is the unchallenged standard in the PC industry today. Multimedia PC Specification 1.0 requires a VGA display.

The first VGA adapter cards had 256K of RAM and provided 16 colors in 640-by-480-pixel images. Who needed more than 16 colors with text-based DOS applications? When Windows 3.0 arrived on May 22, 1990, however, 256-color capability became a necessity, so the new standard for VGA adapters quickly became 512K of RAM. Many Windows users opted to use the 800-by-600 pixel SVGA mode to include more spreadsheet columns or to show the full 8 1/2-inch width of a word processing document in the display. Windows power users with 17-inch display units chose 1,024-by-768-pixel resolution, pioneered by IBM's 8514/a display adapter.

VGA cards soon became a PC commodity, and the street price of 512K models dropped to less than $100. Multimedia Specification 1.0 allows a PC that displays only 16 colors to have the MPC trademark. At the time this book was written, VGA cards with 1M of RAM, providing 256 colors at 1024 by 768 pixels, was on its way to industry-standard status.

This chapter describes how adapter cards and video display units work together to create color images in the three basic resolutions employed by most Windows users. The chapter also explains software and hardware methods of increasing the speed at which Windows applications update the display.

Plasma, LCD, and other display technologies used in portable computers are not covered in this book, because the displays used by laptop and notebook computers are not well-suited to multimedia applications.

VGA Displays and Adapter Cards

Conventional color video display units use cathode-ray tubes (CRTs) similar to those used in television sets. Figure 16.1 shows a diagram of the CRT and associated components required for a computer's VDU or a color television set.

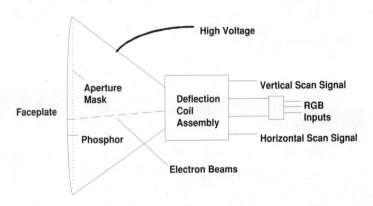

FIG. 16.1

The CRT and deflection components of a VDU or color TV set.

Color images are created from three analog signals, representing the relative intensity of the reds, greens, and blues (RGB) required to create a particular pixel of a specified color. The analog RGB signals control the intensity of three individual electron beams created by a heated filament. The electron beams are accelerated by a high voltage applied to a conductive coating inside the CRT. The three beams then are deflected to impinge on the face plate of the CRT at the location of the desired pixel by a pair of magnetic coils in a deflection yoke assembly; one coil determines vertical position, and the other coil determines horizontal position of the three beams. The signals that drive these coils are derived from vertical and horizontal synchronization signals that originate on the VGA adapter card.

The three deflected electron beams travel through thousands of minute holes as they sweep across a metal plate called an *aperture* (or shadow) mask and then strike a phosphor coating on the inside of the glass face plate of the picture tube. The coating consists of dots made of three different phosphors that emit red, green, or blue light of an intensity proportional to the number of electrons that strike them during the short time that the electron beams pass through a hole in the aperture mask. The three phosphors are arranged so that when the electron beams for each of the colors pass through the holes in the aperture mask, each beam strikes the phosphor dots that correspond to its color. As a result, the position of the aperture mask relative to the phosphor dots must be controlled precisely.

The basic difference between CRTs for television sets and computer VDUs is in the aperture mask and phosphor coating on the face plate of the tube. If you compare an image from a VGA with an image on a similar-size television set, you can see the difference. The distance between the aperture holes (called the *dot pitch*) in the average television set is 0.76mm, whereas the standard for SVGA VDUs is 0.28mm. In other words, the aperture mask of an SVGA VDU has about eight times more holes than the CRT used in a standard color TV set. The smaller the holes and the more of them in a picture tube of constant size, the clearer and sharper the image.

Smaller holes in the aperture mask require smaller and more precisely located phosphor dots. Thus, SVGA VDUs are more expensive than color television sets of the same size, even though a TV set contains many more components (such as those used in tuners, remote controls, and audio circuits) than a VDU. VDUs that comply with the basic VGA standard range in cost from less than $250 to more than $3,000. Display size plays the largest role in determining the price of a VGA monitor. In the common 13-and 14-inch sizes, display resolution (dot pitch) determines the price.

Early VGA displays had a dot pitch of 0.41mm or greater. Subsequently, improved displays with 0.38mm, 0.35mm, and 0.31mm dot pitch were developed. The current standard for quality VGA displays is 0.28mm dot pitch in the normal 13- or 14-inch (diagonal) sizes, which are priced in the $350 range. Dot pitch usually is somewhat greater in 15-, 17-, and 19-inch VDUs.

T   I   P

In an attempt to market computers at the lowest possible price, many retail and mail-order firms supply low-cost, grainy 0.38mm display units. You can substantially reduce the inevitable eyestrain from long hours spent in front of your VDU by purchasing a display with a dot pitch no greater than 0.28mm.

From your computer's central processing unit, VGA adapter cards receive data that represents the color of each pixel of the display in digital form. Data is transmitted over the internal I/O bus that connects all adapter card connectors to the I/O ports of the microprocessor. As display data is received by a conventional VGA card in 2-byte (16-bit) pairs, the card stores the bytes in a specific location (address) in random-access memory (RAM) corresponding to the position of the pixels on the display. In the 16-color mode of an SVGA adapter card or if a standard VGA card is installed, 1 byte of data contains the color information for two pixels. In 256-color mode used by SVGA cards, each pixel requires 1 byte of RAM.

Figure 16.2 shows a simplified diagram of an SVGA display card.

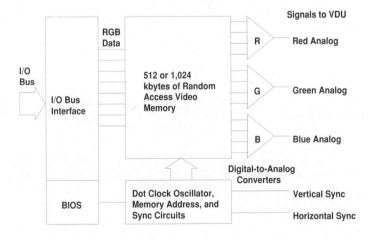

FIG. 16.2

A simplified diagram of a conventional super-VGA adapter card.

After the color data for each pixel is written to the video memory, the digital values for red, green, and blue intensities are sent to three digital-to-analog converters (DACs) that produce the analog color signals required by VGA display units. The rate at which the data is sent to the DACs is controlled by an internal oscillator called the *dot clock*. Each pulse of the dot clock represents one pixel of the display. The dot-clock frequency for the various VESA SVGA modes ranges from 25 MHz to 75 MHz. The horizontal and vertical synchronization signals used to drive the vertical and horizontal deflection coils are derived by using a counter circuit to divide the pulses of the dot clock.

Conventional television signals are interlaced, whereas all VGA operating modes except VESA modes 104, 105, and 106 are not interlaced. *Interlacing* means that the display is created by first drawing all the odd-numbered lines and then filling in the even-numbered lines. Television displays use interlaced images because television's slower vertical sync rate of 29.94 Hz would cause the perception of flicker in a noninterlaced image. The higher scan rates of SVGA displays, however, enable the image to be created in one pass. Non-interlaced SVGA displays have better image quality than their noninterlaced counterparts do.

VGA Operating Modes and VESA Standards

Early VGA adapter cards, which had 256K of memory, were capable of displaying 17 operating modes. These modes were defined by numbers that the card's basic input/output system (BIOS) chip could recognize.

Table 16.1 lists the original standard VGA modes.

Table 16.1. Standard VGA Operating Modes.

Mode	Width	Height	Colors	Comments
00/01	320	200	16	Text, 8x8-pixel cell
00*/01	320	350	16	Text, 8x14-pixel cell, EGA
00+/01+	360	400	16	Text, 8x16-pixel cell
02/03	640	200	16	Text, 8x8-pixel cell
02*/03*	640	350	16	Text, 8x14-pixel cell, EGA
02+/03+	720	400	16	Text, 8x14-pixel cell
04/05	320	200	4	Graphics

continues

Table 16.1. Continued

Mode	Width	Height	Colors	Comments
06	640	500	2	Graphics
07*	720	300	Mono	Text, 9x14-pixel cell
07+	720	400	Mono	Text, 9x16-pixel cell
0D	320	200	16	Graphics
0E	640	200	16	Graphics
0F	640	350	mono	Graphics, EGA
10	640	350	16	Graphics, EGA maximum
11	640	480	2	Graphics
12	640	480	16	Graphics, standard VGA
13	640	200	256	Graphics

Several of these modes were included in the VGA BIOS to make VGA adapter cards and displays compatible with applications designed for the EGA display system that VGA replaced. When you boot your computer with a VGA card installed, mode 00/01 is used to display DOS text. Special drivers used the graphics modes to display more than 25 lines and 80 characters per line for DOS-based word processing and spreadsheet applications.

All the VGA versions of Windows introduced after the VGA display became available were designed to operate in VGA graphics mode 12, which provides 16 colors in a 640-by-480-pixel display. The horizontal scanning frequency for all standard VGA displays is 31.5 kHz (twice the standard for television broadcasting), and the vertical synchronization frequency is 70 Hz except for modes 11 and 12, in which it is 60 Hz (also twice the TV standard, 29.94 Hz). The standard VGA driver supplied with Windows, VGA.DRV, supports mode 12.

After standard VGA cards were entrenched in the market, manufacturers began to develop additional display formats that provided higher display resolution. To avoid the chaos that would result if each manufacturer decided on different numbers of horizontal and vertical pixels and nonstandard numbers of characters and lines for text, the Video Electronic Standards Association (VESA) was formed to coordinate the definitions of modes for SVGA displays.

Table 16.2 lists current VESA standard and extended modes for Super-VGA operating cards.

Table 16.2. VESA Hexadecimal Mode Numbers for SVGA Modes.

Mode	Width	Height	Colors	Comments
100H	640	400	256	Close to TV aspect ratio
101H	640	480	256	Standard for 256 colors
102H	800	600	16	Standard Windows driver
103H	800	600	256	512K VRAM, SVGA
104H	1,024	768	16	512K VRAM
105H	1,024	768	256	1M VRAM required
106H	1,280	1,024	16	High-resolution displays
107H	1,280	1,024	256	High-resolution displays
108H	80 characters	60 lines	16	Text mode
109H	132	25	16	Text mode
10AH	132	43	16	Text mode
10BH	132	50	16	Text mode
10CH	132	60	16	Text mode

SVGA cards use vertical synchronization rates ranging from 56 Hz to 87 Hz and horizontal scanning frequencies of 25 kHz to 56 kHz. The most common vertical sync rates are 56 Hz, 60 Hz, and 72 Hz. Higher vertical sync rates result in less flicker in the display, especially when you view the screen close-up. Accommodating the various vertical sync and horizontal scanning frequencies requires a multisynchronous monitor. Most current SVGA monitors can synchronize to VESA signals for resolutions as high as 1,024 by 768 pixels.

Composition of Color Images

The pitch of sound is determined by the frequency of the sound wave, and loudness is controlled by the wave's amplitude. Similarly, the intensity of color is determined by the frequency of light waves (usually expressed as wavelength, which is the reciprocal of frequency), and brightness is determined by the light wave's amplitude.

The color of a passive object (an object that does not create light waves, such as a painting) is determined by the wavelengths of the colors it absorbs. The pigment used to create the flowers in Vincent van Gogh's *Irises*, for example, absorbs all wavelengths of light other than blue. The apparent brightness of an object is determined by the amount of the light that it does not absorb; the brightness of an object is measured by its reflectivity.

The three primary pigments—red, yellow, and blue—can be mixed in any proportion to create any pigment except pure white, because white is defined as the color of all wavelengths of light. Any colored pigment absorbs some of the wavelengths. When you mix the primary pigments in equal proportions, the pigments absorb all wavelengths and create black. The process of creating colors by mixing pigments is called *subtractive color synthesis*; each primary pigment subtracts colors other than its own from the mixture. A different set of pigments—cyan, magenta, and yellow—are used, along with black, in the ink used to print color images. In four-color printing processes, colors are defined by the CMYK model, in which the percentages of each of the cyan, magenta, yellow, and black (CMYK) inks are specified to define a particular color.

The CRT of your video display unit is an active object; it mixes colors, not pigments. The CRT creates colors by combining light waves of the wavelengths corresponding to red, blue, and green at varying intensities. In this case, your CRT creates the light waves by combining the three primary colors; combining the three light waves to create a particular color is called *additive color synthesis*. Additive color synthesis is the basic method by which computer applications define colors. Advanced drawing and image-editing applications (including CorelDRAW! and Micrografx Picture Publisher) can convert additive colors to their subtractive counterparts in preparing the four-color CYMK separations used to make color lithographic printing plates.

Additive Color Representation Models

Windows operates satisfactorily with the 16 colors that have been standard for the PC since the introduction of the almost-extinct EGA (extended graphics array) display. The standard colors are assigned 16 arbitrary numbers, ranging from 0 (black) to 15 (pure white). Windows calls this color grouping the 16-color standard VGA palette. Each of the 16 colors is defined by the amount of red, blue, and green light required to create it, using a scale of 0 (none) to 255 (maximum intensity).

Table 16.3 lists the red, blue, and green (RGB) values for the 16 standard VGA colors.

Table 16.3. RGB Values of Windows' 16-Color VGA Palette.

Code	Color	R	G	B
0	Black	0	0	0
1	Blue	0	0	128
2	Green	0	128	0
3	Cyan	0	128	128
4	Red	128	0	0
5	Magenta	128	0	128
6	Dark yellow	128	128	0
7	Light gray	192	192	192
8	Dark gray	128	128	128
9	Light blue	0	0	255
10	Light green	0	255	0
11	Light cyan	0	255	255
12	Light red	255	0	0
13	Light magenta	255	0	255
14	Yellow	255	255	0
15	Bright white	255	255	255

The RGB values used to create the colors listed in Table 16.3 follow a distinct pattern. The darker colors (1 through 6) are created by using half the maximum intensity. The lighter colors (9 through 15) are generated by combining maximum intensities. The intensities used to create light and dark gray are arbitrary, but all three RGB values must be equal.

Each of the 256 possible intensities of the three primary colors can be expressed by an 8-bit binary number ranging from 00000000 (0) to 11111111 (255). Theoretically, you can create 256×256×256 colors (16,777,216) through various permutations and combinations of the three 8-bit values; this combination is called 24-bit color. Few VGA adapter cards, however, are capable of displaying 16 million colors; those that can are expensive.

The RGB additive color synthesis model is the standard for Windows, but you also can use a model called hue-saturation-luminance (HSL) to define color. The HSL color model defines the color wavelength (*hue*), the intensity of the color (*saturation*), and the amount of white light added (*luminance*). The HSL model is used exclusively in the television broadcast industry, where it is called *YUV* (luminance, hue, and saturation). The picture controls on your color television set can adjust each of the three HSL values so that they match the corresponding HSL values of the video being transmitted. Luminance (Y) provides the black-and-white signal for monochrome television; hue and saturation are combined to create the chrominance signal that color TV sets require.

Table 16.4 lists the HSL equivalents of the RGB values listed in Table 16.1.

Table 16.4. HSL Values of Windows' 16-Color VGA Palette.

Code	Color	H	S	L
0	Black	160	0	0
1	Blue	160	240	60
2	Green	80	240	60
3	Cyan	120	240	60
4	Red	0	240	60
5	Magenta	200	240	60
6	Dark yellow	40	240	60
7	Light gray	160	0	180
8	Dark gray	160	0	120
9	Light blue	160	240	120
10	Light green	80	240	120
11	Light cyan	120	240	120
12	Light red	0	240	120
13	Light magenta	200	240	120
14	Yellow	40	240	120
15	Bright white	160	0	240

The values of hue, saturation, and luminance range from 0 to 240. Thus, the HSL model that Windows uses can create fewer colors (theoretically, 240×240×240, or 13,824,000) than the RGB model. The HSL values listed in Table 16.2 follow a pattern: basic colors are 40 hue units apart, and dark colors have a luminance value of 60. Light colors are created by increasing the luminance to 120. The hue values for black, light gray, dark gray, and white are arbitrarily set by Windows to blue. Hue values at zero saturation are not significant, which is why the number of colors is calculated by multiplying 240, not 241.

The Colors function of Windows 3.1's Control panel includes a dialog box that displays the RGB and HSL values of colors you select from a spectrum picture box. You can enter numeric RGB or HSL values to see the resulting color. This dialog box is one of the common dialog boxes new with Windows 3.1. Common dialog boxes are "prefabricated" versions of the dialog boxes most commonly used in Windows applications, such as those for opening and saving a file, printing documents, and choosing typefaces.

To experiment with the RGB and HSL definitions of various colors, follow these steps:

1. Start Control Panel from the Main program group.

2. Double-click the Color icon in Control Panel's window. The Color dialog box appears.

3. Choose Color **P**alette. The Color dialog box expands to display 48 basic colors, as shown in figure 16.3.

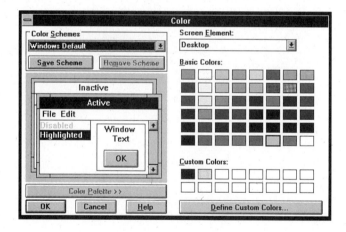

FIG. 16.3

The Color dialog box.

An additional 16 boxes are available, enabling you to create your own bizarre color combinations. Click one of the **B**asic Colors boxes to select a color to edit.

4. Choose **D**efine Custom Colors. The Custom Color Selector dialog box appears (see fig. 16.4).

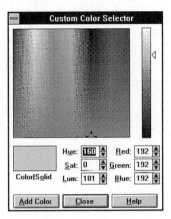

FIG. 16.4

The Custom Color
Selector dialog box.

5. Click the surface of the color picture box (calibrated in HSL). A sample of the hue (left to right) and saturation (bottom to top) you select appears in the Color|Solid box. The HSL values of the color are listed in the **Hue**, **Sat**, and **Lum** boxes, and the corresponding RGB values are listed in the **Red**, **Green**, and **Blue** boxes. You can change the luminance of the hue you selected by moving the arrow at the right of the luminance bar.

6. You can enter values ranging from 0 to 240 in the **Hue**, **Sat**, and **Lum** boxes and values ranging from 0 to 255 in the **Red**, **Green**, and **Blue** boxes. Alternatively, you can click the spin arrows next to those boxes to increase or decrease the values.

7. When you enter the values for the 16 basic VGA colors from table 16.3 or 16.4, the color in the Color|Solid box is a pure solid color. When you change the HSL or RGB values, a color pattern that approximates the true color appears in the Color|Solid box.

8. When you finish experimenting with colors, choose **Close** to close the Custom Color Selector dialog box and return to the Color dialog box. Then click the Cancel button to close the Color dialog box without saving any changes you may have made.

The Windows 256-Color Palette

Creating an image that uses 24-bit RGB values for each pixel requires 3 bytes per pixel. A 640-by-480-pixel image using RGB values needs the CPU to calculate the values of 640×480×3 (921,000) bytes and then send those values to the video adapter card each time the display is updated by (for example) scrolling text. Although a faster CPU can calculate the values more rapidly, the rate at which the data can be sent to the video display card is limited by the speed of the computer's I/O bus: 8 MHz to 10 MHz, which is the same for all PCs of the AT class and above.

Using 24-bit RGB values requires 1M of memory in the video adapter card for 640-by-480-pixel resolution, and you would need more than 2M for a 1,024-by-768-pixel SVGA display.

Windows solves this problem by limiting the range of colors to a 256-color palette. This standardization on 256 colors reduces the number of bytes required to display any of the palette's 256 colors to 1 byte per pixel.

The 256-color palette speeds updating of the display considerably compared with the 24-bit color approach. Instead of specifying an RGB value for each color the display uses, you use the numbers that represent each color's position in the palette (0 to 255). Windows then looks up the RGB values of the numbers in a table. Therefore, palettes often are called color-lookup tables (CLUTs).

Windows has a standard 256-color palette, but you can use applications such as Microsoft's PalEdit (supplied with the Multimedia Development Kit) to create a custom palette. Figure 16.5 shows PalEdit's color-selection window for a 236-color gray-scale palette displayed in 16-color VGA mode. You double-click a color sample in the palette to change it to another color.

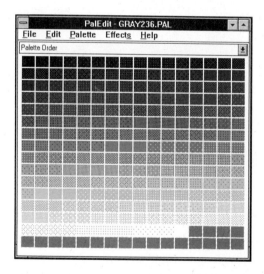

FIG. 16.5

PalEdit's palette-color-selection window.

The palette shown in the figure, GRAY236.PAL (also supplied with the MDK), demonstrates two elements of palettes:

■ The palette provides 236 choices, not 256. If you reserve 20 standard colors as Windows system colors (the 16 standard VGA colors plus 4 special system colors), Windows operates faster. Palettes with 236 colors and 20 system colors are called *identity palettes*.

■ A palette uses patterns to simulate colors not available in a 16- or 256-color display. The display of patterns of differing shades is called *color dithering*. This process is related to the halftone process used in lithography to print continuous-tone images. You can see a similar pattern if you use a magnifying glass to examine a high-quality color image in a magazine.

Figure 16.6 shows dithered colors in a gray-scale palette.

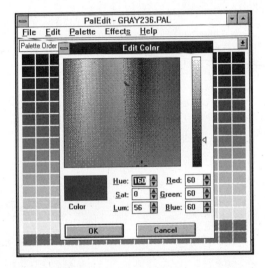

FIG. 16.6

PalEdit's Edit Color
dialog box.

In the figure, 256-color VGA mode was used. No patterns are required to display the gray-scale colors, but dithering is necessary to display the full range of colors available, because that range exceeds the 256-color limit of the adapter card and driver. Color dithering uses combinations of dots of the standard 16 or 256 VGA colors to simulate a color of intermediate hue. Percentages of the hues available in the standard 256-color palette are dithered in the dialog box to create nonstandard colors.

A custom palette is especially useful when you are displaying a video image or a photograph that consists principally of a particular group of colors. For example, a photograph of a forest might consist principally of various hues of green, blue, and brown. The BitEdit application (also provided with the MDK) can analyze a bit-mapped image to determine its range of colors and then create the optimum 236-color identity palette for displaying that image.

Windows' Display Drivers

Windows 3.1 includes an assortment of display-device drivers for the most popular SVGA cards that provide 800-by-600- and 1,024-by-768-pixel displays. SVGA cards with 256K of memory can support 800-by-600-pixel displays with 16 colors, so Windows 3.1 includes SUPERVGA.DRV, a generic driver for VESA mode 102. Windows 3.1 also includes an assortment of drivers for other display formats (including IBM's XGA) and 512K SVGA cards that provide 256-color, 800-by-600-pixel displays (mode 103) and 16-color, 1,024-by-768-pixel (mode 104) displays.

In most cases, you install the display drivers supplied (on floppy disk) by the VGA card's manufacturer. You need special display drivers, however, to take advantage of the 1M of memory in cards that provide a 256-color, 1,024-by-768-pixel display.

If you are using a 256-color driver, you can approximately double Windows' display-refresh rate by changing to the generic 16-color driver supplied with Windows 3.1 for applications that do not require 256 colors.

Many people who purchase VGA cards with the now-standard 512K of memory install the 256-color driver because the card can deliver 256 colors, not because they need the extra colors. Computers in which Windows already is installed invariably use the 256-color driver as the default. Sixteen colors, however, are adequate for virtually all Windows applications except image and video processing applications.

To change drivers, choose Change System Settings from Setup's Options menu and then select the plain VGA driver in the Display list box. (Make a mental or paper note of the name of the current driver so that you can reinstall it when you need 256 colors.) The time you spend rebooting your computer to change display drivers is repaid in the faster performance of your Windows applications.

Software-Based Graphics Accelerators

The VDU drivers supplied by Microsoft are designed to be compatible with a wide range of VGA adapter cards. The drivers provided with conventional SVGA adapters are, for the most part, drivers that can be programmed quickly and easily. You can increase the speed at which Windows updates your display by using a device driver that has been optimized for your VGA card and Windows 3.1.

Panacea, Inc.'s WinSpeed video-device driver can be used with almost any VGA board manufactured after 1988, including boards based on Paradise, Trident, and Tseng Labs ET4000 chips. WinSpeed users report an overall speed improvement of 10 percent to 50 percent for all Windows applications. For example, the driver accelerates text scrolling in applications such as Word for Windows by 30 percent or more.

An obvious advantage of using an optimized display driver is instant gratification. You don't have to take the case off your computer to obtain the driver's benefits; you simply install the driver and begin testing.

WinSpeed gains its best performance ratings in applications that move large amounts of data from memory to the display adapter. WinSpeed accelerates this process by a factor of 2 to 5. You can improve the performance of applications that create Windows device-independent bit maps (DIBs) from vector-based images—for example, the Windows meta files (WMF) created by Microsoft Draw and PowerPoint—by a factor of 4 to 5 if the images contain large areas of color (called *fills*). Other vector-based drawing applications, such as Micrografx Designer, Windows DRAW!, and CorelDRAW!, show similar improvement.

A new version of WinSpeed scheduled for release in late 1992 reportedly will further speed applications, provide 16-bit color (HiColor), and support graphics and mouse operations in DOS windows. HiColor support enables you to use WinSpeed with full-color image editors (such as Micrografx Picture Publisher) or to smooth color-gradient fills in color illustrations created with drawing applications.

The other way to speed the updates of Windows displays is to substitute a Windows graphics accelerator card for your standard VGA or SVGA. (These cards are described later in this chapter.)

Windows Graphics Display Drivers

When you installed Windows 3.1, you probably selected the standard Windows 3.1 generic VGA driver for your display. According to industry reports, more than 85 percent of Windows users now have at least basic (16-color) VGA displays, and more than 60 percent have graphics display adapter boards with at least 512K of memory that can provide 256 colors or more.

If you install a new display adapter card for which Microsoft has not supplied a Windows 3.1 driver, you also need to install a set of special drivers in order to take advantage of all the card's features. Although all current graphics adapter cards support standard VGA operation and virtually all support SVGA mode, special drivers are required for high-resolution displays with more than 16 colors.

Installing display drivers is similar to installing audio adapter card drivers (described in Chapter 5), except that you use Windows Setup instead of Control Panel in the process. Some suppliers include a Windows application that copies the drivers to the hard disk for you, but you still need to install the driver with Setup so that Windows can use the driver.

To install a display driver from the floppy disk supplied with your display adapter card, follow these steps:

1. Double-click the Setup icon in the Main group to start the Windows Setup applet. The Windows Setup dialog box appears (see fig. 16.7).

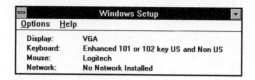

FIG. 16.7

The Windows Setup dialog box, showing primary system drivers in use.

2. Choose **O**ptions from the Main menu and then choose **C**hange System Settings. The Change System Settings dialog box appears (see fig. 16.8).

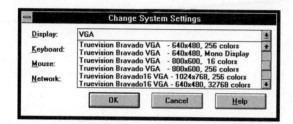

FIG. 16.8

The Change System Settings dialog box.

3. If the installation application copied the drivers to the hard disk, you should be able to find them by scrolling the list box. (Figure 16.8, for example, shows the drivers installed by the INSTDRV.EXE application for the Truevision Bravado video-in-a-window card.)

   If you find the driver you want to use, double-click the driver's name and then skip to step 8. Otherwise, proceed to step 4.

4. Click the down arrow at the right of the **D**isplay box and then use the scroll-bar controls to display the last item in that box, Other Display (see fig. 16.9).

FIG. 16.9

Selecting a VGA driver for the Bravado card.

5. Select Other Display and then click OK or press Enter. The window shown in figure 16.10 appears.

   If you are using drive B:, edit the text box to read B:\.

FIG. 16.10

The dialog box for choosing the drive into which the new driver floppy disk is inserted.

6. Insert the floppy disk that contains the driver you want to install and then click OK. The drivers are copied to your hard disk and their names are added to the Windows' SETUP.INF (setup information) file in your \WINDOWS\SYSTEM directory.

7. When the installation process is complete, the name of the driver you just installed appears in the Change System Settings dialog box. Select that driver and then click OK or press Enter. The dialog box shown in figure 16.11 appears, asking whether you want to use the display driver you just loaded.

FIG. 16.11

The dialog box for choosing an existing driver or adding a new driver on floppy disk.

8. Choose Current (the default) or press Enter. The new driver is installed as the default display driver for Windows. Because you must reboot Windows to make the new driver operational, the Exit Windows Setup dialog box appears (see fig. 16.12).

FIG. 16.12

The Exit Windows Setup dialog box.

9. Choose Restart Windows (the default) or press Enter. You exit Windows (and are given an opportunity to save any document changes), and then Windows reboots automatically. When

Windows runs again, it uses the new display driver. You can confirm this by starting Windows Setup again to redisplay the Windows Setup dialog box, which shows the primary system driver in use.

If you experience a problem in using the new driver, try one of the other drivers for the display adapter card you installed. You may have selected a driver included on the floppy disk but is not applicable to the version of the card you purchased. If you have a basic Bravado card, for example, and select one of the drivers for the 16-bit version (Bravado 16), you may experience display problems.

If none of the drivers appears to operate properly, the drivers may be incompatible with your VDU, or the files may be defective. In this case, reinstall the standard Microsoft VGA driver and then contact the manufacturer's technical-support department for assistance.

Specialty Display Adapters

Windows applications, as a rule, run more slowly than their DOS counterparts do—understandable, when you consider the fact that most DOS applications are character-based. When a character-based DOS display changes, the computer has to send the display adapter a stream of data representing the new characters. Because the standard DOS display is 25 lines by 80 characters, the PC needs to send 4,000 bytes (1 byte representing each character and another byte providing the character's attributes) to update the display. When a full-screen, 256-color Windows display changes, the PC must send 640x480 bytes of data (307,200) to the video display card over the PC bus.

The situation gets worse when you use the SVGA modes. For example, a 600-by-800-pixel display requires 480,000 bytes, and a 1,024-by-768-pixel display needs 786,432 bytes. Sending the bytes to the display adapter is not the only process involved; the computer's CPU also must do a lot of number-crunching to determine which pixel has what color.

As the use of SVGA display adapter cards with 256 and more colors became common, users waited for Windows to update the display. This need created a market for hardware and software that could speed the display response.

Windows Graphics Accelerator Cards

Conventional VGA adapter cards are called *dumb frame buffers* because they simply store one screen of data from the computer's I/O bus and convert the stored digital data to the RGB analog signals that your VGA or SVGA display requires. The I/O bus runs at a speed of 8 MHz to 10 MHz, not at the speed of your computer's CPU chip.

The amount of memory on the card determines the number of colors that you can display in the various VGA operating modes defined by the Video Electronic Standards Association (VESA). Cards with 512K of memory can display 256 colors in 640-by-480- and 800-by-600-pixel modes but only 16 colors at 1,024-by-768-pixel resolution. You need a card with 1M of memory to display 256 colors in 1,024-by-768-pixel mode.

Graphics accelerator cards require the same amount of memory as a conventional VGA card to display the same number of colors. Most accelerator cards use video random-access memory (VRAM), a special type of memory chip that, unlike the conventional RAM in your computer, can be written to and read from at the same time. This feature speeds up video processing.

Some early graphics accelerator cards simply substituted VRAM for conventional RAM and achieved a moderate speedup of Windows and DOS applications. Most graphics accelerator cards designed specifically for Windows perform two specific functions:

- They execute many of the graphics calculations that the CPU normally would perform, but at a much faster rate.

- They eliminate the bottleneck that stems from sending streams of bytes to your graphics adapter card over the computer's relatively slow I/O bus.

Accelerator cards use a special driver that intercepts requests from your application to GUI.EXE—the Windows dynamic link library (DLL) that processes most graphic operations, such as drawing lines, paging displays, and moving blocks of bit-mapped images (the BitBlt function). The processor on the adapter card performs these operations instead. Because the graphics processor and the frame buffer memory are on the same card, the data does not have to travel over the computer's bus and can be stored in the VRAM at a faster rate.

T I P   Purchase a graphics accelerator card from a dealer that provides a money-back guarantee, especially if you have one of the early 80386DX computers. Graphics accelerator cards, especially those that garner the best performance ratings in product reviews, operate at the cutting edge of bus timing. Some cards do not work with certain types of motherboards; other cards are sensitive to certain types of BIOS chips.

S3, Inc.'s 86C911 GUI accelerator chip is the most popular graphics processor for accelerator cards that sell for less than $400. Cards based on the S3 (pronounced S-cubed) 86C911 usually achieve the best price-performance ratings in tests. Other options include Texas Instruments' 34010 and 34020 series of image coprocessors, which are digital signal processors (DSPs) designed for image instead of digital sound manipulation, and proprietary processors such as the Mach 8 (ATI Technologies, Inc.). Accelerator cards that use TI chips and proprietary processors are more expensive than cards that use S3 processors.

Achieving more than 256 colors requires the three digital-to-analog converters (DACs) which create the analog RGB signals that give your display more than 8-bit resolution. Some accelerator boards offer 32,768 (15-bit) colors in 640-by-480 mode by adding a Sierra RAMDAC chip (including 1M of VRAM) and providing another driver for HiColor mode. Adapter cards based on the S3 86C911 chip (with 1M of RAM) and the Sierra HiColor RAMDAC chip are achieving industry-standard status. Many of the computers retail and mail-order dealers offer as "Windows-ready" include one of these standard accelerator cards.

Graphics accelerator cards occupy a range of device addresses often beginning at C000 and ending at C7FF. If you are using an expanded memory manager such as EMM386 (supplied with Windows 3.1) or Quarterdeck's QEMM386, you must exclude the range of addresses from the range the memory manager assigned to expanded memory. Add the line **x=C000-C7FF** (substitute the range of addresses used by your adapter card, if that range is different) after EMM386.SYS or QEMM386.SYS in your CONFIG.SYS file.

You also may find that your SCSI adapter card is using an address in this range (although CC00 is more typical). If so, you usually need to change the SCSI card's address because most graphics accelerator cards and many SVGA adapter cards with 512K or more memory do not offer switches or jumpers that enable you to change their address ranges.

Moderately priced Windows graphics accelerator cards improve overall system performance by a factor of 2 to 5, with the greatest benefit being the tenfold improvement in manipulating large 256-color bit maps in 800-by-600 SVGA mode. Tests of representative S3-based cards show that the cards improve text-scrolling rates by a factor of about 3.5 and line draws by a factor of 5 or more. Advertisements' claims of 20- to 50-time improvements, however, appear to be greatly exaggerated.

Under pressure to keep their prices competitive, some manufacturers of Windows accelerator cards have chosen to omit the VESA feature adapter connector that is standard on virtually all conventional VGA and SVGA adapter cards. If the accelerator card you purchase does not have a feature adapter, you cannot connect the card to most video-in-a-window cards or to VGA-to-NTSC adapter cards. Even if the accelerator card has a feature connector, its synchronization-signal polarity and timing may not match that of the video card to which you intend to attach it.

Local Bus Video

The next-generation method of removing the graphics-data bottleneck is called *local bus video* (LBV). Local bus video enables the CPU to send graphics data to the VGA or SVGA circuits at the CPU's operating speed, 33 MHz or 50 MHz, rather than at the 8-MHz to 10-MHz rate of the I/O bus, resulting in a fourfold to fivefold increase in speed.

With LBV, graphics data can be transferred on a path 32 bits wide instead of the 16-bits-wide path of the standard I/O bus, doubling the data-transfer rate. Thus, LBV has the potential to speed VDU updates by a factor of 8 to 10 without the need for graphics accelerator chips. LBV techniques affect all graphics operations, not just those used in Windows and CAD applications.

As is true of most emerging technologies, no standards have been established for local bus video. The diagram shown in figure 16.13 contrasts conventional I/O bus video with two LBV approaches in current 80486s.

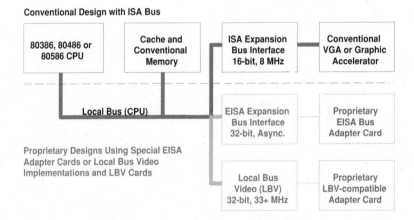

FIG. 16.13

Methods of implementing local bus video.

Both methods of implementing LBV use proprietary expansion-board connections. Some manufacturers have chosen a modified version of the EISA standard; others use a redesigned connection pattern. A few manufacturers add S3's graphics processor to their graphics adapter cards to gain further speed improvement in Windows and AutoCAD. Until VESA establishes a local bus video standard, however (and a standard is not expected until late 1992 or early 1993), anarchy will reign in LBV design.

Several current implementations of local bus video with proprietary graphics adapter cards do not include a VESA feature connector. When LBV is implemented on the motherboard, some manufacturers may sacrifice VESA feature connectors to reduce manufacturing cost.

T I P

If you are considering purchasing an 80486 computer with LBV and plan to add NTSC video-in-a-window or video output capability, make sure that a VESA feature connector is provided. If the feature connector is missing, you cannot add a conventional video-in-a-window card or an internal VGA-to-NTSC card to your system. To convert VGA output to NTSC television signals, you need an external scan converter. Scan converters with genlocking capability are considerably more expensive than their counterparts on adapter cards.

Proprietary LBV implementations on adapter cards are costly because of low production volume compared with standard ISA (industry-standard architecture, the AT bus) graphics adapter and graphics accelerator cards. SVGA is regarded as the standard for today's PCs, and no new technologies threaten to displace it. IBM's XGA graphics standard is used only by PS/2 computers, so it can be classified as one more proprietary technique, not as a threat to SVGA's dominance.

To keep the cost of LBV at or below that of a graphics accelerator card, LBV and the SVGA circuitry must be implemented on the motherboard. Ultimately, local bus video SVGA will be part of the motherboard in most 80486 and 80586 computer systems.

If you purchase a computer with the SVGA circuitry on the motherboard and you plan to use specialty graphics adapter cards for NTSC video applications, make sure that you can disable LBV. For example, Matrox Personal Producer requires that the use of the Matrox Illuminator-16 videographics adapter board. Look for systems that enable you to select LBV or standard ISA-bus graphics with driver software, not on-board jumpers, so that you don't have to open the computer case to switch between the two methods.

T I P

Digital Signal Processing for Images

Digital signal processors (DSPs), represented by the Texas Instruments 320Cxx family described in Chapter 13, are widely used in processing audio signals. Signal compression and digital audio effects, especially in musical applications, are the two primary uses for these processors.

Texas Instruments also produces two DSPs designed for bit-mapped image processing: the 34010 and the 34020.

Because DSP chips contain a microprocessor, they often are called *coprocessors*. DSPs can be programmed to perform a wide range of operations on graphics data without occupying your computer's CPU. These devices also have fast on-chip RAM and special types of multiplier circuits (similar to those used in the 80x87 family of math coprocessors used in PCs) that speed the mathematical operations involved in scaling and rotating images.

Several manufacturers of integrated circuits (including AT&T, IIT, Intel, Motorola, and Texas Instruments) are developing new graphics coprocessor chips specifically for multimedia applications. These DSPs, which offer higher operating speeds and greater flexibility, are expected to be used in real-time image compression and decompression applications and in graphics acceleration applications. One primary use for the new high-speed DSPs is expected to be frame-by-frame rendering of complex three-dimensional animations—a time-consuming process discussed in Chapter 20.

Video Display Units

Reviews of the various SVGA displays are beyond the scope of this book. You can use some general guidelines, however, to determine the SVGA that best combines your multimedia requirements with the limits of your budget.

Those guidelines are as follows:

■ *Display size*, as mentioned earlier in the chapter, is the major factor in VDU prices. Unbranded 13- and 14-inch SVGA VDUs sold for an average $350 at the time this book was written, and prices had been stable for about six months. If you plan to make extensive use of 800-by-600-pixel SVGA mode, however, you should use a 16- or 17-inch VDU. List prices for these larger VDUs range from $1,000 to $3,000. To make effective use of 1,024-by-768-pixel mode, you need a display 19 inches or larger and can expect to spend $3,000 or more.

■ *Dot pitch* is as important in large VDUs as it is in 13- and 14-inch VDUs. If your goal is equal image clarity at equal viewing distance from a larger display, you need the same or smaller dot pitch. The dot pitches of 16-inch VDUs, for example, range from 0.26mm to 0.31mm.

■ *Flat screens* contribute to perceived image quality, even if the improvement is impossible to measure by the techniques used in magazine product reviews. As a rule, the apparent clarity of the image increases in proportion to the radius of curvature of the face plate.

■ *Synchronization rates* are important, but you can get 1,024-by-768-pixel resolution with horizontal scan rates of 35 kHz to 60 kHz. The current standard for SVGA vertical synchronization is 35 Hz to 72 Hz.

■ *Autosizing* adjusts the VDU's vertical and horizontal size controls to maintain image size and position when you switch modes—a significant advantage if you often change display resolution.

■ *Location of controls* is important if the display does not have autosizing capability. Vertical- and horizontal-positioning and size controls should be within easy reach, but these controls are on the backs of many VDUs, and if you have a large display, you may need to use a mirror to make proper adjustments.

■ *BNC connectors* for coaxial-cable connections to the RGB and sync signals from your SVGA adapter card provide lower-loss transmission of these signals. BNC connectors (similar to those used to make connections between TV sets and VCRs) are significant only if the display comes with a coaxial-cable bundle that mates with the 9- or 15-pin mini-D connector that most SVGA adapter cards use. Coaxial-cable connections are a virtual necessity for remote displays.

The best way to determine which VDU meets your requirements, however, is to compare several brands side by side at a computer store. Bring a BMP file containing a large 256-color bit-map image with good detail and contrasting colors to display in Windows Paintbrush.

If you cannot compare images directly, make sure that you obtain a money-back guarantee from the dealer or the mail-order firm from which you buy the VDU. Product reviews in computer magazines are a good source of general guidance and provide list-price information, but the choice of a VDU involves *your* perception of image quality.

Chapter Summary

This chapter introduced you to multimedia graphics. You learned that Multimedia PC Specification 1.0 details requirements for audio adapter cards and CD-ROM drives but virtually disregards the visual aspect of multimedia reproduction. This chapter explained the criteria for selecting VGA displays and adapter cards to obtain the results that you expect from a medium in which graphics play such an important role.

The Windows accelerator cards described in this chapter add snap to your multimedia presentations by speeding the display of large bit maps and complex animations. New techniques for increasing the performance of video displays, including local bus video and digital signal processors for graphic images, were covered briefly, because these techniques have not yet been standardized for multimedia applications.

The remainder of Part V of this book is devoted to the graphics techniques used in creating multimedia titles. Chapter 17 explains how to obtain and process the still images you need for multimedia presentations and title production. Chapter 18 gives examples of commercial presentation applications that combine graphics and sound to create the multimedia equivalent of a slide show. Part V concludes with Chapter 19, which explains how you can add full-motion-video capability to your PC.

Image Acquisitions, Editing, Interchange, and Compression

This chapter introduces the applications and technology involved in manipulating graphic images, whether those images are bit-mapped or vector-based drawings. Creating the graphic images you need to produce a professional-quality multimedia application can be a time-consuming process. This chapter discusses how you can acquire images from a variety of sources and use those images in multimedia productions.

Bit-mapped images, especially with 256 or more colors, can create large files. This chapter discusses image compression and decompression techniques you can use to handle large files.

You seldom can use a photographic image that you scan or copy from a Photo CD-ROM without retouching and cropping. The Windows image-editing applications described in this chapter provide these capabilities and much more. Image editors also are capable of converting graphics from one format to another.

Bit-Mapped versus Vector-Based Images

Graphic images used in Windows multimedia applications are divided into two categories:

■ *Bit-mapped images.* Windows creates bit-mapped images by assigning a color to each pixel inside the image boundary. Most bit-mapped color images require one byte per pixel for storage, so large bit-mapped images create correspondingly large files. A full-screen, 256-color image in 640-by-480-pixel VGA mode requires 307,200 bytes of storage, if the data is not compressed. The standard Windows format for bit-mapped images is a 256-color device-independent bit map (DIB) with a BMP or sometimes a DIB extension. All video images are displayed in the form of bit maps.

■ *Vector-based images.* Drawing applications create vector-based images by defining the images by their end points, thickness, color, and pattern and curvature of lines and solid objects. The definition consists of a numerical representation of the coordinates of the object, referenced to a corner of the image. The standard Windows format for vector-based images is the Windows meta file that carries a WMF extension. You can include DIB bit maps in WMF files, if necessary. If bit-map images are not included, WMF files usually are substantially smaller than BMP files of the same dimensions. Animation applications (such as Autodesk Animator) use vector-based files.

Most Windows presentation applications (including Microsoft PowerPoint, Harvard Graphics for Windows, and Macromedia Action!) also create vector-based files. Although vector images' files are smaller than those of bit-mapped images of equivalent size, complex vector images may take longer to display because the Windows graphic device interface (GDI) ultimately must draw the image as a 256-color bit map on the display. Animation files overcome this obstacle by drawing only the elements of an image that change from frame to frame. This incremental approach to creating moving images is the basis of video-image data-compression techniques (discussed at the end of this chapter).

Sources of Graphic Images

Your basic goal in creating a multimedia application should be to acquire rather than create the necessary graphic images, if possible. Many sources of "stock" images are available; you can use these images alone or in combination, especially in vector formats. You can shoot your own photographs and have them digitized professionally on Photo CD-ROMs, or you can use a color scanner to digitize photographs yourself. Video clips are another source of stock images, as are collections of photographs supplied on CD-ROMs.

This section describes representative sources of graphic images and explains how you can use these images in your multimedia productions.

Vector-Based Images Supplied with Drawing Applications

The richest source of vector-based images, called *clip art*, is the collection supplied by Corel Corporation on the CD-ROM that accompanies CorelDRAW! 3.0. The CD-ROM contains more than 12,000 clip-art images in about 75 different categories.

Figure 17.1 shows 12 of the vector-based images supplied as CDR files in the Art category of the CorelDRAW! CD-ROM. The images are displayed using the CorelMOSAIC! 3.0 image-cataloging application.

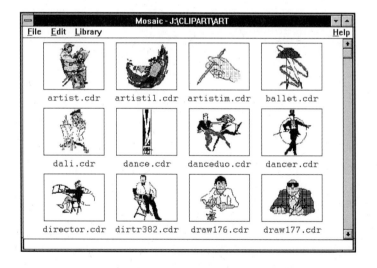

FIG. 17.1

Clip-art images from the CorelDRAW! 3.0 CD-ROM.

Micrografx supplies a collection of vector-based files in DRW format with its Micrografx Designer and Windows Draw! applications. Presentation applications such as PowerPoint, Action!, and Harvard Graphics for Windows include templates for slides and backgrounds and also provide stock images (primarily for use in business presentations).

Kodak Photo CD Images

Kodak introduced its Photo CD process (described briefly in Chapter 3) as a consumer product in August 1992. Initially, a limited group of photo finishers had the processing equipment required to create Photo CD ROMs from 35mm transparencies. Kodak introduced three Photo CD players capable of displaying Photo CD images on television sets at the same time. Kodak Photo CD players now are available at most major electronics stores.

Kodak's Photo CD Access Software application enables you to view Photo CD images on a Windows-equipped computer and to export the images as files in the standard formats supported by Windows and most Windows applications. Kodak has announced several new Photo CD formats and image-editing applications for Windows; these products are scheduled for release in late 1992 and 1993.

The principal advantage of the Photo CD process is that you can take your own photographs and have a photo finisher scan and convert them to Photo CD images at a cost of less than $25 for 24 images. The quality of Photo CD images exceeds that of images produced by color scanners in the under-$10,000 category.

Photo CDs can produce five copies of each image in the sizes listed in Table 17.1. The table also indicates the amount of memory (RAM plus disk cache) required to store those images. If you have 4M of RAM, you need about 24M of space for the temporary or permanent swap file created when you load a Poster-size CD image into the Photo CD Access Software.

Table 17.1. Memory requirements for Photo CD images.

Description	Size	Memory Required
Wallet	2" × 2.5"	98.3K
Snapshot	4" × 5"	393.2K
Standard	8" × 10"	1.5M
Large	11" × 14"	6.2M
Poster	16" × 20"	25.1M

At the time the Photo CD process became available, the following commercially available CD-ROM drives were compatible with the Photo CD image format:

- Magnavox CDD 461
- Sony CDU 535 (with the Sony CDB X10 controller adapter card)
- Sony CDU 541 (with the latest driver software from the Sony BBS)
- Sony CDU 6211

The Photo CD Access Software provides the capability to crop and edit images and to export Photo CD images in BMP, EPS, PCX, Windows RIFF (RDIB), TIFF, and WMF formats. Photo CD images use a proprietary compression technique and are identified by the PCD extension.

Micrografx Picture Publisher 3.1 (discussed later in this chapter) was one of the few Windows image-editing applications that supported the Photo CD format when that format was released.

Scanned Photographic Images

If you have a black-and-white or color photograph and do not have access to a Photo CD-compatible CD-ROM drive, the next-best choice is to use a hand-held or flatbed scanner to convert the images to bit maps. Creating a gray-scale image requires only one scan, but color images usually require three complete scans of the image (one scan for each color).

As you scan the image, the data is stored in memory (RAM and disk cache, as required) by a scanner driver that you load as a conventional Windows device driver. The driver converts the digital data from the scanner's output to a Windows DIB. Windows applications supplied with the scanners provide scanner control, color-balance and calibration adjustment, cropping, scaling, and *stitching*—the process of pasting together two images derived from the same source image to form one image.

Most scanners use a CCD (charge-coupled device) array of photoreceptors that convert light reflected from the image to an electrical signal translated to digital form by an analog-to-digital converter (ADC) in the unit. The CCDs in scanners are similar to those used in camcorders, except that a scanner's CCD consists of a row of photoreceptors instead of a rectangular array.

Scanner resolution is measured in dots per inch (dpi), and almost all scanners support the standard 300-dpi format common to standard laser printers. Some scanners provide resolution of 400 dpi or greater—about four times the resolution (roughly 95 dpi) of a 13-inch 640-by-480 pixel

VGA display. Large, high-resolution scanned images in 16-bit-and-higher color occupy astronomical amounts of disk space. For most multimedia applications, 200 dpi resolution is adequate unless you plan to blow up a small area of an image to occupy the entire display.

A few image-editing applications (including Picture Publisher 3.0) feature Windows drivers for popular scanners that you can add during software installation. The advantage of using a scanner supplied by the publisher of the editing application is that you can scan directly from a menu choice in the editing application rather than start a separate scanning application.

Hand-Held Color Scanners

Hand-held scanners are less costly than full-page scanning devices but can provide equal image quality after you learn to manipulate them properly. For best results, you should clamp a guide to the scanner to ensure that it does not wander during the scanning process. You also need a steady hand and a smooth surface.

Figure 17.2 shows the MusTek ColorArtist, a typical color scanner with 18-bit (262,144) color capability. You can select resolutions of 50 dpi through 400 dpi and 12-bit (4,096) or 18-bit color. You also can choose 64 or 256 shades in gray or black-and-white mode for copying line art.

The MusTek ColorArtist includes a copy of OCRON, Inc.'s Perceive Personal OCR (optical character recognition) application for converting scanned text to ASCII and popular word processing file formats. A limited-features copy of Micrografx Picture Publisher with the MusTek Windows driver also is included. This limited version of Picture Publisher does not, however, support Photo CD files. Both applications are designed for use in Windows 3.x.

Flatbed Color Scanners

A variety of flatbed color scanners can scan images 8-1/2 inches by 11 inches or larger in single or multiple passes to produce 8-bit to 24-bit color. The Hewlett-Packard ScanJet series scanners are most widely used for both gray-scale and color images. Other manufacturers produce flatbed scanners with a slightly different feature set or with bundled OCR and image-editing software from different publishers.

FIG. 17.2

The MusTek
ColorArtist. *(Courtesy
of MusTek, Inc.)*

Scanner sales have increased sharply since Windows 3.1 was released, and new models are being introduced monthly. The best way to select a flatbed scanner is to scan a standard 8-inch-by-10-inch color photograph at a computer store and then compare the image on the screen with the original. The next-best way to select a flatbed scanner is to read the reviews of scanner hardware in computer magazines devoted to the PC. All scanners now include applications that run in Windows 3.x.

Captured Videotape Images

You can use a video-in-a-window (VIW) adapter card to display and capture images from videotape cassettes and (if your VIW card includes a TV tuner) from broadcast television, as described in Chapter 19, "Incorporating Digital Video."

Commercial Images

Sounds and images in commercial videocassettes and broadcast television are copyrighted material. You cannot use copyrighted material in multimedia presentations without obtaining a release from and/or paying a fee to the copyright owner. The fee often depends on the extent to which you use the images in your production and on the number of copies of the title you intend to produce.

Some firms provide royalty-free commercial images on floppy disks and CD-ROMs. These firms usually grant you a paid-up, nonexclusive, limited license to use the images in your own productions and prohibit you from reselling the images.

Still and Animated Images on CD-ROMs

One growing market for multimedia titles (discussed in Chapter 20) is the production of images and sounds on CD-ROM for use in presentations.

Autodesk's Multimedia Explorer CD-ROM includes more than 200 animated clips in FLI format, including 86 FLI and GIF (still background images in graphic interchange format) files designed for business presentations. You can incorporate these FLI and GIF files into your own presentations. Multimedia Explorer also includes Autodesk Animator, a DOS animation application that enable you to edit the files or create your own animation.

Autodesk Animation Player for Windows enables you to view animation, add sound in the form of MID or WAV files, and create scripts that control the playback characteristics of the files. Figure 17.3 shows a window from an FLI animation file being played on this device.

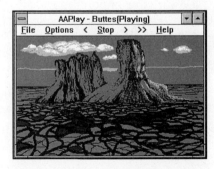

FIG. 17.3

Playing an FLI animation file on Autodesk Animation Player for Windows.

Appendix F lists other publishers that provide images and sounds on CD-ROMs for use in Windows multimedia publications. Some publishers specialize in bit maps of folk-art images from various countries; others provide vector-based clip art in a variety of categories, ranging from decorative borders to religious images and symbols.

Commercial Video Clips

Commercial video clips of historic events, scenes from early movies, famous people, and specialized film leaders and trailers are supplied by a variety of firms located primarily in New York City and Los Angeles. These firms supply high-quality images in Betacam, S-VHS, and Hi8 formats to video hobbyists, advertising agencies, and TV production companies.

Some video-clip firms sell the images for a flat fee with one-time broadcast rights; others charge a royalty based on footage and the number of copies to be produced. Most firms also produce special videotapes by kinescoping motion-picture footage.

Photographic Agencies and Image Archives

Photographic agencies serve as brokers between the users of images and the photographers who created those images. Fees vary, depending on the quality and uniqueness of the photograph, on the intended use of the photograph, and on the number of times the photograph is to be used. If you need a specific type of photograph, an agency will conduct a search for photographers who specialize in that category or in a related category.

Photographic archive firms own the images or have the right to license their use. Both types of still-image suppliers usually send an original photographic print that you scan and then return to the owner. Loss of or damage to an original print can involve a very substantial charge.

CompuServe offers a vast collection of bit-map graphics. The primary archive is the Computer Art Forum (GO COMART), in which most of the images are stored in graphic interchange format (GIF) files. (For more information on GIF format, see "Graphic File Formats" later in this chapter.)

Image Editing and Drawing Applications for Windows

If you intend to edit photographic images and to edit or create vector drawings, you need two distinctly different applications. To use an analogy, the difference between bit-mapped and vector images is similar to that between waveform audio and MIDI files. A bit map is an exact digital representation of the image, whereas a vector file stores information that enables you to use a drawing application to re-create the image. Although you can use the Paintbrush bit-map-editing application (supplied with Windows) or the BitEdit application (provided with the Multimedia Development Kit) to do minor retouching of photographs, you need a full-scale photographic-image editing application to make major changes in bit-mapped color images.

Many Windows image-editing applications are available, each with strong and weak points. All image-editing applications enable you to retouch gray-scale and color images, and most applications include filters that you can use to smooth or sharpen images, increase or decrease contrast, and apply textures. (Textures are used to make photographic images look as though they were painted on canvas, paper, or wood.)

Windows vector-drawing applications range in capability from the basic but easy-to-learn Microsoft Draw (included with Word for Windows 2.x) and Microsoft Publisher to professional-level applications exemplified by Micrografx Designer and CorelDRAW!. A typical midrange product is the Designer-derived Micrografx Windows Draw!, which enables you to create and edit vector drawings.

This chapter uses Micrografx Picture Publisher and CorelDRAW! as examples of high-end image-editing and drawing applications, respectively.

Picture Publisher 3.0

Micrografx Picture Publisher is a full-featured image editor for color and gray-scale bit-map images derived from a variety of sources, including scanning, Photo CDs, and public-domain or shareware files. Because Picture Publisher 3.0 is an OLE server, you can use it in OLE client applications to display and edit bit-mapped images.

Figure 17.4 shows a 24-bit color image enlarged by 300 percent and displayed with the dithered patterns used by Windows' 16-color VGA palette.

FIG. 17.4

A color image displayed in Picture Publisher.

Picture Publisher uses masks to identify the portion of the image to which retouching or other editing functions apply. The mask tool is similar to a frisket knife (X-Acto or equivalent), which retouching artists use to cut paper masks when they airbrush portions of an image. After you create a mask, you can save it for use when you want to modify the area of the image that the mask defines.

CorelDRAW! 3.0

CorelDRAW! 3.0 is the latest release of a vector-based drawing application that has been popular among Windows users since the latter days of Windows 2.x and Windows 386. Like most other drawing applications (with the exception of the Microsoft Draw OLE applet), CorelDRAW! 3.0 uses Bezier curves to define lines and shapes. *Bezier curves* define geometric shapes (including curved line segments) by establishing the end points (nodes) of an arc and two "control handles" that define the curvature of the arc. As you move the handles, you can generate a line of almost any shape imaginable. You connect lines at their nodes to create geometric forms such as triangles and rectangles. This technique was invented by a French engineer, M. Bezier, for use in computer-based design of automobiles.

Drawing applications have a much steeper learning curve than image-editing applications do. Creating sophisticated images by connecting Bezier curves and adjusting their control points takes a great deal of experimentation and practice.

Figure 17.5 shows one of the images supplied with CorelDRAW! 3.0 in the process of being edited.

FIG. 17.5

Editing a CorelDRAW! vector image.

The small black square on the left sleeve of the man in the figure is a selected curve node. The solid arrow moves the control point at the curve node's tip to alter the curvature. When you create a closed surface, you can fill the surface with solid colors or a variety of patterns.

CorelDRAW!'s principal advantages over competing products are the intuitive nature of its user interface, its long-standing reputation for creating logos and other "artistic" text effects, and the inclusion in the application of more than 250 typeface families (now in TrueType format for Windows 3.1) and 12,500 clip-art and animation files.

CorelDRAW! 3.0 features several other applications, including CorelTRACE!, a sophisticated tool that you can use to convert bit-mapped images to vector files that are scalable and do not have the "jaggies" (a serrated appearance, especially in diagonal lines, associated with bit maps displayed at certain scales). The package also includes CorelPAINT!, an image-editing application, created by Z-Soft; CorelSHOW!, an OLE presentation application (described in the next chapter); CorelCHART!; and CorelMOSAIC!, an image-cataloging application.

Graphic File Formats

Windows supports only two basic types of image files: BMPs for bit maps and WMFs for vector images. All other graphic-file formats must be converted to one of these two types for use by Windows' GDI.

The following sections briefly describe the differences between the BMP and WMF formats.

Bit-Mapped Image File Formats

Bit-mapped images are more common than those that use vector-based formats because bit-mapped images have been used on PCs for a longer time and more PC applications have been written for them. Scanners have contributed to the proliferation of bit-mapped images, and most computerized document imaging and archiving systems use compressed bit-map files.

All graphic files are identified by generally accepted file extensions that serve to define most or all of the format's basic characteristics. The following file extensions identify bit-mapped-image file formats that have achieved the status of industry standards for the PC. Almost all commercial bit-map image-editing applications support most of these formats; fewer applications support GIF files.

The most common bit-mapped-image file formats are as follows:

- *BMP*, for Windows bit-map files in 1-, 2-, 4-, 8-, and 24-bit color depths. BMP files contain a bit-map header that defines the size of the image, the number of color planes, the type of compression used (if any), and the palette used.

  Windows DIB format (described in Chapter 16) is a variant of the BMP format that includes a color table defining the RGB values of the colors used.

- *TIF*, an abbreviated form of TIFF (tagged image format file), a format developed by Aldus Corporation and now managed by Microsoft Corporation. TIFF files originally were used primarily to store scanned images but now are the preferred bit-map format of a substantial number of applications, including Windows applications.

  A special version of TIFF that employs file compression is used for FAX transmission. TIFF files for conventional bit maps are found in compressed and uncompressed formats. These files contain a header similar to the header in BMP files.

- *PCX*, for files compatible with Z-Soft Paint applications. The PCX file format is the common denominator for most bit-map file-format conversions. Almost every graphics application created in the past five years (including Windows Paintbrush) can handle PCX files.

- *GIF* (graphics interchange file format), used to archive bit-mapped images on CompuServe. Shareware and freeware GIF file-conversion applications for popular personal computers are available for downloading from the Computer Art forum. GIF is the standard bit-map format for the background images used by Autodesk Animator.

- *TGA*, the TARGA file format developed by Truevision for its TARGA line of graphics adapter cards. TARGA cards were the first to offer relatively high-resolution, wide-spectrum color images for PCs through a separate video monitor. TARGA cards were the unchallenged standard for professional graphic artists until the advent of large-screen super-VGA displays.

Vector-Based-Image File Formats

The file formats for vector-based images on the PC are similar to one another, but different formats store vector data in different ways.

The most common vector-based-image file formats are as follows:

- *WMF*, which identifies a Windows meta file, the standard vector-based file structure of Windows. You can embed bit-mapped images in WMF files.

- *CGM* (computer graphics meta file), the original vector-image file format for Windows. CGM files rarely are used today, but most full-scale drawing packages support the format.

- *DRW*, for Micrografx Designer files. Windows Draw! uses DRW as its native format. These files contain mathematical representations of Bezier curves.

- *CDR*, the native format of CorelDRAW!. CDR is similar to Micrografx's DRW format.

- *EPS* (encapsulated PostScript files), developed by Adobe Systems, Inc. for compatibility with its PostScript page-description language for printers. EPS is the most popular format for commercial clip-art packages not provided by publishers of drawing applications. EPS files can include bit maps, and you can add a low-resolution bit-map header to the basic EPS vector data to provide a rough illustration of the vector image contained in the file.

- *DXF*, for drawing-exchange files created by Autodesk's AutoCAD product. This format is used primarily for architectural and engineering drawings.

- *FLI* and *FLC*, for files are created by Autodesk Animator. Presentation applications that include animation capabilities support these formats.

Most drawing applications can import any of these formats (except FLI and FLC) and convert them (through an application called an *import filter*) to the application's native format. Export filters usually mirror the import filters.

Graphic-Capture and Format-Conversion Applications

Windows graphic-capture applications, such as Collage for Windows and Hijaak for Windows, are useful for creating manuals for commercial software products. These graphic-capture applications can copy all or a portion of your display or the active window of the application you are running. Capture applications also are useful if you are creating a multimedia productivity application designed to show users how to use special-purpose programs such as those created with worksheet macros. (The Windows version of Collage was used to capture all the screen images in this book.) Hijaak can use a wide variety of bit-map and vector-based file formats and can convert images between many of these formats.

Converting vector files to bit-map files in all standard formats is relatively simple, and all drawing packages provide this capability. The reverse process—converting bit-mapped images to vector-based images—requires the use of a tracing application (such as CorelTRACE!). Image-tracing applications are sophisticated; you must practice using these applications before you can set the options for optimal conversion, and even optimally converted files usually require substantial editing.

Still-Image Compression

The size of the files required to store large high-resolution color images resulted in attempts to provide dynamic file compression. Archiving applications such as PKZIP can compress the standard 256-gray-shade TIFF file of a typical Windows screen to about 5 percent of its original size. PKZIP, however, takes more time to compress large files than most users are willing to wait. Stacker is somewhat less efficient at compression, compressing the same files to about 15 percent of their original size, but Stacker compresses and decompresses files as you create or read them; this process is called *real-time* or *on-the-fly compression/decompression*.

Two specialized standards for real-time compression and decompression of still graphic images are as follows:

■ *RLE* (run-length encoding), the standard compression method for Windows BMP and DIB files. (The opening screen of Windows 3.1 is contained in an RLE file.) BMP files can be run-length encoded because RLE is a standard method, but compressed BMP files are the exception rather than the rule. RLE files test for duplicated pixels in a single line of the bit map and store the number of consecutive duplicate pixels rather than data for the pixel itself. The compression ratio depends on the complexity of the image.

■ *JPEG* (Joint Photographic Experts Group) is a group of related standards that provide the choice of *lossless* (no degradation in image quality) or *lossy* (virtually imperceptible to severe degradation) compression types.

JPEG is a *symmetrical* compression system, meaning that the techniques used for compression and decompression of JPEG files (JPG extension) use the same mathematics and take about the same length of time. JPEG compression in software is somewhat slower than RLE, but JPEG's compression ratios for complex images are better than RLE's, especially if you're willing to live with a very minor change in the image.

Hardware JPEG compression, which involves the use of special adapter cards, speeds the process greatly, but the cards currently cost about $1,000. The cost of hardware JPEG compression, however, is likely to decrease as the method becomes the standard for both still-image and video compression.

Video Compression

Related Topics
Nonlinear Editing, p. 611

The ultimate goal of computer-based video systems is to store all the elements of a multimedia presentation (including live-action video) on a hard disk for essentially instant access. Storing full-motion, full-screen video directly as digital data, however, is impractical, because the files are extremely large (23M per second at 30 frames per second and 768K per frame). Data compression in the range of 20:1 to 50:1 must be used to accomplish this goal.

More drastic forms of data compression are required if real-time video images and audio-CD-quality sound are to be available on CD-ROMs. Although space requirements are not a major factor for CD-ROMs, data-transfer rates are an important consideration. The MPC specifications require CD-ROM drives to have a continuous data throughput of only 150K per second—a requirement that calls for compression ratios of 200:1 or more for images of commercial quality.

Software-Based Video Compression

If you have an 80386DX or (preferably) 80486DX computer operating at 33 MHz or faster and need only relatively small video images, you may be able to use software-compression techniques to process video images. This chapter discusses video compression because video compression primarily is an image-compression problem, although the need to process digital audio and images simultaneously contributes to the problem.

The MPC specifications assume that CD-ROM drives are most computer users' primary source of multimedia data. The original set of multimedia extensions for Windows 3.0, however, did not provide for playing live video from CD-ROMs. A driver that controlled one laserdisc player (the Pioneer LD-V4200) was included, but laserdiscs store analog (not digital) video images and sound.

The capabilities of Apple Computer's QuickTime image and sound-synchronization standard for animation and the display of small video images in a window provided with its System 7 operating system caused Microsoft to accelerate the development of the audio video interleaved standard for Windows. Like QuickTime movie files, AVI files are designed to display motion video in a 160-by-120-pixel window accompanied by synchronized sound. AVI was in the beta-testing stage when this book was written, but Microsoft gave demonstrations of AVI's capabilities at most major PC exhibitions starting in early 1992. An AVI video image of William Gates, chairman and CEO of Microsoft Corporation, appears in figure 17.6.

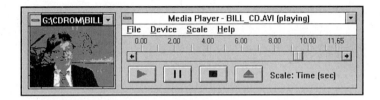

FIG. 17.6

The Media Player applet playing an AVI file created from a segment of videotape.

Related Topics
Using ADPCM Compression Techniques, p. 380

The video and audio data in AVI files are compressed so that the images can be retrieved from CD-ROMs operating at the current standard data rate of 150K per second. Double-speed CD-ROM drives with 300K-per-second data-transfer capability and faster 80486DX computers can come nearer to true "live-motion" (30 frames per second) video with moderate audio fidelity. If a soundtrack is present, the audio data is given priority in decompression, so audio adapter cards with on-board ADPCM decompression capability improve both audio and video performance.

Pixel-doubling is the current method of creating a display larger than 160 by 120 pixels. Pixel-doubling takes every other pixel in the image and creates three duplicates of it, then arranges the four identical pixels into a 2-by-2-pixel square. The effect of pixel-doubling, called *pixelation*, sometimes is used as an artistic effect in image-editing applications (see fig. 17.7).

Hardware Compression of Video Images

The complexity of the computations and the large amount of data that must be converted to display true live-motion video images in moderate-size windows dictates that dedicated microprocessors be used to perform the decompression operation.

FIG. 17.7

Pixelation of an AVI image displayed in larger-than-normal size.

JPEG hardware compression adapter cards and daughterboards for video adapter cards were beginning to appear in the commercial market when this book was written. At the same time, the Windows drivers for Intel's Digital Video Interactive (DVI) standard, developed jointly with IBM, were in the beta test stage, and special-purpose chips that implement the proposed MPEG (Moving Pictures Experts Group) standards were not yet in full-scale production.

JPEG Hardware Compression

The Joint Photographic Experts Group (JPEG) compression standard was adopted recently by most manufacturers of on-line video compression boards for video input cards. Unlike the proprietary RTV compression techniques of the Intel i750-based DVI process, JPEG is an open, international (CCITT CCIR-601) standard that anyone can use for intraframe compression. *Intraframe compression* treats each frame like a still photograph and does not attempt to discard redundant data between frames.

JPEG compression can reduce the disk-space requirement for live-motion video by a factor of 20 to 30 (about 1M per second) without significant loss of image quality. Hard disks with 600M or more of memory capacity are available at affordable prices, and high-speed SCSI interfaces accommodate the fast data-transfer rates required. If you're willing to sacrifice some image quality, you can use a substantially greater compression ratio—as much as 200:1.

JPEG compression at 30 frames per second requires a high-speed dedicated microprocessor. The two major JPEG compression circuits are the C-Cube CL-550 single-chip implementation and the LSI Logic 700-series JPEG chipset. The equally high-speed, video-image data-transfer rates require that these chips be connected directly to the video memory (VRAM) bus on the video input card.

VideoLogic's MediaStation is an example of an adapter card that uses C-Cube's CL-550 chipset to provide JPEG compression and decompression of video images in real time. The MediaStation board attaches to VideoLogic's DVA-4000 series digital video adapter and provides 24-bit video capability with NTSC composite and S-Video formats. VideoLogic uses a digital signal processor chip to compress audio, using CD-ROM XA-compatible ADPCM at rates up to 48 kHz.

MPEG Compression

The Moving Pictures Experts Group (MPEG), an organization similar to JPEG, was in the process of establishing a set of standards for compressing and expanding video, motion picture, and animated graphic images when this book was written. MPEG compression provides increased compression efficiency compared with JPEG and other compression methods designed for still images. The emerging MPEG standards provide data compression for video images in the range of about 200:1.

MPEG compression and decompression techniques use *interframe compression*; interframe compression stores only the differences between successive frames in the data file. Interframe compression begins by digitizing the entire image of a *key frame*. Successive frames are compared with the key frame, and only the differences between the digitized data from the key frame and from the successive frames are stored. Periodically, new key frames are digitized to start the comparison from a new reference point. Interframe compression ratios are content-dependent; if the video clip being compressed contains many abrupt transitions from one image to another (called *cuts*), the compression is less efficient.

The files created by MPEG compression are complex because only the data derived from key frames is of constant length; the data in successive frames varies in length depending on the extent of frame-to-frame changes in the image. Therefore, the data files must include a *frame directory*; frame directories indicate the position of each key frame in the file. The frame directory usually is added in a second step after the images have been compressed and stored in a file. Otherwise, the time required to create the frame directory might cause the compression process to miss a proportion of the frames.

When you need to view one compressed video frame with an application that handles interframe decompression, the application finds the closest key frame in the file and then modifies the key frame images with the data for succeeding frames until the desired frame number is reached. Therefore, a delay occurs when images other than those from key frames must be created; the delay is related to the frequency with which key frames are stored. Reducing the average delay to display a specific frame also reduces the compression efficiency. In most cases, key frames and difference frames are compressed by an intraframe compression method.

Interframe compression is a complex process, requiring hardware compression to compress live video for digital recording and to decompress it for display of full-screen color video images at 30 frames per second. Sound must be recorded simultaneously with the video data, and audio data also must be compressed if file sizes are to be maintained within reasonable limits. MPEG specifies ADPCM because ADPCM currently offers the highest compression ratios that achieve acceptable sound quality. The video and audio data is interleaved in the file so that the images and sound can be synchronized.

MPEG compression provides an average of about 50:1 reduction in the data-transfer rate. If you need a full-screen (640×480 pixels) image with 24-bit color, the required data rate is 30 frames per second $\times$ 2 fields/frame $\times$ (640×480 pixels) $\times$ 24 bits per pixel/8 bits per byte or 27.65M per second. MPEG compression at an average of 50:1 reduces this requirement to 553K per second, not counting the digital audio data stream. This figure is well within the range of today's hard disk drives but not of CD-ROM drives (even double-speed drives).

Bringing full-screen, full-motion video within the data-transfer rate of conventional CD-ROMs (about 150K per second) requires additional compression. C-Cube Microsystems, a firm that has developed a high-speed MPEG decompressor on one chip, uses a process called decimation to further reduce the data-transfer rate. C-Cube's decimation process omits every other pixel in the digitized image and digitizes only alternate frames. When the image is re-created, the missing pixels and frames are reconstructed by *interpolation*. Interpolation estimates the color and position of the pixels from those in adjacent positions and successive frames. Decimation reduces the data rate by a factor of 4 to about 138K per second. Adding compressed audio within the 150K-per-second data-transfer rate of CD-ROMs can be accomplished by reducing the resolution (number of bits) that defines the color.

MPEG compression is *asymmetrical*; the compression process is much more complex than decompression. MPEG compression usually is accomplished through a combination of software and hardware using the equivalent of a VCR's slow-motion mode.

DVI Compression

Intel Corporation's Digital Video Interactive (DVI) standard uses interframe video compression techniques similar to that of the MPEG standard and ADPCM audio compression compatible with the CD-ROM XA standards. Intel's compression method is called RTV 2.0 (real-time video) and is incorporated in its AVK (audio/video kernel) software for its DVI product line. Intel manufactures the adapter cards for DVI under the ActionMedia II trademark. Adapter cards that use DVI technology have sold in the $2,000 range, but VideoLogic announced in mid-1992 that it intends to develop a lower-cost DVI adapter card.

DVI provides different levels of quality of the compressed video and audio data. For high-resolution, full-color digital video with stereo audio quality approaching that of audio CDs, compression becomes so time-intensive and complex that special supercomputers must handle the conversion. In this case, Intel processes the videotaped material at its New Jersey facility and returns to the customer a file containing the compressed data. You can record lower-quality video and sound by adding a capture daughterboard to the basic DVI adapter card.

Microsoft and Intel jointly announced the creation of the DV MCI (digital video media control interface) command set for Windows 3.1 in March 1992. At the same time, Asymetrix Corporation was assigned responsibility for creating the software development kit (DV SDK) for DV MCI. At the time this book was written, the DV MCI command set and the DV SDK were in the final stages of beta testing.

Chapter Summary

This chapter described some of the sources of ready-made still and video images you can add to your multimedia productions and the applications you need to edit still images in bit-mapped and vector formats. You learned about the different file formats used for still graphic images and about some Windows applications that convert files from one format to another. The chapter also described compression techniques for still and moving images.

In the next chapter, you learn how to incorporate the graphics you create into multimedia presentations, using Windows applications specifically designed to combine images and sound.

Presentation Graphics and Animation Techniques

Creating a multimedia presentation requires an application that can combine your graphics and sound files, integrating them into a structure that resembles an animated slide show with a soundtrack. Multimedia presentation-graphics applications represent the simplest and least costly means of creating both linear and nonlinear presentations. Authoring programs used to create commercial multimedia titles are more complex and considerably more expensive than presentation managers, but they have many characteristics in common with the three presentation packages described in this chapter.

Asymetrix Corporation's Multimedia Make Your Point, Corel Corporation's CorelSHOW!, and Macromedia's Action! are used as examples in this chapter because each package takes a different approach to creating a multimedia presentation.

Multimedia Make Your Point

Multimedia Make Your Point (MMYP) is an easy-to-use multimedia presentation application with a list price of less than $100. The product was developed with Asymetrix Corporation's Multimedia ToolBook, a Windows programming application that has been used to create several commercial multimedia titles distributed on CD-ROM.

MMYP provides a collection of templates that you can use to create a presentation—complete with waveform audio narration, MIDI music, CD-ROM tracks, animation, and still graphics—in less than two hours.

Creating Multimedia Slides

MMYP lacks much of the flexibility of full-featured multimedia presentation applications but makes up for its limitations by enabling you to develop a presentation quickly and easily. MMYP presentations consist of a series of slides (Asymetrix calls them *screens*) that you create with templates supplied with the application.

To select a template, choose Template **G**allery from the **E**dit menu. The Template Gallery dialog box appears (see fig. 18.1).

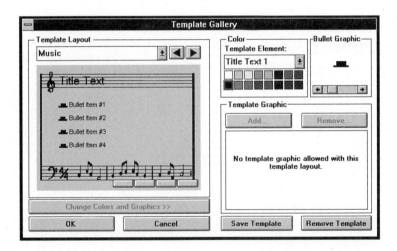

FIG. 18.1

The Template Gallery dialog box.

You can select any of the 32 standard templates provided with the application and change the colors of the template's basic elements to the 16 basic Windows colors. MMYP also offers more than 50 different bullets in the form of individual graphics files of boxes, arrows, and other symbols used to emphasize text. Some templates provide a place-holder for an optional graphic, such as a company logo, that you can add in the form of a bit map or vector graphic. After you edit the template, you can save it for use as the background for the remaining screens of your presentation.

Each template has a text box for the slide title and provides for three to six bullets, arranged in one, two, or three outline levels; each level has its own text box.

Figure 18.2 shows text entries for the four bullets—musical rest symbols, in this case—standard for the Music template.

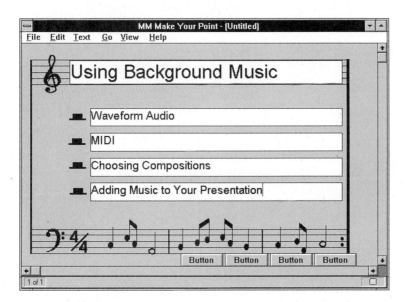

FIG. 18.2

Adding text to the four-bullet Music template.

Large type sizes are the default so as to encourage you to minimize the amount of text in the display. Short, succinct headings add to the legibility and impact of your presentation.

Controlling the Presentation with Events

MMYP is event-driven, rather than controlled by a time line. Event-driven applications rely on mouse clicks or other user input to display graphics, play sounds, or advance to the next screen. When you click a bullet, the event that occurs is determined by the settings in the Bullet Behavior dialog box. To open this dialog box, you place the cursor in the text box of the template screen next to the bullet and choose Bullet Behavior from the Edit menu.

The settings shown in figure 18.3 call for a WMK vector graphic of a guitar to appear when you click the Waveform Audio bullet.

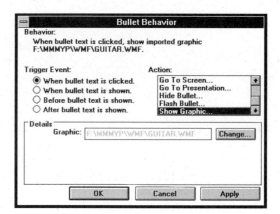

FIG. 18.3

The Bullet Behavior
dialog box.

Related Topics

Graphic File Formats,
p. 483

MMYP can display bit-mapped graphics in BMP, DIB, and TIF formats and vector graphics in WMK, CGM, EPS, and DRW files. You click the Change button to choose the file to be displayed and then choose OK to close the dialog box.

The graphic you selected appears in the upper left corner of your display. You can drag the graphic with the mouse, as shown in figure 18.4, and resize the graphic by dragging one of its corners.

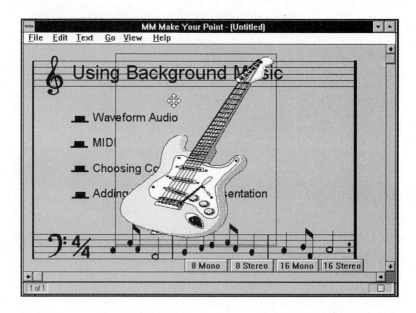

FIG. 18.4

Moving and sizing a
graphic.

Assigning Actions to Buttons

Many MMYP templates feature four buttons to which you can assign different actions. These buttons are shown as 8 Mono, 8 Stereo, 16 Mono, and 16 Stereo in figure 18.4. To assign an action to a button, follow these steps:

1. Click the button to which you want to assign an action and then choose Button **B**ehavior from the **E**dit menu. The Button Behavior dialog box appears.

2. Type a caption, **8 Mono**, for the button in the Caption text box.

3. Choose the event that will trigger the action by clicking the corresponding Trigger Event option button—When Button Is Clicked.

   In figure 18.5, the Button Behavior dialog box is set up to demonstrate differences in the sound quality of four types of waveform audio files that contain recordings from an electric guitar. A different WAV file is assigned to the When Bullet Text Is Clicked trigger event of each of the four buttons by choosing Play Wave File from the Action list box.

4. Enter the path and name of the WAV file to play in the Wave File text box, then click the Change button. The path and name of the file appears under the Behavior caption.

5. Repeat steps 1 through 4 for the remaining three buttons with the captions shown at the bottom of figure 18.4 and enter the paths and names of the WAV files that correspond to the captions.

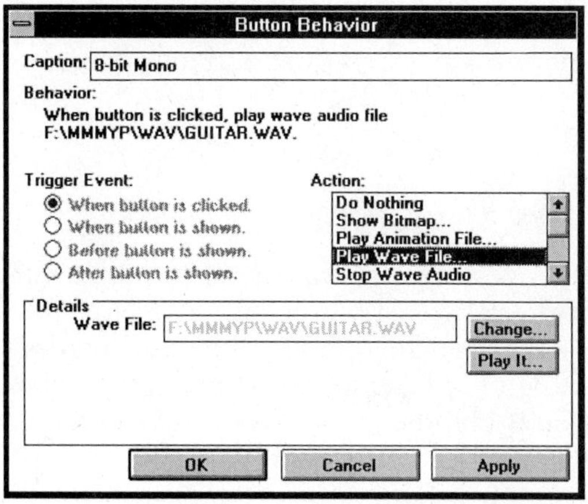

FIG. 18.5

The Button Behavior dialog box.

Saving and Testing the First Slide

To test the presentation during the design phase, choose View **P**resentation from the **V**iew menu. MMYP prompts you to save your presentation when you change from Edit to View mode to prevent accidental loss of your work.

Presentation files use the MYP extension, as shown in figure 18.6.

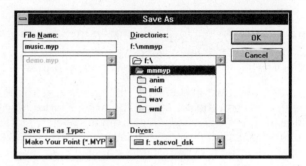

FIG. 18.6

The Save As dialog
box, listing an MYP
file.

By default, MMYP opens with a slide that shows only the basic elements of the template, the title, and the four buttons; the bullets and their associated text are hidden. To display the first bullet and its text, click the title.

In this example, when you click the Waveform Audio bullet, the graphic of the guitar appears on your screen (see fig. 18.7).

When you click the buttons at the bottom of the slide, the WAV file you assigned to each button plays. Buttons can play animations, display graphics, or bring up another screen.

Choosing Presentation Options

Although MMYP is event-driven and designed to be controlled by mouse clicks, you can run your presentation automatically. You also can start your presentation in automatic mode when you load the MYP file and create a loop so that the presentation plays continuously. Another option enables you to run the presentation in full-screen mode so that the Windows title bar does not appear.

To choose presentation options, choose Set **O**ptions from the **V**iew menu. The Set Options dialog box appears (see fig. 18.8).

Viewing the Music
presentation.

The Set Options
dialog box.

The timing and control options of the auto Presentation section of the
Set Options dialog box enable you to use an adjustable-duration timer to
simulate a series of mouse clicks on the title bar and the bullets. If you
check Enter Auto Presentation On **S**tart-up, you don't need to click the
title bar to display the bullets. If you check **A**nimate Bullets, each bullet
will appear after a specified amount of time in the adjacent text box delay.

One characteristic that distinguishes a multimedia presentation from a
conventional slide show is the multimedia presentation's capability to
show different transitions between slides. Conventional presentation-
manager applications simply replace one image on the screen with

another (a procedure called a *cut* in video terminology). If you choose **E**ffects in the Set Options dialog box, MMYP displays the Transition Effect dialog box (see fig. 18.9), which enables you to choose wipes, dissolves, and zooms as transitions.

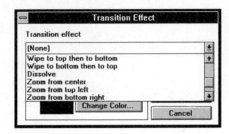

FIG. 18.9

The Transition Effect dialog box.

You also can add speaker notes to your slides and then print these notes for distribution to the audience. MMYP does not print the graphic elements of the slide but can add a title and screen number as a preface to the notes.

To add notes, choose Speaker **N**otes from the **E**dit menu. The Speaker Notes dialog box appears (see fig. 18.10). Enter the notes you want to add in the text box and click the OK button.

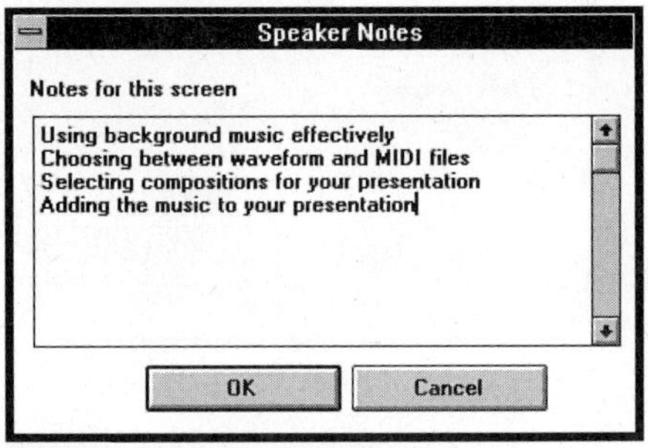

FIG. 18.10

The Speaker Notes dialog box.

Using Related Applications

Despite the restrictions imposed by MMYP's structure, you can use MMYP to create a simple presentation for use in a department store or at a trade show. A computer playing music and narration synchronized with quality graphics, and featuring transition effects such as fades and wipes, is a crowd-stopper.

To create such a presentation, you need the following tools:

- A color scanner
- An image-editing application
- A drawing program
- A waveform-audio-editing or MIDI-sequencing application

Fortunately, MMYP includes a variety of WMK (graphics), WAV, MID, and FLI (animation) files, so you can experiment with MMYP's automated presentations before you make an additional investment in hardware and software.

Related Topics
Scanned Photographic Images, p. 475
Image Editing and Drawing Applications for Windows, p. 480
Using Commercial Wave-form Editing Applications, p. 395
Professional MIDI Sequencers, p. 342

CorelSHOW!

CorelSHOW! takes a different approach to multimedia presentations. CorelSHOW!, included with CorelDRAW! 3.0, is a free-form, linear presentation-manager application that dispenses with buttons and displays a series of slides in any sequence you assign.

Using OLE Servers with CorelSHOW!

CorelSHOW! is an OLE client application that uses OLE servers for all functions except the display of animated FLI files. The application takes full advantage of the OLE capabilities added to Windows 3.1. Figure 18.11 shows the main window of CorelSHOW!.

Instead of a template, you choose a background for the series of slides from those supplied with CorelSHOW!. You can create a new background in CorelDRAW! or any other drawing application that has OLE server capability.

You create graphs, charts, and vector drawings or edit bit-mapped images with Windows Paintbrush or Micrografx Picture Publisher 3.0. As you complete each image, you copy it to the Clipboard and then embed or link the image to a slide in CorelSHOW! You can embed or link as many different OLE images as you can fit on a slide.

You can create graphs and charts with Microsoft Excel, Microsoft Graph, or the CorelGRAPH! application that comes with CorelDRAW! and then add the graphs and charts to a CorelSHOW! slide. If you link an Excel chart, when you update the worksheet that contains the chart's source data, your slide is automatically updated. If you are creating a presentation to be delivered periodically and only the data changes, you need not be concerned about the presentation side; the OLE links update the data automatically.

FIG. 18.11

CorelSHOW!'s main window, showing the OLE server selection tool.

To embed or link a sound object so that it plays when the slide appears, follow these steps:

1. Start Sound Recorder.

2. Open the WAV file you want to use and then choose **E**dit, **C**opy to copy the waveform audio data to the Clipboard.

3. Choose **P**aste from CorelSHOW!'s **E**dit menu to embed the waveform audio data, or choose Paste **L**ink from the **E**dit menu to create a link to the file. In either case, Sound Recorder's icon appears on the slide, as shown in figure 18.12.

Related Topics
Embedding or Linking Source Documents, p. 223

Related Topics
Software-Based Video Compression, p. 487

Media Player is not an OLE server, and although you can package a MIDI file into an OLE object and embed that file in your slide, the file does not play when the slide appears. If you have Lenel Systems' MpcOrganizer or MediaOrganizer application, however, you can embed MIDI files, display video in a window, or link AVI files on CD-ROM to a slide. As new sequencers and other applications appear, providing access to MIDI files and audio CD tracks through OLE, you will be able to add more sounds to CorelSHOW! through OLE.

FIG. 18.12

A sound object
embedded in a slide.

Viewing CorelSHOW!'s Presentation

When you click the camera icon at the left of the tool bar, you get a full-screen presentation of your slide show (see fig. 18.13), together with the music, narration, or animation you added.

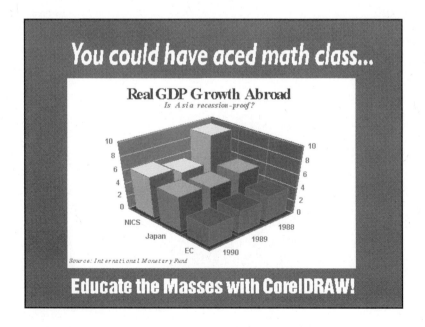

FIG. 18.13

A full-screen slide
presentation.

You can control the appearance of the slides manually by pressing function keys; you also can display the entire sequence at timed intervals.

CorelSHOW! includes a drag-and-drop slide-sorter window that enables you to rearrange your slides with the mouse (see fig. 18.14).

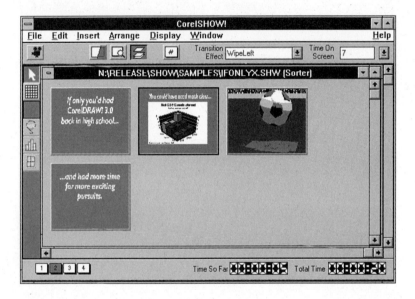

You can select any slide and readjust its time on the screen or select a different transition effect by choosing values from the drop-down list boxes in the tool bar.

Using Related Applications

By dispensing with the bullets-and-buttons idiom of Multimedia Make Your Point, CorelSHOW! gives you more freedom in designing a presentation. On the other hand, CorelSHOW! is not interactive—that is, the application is linear. This linearity makes CorelSHOW! suitable for creating a continuously running product demonstration or creating a videotape that consists of a series of graphic images. As OLE-server capability is added to existing applications, you can use them in conjunction with CorelSHOW! to expand its repertoire of sounds and images.

Another use for CorelSHOW! was mentioned briefly earlier in this section: preparing presentations in which only the data changes, not the structure of the presentation. You can create a series of Excel charts and graphs to display the data and then choose Paste **S**pecial from the **E**dit menu to create a link between each chart or graph and a slide. If you're narrating the data, you can record a new soundtrack over the existing WAV files linked to the slides, a capability that substantially reduces the time you spend preparing weekly or monthly presentations for management. If you have a VGA-to-NTSC card or a video converter, you can easily create a videotape of the presentation.

You can display CorelSHOW! presentations on any computer capable of running Windows 3.1 with at least 2M of memory, but the time required to read and write your Windows swap file may interfere with sound synchronization. If you use large WAV files for music or narration with CorelSHOW!, you should use a fast computer, preferably an 80486DX with 8M of memory.

Exploring Macromedia Action! 2.0

Macromedia's Action! 2.0 application adds animation to your presentations. Instead of static images in the form of slides, your graphics and text in an Action! presentation can move, accompanied by waveform audio sound effects and MIDI background music. Action! enables you to import movies created in Macromedia's Director program for Apple Macintosh computers; you make Director "movies" from the Macintosh compatible with Action! with Macromedia's Windows Player. Action! can create interactive presentations; you designate bullets or other objects on the screen as buttons, then assign actions to the buttons.

Action! on CD-ROM is included in the MPC Upgrade Kits offered by Media Vision and Creative Labs, and is also supplied with Creative Labs' Video Blaster video-in-a-window card. The CD-ROM version of Action! includes a variety of templates, clip art, multimedia movies, and waveform audio files to get you started with animated presentations.

Action! Scenes and Objects

Action! uses the term *scene*, rather than slide or screen, to define the basic display element of the presentation. The scenes that comprise an Action! presentation and the sequence in which they appear are shown in Action!'s Scene Sorter dialog box (see fig. 18.15).

FIG. 18.15

The Scene Sorter
window of Action!
2.0.

The Introduction, Dynamic, and Features scenes automatically follow one another in sequence, so the Scene Sorter displays single-headed arrows between these scenes. The remaining scenes are chosen by clicking buttons created from bullets on the Features scene; scenes that appear as the result of an action that occurs on another screen are indicated by double-headed, circular arrows.

Each scene is composed of objects, such as text, charts, sounds, movies (animations), and imported graphic images. Each scene and the objects it contains are included in a Content List window. A portion of the Content List for scene 4, SOUND, is shown in figure 18.16. Objects are represented by small icons, such as the movie film icon between the 4 and SOUND in the figure. You can create Groups of objects, represented by the icon of a package. Sound is indicated by the icon for a speaker, followed by the name of the waveform audio file (LGHTNESY.WAV) that supplies the sound.

The graphics objects in each scene can appear at any desired time and have the capability of movement. Therefore, you need a method of determining when and how the object is to appear and, if it is to be animated, where and when it is to move. This is accomplished by establishing a *timeline* for each object in the scene. A timeline is a window that includes a scale, calibrated in seconds, and an individual horizontal bar to represent each object in the scene. The beginning of the bar indicates the time that the object enters the scene and the end of the bar indicates the time the object exits. The timeline for scene 4 is shown in figure 18.17.

The scene corresponding to the time selected by the arrows at the 23-second point in the timeline scale at the top of figure 18.17 is shown in figure 18.18. LGHTNESY.WAV has just completed playing, the three graphic logos, CD, MIDI and WAV are displayed, and the Return to Choices button has just appeared.

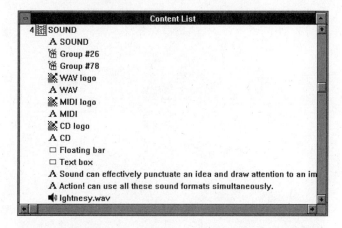

FIG. 18.16

Action! 2.0's Content List window.

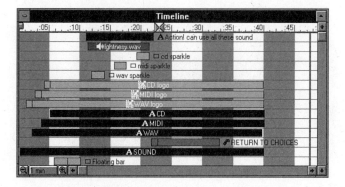

FIG. 18.17

The Timeline window of Macromedia Action!

Action!'s Scene Design Window

You create your presentation in Action!'s design window, shown in figure 18.19. You start by selecting one of the standard background templates included with Action! by choosing **L**oad Template from the **F**ile menu and choosing a TPL template file to provide a consistent background for your scenes. You use the toolbox at the left of figure 18.19 to add objects, represented by icons, to the template. Objects you can add include text boxes, rectangles, polygons, circles, lines, graphs, waveform audio sounds, and MIDI music.

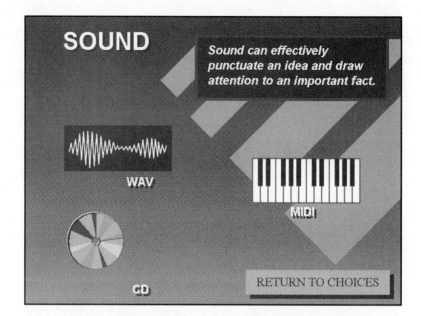

FIG. 18.18

An Action! 2.0 demonstration presentation in full-display mode.

FIG. 18.19

Action! 2.0's scene design window with the CD-ROM image selected.

The Control Panel in the upper right corner of the design window enables you to preview the appearance of your scene with the standard multimedia tape-recorder buttons. You can set the time from which to start playing with the slider in the Control panel or the button with the vertical line in the Timeline window.

After you add an object, you double-click its image on the display or the bar that represents the object in the Timeline window to bring up the Edit Object dialog box shown in figure 18.20. You select an action, such as Enter, from a drop-down list box, and then choose how the object is to behave by making selections from the Transition and Motion drop-down list boxes. You control length of time that the action takes with the slider at the bottom of the Edit Object dialog.

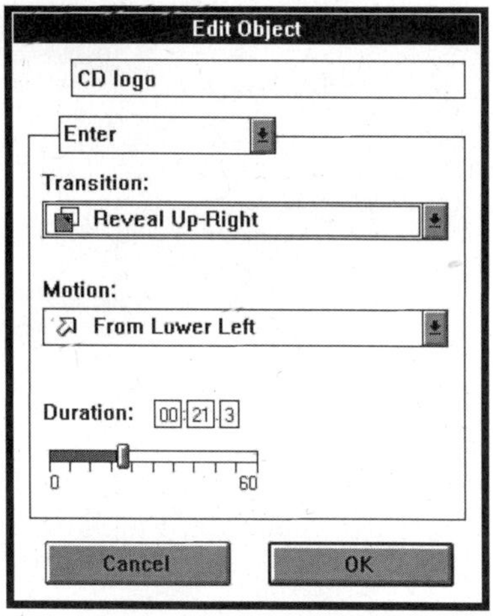

FIG. 18.20

Action's Edit Object dialog box for controlling object animation.

After you have added all the objects needed by your scene, you can drag each object's timeline to fine-tune its entrance, movement, and exit in relation to the other objects in the scene.

Applications for Action! Presentations

You can use Action! to create linear presentations that play from beginning to end and employ the presentations in advertising kiosks or create videotapes from the screens with a VGA-to-NTSC adapter card or converter described in the next chapter. Cleverly animated graphics hold a viewer's interest longer than static images. Synchronizing sound effects with the movement of the graphic objects adds "zip" to your presentation.

Action! presentations that include user interaction can be distributed on floppy disk to those who have Windows 3.1 installed on their computers. Action! 2.0 includes a player for Action! presentation—PLAYACT.EXE—which enables users to run Action! presentations without the need to own the Action! application. You can distribute PLAYACT.EXE with the ACP file that contains your presentation on a royalty-free basis. Because action uses vector files for its graphic images, all but the most complex presentations (or those that involve large bit map or WAV files) will fit on a 1.44M floppy.

Chapter Summary

This chapter has described three commercial presentation applications that employ multimedia techniques. Each was selected because of its unique features: Multimedia Make Your Point for its simplicity and low cost; CorelSHOW! because of its extensive use of object linking and embedding; and Action! for its animation capabilities. Most of the presentation applications that have been introduced or updated subsequent to the release of Windows 3.1 have at least one or two multimedia features added. Ultimately, all graphics presentation applications will include provision for use of the full complement of multimedia devices offered by Windows 3.1 and those devices subsequently added to the Windows multimedia vocabulary by Microsoft and other firms.

The next chapter describes how Windows deals with video images, including the generation of television-compatible signals from your computers display circuitry and how you can display full-motion video images in Windows and its applications.

Incorporating Digital Video

Multimedia PC Specification 1.0 does not mention television-style video input or output capability, even as an option or recommendation. This omission probably is due to a combination of economic and technical factors. The goal of the specification was to define the minimum capabilities of a PC or upgrade kit to qualify for MPC labeling, with the goal of making multimedia affordable. Standards were established, however, for audio cards that exceed the basic specification requirements.

At the time the MPC specification was adopted, Microsoft Corporation offered only one driver for video devices, a driver devoted to a special remotely controlled laserdisc player, the Pioneer LD-V4200. The ubiquitous VCR was ignored altogether. Failure to define an MPC video standard has created a plethora of video adapter cards and related devices that incorporate "multimedia" in their names or advertisements.

This chapter introduces some of the basic technical characteristics of television signals and explains how these characteristics determine the quality of video reproduction. The chapter also describes the three basic types of video cards—still-frame capture, full-motion-video input, and VGA-to-NTSC output—and provides suggestions on choosing and installing the card that meets your requirements. The chapter concludes with a brief discussion of applications designed to use video adapter cards.

Television Broadcast Standards

Incorporating still or full-motion video in a multimedia title requires an understanding of the differences between the images you create on your video display unit and those that appear on a television monitor.

The standard NTSC (National Television Standards Committee) television signal, called RS-170, dates from the 1940s. The NTSC signal, however, has been cast in concrete since its original specification. The only change was made in the 1950s, with the addition of a compatible color signal called RS-170-A. This change did not significantly affect the black-and-white signal.

Despite recent strides in digital technology and integrated circuits, the NTSC signal is locked into the days of vacuum tubes and analog signals. Although the Federal Communication Commission, which controls broadcast-frequency allocation and transmission standards in the United States, is expected to adopt digital methods for high-definition television (HDTV), don't hold your breath waiting for HDTV sets to appear in your local electronics store. Initial transmission of HDTV signals are not expected until the late 1990s, and the first HDTV receivers are expected to cost about $2,000.

By contrast, display technology for PCs has gone through several standards since the first PCs appeared. These standards range from the original (and grainy) CGA graphic displays supplied with IBM's first PCs to today's VESA (Video Electronics Standards Association) standards for 1,024-by-768-pixel high-resolution super-VGA.

The Effect of Bandwidth on Video Quality

Television signals are transmitted on channels spaced 6 MHz apart in the radio-frequency spectrum. The first 1.25 MHz of the 6-MHz band provides for interchannel separation. The video image occupies the next 4.5 MHz band of each channel, and the audio signal occupies a portion of the remaining 250-kHz band up to 6 MHz. The difference between the high and low frequencies of each band constitutes the *bandwidth* of the signal.

The original NTSC black-and-white television signal, RS-170, was a simple combination of amplitude-modulated (AM) video and frequency-modulated (FM) signals, as shown in figure 19.1.

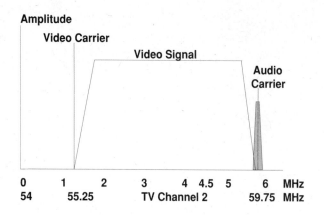

FIG. 19.1

The components of an NTSC black-and-white TV signal.

FM transmission for audio signals was chosen to provide better sound fidelity than conventional AM broadcasting methods could produce. Figure 19.1 shows the actual frequencies of video and audio transmission for a black-and-white signal on TV Channel 2, which occupies the frequency range of 54 MHz to 60 MHz, together with the bandwidth of the signals in MHz.

The amount of information contained in an analog television signal is limited by its bandwidth—a fundamental principle of information theory. The more information you supply about an image, requiring greater bandwidth, the greater the image's clarity.

When the FCC first assigned television channels in the late 1940s, television technology was in its infancy, and the limiting factor in television-image clarity was the receiving set. Thus, the FCC and the television industry thought that the 4.5-MHz bandwidth assigned at that time would be adequate. Time has proven that conclusion wrong, but until high-definition television (HDTV) is introduced in the United States, broadcast-image quality cannot be significantly improved.

Fortunately, VCRs do not have the bandwidth restriction imposed by the 6-MHz channel-frequency separation, so videotapes often provide much better image quality than the broadcast video that appears on television sets.

When color television broadcasting was introduced, millions of black-and-white television sets were in use. Therefore, color television signals had to be compatible with the NTSC RS-170 standards to which existing television sets conformed. The color information, called the *chroma* or *chrominance signal*, was added to the black-and-white signal as a *subcarrier* of the video signal at a frequency 3.579545 MHz higher than the video-carrier frequency. This addition created today's RS-170-A color signal, shown in figure 19.2.

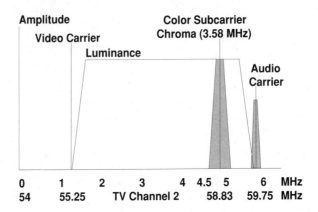

FIG. 19.2

The components of an NTSC-compatible color TV signal.

The chroma subcarrier frequency offset was chosen because 3.58 MHz is the product of the vertical and horizontal scan rates of color television: 59.94 Hz and 15,734.3 Hz, respectively. (Multiply the two, and you get 3,579,545.)

A subcarrier can be likened to narration dubbed over background music; you hear both elements, but the background music may obscure some nuances of the narration. Because the color subcarrier is located in the 4.5-MHz band of the black-and-white video signal—called the *luma* or *luminance signal* in color television—the subcarrier obscures some of the luminance band. This phenomenon is called *intermodulation (IM) distortion*, a term commonly used to describe audio interference between two signals of widely differing frequencies.

The insertion of the chrominance signal results in degradation of both black-and-white and color images whenever the luminance signal includes frequencies at or near 3.58 MHz. If you have a television camera or a camcorder, you may have seen this effect when you panned a scene with multiple bright colors.

VGA versus Television Image Resolution

The perceived resolution of images on your computer's video display unit (VDU) is determined by the following factors:

- The dimensions (in pixels) of the display-graphics adapter card and Windows driver. The standard VGA display is 640 by 480 pixels with a 1.33 ratio of width to height, called the *aspect ratio* of an image. Super-VGA resolutions of 800 by 600 and 1,024 by 768 pixels maintain this aspect ratio. These standard dimensions result in square pixels, assuming that your VDU's horizontal and vertical size controls are set correctly.

- The dot pitch of the shadow (aperture) mask of the cathode-ray tube (CRT) of your VDU. The standard for SVGA VDUs is 0.28mm, which is close to 0.011 inch.

- The size of the image on the display. The size of VDUs, like television sets, is measured in diagonal screen inches. The actual display on a standard 13-inch VDU is 9.6 inches wide by 7.2 inches high. If you measure the image on your VDU with a ruler and do not obtain a ratio of 1.33 between the width and the height, the horizontal or vertical size controls are misadjusted.

- Proper operation of the VDU itself, including focus, convergence, and other internal adjustments.

Thus, a 13-inch SVGA display with 0.28mm dot pitch has a theoretical resolution of 9.6/0.011, or 871 horizontal pixels. A CRT with 0.28mm dot pitch can display a 600-by-800-pixel image without missing pixels. Another quick calculation, 9.6/640, indicates that a dot size of 0.015 inches (0.038mm) or less is required to display a standard 640-by-480-pixel VGA image adequately.

The vertical resolution of a television signal is determined by the total number of scanning lines—525 for NTSC signals. The theoretical aspect ratio of a television image is the same as that of a VGA display: 4:3 or 1.33:1. Broadcast television images have a 1.56:1 aspect ratio, based on an unofficial standard of 756 by 486 pixels for professional digital television equipment. The 486 vertical pixels correspond to the number of lines of "active" video you see on the screen. The unseen 39 lines are masked (blanked) during the *vertical blanking interval,* the period during which synchronization signals are transmitted.

The 756-by-486 pixel dimensions seem to indicate that the quality of a television image should compare with that of a 800-by-600-pixel SVGA image. Placing a television set of similar screen size next to your 13-inch or 14-inch VDU (even displaying a 640-by-480-pixel graphic) and comparing the two displays quickly dispels that theory. Your computer's display is much clearer. The demonstration is even more effective if you use an VGA-to-NTSC card and show the same still image (especially one with many bright saturated colors) on both screens.

If you look closely at the television image, you see that the transitions between colors are slightly smeared and that the image does not have the crispness you have come to expect from your VGA display. Bright colors and thin lines tend to vibrate on a television monitor, a phenomenon called *buzz*.

The primary reasons for loss of television-picture clarity are as follows:

- Bandwidth limitations in television transmission
- Interference (intermodulation distortion) by the color subcarrier
- Degradation caused by less-than-optimum circuitry in the television monitor
- Noise that affects the analog television signals
- Excessively saturated colors that smear or wobble, due to the colors in the original image or to improper setting of the color-saturation control
- Thin vertical or diagonal lines that appear to vibrate in synchronization with alternate frames

The difference in image quality between analog television transmission signals and the digital data that appears on your VGA display is analogous to the relative audio quality of a 78-rpm record compared with an audio CD.

The resolution of a high-quality television monitor is adequate for viewing at a substantial distance from the screen. A rule of thumb is at least 4 inches of viewing distance per inch of tube size. At such distances, the limitations of human vision mask television's reduced image clarity. By contrast, most people work with VDUs at a distance of 18 to 24 inches. Thus, the composition of images (especially type size in titles and text) for presentations designed for television viewing must be different from those intended to be used with a computer.

The resolution of a television image is measured in horizontal lines. Perfect resolution is 768 horizontal lines (the equivalent of square pixels). Current television transmission, with 4.5-MHz luminance bandwidth, produces about 336 horizontal lines—less than half the theoretically perfect resolution.

You measure a television image's vertical and horizontal resolution by using test patterns. Resolution test patterns consist of a series of converging vertical lines, as shown in figure 19.3.

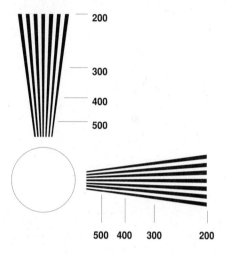

FIG. 19.3

Test pattern for determining vertical and horizontal resolution.

Resolution is determined by inspecting the point at which the lines no longer appear to be distinctly separated and by relating this point to the adjacent legend.

You can obtain test patterns on videotape, or you can generate your own test pattern by using a drawing application.

Differences in Image Aspect Ratio

Aspect ratio is the number of horizontal pixels divided by the number of vertical pixels in the display, assuming that the pixels are square. Figure 19.4 shows the differences in aspect ratio between computer and television images.

In the figure, the NTSC and HDTV (high-definition TV) images have been adjusted to the same vertical dimension to show aspect ratio more clearly. The pixel dimensions of the HDTV image are arbitrary (taken from one of the contenders for the standard system to be chosen in the 1990s), but the FCC made the 16:9 aspect ratio of wide-screen motion-picture images a requirement for HDTV early in the standards process.

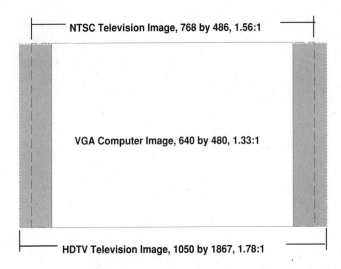

NTSC Television Image, 768 by 486, 1.56:1

VGA Computer Image, 640 by 480, 1.33:1

HDTV Television Image, 1050 by 1867, 1.78:1

FIG. 19.4

Aspect ratios for VGA, NTSC, and HDTV images at constant image height.

VESA Mode 100H for VGA adapters—640 by 400 pixels—has an aspect ratio of 1.6:1. This ratio is equivalent to the aspect ratio of a 768-by-480-pixel image and close to the 1.56:1 aspect ratio used in digital processing of NTSC broadcast signals. The 640-by-400-pixel display, however, is not a standard VGA operating mode for Windows or most Windows applications. On your television set, the aspect ratio of broadcast television is less than 1.56:1 because TV sets use a process called *overscanning*. Overscanning cuts off the left and right edges of the image to prevent vertical black bands from appearing on the screen.

"Wide-screen" TV sets that produce the 16:9 (1.78) aspect ratio to be used with HDTV are expected to appear on the market in 1992 or 1993. This aspect ratio, however, produces an even wider black border on video displays created by conventional 640-by-480-pixel VGA cards. You can eliminate the black bands at the top and bottom of conventional video displays by using adapter cards that include overscan capability (see the section "Video Overscan" later in this chapter).

The Effect of Video-Camera Quality

If you create your own video images rather than capture them from videotapes or laserdiscs, the quality of the camera you use influences the resolution of the image. Modern video cameras use CCDs (charge-coupled devices) to create a color image. A CCD consists of an array of photoreceptor devices on an integrated-circuit chip mounted in a package with a glass porthole through which light strikes the chip.

In consumer devices, the active surface of a CCD array usually is 1/3 inch by 1/3 inch or so.

A *photoreceptor* is an individual photovoltaic cell that generates a minute voltage proportionate to the intensity of the light falling on it. CCDs are the reverse of the monochrome liquid-crystal displays (LCDs) of laptop and notebook computers. In the case of LCDs, the voltage you apply to an element (pixel) of the LCD array determines the pixel's reflectivity (or opacity, in the case of backlighted displays).

A CCD array resembles the arrangement of pixels on your video display (see fig. 19.5).

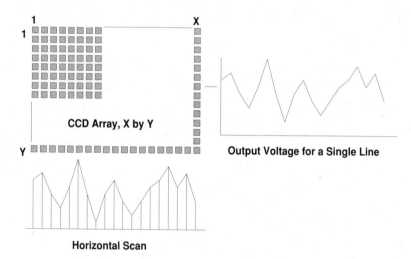

CCD Array, X by Y

Output Voltage for a Single Line

Horizontal Scan

FIG. 19.5

Diagram of the CCD array used in video cameras.

Video cameras use a variety of methods to create color images. Professional cameras, for example, use signals from three separate CCDs, one for each color (red, green, and blue). These CCDs create RGB values for the chrominance signal; in combination, they also provide the luminance signal. Recently, camcorders that use two CCDs—one for green and the other for red and blue—were introduced in the consumer market.

The internal circuitry of the camera selects alternate rows of cells every 1/60 second and scans the columns of the selected row to obtain the output voltage of each cell. Additional circuitry combines the individual voltages to create a video output signal, in much the same way that the output of an audio digital-to-analog converter is used to create an analog sound signal.

A 756-by-486 element array would be required to create a digital video image with square pixels and optimum resolution. Arrays of this size, however, are available only in professional and broadcast cameras that cost several thousand dollars. High-quality industrial video cameras (including most Hi8 camcorders) usually have 400 to 500 horizontal elements, roughly corresponding to the resolution of the recording medium. For commercial videotape production, you should use a Hi8 (high-band 8mm) or S-VHS (Super-VHS) camcorder with a CCD, with minimum resolution of 400 horizontal lines.

Still-image video cameras that record signals from video frames and store those signals on a miniature floppy disk are available for special-purpose applications. These cameras most often are used to capture images of three-dimensional objects in which motion is not a factor—for example, images of homes for use by a real-estate firm. The image quality usually is better than that of a scanned color Polaroid photo but not up to the standards of Kodak's Photo CD.

Color Fidelity and Hue Correction

Conventional video signals are processed by analog circuits, not digital circuits. Analog electronic circuitry is subject to variation with time, a phenomenon called *drift*. Television engineers joke that NTSC is an abbreviation for "Never Twice the Same Color."

Following are some factors that commonly cause errors in hue:

- *Improper color-control settings.* Periodic adjustments can compensate for analog drift. Brightness and color-saturation controls must be set to standard values.

- *Picture-tube phosphor coating.* The dots coated on the inside of the tube fluoresce red, blue, or green when the electron beam strikes them. This coating, however, may not be the same for different brands of picture tubes.

- *Aging of the phosphor coating.* Over time, the phosphor coating burns out, resulting in a washed-out image.

- *Improper convergence settings.* Internal controls set the exact angle of the three electron beams used to excite each phosphor. These beams must align properly with the dots on the face plate of the tube. Convergence adjustments are subject to drift and can change due to mechanical shock.

■ *Magnetization of the aperture mask.* Strong magnetic fields close to the picture-tube face plate may magnetize the shadow mask. To remove a residual magnetic field, use a degaussing wand. (Degaussing wands are available at most Radio Shack stores.)

Color-bar generators that create a signal with precisely controlled hues are used to calibrate the color-control circuitry of television monitors. Many desktop video publishing applications include a built-in color-bar generator. You also can use Windows Paintbrush to create a color-bar generator.

A separate color-bar generator is useful in creating video productions. Fortunately, consumer-grade models are adequate for this purpose and are not too expensive.

Conversion between VGA and Television Signals

Computer graphic images are created and stored in digital format; VDUs and television monitors reproduce analog signals. Thus, analog-to-digital converters (ADCs) are used to convert analog video signals to digital format, and digital-to-analog converters are used to create a composite NTSC analog video signal from digital data. This procedure is the same as the one used to convert analog sound signals to and from waveform audio files.

Although you can use a video adapter card without understanding how the conversion is accomplished, that knowledge may help you understand some of the terms in your adapter card's documentation and interpret the examples provided in this chapter.

The following table shows the conventional format for converting the RGB data used to define the color of a VGA pixel to chrominance (color, abbreviated C or UV) and luminance (brightness, abbreviated Y) television signals.

Component	Symbol	Red ratio	Blue ratio	Green ratio
Luminance	Y	0.30	0.11	0.30
Hue	U	0.30	0.87	0.59
Saturation	V	0.70	0.11	0.59

The first row of the table shows that the luminance signal is created from a value 0.30 times the amount of red in the VGA pixel, 0.11 times the amount of blue, and 0.30 times the amount of green. Hue and saturation, which together make up the television chrominance signal, are derived from the next two rows of RGB ratios. You can use the same values to create a table that makes the conversion in the opposite direction (YUV to RGB).

YUV values commonly are converted to digital data with 7-bit (1 part in 128) resolution. In theory, this conversion results in a final color resolution of 21 bits (2^{21}, or about two million colors) because each encoded value contains information about the color. In practice, far fewer than two million colors can be represented, but the actual number is sufficient for most applications.

The 7-bit value of the luminance signal is stored for every pixel on the display, but the hue and saturation data are averaged for groups of four pixels and then stored. This format is called 4:1:1 YUV, the letters representing luminance, hue, and saturation, respectively. The averaging of color information across four pixels can cause a slight halo around clear images that contrast sharply with their background. This problem does not occur, however, for most television images, which contain about 10,000 colors.

To obtain higher-quality images and eliminate most of the halo effect, increase the encoding or decoding resolution from 7 to 8 bits and average the hue and saturation data for fewer than four pixels. 4:2:2 YUV decoding uses groups of four pixels, but the hue and saturation data for only two pixels are averaged. Using 8-bit resolution with 4:2:2 encoding substantially increases the memory requirements (and thus the cost) of video adapter cards. The Matrox Marvel video-in-a-window card is one of the few video adapter cards that uses 4:2:2 YUV encoding together with 8-bit DACs to produce 24-bit color.

T I P   Most video adapter cards provide two video inputs or outputs. One input is for conventional NTSC composite video signals, which combine luminance and chrominance data; the other input supports Super-video (S-video), which separates the luminance and chrominance signals to improve video image quality. Even if you don't have S-video equipment (such as an S-VHS videocassette recorder), the next TV set or VCR that you purchase is likely to have S-video connectors. If the price difference between a board that offers composite video output only and one that gives you a choice of composite or S-video is not beyond your budget, choose the latter.

Video Output Adapter Devices

The only additional adapter card you need for producing a videotape from an existing presentation is a video output card. Video output cards, called VGA-to-NTSC adapters, decode digital RGB signals from VGA adapter cards to analog NTSC composite video signals. Video output cards also divide the scanning rate of your VGA display—31.5 kHz—by 2 to conform to the 15.75-kHz television standard.

VGA-to-NTSC adapters often are called scan converters, but the generally accepted definition of a scan converter is of a separate device that connects to the output of your VGA adapter card. Scan converters create the synchronization signals required by the NTSC standard, usually include antijitter circuits, and cost substantially more than VGA-to-NTSC adapters.

Conventional VGA-to-NTSC adapter cards include a cable that connects to the feature connector of your VGA adapter card, similar to the connection between VIW and VGA cards (see fig. 19.6).

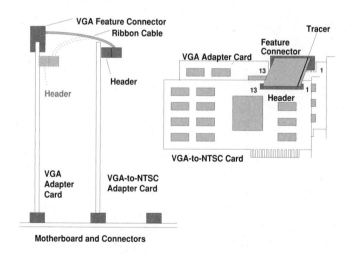

FIG. 19.6

Connections between VGA and basic VGA-to-NTSC adapter cards.

Some VGA adapter cards, especially video accelerator cards, use a multipin header instead of the printed circuit fingers. In figure 19.6, the cables between two headers appear as dotted lines.

T   I   P

Make sure that the VGA-to-NTSC adapter card you buy is compatible with your VGA card's feature connector. The VESA specification for the feature connector describes the function of each pin but does not specify the exact timing of the synchronization signals or synchronization-signal polarity.

Video output cards are more sensitive to differences in timing than video-in-a-window cards. Minor differences, even in the length of the interconnecting cable, can cause compatibility problems between the two cards or severe jitter in the television image. You may want to obtain a money-back guarantee from the dealer or bring your VGA card with you to the dealership for testing when you purchase a VGA-to-NTSC card.

Installing a VGA-to-NTSC adapter card is similar to installing an audio adapter card. As is true of audio cards, you must choose a device address that does not conflict with previously installed adapter cards.

To test the installation of a VGA-to-NTSC card, follow these steps:

1. Connect the composite (NTSC) video output of the VGA-to-NTSC card to the composite video input (usually marked VIDEO IN) of your television set, if your set has one. You need a standard video patch cable with RCA phono plugs on both ends. In a pinch, you can use a standard audio patch cable, but video patch cables are specifically designed to match the 75-ohm impedance of video connectors.

2. If no video input connector is available, connect the cable to the video input of your VCR and make the selection with the VCR/TV button.

3. Use the demonstration or test application that most suppliers include with the card to create your VGA test image. Usually, the application includes a color-bar generator; some applications provide a test pattern.

4. Record a minute or two of the image of your computer's display on a good-quality videotape and then play back the tape to compare the recorded image with the image on your computer's VDU. This procedure gives you a preview of the quality you can expect from your VCR when you use composite video.

5. If your VCR has S-VHS capability, replace the composite cables with S-VHS cables, which have circular mini-DIN connectors on each end.

6. Repeat steps 3 and 4 to compare the recorded S-VHS image with the composite image recorded at the beginning of the tape.

If you have a problem with the installation, the problem probably stems from the card's incompatibility with your VGA card's feature connector, from a conflicting device address (in which case you need to change a jumper to choose a vacant address), or from the monitor or VCR cables.

> When you install video adapter cards, make a list of the device addresses those cards use and tape the list inside your computer (perhaps to the top of the power supply, if the power supply does not have ventilation holes). Add the device address of your sound card, if you have one. Another useful item to add to the list is the installation data for your hard disk drive (type, cylinders, heads, write precompensation, landing zone, and sectors per track). You will need this information if you have to replace the battery in your computer. You can obtain the drive data by running the CMOS setup program when you boot your computer. You may want to keep a copy outside the computer's case for reference.
>
> **T I P**

VGA-to-NTSC Adapter Cards

VGA-to-NTSC adapter cards convert the VGA card's RGB data (received from the VGA adapter's feature connector) to 4:1:1 YUV. Figure 19.7 shows a simplified diagram of the signal paths in a VGA-to-NTSC video output card.

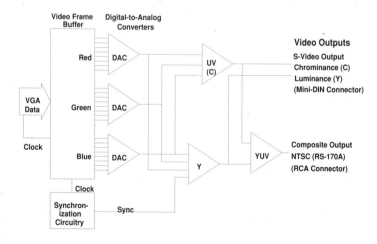

FIG. 19.7

Simplified diagram of a basic VGA-to-NTSC adapter card.

Your VGA display operates at two or more times the horizontal scan frequency of NTSC color television signals, which operate at 15.75 kHz. The VGA display probably also has a higher vertical scan frequency (up to 76 Hz) than NTSC color television signals, which operate at 29.94 Hz.

Figure 19.7 shows that RGB data for one frame of your VGA display card's feature adapter is stored in a frame buffer memory. The content of the frame buffer memory is read at NTSC scan rates and then converted to YUV format. Next, the YUV data is converted to YC (S-video), and synchronization data is added to the Y (luminance) component. Finally, the YC components are combined to create a composite (NTSC) signal. Some cards first convert the RGB signals to YUV data and then store YUV values in the frame buffer memory; the result is the same.

Basic VGA-to-NTSC adapter cards, which do not include video inputs, usually have limited capabilities but sell for a moderate price. External video converters, which do not require an adapter-card slot, and video output cards with genlock capabilities are beginning to appear in larger numbers. Video converters and genlock cards are described later in this chapter.

Related Topics
VGA Operating Modes and VESA Standards, p. 449

Video Overscan

Many VGA-to-NTSC adapters provide a software- or switch-selectable overscan mode that eliminates the black borders around the video screen caused by differences in aspect ratios between the VGA and NTSC television images. Overscan capability is necessary for presentation video because black borders are distracting to viewers. When you turn on the overscan feature, the image size is increased and parts of the top and bottom of your VGA image are lost. The theoretical loss is 96 lines ((768/640 * 480) –480), but 80 lines usually are dropped to conform to 256-color 640-by-400-pixel SVGA (VESA 100H) mode.

Some VGA-to-NTSC adapter cards enable you to specify how many lines are to be dropped from the display, and where: 80 lines from the top or the bottom, or 40 lines from both the top and bottom (the preferred method, because it centers the image).

Video and RF Converters

Video converters are a new category of external VGA-to-NTSC output devices that you can attach directly to the 15-pin output connector of your VGA adapter card. Video converters perform the same function as a basic VGA-to-NTSC adapter card but don't consume a card slot or require you to open your computer's case for installation. The converters accept the RGB analog outputs of your VGA card and use analog-to-digital converters to encode an image, which is stored in frame buffer memory and then converted to an NTSC composite signal.

The output of the converter is an NTSC composite or S-video signal that you can plug into a TV projector or a VCR. If you want to view the output on a TV set and yours does not have a video input connector, you also need an RF converter—a miniature television transmitter that connects between the video output of the VGA-to-NTSC converter and your TV set's antenna connector, and enables you to view the signal on TV Channel 2 or 3. You can use the same RF converter with a video output adapter card, an external video converter, or an external scan converter.

Figure 19.8 shows the connections for a VGA card, a video converter, and a scan converter.

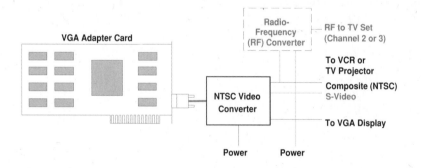

FIG. 19.8

Video output (scan) converter and optional RF converter installation.

The advantages of using a video output converter are simplicity and portability. Video converters enable you to display a laptop-computer multimedia presentation on a large-screen TV monitor or projector. If you have an RF converter, you can use the TV set in your hotel room as a substitute for the laptop's LCD display.

Video converters also enable you to record a computer-based presentation on videotape to simulate desktop video. These converters, however, are not the same as external scan converters, which feature genlocking capability. Chapter 22, "Desktop Video Production," describes some of the changes you may have to make in your presentation to make it satisfactory for video reproduction.

Genlock Cards for Video Titling and Special Effects

Basic VGA-to-NTSC adapter cards and external video converters act like miniature television-broadcasting devices, creating all the synchronization signals that the receiving VCR or television set requires to maintain a stable image (one that does not roll vertically or tear horizontally). The data transmitted to the VCR to TV set is synchronized with your computer's VGA signal.

If you want to add computer graphics to a video image and then record the combination on a VCR, you must synchronize your computer graphics with the source-video signal. This type of synchronization, called *genlocking*, requires a special type of VGA-to-NTSC adapter commonly called a *genlock card*.

Genlock cards need both video input and output connectors and a connection to your VGA adapter card. The video input is connected to the video source (such as a VCR or camcorder), and the output is connected to a video monitor or to another VCR to record the combined images. The most common type of connection to your computer's graphic output is the same as that for basic VGA-to-NTSC cards: a ribbon cable to the feature adapter of your VGA adapter card.

Figure 19.9 shows a simplified diagram of the connections required for a typical genlock card.

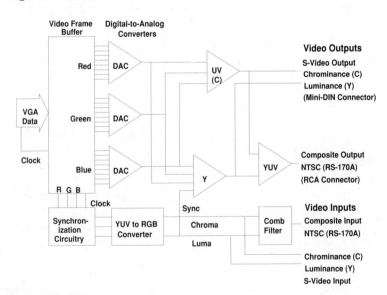

FIG. 19.9

Connections for a video output card with genlock capability.

The composite video input is separated into its chrominance and luminance components (YC) by a circuit called a *comb filter*. These two signals are then converted to YUV format and finally converted to their RGB equivalents for compatibility with the VGA data stored in the frame buffer. Images from the video source are written to the frame buffer in synchronization with the input video signal, and the graphic data you create on your VGA display is written in sync with your computer. Special control circuitry determines how the graphic data replaces the video data in the frame buffer.

Genlocking requires adding a considerable amount of circuitry to a basic VGA-to-NTSC card (see fig. 19.10).

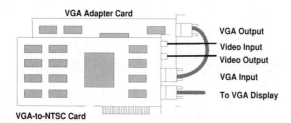

FIG. 19.10

External connections for video input, VGA, and VGA-to-NTSC genlock cards.

The additional circuitry makes genlock cards substantially more expensive than simple scan converters. As desktop video increases in popularity, many individual integrated circuits will be combined in one chip, a change that ultimately will lower the price of genlock cards.

If your VGA adapter does not have a standard VESA feature connector, or if the output signals of the feature connector are incompatible with standard genlock cards, you need a special type of genlock device that accepts analog RGB signals from the output of your VGA card. These genlock devices, which are available in the form of adapter cards or external boxes (such as VideoLogic's Mediator), are even more expensive than conventional genlock cards, but they are the only option for many computer configurations.

Cabling becomes slightly more complex when you install a genlock card that must be attached to the VGA card's feature connector in conjunction with a video card that already is attached to the feature connector. Figure 19.11 diagrams this three-way connection.

Most cards use multipin headers for the connection to the VGA feature connector, but some have printed-wiring-board fingers similar to the feature connector. If your VGA or video accelerator card uses a header instead of printed-wiring-board fingers, use the cabling represented in figure 19.11 by dotted lines. The dealership from which you bought your video adapter cards should be able to provide the proper cable.

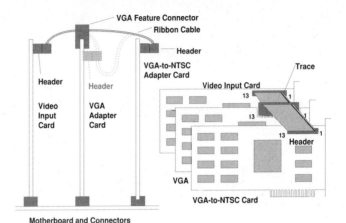

FIG. 19.11

Internal connections for video input, VGA, and VGA-to-NTSC genlock cards.

T I P   Ribbon cables that connect both video input and video output cards to a single VGA feature connector (especially the header type) are not standard catalog items for most card manufacturers. If the manufacturer of the adapter card you are adding cannot supply a three-connector ribbon cable to replace the two-connector version you are using, you may be forced to have a cable custom-made. Cables-to-Go, a firm that fabricates specialty video cable, can supply custom cables. (The company's address and telephone number are listed in Appendix F.)

The cabling between audio and video adapter cards and external audio-visual devices also can become complex, as shown in figure 19.12.

The audio (thin-line) and video (thick-line) connections shown in figure 19.12 perform the following functions:

1. Select video-in-a-window display from three composite video sources: VCR (0), genlock card (1), and a video source such as a camcorder (2).

2. Performing video overlay and titling with the genlock card, using S-video signals.

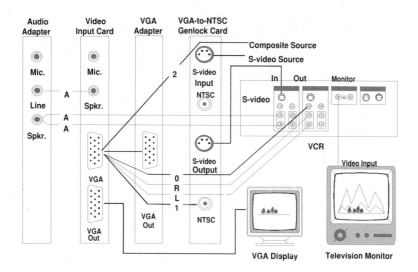

FIG. 19.12

Typical external connections for audio, video input, VGA, and VGA-to-NTSC adapter cards.

3. Mixing two monaural microphone audio inputs with stereo VCR or camcorder audio, FM synthesizer, waveform audio, and CD audio sources.

The cables labeled A in the figure are attenuating cables designed for connecting speaker outputs to consumer-type audio line inputs. If the audio mixer application for both the audio adapter card and the VIW card enables you to adjust the level of the monaural microphone input on the left and right channels, you can record live stereo by using one mixer to record microphone input on the left channel and using the other on the right channel.

If you are considering buying video adapter cards so that you can experiment with desktop video, try to choose products made by a manufacturer that offers compatible VIW cards and genlock cards. The simplest (but not necessarily the least costly) option is a combination VIW and genlock board, such as the Matrox Illuminator-16 board. The next-best alternative is to purchase video adapter cards from a dealer who promises a money-back guarantee that the products are compatible with each other and with your VGA adapter card. Nothing is more frustrating than trying to track the cause of video image distortion that turns out to be the result of incompatible adapter cards.

T I P

Overlay Titling and Chroma Keying

Conventional video titling performed with VIW cards that have overlay capacity and genlock cards replaces the source image's video pixels with the pixels that comprise graphic images on your computer. This process, called *overlay titling*, is used in many consumer-grade, video-titling devices.

Simple overlay titling with images created by Windows applications can be a substantial improvement over titles produced by stand-alone titlers, some of which cost as much as a genlock card or an external scan converter. You can use any of the TrueType faces offered by Windows and typeface suppliers, as well as those included in drawing applications such as CorelDRAW! or the Microsoft WordArt applet included with Word for Windows 2 and Microsoft Publisher.

For more sophisticated graphic effects, you may want to use a special feature of genlock cards called *chroma keying*. Chroma keying is the method used in television broadcasting to make maps appear behind TV weathercasters. Chroma keying enables you to substitute a computer-generated graphic image for one color or for a range of the colors contained in the video input signal.

For example, the TV weatherperson may stand in front of a green backdrop. If you select green as the chroma key for your graphic of a satellite weather map, the map replaces all the green pixels in the source-video image, creating the effect of the weatherperson standing in front of the graphic. If the weatherperson is wearing a green necktie or scarf, however, strange effects can occur, so careful planning is required when you shoot source footage for subsequent chroma keying.

Application Software for Titling and Graphic Overlays

Suppliers of genlock cards and external genlock devices also supply product-specific titling and chroma-key applications of varying capabilities. Many of these applications are for DOS, not for Windows, and some of the Windows applications may not be compatible with Windows 3.1 VGA drivers.

Many applications for video titling and chroma keying are available for Macintosh and Amiga computers, but at the time this book was written, no third-party Windows applications of the same caliber were available except for specific hardware combinations. Matrox Corporation's Personal Producer, which includes titling and chroma-key capabilities, is designed for use only with the firm's Illuminator 16 adapter card and two specific types of edit controllers.

As the size of the Windows desktop video (DTV) market grows, you can expect new third parties to provide applications for video titling, chroma keying, and special effects. In most cases, these elements will be combined in a package similar to desktop publishing products.

Video Display Adapter Cards for Windows

Adapter cards that digitize full-motion television signals for display on computer or television monitors have been available for the PC since the late 1980s. The advent of Windows 3.1 multimedia has changed the market for cards that can display and capture images from TV broadcasts and videotapes. Truevision's TARGA-16 card for the PC was one of the first of these devices and still is widely used by graphics professionals.

Still-Image-Video Capture Cards

Related Topics
Super-Video Devices, p. 602

The simplest and least costly video input cards capture and store frames of video signals directly from television broadcasts, video cameras, or the video outputs of videocassette recorders. Most of these cards, also called *frame grabbers* or *video digitizing cards*, accept conventional NTSC composite video or super-video (S-video) signals; some handle the European broadcast standard, PAL.

Each captured image is saved to a separate file—usually in a choice of standard formats, such as Windows bit map (BMP), tagged image format (TIF), or TARGA (TGA)—in color or in 256 shades of gray.

Figure 19.13 shows an image from a Sony television commercial captured by Digital Vision's ComputerEyes/RT board.

FIG. 19.13

Captured video
image.

Related Topics
VGA Operating Modes
and VESA Standards,
p. 449

Most video-capture cards (including the ComputerEyes/RT) provide a
live video preview window and DOS and Windows applications to
control the capture operation. Some cards include image-manipulation
software that you can use to adjust color balance, contrast, and other
characteristics of the captured video image.

In contrast to the TARGA products, video frame grabbers use your VGA
display; they do not require a separate television or analog RGB monitor.
Video-capture cards store the digital representation of the image in on-
board memory chips and then transmit this data over your computer's
data bus to the VGA display card. This transmission takes time, so you
may see 15 frames or fewer per second in the preview window, depending on the speed of your computer.

The principal difference between frame grabbers is the number of colors
that they support. Analog NTSC video signals theoretically are capable
of displaying an infinite range of colors. Colors displayed by video
adapter cards are limited in number to the resolution (number of bits)
of the analog-to-digital converters (ADCs) used to change the analog
chrominance signal to digital form. Most video-capture cards support
the HiColor standard of 32,768 (16-bit) colors, equivalent to the 16-bit
sampled audio recording resolution offered by high-quality audio
adapter cards. A few video-capture cards extend the range to the 16.7
million colors available in the 24-bit TARGA file format.

If you are running Windows with the now-standard 512K VGA card, you can display 256 of the available colors in VGA (640 by 480 pixels) or SVGA (800 by 600) mode. For all but professional graphics work, 256 colors should suffice. Using SVGA mode offers little advantage because of the relatively low resolution of television images.

The fate of dedicated video-capture cards for multimedia applications depends on the extent to which Windows applications dominate the desktop video market. VIW adapters combine 256-color-video image capture and full-motion-video display functions at a cost comparable to that of some frame grabbers.

T I P

Frame grabbers and other video cards require a device address. Many frame grabbers (ComputerEyes/RT included) have a default base address of 220H, the address used by the Sound Blaster and cards compatible with it. You must choose a device address other than 220H (hexadecimal) for the video adapter card by changing jumper positions on the video card before you install it in conjunction with most audio adapter cards. You also need to alter the installation parameters for the card's software so that the application can communicate with the card at its new address.

Full-Motion VIW Cards

Video-in-a-window (VIW) adapter cards provide a sizable window that displays full-motion video from NTSC or PAL (European) video signal sources. VIW adapters sold in the United States adapt the horizontal scanning rate of NTSC television signals (15,750 Hz) to the usual rate of VGA display units (31,500 Hz).

VIW adapters are compatible with both DOS and Windows, but they are expected to be used primarily with Windows multimedia applications. VIW adapters are available in an 8-bit version with the 256 colors ordinarily used by Windows applications and in a higher-cost 16-bit version (with larger amounts of VRAM) that can display up to 32,768 colors, depending on the resolution selected. Figure 19.14 shows a typical image from a VIW card.

Each video frame is digitized by an analog-to-digital converter and stored in VRAM (video random-access memory.) The more sophisticated (and thus more expensive) versions also incorporate VGA drive circuitry.

Other cards use your existing VGA adapter card to minimize cost. Most VIW cards include a two-channel audio mixer and a small power amplifier designed to drive headphones or small speakers.

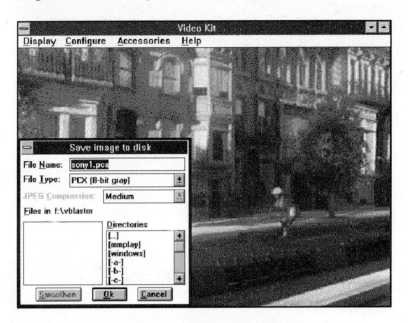

FIG. 19.14

A video image in a window created by a VIW card.

Adding VIW to Existing VGA Setups

Most VIW cards use your existing VGA adapter to drive the VGA display. A ribbon cable connects the VESA feature connector of the VGA card to a header on the VIW card. The feature connector is a set of printed circuit fingers or a multipin connector (header), usually located at the top of the card. You can use one of these VIW cards with a graphic accelerator card, if the card includes a VESA feature connector *and* if the feature connector's signals are compatible with the VIW card that you plan to use.

T I P   If you have a VGA adapter card that was manufactured before 1988 or if you have installed a graphic accelerator card, contact the customer-support number of the manufacturer whose VIW card you intend to purchase to verify compatibility with your current VGA adapter. Incompatibilities between synchronization signals are more likely to occur with older VGA cards, and signal-timing problems often occur with graphic accelerator cards.

Creative Labs' Video Blaster is an example of a moderately priced VIW card that uses an existing VGA card. Most other VIW cards are similar in function, but their video and audio connections differ. You also can use the Video Blaster in DOS applications through a terminate-and-stay resident utility supplied with the board.

Figure 19.15 shows the internal and external video connections for the Video Blaster card and an existing VGA card.

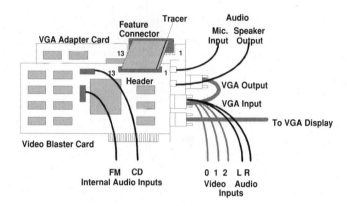

FIG. 19.15

Internal and external connections for the Video Blaster and a VGA card.

The Video Blaster uses the following connections:

■ Composite video input from three selectable sources via RCA phono (RS-170-A) plugs on cables from the A-V (audio-video) breakout connector. S-video input is not supported.

■ Stereo audio input from a single VCR, camcorder, TV set, or other audio source, via RCA phono plugs, from the A-V breakout connector.

■ Monaural audio input from a consumer-type microphone via a 1/8-inch mono minijack. (The Video Blaster is one of the few VIW cards that includes a microphone input.)

■ Two internal audio inputs that require special cables. One input is designed for the audio output of CD-ROM drives; the other input connects to the FM synthesizer output of a Sound Blaster card. The required cables for internal audio connections are not supplied with the Video Blaster, but Creative Labs offers them as accessories.

■ An internal connection between the feature connector of your VGA card and a header on the Video Blaster. The cable supplied by Creative Labs includes connectors for feature connectors with either printed circuit fingers or a multipin header.

■ A VGA input connector terminating a cable that attaches to the output connector of your VGA adapter card; this cable also is part of the A-V breakout cable.

■ A VGA output connector into which you plug the cable from your VGA display.

The cable that connects the Video Blaster to the VGA is used to implement color-keyed video overlay titling, a rare feature among VIW cards. Color keying is the opposite of chroma keying. To color key, you first create a bit-map image with a block of a specific color called the *key color* (black is a good choice). Then you use the overlay application to instruct the adapter card that black (0) is the key color. The black hole you create in the graphic is filled with the video image from the source.

Installing a Video Blaster or similar adapter card is similar to installing a VIW card that combines VIW and VGA capabilities. You leave your VGA card in your computer and connect the ribbon cable between the feature connector of the VGA card and a header on the VIW card.

T I P VIW adapter cards require a device address, and some cards use a bank of memory in your computer as a frame buffer. Thus, you must choose a device address that does not conflict with the addresses of other adapter cards installed in your computer.

A few applications require a vertical blanking interrupt from either the VGA adapter card or the video card. The Video Blaster card requires you to select an interrupt; other cards enable you to disable the interrupt if it is not needed. You must choose an interrupt that does not conflict with that of another adapter card. (Device addresses and interrupt levels are explained in Chapter 4.)

Using VIW Cards with On-Board VGA

The most straightforward way of adding full-motion-video display capability to your Windows-equipped computer is a VIW card with built-in VGA display driver circuitry. The advantages of a card that combines the two functions are simplicity of installation and the assurance that VIW and VGA circuitry is compatible. You also save a precious card slot.

Among the first of these combined-function cards are Truevision's Bravado-series cards, which are used here as examples.

Bravado cards are available as 8-bit devices capable of displaying 256 colors and as 16-bit devices for HiColor applications. The basic 8-bit Bravado card accepts up to three composite NTSC video and two stereo audio inputs; the Bravado 16 handles either composite or S-video signals and adds an internally accessible audio input. You can add more than one Bravado card to your PC to obtain multiple video windows, each of which you can control individually. You can expect to see PCs replace the multiple monitors currently used in building-surveillance applications.

Installing a VIW Card

Although you have to make several connections, installing a Video Blaster or other VIW adapter card is no more difficult than installing a hard disk or CD-ROM drive. The entire process takes an hour or less under normal conditions, including installing the required drivers on your hard disk and testing the card.

Before the advent of graphic accelerator cards, the feature connectors of most VGA cards consisted of gold-plated printed circuit fingers located at the top of the card. Most accelerator cards now use multipin headers for the feature connector. Some manufacturers of VIW cards include two sets of cables or a cable that features both types of connectors. Before you buy a VIW card, determine whether your VGA card has a header or printed circuit fingers so that you can verify that the VIW package you plan to buy includes the proper cable.

T I P

To add a VIW card to your PC, follow these steps:

1. Disconnect the cable that leads from the VGA display from your current VGA adapter card.

2. Turn off your computer and remove the cover.

   If you are installing a VIW card that uses your current VGA card, skip to step 5. Otherwise, proceed to step 3.

3. Remove your VGA adapter card.

4. Install the VIW-VGA card in the adapter slot previously occupied by your VGA adapter card and then skip to step 7.

5. Plug one end of the interconnecting cable onto the fingers (or multipin header) of your VGA card's feature adapter and the other end into the multipin header connector of the VIW card.

6. Install the VIW card in a vacant adapter card socket, preferably adjacent to your VGA adapter card.

7. Replace the computer's cover and connect the cable from your VGA display to the 15-pin VGA connector on the VIW-VGA card or your VIW-only card, if the latter has a 15-pin connector mounted on the bracket (not all VIW-only cards have this connection). For VIW cards with VGA connectors, plug the cable with the 15-pin connector into the VGA card's connector.

8. Most VIW-VGA cards include a breakout cable with a multipin plug on one end and with video and audio connectors on the other end. Breakout cables are required when the number of required video and audio connectors exceeds the number that you can mount on the sheet-metal closure plate on the back of the card. If your VIW-VGA card has a breakout cable, connect its multipin connector to the card's mating connector.

9. Connect a video source (for example, a television set with a composite video output, or the video output of a VCR) to the video input connector of the VIW-VGA card or the appropriate connector from the breakout cable. If your adapter card accommodates more than one video source, use the first video input.

10. Almost all VIW cards include stereo audio level control; some cards enable you to mix from more than one input. Connect the audio input from your TV set or VCR (left and right inputs, if the TV set or VCR has stereo audio outputs) to the RCA phono jacks on the adapter card or breakout cable. RCA phono jacks are used for both composite video and audio signals, so be careful to identify which connectors are audio connectors and which are video connectors.

11. After you make the required connections, turn on your computer.

Now that you have installed the hardware, the next step is to install the application software supplied with the card. This software usually includes a set of Windows drivers for the card and one or more Windows applications to demonstrate the card's VIW capabilities. If you are installing a VIW-only card, you use your existing Windows VGA driver, so you can skip the first four steps.

1. After you finish installing the software, you need to substitute the appropriate VGA driver for the one you currently are using. Start

the Windows Setup applet from the Main group to change the driver for your VGA display.

2. Choose **O**ptions from the main menu and then choose **C**hange System Settings from the drop-down menu. The Change System Settings dialog box appears (see fig. 19.16).

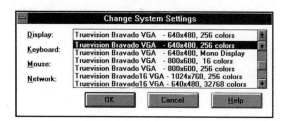

3. Use the vertical scroll bar to find the newly added VGA drivers and select the driver for 640 by 480 pixels and 256 colors. Then choose OK.

4. Before your computer can use the new VGA driver, you must restart Windows. Unless you have a reason to delay installing the driver, click the Restart Now button. Windows restarts, with the new driver installed.

   If you are using a 16-color display, you may notice slight changes in the colors of the title bar and some of the icons displayed by Program Manager.

5. Start the VIW application supplied with the card.

6. Play back a videotape on your VCR or tune your TV set to an active channel. A video image appears in the window.

Problems with installing VIW cards usually are the result of cabling errors. Recheck all your cables before concluding that something is wrong with your VIW card. Streaked, distorted, or nonexistent images often are the result of incompatibilities between synchronization signals or timing requirements.

Using Audio and Video Cables

Audio-video breakout cables for VIW cards come in a wide variety of shapes and sizes, but most breakout cables include at least some of the basic connections shown in figure 19.17.

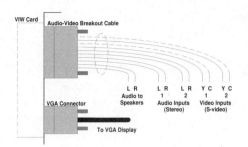

FIG. 19.17

Typical video and audio connections to a VIW breakout cable.

Although your VIW card may accept S-video signals, many cards have only composite video input connectors, so chroma signals are shown as dashed lines in the figure.

Audio connectors may be the RCA phono plugs or jacks associated with stereo components or the newer 1/8-inch stereo miniplugs or jacks used on audio adapter cards. The audio output to speakers, which also can serve as a line output to your audio adapter card's mixer, most commonly is a 1/8-inch stereo minijack.

T I P

If you plan to use S-video with VIW cards that have S-video input capability, ask the manufacturer's customer-service department whether breakout cables with S-video connectors are included with the card. If not, you need to purchase a special cable with the required mini-DIN connectors for S-video connections. You can obtain this cable from the card manufacturer or from a specialty-cable supplier. Special video cables can add $100 or more to the cost of your installation, depending on the source.

Combination VIW and Genlock Cards

Cards that combine VIW, frame grabbing, and genlock capabilities and that occupy only one slot in your PC undoubtedly will dominate desktop video in the future. The Matrox Illuminator-16 is the first multipurpose card that provides guaranteed compatibility between the video input and output and most VGA adapter cards.

The Illuminator-16 includes the following features:

- Two selectable composite or S-video inputs
- One composite or S-video genlocked video output

- 16-bit color for display of 32,768 colors simultaneously (dithering is used to simulate 24-bit color)

- An optional video stabilizer daughterboard that provides time-base correction (TBC) for steady display of images even in fast-forward, rewind, and pause modes

- Applications for special effects including slides, wipes, push/pull, fade transitions, chroma keying, solarization, mosaicing, and kaleidoscoping

- Hardware compatibility with the Truevision TARGA-16 board (for compatibility with the wide range of applications written for the TARGA-16 without the need for a separate NTSC monitor)

The Illuminator-16 card is used in conjunction with the Matrox Personal Producer application (described in Chapter 22), one of the first self-contained applications for DTV production.

More-advanced and lower-cost single-chip video components will enable these cards to include the VGA adapter, providing complete DTV capability with one videographics card and one audio adapter card. RS-422 control of industrial video-editing equipment requires another card, but VISCA and other RS-232 control protocols for semiprofessional video components (described in Chapter 22) work directly from your computer's COM ports.

Video Input Cards and Television Tuners

VIW cards such as New Media Graphics' Super TV Video Windows include an on-board, cable-ready television tuner. Instead of an infrared remote control, you use a Windows application to select a VHF, UHF, or cable channel. You also can purchase a separate adapter card that has a cable or antenna connection and provides a video output signal you can connect to your VIW card.

Tuner adapter cards currently cost as much as a color television set, but the price is expected to decline as VIW cards become more popular. Tuners enable you to watch the World Series, Super Bowl, or your favorite soap opera in a sizable window that you can hide quickly when the boss arrives on the scene. Unfortunately, a separate operation is required to turn off the sound, so you will want to keep the mixer application on-screen, just in case.

Most VIW cards with TV tuners and TV tuner adapter cards have an antenna or RF (radio frequency) input with a 75-ohm, type-F coaxial cable connector. If you want to use an antenna with your tuner rather than connect it to a cable-television hookup, you need a balun. A *balun* is a balanced (300-ohm TV ribbon cable) to unbalanced (75-ohm coaxial cable) transformer, similar in function to the impedance-matching transformers you use when you connect a professional microphone to an audio adapter card input. Baluns also are known as TV-VCR matching transformers; the Radio Shack 15-1253B is a typical example.

Microsoft apparently did not anticipate that PC users would want to watch TV in a window, because the media-control interface (MCI) commands of Windows (see Chapter 23) do not include a standard syntax for setting the channel number. The fact that the MCI commands are file or media-oriented, rather than design for real-time applications such as controlling video cameras or watching television, may have contributed to this omission.

New Media Graphics provides optional development software that uses the MCI to control its TV Video Windows products.

Application Software for VIW Adapters

Most VIW cards come with a basic Windows application that enables you to view the video image and capture selected frames. Most VIW cards also offer applications that enable you to create scalable, movable video windows and to save captured video images in a wide range of graphic file formats. A few products even include image-editing software. Some suppliers, such as New Media Graphics, provide application software as an extra-cost option.

As is true of genlock cards, no generic third-party Windows applications specifically designed for VIW cards are available. In the case of VIW cards, the basic applications are simple enough that you seldom require the versatility that characterizes third-party software.

One exception is the Windows drivers required for use of VIW cards with the multimedia databases described in Chapter 22. If you use a multimedia database such as Lenel Systems' MediaOrganizer, make sure that a compatible driver is available from the manufacturer of the card or from the producer of the database application.

Chapter Summary

This chapter discussed the basic characteristics of the NTSC television broadcast signal and how VGA-to-NTSC converters and adapter cards convert your computer's RGB display signals to NTSC standards. The chapter also discussed adapter cards that display full-motion video in a window.

Chapter 23 shows you how to use the command language built into the media-control interface (MCI) of Windows 3.1 to program multimedia devices.

Authoring Multimedia Productions

PART VI

OUTLINE

The Multimedia Production Process

U p to this point, this book has concentrated on the nuts and bolts of Windows Multimedia. You have learned how to install and use audio adapter cards, MIDI devices, graphics and video cards, and a representative selection of the Windows application software designed to be used with multimedia hardware. Now that you understand the capabilities of your Windows multimedia hardware and software, you are ready to create your first full-scale multimedia presentation.

Microsoft Corporation defines multimedia as "an electronic document" and implies that the production of multimedia is inextricably linked with the use of CD-ROM as the distribution medium. This definition is both too broad and too narrow. An electronic document can be a simple ASCII text file; it need not contain graphic images and sound. Moreover, multimedia presentations can be distributed in a variety of forms, including videocassettes, laserdiscs, and CD-I discs.

In this book, the term *Windows multimedia presentation* means a time-based combination of graphics and synchronized sound you create with applications that run in Windows 3.1. A Windows multimedia presentation is designed to communicate a specific message, and some presentations require a Windows application to deliver the message. The presentation may reside only on your computer; you also can distribute the presentation over a network or on floppy disk, videotape, or CD-WO ROM.

A *Windows multimedia title* is a commercial product created under Windows 3.1 that is designed to be distributed in quantity on CD-ROM or videotape. The purpose of the title may be to inform or entertain the viewer. In most cases, multimedia titles may be purchased, but titles often are distributed free as advertising and promotion tools. If the title is distributed on CD-ROM, the title is assumed to be designed exclusively for use under Windows 3.0 with Multimedia or Windows 3.1.

A *Windows multimedia production* includes both multimedia presentations and multimedia titles. Figure 20.1 shows the hierarchy of Windows multimedia productions.

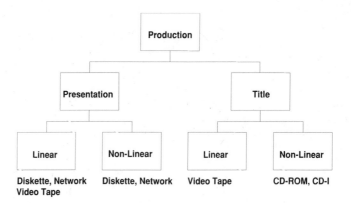

FIG. 20.1

The hierarchy of Windows multimedia productions.

Categorizing Windows Multimedia Productions

When you are learning about a branch of science such as botany or zoology, the first step is to learn the classifications of the objects that the field encompasses. For example, the taxonomy of animals—a hierarchy of species and subspecies—helps you understand zoology as a whole and also individual animals. The same principle applies to multimedia productions.

Multimedia productions can be classified by their structures: *linear* and *nonlinear*.

A linear production is intended to be viewed from beginning to end, usually in a single session. Linear productions have traditional opening, content, and closing sections, similar to books and television commercials. The viewer cannot alter the sequence of events. When viewer interaction is limited to the ability to start and stop the production, the production is suitable for distribution on videotape as a presentation or as a title.

You can add viewer-interaction capability to a linear production by incorporating buttons or other objects that the viewer can click to see additional detail on a subject; this kind of presentation is called a *drill-down* presentation or title. Drill-down presentations and titles must be viewed on a computer or on a special player (such as a consumer CD-I drive), so they must be distributed on CD-ROM or floppy disk.

Figure 20.2 shows the horizontal structure of a linear production, with drill-down detail options shaded.

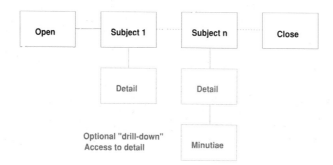

FIG. 20.2

The structure of a linear multimedia production.

Most linear productions are created by applications that use the time-line principle. Macromedia Action! and CorelSHOW! for presentations and Matrox Personal Producer for desktop video production are examples of timeline-based applications. (Action! and CorelSHOW! are described in Chapter 18; Personal Producer is described in Chapter 22.)

Nonlinear productions, by contrast, give the viewer control of the sequence of the presentation. An example of a nonlinear production is a multimedia encyclopedia. The user chooses or enters a search topic, and the application displays a list of topics that match the search term. Each topic may have additional suboptions, such as a bit map of a painting, a video clip, or a selection from a musical composition. Links to other related topics may be provided at the subject-selection level or in the text. The production also offers the user a return path to the preceding image or to the original search level (see fig. 20.3).

The production may make choices for the user automatically, as in the case of multimedia titles used as context-sensitive help systems, such as Lotus SmartHelp for 1-2-3 for Windows and Microsoft's Multimedia

Works. Most nonlinear productions include some degree of structure, often presented as a viewer-guidance option. Because more-complex interaction with the user is required than just starting and stopping the production, nonlinear productions cannot be distributed on videotape.

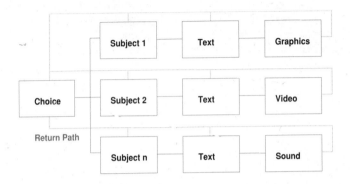

FIG. 20.3

The structure of a typical nonlinear multimedia production.

Applications used to create nonlinear multimedia productions are called *multimedia authoring software*. Multimedia authoring software is *event-driven*, rather than timeline-oriented. In a nonlinear production, an event such as the click of a mouse or the touch of a finger on a control button in a window makes the presentation move forward or backward.

One of the first multimedia authoring packages was Microsoft's Multimedia Viewer, based on the context-sensitive help system of Windows 3.1. Multimedia Viewer includes basic capabilities to incorporate text, still graphics, waveform audio, and MIDI music in nonlinear productions. Multimedia Viewer is designed primarily for the creation of nonlinear multimedia titles comprised mainly of text, such as encyclopedias.

You access additional media device types for which you have the required drivers through the media control interface (MCI) command set described in Chapter 23, "The High-Level MCI Commands of Windows 3.1." Multimedia Viewer, which is oriented to text-based applications, uses files created by a word processing application (such as Word for Windows) that can produce files in Microsoft rich-text format (RTF). Codes embedded in the file are used to incorporate graphics, sounds, and video. If your multimedia title uses devices that Windows 3.1 does not support (such as multimedia movies or AVI video), you must include the MCI drivers for these devices on an installation floppy disk or on the CD-ROM.

A wide range of other multimedia authoring applications for Windows has become available since Windows with Multimedia was introduced in the fall of 1991. One of the most successful of these applications is

Multimedia ToolBook, a derivative of Asymetrix's original ToolBook application. Most new multimedia authoring applications are designed to simplify the creation of nonlinear productions by improving the user interface and by adding sophisticated graphics tools not provided with Multimedia Viewer.

Multimedia Production Categories

Multimedia presentations and titles fall into several basic categories. The following sections present these categories in order of their prevalence.

Business Communication

Business communication is the primary use for Windows multimedia presentations. Business communication includes marketing, research-and-development, production, human-resources, and financial presentations to an audience ranging from one person to all the members of an organization.

An entire class of Windows applications has evolved for this market. Animated presentation-management applications, such as Macromedia Action!, are specifically designed for creating business presentations.

The traditional business-oriented multimedia presentation consists of a series of graphic images, created by drawing and charting applications, that resemble the traditional 35mm slide show with live narration. Most still-image presentation software packages include the capability to create 35mm slides of the images.

Multimedia techniques can lift a business-oriented presentation out of the slide-show rut by including animated graphics, skilled narration, and sound effects apropos to the subject. Full-motion video inserts (using VCRs or AVI video files as the source) add a movement to the presentation and maintain the audience's interest.

Narration usually is prerecorded in WAV files so that the pace of the entire presentation is determined by the duration of the narration, rather than by manual slide changes. Although recorded narration detracts from spontaneity, a recording discourages interruption. If a viewer asks for explanation of a point, you can stop the presentation and add impromptu comments.

Business presentations almost always are linear, so they are good candidates for printing to videotape. You can use large-screen video display units or projectors for presentations to moderate-size audiences, but because presentations to large audiences require large-screen television projection, videotape is the best medium.

When you design a presentation for projection, text must be enlarged and the amount of detail in each image must be limited because of the lower resolution of video projection devices compared with 35mm slide and overhead-transparency projectors and because of the viewers' distance from the projection screen.

Advertising and Promotion

Advertising and promotion is a relatively new use for multimedia productions. This category includes a wide range of formats, ranging from linear desktop television commercials to nonlinear titles for kiosks that display items on sale in department stores.

Advertising and promotion productions fall into the following three categories:

- *Commercials* dedicated to a particular product or to enhancing a firm's image. You can use a multimedia presentation application (such as Action! and CorelSHOW!) if you don't need live video or if you use a video service bureau to combine the graphics and video clips. If you intend to include live video in a commercial (and if you have the VCRs and remote-control hardware described in Chapter 22), you can use an application such as Matrox Personal Producer.

  Commercials are designed for airing on broadcast television or for distribution as videotapes. Demonstration videotapes for computer software, such as the tape NewTek produced to market its Video Toaster, constitute one of the fastest-growing segments of the multimedia industry.

- *Product or service databases* are nonlinear titles that must be viewed on a computer, a consumer CD-I drive, or a Photo CD player so that the user can choose topics.

  An example of a product database is a collection of scaled vector drawings of a firm's office furniture, which a space planner might incorporate in perspective views of the interior of a building. The user copies the vector drawing of the selected item to the Clipboard and then pastes the copy into a drawing created by a Windows application such as AutoCAD for Windows or Micrografx Designer.

  An example of a service database is bit-mapped images of buildings on a Photo CD for use by a real estate agency. (Chapter 17, "Image Acquisitions, Editing, Interchange, and Compression" explains how the images are created.)

- *Informational kiosks* use touch-screen displays so that the user can choose a topic by touching a specific part of the screen.

DOS-based multimedia productions have dominated this sector of the industry, but Windows productions are gaining recognition. An example of a Windows-developed vending kiosk is MusicWriter's NoteStation (described in Chapter 7, "Playing MIDI Files"). The NoteStation plays a portion of a musical composition that you select by making successive choices in various categories and then offers you the opportunity to print the sheet music or obtain a MIDI file on floppy disk.

After business communication, the advertising and promotion market is expected to generate the largest number of new multimedia titles and presentations. Windows is expected to gain an increasing share of the market for the applications used to create these productions (and, where applicable, to present them) because of Windows' ease of use and the lower cost of PCs compared with other kinds of computers.

Training and Productivity

Organizations use *training and productivity* productions to refresh employees' old skills and impart new ones. Training productions usually cover a broad subject, such as "Basic Electricity." Productivity productions tend to focus on a specific subject, such as Lotus 1-2-3 macros.

Training courses were among the first industrial applications for laserdisc titles. Several proprietary videodisc players are available that provide for user interaction, such as reviewing particular subjects and completing multiple-choice tests. Now that computers equipped with CD-ROM drives are within the same price range as remotely controllable laserdisc players, many of these laserdisc titles have been converted to CD-ROMs.

Computer-based training productions designed to upgrade employees' skills in subjects such as mathematics, accounting, and technical specialties have become a major multimedia industry. Training productions are closely related to education productions but are directed to employed adults rather than students. Most training productions are created by firms that specialize in the field.

Productivity productions that focus on specific products are much more common than broad-scope training productions. In addition to user-assistance titles on CD-ROMs designed to replace or supplement disk-based help files, many software packages (including those produced by Macromedia and Corel Corporation) now include linear productivity productions on videotape. Some of these videotapes also are distributed as commercials for the product.

Another category of productivity productions instructs an organization's employees on new or rarely used procedures. For example, when a bank implements a new procedure (perhaps involving new software) for processing letters of credit, it provides a CD-ROM describing the procedure to its clerical personnel. As a related example, American Airlines plans to convert its aircraft maintenance procedures, which now are stored in bound manuals, to CD-ROMs so that aircraft mechanics can access the procedures through laptop computers.

Other Categories

Education is a substantial market for multimedia productions. Education productions commonly are used in elementary and secondary schools and in colleges and universities. Professional organizations also use these productions to help members brush up their skills, either voluntarily or as part of a continuing-education program for compliance with professional licensing requirements.

Education productions usually are linear but enable users to move to specific subjects based on the correctness of answers to multiple-choice questions.

Encyclopedias and databases provide indexed information designed for easy retrieval. An example of a multimedia database production is a CD-ROM listing of automotive parts, together with AVI video clips showing how to install the parts.

Encyclopedia and database productions are nonlinear but may incorporate linear subtopics. For example, an encyclopedia production may provide indexing by dates to create a linear "What happened in 1992?" topic.

Multimedia sources include categorized sounds, still images, animation, and video clips, usually distributed on CD-ROM. Material from video archives supplied on videotape qualifies as a multimedia source under the definition used in this book.

Multimedia sources have no structure; they consist solely of files that you incorporate in your own multimedia productions.

Entertainment productions are delivered on CD-ROM and usually are highly nonlinear. As a rule, substantial user interaction is required to qualify a CD-ROM production as entertainment, because the production values (quality of content) of entertainment CD-ROMs are far below the standards established by broadcast television. Clever entertainment productions are structured by user choices during the session.

Productions that combine education and entertainment are called "edutainment" productions. Only a few of these productions, such as Multimedia Beethoven, have achieved commercial success.

Developing Multimedia Productions

The steps involved in developing a multimedia production are basically the same for productions in all categories. You define the need and the audience for the production, form a team to do the work, and then create the production. The following sections describe these steps in detail.

Defining the Need and the Audience

If you are creating a business presentation, the need is established by the organization's management or policy, and your audience is predefined (and likely to be familiar with the subject of the presentation).

Business presentations, such as performance reports, are repetitive and often involve only changes in graphs and charts. The information ultimately may be summarized and presented to a larger audience of employees or shareholders; in such a case, audience members may have widely differing levels of acquaintance with the subject. The information must be presented in simplified form, and the presentation must incorporate higher production values to maintain audience interest.

Productivity titles have a precisely defined need and audience, but viewers' familiarity with the product, service, or operation these productions describe may vary widely. Advertising and promotional productions may be designed to reach a diverse audience, such as viewers of a television broadcast, whose members know little or nothing about the product or firm. Productions designed for kiosks are designed for the latter type of audience.

The need for commercials and kiosk productions is determined by projected cost-benefit analysis, which is a marketing function. The purpose of commercials is to give the viewer a sense of necessity—first the necessity to pay attention to the commercial and then the necessity to purchase the product or service.

To be successful, a commercial must have high production values—that is, graphics and audio that capture the viewer's interest in the first second or two, retain that interest, and close in such a way that the viewer remembers the commercial's content. Short commercials that meet this test are the most difficult multimedia productions to create.

Creating the Multimedia Team

Creating multimedia presentations and titles usually is a team effort. Small-scale business presentations are a possible exception, but the contributions of many people to the production of a business presentation can result in major improvement.

A typical multimedia team includes the following:

- A *producer*, who is in charge of the entire process, including selecting the other members of the team. The producer is responsible for establishing—and maintaining—a budget and schedule for the production. The producer also makes contracts with outside consultants, authors, composers, and artists. Finally, the producer obtains any necessary copyright permissions and licenses. Lawyers who specialize in copyright and contract law often are consultants to multimedia producers.

- *Graphic artists*, who create or edit the still and animated images to be used in the production. Graphic artists usually select the video clips to be used, especially if those clips are to be integrated with titles and overlays.

- A *writer*, who creates the text and the narration script. The writer also may specify the background music (or perhaps specific compositions) to accompany the narration. The narration determines the transitions between images if you are using a timeline-based application.

- An *audio engineer, specialist, or studio* to record the soundtrack, on audiotape or in waveform audio files. Most sound studios employ or have relationships with professional narrators, musicians, and composers whom you can hire on an hourly or fixed-fee basis.

- A *video service bureau* to perform on-line editing of video material, if you do not have professional-quality video-editing hardware and software. (Chapter 22 describes the video-editing process.) If you distribute your production on videotape, the video service bureau will create your master tape.

- A *CD-ROM premastering service bureau*, if your title is on CD-ROM, to create the final test CD-ROM and to prepare the master tape from which the production is to be duplicated. Most service bureaus are equipped to produce CD-WO discs for limited-quantity distribution.

- A *duplicating facility* to duplicate the production on CD-ROMs and videocassettes.

If you do not have the time to serve as producer and cannot assign an employee to that role, you can hire an independent producer. Independent multimedia producers ordinarily have a background in video production and an interest in computers.

> A Windows project-management application, such as Microsoft Project 2.0, can make your life as a producer much happier and productive. Project-management applications enable you to break down a project into individual tasks on a time line. You can use one of these applications to assign a cost, starting date, and completion date to each task; you also can use the application to assign certain people to certain tasks. The application then organizes the data in the form of a time line and warns you if a conflict occurs. Project-management applications enable you to produce periodic reports on completion of tasks, adherence to the budget, and resources used.
>
> **T I P**

If you have a flair for design, an image-editing application for bit-mapped graphics, and a vector-based drawing application, you can serve as your own artist. Most presentation applications include templates that you can use in your own presentations. Graphics and drawing applications like CorelDRAW! and Micrografx Designer include a variety of vector images you can edit to suit your needs.

Audio and video editing require greater technical expertise than most beginning multimedia producers possess, so you may want to hire and learn from an expert in the field before you attempt to do your own recording. If you have quality audio and video components, practice can give you the experience you need to create respectable soundtracks for your productions.

Designing the Structure and Content

Designing a multimedia production requires creativity and technical skill. Without creativity, your production will not capture viewers' interest. As for technical skill, poorly chosen color combinations, unattractive graphics, and amateurish sound kill multimedia productions, no matter how interesting or important the content.

If you are creating a production for use on PCs, your authoring application must be capable of producing a title responsive to user input, even on a 16-MHz 80386SX. Sluggish performance offends users of interactive titles, and CD-ROMs have slow seek times. You may need to offload a substantial part of the title onto the user's hard disk drive to achieve an acceptable response speed.

The best way to design a multimedia production is to create a map of its elements or functions (similar to the diagrams shown in figures 20.2 and 20.3 at the beginning of this chapter).

If your title is primarily linear, you can use the PERT (project evaluation and review technique) charting capabilities of a Windows project-management application to create a useful map or flow chart and simultaneously create a database-like structure containing the elements that make up the content. Several Windows flow-charting applications are available. The advantages of using a flow-charting application are that many of its standard symbols are suitable for mapping multimedia productions and that you can edit a flow chart easily on-screen.

Establishing Uniform Design Standards

If you plan to create more than one production for an organization, you should develop a set of uniform design standards for backgrounds, graphics (including logos and charts), animations, and music before you create the first production. Uniform standards create a perception of consistency in your work.

Another advantage to uniformity in design is that you can use backgrounds and graphics as templates for future productions. Making minor edits in a template or changing the legends in a graph or chart is a much faster process than re-creating images from scratch.

Designing Productions for the Method of Display

A topic touched upon earlier in this chapter is repeated throughout this book: design your images to fit the method that you intend to use to display them. Graph and chart legends easily readable on a VGA display are likely to become totally illegible on a large-screen television set or RGB display, or projected on a wide screen and viewed from a distance of 6 feet or more.

Most VCRs and television monitors have problems displaying contrasting, highly saturated colors and thin horizontal lines, which create buzz (vibration) in the image. Highly contrasting primary colors are the defaults for charts and graphs created by applications such as Excel and Microsoft Chart; you should avoid using these colors for large-screen or RGB displays.

Chapter 22 provides tips on selecting typefaces, type sizes, and colors for desktop video productions. These recommendations also apply to presentations designed for large-screen RGB displays and LCD (liquid-crystal display) projection panels used with overhead projectors.

Creating CD-ROM Titles

If you plan to produce a title on CD-ROM, a short description of how commercial CD-ROM titles are produced may be useful, especially in terms of understanding the hardware you need to use. You are responsible for creating the logical file structures required by the operating system you intend to use. All still images are supplied as 256-color Windows device-independent bit maps. Sound is recorded in WAV format or supplied in MIDI files, and video clips are captured in AVI files. All files must conform to one of the Microsoft RIFF file formats or must be created in a format (such as FLI for animation files) that your application's drivers can translate.

After you have your text, images, and sound stored in files on floppy disk (or in another machine-readable format, such as a tape from a disk backup tape drive), your next step is to organize the data for creation of the CD-ROM.

Premastering

Premastering involves preparing and organizing the data in CD-ROM format. This process requires a major investment in hardware, software, and training, so unless you intend to produce a substantial number of CD-ROM titles, you should have a premastering service bureau do this work.

Premastering involves the following tasks:

1. Creating a disk file that contains an image of the files as they will appear in the tracks of your CD-ROM. When CD-ROM XA (see Chapter 4) becomes an established standard, this step will include interleaving the graphic images and audio tracks. AVI files contain audio and video images interleaved in a single track. MCI files are described in Chapter 17.

2. Dividing the disk file into blocks in accordance with the premastering facility's requirements.

3. Providing the file blocks on tape or CD-WO ROM (see Chapter 4) in a format that the premastering facility uses.

The premastering facility provides you an initial test CD-ROM from a write-once drive. You must then test this CD-ROM, as the following section explains.

Testing

Testing the CD-ROM for adherence to performance specifications is your responsibility. An especially critical responsibility is testing the product in CD-ROM drives like those that your intended audience will use.

T I P   Testing a CD-ROM's performance on a double-speed CD-ROM drive masks synchronization and response problems that occur when the CD-ROM is played by a conventional drive with a 300- to 400-ms (millisecond) seek time and 150K-per-second data-transfer rate. If possible, test the CD-ROM in a drive that conforms to the lowest common denominator of Multimedia Specification 1.0: a 1-second maximum seek time. Although drives with this glacial seek time now are uncommon, these drives do qualify for MPC status under the current specification.

You may be able to correct performance problems caused by long seek times by having the service bureau restructure your data so as to minimize the distance that the drive head must travel to access successive blocks of data. If this restructuring fails to solve the problem, you may have to relocate some of the data to the user's hard disk. Most users, however, are put off by an application that requires them to copy many megabytes' worth of data from the CD-ROM to their hard disk.

Mastering and Duplication

The last step in the CD-ROM production process is the creation of the final CD-ROM. Although some premastering service bureaus also have CD-ROM production capability, CD-ROM production requires a large investment in equipment and thus usually is performed by large firms.

A CD-ROM production facility performs the following tasks:

- Reads the data from the premastering service bureau's tape or CD-WO ROM to a hard disk drive.

- Adds the necessary synchronization and header data to make the production conform to Yellow Book CD-ROM standards (see Chapter 4), and then adds the error-detection codes and error-correction codes necessary to preserve data integrity.

- Creates a "glass master" of the CD-ROM through a photoetching process that creates a mechanical image of the pits on the disc that store the data.

- Evaporates a metal film onto the surface of the glass master to create the metal stamper used to press the pits into the plastic CD-ROM blanks.

- Silkscreens a label on the side of the disc opposite the side in which the pits are located. (You supply the label artwork to the production facility in the form of a file positive or negative.)

■ Packages the disc in a standard plastic housing called a jewel case, inserting a label and any other printed matter you supply.

Many CD-ROM production facilities also have fulfillment capabilities and can package and ship CD-ROMs in response to the orders you receive.

Understanding Multimedia Hardware Recommendations

The Microsoft Multimedia Development Kit (MDK) includes a set of recommendations for computers to be used in producing multimedia titles (assuming that these titles will be produced in the form of CD-ROMs). The minimum recommendations do not apply to full-motion video applications that use audio-video interleaved (AVI) or digital video interactive (DVI) techniques, because neither these techniques nor Windows 3.1 was available when the documentation for the original MDK was written.

Table 20.1 lists the MDK's hardware recommendations. The listings in the "Recommended for CD-ROM" column are based on the assumption that you want to incorporate full-motion video into your applications.

Table 20.1. Multimedia Hardware Recommendations.

Component	Microsoft Minimum	Recommended for CD-ROM
Computer CPU	80386SX or DX	80486DX
CPU speed	Not specified	33 MHz for 80386, 25 MHz for 80486
VGA graphic adapter card	4-bit, 16-color (8-bit, 256-color, 512K recommended)	32K color (1M RAM), preferably with A 72-MHz monitor, noninterlaced display (Windows accelerator card optional
Scanner	Color, hand or full-page type	Same, plus optional 35mm transparency scanner or CD-ROM drive with Photo CD capability
Drive for CD-ROM image files	Tape	Tape with 640M capacity or (preferably) a CD-WO (writable) CD-ROM drive
Memory	4M	8M minimum

continues

Table 20.1. Continued

Component	Microsoft Minimum	Recommended for CD-ROM
Hard disk	70M (80M also is mentioned)	600M, SCSI interface, 18-ms or faster seek time
Audio adapter card	MPC base level, mono, 22.1-kHz waveform audio reproduction and 11.025-kHz recording capability	Professional-quality 16-bit stereo sound card, 44.1-kHz, preferably with PCM-sampled synthesized sound
CD-ROM drive	MPC base level, 150K/second data transfer, 1-second maximum seek time	Double-speed drive (300K/second) with 180-ms or faster seek time, 300-400-ms drive for testing, full CD-XA recommended but available only from a few firms
Video input card	Frame grabber (video-capture card for still images)	Full-motion VIW input card, NTSC and S-VHS inputs, frame-grabbing option
VGA-to-NTSC adapter card	No recommendation	NTSC and S-VHS outputs, genlock capability for overlaying, chroma-keying, and mixing with external video signals
I/O adapter card	No recommendation	Minimum 1 bidirectional parallel and 2 COM ports; board with 4 COM ports recommended for video-device control
Multimedia authoring application	Multimedia Viewer (supplied with the MDK)	Any of the multimedia authoring applications described in this book
Compiler for multimedia programming	Microsoft C, Version 5.1 or later	Not required when you use a multimedia authoring application (Visual Basic with the Professional Toolkit is a good choice for creating special multimedia applications
Windows development libraries and utilities	Microsoft Software Development Kit (SDK)	SDK for Windows 3.1, if SDK data is not included with the compiler (SDK is required only if you use a C compiler but is recommended if you use Visual Basic)

Component	Microsoft Minimum	Recommended for CD-ROM
	Microsoft Multimedia Development Kit (MDK)	MDK (Windows 3.1 version) essential if you plan to use the MCI command strings or if you are writing Windows multimedia applications in Visual Basic or C, regardless of the documentation provided with your compiler
Text processor	Microsoft Word for Windows text processor that can create rich-text format (RTF) files	Word for Windows 2.0a or later, or other Windows word processing application with the capability to create RTF files
Microphone(s)	No recommendation	At least one professional- or semiprofessional-quality dynamic microphone with impedance converter for audio adapter card
Audiotape recorder	No recommendation	Semiprofessional-quality, four-channel cassette recorder with mixer (minimum); digital audiotape (DAT) recorder preferred

The major system components listed in this table are discussed in later chapters. (Some components, such as graphic and video adapter cards, have their own chapters.)

You can use any of the applications described in this book with a 16-Mhz 80386SX computer, but you may not be able to fully exploit full-motion video, especially in combination with synchronized sound.

All references to the speed of applications described in this book are based on the use of a 33-MHz 80386DX computer equipped with a 256K memory cache and a hard disk with 18-ms average access time.

CPUs and Motherboards

If you are purchasing a PC to use in creating Windows multimedia productions, choose a 33-MHz 80386DX or better, not an SX model. Speed is particularly important for full-motion digital video productions. The cost difference between 80386SX and DX clones diminished in early 1992 and is expected to continue to decrease into 1993.

You should use at least a 25-MHz 80486DX with an SCSI adapter card that includes disk-caching capability if you plan to capture motion video images to create AVI files.

Install at least 6M and preferably 8M to 12M of RAM; 4M is barely adequate to run many graphics applications with large bit-mapped images. If you plan to try software-based full-motion-video image compression and decompression in order to save storage space, your best choice is a 25-MHz 80486DX motherboard with 8M of RAM, especially if you want to decompress the images in real time. The 80486DX includes an on-chip math coprocessor that some applications use to speed the decompression process.

For more sophisticated applications, such as any form of video work, make sure that your computer's motherboard has enough slots to accommodate the number of adapter cards you need. Five open slots is the minimum for video; you probably need one slot for video input and another for sending video signals to a videocassette recorder.

Bear in mind that you undoubtedly will need to install a scanner, an audio card, and a fax-modem combination at some point. An external fax-modem is the better choice, because an external modem doesn't require a slot. Most multipurpose I/O cards have two serial ports: one for the mouse and another for a modem.

T I P Choose a serial mouse or trackball so that you need not use a valuable slot for a bus mouse adapter card. This card requires two serial ports (now the usual complement). Try to buy a PC with serial port mounting slots in the rear panel so that you can mount the serial port connectors directly in the slots instead of on a bracket that occupies a slot. You can use the other serial port for an external modem or for remote control of video devices. Although the MPC specifications require a bus mouse be used, the performance difference between the two types of pointing devices is insignificant.

Disk Drives and Computer Cases

A 300M hard disk drive is the smallest you should consider for creating multimedia applications. Multimedia sound and graphics devour hard disk space. Make sure that the drive you select has 20-ms or less average access time. You can use a disk-compression utility such as Stacker to increase the capacity of a 300M driver to more than 600M. Bear in mind that Stacker does not reduce the size of WAV files significantly, but most other types of files shrink by a factor of about 2.5.

If you choose an IDE (Integrated Device Electronics) disk drive, specify a drive adapter card that includes two floppy-disk interfaces, one parallel port, and two serial ports. You can use one SCSI (Small Computer Systems Interface) adapter card for multiple hard disk and CD-ROM drives and also for some scanners (usually the flatbed variety) and some tape drives. You must buy a SCSI adapter card if you purchase a Turtle Beach MultiSound card, because this card does not include a CD-ROM connector.

T I P

Verify that the SCSI adapter card you purchase is compatible with each device with which you plan to use it. SCSI is implemented in many ways, some of which are not compatible with specific types of SCSI devices. Some manufacturers of SCSI adapter cards (including Adaptec and Trantor) provide a list of devices that have been tested with the card.

If you choose to use SCSI for your drives, you need a separate adapter card for your floppy disk drives unless you purchase a combined SCSI/floppy-disk-drive board. Some SCSI adapters include connectors for two floppy disk drives. A typical combined SCSI/floppy-disk-drive adapter card is the Trantor T148F.

You also need a tape backup drive (such as the drives supplied by Exabyte) with 600M or greater capacity to provide an image of the CD-ROM for premastering operations. Selecting a model with a SCSI interface saves an adapter-card slot. You also use the tape drive to back up your hard disk drives.

Both 5.25-inch and 3.5-inch high-density floppy-disk drives are standard in modern PCs. Internal CD-ROMs and tape drives are less expensive than their external cousins. Thus, you should specify a tower or mini-tower case that accommodates at least five half-height devices (two floppy disk drives, one hard disk drive, a CD-ROM, and a tape drive). Six or more half-height device bays in a tower case are recommended for authoring applications, because you may want to add an internal CD-WO write-once drive for creating your own test CD-ROMs.

You can never have too many open adapter slots and device bays in your computer. Changing to a larger case to accommodate another hard disk drive is a major mechanical exercise.

Remotely controlled Hi8 (8mm) videocassette recorders are likely to become available as early as 1993 in the standard 5 1/4-inch format.

Graphic Displays and Adapter Cards

If you are buying a new system, you should consider a multisynchronous Super-VGA (SVGA) video display with dot pitch 0.28mm or smaller. You may want to use a display with higher-than-normal vertical sync speed, such as 72 Hz, because such a display is easier on the eyes. A noninterlaced display further minimizes flicker and eyestrain, but if you are creating multimedia titles to be distributed on CD-ROM or floppy disk, remember that your users probably use conventional VGA displays, perhaps with only 16 colors. You should use a plain-vanilla VGA display to test titles that feature digital video and animation sequences before you make the master copy for distribution. See Chapter 16 for detailed information on graphic displays and adapter cards.

If you decide not to buy a video accelerator card when you purchase the computer, consider buying a low-cost 1M adapter card to start. If you later purchase a video adapter card that includes VGA capability (such as Truevision's Bravado), you will not make a major investment obsolete.

Make sure that you purchase a graphic adapter card with a feature connector (a series of printed-circuit-board contact fingers on its top edge), because most digital video input cards (including some frame grabbers) and video output adapters require a connection to this connector.

Several PC manufacturers are incorporating Local Bus Video (LVB) into their motherboards to speed data transfer to the video card. (LVB is discussed in Chapter 16, "Graphic Displays and Adapter Cards for Windows.") The abbreviation implies some form of standardization, but none exists.

In mid-1992, the Video Electronics Standards Association (VESA), which maintains specifications for the feature connector of VGA adapter cards, met to evaluate current and proposed LVB designs, including data paths, signals, and connectors. Unless you are very sure that the combination of LVB motherboard and graphic adapter card is compatible with other adapter cards (such as video-in-a-window and genlock video output cards, which are described in Chapter 19, "Incorporating Digital Video"), you may want to take the conservative approach. Wait for the VESA committee to establish at least a tentative LVB standard and then purchase a motherboard and video adapter card that conform to the specification.

Chapter Summary

This chapter provided basic guidelines for creating multimedia productions, either as presentations or as titles on CD-ROM or videotape. The chapter explained the differences between multimedia presentations and titles, and compared linear and nonlinear multimedia productions. The chapter listed the steps involved in creating a multimedia title, from assembling the team that creates the content of the title to duplicating a CD-ROM in production quantities. The chapter ended with recommendations for the computer hardware necessary to produce CD-ROM titles.

The remaining chapters in Part VI are devoted to advanced techniques for multimedia production. The next chapter deals with synchronizing MIDI music and WAV files or prerecorded material on tape, and with the structure of MID and WAV files. The final chapter of Part VI describes desktop video production and the hardware and software you need to create professional-quality videocassette tapes with your computer.

Advanced MIDI and Waveform Audio Techniques

After you create or collect the graphic images, record the narration, and acquire the background music you intend to use, you must orchestrate these elements into your multimedia production. In essence, you must become a conductor, using the computer's mouse or keyboard as your baton.

As is true of acting and music, timing is critical. Your narration must fit the images, and your background music must evoke the desired emotional responses. Sound effects, if you use them, must occur at just the right time.

If you create a musical composition designed to elicit a specific emotional response in conjunction with a graphic image, the music, rather than the time line of your presentation, becomes the controlling factor in the timing of your presentation. When narration must be keyed to the music, your MIDI sequencer is the keeper of the master clock for audio.

MIDI System Exclusive (SysEx) messages are important elements of the MIDI standard because they allow you to send special messages to individual MIDI devices to control how they respond to conventional MIDI messages. SysEx messages are complex and not easy to create without help from special applications designed to create these messages for MIDI devices. This chapter describes how you can use MIDI SysEx messages to alter the behavior of MIDI devices.

This chapter also describes the Resource Interchange Format Files (RIFF) that the Windows media control interface uses. You need not know the structure of these files to use them, but understanding how RIFF files work helps you understand multimedia processes in the Windows environment.

Using Audio and Video Synchronization Techniques

If you combine sound composed on a MIDI sequencer with other recorded sounds or graphics, all related events must occur at the proper time. Each element of the production must coincide with the other elements. Similarly, music created for a television production must underlie the appropriate video frames. If you are creating a presentation, your narration and background music must coincide with the presentation's still or animated images. The process of combining sounds and images reproduced by multiple devices or computer applications at the proper instant is called *synchronization* (or *sync*).

Audiotape or videotape and the sequenced MIDI music are *time-independent*—that is, the rate at which the images or sound of the two sources is reproduced by a tape recorder and a computer may vary, sometimes substantially. This variance may occur for any of the following reasons:

- The speed of the tape drive may vary due to fluctuations in the capstan drive motor speed.

- The tape may stretch after many plays, especially if you have rewound and fast-forwarded the tape many times.

- The tape may have been edited, or a new set of synchronization signals may have been recorded over the old sync track.

- You may have changed the tempo of the MIDI sequence by changing the tempo of part or all of the sequence.

The principle of synchronization is simple: a master source maintains a clock used by all other sources of sound, called *slaves*. Each added source of sound, whether that source is the original soundtrack for a video presentation or a track added to an audiotape, substitutes the master clock for the internal clock that the slave uses independently. But as simple as the principle may be, implementing it in multimedia projects can be a complex process.

The master clock that establishes the speed at which the slave sound sources are reproduced by MIDI devices, audio adapter cards, and tape recorders may be *relative* or *absolute, tempo-dependent* or *fixed*:

- *Relative clocks* are dependent on the speed of the device that generates the clock signal. The speed of your computer, measured in MHz, is a relative clock.

- *Absolute clocks* are based on the position of the medium on which the sound or video data is recorded. An absolute clock enables you to find a specific frame of a videotaped image or the measure and beat of a MIDI performance.

- *Tempo-dependent clocks* are relative clocks that vary in accordance with the speed at which the beat of a musical performance is maintained. Tempo often changes during a performance.

- *Fixed clocks* are relative clocks that do not change over time. If all your MIDI files have a tempo of 60 beats per minute, you create a fixed clock.

- *MIDI synchronization* maintains synchronization of devices connected by MIDI cables, based on the values of the MIDI Song Position Pointer (SPP). MIDI synchronization does not apply to audiotape or videotape synchronization. MIDI synchronization is absolute (because the synchronization is based on the precise numeric value of the measure and beats incorporated in the SPP) and tempo-dependent (because the relationship to time in minutes and seconds depends on the tempo of the master control device in the MIDI chain).

- *FSK* (Frequency Shift Keying) is a method of synchronizing MIDI sequencers with prerecorded tracks played on audiotape recorders. FSK sync is both relative and tempo-dependent—relative because it is based on the tempo, and relative because it consists only of clock pulses and does not provide a numeric representation of tape position relative to the prerecorded sequence or to 24-hour-clock time.

- *CLS* (Chase Lock Sync) also is used to synchronize MIDI sequencing applications and tracks played on audiotape recorders, and is a considerable improvement over FSK sync. CLS is absolute but still tempo-dependent—absolute because it transcribes the value of the MIDI SPP on the sync track of the audiotape and tempo-dependent because the SPP values are absolute.

- *LANC* (Local Application Numerical Control) is a time code synchronization method used by high-end, remotely controllable VCRs. LANC time code often is based on a linear position counter whose time values are calculated by the VCR.

In this case, LANC time code derived from linear position counters is subject to errors resulting from tape stretching but not from changing capstan speed. LANC time code can be derived from an initial time code recorded on the audio track in the leader portion of the tape and then by counting frames. SyncMAN Pro (described in Chapter 11, "Accessories for MIDI Systems") is one of the few VCRs that uses this method. LANC code and its derivatives are fixed to the 24-hour clock, providing elapsed-time data in hh:mm:ss:ff format (hours:minutes:seconds:frames), but the elapsed time data is not recorded on the videotape.

■ *RC* is an abbreviation for the proprietary Sony Rewritable Consumer time code used by the firm's Hi8 camcorders and VCRs. RC time code is written on the tape in hh:mm:ss:ff format. Like LANC time code, this code is absolute and fixed. You can use RC time code to search for a frame in an Hi8 videotape.

■ *SMPTE* (Society of Motion Picture and Television Engineers) synchronization is used for professional audio and video work and with MIDI sequencer applications. SMPTE synchronization, which is absolute and fixed, is recorded on an individual track of both audiotapes and videotapes. A tape encoded with SMPTE time signals in hh:mm:ss:ff format can be positioned to 1/30th of a second—the display duration of a video frame.

■ *MIDI Time Code* (MTC) synchronization is a shortened version of the SMPTE time code that can be transmitted in the form of MIDI messages to devices connected in a MIDI daisy chain. MTC and SMPTE are identical in terms of time code format (hh:mm:ss:ff) and accuracy (single-frame).

The following sections discuss the merits and deficiencies of each of these time codes when they are used for synchronization purposes.

Synchronization Systems for Sequencers

You use MIDI timing signals, sequencer applications, and sometimes MIDI synchronization hardware to keep multiple sound sources in sync. Audiotape recorders, for example, do not play back at exactly the same rate at all times; tapes stretch and transport-motor speeds vary slightly, causing variations in playback speeds. Playback variation usually is on the order of seconds per hour of music, but a variation of as little as 0.1 second is evident to an audience, especially if your production synchronizes a vocal track with video images of a singer. Exact synchronization, preferably in the range of thousandths of a second, is required.

T I P

Audio adapter cards, whether or not they are MPC-compatible, do not provide synchronization capability. The only exception is Roland's LAPC-1 equipped with the MCB-I MIDI breakout box, which duplicates the FSK synchronization functions of the IPC breakout box supplied with the Roland MPU-401. If you plan to synchronize your MIDI sequences with material played back on audiotape or videotape recorders, you need a MIDI adapter card or a MIDI sync box (described in Chapter 11) in addition to your sound card. Make sure that the MIDI adapter card you buy has SMPTE synchronization capability.

Tempo-Dependent Synchronization

The rate at which MIDI note messages are sent is based on the tempo (beats per minute) you specify. In most cases, your computer's internal clock inserts basic MIDI Clock messages into the MIDI message stream through a division process. The multimedia functions included in Windows 3.1 provide a driver called Timer (which appears in the Driver applet's list of installed drivers) to generate timing pulses for Windows applications.

Your Windows sequencer application instructs the Windows Timer driver to provide tick pulses based on the resolution you select—for example, 96, 120, 144, 192, or 384 pulses per quarter note (*ppqn*). The number of tick pulses per quarter note always are multiples of 24 (24 is the MIDI clock rate in ppqn); the most commonly used tick pulse rates are 96, 120, 192, and 384 ppqn. The tick pulses are divided by the appropriate integer (4, 5, 8, or 16 for the examples shown) to provide the 24-ppqn MIDI clock. The higher the number of tick pulses per quarter note, the more precisely you can specify the beginning and ending time of a note; this is called *timing resolution* or *resolution*. Regardless of the resolution you choose, the MIDI clock rate remains fixed at 24 ppqn.

When you choose high tick-pulse resolutions, MIDI Note On messages occur at the same intervals in which they were recorded, giving the music a less mechanical, more natural sound. You need a fast computer to use high resolutions, and you may find that you must use a lower-than-desired resolution so that other portions of a multimedia presentation (such as animated graphics) obtain their share of the computer's resources.

MIDI Synchronization

MIDI sync consists of MIDI clock messages (and the ticks from which they are derived) that occur at a tempo-dependent rate. MIDI clock messages are transmitted by your sequencer (set to internal sync) or by an outboard device such as a drum machine, which can send MIDI clock messages to both your sequencer (set to external sync) and other devices in the chain.

Drum machines often are used as the source of MIDI clock pulses during recording sessions, because the internal sequencer included with these devices can provide an audible rhythm track to keep the performers on the beat. You set the tempo with push buttons on the drum machine, and you use the machine's Start and Stop buttons to control the recording of MIDI note messages by your sequencer application.

Figure 21.1 shows the connections for this MIDI setup.

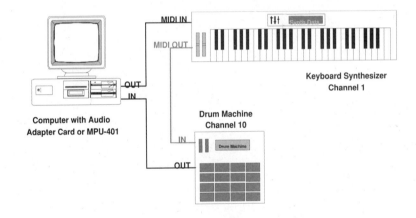

Computer with Audio Adapter Card or MPU-401

Keyboard Synthesizer Channel 1

Drum Machine Channel 10

FIG. 21.1

A MIDI setup in which the drum machine serves as the master MIDI clock controller.

If you use this configuration for recording, your drum machine must be capable of merging MIDI messages from the keyboard synthesizer. If not, you need a special-purpose MIDI adapter card or a separate MIDI merger (both described in Chapter 11) to combine the MIDI OUT signals properly.

If you set your tempo at 120 beats per minute, 48 MIDI clock messages are generated per second. If you increase the tempo to 180 beats per minute, 72 messages are generated per second.

Using tempo-dependent MIDI clock messages when all the devices use MIDI synchronization usually is satisfactory. You can use MIDI sync in multimedia applications because its clock is derived from the one used to display accompanying graphic images. Remember not to change the MIDI tempo after you combine the music with the images.

FSK Synchronization for Audiotape Recorders

In the early days of MIDI, synthesizers had limited polyphonic capability and were quite expensive. Recording a song on tape required multiple recording sessions in which different instrument voices were recorded on the same tracks—a process called *overdubbing*—and vocals were synchronized with the music.

As you learned earlier in this chapter, however, tape recorders are subject to playback timing variations. Thus, some method had to be developed to ensure that overdubbed material stayed synchronized with the rest of the recording. The first truly successful method of accomplishing this with MIDI was *frequency-shift keying (FSK) sync*.

FSK sync devotes one track to clock pulses recorded at two frequencies: one frequency representing the clock's on (or 1) state and another representing the off (or 0) state. Different frequencies are used because audiotape recorders have difficulty recording and reproducing the clock pulses themselves.

Most MIDI adapter cards include FSK inputs and outputs connected to the output and input, respectively, of one track of the recorder, as shown in figure 21.2.

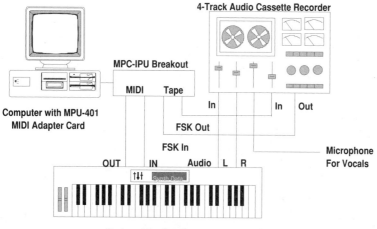

FIG. 21.2

A simple MIDI setup for FSK sync with a four-track audiocassette recorder.

When the first instrument part is recorded, the sequencer application is set to *internal synchronization*, meaning that the computer's internal clock controls the rate of playback. FSK synchronization signals are recorded on another track simultaneously. When you overdub the second instrument part, the sequencer is set to *external synchronization*. In external synchronization, the first FSK signal that the recorder plays back starts the sequencer. The FSK signals regenerate MIDI clock pulses, which control the rate at which the sequencer operates.

After you record the instrumental tracks, you record the vocals on another track, with the vocalist listening to a playback of the instrumental tracks over headphones so as to perform at the same tempo.

The MPU-401 MIDI adapter card features a breakout box (called an MPU-IPC) that includes the FSK synchronization connectors and electronic circuits required for FSK synchronization. Other MPU-compatible cards provide FSK, but the more-sophisticated versions substitute chase-lock and clock-time synchronization for the older FSK method.

The MIDI Song Position Pointer

MIDI clock messages are satisfactory for synchronizing various devices, but you need to make sure that each device starts and stops at the same relative time. You also may need to start a MIDI sequence in a particular measure of a song or even on a specified beat in a measure. The MIDI Song Position Pointer (SPP) gives you this capability.

The SPP itself is not a MIDI message but a value related to the number of beats that have occurred since the beginning of the sequence. The SPP value is calculated by the sequencer application and by the microprocessors used in MIDI devices. The value of the SPP is 0 for the first beat of the first measure of a sequence and increases by 1 every six MIDI clock intervals (a quarter of a beat, or a sixteenth note in ¼ time). The maximum value of the SPP is 16,383, so the maximum length of a ¼ song using SPP is 1,024 bars. At a tempo of 120 beats per measure, the maximum duration of such a song is 34.13 minutes (2,048 seconds).

The MIDI adapter card in your computer normally transmits a MIDI SPP System Common message when it receives a MIDI System Common Stop message from any source. The SPP System Common message contains the measure and beat value (in ppgn) of the position in the sequence at which the stop command occurred. An SPP message causes all devices in the chain that can respond to SPP messages to go to the same measure and beat location corresponding to this value.

The most common use of the SPP message is to position the internal sequencers included with drum machines to the proper measure and beat and to position a tape recorder to a specific location in a recorded MIDI sequence. Using SPP for tape positioning requires a special MIDI synchronizing device connected to the tape recorder's controls and to the inputs and outputs of one audio channel. SMPTE synchronization (discussed later in this chapter) has virtually replaced SPP synchronization for this purpose.

Chase-Lock Synchronization

Chase-lock synchronization (CLS) is an improvement over FSK sync because it encodes the actual values of the SPP and MIDI clocks on one of the tape's tracks. This code uses the equivalent of the characters 39:3, for example, for the third beat of measure 39 (the actual number is 4 beats/measure×39 measures+3 beats=159), enabling the sequencer, when set up for external CLS, to move to the positions written on the tape. You position the tape at or slightly before the point at which you want to begin overdubbing and start the tape. Your sequencer then positions itself (*chases*) to the SPP location corresponding to the music on the tape.

Chase-lock sync is popular because it uses the SPP, which is familiar to all MIDI musicians, and does not require expensive, professional-type recording equipment.

To use chase-lock synchronization, you need a specialized MIDI adapter card (for example, a card in Music Quest's MQX series) and a sequencer application that responds to the card's CLS messages. You also must *stripe* the audiotape with the tempo data before you use it for synchronization. Striping the tape means to prerecord the MIDI SPP (tempo) data on the tape before you use it to record a performance. If you are recording multiple instrument parts on parallel tracks, striping is no problem; simply record the first sequencer track and CLS information on another track.

In standard MIDI files, the first sequencer track must include the tempo information and must be as long as (or longer than) any other sequencer track. If you decide to change the tempo anywhere in the sequence, you must restripe tapes that use CLS and start over, because the time code is tempo-dependent. Clock-based synchronization, described in the following section, averts this problem.

Clock-Based Synchronization

Music produced for motion pictures and television must be synchronized precisely with the accompanying images, which appear in frames. The Society of Motion Picture and Television Engineers (SMPTE) has established a standard method of coding the times at which frames occur, relative to conventional 24-hour time measurement.

Synchronization of devices implies that one device—the master—is in total control and that the other devices are capable of following the master device's synchronization instructions. The two clock-based synchronization methods commonly used by professional recording engineers and MIDI musicians are based on SMPTE and MIDI time codes.

SMPTE Time-Code Synchronization

SMPTE time code measures elapsed time in hours, minutes, seconds, and frames. The time data is recorded on one track of a multitrack audiotape or videotape recorder in a format of 20 characters in three groups, as follows:

1. Eight digits represent elapsed time before a particular frame appears. Time is recorded in hh:mm:ss:ff format, with hh representing hours, mm minutes, ss seconds, and ff frames.

2. Eight characters are used for identification purposes, representing (for example) a reel number or date.

3. Four more digits are added at the end of the code for synchronization purposes. These synchronization signals can be used, for example, to indicate whether the tape is going forward or backward.

The advantages of clock-time and time-code synchronization methods are that all locations on a tape or in a MIDI sequence are designated precisely and that you can position the recorder and the sequencer on the basis of elapsed or clock time, not tempo.

SMPTE and Windows' multimedia extensions provide for the following types of time codes:

- 24 frames per second for U.S. motion pictures

- 25 frames per second for European (PAL and SECAM) television

- 30 nondrop frames per second for worldwide audio applications and for old U.S. black-and-white television

- 30 drop frames per second for U.S. color television

Black-and-white television signals were originally transmitted at exactly 30 frames per second. Because additional information must be transmitted for color television, the National Television Standards Committee (NTSC) chose to drop a frame periodically from the 30-frames-per-second standard for black-and-white TV, resulting in transmission of approximately 29.97 frames per second. This event is the origin of the term *drop frame*. The original rate of 30 frames per second is convenient for calculations, so the term *non-drop* is used to describe it. Although audio signals are not transmitted in frames, division of seconds into 30 intervals is useful for synchronizing sound. The European Broadcast Union uses 25 frames per second for both black-and-white and color television. Frame rates are based on power-line frequency, which in Europe is 50 Hz.

Most professional-level sequencer applications provide SMPTE synchronization capability, which also is the preferred method of synchronizing multimedia sound and graphics. Special versions of MPU-compatible MIDI adapter cards (described in Chapter 11) provide SMPTE synchronization capability.

Figure 21.3 shows the connections for a Music Quest MQX-32M that provides SMPTE sync.

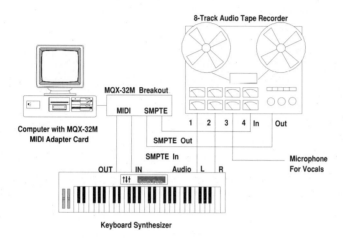

FIG. 21.3

A simple MIDI setup using SMPTE synchronization.

Adapter cards like the MQX-32M can write SMPTE time code on one track of an audiotape or videotape, a process called *striping*. The connections for an SMPTE track on a videotape recorder are similar to those shown in figure 21.3, except that only the SMPTE In connection to the MIDI adapter card is used.

The format of the audio signals used to write SMPTE time code on analog tracks of audiotape and videotape is defined in the SMPTE standard. As a result of this standard, the audio signal from any SMPTE-compatible recorder can be read by a SMPTE time-code interface, such as the interface provided on specialized MIDI adapter cards.

LANC and Sony RC time codes are not recorded to SMPTE standards, however, so you cannot connect the time code output of a LANC- or RC-equipped VCR to your MIDI adapter's time-code input. Furthermore, LANC and RC time codes are not designed for continuous transmission to a synchronizing device; the LANC or RC time-code position of a tape is transmitted over the RS-232-C or RS-422 connection only when the computer sends a message requesting the time code data.

External devices that create SMPTE time signals in conventional audio formats were being developed when this book was written. As the use of semiprofessional and prosumer video equipment proliferates, you can expect to see a variety of devices that can generate SMPTE signals from LANC and RC VCRs and, perhaps, strip RC code on Hi8 tapes. Until these devices appear on the market, however, you are likely to need a device such as the SyncMAN Pro and to sacrifice one channel of your VCR's stereo analog audio to a SMPTE synchronization track.

MIDI Time Code Synchronization

MIDI Time Code (MTC) is a relatively new development designed to make SMPTE time codes compatible with MIDI messages. MTC messages contain the equivalent of the HH:MM:SS:FF portion of the SMPTE time code broadcast (as MIDI clock pulses are) to all devices in the chain. MIDI Time Code consumes about 8 percent of the time available for sending messages in a sequence.

To use this synchronization method, you need a MIDI adapter card and a sequencer that implements MTC. All Windows sequencers that support SMPTE synchronization capability can generate MIDI Time Code messages.

In addition to time information, MTC messages can include MIDI Cueing messages that provide for up to 128 different actions, such as instructing a tape recorder to play, record, or stop. You can cue a person to make an announcement or a device to play a tape. Cueing messages include a unique cue number, the time at which the cue is to take place, the name of the cue, the action to be performed, and additional information about the cue.

Embedding Waveform Audio as a MIDI Meta Event

MIDI sequencing applications for Windows time events precisely. In this respect, MIDI sequencing applications are closely related to time-based multimedia presentation applications (described in Chapter 18).

Related Topics
Understanding Standard
MIDI File Meta Events,
p.313

You could use the capability of Standard MIDI Files (SMFs) to incorporate non-MIDI information as meta events to create a complete presentation application in a MIDI sequencing application. Any type of data, including graphic images and OLE objects, can be embedded in an SMF as a meta event, so a sequencer application that can display graphics and act as an OLE client could display graphic images and play music simultaneously.

Twelve Tone Systems took the first step in this direction with its Cakewalk Professional for Windows sequencer. Cakewalk can embed waveform audio files as meta events in its own WRK files (but not in MID files) and then play those files in synchronization with music. In this case, you want the music to play continuously, because maintaining a tempo is difficult when individual MIDI files must be loaded and played to correspond with the appearance of specific graphic images or animation sequences.

Narration and sound effects are the most common types of embedded waveform audio data. The advantage of embedding waveform audio data is that you eliminate the risk of interruption of the MIDI music or loss of synchronization as a result of the time Windows and your presentation application need to open a WAV file and load its content into buffer memory. The delay can become a serious problem if you attempt to open a large WAV file and simultaneously display images in an animation file.

Related Topics
Examining Commercial
MIDI Sequencers for
Windows, p.343

Embedding waveform audio data as a MIDI meta event is closely related to embedding OLE objects in compound documents; you copy the desired audio data to the Clipboard and then paste the data into Cakewalk as a MIDI event. Version 1.0 of Cakewalk is not an OLE server, so you cannot use an OLE client presentation application such as CorelSHOW! to play back a WRK file that contains embedded waveform audio data. You can record the combined sound, however, as a video soundtrack that is SMPTE-synchronized to a videotape recorder.

Related Topics
Embedding or Linking
Source Documents, p.223

All new professional-level Windows sequencer applications are likely to include OLE server and client capabilities by the end of 1993.

To embed waveform audio data in a Cakewalk Professional for Windows WRK file, follow these steps:

1. Start Sound Recorder or your waveform-audio-editing application.

2. Open the waveform audio file that you want to embed.

   If you are using a waveform audio editor, select the portion of the file you want to embed. (You cannot use Sound Recorder to select parts of a file.)

3. Choose **C**opy from the **E**dit menu to create a copy of the data in the Windows Clipboard.

4. Start Cakewalk Professional for Windows.

5. Choose **O**pen from the **F**ile menu and open the MIDI file in which you want to embed the waveform audio data.

   You can embed audio data in an existing track or add a new track that contains only waveform audio. In this example, the audio data will be incorporated into track 1 of the DEMO.WRK file supplied with Cakewalk.

6. Choose **N**ew from the **W**indow menu and open a new Event List window for track 1.

7. Position the cursor at the entry corresponding to beat 1 of measure 2 in the Event List window and press Insert to create a new MIDI event. The data in the inserted event duplicates that of the event on which you positioned the cursor.

8. Move the cursor to the Kind column and select Note. The Kind of Event dialog box appears (see fig. 21.4).

9. Choose the Wave Audio option in the Special column of the dialog box and then choose OK. The Wave Event dialog box appears (see fig. 21.5).

10. Choose **P**aste Wave From Clipboard and then choose OK. Waveform audio data is embedded as a MIDI meta event in the computer's memory.

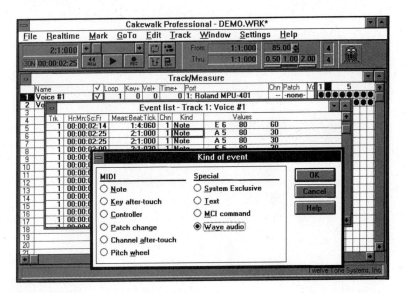

FIG. 21.4

The Kind of Event dialog box.

The Wave Event dialog box also offers you the option of loading all the data in a WAV file. The wave event in the Event List window now includes data on the audio data you loaded (9.47 seconds, 11-kHz sampling rate, 8-bit mono format, 102K file length), as shown in figure 21.6.

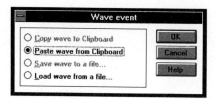

FIG. 21.5

The Wave Event dialog box.

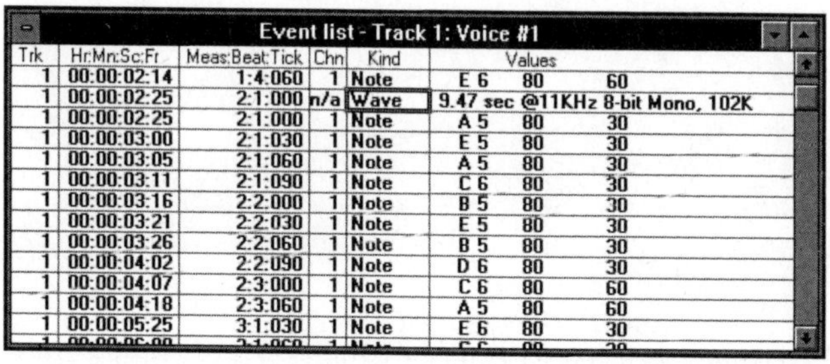

Trk	Hr:Mn:Sc:Fr	Meas:Beat:Tick	Chn	Kind	Values		
1	00:00:02:14	1:4:060	1	Note	E 6	80	60
1	00:00:02:25	2:1:000	n/a	Wave	9.47 sec @11KHz 8-bit Mono, 102K		
1	00:00:02:25	2:1:000	1	Note	A 5	80	30
1	00:00:03:00	2:1:030	1	Note	E 5	80	30
1	00:00:03:05	2:1:060	1	Note	A 5	80	30
1	00:00:03:11	2:1:090	1	Note	C 6	80	30
1	00:00:03:16	2:2:000	1	Note	B 5	80	30
1	00:00:03:21	2:2:030	1	Note	E 5	80	30
1	00:00:03:26	2:2:060	1	Note	B 5	80	30
1	00:00:04:02	2:2:090	1	Note	D 6	80	30
1	00:00:04:07	2:3:000	1	Note	C 6	80	60
1	00:00:04:18	2:3:060	1	Note	A 5	80	60
1	00:00:05:25	3:1:030	1	Note	E 6	80	30
1	00:00:06:00	3:1:060	1	Note	C 6	80	30

Event list - Track 1: Voice #1

FIG. 21.6

A waveform audio event embedded in measure 2, beat 1.

This information is used to create the header information Windows needs in order to play waveform audio.

11. Choose Save **As** from the **File** menu and save the file under a descriptive name such as DEMOEMBD.WRK.

If you use File Manager to compare the original DEMO.WRK file with the new file, you see that the file has grown by the indicated size of the waveform audio data (plus a few extra kilobytes).

If you save DEMOEMBD.WRK as a MID file, the waveform audio data is not included as a MIDI meta event and the MID file is smaller than the DEMO.WRK file that originated it. This problem is not serious at this point in the development of Windows multimedia because Media Player, for example, disregards MIDI meta events.

Unlike an OLE waveform audio object, you cannot edit the audio data that you embed in Cakewalk Professional for Windows. You can, however, copy the embedded data to the Clipboard by selecting the Wave entry in the Kind column of the Event List window and then choosing the Copy Wave To Clipboard option in the Wave Event dialog box. If you have a waveform-audio-editing application, you can paste the data to the editing window, edit the data, and then paste the edited data from the Clipboard to Cakewalk.

Ultimately, most Windows sequencer applications will be capable of embedding data as meta events of MID files. More advanced versions will store the data as OLE objects that you can play and edit with the application that you used to create them.

Using MIDI System Exclusive Messages

MIDI System Exclusive messages transmit program data and voice parameters to and from synthesizers and also send new digital waveform samples to sample-playback synthesizers in a special format defined by the MIDI Sample Dump standard. You modify the digital FM voice parameters of Sound Blaster, Pro AudioSpectrum, and other audio adapter cards that use the Yamaha OPL-II and OPL-III chipsets by sending SysEx messages to the cards. The Roland SCC-1 card has an extensive vocabulary of SysEx messages that enable you to alter the characteristics of each of its voices, as well as the effects it offers.

SysEx messages are specific to individual MIDI devices. Each manufacturer that wants to use SysEx messages in its products receives an identification number from the International MIDI Association (IMA), and thereafter, the data in the SysEx message is defined by the manufacturer, not by MIDI Specification 1.0.

Data in SysEx messages traditionally appears in hexadecimal format (a number system that uses a base of 16, instead of the Arabic system's base 10). Appendix E explains binary and hexadecimal numbers.

The Structure of SysEx Messages

All SysEx messages begin with the hexadecimal value F0, the SysEx status byte (sometimes called SOX for start of exclusive), followed by the manufacturer's ID number. Manufacturers usually use the next byte or two to identify the product category and model number. The F0 status byte and product ID bytes are called the header of the SysEx file. Any number of data bytes can follow the header. The SysEx message ends with an F7 byte called EOX (end of exclusive).

Figure 21.7 shows a short SysEx message in the SysEx editing window of Cakewalk for Windows.

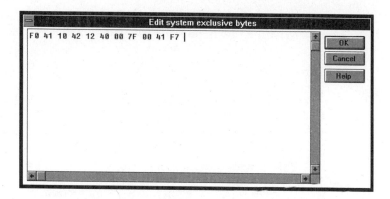

FIG. 21.7

A MIDI SysEx
message.

The 11-byte SysEx message shown in the figure instructs the system to reset the Roland GS-series synthesizers. The parts of this message are as follows:

■ F0 indicates that the following bytes constitute a SysEx message.

■ 41 is the hexadecimal code assigned to Roland Corporation. This number (which would be 65 in a decimal system) is part of the SysEx file's header.

■ 10, 42, and 12, also part of the header, identify the product as a synthesizer (10) of the General MIDI type (42) in the Sound Canvas line (12). These values are identical for the Roland SCC-1 adapter card and for the SC-55 and SC-155 Sound Canvas modules, but circuits in each MIDI device respond only to SysEx messages that match the device's assigned header code.

■ 40, 00, 7F, and 00 are the data bytes that cause the device to be reset to its initial state, restoring the factory settings that previous SysEx messages may have changed.

■ 41 is a check-sum byte used to verify that the SysEx data that the device received is identical to the data stored in your computer. SysEx check sums resemble the check sums that communications applications use to download files by modem.

■ F7 indicates the end of the SysEx message.

Bulk SysEx Dumps

All keyboard synthesizers and sound modules can transmit SysEx data that represents their current status. You select the type of data you want to transmit to your computer—for example, the editing parameters for a voice or group of voices, a program, or a performance—and then set your sequencer application or librarian to receive the data and press the Send button on your synthesizer. You store the data in a file on your hard disk so that you can re-create the setup later.

Audio adapter cards do not have Send buttons, so most of these cards are designed to recognize a special type of SysEx message called a SysEx Dump Request. The Dump Request message includes data that indicates the type of SysEx information desired. At the end of the message, the receiving device pauses before sending the requested data to a buffer in your computer. You save the data to a file for later reuse.

Cakewalk Professional for Windows includes a collection of Dump Request Macros (DRMs) for popular synthesizers. To send and receive SysEx data from your synthesizer or audio adapter card, follow these steps:

1. Choose **5** Sysx from Cakewalk's **W**indows menu.

2. Select an empty SysEx bank in the Sysx window, as shown in figure 21.8, and then click the Receive button. The Dump Request Macro dialog box appears.

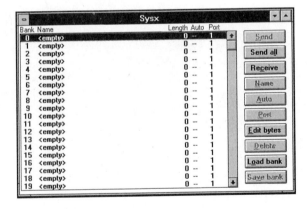

FIG. 21.8

Cakewalk's Sysx window.

3. Select the make and model of your synthesizer or audio adapter card in the Dump Request Macro list box, as shown in figure 21.9.

4. Click the OK button. Cakewalk sends the dump-request message to your synthesizer, and the resulting SysEx message transmitted by the synthesizer is stored in the SysEx bank you selected in step 2.

The version of Cakewalk Professional for Windows used in this example did not include DRMs for audio adapter cards that support SysEx or popular sound modules such as the Yamaha TX-81Z. You can create your own DRMs by adding them to the WINCAKE.INI file with Windows Notepad. DRMs for many additional MIDI devices are available for downloading from the Twelve Tone Systems library of the MIDI forum's MIDI Vendor A division (GO MIDIVENA).

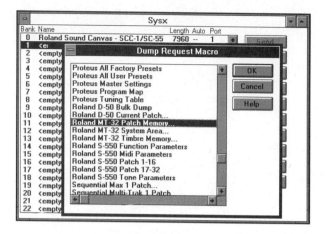

FIG. 21.9

Choosing a MIDI
SysEx dump-request
message in Cakewalk.

T I P

Although you can edit the SysEx data received via a dump from your sound card or synthesizer, you must also change the value the check-sum byte that precedes the F7 byte at the end of the file.

The procedure for calculating the check-sum byte varies by manufacturer and product; a few products do not use check sums. If you send the wrong check-sum value, the entire SysEx message is ignored, and you may receive an error message. Some manufacturers' SysEx documentation explains how to calculate the correct check sum.

Using RIFF Files

The Resource Interchange File Format (RIFF), developed by Microsoft and IBM, is the standard structure for all multimedia files intended for use with Windows. RIFF is a tagged format similar to the IFF structure developed by Electronic Arts and related to the TIFF (tagged image format) files used to store still graphic images. A tagged format file identifies individual types of data in the file by preceding the data with a short header called *tag*.

Microsoft's documentation for the Multimedia Development Kit (MDK) defines four types of RIFF files. An additional RIFF file format was added when Microsoft developed the Audio Video Interleaved format. The RIFF file formats are as follows:

- ■ *RAVI* (RIFF AVI) format is used by applications that support the Microsoft Audio Video Interleaved file format, designed to display full-motion video in a small window accompanied by an audio soundtrack. The AVI extension is used for these files, which because of their size usually are distributed on CD-ROMs. To play AVI files, you need the device driver MCIAVI.DRV.

■ *RDIB* (RIFF DIB) format stores Windows device-independent bit maps in RIFF format. The format supports the standard DIB formats (1, 4, 8, and 24 bytes per pixel) and compression by run-length encoding (RLE) to reduce the size of the files. (The DIB format and RLE encoding are discussed in Chapter 17, "Image Acquisition, Editing, Compression, and Interchange.")

■ *RMID* (RIFF MIDI) format adds RIFF header information to a Standard MIDI File. Windows also uses SMFs without the header. No sequencer applications store data in RMID format, but most can import RMI files.

■ *RMMP* (RIFF Multimedia Movie Player) formats use the extension MMM. These files are created by Macromedia's Director application on Apple Macintosh computers and then converted to RMMP format by Microsoft's CONVERT.EXE application (supplied with the MDK). To play MMM files, you need the Multimedia Movie Player (MMP.DLL) and the device driver MCIMMP.DRV, which are not included in Windows 3.1.

■ *WAVE* (RIFF waveaudio) format includes a header that describes the recording parameters of the waveform audio data that follows.

Device manufacturers and software publishers can develop their own RIFF file formats. Each such format is assigned a four-letter code (called a four-character code or FourCC) that identifies the type of data it contains. To ensure that the code for each type of RIFF file is unique, Microsoft provides a registration service (similar to that for manufacturer codes provided by the IMA) to assure the assignment of unique FourCCs. Firms that develop new RIFF formats provide the necessary Windows applications and MCI device drivers.

RIFF files are constructed from chunks of specific types of data. Each element of a RIFF file is contained in a chunk, starting with the Form Chunk that begins with RIFF and is followed by the type code for the file. (You can identify a RIFF file, if you have a question about its structure, by reading it with a Windows text-editing application; Notepad suffices if the file is less than 64K long.) The first four ASCII characters of the file read RIFF. Sound Blaster VOC files, for example, begin with Creative Voice File, but other types of waveform audio files have no readable header data. Other RIFF header chunks define copyright information, artist's name, dates, product names, and so on.

Data chunks follow the header chunks. Chunks containing different types of data can be intermingled in the file, providing that the type of data in each chunk is identified.

RMMP files have 17 different types of data chunks arranged in the sequence in which the data is required. Alternating chunks that contain different types of data is the principle of interleaving graphic images and sound in AVI files and of the data format of the CD-ROM XA standard. The advantage of interleaving the data is increased speed of access to different types of data that must be played in synchronization, because CD-ROM drives are notoriously slow in changing from one track to another.

As Windows multimedia matures and multimedia applications for Windows capture a larger share of the multimedia market, you can expect RIFF files to proliferate. Meanwhile, producers of software that uses pre-RIFF formats (for example, Autodesk's Animator products) provide DLLs and drivers that make DOS files act like RIFF files in Windows.

Chapter Summary

This chapter has provided a part of the technical background that you need when you create multimedia presentations or titles that involve MIDI music. This chapter describes the synchronization of MIDI sound with previously recorded data, both audio or video. Embedding waveform audio data in MIDI music files is shown as an example of an advanced synchronization technique that does not require special sound cards or other outboard devices. Entire books have been written on audio and video synchronization technology, and should be consulted if you need a full understanding of SMPTE, LANC, or RC sync. Sources of publications that cover advanced synchronization methods are listed in Appendix F.

The MIDI System Exclusive messages described in this chapter only scratch the surface of the capabilities of SysEx techniques that you can employ with sophisticated sound cards and extended MIDI devices. The explanation of the structure of RIFF files provided in this chapter demonstrates how interleaved sound and images are combined in a single file.

Chapter 22 introduces you to desktop video publishing, a new technology in which Windows multimedia will play a major role. Chapter 22 shows you how to create videotape productions with video applications, using approaches that originated in desktop publishing.

Desktop Video Production

D esktop video production (DTV) is in the same stage today that
desktop print publishing was in the late 1980s. Just as the laser
printer made desktop publishing (DTP) a reality, VGA-to-NTSC converters, camcorders, and remotely controllable VCRs are bringing DTV
capability to PC users. The similarity between DTP and DTV extends to
the terms used; you "print" DTV productions on tape.

Although PCs have achieved a substantial presence in the consumer
market, they still are less common in homes than television sets, VCRs,
and microwave ovens. Microsoft Corporation estimates that only 15
million of the 60 million or so PCs in use in North America have the VGA
displays and 80386SX or better CPU required for multimedia applications. Of these PCs, perhaps 10 percent are equipped with sound cards
or CD-ROM drives, and many do not have Windows installed. The
percentages will change in favor of multimedia-capable, Windows-
equipped PCs in the future, but you must deal with the equipment your
prospective audience has available now.

Following are a few reasons why DTV will rival DTP:

■ Industry sources report that 80 million Americans regularly use
videocassette recorders.

■ Four out of five U.S. households are believed to possess at least one
VCR.

■ Many observers believe that the number of VCR users exceeds that of regular readers of books, magazines, and newspapers combined.

■ Large-screen or projection television systems are becoming standard equipment in corporate and hotel conference rooms.

■ Market research conducted by Autodesk, Inc. shows that most computer owners also own a video camcorder.

To experiment with DTV, you need a VGA-to-NTSC adapter card (or one of the new video translators that plug into the output of your VGA display adapter) and a consumer-grade VCR. Video-in-a-window (VIW) capability is helpful but not necessary.

Creating a commercial-quality videotape from a computer-based multimedia production, however, calls for higher-quality equipment. You can obtain commercially acceptable results with the new breed of "prosumer" or semiprofessional video components, designed specifically for DTV and now beginning to appear in electronics stores. Prosumer devices add remotely controllable editing—a feature normally found only in professional-grade video equipment—to consumer-level products.

Understanding Desktop Video Productions

Desktop video production breathes new life into conventional slide-show and overhead-projector presentations. Adding appropriate background music and lively animation to a presentation, no matter what its subject, catches your audience's attention and maintains interest. You can package your DTV presentation with recorded narration and distribute multiple copies, or you can narrate the presentation in person. The basic principles of DTV outlined in this chapter apply in either case.

Packaged DTV productions lack one of the critical elements that ordinarily define a multimedia title: interactivity. Desktop video is a linear medium—that is, a presentation runs from beginning to end, and the user's only option is to rewind and replay portions of particular interest. Although you must give up interactivity with DTV, you gain the comfort factor of a medium that people understand and use regularly. The viewer need not make any effort to learn how to install and then use your presentation effectively, as is required for an interactive presentation on a CD-ROM. Another benefit of using DTV is that you are in complete control of the presentation.

Before DTV, producing a videotape was a major undertaking that involved a substantial budget. A simple 15-minute production created by a professional video organization using traditional video techniques might cost $15,000 to $30,000. Glossy videotapes with custom-designed graphics and special effects could cost $2,500 to $5,000 or more per minute. DTV can cut these costs by a factor of 5 or more. If you do most of the work yourself on your own computer, you can divide these costs by 10 or 20.

A few of the multimedia productions that you can create with low-cost DTV technology are as follows:

- *Corporate communications.* Image-oriented productions and introductions of new products, including interviews with the employees involved in developing those products, are better suited to video than to CD-ROM. You can produce videos for conferences and exhibitions in much less time when you do most or all of the production work in-house. Another benefit of in-house production is that you can maintain secrecy until the announcement date.

- *Product demonstrations and video brochures.* Some products, including heavy equipment, demand action shots to demonstrate their true capabilities. If one major feature of your product involves movement, video is the logical medium in which to depict that movement.

- *Real-estate sales aids.* Many potential buyers of expensive homes don't have time to visit all the homes listed by real-estate firms. A videotape of current offerings is the ideal way to present a specific group of homes to a client. You can use DeLorme Mapping's Street Atlas USA CD-ROM to add maps to the videotape; you can even personalize the videotape by adding the client's name.

- *Architectural and engineering presentations.* Architectural and engineering drawings created with AutoCAD and other computer-aided-design programs can be animated for videotape with applications such as Autodesk 3D Studio and Autoshade. A&E firms can create client presentations in-house, ensuring that the final product truly represents the firm's design concepts.

- *Broadcast advertising.* Most small firms that advertise on local television stations and on cable TV can't afford agency-produced commercials. DTV enables these firms to produce their own commercials and even to update agency-produced commercials.

- *Animated documentation.* Few people read thick software manuals, and even fewer use the extensive tutorials supplied with advanced computer applications. A short videotape can show purchasers how to use the product. The demonstration videotape included with Macromedia's Action! animation application is an example of video documentation at its best. A well-done video manual also can be used as a sales tool. Borland International, for example, sells DTV manuals for its programming-language applications.

■ *Litigation support.* Videotape has become an accepted method of presenting evidence in court and sometimes has a more profound effect on the jury than expert witnesses' opinions do. DTV can significantly reduce the cost of creating a videotape to establish damages in a tort case, for example.

■ *Conference proceedings.* Traditionally, papers presented at technical conferences also have been offered on audiotape. DTV extends this capability. A videotape can include still images of the graphics used by the speaker and show the speaker in a small window.

All the productions in the preceding list are multimedia presentations. Most of these productions are not suited to presentation on floppy disks or CD-ROMs, or would not be enhanced significantly by interactivity.

Related Topics
VGA-to-NTSC Adapter Cards, p. 527

Examining What You Need for DTV

The only additional pieces of equipment you need to experiment with desktop video are a VGA-to-NTSC adapter card or plug-in adapter (described in Chapter 19), a VCR, and a TV set, if you have an audio adapter card. You don't even need an audio adapter card if your VCR has audio-overdub capability; a microphone input enables you to create a soundtrack.

Figure 22.1 shows the connections for the basic DTV hardware components.

Although a video output card (VGA-to-NTSC) with genlock capability is more versatile, you can substitute the simple outboard VGA-NTSC adapter shown in dashed lines in the figure. These adapters are available at computer stores for about $250 to $350. (With the lower-cost versions, however, you may find that your TV set displays images with substantial amounts of flicker.) You don't have to open your computer or use a card slot for this adapter, which converts your VGA output to a video signal.

If you want to add animation and waveform audio or MIDI music to your graphics, you also need a Windows multimedia presentation manager like Macromedia Action! (see Chapter 18).

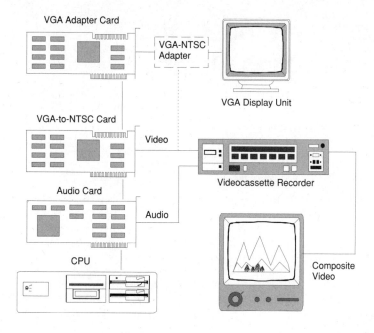

FIG. 22.1

Connections for basic
DTV hardware.

If you have a computer-based presentation and an audio adapter card
that enables you to play waveform audio narration or background music,
you're ready to create a test videotape. Follow these steps:

1. Plug the VGA-to-NTSC adapter card's output into the VCR's composite video input.

2. Plug the audio adapter card's output into the VCR's audio input.

3. Simultaneously start your presentation and start recording on
   the VCR.

4. Stop recording at the end of the presentation.

5. Play back the videotape.

The tape will not be commercial-quality; the recorded images may not
look the way you want an audience to see them, and you may need to
adjust the master volume control of your audio card's mixer to get the
sound level right. Still, you now have a videocassette of your presentation.

The rest of this chapter explains how to create a professional-quality
DTV production.

Examining Videotape Reproduction Quality

The pivotal element of DTV production is the videocassette recorder. When this book was published, the VHS format invented by Japan Victor Company (JVC) was 16 years old. VHS is firmly established as the premier videotape format, especially for mass-produced tapes such as movies and educational programs.

No matter what videotape format you use or how you acquire your images, the final product undoubtedly will be on standard VHS cassettes. You must design presentations and other types of multimedia productions that take into account the limitations of consumer-grade VHS videocassette recorders and ordinary TV receivers.

Related Topics
The Effect of Bandwidth on Video Quality, p. 514

Broadcast and Industrial Videotape Drives

The first videotape recorders for broadcast television were introduced in the 1950s by Ampex Corporation, a manufacturer of audiotape drives. These devices used two-inch-wide tape and had a rotating head that recorded each video field as one track that ran diagonally across the tape—a process called *helical scanning*. A control track synchronized the scanning of the video heads during playback. Audio was recorded in a conventional track at the edge of the tape. This technique accommodated the bandwidth of both video signals (4.5 MHz) and audio signals (20 kHz).

Figure 22.2 illustrates the tracks created by helical scanning.

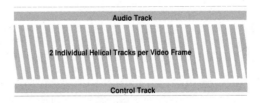

Audio Track

2 Individual Helical Tracks per Video Frame

Control Track

FIG. 22.2

Tracks recorded on magnetic tape by helical scanning.

Videotape recorders revolutionized the television industry by enabling broadcasters to record images photographed by multiple cameras on one reel of magnetic tape, eliminating the time required to combine sequences into a production. Like audiotapes, videotapes can be cut and spliced to eliminate mistakes. Videotape sounded the death knell for most live television productions, and TV programs lost much of their former spontaneity.

Early videotape recorders are analogous to the first mainframe computers, in that technology improved rapidly during the next 30 years. For example, the early reel-to-reel video recorders used wide tape on horizontally mounted reels (leading to the term "deck," which still is used to describe audiotape recorders). But recording heads later were miniaturized to accommodate lower-cost, 1-inch tape drives that used digital D-1 format, generating better-quality images (540 horizontal lines) than the original 2-inch-tape recorders. Then videocassette recorders that used 3/4-inch tape were developed for use in low-cost industrial productions. The 3/4-inch machines (typified by Sony's U-Matic series) correspond to today's high-powered minicomputers.

Videocassette Recorders

Most companies have at least one VCR-monitor combination, and almost all hotels and convention centers have meeting rooms equipped with VCRs and large-screen or projection-television equipment. A wide variety of equipment also is available from audiovisual rental firms.

VCRs differ widely in terms of image-reproduction quality. Table 22.1 compares the resolution (in horizontal lines) produced by broadcast, industrial, and consumer videotape and VCRs.

Table 22.1. Videotape Resolution.

Technology	Resolution	Recording medium
Broadcast (digital)	768	1-inch tape
Broadcast (analog)	500-600	1-inch tape
Industrial	400-500	3/4-inch cassette
Hi8 8mm Hi-band	450	8mm metal-film cassette
VHS-C and 8mm	350	8mm oxide-coated cassette
S-VHS	325	Quality 1/2-inch cassette
VHS	300	Economy 1/2-inch cassette

VHS Videocassette Recorders

Early consumer VCRs are the video equivalent of the first 8086-based IBM PCs, with their grainy CGA graphic monitors. Conventional 1/2-inch VCRs were designed to reproduce video images at broadcast-quality resolution. Such devices need a luminance bandwidth (the range of frequencies required to transmit a video signal) of only about 4.5 MHz. Consumer-grade VCRs are acceptable for amateur recordings, but not for creating commercial videotape productions, because their signal quality is inadequate for creating master tapes.

Even moderately priced consumer VCRs now provide stereo audio-recording capability by dividing the linear audio track into left and right channels. Most stereo decks also decode the MTS signals used to create TV stereo sound and SAP (second audio program) multilingual audio broadcasts. If you are recording stereo tracks, check the sound on a monaural VCR and TV set before you finalize the audio portion of your tape. Some VCRs can combine the stereo signals to dub a conventional monaural audio track; others cannot.

T   I   P   Conventional VCRs use a fixed head to erase previously recorded materials, so a short signal (between the erase head and the record head) is not fully erased when new video is recorded over old. VCRs with flying erase heads incorporate the erase head in the rotating-head assembly to eliminate this problem. Make sure that the VCR you use as an editing deck has flying erase heads.

Super-Video Devices

Conventional video devices combine the luminance (brightness, luma, or Y) and chrominance (color, chroma, or C) components of a television image into a composite video signal. Video devices with Super-video (S-video) capability send the luminance and chrominance data as two separate signals through a four-pin mini-DIN (circular) connector. Separating the two signals improves image quality by reducing the flicker and color blur that result from interference between the two components of a composite color video signal (described earlier in this chapter).

Most high-quality television sets and videocassette recorders (S-VHS, VHS-C, and Hi8 formats) provide S-video capability. If you are purchasing video equipment for multimedia applications, S-video capability is mandatory because S-video helps maintain the image quality of your master tape.

Price differences between conventional and S-VHS devices, dictated by marketing policies instead of manufacturing costs, have restrained S-VHS acceptance. S-video capability is available in a small minority of the VCRs in current use. JVC and Panasonic now offer S-VHS decks at lower prices, however, and other manufacturers are expected to follow suit.

VHS-HQ

VHS videocassette recorders, which record high-fidelity stereo audio tracks next to the video information on helical tracks, are labeled VHS-HQ (high-quality).

Figure 22.3 shows the recording pattern on a standard 1/2-inch VHS cassette.

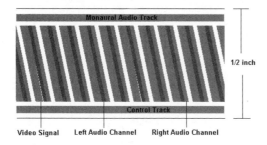

FIG. 22.3

VHS-HQ helically recorded stereo audio tracks.

You can play standard VHS cassettes on VHS-HQ decks, but conventional VHS recorders cannot play VHS-HQ tapes.

Camcorders and 8mm Videotape

Recording live video material formerly required a separate camera and recorder (and a substantial amount of electrical power to run both devices). Camcorders, originally developed for TV journalism, now are available as consumer-grade devices at prices starting at around $500.

Conventional 1/2-inch videocassettes were considered to be too large to make camcorders practical for hand-held shooting by consumers. Today, however, miniaturization of magnetic recording heads and improvement in magnetic storage media mean that camcorders can store video images on smaller cassettes with narrower tape.

Camcorders are available in two formats: Compact VHS or VHS-C format, a scaled-down version of conventional VHS technology; and the 8mm format pioneered by Sony Corporation. The advantage of using VHS-C is that you can play these tapes back on standard VHS decks by using an adapter device. The 8mm format, however, appears to be more popular, capturing about 85 percent of the current camcorder market. You must either purchase an 8mm deck or play back the tapes by plugging the video output of the 8mm camcorder into video input of your TV set.

The 8mm devices record luminance information as an FM signal rather than use the AM signals of broadcasting and standard VHS. Because interchannel separation is not required for recording, these camcorders shift the chroma and audio signals below the frequencies used in broadcasting.

Figure 22.4 shows the frequencies allocated to video and audio signals in conventional 8-mm format.

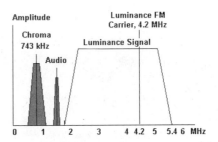

FIG. 22.4

The frequency allocations for conventional 8mm camcorders and VCRs.

VHS-C and 8-mm camcorders and VCRs can record high-fidelity stereo audio on two separate tracks, although not all camcorders have stereo microphone inputs. Most camcorders have a built-in microphone next to the lens.

NOTE Camcorders are lightweight devices. If you plan to shoot commercial-quality footage with a camcorder, you must stabilize the device by using a sturdy tripod equipped with a damped panning head. You can purchase a consumer version of Cinema Products' Steadicam JR, a stabilizing device used for motion-picture and professional television cameras.

Hi8

Sony Corporation took 8mm, S-video, and VHS-HQ technology one step further with Hi8 format (short for high-bandwidth 8mm). Hi8 increases the luminance signal's bandwidth by about 0.8 MHz, as you can see by comparing figures 22.4 and 22.5.

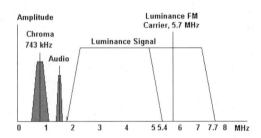

The luminance frequency allocation for Hi8 camcorders and VCRs.

Because the resolution of a television image increases with increased luminance bandwidth, the Hi8 format can produce horizontal resolution of 400 lines by using special high-output tape. Hi8 tape is coated with evaporated metal instead of the metallic (usually a mixture of iron, cobalt, and nickel or chromium) oxide particles that coat standard audiotapes and videotapes.

Evaporated-metal (also called "sputtered") film is used in high-capacity, 3.5-inch-and-smaller hard disk drives and for creating CD-ROM production masters (described in Chapter 20). Metallic tape largely eliminates dropout—the loss of portions of images when metallic oxide particles are dislodged during the recording and editing of conventional 8-mm tapes.

Figure 22.6 shows the recording pattern on a Hi8 tape.

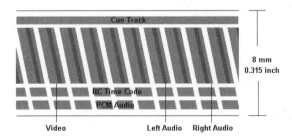

The recording pattern used on Hi8 8-mm format tape.

Hi8 format provides an additional pair of tracks on which you can record stereo digital audio signals in pulse-code-modulated (PCM) format, similar to the format used for recording waveform audio files. (You don't record PCM tracks during camcorder shooting, however; you add them later in the production process.) Hi8 also adds a control track that identifies a frame in Sony's proprietary rewritable consumer (RC) time code, which translates to hours:minutes:seconds:frames (similar to MIDI and SMPTE time codes). The cue track provides tape-location information for high-speed searching.

Hi8 camcorders and remotely controllable VCRs are priced in the $2,000 range, compared with $6,000 or more for their industrial-grade counterparts. As DTV expands the market for Hi8 video equipment, you can expect prices to fall to slightly below $1,000.

Editing Videotape

Television production techniques determine how video presentations are created. The three phases of TV production are as follows:

- *Preproduction* involves creating an outline of the presentation and specifying graphic and audio elements. If you have an existing computer-based presentation, much of the preproduction work already is done.

- *Production* consists of obtaining images, preparing or modifying graphics, and recording narration. The images may be still or animated graphics stored on your hard disk, camcorder footage on Hi8 cassettes, and stock video clips in S-VHS format. Sound may have been recorded during a camcorder shooting session or recorded later on an audio cassette.

- *Postproduction* involves creating the master videotape from which duplicate tapes will be made (usually by a videotape-duplication service). You add background music to your presentation at this point.

The process of creating the master videotape is called *editing*, a term that originated in the motion-picture industry. Although editing is one of the last steps in the production process, this chapter describes it first because the editing techniques you use for DTV determine how you will carry out the preproduction and production phases.

Your guiding principle in postproduction editing is to minimize the number of *generations* between your original videotape sources and the master tape. Each time you rerecord video and audio material, you create a new generation, and the quality of the images and sound deteriorates, even when you are using the highest-quality equipment. Duplicated videotapes are, at best, second-generation versions of computer-based images (master, duplicate) and third-generation versions of videotape footage (original, master, duplicate).

> Buy the highest-quality tape you can find that is compatible with your conventional VHS videocassette recorder, especially if you plan to present your video production repeatedly from the master tape. Lower-cost metallic-oxide tapes tend to shed particles, which create interference (usually in the form of streaks) and build up on the recording and reproduction heads. Make sure that you use a head-cleaning kit regularly (every 10 to 20 hours of use) to prevent blurred and jagged effects caused by foreign substances stuck to the heads.
>
> **T I P**

Append and Insert Editing

The simplest form of video editing is *append* (or assemble) *editing*. Append editing enables you to create the master edit tape on the destination VCR by recording scenes from a source VCR or camcorder in sequence. You can perform append edits by connecting the source and destination VCRs' pause controls to a Control-S cable.

To perform an append edit, follow these steps:

1. Insert the source videotape into the source VCR and position the tape at the beginning of the desired scene.

2. Press Play and then press Pause.

3. Press the destination VCR's Record button. The VCR does not begin recording, however; when you paused the source VCR, you also paused the destination VCR through the Control-S cable.

4. To start both VCRs simultaneously, press the source VCR's Pause button again.

5. When the end of the scene appears, press the source VCR's Pause button to stop playback and recording.

6. Disable Record mode on the destination VCR so that you do not record while you are searching for the next segment on the source videotape or inserting the next source videotape.

7. Repeat steps 1 through 6 for each video sequence.

The exact sequence of steps depends on the controls of your source and destination VCRs. The soundtrack accompanying the scenes you record can come from the source VCR, your computer, or an audiotape recorder (or all three sources, if you have an audio mixer).

Higher-priced consumer VCRs and dedicated edit controllers are designed for *insert editing*, in which you replace video footage with footage of equal length. Accurate insert editing requires a destination with a specially wired remote control connector so that you can set the master edit tape to the proper position for the edit.

You can perform the following types of insert edits:

- *Video insert* substitutes a new video segment for an existing one on the edit tape without affecting the existing soundtrack.

- *Audio insert* substitutes a new audio segment for an existing one.

- *Audio/Video (A/V) insert* substitutes new video and audio segments for the existing ones.

If you use a conventional VHS-C or 8mm camcorder or a VCR with Control-L, you can perform insert editing with 10- to 15-frame accuracy (1/3 to 1/2 second of video). VISCA control reduces frame uncertainty (how close you can set the position of the tape to the desired frame) to fewer than 3 or 4 frames. Some users have reported one-frame uncertainty with computer-controlled VISCA insert editing.

Edit Decision Lists

The types of video editing described in this chapter are based on information from an edit decision list (EDL) that orchestrates the editing process. You can prepare an edit decision list on paper or with a spreadsheet application.

An EDL contains the following information for each segment of the production:

- The sequence of the video scene or segment (called an *edit event*) in the final production

- The name or a brief description of the edit event

- The type of edit (append, video insert, audio insert, and so on)

- The type of transitions between edit events (cut, fade, dissolve, and so on)

■ The start (edit in) and stop (edit out) times of the edit event, expressed in hours:minutes:seconds:frames format if you are using a remote-control protocol (otherwise, you must depend on the footage counter, which is inaccurate)

■ The edit in and edit out times of the edit master for insert editing (if your equipment can handle insert editing)

Windows applications that create edit decision lists range from relatively simple text-based applications to sophisticated systems such as PalTex International's EDDI ProVision Editor, shown in figure 22.7.

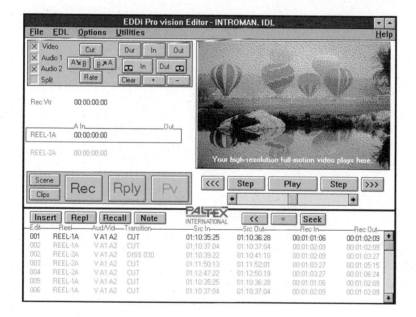

FIG. 22.7

Creating an edit decision list with EDDI ProVision.

A-B roll editing requires a combination of adapter cards and external devices to control the VCRs involved. In most cases, Windows video editors are published by manufacturers that also produce video-display and VCR-control hardware. The PalTex applications described in this chapter, for example, are designed around the company's EDDI hardware for PC video editing.

A-B Roll Editing

The traditional description of A-B roll editing is the use of two VCRs in playback mode whose video outputs are alternately switched to the input of a third VCR (called the edit deck) used for recording the master edit tape. A-B roll editing differs from append and insert editing because the edit out of one playback VCR can overlap the other playback VCR's edit in. This editing technique enables you to use sophisticated effects such as laps, dissolves, and wipes.

All three VCRs must be equipped with Control-L or VISCA, or an equivalent bidirectional control interface.

Dedicated edit controllers, which can be programmed to locate and play portions of the tapes on the two playback VCRs, are commonly used in industrial editing. When you use DTV techniques, however, your computer takes the place of the edit controller and one playback VCRs. You still will be performing A-B editing, although the DTV technique might better be called A-C.

If your camcorder has remote-control capabilities, you can use it as a playback device for editing, as shown in figure 22.8.

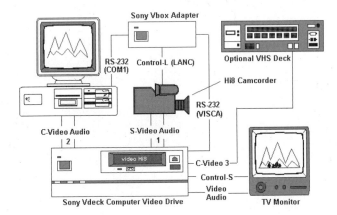

FIG. 22.8

A-B editing with computer and camcorder video and audio inputs.

Composite NTSC video signals are called C-video in the figure. The Sony Vbox adapter is used to convert the serial (RS-232-C) output of your computer's COM port to the Control-L signals that most camcorders require.

Sony V-series Hi8 computer-controlled video components are used as examples in figure 22.8. V-series video devices are available through distributors of Sony's industrial video products. Other video devices can be substituted, provided that both the editing VCR and the camcorder or playback VCR have the following capabilities:

■ Remote control of basic start, stop, pause, continue, fast-forward, and rewind functions.

■ Remote positioning of the tape to an accuracy of at least 3 to 5 frames. This capability requires that a frame-accurate time code be written to the tapes. Professional editing decks are *frame-accurate*— that is, you can position the tape on any specified frame.

■ At least two individual video inputs on the edit VCR (preferably both composite and S-video), switchable by remote control.

■ Fade for each live video input in the edit VCR to avoid abrupt transitions between contrasting image types. Additional special effects, such as dissolves and wipes, are desirable.

■ Remotely controllable audio dubbing capability in the edit VCR. The capability to mix live recorded sound effects (such as traffic noise) with music and narration is desirable. (Alternatively, you can use your audio adapter card for mixing.)

Because the Sony Vdeck enables you to mix one S-video signal and two composite video signals, figure 22.8 shows an optional composite video input from a VHS VCR that provides A-B-C editing capability. (You might use the VCR to insert stock video images unavailable in Hi8 format. You can purchase almost any video image you can imagine from stock-video firms.)

Full-roll editing requires that the source VCR have Control-L, VISCA, or another remote-control protocol of equivalent accuracy.

In figure 22.8, the S-video output of the Hi8 camcorder is connected to the Vdeck's S-video input. You can control the images you create on your computer to minimize color buzz and other problems caused by chroma intermodulation distortion with composite video, so the computer's output can be routed to the first composite input. Live video shooting with a camcorder does not offer this flexibility.

In mid-1992, the cost of a remotely controllable editing VCR and camcorder, an interface for computer control of the camcorder, and a VHS-to-NTSC adapter card ranged from $4,000 to $4,500. The cost (which does not include the optional VHS VCR or an audiotape recorder) compares with that of the first laser printers for the Macintosh and PC.

Nonlinear Editing

Nonlinear editing describes computer-controlled creation of video productions in which video segments, still and animated graphics, narration, and background music are represented by icons. Each icon is treated as an object that includes all the necessary information about the sound or image it represents.

A typical icon could represent any of the following objects:

- A video object, including the name of the videotape containing the segment, the beginning and ending points of the segment (expressed as times from the start of the tape), and any special transitions or effects to be used.

- A graphic image, including the file name, hard disk directory location, and information about the size of the image, if it is to be scaled. Both video and graphic icons may appear as small-scale versions of the actual images.

- Waveform audio, including the file name, sound level, duration, loops for repetition, and timed fades, as required.

- MIDI background music, including volume, start point, end point, loops, and fades by time (MIDI or SMPTE time code) or measure/beat (Song Position Pointer).

After you create the icons with the EDDI application, you use the mouse to drag them to positions on the screen that represent their playing time in the final presentation. You can double-click an icon and change any of its properties, such as beginning and ending points or sound levels. In this respect, the icons behave much like Sound Recorder OLE objects embedded in the compound documents (discussed in Chapter 8).

Nonlinear editing systems use database techniques to catalog images. Figure 22.9 shows a window from a video-clip database application, PalTex International's ClipLog, a component of the firm's Vision video overlay option for its EDDI application.

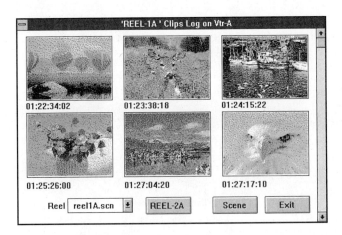

FIG. 22.9

A ClipLog window for storing data on video segments.

Figure 22.10 shows a window from PalTex's SceneLog application, which creates the bit-mapped still images of clips that appear in figure 22.9.

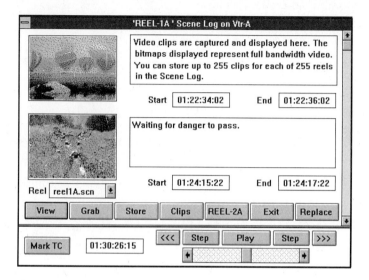

FIG. 22.10

Creating a video clip database entry with starting and ending times.

You specify the beginning and ending times of each clip and then click the Grab button to capture a bit-mapped sample frame. You then complete the entry by adding text that describes the clip.

After you catalog the video clips you need for your presentation, the clips become the equivalent of video objects that you can insert into your edit decision list.

Controlling VCRs with Your Computer

If you own a camcorder and a remotely controllable VCR, you can use your PC to edit your camcorder's videotapes if the camcorder has a remote-control connector. This procedure requires a certain amount of ingenuity and enthusiasm, but as the DTV industry matures, the process undoubtedly will become simplified and editing videotapes on PCs will become as common as creating DTP publications.

Unfortunately, no DTV standards have achieved the dominance that Hewlett-Packard's Printer Control Language (PCL) and Adobe's PostScript enjoy in the DTP field. Competitors in the advanced-amateur and low-end industrial-quality video market have created the video remote-control protocols.

A protocol defines a combination of cabling and electronic signals and control functions that the hardware can perform. Most of the earlier-remote control protocols were designed for consumer VHS decks. When the 8mm format was introduced, camcorder and VCR manufacturers adopted a more advanced remote-control protocol, Control-L, for these products. Recently, Sony Corporation introduced the VISCA protocol, an extension of Control-L for computer control of Hi8 tape decks and camcorders.

Remote-Control Protocols for VCRs and Laserdisc Drives

The most common remote-control protocols for consumer and prosumer video equipment appear in ascending order of capability in the following list:

- *Synchro-edit* or remote pause control enables you to stop and start two VCRs alternately by connecting them with a two-wire cable. This rudimentary control method usually does not compensate for the time required to engage and start the tape.

- *Infrared remote-control simulators* incorporate the equivalent of a universal hand-held wireless remote control that activates a VCR's play, record, fast-forward, and rewind functions. Most of these controllers connect to one of the serial ports of your computer.

- *Control-S* was one of the first wired remote-control protocols for 8mm camcorders and VCRs. This protocol duplicates the operation of an infrared remote-control device by using one-way communication over a cable. Control-S now is used primarily for controlling television monitors, not VCRs.

- *Control-L* or LANC (Local Application Numerical Control) is an improvement over Control-S that provides two-way communication among camcorders, VCRs, and edit-controlling devices (such as your computer). Control-L can send tape-position information back to the edit controller.

Other proprietary protocols, such as Panasonic's five-pin system for its S-VHS decks and the RS-232-C serial protocol for NEC's PC VCR, provide Control-L capabilities.

■ *VISCA* is a new protocol developed by Sony Corporation for its Hi8 camcorders and VCRs. VISCA, which was designed specifically for computer control of videotape devices, plugs into a RS-232-C serial (COM) port on your computer. You can connect up to seven different devices in a daisy-chain configuration similar to that used for MIDI equipment. VISCA offers all the features of Control-L and a few new functions of its own (described later in this chapter).

If you want to use your existing video equipment for any purpose other than experimentation, you need at least the equivalent of Control-L capability in your playback and edit VCRs.

VISCA Products

Sony Video System Control Architecture (VISCA) was designed for computers, rather than dedicated edit controllers. Although Sony offered only one video product that incorporated a VISCA interface when this book was being written, other products are sure to follow. Whether other manufacturers replace their Control-L connectors with VISCA will depend on the new protocol's acceptance in the commercial video market. The VISCA control protocol and two of the first products that use it are described in the following sections.

VISCA Serial Protocol

VISCA protocol uses the standard serial I/O connector of one of your computer's COM ports (RS-232-C). The standard VISCA cable is an eight-pin mini-DIN connector similar to that used for the serial ports of Apple Macintosh computers. You can use one COM port connection to install up to seven VISCA-compatible devices in a VISCA-Out to VISCA-In series.

The daisy-chain connection is similar to that used for MIDI devices, except that no equivalent to the MIDI THRU port exists. You don't need an adapter card to use VISCA-controlled products, but you do need an 8-pin male DIN to female DB-9 (Sony SMF-533 for the AT 9-pin serial port) or DB-25 (Sony SMF-534 for the standard 25-pin serial port) cable with cross-connections.

Cross-connected serial cables are similar to the null-modem cables used to connect two computers through their COM ports. The receive signal on one end of the cable is connected to the transmit signal on the other, and vice versa. You can purchase these cables from Sony dealers or from firms such as Cables-to-Go (see Appendix F).

Figure 22.11 shows the connections for a typical VISCA setup.

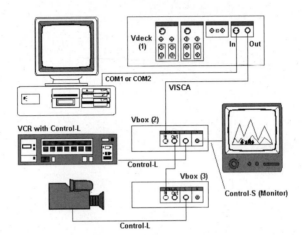

FIG. 22.11

Typical control connections for Sony VISCA and other video components.

Each VISCA device in the chain carries an automatically assigned address ranging from 1 to 7 (the computer is considered to be address 0). VISCA messages are similar to MIDI messages, preceded by a destination (channel) address.

Unlike MIDI, which requires you to set channel addresses on chained devices by pushing buttons, a software command (similar to a MIDI SysEx message) broadcasts addresses to all VISCA. The VISCA protocol implements the two-way Control-L command set for VCRs and video cameras and the one-way Control-S command sets for VCRs, monitors, audio-video selectors, and projectors.

Vdeck Hi8 VCR

The Sony VCD-1000 Vdeck is the first videocassette recorder to implement the VISCA command set. The Vdeck can be remotely controlled to select one of three different video signals (one S-video and 2 NTSC) and two separate audio sources. A microphone connector is included so that you can add narration to a video presentation, if you choose not to use waveform files for the audio track. The Hi8 format provides up to 400 lines of horizontal resolution. The Vdeck also plays conventional 8 mm videocassettes. Figure 22.12 shows the Vdeck.

FIG. 22.12

The Sony VCD-1000 Vdeck Hi8 VCR for VISCA computer control. (*Courtesy of Sony Corporation*)

Sony chose to add the Rewritable Consumer (RC) format, which enables you to search for a specific video frame with approximately two-frame accuracy. An advantage of the RC code is that the Vdeck can read RC time code in fast-forward or rewind mode, so you don't have to switch to playback to locate frames. This feature makes the editing process considerably faster with a Vdeck than with prosumer decks that use the Control-L time code. The hours:minutes:seconds:frames format of RC time code is compatible with SMPTE's time-code format. Devices available from firms such as Future Vision synthesize SMPTE time-code signals from Sony RC time code to synchronize MIDI synthesizers with Vdecks and other VISCA devices.

At the time this book was written, Sony was developing a driver for VISCA devices in conjunction with the Windows media-control interface. Other manufacturers already offer drivers that enable you to use VISCA protocol with their DTV applications.

Vbox Video-Control Interface

If you decide to use the VISCA protocol and if you own remotely controllable video equipment that uses the Control-S or Control-L protocols, you need a Sony Vbox to translate the VISCA instructions to instructions that your other equipment can understand (see fig. 22.13). Although Sony's Hi8 camcorders and VCRs ultimately will incorporate VISCA connectors, the Vdeck was the only VISCA-equipped video peripheral available when this book was written. Fortunately, the Vbox is moderately priced, at least compared with semiprofessional video gear, so the cost of protocol conversion is not excessive.

FIG. 22.13

Sony's Vbox controller for converting VISCA to Control-S and Control-L. *(Courtesy of Sony Corporation)*

Other Computer-Driven Video-Control Devices

An alternative to VISCA devices is an external edit controller that connects to your computer's RS-232-C COM port and supplies the necessary RS-422 control signals in Control-L or Panasonic five-pin protocol. An example is the Future Video EditLink 2000-DT, which is used with the Matrox Personal Producer DTV application. The Future Video EditLink 2200/TCG can read and write SMPTE time code on the audio channels of VCRs and camcorders with stereo audio tracks and generates SMPTE signals from RC time-code tracks or from linear tape counters.

A-B edit controllers also are available on PC adapter cards. In addition to an edit controller, you need video switching capability unless you are satisfied with simple cuts between segments. Video switchers are available as stand-alone devices or as PC adapter cards. PalTex International, for example, produces a seven-input, two-output switcher that incorporates a generator for creating leaders and fade-to-black transitions. You can add an eight-channel audio mixer to the switcher card as a daughterboard.

Some video adapter cards, such as the Matrox Illuminator-16, have self-contained A-B video source switching with slide, wipe, push, and fade transitions (among others), eliminating the need for a separate video switcher if two source-video inputs are sufficient.

Generating Special Video Effects

No discussion of desktop video would be complete without at least a brief discussion of New Tek's Video Toaster. The Video Toaster is a Commodore Amiga computer modified to create a video workstation. The Video Toaster includes a four-input video-source switcher, a frame grabber, and genlock output. The workstation includes 3-D animation and modeling applications and a character generator for titles.

New Tek expects to introduce a Video Toaster adapter card for the PC in 1993. This card set will enable you to control all Video Toaster functions from within a Windows application.

The Video Toaster workstation, which includes the Amiga computer but not the PC adapter card, sells for $4,595. You also need a time-base corrector if your playback VCR doesn't have one. If you have a Video Toaster workstation, you don't need a video-capture, live-motion-video, or VGA-to-NTSC card in your PC; these cards are included in the workstation. According to industry sources, the Video Toaster performs the same functions with similar quality to studio equipment that costs $60,000 or more.

In mid-1992, PalTex International introduced a PC adapter card that can control the Video Toaster's video switching and digital video effects from within the EDDI application running under Windows. The painting and character-generation functions of the Video Toaster cannot be controlled with your PC by the PalTex adapter card, however.

You can obtain a demonstration tape of the Video Toaster from New Tek (see Appendix F).

Creating a DTV Production

Video production traditionally is a team effort involving writers, artists, and camera operators. If you have a flair for writing and graphic design and the technical savvy to make the required connections between the video components and your computer, you can create a DTV production by yourself. After you create the video and audio and perform the off-line (rough) edit, you can give a copy of that edit (and your edit decision list) to a video service bureau, which will use professional-grade equipment to perform the on-line (final) edit.

Figure 22.14 shows the activities involved in creating a 10- to 15-minute DTV production. The diagram is derived from *Desk Video-Video,* a commercial videotape produced by Jon Leland of Communication Bridges to demonstrate the capabilities of DTV.

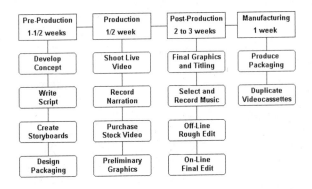

FIG. 22.14

The tasks involved in creating a 10- to 15-minute DTV production.

You can produce a short DTV production in five to six weeks, even if you do most of the work yourself. The first one or two presentations you create usually take longer than six weeks, however, because you still will be learning the procedure.

> **CAUTION:** Most television broadcasts are copyrighted. You cannot reproduce them, either as full-motion or still images, for distribution without the written permission of the copyright owner. The same restriction applies to videotapes of motion pictures. Some stock video images on videotapes or laserdiscs are copyrighted, but you can obtain a license to use all or limited portions of those images in your productions.

Video Storyboards

A storyboard consists of a series of sketches and notes that define each segment of a production. A segment is one still image or video scene, together with narration, that conveys one idea or point to the audience. For example, a 15-second television commercial might consist of the following 2- to 3-second segments:

- An opening that attracts attention

- An explanation of why you need the product

- A description of the product

- A closing that tells you where you can purchase the product

A storyboard for a commercial might look like figure 22.15.

Intro, 2 seconds   Fade to birthday, 2 seconds   Cut to XYZ-30, 3 seconds

Pick up your own
XYZ-30 at -
(Cooperating Dealers)

Cut to viewfinder, 3 secs.   Fade to TV image, 3 secs.

FIG. 22.15

A storyboard for a 15-second commercial.

Information about narration, background music, and special effects usually accompanies each image in a storyboard. When you create a storyboard on a computer instead of on paper, you can insert new or different segments.

> You can use a multimedia presentation application such as Macromedia Action! to create timed storyboards for your video presentation. Create rough graphics or use stock clips with simple text for the storyboard, and make the graphics or clip objects in the application's script. Then you can add the on-screen time of each graphic or clip and preview the off-line edit of your presentation.

T I P

Live-Video Titling

Titling requires a video output adapter that can synchronize the VGA signals containing the title text with the NTSC video signal from a playback VCR. Most commercial DTV applications include overlay and chroma-key titling capability; some applications, including Matrox Personal Producer Titler, require a specific type of genlocking video output adapter card.

Titling applications usually provide least-roll (vertical) and crawl (horizontal) movement of text in a variety of typefaces, color gradient (fill), drop shadows, and outlines of various thicknesses. You can have the titles appear over a solid-color background or overlay them on live video.

Unless you use live titling—adding title graphics to the images during on-line editing—you must add a new generation to titled video segments. The added generation is created when you combine your source video with the title graphics on a new segment inserted into your master tape. You do not want to take the risk of titling your source video, because you cannot correct the source video if you make a mistake.

You may want to hire a video service bureau to do your titling during on-line editing. Make sure that you supply your titling graphics on floppy disk in a format that the service bureau's computers can read. Many video-editing firms use Apple Macintosh computers, and although newer Macs can read 3 1/2-inch DOS floppy disks, a particular format may be required.

Most Macintosh applications can read files stored as color TIF images and in the Graphic Interchange format (GIF) that CompuServe uses. If you use vector-based images created by a drawing or illustration application, you may have to convert the images to TIF or GIF bit maps.

Off-Line and On-Line Editing

Even if you don't have prosumer or professional-level video recording equipment, you can prepare an off-line edit of your presentation and then hire a video editing service to perform the final on-line edit. You can save much of the cost of producing a professional-appearing video presentation by producing the graphics, the narration, and the edit decision list yourself.

Whether or not you intend to perform your own on-line edits, you should back up your original videotape and use the backup tape for the off-line edits. This procedure prevents deterioration of the original tape from repeated replays and (especially) pauses.

You supply the original video footage, narration tapes or sound files, and still graphics to the video service bureau. Most service bureaus offer narration services, so you might want to have the bureau dub the final audio track. Supplying an off-line-edited video minimizes the amount of time you and the service bureau spend coordinating the production and doing retakes.

If you are using background music created as MIDI files, don't count on video service bureaus to have the same audio card or outboard synthesizer setup that you use. Many editing services use Macintoshes and may not be able to use your waveform audio files or duplicate the voices used in your sound production. In such a case, you need to record the music on audiotape. (You can rent a high-quality reel-to-reel or cassette tape recorder from an audiovisual-equipment rental company.) Make sure that your service bureau can reproduce the audio format you choose for your recording.

T I P

Presentation Graphics for DTV

Still graphics for display on television sets and projectors must be large and simple. Television viewers do not have the benefit of the resolution of a 35-mm slide or an 8 1/2-by-11-inch transparency displayed by a projector. Another problem is that unlike interactive multimedia presentations created from still graphics and animation, video presentations require continuous playback. Television images often break up or streak when consumer-grade and even prosumer VCRs are paused.

Some guidelines for creating and editing graphics follow. These points are especially important for graphs and charts that contain numerical information, such as those used in marketing and financial presentations.

- Minimize the amount of text in images, substituting narration as required.

- The minimum type size should be 36 points (preferably 48 or 60 points).

- Use bold sans-serif typefaces, such as Helvetica and Ariel, rather than serif typefaces that incorporate thin lines in the characters.

- If you are using line art and the lines are less than 3 points wide, increase their thickness to about 6 points. You may have to reduce the detail in images and to refine the graphics to balance the heavier lines.

- Use bar and pie charts to display numerical information whenever possible. Line charts should use solid colors to represent the areas below lines. Most spreadsheet and presentation packages provide these chart types.

- Avoid bright, highly saturated colors in your images to avoid color buzz. If your application supports hue-saturation-luminance (HSL) palettes, do not exceed 75 percent or 80 percent saturation.

- Minimize the use of black areas in your graphics, which appear as holes in your television image. You can use black outlines for emphasis, but 70 percent to 80 percent gray is a better choice.

- Alter the width-to-height ratio of graphics, to the extent possible, to correspond to the 1.56 aspect ratio of commercial television or to suit the overscan capabilities of your NTSC-to-VGA adapter card.

- If your NTSC-to-VGA adapter card has overscan capability, provide a 1-inch margin at the top and bottom of the content (not background fill) of your image. Overscanning enables you to create an image that fills the television screen horizontally, with portions of the top and bottom of the image being cut off.

- Adjust the on-screen time of each image in proportion to the significance and quantity of the information it contains. Longer viewing times are required for images that introduce new subjects. Don't depend on the viewer to pause the presentation or to rewind and replay segments on complex subjects.

T I P When you are editing graphics for videotape, keep the video monitor in operation while you are working on the project. Glancing at the monitor occasionally while you are creating a still graphic image or performing off-line editing can save you many retakes.

DTV Applications for Windows

Video display capability has only recently become available for Windows, so few full-featured DTV applications were available when this book was written. Self-contained DTV applications for Windows (created by adapter-card manufacturers as sales aids for their hardware) and general-purpose applications that accommodate a variety of adapter cards and external video devices are expected to gain mainstream status in the mid-1990s. Windows NT, with its 32-bit architecture and multi-tasking capabilities will make the next generation of Windows DTV applications faster and even more versatile.

Personal Producer

Matrox Personal Producer is one of the first contenders for mainstream-DTV-application status. Aside from its capabilities, Personal Producer's principal advantage is that it requires only one adapter-card slot for the Illuminator-16 board that it uses.

The Illuminator-16, which provides video display and video output capabilities, attaches to the feature connector of your VGA adapter. To manipulate one or two VCR source decks and the destination VCR that records your master, you need a video edit controller (either a stand-alone device or an internal adapter card).

Matrox Personal Producer uses icons in a time-line format similar to that used by multimedia presentation applications. Video clips, waveform audio, MIDI music, and graphics (including titles) are displayed on separate time lines. A-B transitions such as fades, slides, and wipes are available, and you can make an A-B transition between two segments on one VCR. Digital video effects such as solarization, mosaic, and chroma keying also are included.

Another advantage of Matrox's approach to DTV production is the integration of video-adapter-card hardware and software in a complete package. Until video display and genlock cards take their place beside VGA and printer adapters as standard computer equipment and industry-wide standards are in place, integrated hardware-software DTV packages are the safest (and often the least expensive) approach.

MediaOrganizer

Multimedia presentations that incorporate video contain many other types of media, such as waveform audio and MIDI sound, bit-mapped images, vector-based drawings, and animation files. Video sources include 8- and 12-inch laserdiscs and the new 5 -1/4-inch compact laserdiscs. Keeping track of the locations of the latest versions of all of the sources for a multimedia production can be a major administrative problem, especially if many of the files are located on network file servers. As you produce more DTV presentations, finding an image or video clip that you recall using a year ago can be a daunting task.

Chapter 16 introduced Lenel Systems International, Inc.'s MpcOrganizer application. The firm's full-featured product, MediaOrganizer, adds device control and OLE server capability to MpcOrganizer. Both products use an object-oriented approach to multimedia cataloging, treating still images, video, animation, and sound as classes of objects. The applications treat clips from VCRs and laserdiscs and AVI video sequences on CD-ROMs as subclasses of the video object.

MediaOrganizer can display video images in a window, using video-in-a-window cards. You enter each of the properties applicable to a multimedia object in an object-description window, like the one shown in figure 22.16.

In addition to its basic function of cataloging multimedia objects, MediaOrganizer can create and play a presentation. You can group various multimedia objects and then establish the sequence and timing of their appearances. The advantage of this application is that it can control a NEC PC VCR or a Sony VISCA-equipped VCR and automatically search for and display a particular video segment. MediaOrganizer also supports remotely controllable laserdisc players (including the Pioneer LDV-4200 and the Sony LaserMax) and can display selected images from Photo CDs.

Learning Desktop Video Techniques

Although you can learn to create DTV productions by reading books and by experimenting with DTV hardware and software, you can save a great deal of time by taking a video-production course. Many two-year colleges offer day and night courses in video production, and four-year universities are establishing video programs. These courses offer at least some hands-on training in camera work and editing.

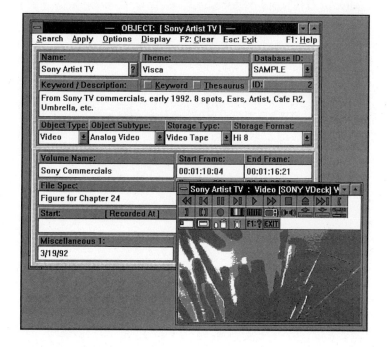

FIG. 22.16

MediaOrganizer's multimedia-object data screen.

Although many college and university courses focus on DTV, you probably will use an Apple Macintosh or a Commodore Amiga instead of a PC running Microsoft Windows. The Amiga and the Macintosh have been used for DTV purposes longer than the PC has, and many more DTV applications are available for those computers than for PCs. As Windows multimedia becomes more widely accepted in the DTV industry, however, you can expect more schools to offer courses in PC-based video production.

Chapter Summary

This chapter gave you insight into a fledgling technology, desktop video publishing, which most industry experts expect to take its place beside desktop print publishing as one of the major applications for personal computers. You learned what adapter cards and video equipment you need for DTV; you also learned some fundamental editing techniques for creating a quality DTV production.

DTV is a new and expanding field, and only a few commercial applications are available for Windows 3.1. This chapter briefly described one of the first entrants into the filed: Matrox Personal Producer, designed specifically for DTV applications.

The next chapter, "The High-Level MCI Commands of Windows 3.1," describes how you control multimedia devices with programming languages for Windows. The MCI command, described in Chapter 23, also can be used with other Windows multimedia applications, as demonstrated in Chapter 24.

Multimedia Programming Techniques

PART

VII

OUTLINE

The High-Level MCI Commands of Windows 3.1

The Windows Media Control Interface (MCI) is a set of high-level commands that provides a device-independent method of controlling multimedia devices and the files those devices use, called *resources*. Resources can be hard-disk or CD-ROM files, videodiscs and audio CD tracks, or VCR tapes.

MCI is a platform-independent layer between your multimedia applications and the underlying system software. *Platform-independent* means that the MCI commands can be used with a variety of applications and multimedia hardware. MCI's purpose is to simplify the programming code for the basic operations of the audio multimedia devices supported by Windows 3.1. Other types of devices are supported by extensions to the basic set of MCI commands included with Windows 3.1 audio device drivers.

Using MCI, you can use simple command strings such as open, play, and close to control multimedia devices. These strings are used as arguments in a single Windows function, mciSendString(), contained in MMSYSTEM.DLL, the Windows dynamic link library that provides the core of the multimedia extensions.

Related Topics
Integrating Sound with
Windows Applications,
p. 142

Related Topics
Examining Commercial MIDI
Sequences for Windows,
p. 343

You don't need to be a programmer to use the MCI functions with some new multimedia applications for Windows. Twelve-Tone Systems' Cakewalk Professional for Windows, for example, enables you to embed MCI commands in MIDI files as meta events. You can expect other publishers of sequencing applications to follow Cakewalk's lead. Presentation applications that enable you to enter MCI command strings in plain English text are expected to be available in late 1992 or early 1993. You can use MCI command strings with any Windows programming language, such as Visual Basic, Turbo Pascal for Windows, C, and C++.

Appendix D covers the MCI command strings implemented in Windows 3.1 and Windows 3.0 with Multimedia and also covers Media Vision's proposed standard MCI command set for the mixer used by MPC-compliant audio cards. A full description of the basic MCI commands is provided in Microsoft's Multimedia Development Kit (MDK), which was updated to a Windows 3.1 version in late 1992.

Multimedia Programming Interface and Data Specification 1.0

Much of this chapter is based on Multimedia Programming Interface and Data Specification 1.0, issued as a joint IBM-Microsoft standard and applicable to both Microsoft Windows and the OS/2 operating system.

Related Topics
Video Compression
Methods, p. 487

Until late 1991, Microsoft and IBM collaborated in the development of the OS/2. One goal of this cooperative effort was to create a set of application programming interface (API) standards for multimedia applications that would share common programming methodology under OS/2 or DOS-based Windows. The companies achieved this goal but went separate ways in their approaches to animation and digital video techniques. IBM adopted Intel Corporation's DVI technology, based on the Intel i750 video processor chip. Microsoft announced in March 1992 that it would support DVI within the multimedia control interface and also announced its Audio Video Interleaved (AVI) driver.

One basic principle of the MCI is that new commands can be added to support new devices. The MCI command set can be extended in two ways:

■ New commands and command options can be added to support special features or functions that new multimedia devices or file formats require. (Microsoft's addition of the Audio Video Interleaved MCI commands and support of the Intel DVI standard are examples.)

■ Developers can incorporate new multimedia devices and file formats in the MCI command set by creating new MCI drivers to interpret the commands. (The MCI standard for audio mixers proposed
by Media Vision, Inc. is an example of third-party extensions.) A
Windows DLL is created to interpret the new command syntax, and
drivers are written to support the specific hardware devices that
accept the new commands.

Multimedia Programming Interface and Data Specification 1.0 also includes detailed information on the Resource Interchange File Format
(RIFF), described in Chapter 21.

In addition to issuing instructions in the form of strings, you can execute
MCI commands by sending combinations of numeric values (expressed
as symbolic constants) and strings containing file names with the
`mciSendCommand()` function. Lower-level MCI functions also are available
for use in creating MIDI files. These MCI functions, which are used primarily by C-language programmers, are beyond the scope of this book.

Command-Syntax Conventions

This chapter departs slightly from the conventions described in the
introduction of the book, using the documentation conventions of
Multimedia Specifications 1.0. Table 23.1 lists these conventions.

Table 23.1. Conventions for MCI-Command Tables.	
Convention	**Description**
boldface	MCI command or flag keyword
italic	Command parameter to be replaced with a valid string, number, or rectangle specification
""	Parameter text to be typed exactly as shown
|	Separates flags or parameters in lists from which one flag or parameter is to be chosen
[]	Optional flags or parameters that can be omitted without creating an error

MCI Command Strings

The MCI commands provide a generic interface to different multimedia
devices, reducing the number of commands that a multimedia developer

or author needs to learn. A multimedia application might even accept MCI commands typed by the end user and pass those commands unchanged to the MCI driver, which parses the command and performs the appropriate action. This technique is the one that Twelve-Tone Systems uses to implement end-user MCI command capability in Cakewalk Professional for Windows.

Figure 23.1 shows an embedded MCI command to play TADA.WAV at the end of a MIDI performance. (Chapter 24 discusses embedded MCI commands in detail.)

FIG. 23.1

An embedded MCI command in Cakewalk for Windows.

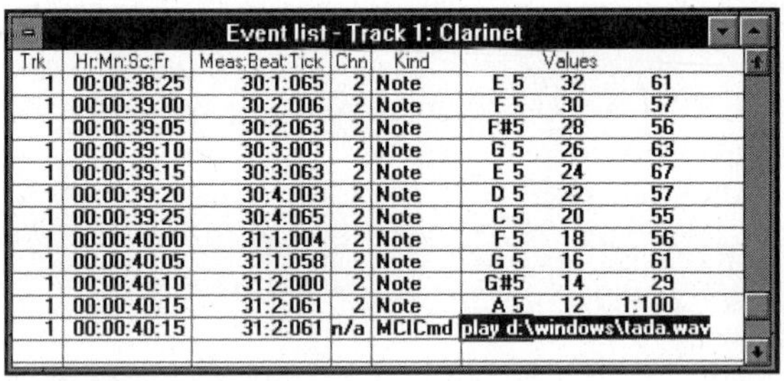

Event list - Track 1: Clarinet

Trk	Hr:Mn:Sc:Fr	Meas:Beat:Tick	Chn	Kind	Values		
1	00:00:38:25	30:1:065	2	Note	E 5	32	61
1	00:00:39:00	30:2:006	2	Note	F 5	30	57
1	00:00:39:05	30:2:063	2	Note	F#5	28	56
1	00:00:39:10	30:3:003	2	Note	G 5	26	63
1	00:00:39:15	30:3:063	2	Note	E 5	24	67
1	00:00:39:20	30:4:003	2	Note	D 5	22	57
1	00:00:39:25	30:4:065	2	Note	C 5	20	55
1	00:00:40:00	31:1:004	2	Note	F 5	18	56
1	00:00:40:05	31:1:058	2	Note	G 5	16	61
1	00:00:40:10	31:2:000	2	Note	G#5	14	29
1	00:00:40:15	31:2:061	2	Note	A 5	12	1:100
1	00:00:40:15	31:2:061	n/a	MCICmd	play d:\windows\tada.wav		

All MCI devices support a set of basic commands. Developers can define their own MCI commands and command options for a particular multimedia device or file format. You need device-specific commands and command options only when the basic command set does not support a feature specific to the device or file format. (Appendix D includes an example of device-specific MCI commands created by Media Vision for audio mixer applications.)

Three components are associated with each command string: the command, the name or identification number of the device receiving the command, and the command arguments. A command string takes the following form:

command *device_name arguments*

The **command** component includes a command from the system, required, basic, or extended command set. Examples of commands are **open**, **close**, and **play**.

The *device_name* component designates the target of **command**. MCI accepts the names of MCI device types and names of media elements for *device_name*. An example of a device name is *cdaudio*.

The *arguments* specify the flags and parameters used by **command**. **Flags** are keywords recognized by the MCI command, and *parameters* are variables associated with the MCI command or flag. Parameters specify variable values such as file names, track and frame numbers, and speed values. You can use the following types of data for the parameters in the string used to create an MCI command:

- *Strings.* You can delimit string data types by using leading and trailing white space (blanks) or by matching quotation marks. If MCI encounters one unmatched quotation mark, it ignores the quotation mark. To embed a quote in a string, use two quotes (""). To specify an empty string, you can use double quotes ("") for the string.

- *Signed long integers.* Signed long integer data types are delimited by leading and trailing white space. Unless you specify otherwise, long integers can be positive or negative. If you are using negative integers, do not embed white space between the negative sign (–) and the first digit.

- *Rectangle.* Rectangle data types are an ordered list of four signed integer values that describe the position and size of a window. White space delimits this data type and separates each integer in the list.

For example, the **play** command uses the arguments **from** *position* **to** *position* to specify starting and ending points for the playback. The **from** and **to** arguments are flags, and the two *position* values are parameters.

The following command string instructs the CD audio player **cdaudio** to play from the start of track 6 to the beginning of track 7:

> **play cdaudio from** 6 **to** 7

Unspecified command arguments assume a default value. For example, if the flag **from** were unspecified in the preceding example, the audio player would start playing at the current position.

Typical MCI Command Strings

The following set of MCI commands play track 6 of an audio compact disc:

```
open cdaudio
set cdaudio time format tmsf
play cdaudio from 6 to 7
close cdaudio
```

The following MCI commands play the first 10,000 samples of a waveform audio file:

```
open c:\mmdata\redrobin.wav type waveaudio alias robin
set robin time format samples
play robin from 1 to 10000 wait
close robin
```

These commands demonstrate the following properties of MCI command string sets:

- The same basic commands (**open**, **play**, and **close**) are used for both devices.

- The **open** command for the **waveaudio** device includes a file-name specification. The **waveaudio** device is a compound device (one associated with a media element); the **cdaudio** device is a simple device (one that lacks an associated media element).

- The **set** commands specify time formats, but the time-format options for the **cdaudio** device are different from those for the **waveaudio** device.

- The parameters used with the **from** and **to** flags are appropriate to the devices. For the **cdaudio** device, the parameters specify a range of tracks; for the **waveaudio** device, the parameters specify a range of samples.

Categories of MCI Command Strings

MCI command strings are divided into the following general categories:

- *System commands* are processed directly by MCI instead of being relayed to a supported device.

- *Required commands* are recognized by all MCI devices. If a device does not support a required command, the device can return "unsupported function" in response to the message.

- *Basic commands* are optional commands. If a device uses a basic command, the device must respond to all options for that command. If a device does not use a basic command, the device can return "unrecognized command" in response to the message.

- *Extended commands* are specific to a device type (waveaudio) or device class (for example, videodisc players of various types). Extended commands contain both unique commands and extensions of the required and basic commands.

System Commands

Table 23.2 summarizes the system commands. MCI supports these commands directly rather than passing them to MCI devices.

Table 23.2. MCI System Commands.

Message	Description
sound	Plays system sounds defined in a system setup (WIN.INI) file
sysinfo	Returns information about MCI devices (Table 23.10 shows the items for **sysinfo**)

Required Commands

Table 23.3 summarizes the required commands. All devices recognize these messages. If a device does not support a required command, the device can return "unsupported function" in response to the message.

Table 23.3. Required MCI Commands.

Message	Description
capability	Obtains the capabilities of a device
close	Closes the device
info	Obtains text information from a device
open	Initializes the device
status	Obtains status information from a device

Basic Commands

Table 23.4 summarizes the basic MCI commands. MCI devices are not required to recognize these commands, but most devices do accept them. If a device does not recognize a basic command, the device can return "unrecognized command" in response to the message.

Table 23.4. Basic MCI Commands.

Message	Description
load	Recalls data from a disk file
pause	Pauses playback

continues

Table 23.4. Continued

Message	Description
play	Starts transmitting output data
record	Starts recording input data
resume	Resumes playback or recording after a pause
save	Saves data to a disk file
seek	Searches forward or backward
set	Sets the operating state of a device
status	Obtains status information from a device (the flags for this command supplement the flags for the command in the required command group)
stop	Stops playback

Extended Commands

MCI devices can recognize additional commands or extend the definitions of the required and basic commands. Although some extended commands apply only to a specific device driver, most extended commands apply to all devices of a particular type. For example, the MIDI sequencer command set extends the **set** command to add the time formats that MIDI sequencers use. (Descriptions of extended commands appear later in this chapter and in Appendix D.)

Table 23.5 lists reserved extended commands. With the exception of the **delete** command, these commands are not currently defined for any MCI devices.

Table 23.5. Extended MCI Commands Reserved for Future Use.

Message	Description
copy	Copies data to the Clipboard (parameters and flags for this message vary from device to device)
cut	Moves data from the MCI element to the Clipboard (parameters and flags for this message vary from device to device)
delete	Removes data from the MCI element (parameters and flags for this message vary from device to device)

MCI Device Types

Your application identifies an MCI device by specifying an MCI *device type*. Table 23.6 lists the MCI device types currently defined by Windows 3.1 and Windows 3.0 with Multimedia, plus additions of device types made by Microsoft and other manufacturers after the release of Windows 3.1.

Table 23.6. Current MCI Device Types.

Device type	Description	MCI driver
AVIVideo	Microsoft Audio Video Interleaved	MCIAVI.DRV
cdaudio[1]	Audio CD player	MCICDA.DRV[2]
dat	Digital audiotape player	Named by supplier
digitalvideo	Digital video in a window (not GDI)	Named by supplier
mixer	Media Vision MMMIXER.DLL	MVMIXER.DRV
MMMovie[3]	Multimedia movie player	MCIMMP.DRV
other	Undefined MCI device	Named by supplier
scanner	Image scanner	Named by supplier
sequencer[1]	MIDI sequencer	MCISEQ.DRV[2]
vcr	Videotape recorder or player	Named by supplier[4]
videodisc[1]	Pioneer LD-V4200 videodisc player	MCIPIONR.DRV
waveaudio[1]	Digitized waveform audio device	MCIWAVE.DRV[2]

[1] *An extended command set is provided for these devices.*

[2] *These drivers are included with Windows 3.1. Other drivers are included with Windows with Multimedia unless shown as drivers provided with device hardware.*

[3] *MMMMovie (animation) and Audio Video Interleaved (DVI digital video) are not part of the joint IBM-Microsoft Multimedia Specifications 1.0.*

[4] *An MCI command set DLL and driver for the Sony Vdeck and Vbox products using VISCA protocol were in the beta-testing state when this book was written.*

If you have installed more than one device of a particular type, the device-type names in the system setup file are numbered by Windows. For example, if the **cdaudio** device type is installed twice, the names **cdaudio1** and **cdaudio2** are used. Each name usually refers to a different audio CD player in the system.

Uses for MCI Command Strings

The tables at the end of this chapter describe command strings for basic MCI devices. The following sections describe command strings for the most commonly used devices, including **cdaudio**, **waveaudio**, and **sequencer**.

Opening a Device

Before you use a device, you must use the **open** command to initialize the device. The number of devices you can open depends on the amount of available memory. The **open** command has the following syntax:

> **open** *device_name* [**shareable**] [**type** *device_type*] [**alias** *alias*]

Table 23.7 shows the parameters for the **open** command.

Table 23.7. MCI Open Command Parameters.	
Parameter	**Description**
device_name	Specifies a destination device or MCI element
shareable	Enables applications to share a device or device element
type *device_type*	Specifies a device when *device_name* refers to an MCI element
alias *alias*	Specifies an alternative name for a device

MCI classifies device drivers as *compound* and *simple*. Compound device drivers use a *device element* (a media element associated with a device) during operation. For most compound device drivers, the device element is the source or destination data file. For file elements, the element name references a file and its path.

Simple device drivers do not require a device element for playback. For example, audio CD device drivers are simple device drivers.

Opening Simple Devices

Simple devices require only *device_name* for operation. You don't need to provide any additional information (such as the name of a data file) to open these devices. For these devices, substitute the name of a device type from the system setup file. For example, you can open a laserdisc device by using the following command:

open videodisc1

Opening Compound Devices

You can open a compound device in the following ways:

- By specifying only the device type
- By specifying the element name and the device type
- By specifying only the element name

To determine the capabilities of a device, you can open a device by specifying only the device type. When you use this method, you can determine the capabilities of most compound devices and then close the devices. For example, you can open the sequencer with the following command:

open sequencer

To associate a device element with a particular device, you must specify the element name and device type. In the **open** command, substitute the element name for *device_name*, add the **type** flag, and substitute the name of the device you want to use for *device_type*. This combination enables your application to specify the MCI device it needs to use. For example, you can open a device element of the waveaudio device with the following command:

open right.wav type waveaudio

To associate a default MCI device with a device element, you can specify only an element name. In this case, MCI uses the file-name extension of the element name to select the device type.

Using the Shareable Flag

The **shareable** flag enables multiple applications or tasks to concurrently access the same device (or element) and device instance. Applications that use device drivers, such as Sound Recorder, may have several windows open at one, provided that a different WAV file is loaded. Each window is called an instance of Sound Recorder.

If your application opens a device or device element without the **shareable** flag, no other application can access that device or device element simultaneously. If your application opens a device or device element as shareable, other applications can also access that device or device element by opening it as shareable. The shared device or device element enables each application to change the parameters that govern the operating state of the device or device element. Each time that a device or device element is opened as shareable, a unique device identification number is returned (even though the device numbers refer to the same device instance).

If you make a device or device element shareable, your application should not make any assumptions about the state of a device. When working with shared devices, your application might need to compensate for changes made by other applications using the same services.

If a device can service only one application or task, you cannot use the **shareable** flag to open that device. MIDI Mapper and the MPU-401 driver supplied with Windows 3.1, for example, are not shareable. If you try to open the MPU-401 driver as shareable, an error message appears (see fig. 23.2).

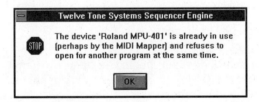

FIG. 23.2

A nonshareable-driver error message.

Although most compound device elements are not shareable, you can open multiple elements (if each element is unique), or you can open one element several times. If you open a file element several times, MCI creates a device instance for each open device.

Each file element opened within a task must have a unique name. The **alias** flag, described in the following section, enables you to use a unique name for each element.

Using the Alias Flag

The **alias** flag specifies an alternative name for a device and allows you to substitute a short name for compound devices with long path names. If your application creates a device alias, the application must use the alias rather than the device name for all subsequent references.

Opening New Device Elements

To create a new device element for a task such as capturing a sound as a waveform recording, specify **new** for *device_name*. MCI does not save a new file element until you use the **save** command. When you create a new file, you must include a device alias with the **open** command.

The following commands open a new waveaudio device element, start and stop recording, save the file element, and close the device element:

```
open new type waveaudio alias capture
record capture
stop capture
save capture orca.wav
close capture
```

Closing a Device

The **close** command releases access to a device or device element. To help MCI manage the devices, your application must explicitly close each device or device element after using that device or device element.

Using Shortcuts and Variations for MCI Commands

The MCI string interface enables you to use several shortcuts when you work with MCI devices.

You can specify **all** as a *device_name* for any command that does not return information. When you specify **all**, the command is sent to all devices opened by your application. For example, **close all** closes all open devices, and **play all** starts playing all devices opened by the task. Because MCI sends the commands to each device, a delay occurs between the first device's receipt of the command and the last device's receipt of the command.

You can eliminate the **type** flag in the **open** command if you combine the device type with the device element name. MCI recognizes this combination when you use the following syntax:

> **device_type!element_name**

The exclamation point separates the device type from the element name. The following example opens the right.wav element with the waveaudio device:

> **open waveaudio!right.wav**

Using Automatic Open

If MCI cannot identify *device_name* as an already open device, MCI tries to open the specified device automatically. Automatic open does not enable your application to specify the **type** flag. If the device type is not supplied, MCI determines the device type from the element (file-name) extensions listed in the system setup file. If you want to use a specific device, you can combine the device type name with the device element name, using the exclamation point syntax, as shown in the preceding section.

Only the command-string interface supports automatic open. Automatic open fails for device-specific commands. For example, a command to unlock the front panel of a laserdisc player fails on automatic open because this capability is specific to the particular laserdisc player.

A device that was opened with automatic open does not respond to a command that uses **all** as a device name.

Using Automatic Close

MCI automatically closes any device opened with the command-string interface. MCI closes a device when the command ends, when you abort the command, when you request notification with a subsequent command, or when MCI detects a failure.

Using Wait and Notify Flags

Normally, MCI commands return to the user immediately, even if the action that the command initiates runs for several minutes. For example, after a VCR device receives a rewind command, the command returns before the tape finishes rewinding. You can use either of the required MCI flags shown in Table 23.8 to modify this default behavior.

Table 23.8. MCI Wait and Notify Flags.

Flag	Description
notify	Directs a device to send an MM_MCINOTIFY message to a window when the requested action is complete
wait	Directs a device to wait until the requested action is complete before returning to the application

The **notify** flag directs a device to post an MM_MCINOTIFY message when the device completes an action. Your application must have a window procedure to process the MM_MCINOTIFY message.

Although the results of a notification are application-dependent, the application's window procedure can act on four possible conditions associated with the notify message:

- Notification occurs when the notification conditions are satisfied. A successful notification occurs when the conditions required for initiating the callback are satisfied and the command is completed without interruption.

- Notification can be superseded. A notification is superseded when a device has a notification pending and you send the device another notify request. When a notification is superseded, MCI resets the callback conditions to correspond with the notify request of the new command.

- Notification can be aborted. A notification is aborted when you send a new command that prevents the callback conditions set by a previous command from being satisfied. For example, sending the **stop** command cancels a notification pending for the **play to 500** command. If your command interrupts a command that has a notification pending and your command also requests notification, MCI aborts the first notification immediately and responds to the second notification normally.

- Notification can fail. A notification fails if a device error occurs while a device is executing the MCI command. For example, MCI posts this message when a hardware error occurs during a **play** command.

Obtaining Information from MCI Devices

Every device responds to the **capability**, **status**, and **info** commands, which obtain information about the device. For example, your application can determine whether a laserdisc requires a device element by using the following command:

```
capability videodisc compound file
```

For most laserdisc devices, this example would return false.

The flags listed for the required and basic commands provide minimal information about a device. Many devices supplement the required and basic flags with extended flags to provide additional information about the device.

When you use the **capability**, **status**, or **info** command to request information, the argument list can contain only one flag requesting information. The string interface can return only one string or value in response to a **capability**, **status**, or **info** command.

Using the Play Command

The **play** command starts playing a device. Without any flags, the **play** command starts playing from the current position and plays until the command is halted or until the end of the media or file is reached. For example, **play cdaudio** starts playing an audio disc from the position at which it was stopped.

Most devices that support the **play** command also support the **from** and **to** flags. These flags indicate the positions at which the device should start and stop playing. For example, **play cdaudio from 0** plays the audio disc from the beginning of the first track. The units assigned to the position value depend on the device. For example, the position normally is specified in frames for CAV (constant angular velocity) laserdiscs and in milliseconds for digital audio.

As an extended command, devices add flags to use the capabilities of a particular device. For example, the **play** command for laserdisc players adds the flags **fast**, **slow**, **reverse**, and **scan**.

Using the Stop, Pause, and Resume Commands

The **stop** command suspends the playing or recording of a device. Many devices include the basic command **pause**, which also suspends these sessions. The difference between **stop** and **pause** depends on the device. Usually, **pause** suspends operation but leaves the device ready to resume playing or recording immediately.

Using **play** or **record** to restart a device resets the **to** and **from** positions specified before the device was paused or stopped. Without the **from** flag, these commands reset the start position to the current position. Without the **to** flag, the commands reset the end position to the end of the disc or tape. If you want to continue playing or recording but want to stop at a previously specified position, use the **to** flag with these commands and repeat the position value.

Some devices include the **resume** command to restart a paused device. This command does not change the **to** and **from** positions specified with the **play** or **record** command, which preceded the pause command.

MCI Open Error Processing

If MMSYSTEM.DLL or the driver for the specified device type cannot execute a command, mciSendString() returns an error value. You can use the error value as the argument of mciGetErrorString() to request an explanation of the problem in the form of a string. Applications use this string to create a message that identifies the problem.

Table 23.9 shows the decimal values of errors returned by mciSendString(), the constants corresponding to these values, and the error strings provided by mciGetErrorString() that are specific to the MCI **open** command.

Table 23.9. Error Values and Strings for the MCI Open Command.

Value	mciSendString Return Constant	mciGetErrorString Response
266	MCIERR_CANNOT_LOAD_DRIVER	Error loading media device driver
265	NCIERR_DEVICE_OPEN	The device name is in use; use a unique alias
289	MCIERR_DUPLICATE_ALIAS	The specified alias is an open device
281	MCIERR_EXTENSION_NOT_FOUND	A device name cannot be deduced from the specified extension
304	MCIERR_FILENAME_REQUIRED	A valid file name is required
273	MCIERR_MISSING_PARAMETER	A required parameter is missing
291	MCIERR_MUST_USE_SHAREABLE	The device already is open; use the **shareable** flag with each **open** command
301	MCIERR_NO_ELEMENT_ALLOWED	An element name cannot be used with this device

MCI Command Tables

The tables in the following sections list all currently defined MCI commands for devices supported by Microsoft Windows and the parameters that apply to those commands.

MCI System Commands

Some commands are executed directly by MMSYSTEM.DLL or an installed driver and do not use the standard syntax for MCI commands. Table 23.10 shows commands that MCI interprets directly.

Table 23.10. MCI System Commands.

Command	Description
sound	The *device_name* portion of this command specifies a sound defined in a system setup file; if MCI cannot find the sound, MCI uses a default system sound
sysinfo *device_name* *item*	Obtains MCI system information, with one of the following *item*s modifying **sysinfo**:

	installname	Returns the name used to install the device
	quantity	Returns the number of MCI devices of the type specified by the *device_name* field. The device name must be a standard MCI device type. Any digits after the name are ignored. The special device name **all** returns the number of MCI devices in the system.
	quantity open	Returns the number of open MCI devices of the type specified by the device name. The device name must be a standard MCI device type. Any digits after the name are ignored. The special device name **all** returns the number of MCI devices open in the system.
	name *index*	Returns the name of an MCI device. *Index* ranges from 1 to the number of devices of that type. If **all** is the device name, *index* ranges from 1 to the number of devices in the system.

Command	Description
name *index* **open**	Returns the name of an open MCI device. *Index* ranges from 1 to the number of devices of that type that are open. If **all** is the device name, *index* ranges from 1 to the number of open devices of all types in the system.

Required Command Sets for All Devices

All devices recognize the command sets listed in Table 23.10. Extended commands can add other options to these commands. Table 23.11 lists the required MCI command sets.

Table 23.11. Required MCI Command Sets for All Devices.

Command	Description
capability *device_name item*	Requests information about a particular capability of a device.
	Although other capabilities are defined for specific devices and device types, the following *item*s always are available:
	can eject Returns `true` if the device can eject the medium
	can play Returns `true` if the device can play
	can record Returns `true` if the device can record
	can save Returns `true` if the device can save data
	compound device Returns `true` if the device requires an element name
	device type Returns `audio tape`, `cdaudio`, `digital audio tape`, `scanner`, `sequencer`, `videodisc`, `videotape`, or `waveaudio`

continues

Table 23.11. Continued

Command	Description
	has audio Returns true if the device supports audio
	has video Returns true if the device supports video
	uses files Returns true if the element of a compound device is a file path name
close *device_name*	When sent to a simple device, closes the device. When sent to a compound device element, closes the element and any resources associated with it. MCI unloads a device when the device no longer is being used.
info *device_name item*	Fills a user-supplied buffer with a null-terminated string containing text. The following *item* modifies **info**:
	product Returns a description of the hardware associated with the device (usually including manufacturer and model information)
open *device_name item*	Initializes a device. The following optional *item*s modify **open**:
	alias *device alias* Specifies an alternative name for a device. If specified, the alias must be used in subsequent references to that device.
	shareable Initializes a device or device element as shareable. Later attempts to open the device or device element fails unless you specify **shareable** in the original and subsequent **open** commands. MCI returns an error if the device or device element already is open and is not shareable.

Command	Description	
type *device type*	Specifies the compound device that controls a device element. As an alternative to **type**, MCI can use the file-name extension entries to select the device based on the extension used by the device element.	
status *device_name item*	Obtains status information for the device. One of the following *item*s modifies **status**:	
	mode	Returns the current mode of the device. Common modes are `not ready`, `paused`, `playing`, `stopped`, `open`, `recording`, and `seeking`.
	ready	Returns `true` if the device is ready

A special set of error values and error explanation strings are used with the required MCI command sets. All devices must be capable of returning the values shown in Table 23.12.

Table 23.12. Error Values and Strings for Required MCI Command Sets.

Value	mciSendString Return Constant	mciGetErrorString Response
293	MCIERR_BAD_TIME_FORMAT	Illegal value for time format
279	MCIERR_CANNOT_USE_ALL	The device name **all** cannot be used for this command
347	MCIERR_CREATEWINDOW	Could not create or use window
288	MCIERR_DEVICE_LOCKED	The device is locked until it is closed automatically
276	MCIERR_DEVICE_NOT_READY	The device is not ready
287	MCIERR_DEVICE_TYPE_REQUIRED	The device name must be a valid device type
278	MCIERR_DRIVER	Unspecified driver error
272	MCIERR_DRIVER_INTERNAL	Internal driver error

continues

Table 23.12. Continued

Value	mciSendString Return Constant	mciGetErrorString Response
275	MCIERR_FILE_NOT_FOUND	The requested file could not be found
286	MCIERR_FILE_NOT_SAVED	The requested file was not saved
348	MCIERR_FILE_READ	A read from the file failed
349	MCIERR_FILE_WRITE	A write to the file failed
284	MCIERR_FLAGS_NOT_COMPATIBLE	The specified parameters are incompatible
262	MCIERR_HARDWARE	Hardware error
277	MCIERR_INTERNAL	Internal error
257	MCIERR_INVALID_DEVICE_ID	Invalid device identification number
263	MCIERR_INVALID_DEVICE_NAME	The device is not open or is not known
296	MCIERR_INVALID_FILE	Invalid file format
280	MCIERR_MULTIPLE	Errors occurred in more than one device
346	MCIERR_NO_WINDOW	No display window
297	MCIERR_NULL_PARAMETER_BLOCK	Parameter block pointer is null
264	MCIERR_OUT_OF_MEMORY	Not enough memory is available for requested operation
282	MCIERR_OUTOFRANGE	Parameter value is out of range
298	MCIERR_UNNAMED_RESOURCE	Attempt to save an unnamed file
261	MCIERR_UNRECOGNIZED_COMMAND	Unknown command
274	MCIERR_UNSUPPORTED_FUNCTION	The requested action is not available for the specified device

Commands for Specific Device Types

In addition to the commands described previously, each device supports
a set of commands specific to its device type. Where possible, these
type-specific commands are identical between types.

Basic Commands for Multiple Device Types

When type-specific commands are common to multiple devices, these commands are considered to be basic commands. For example, the basic **play** command is identical for laserdisc and videotape players. Although basic commands are optional for a device, if a basic command is used, the command must recognize all command options. The options generally provide for a minimum set of capabilities, but some devices may return "unsupported function" if an option clearly does not apply.

Table 23.13 lists the basic MCI command sets for multiple device types.

Table 23.13. MCI Device-Specific Commands for Multiple Device Types.

Command	Description
load *device_name item*	Loads a device element from disk. The following optional *item* modifies **load**:
	file name — Specifies the source path and file
pause *device_name*	Pauses playback or recording
play *device_name item*	Starts playing the device. The following optional *item*s modify **play**:
	from *position* — Specifies the position from which to start playback. If **from** is omitted, playback starts at the current position.
	to *position* — Specifies the position at which to stop playback. If **to** is omitted, playback stops at the end of the disk or tape.
record *device_name item*	Starts recording data. All data recorded after a file is opened is discarded if the file is closed without being saved. The following optional *item*s modify **record**:
	insert — Specifies that new data are added to the device element at the current position
	from *position* — Specifies the position from which to start recording. If **from** is omitted, recording starts at the current position.

continues

Table 23.13. Continued

Command	Description
	to *position* — Specifies the position at which to stop recording. If **to** is omitted, recording continues until a **stop** or **pause** command is issued.
	overwrite — Specifies that new data are to replace data in the device element
	The default recording mode (**insert** or **overwrite**) depends on the specific device. Each device should define a default recording mode.
resume *device_name*	Resumes playback or recording after a pause
save *device_name item*	Saves the MCI element. The following optional *item* modifies **save**:
	file name — Specifies the destination path and name
seek *device_name item*	Moves to the specified position and stops. One of the following *item*s modifies **seek**:
	to *position* — Specifies the position from which to start the search
	to start — Searches to the start of the disc, tape, or device element
	to end — Searches to the end of the disc, tape, or device element
set *device_name item*	Sets the various control *item*s, which follow:
	audio all off| **audio all on** — Enables or disables audio output
	audio left off| **audio left on** — Enables or disables output to the left audio channel
	audio right off| **audio right on** — Enables or disables output to the right audio channel
	door closed — Loads the disc or tape and closes the device door, if possible
	door open — Opens the device door and ejects the disc or tape, if possible

Command	Description	
	time format milliseconds	Sets time format to milliseconds (ms). All position information appears in this format after this command.
	video off | video on	Enables or disables video output
status *device_name item*	Obtains status information from a device. One of the following *item*s modifies **status**:	
	current track	Returns the current track
	length	Returns the length of the segment
	length track *track_number*	Returns the length of the serial track specified by *track_number*
	start position	Returns to the starting position of the disc, tape, or device element
	time format	Returns the time format
stop *device_name*	Stops a device.	

Specific Device Command Sets

Appendix D lists the complete mciSendString() command set for conventional MCI devices supported by Windows 3.1 and Windows with Multimedia, plus the Media Vision Mixer device types. Table 23.14 lists those devices for which command sets are provided in the appendix.

Table 23.14. MCI Commands for Specific Devices.

Table	Command description	Driver
D.1	Waveform audio commands	MCIWAVE.DRV
D.2	MIDI sequencer commands	MCISEQ.DRV
D.3	Audio CD (Red Book audio) commands	MCISEQ.DRV
D.4	Laserdisc player commands	MCIPIONR.DRV
D.5	Animation and movie player commands	MCIMMP.DRV

continues

Table 23.14. Continued

Table	Command description	Driver
D.6	Video overlay commands	Named by supplier
D.7	Audio mixer commands (standard proposed by Media Vision, MMMIXER.DLL)	MCIMIX.DRV

The syntax of these commands is provided in the appendix so that you can use embedded MCI commands in applications that currently support the `mciSendString()` function. Full MCI command-string syntax seldom is included in the documentation for these applications. The documentation accompanying the Microsoft Multimedia Development Kit (MDK) includes additional information on the use of the `mciSendString()` function.

Chapter Summary

The MCI command strings described in this chapter are a very powerful feature of the multimedia extensions to Windows. The syntax of MCI command strings, as outlined here, is almost plain English and therefore is easy to follow. Applications that allow you to embed MCI command strings have the advantage of supporting all of the presently available multimedia devices for which MCI drivers have been created. In addition, such applications enable you to use new additions to the MCI command set, created by Microsoft and other firms, without the necessity of waiting for or purchasing an upgrade to the software.

Chapter 24 provides examples of the use of MCI command strings in a typical commercial application, Cakewalk Professional for Windows, and examples of the use of MCI command strings in Visual Basic programming.

Programming with MCI Commands

The mciSendString() function of Windows 3.1's MMSYSTEM.DLL is designed to make MCI functions easily accessible to beginning programmers. The use of English-language descriptions for the actions to be performed contributes to readable source code in your programs. Another advantage of using mciSendString() is that you are not required to declare the extensive group of symbolic constants (such as WAVE_FORMAT_1S08, which represents an 11.025-kHz 8-bit stereo format for a waveform audio file as a numeric value) and data structures necessary to use the mciSendCommand() function.

This book is not intended to be a guide to programming techniques for multimedia applications, so only a few examples of using the MCI commands with Windows applications and programming languages are presented in this chapter. An example of embedding MCI command strings in files created by Windows multimedia applications is included, however, because this methodology is expected to be implemented in many future applications (especially multimedia presentation packages).

Visual Basic is used in the programming examples because Visual Basic is the most popular Windows programming language for beginning and intermediate-level programmers. C-language function prototype declarations are provided for programmers who do not have the Windows 3.1 Software Development Kit or the Multimedia Development Kit.

Embedding MCI Command Strings As MIDI Meta Events

Cakewalk Professional for Windows is one of the few commercial software products that enables you to use the mciSendString() function to complement its own use of the MCI functions of Windows 3.1. (Cakewalk's capability to embed waveform files as MIDI meta events was described in Chapter 21, "Advanced MIDI and Waveform Audio Techniques.")

The problem with embedding waveform audio files is that the size of your MIDI file expands by the length of each waveform audio file you embed. If you use a waveform audio file repeatedly in a production, you need to embed a copy of that file at each location in the production where that file is to be used. Linking the waveform audio file by embedding the appropriate mciSendString() commands saves valuable disk space because you don't need duplicate copies of the WAV file in your MIDI file.

You can take advantage of Cakewalk's capability to execute MCI command strings when you program sequences of sounds from a wide range of sources other than MIDI files. For example, you can create a MIDI file that consists solely of MCI command strings that play waveform audio files and audio CD tracks, and even display video in a small window with AVI files at precisely timed intervals.

To create a Cakewalk Professional for Windows MCI command track that plays waveform audio files, follow these steps:

1. Copy the WAV files you plan to use to your \WINCAKE directory so that you don't have to enter paths. For this exercise, you can use the standard system sound files DING.WAV, CHORD.WAV, CHIME.WAV, and TADA.WAV in your \WINDOWS directory or any other short (1 to 10 seconds long) WAV files.

2. Launch Cakewalk for Windows. Then choose **O**pen from the **F**ile menu and open DEMO.WRK, a demonstration file supplied with Cakewalk.

3. Click the down arrow in the text box to the right of the From text box to decrease the tempo from 85 to 60 beats per minute so that a new measure begins every four seconds.

4. Type **MCI Commands** in the Name column of track 3 (under Voice #2), as shown in figure 24.1. Double-click track 3's check column to remove the mute (m) symbol and substitute a check to indicate that the track plays.

5. Select track 1. Choose **N**ew from the **W**indows menu and click Event List in the submenu to open the Event List window. This displays the timing of the MIDI events for the right-hand piano notes, as shown in figure 24.1. The purpose of displaying this event list is to provide an example of the appearance of a typical Cakewalk event list for MIDI Note messages.

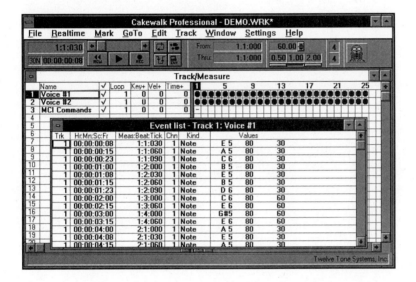

FIG. 24.1

Cakewalk's MIDI Event List window.

6. Rewind the file to beat 1 of measure 1 by clicking the Rew button.

7. Select new track 3 in the Track/Measure window. Then choose **N**ew from the **W**indows menu and click Event List in the submenu to open a new event-list window for track 3.

Now you're ready to enter the MCI command strings to open the waveaudio devices for each of the four WAV files. Follow these steps:

1. Press the Ins key to insert an event at measure 1, beat 1.

2. Edit the Meas:Beat:Tick column to set the Tick value to 000, if necessary.

3. Click the default event, Note. The Kind of Event dialog box appears (see fig. 24.2).

4. Select **M**CI Command in the Special column and then choose OK.

5. In the Values column, type **open DING.WAV type waveaudio alias Waves1** as the first (and only parameter) to open the waveform audio device, as shown in the first row of the Values column in figure 24.3.

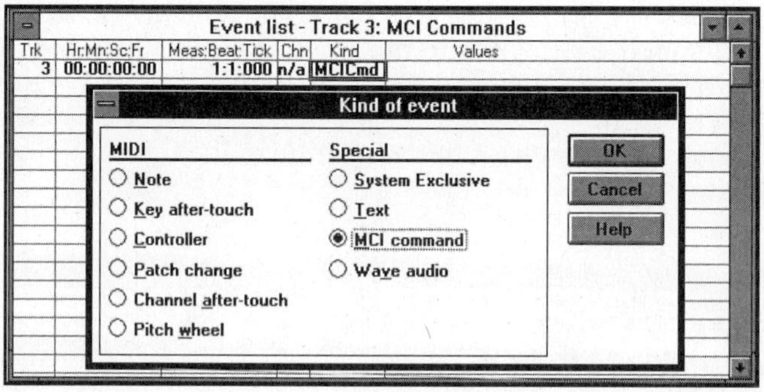

FIG. 24.2

The Kind of Event
dialog box.

You must use the full command syntax with the **open** command
and specify the device type. Make sure that you type **Waves1**; because Wave is a default alias, an error message appears if you type
Wave1. You use the **open** command before using the file because
this command loads the waveform audio data into a buffer so that
the sound is not delayed by the time required to open the file.

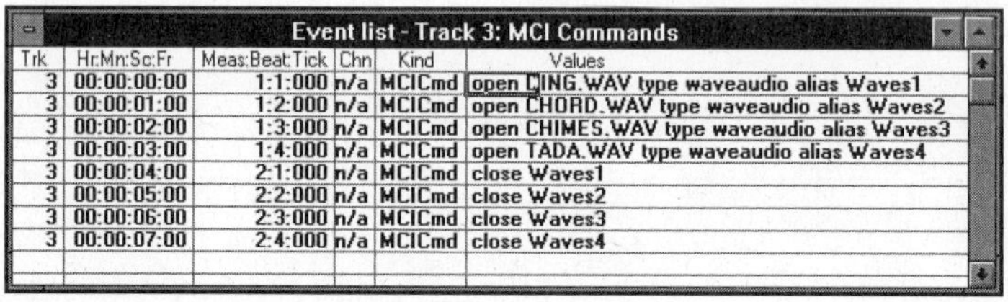

FIG. 24.3

The MCI commands
for opening and
closing waveform
audio files.

6. Repeat steps 1 through 5 for each WAV file that you plan to use,
   assigning each file the alias Waves2, Waves3, and Waves4 in sequence. Each file opens on a separate beat in the measure so that
   you can detect syntax errors in a specific command. Edit the Beat
   entry in the Meas:Beat:Tick column so that Waves2 occurs on beat
   2, Waves3 on beat 3, and Waves4 on beat 4, as shown in figure 24.3.

You must close each device that you open so that you can repeat the
performance. If you attempt to reopen a device already open, an MCI
error message appears in the status bar at the bottom of Cakewalk's
main window.

To close devices, follow these steps:

1. Type **close Waves#**, with **#** representing the number of each alias.
   For the moment, use measure 2, beats 1 through 4 for these entries
   so that you do not have to play the entire sequence to close the
   devices. Your entries should resemble figure 24.3 when you finish.

2. Save your file under a unique file name such as DEMOWAVE.WRK. Then save any files open in other applications, because errors in MCI syntax may cause crashes in Windows 3.1 from which you cannot recover; you are unceremoniously dropped out of Windows to the DOS prompt.

3. Play DEMOWAVE to test your entries to this point. As each file opens, an MCI Result value appears in the status bar. If your syntax contains errors or a file is missing from your \WINCAKE directory, your computer beeps and an error message appears in the status bar. You must play the file to at least measure 3 to ensure that each device is closed before you rewind and play DEMOWAVE again.

At this point, you're ready to make the entries that play the WAV files by following these steps:

1. Edit the measure of the **close Waves#** entry so that the close operations occur later in the sequence. Normally, you would close the files after the last measure of the sequence (measure 25, in this case). This example plays Wave1 to Wave4 in measures 2 to 5, so the devices are closed in measure 6.

2. Select the event with **close Wave1** as the command, and press Ins key to add an event.

3. Edit the measure and beat to select the location at which the device is to play, and then type **play Waves1** as the parameter.

4. Repeat steps 2 and 3 for Wave2, Wave3, and Wave4. When you finish, your Event List window should resemble figure 24.4.

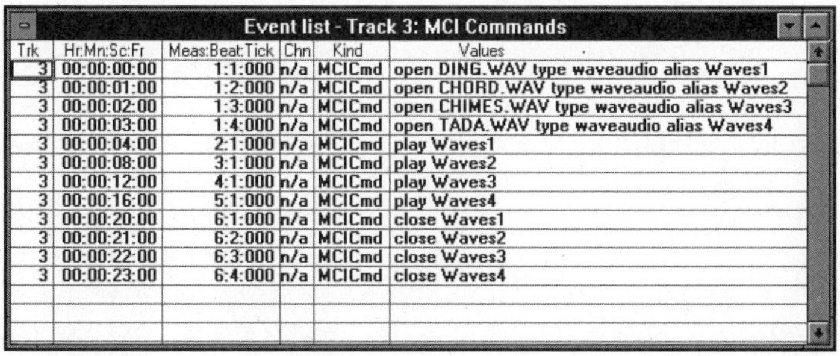

Trk	Hr:Mn:Sc:Fr	Meas:Beat:Tick	Chn	Kind	Values
3	00:00:00:00	1:1:000	n/a	MCICmd	open DING.WAV type waveaudio alias Waves1
3	00:00:01:00	1:2:000	n/a	MCICmd	open CHORD.WAV type waveaudio alias Waves2
3	00:00:02:00	1:3:000	n/a	MCICmd	open CHIMES.WAV type waveaudio alias Waves3
3	00:00:03:00	1:4:000	n/a	MCICmd	open TADA.WAV type waveaudio alias Waves4
3	00:00:04:00	2:1:000	n/a	MCICmd	play Waves1
3	00:00:08:00	3:1:000	n/a	MCICmd	play Waves2
3	00:00:12:00	4:1:000	n/a	MCICmd	play Waves3
3	00:00:16:00	5:1:000	n/a	MCICmd	play Waves4
3	00:00:20:00	6:1:000	n/a	MCICmd	close Waves1
3	00:00:21:00	6:2:000	n/a	MCICmd	close Waves2
3	00:00:22:00	6:3:000	n/a	MCICmd	close Waves3
3	00:00:23:00	6:4:000	n/a	MCICmd	close Waves4

Event list - Track 3: MCI Commands

FIG. 24.4

The additional commands required to play waveform audio files.

5. Save DEMOWAVE.WRK again, and then click Rewind and play the file again. If you use the Meas:Beat:Tick values shown in figure 24.4, each WAV file plays in sequence on beat 1 of measures 2 through 5.

The preceding example is intended only to demonstrate the versatility of the MCI commands. If you record vocals for a MIDI-orchestrated song as WAV files, you can play the vocals over the MIDI accompaniment. Using a waveform audio file editor such as Wave for Windows, you can create individual WAV files that contain specific phrases in the vocals, and then rearrange the vocals and accompaniment. You also can make fine alterations in the tempo of the accompaniment to keep the vocals on the beat, compress or expand the vocals without changing the pitch, and even change the pitch of portions of the vocals if your vocalist is off-key. Embedding MCI commands in MIDI sequencers creates the ultimate user-programmable karaoke player.

Embedded MCI commands in Windows sequencer applications are not limited to WAV files. You can play MIDI music over tracks of audio CDs, specifying the beginning and ending times of the music on the CD track. For example, you could use the command **play from 02:10:15 to 03:09:22** to play an audio segment from 2 minutes, 10 seconds, 15 frames to 3 minutes, 9 seconds, 22 frames. If you have the Microsoft AVI driver (MCIAVI.DRV), you can play video clips and audio tracks stored in the form of AVI files on your hard disk or CD-ROM, as shown in figure 24.5.

FIG. 24.5

MCI commands that open and play an AVI file from a CD-ROM.

Although you need Cakewalk Professional for Windows to perform the exercise in this section, the MCI commands used in the exercise are typical of those that you can embed in any Windows application that provides MCI command capabilities. The implementation may be different—some applications write the commands for you when you use option buttons to choose the command and its parameters—but the basic principles are the same.

Using Visual Basic MCI Applications

Visual Basic is the most successful of Microsoft's programming languages, if you measure success by the number of copies sold in the first year of a language's life. Although C programmers scorn dialects of BASIC as beginners' languages, the object-oriented, event-driven implementation of QBasic and QuickBasic in Visual Basic 2.0 offers a set of instructions more than adequate for use in most Windows applications.

Visual Basic's forms-design functions, which create the windows in which control objects such as text and picture boxes appear, are intuitive and easy to use. Visual Basic offers access to almost all Windows 3.1 functions through its **Declare Function** and **Declare Sub** keywords. You can create multimedia presentations and related applications in Visual Basic by using the mciSendString() function of MMSYSTEM.DLL.

Visual Basic Function Prototype Declarations

Using a Windows function in a Visual Basic application requires you to register the function in the global module of your application. This procedure is similar to registering function prototypes in the header files of C++ applications.

The following function prototypes are declared in the global module of your Visual Basic application.

```
Declare Function mciExecute Lib "MMSYSTEM.DLL"
  (ByVal mciCommand As String) As Integer

Declare Function mciSendString Lib "MMSYSTEM.DLL"
  (ByVal mciCommand As String,
  ByVal mciReturn As String,
  Byval mciReturnLength As Integer,
  ByVal mcihWnd As Integer) As Long

Declare Function mciGetErrorString Lib "MMSYSTEM.DLL"
  (ByVal mciError As Long,
  ByVal mciErrString As String,
  ByVal mciErrLength As Integer) As Integer
```

NOTE   For clarity, declarations appear in multiple lines in this section, but you must type declarations on one line in order to comply with Visual Basic's line-oriented interpreter. You need not include these prototypes if you are using the MCI custom control, MCI.VBX, to implement MCI commands with the MMControl object. (MCI.VBX is included in the Microsoft Professional Toolkit for Visual Basic, described later in this chapter.)

The mciExecute() function is a simplified substitute for the combination of mciSendString and mciGetErrorString. mciExecute() returns true (–1) if it executes successfully and displays a message containing the appropriate return value of mciGetErrString() when an error occurs. You need not include the global constants for the long integer error codes returned by mciSendString() in either case, because the error values can be converted to their text representations by mciGetErrorString().

Typical Visual Basic Applications Using MCI Commands

You can use the MCI command strings to write simple to complex multimedia applications in Visual Basic. One advantage of using Visual Basic is that you can easily write a simple application to test the use of the mciSendString() command with a waveaudio device, and then expand the capabilities of the application by substituting additional MCI command strings for a sequencer device as arguments of mciSendString(). You can add still graphics to your Visual Basic application with the language's native commands; you can display animated graphics with the mmmovie device. Visual Basic **Timer** objects are used to synchronize the images and sounds.

Figure 24.6 shows a window from a complex Visual Basic application (approximately 1,200 lines of code) that demonstrates the individual voices available with the Roland SCC-1 GS Sound Card.

The application shown in figure 24.6 makes extensive use of mciSendString() to play MIDI files. The application also uses some lower-level MCI commands to send MIDI Program Change, Continuous Controller, and SysEx messages to the MPU-401 driver to demonstrate different sounds and how the SCC-1's built-in effects alter the quality of the sounds.

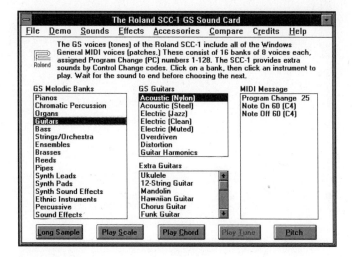

FIG. 24.6

A Visual Basic
application that uses
MCI commands.

A Test Application for mciSendString in Visual Basic

Microsoft's Multimedia Development Kit (MDK) includes the MCITest application, which enables you to experiment with MCI command strings. If you own Visual Basic but not the MDK, you can create a similar test application except for the callback functions provided in MCITest that you use when you specify the notify item.

Figure 24.7 shows the Visual Basic form for the MCITest application you create with the code example that follows. You type an MCI string in the top text box, and the return string (if any) appears in the middle text box. Error strings appear in the bottom text box if an error occurs; otherwise, the message OK appears. A history of all of the commands you type appears in the text box on the right side of the form. This example assumes that you are familiar with Visual Basic and the procedures used to create new applications.

To create the mciSendString() test application in Visual Basic, follow these steps:

1. Starting with a new project, type the following code in the GLOBAL.BAS module (typing each Declare Function entry in one line):

```
Declare Function mciSendString Lib "MMSYSTEM.DLL"
  (ByVal mciCommand As String,
  ByVal mciReturn As String,
```

```
        ByVal mciReturnLength As Integer,
        ByVal mcihWnd As Integer) As Long

    Declare Function mciGetErrorString Lib "MMSYSTEM.DLL"
      (ByVal mciError As Long,
       ByVal mciErrString As String,
            ByVal mciErrLength As Any) As Integer

    Global mciCommand        As String
    Global mciReturn         As String
    Global mciReturnLength   As Integer
    Global mcihWnd           As Integer
    Global mciErrString      As String
    Global mciErrLength      As Integer
    Global mciError          As Long
```

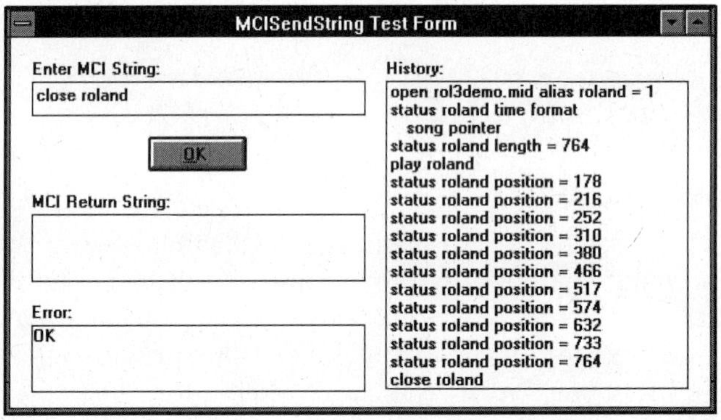

FIG. 24.7

The Visual Basic form for the MCITest application.

2. At the top of the form, add a text box called Text1 in which to enter the MCI command string, sized as shown in figure 24.7.

3. Add five labels to Form1, sized as shown in figure 24.7. These labels, from top to bottom, are Label1 through Label5. Assign captions to Label1 and Label5 as shown and set their **BorderStyle** property to 1.

4. Add the Command1 button in the position shown and assign &OK as its caption.

5. Add the list-box control object List1 in the position shown in the figure and add Label6 to identify the list box.

6. Select Command1 and enter the following event-handler code:

```
Sub Command1_Click ()          'Command1 is the OK button

    Label3.Caption = ""    'Label 3 receives the return string
    Label5.Caption = ""    'Label 5 receives the error string
```

```
mciReturn = String$(256, " ")
mciReturnLength = 256
mciErrString = String$(256, " ")
mciErrLength = 256
mciCommand = Text1.Text
mcihWnd = 0
mciError = mciSendString(mciCommand, mciReturn, mciReturnLength, mcihWnd)

Label3.Caption = Left$(mciReturn, (mciReturnLength [ms] 1))

If mciError > 0 Then
  Success% = mciGetErrorString(mciError, mciErrString, mciErrLength)
  Label5.Caption = LTrim$(Str$(mciError)) + "   " +
    Left$(mciErrString, (mciReturnLength [ms] 1))
  List1.AddItem mciCommand + " Err:" + Str$(mciError)
Else
  Label5.Caption = "OK"
  If Val(Label3.Caption) > 0 Then
   List1.AddItem mciCommand + " = " + Label3.Caption
  Else
   List1.AddItem mciCommand
   If Len(RTrim$(Label3.Caption)) > 0 Then
    List1.AddItem "    " + Label3.Caption
   End If
  End If
 End If
End Sub
```

7. Save the project under an appropriate name such as MCI_TEST.MAK.

8. Run the application. Enter your MCI test string in Text1, then click Command1. If your syntax is correct, the function is executed, and OK appears as the caption of Label5. If not, you receive the error number and the text description from mciGetErrorString() in Label5. Each MCI string you enter is shown in the text box, followed by the result value or text or the error that occurred.

This application demonstrates the principal advantage of Visual Basic over other programming languages for Windows: quick and easy generation of Windows applications. Creating the form, writing the code, and testing the application with several different types of devices takes less than an hour.

Multimedia Custom Control

Visual Basic with Professional Extensions and the Professional Toolkit for Visual Basic provide the MCI custom control (MCI.VBX) and a sample application (MCITest) that demonstrates use of the Animation, MIDI Sequencer, WaveAudio, and other MCI device types. The animation drivers (MCIMMP.DRV and MMP.DLL), which are not included with Windows 3.1, are provided in the Toolkit.

Figure 24.8 shows a MMMovie Player animation using the MCITEST.MMM file.

The command buttons at the bottom of the screen shown in the figure are created by the MMControl object. The buttons duplicate the functions of an audiotape or videotape recorder: (from left to right) rewind, fast forward, play, pause/resume, step backward, step forward, and stop.

The advantages of using the MCI.VBX custom control are its capability to create the command syntax for commonly used device types for you and its command buttons.

The version of MCI.VBX that was available when this book was written did not include all the properties for newer MCI device types such as AVIVideo. To display Audio Video Interleaved images in specific sizes at specific locations on your display using the *rectangle* item, for example, requires that you declare and use the mciSendString() function.

Using C and C++ Declarations

You must declare two function prototypes (included in the
MMSYSTEM.H header file of the Windows 3.1 Software Development
Kit and the Multimedia Development Kit) in order to implement MCI
command-string capability in your C or C++ application. Those declarations are as follows:

```
DWORD WINAPI mciSendString        (LPCSTR lpstrCommand,
                                   LPSTR lpstrReturnString,
                                   WORD wReturnLength,
                                   HWND hwndCallback);
BOOL WINAPI mciGetErrorString (DWORD wError,
                                   LPSTR lpstrBuffer,
                                   WORD wLength);
```

The Windows 3.1 SDK adds the LPCSTR type and substitutes WINAPI for
the conventional FAR PASCAL calling convention of SDK Version 3.0. SDK
Version 3.0 includes the following header entries in WINDOWS.H:

```
typedef const char FAR*        LPCSTR;

#define WINAPI                 _far _pascal
```

The conventional prototype declarations, WORD FAR PASCAL
mciSendString and DWORD FAR PASCAL mciGetErrorString, are
needed if you do not use the Windows 3.1 SDK.

```
BOOL WINAPI mciExecute         (lpstrCommand)

DWORD WINAPI mciSendString     (LPCSTR lpstrCommand,
                                LPSTR  lpstrReturnString,
                                WORD   wReturnLength,
                                HWND   hwndCallback);
BOOL WINAPI mciGetErrorString (DWORD  wError,
                                LPSTR  lpstrBuffer,
                                WORD   wLength);
```

wError is a long integer that contains the return value of an error
that occurs when the command is executed. This value is passed
to mciGetErrorString() to return the text version of the error in
lpstrBuffer. hwndCallback is a handle to the window to receive the
callback message if you use the **wait** parameter in your command string.

C and C++ programmers who are familiar with programming Windows
applications can add these function declarations to their header file
and create multimedia applications that use any valid MCI command
string by appropriate calls to mciSendString() and (optionally)

mciGetErrorString(). You can create more efficient C or C++ code by using mciSendCommand() and the symbolic constants declared in header files supplied with Version 3.1 of the SDK.

Chapter Summary

This chapter showed you how to use the MCI command strings to create multimedia applications that you cannot implement with commercial software. The chapter presented an example of the use of MCI command strings with a commercial application, Cakewalk Professional for Windows. The simple Visual Basic application presented in this chapter demonstrated how mciSendCommand() is used with programming language for Windows. The chapter also provided C type definitions and function prototype declarations for the basic MCI functions.

Chapter 25, the last chapter of this book, includes sales forecasts for the multimedia market and looks ahead to the new multimedia hardware and software you can expect to see in the mid-1990s.

Multimedia in the Future

M aking predictions about a technology as all-encompassing as multimedia is risky at best. Research firms are churning out reports at a furious pace, projecting multibillion-dollar markets for multimedia-related products in 1993 and later. Marketing professionals are creating plans designed to help their firms obtain (and maintain) a significant share of the multimedia market. The rate of multimedia-hardware development in the United States and Japan has accelerated greatly since the introduction of Windows 3.1, and new multimedia-product announcements appear weekly.

At the time this book was written, several competing standards for full-motion-video image compression existed. Moderately priced double-speed CD-ROM and CD-ROM XA drives were just beginning to emerge. Photo finishers were receiving the equipment they needed to create Kodak's Photo CD-ROMs. Prices of prosumer video equipment with remote-control capability remained in the $2,000-and-up range. Only a few applications for full-scale multimedia title authoring and professional desktop video production were out of beta testing and into shrink-wrapped packages. Only the future will tell what standards and applications will reign over DTV.

For nearly 10 years, the computing power of PCs has doubled every 18 months or so, but the price of the PC hardware that provides this increased power has remained constant or even declined. Whether the firms producing 80x86 microprocessors and their clones can continue this pace indefinitely is open to question, but prices of PCs with today's constant computing power will probably continue to decline. Multimedia hardware will follow the same pattern. Double-speed, 300K-per-second CD-ROM drives will be available in 1993 for about $350—the current price of a conventional drive (or even less).

MPC-compliant computers soon will be appearing alongside stereo equipment, VCRs, and camcorders in electronics stores. MPC computers will become essential home appliances, as microwave ovens are today. A computer, in fact, will control many of your other appliances. Your children will bring home CD-ROMs instead of books and prepare their homework on 3 1/2-inch floppy disks.

The Driving Force in Multimedia

John Walker, one of the founders of Autodesk, Inc., observed in the May 11, 1992 issue of *Microtimes* magazine that availability creates new computer markets and destroys old ones. Not long ago, one group of firms made specialty graphics adapter cards; another group made expensive video display units. But when Microsoft Corporation made a colorful graphical user interface available to the 10 million or more purchasers of Windows 3.0, Microsoft singlehandedly killed what used to be called the graphics market. Since the introduction of Windows 3.0, 256-color 800-by-600 adapters and SVGA monitors have been components of virtually all the new PCs sold. Now you buy a graphics adapter card only if the one in your computer fails, or you replace it with a graphics accelerator or a video-in-a-window (VIW) card. Ultimately, most of the components of today's graphics adapter cards will be built into the 80x86 microprocessor chip.

Windows 3.1 added a sound user interface. The mere availability of the Sound Recorder and Media Player applets enable you to play a death knell for the basic audio adapter card. Adding digitally sampled and FM-synthesized sound capability to a PC requires only a few chips, so these capabilities will be moved to the motherboard no later than 1993. Compaq added waveform audio capability to the motherboard in mid-1992. No wonder that Creative Labs announced a new, low-priced VIW card in April 1992.

Future versions of Windows will add full-motion video to Media Player's repertoire and perhaps add an applet or two to the Accessories group for more sophisticated video operations, probably in early 1993. By mid-1993, 15 million to 20 million people will be using Windows 3.x (including Windows NT), and Windows applications will constitute close to 40 percent of the personal-computer-software market, as projected in figure 25.1.

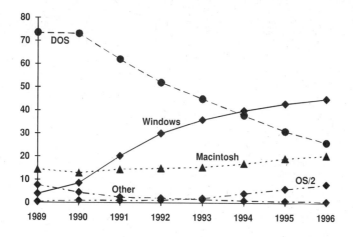

FIG. 25.1

Historical and
projected software-
market percentages.

The market percentages shown in the figure (which exclude operating systems and environments) are based on information furnished by the Software Publishers Association. The projections for 1992 through 1996 are derived from industry sources.

Windows 3.x will wreck the VIW card market. The standard graphic adapter cards in 1994 computers will have composite and S-video inputs and outputs, too. A set of connectors on the board, similar to the connectors now used for CD-ROM drives, will be provided for internal 5 1/4-inch Hi8 or VHS-C cassette VCRs.

Operating environments make the market for hardware, and hardware makes the market for applications. Windows opened the door to desktop publishing on the PC, but where would DTP be today without the low-cost laser printer? Multimedia technology predated the CD-ROM drive, but inexpensive CD-ROM drives will turn MPCs into home appliances. Tens of millions of VCRs and camcorders provide the impetus to create easy-to-use DTV applications. On the day you can buy a shrink-wrapped video-editing equivalent of Aldus Corporation's PageMaker, DTV can be said to have arrived.

The CD-ROM Drive Market

A CD-ROM drive is the most expensive component of an MPC computer. In most MPC installations, CD-ROM drive prices will pace the adoption of MPC capability on U.S. desktops and in home-based PCs. Certainly, the variety and quality of multimedia titles available in CD-ROM format will affect purchases, as will the proliferation of database and full-text discs. Hardware cost, however, traditionally has been the major factor in the acceptance of new PC technology.

Frost & Sullivan, Inc., a major market research firm, has prepared a study titled *The U.S. Market for CD-ROM Players and Prerecorded Media*, which forecasts sales of these products through 1996. The study projects that from the 350,000 units delivered in 1991, sales of CD-ROM drives will reach 5.4 million units annually by 1996, with sales volume approaching $1.7 billion in 1991 dollars. (Not all the CD-ROMs sold will be sold specifically for multimedia applications, but all will be capable of playing audio CD media.) Simple division results in an average price of $315—not substantially less than the cost of a discounted drive in mid-1992. By 1994, however, simple Red Book CD-ROM drives will sell for $200 or less. Average prices will be raised by high-end drives that provide CD-ROM extended architecture (XA), multiple-format playback capability, cartridge and changer functions, and other technological accouterments.

Figure 25.2 shows the Frost & Sullivan data for 1985 to 1996.

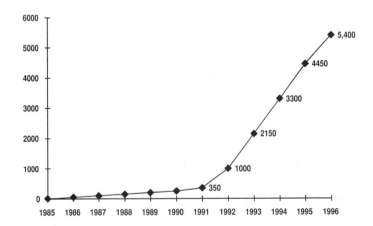

FIG. 25.2

Reported and projected sales of CD-ROM drives.

CD-ROM Formats and Titles

The cost of CD-ROM drives and the availability of double-speed CD-ROM XA drives will determine the size of the PC market for consumer CD-ROM titles and the formats in which those titles are available. Multimedia titles, like multimedia applications, depend on the widespread adoption of standardized hardware and the necessary Windows drivers. Following are some short-term trends for CD-ROM drives and the formats they will support:

- By the end of 1992, Kodak will have supplied most major photo finishers the equipment they need to produce Photo CDs. High-end CD-ROM XA drives compatible with the Photo CD format will be available from several sources—one of the few cases in which the software drives the hardware.

  Most of these drives will accommodate multiple-session Photo CDs, but few will provide CD-ROM XA audio compatibility. Avoid drives that don't support CD-ROM XA unless the manufacturer commits to an upgrade.

- By mid-1993, most CD-ROM drives sold will have full CD-ROM XA capability, including ADPCM audio compression. The Sony Multimedia Player will be in full production, extending CD-ROM XA benefits to the high-end consumer market. A Sony Multimedia Player with a 256-color display will be announced in 1993 or early 1994. By the end of 1994, or even sooner, a future version of Windows will be built into the Multimedia Player.

- Personal digital assistants and notebook computers will include a low-power-consumption CD-ROM XA drive similar to that used in the Sony Multimedia Player.

- By the end of 1993, the fate of Philips' CD-I format will be determined. Whether CD-I fades into oblivion (like Sony's consumer Beta video format) or becomes the VHS of the video CD market is anyone's guess at the moment, including Philips'. CD-ROM XA drives, however, that include CD-I bridge capability (necessary for playing CD-I titles on your computer) should be available in 1993.

- By late 1993, photo finishers will be able to add narration and music to Photo CD albums. Can Photo CDs with video capability be far behind?

- The CD-ROM will replace videotape as the distribution medium of choice for video clips. By 1994, video clips for DTV will be as common as clip art is for DTP. CD-ROMs will include video clips in AVI and DVI formats. Adapters and applications will enable you to play QuickTime CD-ROM animations and video clips in Windows.

Interactive CD-ROM titles designed for classrooms will have a profound influence on education. Classrooms of the future will be equipped with multiple large-screen or projection-TV displays attached to the teacher's PC. Pupils' desks will have built-in keyboards and trackballs. As budgets permit, displays and CD-ROM drives will be added to the desktop keyboards to permit students to learn at their own pace. Textbooks will become supplemental references, not primary learning devices.

What's in Store for Sound

The audio quality that will be implemented in the motherboards of most 1993 MPC computers will equal today's standard audio adapter card: four-operator FM synthesis, 8-bit and 16-bit stereo waveform audio, and a connector for a MIDI breakout box. Musicians undoubtedly will continue to use professional outboard MIDI equipment until equivalents become available on PC adapter cards. The wait will not be long, because Roland has announced an MPC-compliant version of its renowned SCC-1 Sound Canvas adapter card. Creative Labs' license for E-mu's Sound Engine technology will result in a new "music blaster" standard.

Multimedia title producers will opt for sophisticated audio adapter cards with 16-bit resolution and 44.1-kHz sampling (and the different sampling rates required for CD-ROM XA and digital audiotape). These cards will include 16-bit multisampled instrument sounds and will use digital signal processors to provide the digital audio effects that today require an outboard box. The Turtle Beach MultiSound card includes hardware that can produce these effects, but the software needed to program its on-board digital signal processor currently is missing. Turtle Beach and other manufacturers undoubtedly will fill this gap soon.

Desktop Audio Production

The major changes in multimedia audio will occur at the "prosumer" quality and pricing levels. Much of the audio work normally performed by studios for fees of hundreds of dollars per hour will be done on the desktop. Windows applications that make waveform audio files easy to edit have begun to appear, and you can expect improved multichannel editing applications to arrive in 1993.

Digital Audio Processing

Digital audiotape (DAT) is off to a slow start in the consumer market. Audio professionals are using DAT as a backup for reel-to-reel audio recordings, and some are adopting it as their primary audio-production medium.

Audio DAT drives for 5 1/4-inch computer bays are sure to appear in 1994 or sooner. These drives may do double duty for audio recording and reproduction; they also may serve as backup devices.

One change you can expect in professional audio adapter cards is full digital processing of the audio signals inside your computer. DAT drives and many audio CD drives have AES/EBU (professional) or S/PDIF (consumer) three-pin serial connectors that transmit stereo digital data from the tape or disc. Yamaha Corporation and other manufacturers have developed integrated-circuit chips to decode the serial data into the standard 16-bit PCM format required for CD-quality waveform audio files. This development opens the door for digital audio mixing, much as Sound Recorder enables you to mix two audio files with no significant loss of sound quality.

Figure 25.3 shows how a digital audio mixer might be implemented.

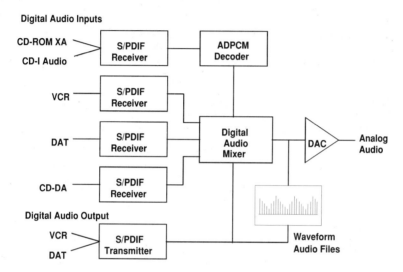

FIG. 25.3

A future digital-audio mixing system.

The professional audio adapter card of the 1993-94 period probably will resemble figure 25.4.

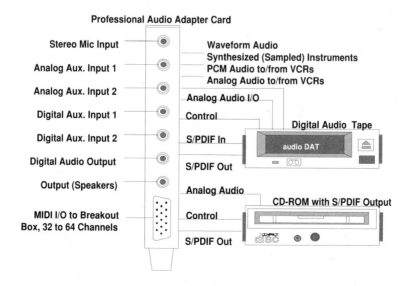

FIG. 25.4

A future professional audio adapter card.

Internal S/PDIF connectors will be provided for input from CD-DA signals and for inputs from and outputs to DATs and VCRs that have PCM sound-recording capability. External S/PDIF connectors will connect to outboard devices. You also can expect additional analog mixer inputs. Future audio adapter cards won't replace your MIDI-controlled 16-channel stereo mixer for mastering music, but these cards will be capable of handling all the audio inputs from internal and external audiovisual drives.

New mono and stereo sampling rates—18.9 kHz and 37.8 kHz for CD-ROM XA audio and 32 kHz and 48 kHz for digital audiotape—will be added to the 11.025-kHz, 22.05-kHz, and 44.1-kHz rates you use today with waveform audio files.

Fiber Optics for Audio Cabling

After digital audio transmission takes over, fiber-optic cabling will replace today's RCA phono jacks. Audio CD players and DAT decks designed for audiophiles include fiber-optic transmitters for the S/PDIF signals.

Fiber-optic cabling eliminates grounding problems but primarily is used to prevent crosstalk (signal interference). No standard similar to RS-170A exists for fiber-optic connectors, but the AT&T cabling system appears to be gaining ground in the consumer market against the more common Toslink and EIAJ fiber-optic connectors. By 1994 or 1995, some form of fiber-optic transmission undoubtedly will be used for audio and video I/O connections in your computer.

Another problem with fiber-optic connections is the communication protocol to be used. The Alesis ADAT eight-channel digital audio recorder (described in Chapter 11) uses EIAJ fiber-optic connectors and a proprietary multichannel protocol. Alesis plans to introduce several new products (including the S4 QuadraSynth sound module and a keyboard version called the S5) that take advantage of fiber-optic capabilities. Other manufacturers of professional audio equipment may license the protocol if ADAT's optics become a studio standard.

Sound Synthesizer Cards

The expanding market for quality sound in multimedia titles and presentations will result in the availability of a broad selection of sound modules on a card. The Roland SCC-1—a complete Sound Canvas GS Sound Module on a half-length PC adapter card—is one example; Turtle Beach's MultiSound (with a built-in E-mu Proteus/1 XR) is another example.

Manufacturers of conventional keyboard synthesizers and sound modules (including Yamaha, E-mu, and Ensoniq) supply low-cost integrated-circuit chips to manufacturers of audio adapter card manufacturers. These firms, however, are losing brand recognition to Media Vision and Creative Labs in the fastest-growing market for electronic musical instruments. The traditional synthesizer manufacturers are unlikely to allow this trend to continue. Agreements between manufacturers of adapter cards and synthesizers, such as the alliance between Creative Labs and E-mu, are likely to proliferate.

When you program a sound module with a computer, all you need is the basic electronics of the module connected to your PC's bus. The case, power supply, voice-programming push buttons, and mini-LCD display required for stand-alone modules become superfluous. Disk files, not plug-in ROM cards, hold PCM samples and preprogrammed performance setups. These unneeded components contribute several times the manufacturing cost of the printed-wiring board and the chips mounted on it. A Korg Wavestation on a PC adapter card, with all programming done in a Windows application on a 13-inch or larger SVGA display, would be an interesting product.

Several additional benefits will accrue when sound modules are supplied on adapter cards instead of in 19-inch rack mounts. Those benefits are as follows:

- The speed limit imposed by MIDI's serial transmission technique will be eliminated. Data from MIDI files will be sent to the appropriate devices over the PC bus, not over MIDI cables.

- A virtually unlimited number of MIDI channels will be available. The new breed of Windows sequencers, such as Cakewalk for Windows, enable you to assign individual tracks to any synthesizer device for which a Windows driver is loaded.

- The rat's nest of MIDI cables and MIDI patch bays will be eliminated. This change will be a boon to performing musicians, because computers are inherently more reliable than MIDI cables and connectors.

- The five-pin mini-DIN connector, which will fit in a PC's rear-panel adapter card slot, will become the new standard for MIDI connections. The Roland SCC-1 was the first adapter card to use mini-DIN MIDI connectors. You will use a female mini-DIN to male standard-DIN adapter during the transition to conventional MIDI connectors.

Because all the internal audio signals in synthesizers are processed in serial digital form, they are ideally suited to be the all-digital audio systems of the future. Figure 25.5 shows how two sound module cards and one drum-machine synthesizer card might be connected via S/PDIF digital audio to a multitrack DAT recorder, the Alesis ADAT.

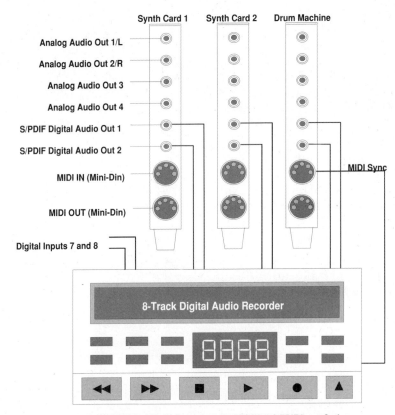

Digital outputs of audio
adapter cards
connected to a
multitrack DAT
recorder.

You can expect new methods of synthesizing the sounds of acoustic musical instruments to appear in 1993 and 1994. High-speed digital signal processors on an audio adapter card provide the computing power to simulate the sound of virtually any musical instrument without the limitations of FM synthesis. The Turtle Beach MultiSound card, with on-board DSP, is the first of these devices to provide MPC capability.

When you combine DSP hardware with Stanford University's WaveGuide programming techniques, you can define your own woodwind instrument, for example, by specifying the material of which the instrument is made, the geometry of its bore, the type of reed it uses, and the locations of its pitch holes. Media Vision is working with Stanford to develop the first commercial implementation of WaveGuide synthesis on an MPC-compliant audio adapter card. Production quantities of the card are expected to be available in 1993. DSPs enable you to program virtually any acoustic effect, so DSPs will become integral components of all high-end sample-playback synthesizer adapters. Programming a DSP to provide a serial digital signal is easy, so S/PDIF or related digital audio signals will become common as synthesizer outputs.

As digital audio components with S/PDIF copper or fiber-optic connectors and digital amplifiers become more common, the only analog signals in the entire audio chain will be inputs from microphones and outputs to speakers.

Sequencer Applications

No sequencer applications were OLE-compliant when this book was written. Passport Designs and Midisoft Corporation had made major upgrades to their Windows sequencer applications to adapt them for use with the multimedia extensions and to incorporate General MIDI features. Twelve Tone Systems had just released a Windows version of Cakewalk Professional. Big Noise Software's Cadenza, which originally used the Gem graphic interface, appeared in a Windows version. These firms are likely to have set their programmers to work making their sequencers OLE-compliant. After OLE-compliant sequencers appear on the market, manufacturers of MPC audio adapter cards and synthesizers (and third-party music-software authors) can create OLE server applications that add new functions and convenience to sequencers.

You may wonder how OLE could be used effectively with MIDI sequencers. Following are a few examples of OLE applications that currently are being developed by manufacturers of adapter cards and sequencer applications:

- *SysEx-editor objects* that enable you to create or edit MIDI SysEx messages to send to sound modules or accessories when you start the track. Double-click the SysEx icon, and the editor pops up, with embedded data stored in the file or linked to a separate SysEx file in MIDIEX format. Professional sequencers provide this capability now, but OLE enables you to use the SysEx editor of your choice.

- *Voice-editor objects* to modify the instrument's sound when you load a MIDI file. Insert a voice-editor object in the first measure and then double-click its icon to bring up an image of the front panel of your sound module.

  Create a patch in a familiar environment and save it in the file as a MIDI meta event, and you don't have to worry about assigning the patch the next time you play the tune.

- *Parameter-adjustment objects* for specific sound cards or modules that send short SysEx messages to change master values, alter reverberation macros, or adjust the chorus effects.

■ *Audio-mixer objects* that mix in waveform audio, CD audio, or audio-tape tracks. All that's needed is to add OLE server capability to the mixer application for your audio adapter card. Cakewalk Professional for Windows provides this capability through its MCI command events.

■ *Waveform-audio objects* that enable you to add vocals or sound effects (embedded in the file or linked from a separate file) wherever you want. Sound Recorder or a more sophisticated waveform audio editor such as Wave for Windows or AudioView might be used. Version 1.0 of Cakewalk for Windows enables you to insert waveform audio data, but not by using OLE.

■ *Clipboard operations* that enable you to paste selected portions of a MIDI file into a document created by an OLE client application.

Figure 25.6 shows how these objects might appear in the Staff window of Cakewalk for Windows.

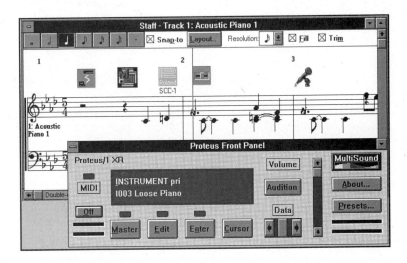

FIG. 25.6

One method of implementing a future OLE server voice editor with an OLE client sequencer.

Each OLE client is represented by its icon at the measure and beat at which its data is required. You double-click the Proteus icon to edit the Acoustic Piano voice of your Turtle Beach MultiSound card. The MultiSound Proteus Front Panel window appears, and you edit the data by clicking replicas of the buttons that appear on the front panel of the Proteus/1 XR sound module. Close the window, and your changes are saved as a patch inserted at beat 3 of measure 2. If you double-click the patch number in the Track/Measure window, the edit applies to the track as a whole.

Windows-based sequencers can be expected to increase in sophistication when Microsoft releases Windows NT in 1993. OLE Version 2, which is expected to be incorporated into Windows NT, will give sequencers expanded interapplication-communication capabilities. Windows NT should eliminate many of the timing problems involved in playing back complex MIDI files and simultaneously recording or reproducing waveform audio.

Desktop Video Publishing

Desktop video, like desktop publishing, depends on the availability of moderately priced but sophisticated hardware for its ultimate success. Following are some of the devices currently under development:

- A combination SVGA and video adapter card with both video inputs and video outputs, creating the equivalent of today's Truevision Bravado card with added genlock capability for video mixing, overlays, and chroma keying. Control-L or VISCA connectors will be included for A-B roll editing. This card will enable you to plug your camcorder into the video input port and attach your VCR to the card's video output for editing and titling.

- VCRs that will mount in standard 5 1/4-inch disk bays and are priced similarly to mid-level consumer VCRs. A basic daughterboard with a serial output port and video mixing capability is required to make the internal connections. Simple fades, dissolves, and wipes would be included.

- Optional daughterboards that provide JPEG, MPEG, ADPCM, and other compression methods for the video and audio signals so that you can store graphics, video segments, and compressed audio data on your hard disk, opening the door for nonlinear editing.

- Special video effects, such as those now offered by New Tek's Video Toaster, will be added as custom chips are developed for this purpose. The basic videographics board will destroy the video-in-a-window and genlock market for the original producers, but special-purpose daughterboards will open a new and lucrative specialty market. Conventional 7-bit 4:1:1 YUV encoding probably will be satisfactory for most applications, keeping memory costs to a minimum.

Figure 25.7 shows a videographics adapter card that may be available near the end of 1993.

When you can install a videographics adapter card, slide an internally mounted VCR into a drive bay, and install the required Windows drivers as easily and inexpensively as you can add a multimedia upgrade kit, desktop video truly will have arrived.

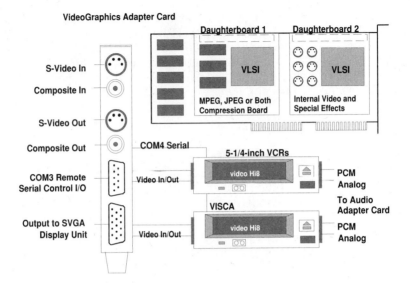

VideoGraphics Adapter Card

FIG. 25.7

A future videographics
adapter card.

As soon as the hardware is available, the software will follow. You will be able to cut and paste video segments into a DTV production as easily as you can place still graphics in PageMaker. Dragging and dropping video and audio files will become as commonplace as moving text in Word for Windows 2 and its successors. Software that offers these capabilities should be available in 1993.

Multimedia Computers in the Future

The pace of multimedia-hardware development will parallel the development of higher-speed computers with new features such as local bus video. When VCRs and DAT drives are available in 5 1/4-inch format, these components will sell for prices comparable to those of today's CD-ROM drives. The following sections discuss a few trends in computer technology.

MPC Computers for Consumers

Multimedia Specifications 1.0 essentially was obsolete after less than one year in existence. No base-level MPC-compliant audio adapter cards are available. No such cards were produced because no one would purchase a monaural, eight-note-polyphonic, five-simultaneous-timbre card for $60 to $75 when 11-voice stereo cards are available for about $100 and 16-voice products sell for about $150.

The specifications' CPU standard also is obsolete. About four months after the specifications were issued, MPC Marketing Council members determined that the specified 80286-based computers are unsatisfactory for running Windows, let alone Windows with the multimedia extensions. You will not be pleased by the performance of AVI video clips played on a CD-ROM with a 16-MHz 80386SX PC. Price wars in the 80386DX market have reduced the price difference between 20-MHz SX and 33-MHz DX PC clones to $100 or so.

The consumer MPC computer probably will have the following features in 1993:

- A ISA motherboard with a 33-MHz 80386DX CPU, 4M of RAM, an on-board SCSI interface, stereo FM-synthesized sound (Yamaha OPL-III), 8-bit stereo waveform audio record/playback capability up to 44.1 kHz, and standard MIDI IN and OUT connectors (the requirement for a MIDI THRU connector will be abandoned)

- A pair of speakers, either built into the computer's case or supplied separately

- A standard 150K-per-second CD-ROM drive with an average seek time of 350 milliseconds or less

- A 120M-or-larger, 18-millisecond-or-faster IDE hard disk drive

- One 3 1/2-inch high-density floppy disk drive (space for at least two additional 5 1/4-inch drives will be provided, but the 5 1/4-inch floppy disk drive will be obsolete)

- A graphics adapter card with 1M of memory to provide 256 colors at 1,024-by-768 pixel resolution

- 14-inch multisynchronous, noninterlaced VGA display with a dot pitch of 0.28mm or smaller

- An external SCSI connector for scanners, additional CD-ROM drives, and similar accessories

- At least four free adapter-card slots

- A version of Windows and all drivers for the standard hardware configuration installed on the hard disk

Figure 25.8 shows price projections for MPC-compliant computers with the preceding features.

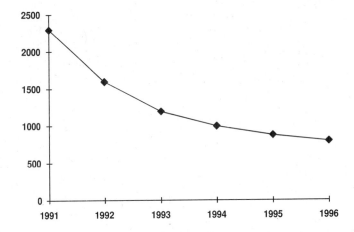

FIG. 25.8

Projected prices of
unbranded MPC-
compliant 80386DX
(or equivalent)
computers.

Options will include substitution of a double-speed CD-ROM XA drive
for the standard drive ($100 or so by mid-1993) and replacement of the
VGA adapter card with a combination VGA-video I/O card (basic version,
about $200 additional in 1993-94).

MPC Specifications 1.0 may continue to assure consumers that the computers or upgrade kits they purchase will be compatible with conventional CD-ROM titles. The upgrade-kit specification will suffice for some
time because market forces, not the specification, have dictated the capabilities of audio adapter cards. But consumers who purchase a mini-
mally compliant MPC computer are bound to be disappointed by its
performance. The failure to include video I/O requirements in MPC
Specifications 1.0 is understandable, considering that the specifications
were published in the fall of 1991. If all goes well, an MPC-II, MPC-V, or
similar standard will be produced for multimedia DTV computers, upgrade kits, and applications.

Multimedia Authoring Computers

A multimedia authoring computer will have the following features by
1994:

- ■ A 50-MHz or faster P5 (80586DX) motherboard with 12M or more
  of RAM

- ■ A built-in SCSI interface for hard disks, CD-ROM drives, and scanner

- ■ One or two 600M-or-larger 3 1/2-inch SCSI hard disk drives

- ■ A 20M to 30M 3 1/2-inch magneto-optical (floptical) disk drive compatible with current 3 1/2-inch magnetic floppy disks

- A stack of 5 1/4-inch multimedia audiovisual devices similar to that shown in figure 25.9.

- A 16-bit hand-held or flatbed color scanner with resolution of 400 dots per inch or greater (to match that of Hi8 videotape)

- Hardware JPEG compression of still images and MPEG compression of video segments

- A 21-inch high-resolution monitor (1,280 by 960 pixels)

- Studio-quality near-field monitor speakers

Figure 25.9 shows the drive bays of a future multimedia authoring computer.

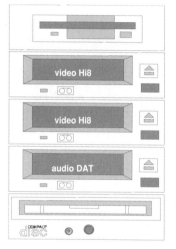

3-1/2-inch Compatible Floptical/Diskette Drive

5-1/4-inch Hi8 VCR

5-1/4-inch Hi8 VCR

Digital Audio Tape Drive with File Backup Capability

Writable CD-ROM Drive with XA and audio CD

FIG. 25.9

The drive bay of a future multimedia authoring computer.

By 1994, write-once CD-ROM drives should be available for about $1,000, and DAT drives should sell for about the same price as mid-level VCRs. The cost of a multimedia authoring computer with the features listed in this section should fall to between $5,000 and $10,000 (depending on the number and types of drives and on the type of monitor).

The widespread use of internal multimedia source and destination drives does not mean that external VCRs, DAT and multitrack digital audio drives, and other audiovisual components will become obsolete overnight. Most on-line editing of commercial DTV presentations and mastering of CD-ROM titles will continue to be done in studios with professional equipment. But today's quality gap between prosumer and industrial-quality or even broadcast-grade equipment will continue to decrease. You will be able to create sample CD-ROM titles for beta and consumer testing, DTV presentations for your firm, and edit decision lists to reduce the cost of on-line editing.

Multimedia Authoring Applications

Professional multimedia authoring applications currently are available from several publishers. Ease of use will be improved, and these applications will be expanded to include a wide range of input devices. By 1993 or 1994, almost all multimedia authoring packages will enable users to produce titles in CD-ROM XA format and in CD-I format (if CD-I succeeds in the marketplace). These improvements will be incremental, not revolutionary.

The major trend in new multimedia authoring applications will be DTV editing. Nonlinear editing applications will enable you to drag and drop video segments, audio narration, background music, and still images into a computer-generated production preview with a tentative edit decision list. After you preview your production, you can send it to tape.

Matrox's Personal Producer is a harbinger of the easy-to-use DTV editing applications that will appear in 1993 and 1994. The size of the market for DTV will exceed that of the market for multimedia CD-ROM titles, but a new market will appear for full-motion, high-resolution video clips supplied on CD-ROMs.

A new class of multimedia applications (the multimedia databases discussed briefly in Chapters 20 and 22) will become necessary as your sources of multimedia images and sounds proliferate. Major DTV producers will need to catalog thousands of still and animated images, video segments, background music, and other multimedia source elements. As multimedia database applications and multimedia network server systems mature, the combination will evolve into large-scale nonlinear multimedia editing systems.

New OLE applets will appear, enabling you to drop video, animation, and sound clips into word processing documents and spreadsheets, much the way that you can use Sound Recorder to add voice notes to spreadsheets and E-mail messages today. Floptical drives can hold up to a few minutes of video in Microsoft AVI format, depending on the content, so the recipient of a floppy disk with a video clip embedded in a worksheet file need not have a VCR attached.

Chapter Summary

You're on your own. Publishing limitations prevent any book on multimedia technology in the Windows environment from being truly all-inclusive. This book concentrated on sound in the Windows 3.1 environment, because adding moderate- to high-quality audio to the PC will be the first step into multimedia for most Windows users, a fact proved by the phenomenal growth in sales of MPC-compliant audio adapter cards since the advent of Windows 3.1. Sales of CD-ROM drives, in MPC Upgrade Kits and as separate devices, were climbing when this book was written.

Desktop video production and the hardware to support it received considerable coverage in this book because of the lack of industry-wide standards. After you add an audio card and a CD-ROM drive, the next logical step is to connect your PC to your VCR and camcorder. NTSC and S-video are standards enough for the more than 60 million owners of VCRs.

Read multimedia periodicals such as *MPC World* and *New Media* to keep pace with multimedia developments, and read magazines such as *AV Video*, *Electronic Musician*, and *Keyboard* to follow trends in more specialized areas. These publications are invaluable sources of up-to-date information on multimedia trends, techniques, and new products. Perhaps as early as mid-1993, the multimedia authoring and DTV equivalents of WordPerfect and Lotus-1-2-3 will emerge. With the assistance of *Discover Windows 3.1 Multimedia*, you could be creating your own multimedia titles or DTV presentations before then.

Glossary

1-bit conversion. A term used in digital audio and video recording and reproduction to describe analog-to-digital (ADC) and digital-to-analog (DAC) converters using an oversampling technique and sigma-delta modulation for coding and decoding.

80x86. A term describing any of the Intel 16- and 32-bit processors used in PCs, including the 16-bit 80286 used in the original AT computers and the 80386 and 80486 32-bit chips. The P5 (80586) microprocessor is expected to be introduced by Intel Corporation in late 1992.

A-B roll editing. A method for creating a master-edited videotape by directing selected portions of video signals from two video sources (computers, VCRs, or camcorders) to a destination recording device, usually a VCR. Also called A-B editing.

Accelerando. A musical term indicating a gradual increase in the tempo of playing.

Accelerator key. A key combination providing access to a menu choice, macro, or other function of an application. The accelerator key replaces selection with the mouse. Also called a shortcut key.

Accent. In music, additional volume given to a particular note for emphasis.

Accidental. In musical notation, a symbol indicating a note should be played either a half tone above (sharp symbol, #) or a half tone below (flat symbol, reverse b) the standard pitch of the note. A natural symbol (similar to the sharp symbol) cancels either a previously assigned sharp or flat accidental for the balance of the measure.

Active. In Windows, the currently running application or the window capable of receiving user input. The title bar of the active window has a colored background.

Active sensing. A MIDI message commanding a MIDI instrument or device to monitor its channel(s) to determine whether messages occur on the channel(s) within a predetermined, maximum time period (called a "time window"). If no messages are received within the time window, the device creates its own All Notes Off MIDI message to assure no notes remain.

Adapter card. A printed wiring board with digital circuitry that plugs into connectors on the motherboard of a personal computer, usually performing input/output functions. *See* Motherboard.

ADC. An abbreviation for Analog-to-Digital Converter. The electronic device converting conventional analog audio and video signals to digital form. The digital form can be processed by computer and stored as data on a computer's hard disk driver.

Address. The numerical value, usually in hexadecimal format, of a particular location in a computer's random-access memory (RAM).

ADPCM. An abbreviation for Adaptive Differential Pulse Code Modulation. A method of digital waveform sampling encoding the difference between successive samples rather than encoding their actual values (DPCM). The differences are assigned different values based on the content of the sample. ADPCM is the storage format used by CD-ROM XA and CD-I discs. *See* CD-I, CD-ROM XA, ADPCM, and PCM.

ADSR. An abbreviation for Attack, Decay, Sustain, and Release. Four elements that describe a conventional musical synthesizer's sound envelope. *See* Attack, Decay, Sustain, Release, and Envelope.

AES. An abbreviation for Audio Engineering Society (U.S.), a professional association that helps establish standards for audio equipment.

AES/EBU. An abbreviation for a standard (ANSI S.4.40-1985) for the transmission of stereo digital audio signals via a shielded, three-conductor cable terminated by XLR (microphone) connectors between professional digital audio components. S/PDIF, the Sony/Philips standard for consumer products, is similar.

Aftertouch. The amount of pressure remaining on the key of a synthesizer keyboard once the key has been depressed. Some keyboards translate aftertouch as a continuous stream of MIDI aftertouch messages.

Algorithm. A set of instructions carrying out a single function, such as the calculation of a single value in a computer program. In electronic music, an algorithm describes how a sound is created. FM synthesizers use algorithms to determine how carriers and modulators interact to form voices.

Aliasing. An occurrence in sampling analog signals where the sampling rate and the frequency of the sampled wave are congruous. Thus, the sample values do not properly represent the original waveform. Aliasing is most pronounced when the fundamental frequency of a sound is more than half the sampling rate. In video images, aliasing causes straight lines (especially diagonal ones) to appear jagged. *See* Anti-aliasing filter.

All notes off. A MIDI message signaling an instrument assigned to a designated channel to be silent.

Amplitude. The volume or intensity measure of a sound or radio wave.

Amplitude modulation. A term describing the interaction of two signals—a carrier and a modulator. The modulation signal varies the amplitude (intensity) of the carrier. In AM radio transmission, the carrier is a medium-frequency signal (550 - 1550 kHz), and the modulator is the sound signal. In sound synthesis, a low-frequency oscillator modulates a carrier that is the sound's fundamental frequency.

Analog. A representation of a sound (or video) by an electrical signal where the amplitude is proportional to the signal voltage and the frequency of the sound or variations in brightness are represented by the signal's rate of change of voltage.

Analog-to-digital conversion. *See* ADC.

ANSI. An abbreviation for the American National Standards Institute. ANSI, in the Windows context, refers to the ANSI character set that Microsoft uses for Windows.

Anti-aliasing (filter). A hardware device or software algorithm that prevents or minimizes aliasing affects, specific sound frequency losses, or unwanted sound additions that occur during sampled audio recording or playback. *See* Aliasing.

Aperiodic. An event that occurs at random intervals, such as noise in an audio or video system.

API. An abbreviation for Application Programming Interface. Generically, a method of accessing or modifying the operating system for a program. In Windows, the API refers to the functions provided by Windows 3.x allowing applications to open and close windows, read the keyboard, interpret mouse movements, and so on. Programmers call these functions hooks to the operating system.

Applet. A Windows application designed to accomplish a single, often simple task. The applet is usually included with a commercial product, but it's not sold as a product by itself. The Packager and Character Map applications supplied with Windows 3.1 are applets.

Application. The software product resulting from the creation of a program. Application is often used as a synonym for program. Microsoft Word for Windows, Microsoft Excel, Adobe Type Manager, and Lotus 1-2-3 are Windows applications. Applications are usually distinguished by the operating system for which they are designed (Windows, DOS, Macintosh, UNIX, and so on).

Argument. Data supplied to and acted upon or used by a function to perform its task. Arguments are enclosed in parentheses. Additional arguments, if any, are separated by commas. Arguments of functions are equivalent to parameters of instructions and procedures.

Array. In mathematics and computer programming, an ordered sequence of values (elements) stored within a single, named variable. Individual elements of the array are accessed by referring to the variable name with the element's number (index or subscript) in parentheses. An example is the BASIC statement: `Value$ = Array$(3)`. Arrays may have more than one dimension. If so, access to the value includes indexes for each dimension, such as `Value$ = Array$(3,3)`.

Artifact. An extraneous sound or affect on an image not present in the source signal and introduced by one of the components in the recording or reproduction chain.

ASCII. Abbreviation for the American Standard Code for Information Interchange. A set of standard numerical values that correspond to sets of printable (letters, numbers, and punctuation), control (created by control-key combinations with characters), and special characters (graphic symbols) used by PCs and most other computers. Other commonly used codes for character sets are ANSI (used by Windows) and EBCDIC (Extended Binary Coded Decimal Interchange Code, used by IBM for mainframe computers).

Aspect ratio. An image's ratio of width to height. Aspect ratio is usually expressed as W:H—W being the width and H being the height of the image. The aspect ratio of digital images is expressed as the ratio of the number of pixels in each dimension (640:480 for VGA images).

Assembler. An application that creates machine-readable (object) code from source code written in assembly language. MASM (the Microsoft Assembler) is the PC application most commonly used to write assembly-language code.

Assembly language. A low-level language that provides direct manipulation of PC hardware. *See* Assembler.

Assign. To give a value to a variable.

Attack. The rate at which a sound reaches its maximum specified amplitude from an initial silent condition. One of the elements of a sound envelope.

Auxiliary audio. A set of multimedia functions used to control the audio mixer of MPC-compatible, sound-adapter cards. The term is also used to describe audio devices whose output may be mixed with WaveAudio or MIDI audio outputs to form a composite sound source.

AVI. An abbreviation for Audio Video Interleaved. The Microsoft Application Programming Interface (API) designed to compete with Apple's QUICKTIME methodology. AVI techniques provide a software synchronization and compression standard for audio and video signals competing with DVI. *See* DVI, Interleaved, Full-motion video, and QuickTime.

Background. In multitasking operations, the application or procedure that is not visible on screen and that will not receive user-generated input. In Windows, background is an application that is minimized and does not have the focus. In multimedia animation, images (usually static) that are shown behind other images (usually animated) are called background.

Balanced. A term describing the transmission of an audio signal over a three-conductor cable including two signal and one ground (earth or return) conductors. The signal conductors carry voltages that are 180 degrees out of phase with one another. The imbalance enables the signals to be recombined with one another at the receiving end of the cable. This type of transmission cancels most of the noise that might have been added to the signal during the cable run. Most balanced audio cables have 600-ohm impedance. Balanced signals are often referred to as "double-ended." *See* Unbalanced.

Bandwidth. The rate information can be transmitted through an electronic channel. Bandwidth is usually expressed in kHz or MHz. In the MPC specifications, bandwidth refers to the rate at which instructions can be passed over the PC bus by the base-level, 16-MHz 80386SX microprocessor. Consumption of processor time by the audio adapter card and CD-ROM drive must not (but often does) exceed the specified percentages of this capacity.

Bar. In musical notation, a synonym for measure. Bar is a grouping of notes corresponding to the number of rhythmic beats corresponding to the denominator of the time signature. *See* Beat and Time signature.

Basic synthesizer standard. The minimum sound synthesis capability of an MPC-compliant, audio-adapter card. The basic synthesizer standard was established by MPC specification 1.0 issued by the Multimedia Marketing Council. The basic requirement is three, melodic timbres assigned to channels 13 through 15 and two, percussive timbres assigned to channel 16 be playable simultaneously. *See* Extended synthesizer standard.

Baud. A term used to describe the rate that teletype signals are transmitted over the switched telephone network. Baud was named for M. Baudot, a French engineer who invented the serial transmission method and the code to implement it. The transmission speed of modems is often expressed in baud, but the baud is applicable to speeds of 300 and 600 only. 1,200 and higher rates are expressed in bps.

Beat. In musical notation, the basic unit of rhythm. The tempo of music is determined by the number of beats per minute. In standard 4/4 (fox-trot) time, one beat is represented by a quarter note.

Bed. A term used in television production to describe the instrumental portion of the music (the underscore) for a program or commercial. *See* Underscore.

Bidirectional. A type of microphone reproducing sound impinging on it from two opposite sides.

Binary file. A file whose content does not consist of lines of text. Executable (EXE), dynamic link library (DLL), and most database files are stored in binary format.

Bit. The smallest piece of information that can be processed by a computer. A bit, derived from the contraction of BInary digiT, has two states: on (1) or off (0). Eight bits make up a byte, and sixteen bits combined are called a word. *See* Byte.

BitBlt. Abbreviation for Bit Block Transfer. An assembly-level function used for copying graphic images in Windows applications from a source to a destination graphic context.

Bit-field. *See* Mask.

Bit map. The representation of a screen or printed image, usually graphic, as a series of bytes containing information on the color of each pixel that comprises the image. *See* Pixel.

Bit-wise. A process evaluating each bit of a combination, such as a byte or word, rather than processing the combination as a single element. Logical operations and masks use bit-wise procedures.

Blitting. The process of using BitBlt functions to copy a bit map from a source to a destination. *See* BitBlt.

Boolean. A type of arithmetic in which all digits are bits. The numbers may have two states only: on (true or 1) or off (false or 0). This type of arithmetic is widely used in set theory and computer programming. Boolean, named after the mathematician George Boole, is also used to describe a data type that may have two states only: true or false.

Break. To cause an interruption in program operation. Ctrl+C is the standard DOS break key combination, but it will seldom halt the operation of a Windows application. In Windows, Esc is more commonly used to cause an operation to terminate prior to completion.

Breakpoint. A designated statement causing program execution to halt after executing the statement preceding it. Breakpoints may be toggled on or off by a Visual Basic menu selection, Run/Toggle Breakpoint, or the F9 function key.

Bridge. An electronic device or software used to connect one type of network or communication system protocol with another. In multimedia, a bridge is a standard enabling CDs created in different formats to be read by a single drive.

Buffer. In memory, a reserved area of a designated size (number of bytes). A buffer is typically used to hold a portion of a file or the value of a variable. When you record waveform audio, for instance, a buffer is created to hold the digital representation of the sound. When you complete the recording and decide to save it, the content of the buffer is written to the hard disk, and the memory reserved by the buffer is freed.

Bulk dump. In MIDI terminology, a long series of System Exclusive (SysEx) messages that may represent the setup information (patches) for a group of voices on a synthesizer or one or more sound samples in PCM format. *See* MIDI sample dump standard, PCM, and System exclusive.

Bus. In PC terminology, a group of conductors (printed circuit wires) to which connectors are attached, allowing multiple adapter cards to have access to the microprocessor. *See* EISA, ISA and MCA as examples of PC bus structures.

Byte. Eight bits of data treated as a group. The minimum decimal value of a byte is 0 (00000000, shown as 0x00, H00, or 00H in hexadecimal notation), and the maximum is 256 (11111111, 0xFF, HFF, or FFH). The byte is the most common form of binary information used by microcomputers and is the basic unit of MIDI messages. The byte is also the unit of RAM memory size in PCs, representing storage capacity for a single character. The most common scaled units are kilobytes (1,024 bytes) and megabytes (1,048,576 bytes).

Camcorder. A contraction of camera and recorder. The term describes a video camera and videocassette recorder combined into a single, hand-held unit. Consumer camcorders record on 8-mm or VHS-C (compact) video cassettes.

Caption. The text appearing in the title bar of a window.

Cardioid. A microphone with a heart-shaped response pattern having maximum sensitivity to sounds arriving from a 180-degree angle and some response to sounds beyond this angle. Microphones with a cardioid pattern are the most common in professional audio work.

Caret. The term used by Windows indicating that the mouse cursor, usually in the shape of a structural steel I-beam, is used in a text field.

Carrier. The fundamental wave of an audio or radio signal that may be modulated by another signal. *See* Modulation, Amplitude modulation, and Frequency modulation.

Case sensitivity. A term defining whether an interpreter or compiler treats lowercase and uppercase letters as the same character. Most interpreters and compilers are case-insensitive. C is an exception; it is case-sensitive, and all its keywords are in lowercase. Many interpreters, such as Visual Basic, will reformat keywords to their standards: all uppercase for BASIC and a combination of upper- and lowercase letters in Visual Basic.

Cast. In the Multimedia Movie Player, a collection of individual images displayed during movie playback.

Cast-based animation. An animation methodology treating each object in an animated production as an individual graphic image (cast member) that may be independently manipulated. Modifications to the object are controlled by a script.

CAV. An abbreviation for Constant Angular Velocity devices. These devices, such as computer-hard disks and CAV video laserdiscs, have a varying data transfer rate depending on the distance of the read-write head from the drive spindle.

CCD. Abbreviation for Charge-Coupled Device. An integrated circuit consisting of a linear array of semiconductor photoreceptor elements. CCDs are used to create a bit-mapped image. Each photoreceptor creats an electrical signal representing the luminance of one pixel. CCDs are primarily used in scanners, color xerographic printers and video cameras. *See* Photoreceptor.

CCITT. An abbreviation for the Consulative Committee International for Telephone and Telegraph communication. CCITT establishes standards for telephone interchange and modems in Europe. Several CCITT standards for communication between modems over telephone networks have been adopted in the United States.

CD. An abbreviation for compact disc. CDs are the original format for distributing compact optical disks for audio reproduction (CDAudio). This early format was jointly developed by Philips N.V. and Sony Corporation and is described in Philips N.V.'s Yellow Book. Control of Yellow Book CD-ROMs, such as starting and stopping the drive and file selection with your computer, requires Microsoft's MSCDEX.DRV driver.

CD-DA. An abbreviation for Compact Disk-Digital Audio, also called "Red Book" audio. CD-DA requires compatibility with MPC specification 1.0. It enables interleaving of audio with other types of data, so recorded sound can accompany images. Playing CDs with CD-DA audio requires Microsoft's MSCDEX.DRV, version 2.2 or higher, which is not provided with Windows 3.1. It is usually supplied with the CD-ROM drive when purchased as a component of an MPC upgrade kit. The CD-DA format is defined in the International Electrotechnical Commission's (IEC) Standard BNN15-83-095.

CD+Graphics. A format in which the subchannel(s) of an audio CD contain graphic images that may be displayed on a computer or a television set.

CD-I. An abbreviation for Compact Disk-Interactive. CD-I refers to a class of CDs primarily designed to be viewed on conventional television sets by means of a CD-I player. CD-I players incorporate at least 1M of memory (RAM), special pointing devices, and remote-control systems. CD-I players also may be used for training and other commercial and industrial applications. CD-I formats are covered by Philips N.V.'s Green Book specification.

CD+MIDI. A format in which the subchannel(s) of an audio CD contain data in standard MIDI file format that may be routed to a MIDI OUT connector and played on external MIDI synthesizers or internally by audio-adapter cards.

CD-MO. An abbreviation for Compact-Disk Magneto-Optical. Magneto-Optical CDs and CD-ROMs are capable of multiple use because they can be erased and re-recorded. The standards for CD-MOs are incorporated in Philips N.V.'s "Orange Book 1" specification. CD-MO technology is used for high-capacity, 3-1/2-inch "floptical" floppy disks.

CD-ROM. An acronym for Compact Disk Read-Only Memory. CD-ROMs can incorporate both audio and graphic images as well as text files. Philips N.V.'s documentation for this standard has a yellow binding, hence the term Yellow Book audio. MPC Specification 1.0 requires multimedia PCs to include a CD-ROM.

CD-ROM XA. An abbreviation for CD-ROM eXtended Architecture, jointly developed by Philips N.V., Sony Corporation, and Microsoft Corporation in 1989. CD-ROM XA provides storage for audio and other types of data interleaved on a CD-ROM, enabling access simultaneously. The "Extended Yellow Book" standard determines the method for storing and reading data from the disk (audio storage uses ADPCM). CD-ROM XA drives that support the CD-I Bridge standard established by Philips are able to read CD-I discs. CD-ROM XA capability is optional under MPC specification 1.0. Reading Kodak's Photo CD discs requires a CD-ROM XA or CD-I drive. *See* ADPCM and Photo CD.

CDTV. An abbreviation for Commodore Dynamic Total Vision. CDTV is a proprietary audio and video CD format developed by Commodore International for its CD-1000 CDTV player, which also can play CD-DA, CD+Graphics, and CD+MIDI formats.

CD-WO. An abbreviation for a Write-Once CD or CD drive. CD-WO also is referred to as CD-ROM WO or Orange Book 2 CD and may be created in a special CD-ROM drive designed specifically for this medium. CD-WO drives are used for premastering multimedia titles, as well as archival back up of networked file servers. *See* Premastering and Title.

CGA. The abbreviation for Color Graphic Adapter. CGA is the original graphic display standard for personal computers. Its devices have very low resolution and few (in some cases only four) colors. They are now considered obsolete.

CGM. An abbreviation for Computer Graphics Meta file. CGM is also used as the extension for these files. It is a vector-based description of graphic images. *See* Vector.

Channel. In Windows, channel ordinarily refers to a unique task ID assigned to a dynamic data exchange (DDE) conversation. Some applications, such as Word for Windows and Excel, assign integer channel number aliases. Starting with 1 for the first DDE channel opened, the applications number sequentially thereafter. Channel is also used to identify an Input or Output (I/O) port in mini- and mainframe computers. MIDI provides 16, individual channels, one which may be used to direct messages to a specific device or, if the device is multitimbral, one or more voices on separately assigned channels.

Channel map. A device used to assignment MIDI messages received on one of 16 MIDI channels to another channel, often on another device. The MIDI Mapper applet on Windows 3.1's Control Panel creates a channel map for multimedia sound applications.

Check box. A Windows dialog-box object consisting of a square box and an associated caption. An X in the box is created or erased (toggled) by alternate clicks on the box with the mouse or an assigned hot key.

Child. In Windows, usually an abbreviation for an MDI child window. In general, Child is used in computer programming to describe an object related to, but lower in hierarchical level than, a parent object.

Chorus. An electronic effect that combines multiple copies of a sound to create the illusion of multiple instruments playing simultaneously. *See* DSP.

Chroma key. The color or key of a video signal omitted when sending genlocked signals to a television set or VCR. The chroma key can then be replaced by a computer-generated overlay, much like weather maps are shown on commercial television.

Chrominance. A term used in television broadcasting to describe the signal (a subcarrier of the basic black-and-white signal) containing the color information in a composite video signal. Chrominance has two components: hue (tint) and saturation (the degree to which the color is diluted by white light). Chrominance is also called chroma and abbreviated as C. *See* Composite video, NTSC, and S-video.

Chunk. A part of either a RIFF or MIDI file assigned to a particular function. A chunk may be treated as a single element by an application. Chunks are the basic elements of a RIFF file.

Clef. In musical notation, a symbol representing the range of notes falling on the staff lines on which it appears. The most common clefs are the treble or G clef and the bass clef. Some instruments, such as the viola, use the alto clef.

Click track. Metronome-like sounds recorded on one track of a multi-track audio recording to indicate the tempo of the recording when making multiple-track recordings in sequential fashion.

Client. The device or application receiving data from a server device or application. The data may be in the form of a file received from a network file server; an object from an OLE server; or values from a DDE server assigned to client variables. *See* Server.

Clipboard. Windows temporary storage location for text and graphic objects. The Clipboard is the go-between in all copy, cut, and paste operations. You may view and save the contents of the Clipboard using the Program Manager's Clipboard applet.

Clock. The basic timing device in a computer. The most common clock frequencies for 80386-based computers are presently 25 MHz and 33 MHz. In MIDI, clock messages provide the basic synchronization between instruments in a chain. The master MIDI system provides the clock signals. *See* Master.

Clock doubling. A term used to describe the new 80x86 CPU chips created by Intel. The chips double the frequency of the clock for internal, central-processing, unit operations while maintaining the original clock frequency for other functions. This capability provides an improvement in computer-processing speed without requiring expensive, ultra-high-speed DRAM chips.

Cluster. Two or more sectors of a disk drive treated as a group. With current versions of DOS, the standard cluster size for hard disks is 2,048 bytes, made up of four 512-byte sectors. The cluster size determines the minimum disk space taken up by a file. For instance, a short 302-byte text file consumes 2,048 bytes, leaving 1,746 bytes unusable. The unusable bytes are called "slack." *See* Defragmentation and Sector.

CLUT. Acronym for Color Look-Up Table; a synonym for palette. *See* Palette.

CLV. An abbreviation for Constant Linear Velocity. The recording technique used with CD-ROMs (and other CD devices) specifying that the velocity of the media at the point of reading or writing remain constant, regardless of the distance from the spindle. CLV devices have a constant data transfer rate. To achieve CLV, the rotational speed of the spindle motor must be inversely proportional to the distance of the read or write point on the media from the spindle. Video laserdisc drives are produced in CLV and constant angular velocity models. *See* CAV.

Code. An abbreviation for Source Code. The text you enter in a computer program to create an application. Code consists of instructions and their parameters; functions and their arguments; objects and their events; properties and methods; constants, variable declarations and assignments; expressions and comments.

Code template. Self-contained groups of modules and resources performing a group of standard functions. Code templates may be incorporated, usually with little or no modification, into other applications requiring these functions.

Color Palette. In Windows, a means of establishing a foreground or background color by selecting a color displayed with the mouse. The Color Palette then converts the selection to the standard Windows red/green/blue (RGB) color format.

Combo box. A Windows object that combines a text box and list box into a single element. The list portion of a drop-down combo box appears when a downward-pointing arrow to the right of the text box is clicked.

Command button. A Windows object causing an event when clicked. Command buttons are ordinarily gray rectangles with rounded corners surrounded by a border.

Command message. In Media Control Interface terminology, a symbolic constant, usually in hexadecimal format, defining a specific MCI command (such as Pause) to be executed by a device.

Command string. A Media Control Interface term defining a specific MCI command (such as Pause) to be executed by a device. A command string is expressed as a string of English words describing the command to be executed, such as "Play CDAudio."

Comment. Explanatory material within source code. A comment isn't designed to be interpreted or compiled into the final application. In Visual Basic, for example, they are usually preceded by an apostrophe (') but can also be created by preceding them with the REM keyword at the beginning of a line. Comments in C are enclosed within pairs of /* ... */ and in Pascal between curly braces, { ... }.

Common User Access. *See* CUA.

Compile. To create executable or object (machine-language) files from source (readable) code.

Composite video. Describes the method by which color information (chrominance) is added to a conventional black-and-white (luminance) signal to create a standard NTSC television signal. *See* NTSC and PAL.

Compound. In computer programming, a set of instructions or statement requiring more than one keyword to complete. `Select Case ... Case ... End Select` is an example of a compound statement in Visual Basic.

Compound device. In multimedia applications, a device requiring a device element, usually a file, to completely describe the destination of an MCI command.

Compound document. A file or representation of the contents of a file created by two or more applications, usually by the OLE protocol. An example is a Microsoft Word for Windows document containing an Excel spreadsheet or a graph created by Microsoft Chart. The elements of the document created by a foreign application may be embedded in the compound document, becoming an integral component of that document. Alternatively, these elements may be linked to a file from another application and simply contain a reference to the file and the application that created it.

Compound file. A file containing multiple individual (logical) files or file elements within a single physical file, each reading as if it were an individual file. RIFF and Microsoft SQL Server files are compound files.

Constant. A variable name assigned to a permanent value by your source code. When declared, the value of a constant cannot be changed while your application is running.

Contrast. The measure of the range of light and dark values in an image.

Control. In MIDI terminology, a device on a keyboard or a front panel that alters the expression of the sound. It is also called a controller. Controllers may be continuous (modulation wheel) or on-off (sustain).

Control-L. *See* LANC.

Control-S. A wired, video-component control system developed by Sony Corporation for its VCRs and camcorders. Control-S duplicates the functions of a conventional infra-red remote control device by a standard control signal protocol. It is often used to supervise multiple monitors in group presentations because it can be daisy-chained through Control-S In and Out ports.

Conversation. In DDE operations, the collection of Windows messages that are passed between two different applications, the client and server, during an interprocess communication.

Coprocessor. A special chip designed for high-speed number crunching or numeric calculation. A coprocessor can be added to your computer to speed the operation of some applications, such as computer-aided design. Intel coprocessors for the PC include the 8087 (for the original PC), the 80287 for ATs, and the 80387 for 80386-based computers. The Intel 80486DX and 80586DX (P5) chips have built-in numerical coprocessors.

Count-in. A term used in musical sequencing. Count-in provides one or two measures of metronome clicks or drum beats establishing the rhythm prior to recording a performance with a MIDI instrument and a sequencer application. *See* Metronome and Sequencer.

Crescendo. A musical term indicating a gradual increase in the volume of playing.

Cross-talk. Electrical interference between two signals, often related (such as left and right stereo audio signals). Cross-talk occurs in cables carrying more than one signal and in audio mixers. Cross-talk is specified in dB—the larger the negative number the better.

CUA. An abbreviation for Common User Access. An element of IBM's Systems Application Architecture (SAA) specification establishing a set of standards for user interaction with menus, dialog boxes, and other interactive portions of an application. The CUA was first implemented in Windows and OS/2 and has been an integral part of these graphical user interfaces (GUIs) since their beginning.

Cue. A musical or sound effects element occuring in synchronization with a visual event in a multimedia, television or motion-picture production.

Current statement. The statement or instruction executed at a particular instance in time. In debugging or stepwise operation of interpreted applications, such as Visual Basic, the current statement is the next statement executed by the interpreter when program operation is resumed.

Cutoff frequency. The sound frequency at which an audio high-pass or low-pass filter no longer allows the signal to pass through it.

DAC. An abbreviation for digital-to-analog converter. DAC is the electronic device used to convert digital audio and video signals stored on CD-ROMs, DAT, or in computer files to analog signals that can be reproduced by conventional stereo and television components.

DAT. Acronym for Digital Audio Tape. DAT is a process of recording sound in helical bands on a tape cartridge. This process is similar to recording video signals.

Data type. The description of how the computer is to interpret a particular item of data. Data types are generally divided into two families: strings, usually having text or readable content, and numeric data. The types of numeric data supported vary with the compiler or interpreter used. Most programming languages support a user-defined, record, or structure data type that can contain multiple data types within it.

Daughterboard. A small, printed wiring board plugged into a multi-pin connector (header) on an adapter card or your computer's motherboard. A daughterboard performs a function that is not a standard feature of the adapter card or computer.

dB. Abbreviation for decibel. The decibel, one tenth of a Bel, is the fundamental unit of audio-sound intensity. It is a logarithmic unit corresponding numerically to perception of sound intensity by humans. Sound at 40 dB is perceived to be twice as loud as sound at 20 dB. The form db is also used in some publications.

DDE. An abbreviation for Dynamic Data Exchange. DDE is an Interprocess Communication (IPC) method used by Windows and OS/2 to transfer data between different applications.

Debug. The act of removing errors in the source code for an application.

Decay. The rate a sound reduces in amplitude from its initial maximum volume. Decay follows Attack and precedes Sustain.

Declaration. A statement creating a user-defined data type, naming a variable, or creating a constant.

Declare. As a term used in text and not as a keyword in programming, to create a user-defined data type, data holder for a variable, or constant. As a keyword in BASIC languages for writing Windows applications, to register a function contained in a dynamic link library in a code module.

Default. A value assigned to a variable, argument of a function, or parameter of a keyword if not explicitly declared in the statement containing it.

Defragmentation. The process of moving hard-disk data clusters. Defragmentation physically locates the content of files on the drive in the sequence of the data it contains. Defragmentation applications, such as Symantec's Norton SpeedDisk and Allen Morris's DOG, are also called disk organizers.

Delta-sigma modulation. *See* Sigma-delta modulation.

Design mode. One of two modes of operation of Visual Basic, also called design time. The design mode enables you to create and modify forms and control objects, enter code, and execute the application. The other mode is run, the executing of the application.

Device Context. A Windows term describing a record or structure containing a complete definition of all the variables required to fully describe a window with a graphic object. Variables include the dimensions of the graphic area (viewport), drawing tools (pen, brush) in use, fonts, colors, drawing mode, and so on. Windows provides a handle (hDC) for each device context in use.

Dialog box. A pop-up, modal child window requesting information from the user. Dialog boxes include message boxes, input boxes, and user-defined dialog boxes for applications such as choosing files to open.

DIB. An acronym for Device-Independent Bit map, a Windows-specific bit map format designed to display graphic information. DIB files take the extension DIB and are similar to the BMP format.

Digital signal processing. *See* DSP.

Digital-to-analog conversion. *See* DAC.

Digitize. To convert an analog electrical signal to digital form. Digitizing is usually applied to audio or video signals. It is also used to describe the process of scanning a photograph or other graphic image and converting the image to a bit-mapped representation stored in a file. *See* ADC.

Diminuendo. A musical term indicating a gradual decrease in the volume of playing. Sometimes called decrescendo.

DIN. An acronym for Deutches Institute fur Normalization. DIN is an organization similar to ANSI that establishes and coordinates standards for Germany. It has become the de facto standards bureau for Europe.

Directional. A term used to describe the capability of a microphone to reproduce sounds impinging on it from different directions. Microphones are classified as omnidirectional, bidirectional, unidirectional and cardioid.

Directory list box. An element of a file selection dialog box. This element selectively lists the subdirectories of the designated directory of a specified logical drive.

Disk organizer. A synonym for a disk defragment application. *See* Defragmentation.

DLL. An abbreviation for Dynamic Link Library. DLL is a file containing a collection of Windows functions designed to perform a specific class of operations. Functions within DLLs are called (invoked) as necessary by applications to perform the desired operations.

Donut. Music, usually for a television commercial, beginning and ending with a vocal and having an instrumental underscore for narration in the middle.

DPCM. An abbreviation for Differential Pulse-Code Modulation. DPCM is the process used by 1-bit converters to encode and decode digital sound or video data based on the difference between successive samples rather than the actual value of the sample. DPCM provides better sound quality for the same number of bits per sample or enables digitized sound or video data to be stored in smaller files by compression. *See* ADPCM.

Drag-and-drop. A Windows process whereby an icon representing an object, such as a file, can be moved (dragged) by the mouse to another location, such as a different directory, and placed (dropped) in that location. Visual Basic provides drag-and-drop capabilities for control objects.

DRAM. Acronym for Dynamic Random-Access Memory, integrated-circuit devices that store data as the charge in a capacitor. DRAM must be continuously refreshed to restore the charge that would otherwise decay with time. DRAM, the most common form of memory chip used in PCs, are commonly supplied in the form of multiple chips mounted on a small, printed circuit board in banks of 1M capacity (1M x 9).

Drive list box. An element of a file selection dialog box (usually a drop-down list box) that selects the logical drive for subsequent display of directory and file lists.

Drum machine. A synonym for a percussion synthesizer. Drum machines have special features for percussionists, including small, rubber-covered pads that play drum sounds and an internal sequencer to store patterns and songs. Drum machines can be used as a source of MIDI synchronization. They cause the melodic tracks of a composition to be played back at a rate established by the drum machine's tempo.

DRW. The file extension for files created with Micrografx Designer, Draw Plus, and Windows Draw applications. DRW files are vector-based rather than bit-mapped image representations.

Dry. A term used by audio engineers to describe sound freed from added effects, such as reverberation, and equalization. The antonym of Wet.

DSP. An abbreviation for Digital Signal Processing. Although all synthesized sound involves DSP, the term is usually applied to the creation of electronic, acoustic effects such as reverberation, chorusing, flanging, and panning.

DTP. The abbreviation for desktop publishing. DTP is the process of creating commercially-printed material by combining word processing and graphic-manipulation capabilities. It produces a file consisting of digital representations of images required to make lithographic plates. DTP implies the use of a page-oriented, graphic-manipulation application (such as Aldus PageMaker), but many word processing applications also provide DTP capabilities.

DTV. The abbreviation for desktop video. The term describing the production of videotape presentations using the multimedia capabilities of personal computers. DTV implies the capability to edit videotapes by using the playback and record functions of VCRs that can be remotely controlled by a computer. *See* Edit.

Dub. In audio recording, the process of adding new sounds to an existing audio or videotape track from another sound source without erasing the existing track. *See* Mix and Over-dub.

DVI. An abbreviation for Intel's Digital Video Interactive standard. DVI simultaneously displays compressed video images and sound files. IBM has adopted the DVI standard for its Ultimedia product line. Microsoft adds DVI capability through its DVMCI extensions.

DXF. The standard file extension storing the vector images created by or for Autodesk's Autocad applications.

Dynamic Data Exchange. *See* DDE.

Dynamic Link Library. *See* DLL.

EBU. An abbreviation for the European Broadcast Union. EBU is an organization establishing audio and video standards for Western Europe. EBU performs functions similar to those of the NTSC and AES in the U.S. The EBU is affiliated with DIN and CCITT. *See* AES/EBU and NTSC.

Edit. A term used in video production to describe the process of creating a master tape by combining individual video sequences from sources such as videotape, conventional and still video cameras, and still and animated graphics from computers. The master tape is ordinarily used to duplicate multiple videocassettes for distribution.

Edit controller. A video device connecting two or more videotape playback devices with a videotape recorder and controlling the operation of each device to which it is connected. Edit controllers are programmed from an edit decision list (EDL). In desktop video production, the computer usually takes the place of a dedicated edit controller.

EDL. An abbreviation for Edit Decision List. An EDL lists the individual items included in the editing process to create a master videotape. Edit decision lists can be prepared by hand or created and stored on a computer.

Effects. An audio term describing the addition of echoes and other artificially generated modifications to increase a sound's acoustic realism or to create a particular ambiance. In the video field, effects are modifications to an image to increase its visual impact, such as solarization and pixelation. Effects is often abbreviated as FX. *See* Reverberation and Chorusing.

EGA. An abbreviation for Enhanced Graphic Adapter. EGA is a color standard capable of displaying up to 640 by 350 pixels with a maximum of 16 colors. EGA displays and adapter cards are now becoming obsolete and have been replaced by the VGA standard. Windows supports EGA devices.

EIA. Abbreviation for Electronic Industry Association. The EIA maintains standards for consumer and some commercial/industrial electronic products in the U.S., including the RS- series of standards for interconnection between system elements. The most common standards are RS-232-C, a connection between computers or terminals and modems; RS-422, a more robust version of the RS-232-C standard; and RS-170-A, the consumer standard for connection of color NTSC television signals.

EISA. An abbreviation for Extended Industry Standard Architecture. A bus specification used to interconnect adapter cards employing 32-bit memory addresses or providing multiprocessor capabilities. The EISA standard was declared by a group of PC-compatible hardware suppliers to compete with IBM's MicroChannel Architecture. *See* ISA and MCA.

Enabled. The capability of a control object to respond to user actions (such as a mouse click) expressed as true or false.

Engraving. A musical term meaning a musical score printed in a professional manner. High-quality, musical printing programs are referred to as engraving applications.

Entry-level. A term used to describe an application or component having fewer features than a professional version but easier for a beginner to use.

Envelope. A graphic description of the change of a sound's characteristic over time. An envelope is created by an electronic device called an envelope generator. An amplitude or volume envelope describes the intensity of the sound from its beginning to end. *See* ADSR.

Environment. A combination of the computer hardware, operating system, and user interface. A complete statement of an environment is a 386-DX computer with a VGA display and two-button mouse, using the DOS 5.0 operating system, and running the Windows 3.1 Graphical User Interface in its Enhanced Mode with the Multimedia Extensions 1.0.

Environmental variable. A DOS term for variables that are declared by PATH and SET statements, usually made in an AUTOEXEC.BAT file, and stored in a reserved memory location by DOS. These variables may be used by applications to adjust the application's operation for compatibility with user-specific hardware elements or directory structures.

EPS. An abbreviation for Encapsulated PostScript files, also used as the extension for these files. EPS files describe an image in Adobe Corporations's PostScript page-description language and usually incorporate a TIFF bit-mapped image in the header of the file, so a representation of the EPS image can be displayed. Some applications provide a Windows Meta File (WMF) header to be compatible with OLE 1.0 applications. *See* PostScript and WMF.

Error Correction Code (ECC). A coding system that, in conjunction with an Error Detection Coding scheme, can reconstruct erroneous data to its original value.

Error Detection Code (EDC). A coding system that can detect errors in a single byte or in blocks of data. Single-byte errors are caught by parity checkers such as the ones employed in the PC's memory system. Errors in blocks of data are commonly determined by using techniques such as the Cyclic Redundancy Codes (CRC) used for data transfer by modem. More sophisticated EDC methods are employed when error correction is required, such as with CD-ROMs. *See* Error Correction Code.

Error trapping. A procedure by which errors generated during the execution of an application are re-routed to a designated group of code lines called an "error handler." These code lines perform a predefined operation, such as ignoring the error. If errors are not trapped in Visual Basic, the standard modal-message dialog box with the text message for the error that occurred will appear.

Event. The occurrence of an action resulting in a Windows message. Events are usually related to mouse movements and keyboard actions. Events can be also generated by other external hardware devices, such as a MIDI sequencer or a communications modem.

Event-driven. The property of an operating system or environment implying the existence of an idle loop. When an event occurs, the idle loop is exited, and the event-handler code, specific to the event, is executed. After the event handler has completed its operation, program execution returns to the idle loop, where it awaits the next event.

Event handler. A block of program code invoked upon the occurrence of a specific event.

Executable. Code, usually in the form of a disk file, that can be run by the current operating system to perform a particular set of functions. Executable files in Windows carry the extension EXE and may obtain assistance from dynamic link libraries (DLLs) in performing their tasks.

Expander. A musical synthesizer without a keyboard. An expander is usually provided in a rack-mountable enclosure. Expanders are universally controlled by MIDI messages.

Exponent. The second element of a number expressed in scientific notation. The exponent is the power of 10 by which the first element, the mantissa, is multiplied to obtain the actual number. For +1.23E3, the exponent is 3. Multiply 1.23 by 1,000 (10 to the third power) to obtain the result: 1,230.

Expression. A combination of variable names, values, functions, and/or operators returning a result, usually assigned to a variable name. A function may be used in an expression, and the expression may return the value determined by the function to the same variable as the argument.

Extended synthesizer standard. The recommended sound synthesis capability of an MPC-compliant, audio-adapter card. The extended synthesizer standard was established by the MPC specification 1.0 issued by the Multimedia Marketing Council. The extended requirement is that at least nine melodic timbres assigned to channels 1 through 9 and 16 percussive timbres assigned to channel 10 be playable simultaneously. *See* Basic synthesizer standard.

Extended VGA. A description applied to graphic adapter cards capable of displaying 800 by 600 pixels with 256 colors.

Fader. An audio term generally applied to a volume control. A fader is usually in the form of a slider but could also be a rotary knob. Faders are implemented in Windows applications by vertical or horizontal scroll bars and can be used to change the degree of application of digital effects, such as reverberation and chorusing.

Field. In video terminology, one half of a television image. A field consists of either the even or odd lines of a frame. When used in conjunction with computer databases, a field is a single, distinct element of a complete database record.

File element. A complete, independent logical file contained within a RIFF physical file.

File handle. A number assigned, usually by DOS, to a disk file when it is opened. The application may then refer to the integer file handle, instead of the file name, in subsequent file operations.

File list box. A special type of Windows list box displaying the file names, usually having predetermined file extensions, of the files within a selected directory of a specified file.

Fill. In music, the percussion part acting as a transition between two rhythmic patterns. The fill is usually between the verses and the chorus of a song.

Filter. An electronic device removing portions of a sound. The most common types of audio filters are low-pass (removing high-frequency sounds), band-pass (removing low- and high-frequency sounds below and above the band), and high-pass (removing low-frequency sounds). In MIDI terminology, a filter removes certain types of messages (usually continuous signals such as aftertouch or pitch bend) from the MIDI message stream. *See* Cutoff frequency.

Flag. A variable, usually Boolean (true/false), determining the status of a particular condition within an application. The term set often indicates turning a flag from false to true. Reset indicates the reverse.

FLI. One of the two standard file extensions (FLI and FLC) for animation files created by Autodesk, Inc.'s Autodesk Animator application. Both extensions are derived from the slang term "flic."

Flow control. In general usage, conditional expressions controlling the execution sequence of instructions or statements in an application's source code. If...Then...Endif is a flow-control statement. The term is also used to describe diagrams that explain an application's mode of operation.

FM synthesizer. A device creating electronically-synthesized music. An FM synthesizer combines carrier and modulator waveforms of various types and frequencies to create a new waveform. This new waveform contains the overtones that simulate the sound of a conventional musical instrument. *See* Frequency modulation.

Focus. A Windows term specifying the currently selected application, or one of its windows, to which all user-generated input (keyboard and mouse operations) is directed. The title bar of a focused window is colored blue.

Font. A display or printer typeface in a particular size, usually specified in points (1/72 of an inch).

Foreground. In multitasking operations, the application or procedure visible on screen and to which user-generated input is directed. In Windows, the application that has the focus is in the foreground. In the Multimedia Movie Player, images displayed in front of other images have the foreground.

Form type. A FOURCC identifying the type of data contained in an individual RIFF chunk. *See* Chunk, FOURCC, and RIFF.

FOURCC. Abbreviation for Four-Character Code. FOURCC is a set of four ASCII characters defining the content of a RIFF chunk. WAVE, for example, indicates the chunk contains WaveAudio data.

Fragmentation. A term describing disk files that have parts scattered about in different drive locations rather than in a continuous sequence of clusters. Fragmented files slow the transfer of data to and from the disk because the disk drive head must seek too many different locations. *See* Cluster and Defragmentation.

Frame. In Windows, an enclosure (generally with a single-pixel-wide border) surrounding a group of objects (usually of the dialog-box class). When referring to SMPTE timing with MIDI files, the frame is one image of a motion picture film or one complete occurrence of a television image (1/30 of a second). Frame-based animation uses the term to define an image statically displayed for a specified period of time.

Frame capture. Graphic computer hardware and software enabling a selected broadcast or recorded television images to be displayed and stored by a PC. Also called a frame grabber.

Frequency modulation. A term describing the interaction of two signals, a carrier and a modulator, in which the modulation signal varies the frequency of a carrier. In FM radio transmission, the carrier is a high-frequency signal (88-108 MHz), and the modulator is the sound signal. In FM synthesis, a low-frequency oscillator modulates a carrier that is the fundamental frequency of the sound.

FSK. An abbreviation for Frequency-Shift Keying. FSK is an audio signal varying in frequency at a fixed rate. FSK signals are recorded on one track of a multitrack recording for synchronization and were the first form of MIDI recorder synchronization commonly used.

FTP. An abbreviation for File Transfer Protocol. FTP is an Internet communication protocol for performing file transfer operations on a UNIX host.

Full-motion video. A name for presenting video images in a window with accompanying sound. If you have a sufficiently high-speed computer and disk drive, each frame of video comprising the sequence will be displayed and all the sound will be heard. Slower computers and data sources (such as CD-ROM drives) drop as many video frames as required when attempting to provide intelligible sound from waveform audio files. Full-motion video files must be compressed, either by hardware or software techniques, to prevent even short video segments from occupying all available hard disk space.

Function. A subprogram called from within an expression in which a value is computed and returned to the program that called it through its name. Functions are classified as internal to the application language when their names are keywords.

FX. An abbreviation for effects. *See* Effects.

General MIDI (GM). A specification for consumer melodic and percussion synthesizers developed by the MIDI Manufacturers Association. GM defines a group of 96 standard voices, duplicating those voices of an arbitrary collection of musical instruments and a group of MIDI note assignments representing specific nonmelodic percussion instruments (drums). The General MIDI synthesizer specification (GS) is incorporated within the Multimedia Extensions to define its standard patch numbers. *See* GS.

General Synthesizer (GS). A standard for assigning sounds to patch numbers. Any synthesizer conforming to the GS standard will play the same or a similar voice when it receives a particular patch number for one of 128 capital (main) tones. The GS standard provides for 127 additional sets of complementary tones, related to the capital tones in the basic set. Additional tones may be available on more sophisticated expanders or synthesizers.

Generation. A term used in video production indicating the number of successive re-recordings of original video material, such as that created with a camera or by computer. A videotape created by a camcorder is first generation. If edited directly to a master tape, the master tape is second-generation. Duplicates produced from the master tape are third-generation. The number of generations causing visible deterioration in the video image is determined by the quality of the videotape equipment used.

Genlock. A process for synchronizing the video display of a computer to the frame synchronization signal of NTSC, PAL, or SECAM video. This process allows computer-generated graphics to be viewed on a television set or recorded with a VCR. Genlock capability is required to add computer-generated titling to video productions.

GIF. Acronym for Graphic Interchange Format. GIF is the file format (and extension) storing most graphic images in the CompuServe forum libraries.

Global. Pertaining to a computer program as a whole. Global variables and constants are accessible to, and may be modified by, program code at the module and procedure level.

Gray-scale. A description for monochrome (black and white) images displayed in various intensities of black. The most common format is an 8-bit gray-scale providing 256 shades of gray. Four-bit gray-scale images with 64 shades are also used.

Green Book. *See* CD-I.

Grid. A preset group of imaginary vertical and horizontal lines used to assist in aligning the position of graphic objects. In Visual Basic, the intersection of the imaginary lines are shown as dots on forms in design mode. Control objects will automatically align their outlines to these dots if the snap-to-grid option is implemented.

Half-tone. The pitch interval between a note with a sharp or a flat and the adjacent whole tone. The difference between G# and A is a half-tone, also called a half step.

Handle. An unassigned integer assigned by Windows to uniquely identify an instance (occurrence) of a module (application, hModule), task (hTask), window (hWnd) or device context (hDC) of a graphic object.

HDTV. Abbreviation for High-Definition Television, a form of television transmission that results in clearer images, especially on large-screen sets. Japanese television producers have established a standard for HDTV under PAL. A standard for the U.S. version of HDTV, using digital sampling techniques related to techniques for audio sampling, was under study at the time this book was written.

Header. An electrical connector, usually consisting of two rows of gold-plated pins on 0.2-inch centers. A header is primarily used with ribbon cables (such as the cables used to connect an internal CD-ROM drive) or to accommodate daughterboards. Headers are also used as jumper blocks allowing you to select the device address, interrupt level, and other options offered by adapter cards. *See* Daughterboard and Jumper.

Header file. A file type used by C programs to assign names to user-defined data types and symbolic constants and to declare prototypes of the functions used in the application. C header files carry the extension H. The term "include file" is often used synonymously.

Hi8. An abbreviation for High Band 8-mm, a format developed by Sony Corporation for camcorder videotapes. Hi8 provides the capability of recording PCM digital audio- and time-code tracks in addition to conventional analog audio and enhanced-Quality video information. Hi8 format is found on Sony commercial and industrial equipment but not consumer devices.

Hierarchical menu. A menu with multiple levels. The menu consists of a main menu leading to one or more levels of submenus from which choices of actions are made. Almost all Windows applications use hierarchical menu structures.

High Sierra format. A name assigned to the predecessor of ISO standard 9660 defining the table of content and directory structure of CD-ROMs for computer applications. Microsoft's MSCDEX.DRV driver reads the table of content and directory structure and converts the latter to the structure used by DOS. This function enables you to treat CD-ROM files as if they were located on a conventional hard disk drive. *See* ISO and MSCDEX.

HMS Time. Time expressed in hours, minutes, and seconds, usually separated by colons.

HMSF Time. Time expressed in hours, minutes, seconds, and video or motion picture frames. SMPTE time code is an example of HMSF.

Hot-link. A term describing a dynamic data exchange (DDE) operation in which a change in the source of the DDE data (the server) is immediately reflected in the object of the destination application (the client) to which it is linked.

HPGL. An abbreviation for the Hewlett-Packard Graphics Language. HPGL, designed for use with Hewlett-Packard plotters, is a vector format for graphic images. *See* Vector.

HPPCL. An abbreviation for the Hewlett-Packard Printer Control Language. HPPCL was designed to create and manipulate images to be printed by HP LaserJet printers. Several numbered versions of HPPCL implemented by specific LaserJet models exist.

HSG. An abbreviation for High Sierra Group. HSG indicates the directory format of a CD-ROM in High Sierra format rather than ISO-9660 format. *See* High Sierra.

Hum. An unwanted signal induced, usually in an audio input circuit, from surrounding power lines or other electromagnetic fields. Hum in the U.S. is 60-Hz. In most other regions of the world, hum is 50-Hz. It is minimized by proper shielding and grounding of audio and video components.

Humanize. *See* Randomize.

Hz. An abbreviation for Hertz, the fundamental unit of frequency of audio and radio waves. Hertz was previously called cycles per second (cps). Most people can discern sounds that range in frequency from about 20 to 18,000 Hz. KHz (1,000 Hz) and MHz (1 million Hz) are commonly used units.

Icon. In Windows, a 32- by 32-pixel graphic image, usually in color. An icon identifies the application in the program manager window when the application is minimized and in other locations in the application chosen by the programmer (such as the Help/About dialog box).

Identifier. A synonym for "name." An identifier is usually applied to variable names in program source code.

Identity palette. A 256-color palette. The palette's first and last 10 colors are the standard system colors. The remaining 236 colors are used as a color lookup table to increase the speed of loading bit maps into the display. *See* CLUT.

Idle. In Windows, the condition or state in which both Windows and the application has processed all pending messages in the queue from user- or hardware-initiated events and is waiting for the next to occur.

IEC. Abbreviation for the International Electrotechnical Commission. IEC is an organization establishing international standards for electronic components and systems. The IEC is the international equivalent of the RETMA organization in the United States.

IM. Abbreviation for Intermodulation. *See* Intermodulation distortion.

IMA. Abbreviation for the International MIDI Association. IMA is a trade association that creates and maintains the collection of standard MIDI specifications.

IMA. Abbreviation for the Interactive Multimedia Association. IMA is an affiliation of hardware and software producers that establishes standards for computer-based multimedia applications, principally related to cross-platform (for example, Macintosh and IBM) compatibility, such as the *Recommended Practices for Multimedia Portability*, Release R 1.1, published in 1990.

IMD. *See* Intermodulation Distortion.

Index. With arrays, the position of a particular element with respect to others, usually beginning with 0 as the first element. When used in conjunction with database files or tables, index refers to a lookup table, usually in the form of a file, that relates the value of a field in the indexed file to its record number. The record number is similar to the index of an array. It indicates the position of the record within a database file, usually the sequence in which the records were originally created and most often starting with 1.

Infinite loop. A looping program, flow-control structure in which the condition to exit the loop and continue with succeeding statements is never fulfilled. In For...Next loops, this process occurs by internally resetting the loop counter to a value less than the original limit.

Initialize. In programming, setting all variables to their default values and resetting the point of execution to the first executable line of code. Initialization is accomplished automatically in Visual Basic when you start an application.

Insertion point. The position of the cursor within a block of text. When the cursor is in a text field, Windows calls it a caret.

Instance. A term used by Windows describing the temporal existence of a loaded application or one or more of its windows.

Integer. A whole number. In most programming languages, an integer is a data type occupying two bytes (16-bits). Integers may have signs (taking on values from −32,768 to +32,767) or be unsigned. In the latter case, they are called a word and can represent numbers up to 65,535.

Interface. A noun describing a connection between two dissimilar devices. A common phrase is "user interface," meaning the connection between the display-keyboard combination and the user. Use of interface as a verb is jargon.

Interlaced. The method of displaying television signals on conventional TV sets and computer images on video display units. Alternate fields of images, consisting of the even or odd horizontal lines comprising the image, are displayed in succession.

Interleaved. A method for containing sound and video information in a single file but in separate chunks, so digital images and audio signals may be transferred from a file to the computer's memory without the delays incurred by CD-ROM seek operations. *See* Chunk.

Intermodulation distortion. The measure of an audio or video component or system to pass or amplify a signal consisting of two superimposed frequencies (for example, 60 and 400 Hz) without changing the basic waveforms, other than in amplitude. Intermodulation distortion is often abbreviated IM or IMD and is expressed in dB (a large negative value being desired).

Invocation path. The route used to invoke an object or a routine in a computer program. If the routine is deeply nested, the path may be quite circuitous and involve many conditions in its course.

Invoke. To cause execution of a block of code, particularly a procedure or subprocedure.

I/O. A symbolic abbreviation for an Input/Output port. I/O ports are either capable of simultaneous, two-way communication through a single connector, such as the 25-pin RS-232-C serial (COM) ports on PCs, or have two separate ports: one for input and one for output (as with 4-pin DIN MIDI IN and MIDI OUT ports).

ISA. An abbreviation for Industry Standard Architecture, the specification of the connections to plug-in adapter cards with 16-bit memory addressing capability. ISA is the bus structure used in conventional, IBM-compatible computers using Intel 8088 (PC), 80286 (AT), 80386, and 80486 CPU chips. *See* Bus, EISA and MCA.

ISO. An abbreviation for the International Standards Organization. The ISO is a branch of the United Nations headquartered in Geneva. ISO coordinates international standards for a wide variety of products and equipment. The CD-ROM standard for tables of content and file directory entries, originally called the High Sierra Format, has been established as the ISO-9660 standard. *See* High Sierra.

Items. The name given to the elements of a list box.

JPEG. An acronym for the Joint Photographic Experts Group that has established an industry standard for photographic image compression.

JPG. The file extension for graphic image files stored with JPEG compression. *See* JPEG.

Jump. In programming, execution of code in a sequence different from how it appears in the source code. In most cases, a jump will skip over a number of lines of code as the result of the evaluation of a conditional expression. In some cases, a jump will cause another subroutine to be executed.

Jumper. A small, plastic-enclosed spring clip making an electrical connection between two adjacent square metal pins, usually in the form of a header. Jumpers are used to set device addresses, interrupt levels, and select other optional features of adapter cards. They are also found on motherboards. *See* Header.

K. An abbreviation for kilobyte. One kilobyte equals 1,024 bytes. Similarly, k (lowercase) is an abbreviation for kilobit, 1,024 bits per second. *See* Byte.

Karaoke. A musical arrangement designed to accompany an added singing voice, also spelled Ka-ra-oke. A karaoke can be used to describe a consumer audio or audio-video component equipped with a microphone (and often with digital signal processing). The added singer's voice is combined with the accompaniment and heard through the same speakers. Karaoke devices are especially popular in Asia and Southeast Asia.

Key. In musical notation, the number of sharps and flats (accidentals) applied to notes. Key is indicated by the key signature following the clef symbol. Keys are expressed as note letters followed by the terms major and minor. *See* Accidentals.

Keyword. A word that has specific meaning to the interpreter or compiler in use and will cause predefined events to occur when encountered in source code. You may not use keywords as variable, procedure, or function names.

kHz. An abbreviation for kiloHertz. One kiloHertz equals 1,000 hertz. *See* Hz.

LANC. An acronym for Local Application Numerical Control. LANC is the method used by Sony Corporation and some other VCR and camcorder producers to remotely control video products—especially for editing purposes. LANC provides two-way communication and other remote control methods, such as Control-S (send control signals only). Information received through the LANC protocol includes HMSF time code information in Sony RC format and tape counter data. Control-L and "5-pin remote" are synonyms for LANC. *See* HMSF, RC, and VISCA.

Late binding. A method by which a portion of an application, such as a collection of objects or functions, resides in a separate file and is available to the main application when the application is run instead of when it is compiled into an executable file. Windows Dynamic Link Libraries (DLLs) are an example of late binding.

Launch. To start a windows application. The Windows Program Manager is an application launcher.

LFO. An abbreviation for Low Frequency Oscillator. LFOs are used in musical synthesizers to modulate a carrier oscillator providing audio effects such as vibrato (frequency modulation) and tremolo (amplitude modulation).

Library. A collection of functions compiled as a group and accessible to applications by calling the function name and any required arguments. Windows DLLs is one type of library. A library used by compilers to provide specialized functions, such as floating-point mathematical routines, is another type.

Link. To combine one or more object files into a single, executable file structure. This process is called static linking because the object files are made a permanent part of the executable file structure. In DOS, the executable file structure may consist of an executable element and one or more overlay files. Windows dynamic link libraries, on the other hand, are linked to executable files when the executable file is loaded in memory—not when it is created by linking one or more object files. *See* Late binding. Link also is used to indicate a DDE or OLE connection between a client and server application. *See* DDE and OLE.

List box. A dialog-box object providing a list of items from which the user may choose with the mouse or the cursor keys.

LIST chunk. A RIFF chunk identified by the FOURCC LIST type. A LIST chunk contains a series of "subchunks" with FOURCCs (such as INFO) listing information about a file (such as the author's name and the creation date). *See* FOURCCC and RIFF.

Local. The scope of a variable declared within a procedure rather than at the form, module, or global level. Local variables are only visible (defined) within the procedure in which they were declared.

Logical. A synonym for Boolean. Logical is a data type having only true or false values. Logical is also used to define a class of operators whose results are only true or false.

Logical palette. A windows GDI data object that provides a list of the individual colors required by a specific application. *See* GDI and Realizing the palette.

Loop. A compound-program flow-control structure causing statements contained between the instructions designating the beginning and end of the structure to be repeatedly executed. When a given condition is satisfied, program execution continues at the source-code line after the loop-termination statement. In musical terminology, looping means the repetition of a particular group of measures of a composition.

Luminance. One of the characteristics defining a color in the Hue-Saturation-Luminance (HSL) system. Luminance is the collective intensity (lightness) of the color defined by hue and saturation. In television broadcasting, the signal containing the black and white image is referred to as the luminance signal.

M. An abbreviation for megabyte. One megabyte equals 1 million bytes. M is sometimes used as an abbreviation for megabit, especially when describing data rates (such as Mb/s, standing for megabits per second). *See* Bit and Byte.

Machine language. Program code in the form of instructions that has meaning to and can be acted upon by the computer hardware and operating system employed. Object files compiled from source code are in machine language. Executable files consisting of object files linked with library files are also in machine language.

Mantissa. The first element of a number expressed in scientific notation that is multiplied by the power of 10 given in the exponent to obtain the actual number. For +1.23E3, the exponent is 3. Multiply the mantissa, 1.23, by 1,000 (10 to the third power) to obtain the result, 1,230.

Marker. A text label contained in a meta event within a standard MIDI file used to indicate a specific point in a musical composition. Markers are used to assist in synchronizing music with visual events.

Master. The controlling or primary (first) element of a system or sequence of events, such as a master recording. A MIDI master is the controlling element (such as a computer or keyboard's MIDI OUT) in a chain of MIDI instruments. Masters for stamping CD-ROMs consist of a glass disk into which pits are etched. These pits correspond to the digital representation of the information stored. A videotape master is the tape used to broadcast a program or create duplicate tapes for distribution.

MBIG. A video image compression standard under consideration for adoption by ISO when this book was written.

MCA. A registered trademark of IBM Corporation and an abbreviation for MultiChannel Architecture. MCA is a proprietary bus structure used by the IBM PS/2-series computers to provide 32-bit address capabilities for plug-in adapter cards. Like the EISA bus standard, MCA lets more than one microprocessor share the bus, providing multiprocessing techniques for applications requiring them. *See* EISA and ISA.

MCI. Abbreviation for Media Control Interface. MCI is a high-level Application Programming Interface (API) created by Microsoft for Windows multimedia programming. MCI provides an intermediate layer between Windows. The individual function calls included in the MCI API greatly simplify the programming of simple commands such as Play, Stop, and Record. *See* API.

MDK. Abbreviation for the Microsoft *Multimedia Development Kit*. MDK is a product designed to provide programmers and multimedia authors with the basic tools required to create multimedia titles and applications. Developing C-language applications to run under Microsoft Windows also requires the Microsoft *Software Development Kit* or its equivalent. *See* SDK.

Medium. In computer terminology, a substance or object storing information, usually defined as read-write or read-only. Hard disk drives and audio and videotapes have a read-write magnetic film or particle medium. CD-ROMs are read-only devices using optical media.

Menu. A set of choices from which the user determines the next set of actions to take. The design of menus in Windows is governed by the Common User Access (CUA) specification developed by IBM.

Meta event. In MIDI terminology, non-MIDI data, usually text, contained within a standard MIDI file.

Meta file. A type of graphics file used by Windows and other applications. A meta file stores the objects displayed in the form of mathematical descriptions of lines and surfaces. Windows meta files using the extension WMF are a special form of meta file used only by Windows and its applications.

Meter. In musical terminology, the rhythmic pattern of a composition. *See* Tempo.

Metronome. A clock-like device emitting an audible click on each beat at an adjustable tempo. Computer-based sequencer applications often include a metronome feature that plays on the PC's speaker or through a small speaker on the MIDI breakout box.

MHz. An abbreviation for megahertz. One megahertz equals 1 million hertz. *See* Hz.

Microsecond. One millionth of a second, usually abbreviated μs.

MIDI. An acronym for Musical Instrument Digital Interface. MIDI is a standardized method (protocol) for interconnecting electronic musical instruments and controllers, such as keyboards and computers, so they play in synchronization. The basic hardware and protocol is defined by the MIDI Detailed Specification 1.0 published and maintained by the International MIDI Association.

MIDI Cuing. A set of MIDI messages used to determine the occurrence of events other than the playing of musical notes. MIDI Cuing uses the MTC to determine when events occur in absolute rather than relative times. MMC and MSC operations use MIDI Cuing to determine when devices (such as recording, playback, or lighting devices) are to be triggered. *See* Cue.

MIDIEX File. A file consisting of raw MIDI message information without a header or other identifying elements. A MIDIEX file is usually used for saving and loading patches and other MIDI System Exclusive (SysEx) messages.

MIDI File. A file with a MID extension containing MIDI song or system-exclusive data and complying with the IMA's specifications for Standard MIDI files. RIFF MIDI files use the extension RMI. *See* SMF (Standard MIDI File).

MIDI Machine Control (MMC). A set of standard MIDI messages used to control the operation of devices such as audio tape, digital audio tape, audio CD, videotape, or videodisc recorders and playback units. The MMC specification was under development by the IMA at the time this book was written.

MIDI Mapper. A Windows applet enabling standard MIDI files written for a nonstandard synthesizer to play the proper sounds on a General MIDI synthesizer. A MIDI map created by MIDI Mapper intercepts incoming MIDI program-change messages and alters their value before sending them to the MIDI device. A completed MIDI map is called a MIDI setup. *See* General MIDI.

MIDI Real-Time Messages. MIDI messages such as start, stop, continue, clock, MIDI show control (MSC), MIDI time code (MTC), and song position pointer (SPP) codes. These messages are used to synchronize the MIDI message stream with other devices or production elements.

MIDI Sample Dump Standard. A standardized set of MIDI system-exclusive messages used to transfer PCM data from sampled sounds supplied on floppy disk or CD-ROM to the random-access memory (RAM) in a sample-playback synthesizer.

MIDI Show Control (MSC). A set of standardized MIDI codes used to control lighting effects by sending MIDI messages to a compatible controlling device. The MSC specification is maintained by the MMA.

MIDI Time Code (MTC). A set of MIDI synchronization messages corresponding to the SMPTE time-code standard. *See* SMPTE.

Millisecond. One one-thousandth of a second, abbreviated ms.

Mix. In audio and video technology, the combining of two or more signals representing sounds or images into a single, composite sound or image.

MMA. Abbreviation for the MIDI Manufacturers Association. The MMA is a group of U.S. manufacturers of MIDI hardware and software applications. It is affiliated with the International MIDI Association whose other principal member is the Japan MIDI Association. Many of the members of the MMA are off-shore subsidiaries of Japanese manufacturers.

MMC. An abbreviation for the Multimedia Marketing Council. The MMC is a group of hardware and software suppliers establishing and maintaining specifications for the capabilities of IBM-compatible microcomputers used for multimedia applications. The specifications are intended to make PCs suitable for use with multimedia hardware and applications. *See* MPC.

MMM. The extension for files created for display using the Multimedia Movie player. MMM files are created by Macromind's Director application that runs on Apple Macintosh computers. The Microsoft Multimedia Development Kit (MDK) provides an application that can convert Macintosh Director files to MMM files for use on PCs.

MMP. The extension for files created and used by IBM's M-Motion applications. These files use YUV encoding that can reproduce about 2 million colors using a 12-bit format (data for four pixels is stored in six bytes). *See* YUV.

Modal. A Windows dialog box that must be closed before further action can be taken by the user.

Mode. In MIDI terminology, the way a MIDI instrument responds to MIDI channel messages. In Omniphonic mode, the instrument will respond to note messages on any channel. In Polyphonic mode, the instrument will play multiple notes on one MIDI channel simultaneously. Multi mode, which is not included in the MIDI specification, is used to describe a multitimbral device that can respond to more than one channel. In Monophonic mode, the instrument will play only a single note on its assigned channel. Mono and Omni modes are implemented but seldom used in professional MIDI equipment.

Modeless. A window or dialog box that can be closed or minimized by the user without taking any other action. The opposite of modal.

Modem. An acronym for modulator-demodulator. A modem is a device converting digital signals to sound signals of varying frequency. The sound signal can be sent over the switched telephone network and converted back to digital form by a similar device at the destination.

Modulation. The process of one wave interacting with another to create a third (resultant) waveform. *See* Amplitude modulation and Frequency modulation.

Module. A block of code consisting of one or more procedures for which the source code is stored in a single file. In compiled language, a code module would be complied to a single object file.

Monaural. A synonym for monophonic or single-channel audio, usually shortened to mono.

Monitor. A name often used in place of the more proper terms display or graphic display.

Motherboard. The main printed wiring board of a personal computer. A motherboard usually includes the central processing unit (CPU), the system clock, random-access memory (RAM), the Basic Input-Output System (BIOS) in read-only memory (ROM), keyboard controller and connector, and other electronic circuitry essential to the basic operation of the computer. The remaining functions, such as input/output for disk drives and sound and output to a video display unit, are provided by adapter cards plugging into connectors on the motherboard.

MPC. The trademarked abbreviation for Multimedia Personal Computer or Multimedia PC. The MPC was originated by Microsoft Corporation and is now owned by the Multimedia Marketing Council (MMC). Computers, multimedia upgrade kits, and individual multimedia hardware components, such as audio-adapter cards, meeting a set of specifications established by the MMC may be marked with the MPC trademark.

MPEG. An acronym for the Moving Pictures Experts Group. The MPEG establishes standards for compression of moving graphic images.

MPU-401. A trademark of Roland Corporation for its MIDI adapter card for the PC. This trademark has become a de facto standard in the musical industry. "MPU-401-compatible" is a term indicating that a device serves the same purpose as an MPU-401 card or that an application uses an MPU-401 adapter card.

MSCDEX. An abbreviation for Microsoft Compact Disc Extensions. MSCDEX is a driver (MSCDEX.EXE) that is loaded as a DOS terminate-and-stay-resident (TSR) application, not a Windows DLL. MSCEDX allows a CD-ROM to be accessed through the conventional DOS commands applicable to hard disk and floppy disk drives. MSCDEX.DRV version 2.0 or higher is required for PCs to access CD-ROM drives with High Sierra or ISO-9660 directories. Version 2.2 or higher is recommended by the MPC specifications.

MSF. A multimedia (MCI) time format expressing times in Minutes, Seconds, and Frames. MSF is principally used by the CDAudio commands.

Multimedia. The combination of sound and graphic images within a single application for the purpose of selling new computer hardware, software, and books. One related outcome is the creation of animated presentations, some including full-motion video, that incorporate sound effects and graphics. A second is the market's expansion for PCs in the music industry.

Multiprocessor. In PC terminology, two or more microprocessors sharing a common bus. Additional microprocessors are usually assigned to specific functions such as input/output (I/O) operations or high-speed video processing. Multiprocessing PCs are most frequently employed as network file servers, but they will become more common for multimedia applications requiring high-speed animation or digital video presentation. *See* Bus, EISA and MCA.

Multisynchronous monitors. Video display units that are capable of accepting a wide range of horizontal and vertical scan rates and that automatically adjust to the incoming scan rates determined by the graphic adapter card used with them. Also called multiscan rate monitors.

Multitasking. The capability of a computer with a single CPU to simulate the processing of more than one task at a time. In its enhanced mode, Windows is a multitasking application. Multitasking is most effective when one or more of the applications in simultaneous use spends most of its time in an idle state waiting for a user-initiated event such as a keystroke or mouse click.

Multitimbral. MIDI synthesizers responding to MIDI messages on multiple channels playing a different voice for each channel.

NAB. An abbreviation for the National Association of Broadcasters. NAB is an organization comprised of radio and television station owners, equipment suppliers, and other firms involved in the broadcasting industry.

NAMM. Abbreviation for the National Association of Music Merchants. NAMM is an industry association of music dealers and musical instrument manufacturers. NAMM holds a yearly exhibition where new MIDI devices and audio components are introduced.

Nanosecond. One billionth of a second, abbreviated ns. The speed of memory chips is measured in nanoseconds, usually ranging from about 30 to 100. Faster computer clock speeds require memory chips with lower nanosecond response times. 33 MHz computers, for instance, use 70-80 ns memory chips.

Near-field. A term describing a set of speakers designed to be located very close to the listener rather than to fill a room with sound. Near-field audio monitors have the advantage of minimizing the extraneous effects of room acoustics on the reproduced sound.

Needle drop. Use of a short piece of existing recorded music rather than an original composition for a video or audio production. The term derives from the days of vinyl records and phonograph needles. Needle-drop charges are paid to copyright owners for the music's use.

Nested. An expression applied to procedures calling other procedures within an application. The called procedures are said to be nested within the calling procedure. When many calls to subprocedures and sub-subprocedures are made, the last one in the sequence is said to be deeply nested.

Newline. A combination of a carriage-return (the Enter key, CR for Carriage Return, or ASCII character 13) and line feed (LF or ASCII character 10) used to terminate a line of text on screen or within a text file. Other characters or combinations may be substituted for the CR/LF pair to indicate the type of newline character (soft, hard, deletable, and so on).

Noninterlaced. The preferred method of displaying computer images, usually on a multisynchronous video display unit, in which the image is created by displaying consecutive rather than alternate scanning lines. *See* Interlaced.

Note Off. A MIDI message instructing a MIDI instrument to stop playing a specific note on an assigned channel. This message corresponds to the release of a key on a keyboard. The sound may continue for a short time after the Note Off signal. *See* Release.

Note On. A MIDI message instructing a MIDI instrument to start playing a specific note on an assigned channel. This message corresponds to depressing a key on a keyboard. The intensity of the note is determined by the force applied to the key. The force is translated into a MIDI Velocity byte that is added to the channel and note number bytes to form a complete Note On message set.

NTSC. Abbreviation for the National Television Standards Committee. The NTSC establishes standards for television broadcasting in the Western Hemisphere (except Argentina, Brazil, Paraguay, and Uruguay), Japan, and Korea. NTSC television uses 525-line frames and displays full frames at 30 per second. Frames consist of two interlaced fields displayed at about 60 per second corresponding to the U.S. power-line frequency of 60 Hz. NTSC video connections of consumer video products use RCA phonograph plugs and jacks. Most Western European countries (except France) use the PAL standard based on their 50-Hz power-line frequencies. *See* PAL, RS-170-A, and SECAM.

Null. A variable of no value. 0 for numeric variables; an empty string ("") for string variables; or a long-integer 0 for pointers.

Object. In programming, elements combining data (properties) and behavior (methods) in a single container of code called an object. Objects inherit their properties and methods from the classes above them in the hierarchy and can modify these properties and methods to suit their own purposes. The code container may be part of the language itself, or you may define your own objects in source code.

Object code. Code in machine-readable form that can be executed by your computer's CPU and operating system. This code is usually linked with libraries to create an executable file.

Octave. In music, the grouping of a series of notes consisting of 13 semitones; the last note of an octave is twice the frequency of the first. In Western music, octaves begin and end with the same note letter and are divided into eight basic pitches (CDEFGABC, in the C-major scale) or tones. These pitches have five additional half steps (semitones: A#, C#, D#, F#, G#) added to create the chromatic scale.

Off-line. A term used in video production to describe a "rough cut" or rough draft of a videotape production. An off-line edit is usually produced with "prosumer" or less-expensive, industrial-grade video equipment. In DTV, an off-line edit may be used to create the final edit decision list (EDL) for the final, on-line edit. *See* DTV, Edit, and On-line.

Off-screen buffer. An area in memory reserved for the preparation of Multimedia Movie Player images before they are displayed. The off-screen buffer improves the speed of operation of the application. The process of building the off-screen buffer data is called pre-imaging.

Offset. The number of bytes from a reference point, usually the beginning of a file, to the particular byte of interest. When offset is used for location, the first byte in a file is always 0. In MIDI terminology, offset is the difference in time between two events, usually applied to SMPTE time code.

OLE. An acronym for Object Linking and Embedding. OLE is a Windows protocol developed by Microsoft Corporation. It provides for the creation of compound documents in which elements of a document in an OLE client application are created and edited (embedded) by or linked to a file (linking) in another application acting as an OLE server. Applications such as Word for Windows 2.0 and Excel 4.0 may act as either OLE clients or servers. Applets such as Media Player and Microsoft Draw and Chart are OLE servers only. OLE is an extension of the Windows Dynamic Data Exchange (DDE) protocol. The Apple System 7.x for the Macintosh series of computers also supports the OLE protocol. OLE 1.0 accommodates BMP, DIB, and WMF formats for graphic images. *See* Compound document and DDE.

Omnidirectional. A type of microphone responding equally to sound waves impinging on it from all directions. Most omnidirectional microphones are characterized by a rounded cylindrical or hemispherical shape.

One-bit conversion. *See* 1-bit conversion.

On-line. A term used in video production to describe the final step in the editing process that creates the master videotape for duplication. *See* DTV, Edit.

Opens. Musical introductions (cues) at the beginning or in particular sections of a video production used to identify or emphasize new subject matter.

Operand. One of the variables or constants upon which an operator acts. In 1 + 2 = 3, both 1 and 2 are operands; + and = are the operators.

Operator. A keyword or reserved symbol that, in its unary form, acts on a single variable, otherwise on two variables, to produce a result. Operators may be the conventional mathematical type such as +, − (difference), /, and * (multiply) or the logical operators such as And or Not. When applied to a single variable in a statement, the unary minus (−) inverts its sign from − to + or + to −.

Option button. A synonym for radio button, the original terminology in the CUA specification. Option buttons are circular control objects whose center is filled when selected. If grouped, only one option button of a group may be selected.

Orange Book. *See* CD-WO.

Oscillator. A circuit generating a continuous series of waves, usually at a constant frequency. Oscillators are used to create carrier signals and, in sound synthesis, modulation signals.

Outro. A musical ending (finale) in a video production. The complement to intro.

Over-dub. In audio recording, a new sound track created to replace an prerecorded track (erase-before-record).

Oversampling. A term describing conversion of analog audio signals to digital form using a sampling rate much higher than theoretically required to reproduce the highest frequency (a sampling rate of twice the highest frequency to be converted). Oversampling is usually expressed as a multiple (16x, 64x) of the required sampling rate.

PAL. An acronym for Phase-Alternative Line system. PAL is the television transmission standard of Western Europe (except France). PAL displays 625 lines per frame at a rate of 25 frames per second.

Palette. A Windows data structure defining the colors of a bit-mapped image in RGB format. *See* RGB.

Pan. The capability of a synthesizer or sound board to alter the volume on the left and right stereo audio channels creating the illusion of movement of the sound's source. *See* DSP.

Parameter. The equivalent of an argument but associated with a procedure not a function. The terms parameter and argument are often used interchangeably. A parameter is a variable required by a procedure to perform its function and is passed to the procedure by the calling statement. Parameters may be passed by reference, in which case the procedure using it may change its value; or they may be passed by value, in which case its value as seen in the calling program is unchanged by any action by the procedure. The distinction is made between arguments of functions and parameters of procedures in this book because Windows API functions often change the value of arguments passed to them. When applied to sound synthesizers, a parameter is an element that varies one of the properties of a sound.

Patch. When used in conjunction with MIDI terminology, a numerical value from 0 to 127. This value indicates to the receiving device that a specific voice is to be used to play notes transmitted by MIDI Note On messages on the device's MIDI channel. In other programming usage, patch means fixing an error in an executable file by modifying its code directly rather than by recompiling it from the original source code. Patch also describes correcting a bug in an application's executable file without the necessity of recompiling the source code.

Pattern. A MIDI-related term describing a sequence of percussion sounds, usually one or two measures in length. Different patterns are then combined into songs by percussion synthesizers called drum machines. Patterns are usually repeated for a number of bars, often interrupted with a break or drum solo, and followed by another repetitive set of patterns creating a percussion track to back a tune.

PCM. An abbreviation for Pulse Code Modulation. PCM is the technique used for digital sampling of sounds and the method used to create WaveAudio files.

PCX. The file extension created by ZSoft Corporation for storing images created by its PC Paintbrush application. PCX bit-map files can be monochrome or color and are used by many other bit-mapped image-creation (paint) and display applications.

Persistent (graphics). A Windows graphic image that survives movement, resizing, or overwriting of the window in which it appears. Persistent images are stored in global memory blocks and are not released until the window containing them is destroyed.

Photo CD. A trademark of the Eastman Kodak Company for its technology and CDs that provide copies of photographic color images in a format compatible with CD-I and CD-ROM XA drives. Photo CDs are produced from 35-mm film images by licensed photofinishing facilities. These facilities have equipment that can write to the special Photo CD media. The Photo CD media is rewritable. Additional images and, ultimately, sound may be added to the special CD media. A special CD-ROM XA player is required to read subsequent additions to a Photo CD ROM. Photo CD-ROMs with added material are said to have "multiple sessions." *See* CD-I and CD-ROM XA.

Photoreceptor. A light-sensitive semiconductor device creating an electrical charge in proportion to the amount light falling on its surface. Video cameras use arrays of these devices to create video signals. *See* CCD.

Piano-roll sequencer. A musical sequencing application displaying the notes to be played as bars. The bar's length represents the note's duration, and its vertical position on-screen represents the note's pitch. The appearance is similar to a player-piano roll rotated 90 degrees.

Pica. A unit of typographic measurement equal to 12 points (1/6 inch). This unit is generally used for horizontal measurement by printers.

Picon. An icon representing a still image, animation, or video sequence. The representation is usually a size-reduced version of the original video image.

PICT. The favored graphics file format of the Apple Macintosh computer line. Some Windows graphics applications are capable of reading PICT files from DOS-formatted floppy disks or PICT files downloaded from CompuServe and other information utilities.

Pitch bend. The capability to continuously alter the frequency of a synthesized voice to duplicate vibrato or slide effects.

Pitch scale factor. A WaveAudio function scaling the playback rate of a WAVE file.

Pixel. The smallest unit of measurement for video displays. A pixel represents the grain of the screen. Standard VGA color displays measure 640 by 480 pixels. Advanced (super) VGA displays are capable of displaying 800 by 600 pixels (and often 1,024 by 768 pixels). Bit-mapped displays control the color and intensity of each pixel to create the image.

Pixelation. A term indicating graininess in a video image. Pixelation happens when camcorders are operated at extremely low light levels or an excessive number of generations (re-recordings) of images has occurred with digital videotape recorders. Pixelation is often deliberately introduced as a special video effect.

Platform. A term used in computing to describe a particular brand or model of a computer. PCs, Macintoshes, NexTs, and Amigas are individual platforms.

Playlist. A group of musical compositions, usually in MIDI format, to be played in sequence. Playlists are commonly implemented by juke-box applications.

Pointer. A data type that comprises a number representing a memory location. Near pointers are constrained to the 64-K default, local data segment. Far pointers can access any location in the computer's memory. Pointers are used extensively in C-language applications to access elements such a arrays, strings, and structures.

Port. As a noun, the term represents a connection from the computer to external hardware such as a communications (COM) port. As a verb, the term port describes an application designed for one type of computer, operating system, or operating environment to another—as in "... porting a product from a Macintosh to Windows."

PostScript. A registered trademark of the Adobe Corporation. PostScript represents the page description language first used to print images with printers incorporating a PostScript interpreter and rasterizer. Adobe has developed Display PostScript to create video display images using the PostScript language.

PPQN. An abbreviation for Pulses Per Quarter Note. PPQN is the measure of resolution of a MIDI timing signal. The standard MIDI clock messages occur at 24 PPQN corresponding to 32nd-note triplets. At 120 beats per minute (BPM) in 4/4 time, 48 MIDI clock messages per second are transmitted.

Precedence. The execution sequence of operators in statements containing more than one operator.

Premastering. The process of creating a sample CD-ROM for review prior to creating the master disc used to stamp production quantities of CD-ROMs. Premastered samples are created on CD-WO drives. *See* CD-WO.

Presentation. In this book, a multimedia production consisting principally of still images or simple animation covering a single topic. These productions are usually produced with presentation applications such as Microsoft PowerPoint, Software Publishing, Harvard Graphics, or Aldus Persuasion. Presentation files are designed for storage and distribution on floppy disks rather than on CD-ROMs.

Print zone. The area on a sheet of paper where a printer can create an image. For most laser printers and standard dot-matrix printers, this area is 8 inches wide. The vertical dimension is unlimited for dot-matrix printers and is usually 13.5 inches for a laser printer with legal-size paper capabilities.

Procedure. A self-contained collection of source-code statements assigned a name and executable as an entity.

Program. The code required to create an application consisting basically of declarations, statements, and, in Windows, resource definitions and help files.

Program (MIDI). A numbered definition of a combination of instrument voices and their MIDI channel assignments, volume levels, and other parameters chosen by the manufacturer of the synthesizer. This definition is similar to a user-defined record in computer programming. Programs, also called patches, are stored in the synthesizer's memory and are selected by MIDI program change messages.

Property. The other principal characteristic of objects (the first is methods). Properties may be defined for an object or for the class of objects to which the particular object belongs. If the latter occurs, the properties are said to be inherited.

Prosumer. A contraction of professional and consumer. Prosumer describes video components, such as camcorders and VCRs, bridging the gap between consumer-grade products and industrial-quality devices. Prosumer video equipment is usually capable of being remotely controlled by a computer or edit controller.

Punch-in recording. A feature of MIDI sequencers and audio tape recorders enabling you to rerecord only a particular segment of a performance, usually by live musicians.

Quantize. A process in a MIDI sequencer application causing notes to be precisely aligned at fractional intervals of a measure (such as exact quarter, eighth, sixteenth, or thirty-second notes). Excessive quantizing of music leads to a mechanical sound and may result in MIDI choke, a condition caused by a controller attempting to send an excessive number of MIDI messages at a single instance.

QuickDraw. A trademark of Apple Computer, Inc. QuickDraw describes graphical objects created on Macintosh computers. The Multimedia Movie Player can use most QuickDraw images but requires conversion with an application supplied with the MDK.

QuickTime. A trademark of Apple Computer, Inc. QuickTime is the method employed for digital imaging and audio multimedia. This method is used to produce animated and video movies in the System 7+ operating system for the Macintosh computer line. QuickTime implements a set of timing services that maintain synchronization between images and the sound intended to accompany them. The Microsoft AVI Development Kit includes a QuickTime-to-AVI conversion application. *See* AVI.

RAM. An acronym for random-access memory. RAM is used to store instructions and data executed by a computer or sampled sound information in more sophisticated sample-playback synthesizers.

Random-access files. A file category with records consisting solely of the user-defined (record or struct) data type. Each record has a fixed length, and individual records are located by calculating their position from the beginning of the file. dBASE files are an example of a random-access file.

Randomize. In MIDI sequencing, the opposite of quantizing. Randomizing moves each note off the beat by a random time interval whose range of times is adjustable. Randomizing is used to reduce the mechanical ambiance of music that is sequenced exactly on the beat. Also called humanizing.

RC. An abbreviation for Rewritable Consumer time code. RC is a format developed by Sony Corporation and implemented in its VISCA-compatible products such as the Vdeck Hi8 VCR. RC is similar to SMPTE time code and uses Hours:Minutes:Seconds:Frames (HMSF) data to locate a specific frame for editing or synchronization purposes. *See* VISCA and LANC.

Realizing the palette. The process of assigning a set of colors in the application's logical palette to the system palette, so they appear on the display.

Real time. A term used to describe actions that occur while a process, such as recording, is in operation, rather than actions taken on a stored representation of the process, such as a file. MIDI System Real-Time messages are used to synchronize instruments based on the MIDI clock.

Record. A synonym for a user-defined data type. Also used in database applications to define a single element of a relational database file containing each of the fields defined for the file.

Recursion. A condition in which a procedure or function calls itself during its execution.

Red Book audio. The audio storage and CD-ROM output specification defined in Philips N.V.'s red-bound book and incorporated in the Windows Multimedia extensions as the standard for CD-ROM audio processing. *See* CD-DA.

Relational operators. Relational operators consist of operators such as >, <, <>, and =. They compare the values of two operands and return true or false depending on the values compared. They are sometimes called comparative operators.

Reserved word. A synonym for keyword. A reserved word sometimes indicates a subset of keywords that do not include embedded keywords.

Resolution. The measure of the division of the duration of an event into smaller parts. The resolution of the timing of MIDI messages is determined by the MIDI clock rate in ppqn. The resolution of a digital sample is measured in bits—the higher the number of bits in the sample, the greater the possible fidelity of its reproduction (and the greater the amount of storage space required).

RETMA. An abbreviation of the Radio Electronics and Television Manufacturers Association. RETMA was originally the RMA (Radio Manufacturers Association) of the U.S. RS-170, RS-170-A, and RS-232-C cabling standards and the color codes for the values of resistors and capacitors were originally developed by RETMA. Most of the standardization activities of RETMA now have been taken over by the IEC.

Reverberation. Acoustic echoes changing the nature of sound when heard in different environments. Higher reverberation levels result from live acoustic environments characterized by hard surfaces such as plastered walls. Longer reverberation delays occur with larger enclosures such as concert halls. Reverberation effects can be duplicated by digital signal processing. *See* DSP.

RGB. A method of specifying a color by using numbers to designate the individual intensities of the red, green, and blue components of the color created by the three guns of the CRT of a color display. Guns are the elements of a CRT that create the electron beam that is converted to light on the CRT's surface by a phosphor.

Ribbon cable. A flat multiconductor cable having parallel individual conductors that are molded together. One side of the ribbon cable is marked with a printed line, usually blue or red. This line identifies the conductor corresponding to pin 1 of the attached connectors. *See* Header.

RIFF. An acronym for the Windows Resource Interchange File Format. RIFF is used in conjunction with Multimedia Extensions. Depending upon their definition, these files may contain MIDI sequence, sample dump, or system exclusive data; waveform audio files; or data to create graphic images. RIFF is the preferred file format for Windows multimedia files; however, few third-party applications currently create RIFF files, except in WAVE format (WAV files).

RIFF chunk. *See* Chunk.

RIFF files. An acronym for Resource Interchange File Format. A RIFF file is created in a format compatible with the joint IBM-Microsoft specification for RIFF files. Examples are WAVE (WAV) files for WaveAudio sound, RMID (RMI) files for MIDI applications, and RMMP (MMM) files for the Multimedia Movie Player.

Ritardando. A musical term indicating the playing tempo is gradually slowing. Ritardando is the antonym of accelerando. Often abbreviated as ritard.

Rock Ridge format. A proposed standard for CD-WO (write-once CDs) to provide directory structures that may be updated as additional files are added. Rock Ridge directory format is used for multiple-session Photo CD-ROMs.

ROM. An abbreviation for Read-Only Memory. ROM stores data that does not change over time. ROM is most commonly used to store the BIOS (Basic Input-Output System) for microcomputers and to store prerecorded, digitized sound samples in sample-playback musical synthesizers.

Routine. A synonym for a procedure in computer programming. Also describing a choreographic sequence shorter than a full dance production.

RS-170. The Electronic Industry Association (EIA) standard for monochrome, NTSC television signals. RS-170-A is the color signal standard. The standard specifies RCA phonograph plugs and jacks (75-ohm impedance) for consumer video signal connections. *See* NTSC.

RS-232-C. An EIA standard intended to define the cabling between the serial I/O port of a data terminal (such as a PC) to a data set, originally a modem. The designation is now used to describe the PC's serial I/O port(s), COM1 through COM4, and any device or cable connecting to them. RS-232-C serial communications are used to control many types of devices (such as Sony's VISCA-compatible camcorders and VCRs). The -C suffix is often dropped when referring to RS-232-C.

RS-422. An updated version of the RS-232-C standard. The RS-422 was principally designed for use with high-speed modems. Some VCRs with remote control, such as the Panasonic AU-series products use RS-422 connections for their control signals.

Sample. In audio terminology, a digital representation of a sound created by a combination of microphone, amplifier, and analog-to-digital converter. Samples are stored in the form of a PCM file or memory block. They are usually of relatively short length and are then digitally processed by looping or other forms of repetition to create sounds of longer duration. Digital signal processing is used to change the pitch and other characteristics of samples, so a single sample may be used to create a range of notes.

Sample-playback synthesizer. A synthesizer capable of using digitally recorded, instrumental waveform samples to create voices. More sophisticated sampling synthesizers combine the capability to record as well as play sampled sounds. *See* Synthesizer and Wavetable.

Sampling rate. The recording speed of a sound's successive digital samples. Sampling rate is another measure of a digital sound sample's resolution. Standard sample rates are 11.025, 22.05, and 44.l KHz. The potential reproduction fidelity of a sample improves with increasing sampling rate or frequency, but storage requirements also increase. *See* Oversampling.

Scope. In programming terminology, a variable's extent of visibility (definition). The variable's scope depends upon where it is declared. *See* Global, Public and Local.

Scroll bar. Vertical and/or horizontal bars at the right side and bottom, respectively, of a multiline text box or list box. The scroll bar enables the user to scroll the window exposing otherwise hidden text.

SCSI. An acronym (pronounced "scuzzy") for the Small Computer Systems Interface. SCSI is a standard for attaching multiple peripheral devices to a single connector that, in turn, connects to the internal bus of a microcomputer. SCSI is used principally for storage devices, such as hard disks and CD-ROM drives. It is also employed for connection of some scanners and other image-related hardware. Sampling synthesizers may use SCSI connections to store and retrieve digitized sound samples. The Apple Macintosh computers use SCSI to connect many types of peripheral hardware.

SDK. Abbreviation for the Microsoft *Software Development Kit* for Windows. The SDK includes the files and documentation necessary for Windows programming in the C language.

SECAM. The acronym for Systeme Couleur avec Memoire. SECAM is the French standard for television transmission (819 horizontal lines per frame displayed at 25 frames per second). SECAM is the standard for most of Eastern Europe, including the former USSR and in African countries where French is the most common second language.

Sector. The basic unit for data storage on a hard disk or floppy disk. DOS reads one or more sectors from a disk and writes their data to buffer memory. Data from the buffer is written to the disk as necessary (always when the file is closed). Modern versions of DOS use 512-byte sectors. *See* Buffer and Cluster.

Seek. To locate a specific byte, sector, cluster, record, or chunk within a disk file.

Segue. A combination of or transition between two sounds without intervening silence. Segue (pronounced "seg-guay") is sometimes applied to transitions between video images with or without special effects, such as dissolves or wipes.

Sequencer. A device or application that records and plays back musical compositions in MIDI message format. Computer-based sequencer applications enable MIDI scores to be composed and edited. Sequencers are often incorporated within high-end keyboard synthesizers. Stand-alone sequencers are also available. They can record a performance from a MIDI keyboard and then be transported to a computer site and played into a sequencing application for editing.

Sequential access file. A file having one record follow another in the sequence applying to the application. Most text files are sequential.

Serial communication. A process transmitting information as a stream of bits in a specified length, usually over one or two pairs of wires such as a telephone line. Modems and the COM ports of PCs are serial communication devices.

Server. The device or application providing data to a client device or application using the data. The client may modify and return the data to the server. The data may be in the form of a file on a network file server, an object in an OLE server, or the topic values of a DDE server.

Shortcut key. A key combination providing access to a menu choice, macro, or other application function. A shortcut key is used in place of the mouse. Also called an accelerator key.

Shotgun microphone. A highly directional microphone frequently supplied with camcorders.

Sigma-delta modulation. A type of differential pulse code modulation (DPCM). With sigma-delta modulation, the difference (delta) used to convert to and from digital and analog signals is based on the sum (sigma) of a number of preceding samples rather than the preceding sample itself. Sigma-delta (also called delta-sigma) modulation is used with 1-bit converters and requires high values of oversampling. 64x is common in consumer, audio CD drives.

Signal-to-noise ratio (SNR). The ratio between an audio or video signal of a specific amplitude (level) and the underlying noise contributed to the signal by a component. Signal-to-noise ratio is expressed in dB or dBr (relative)—a large negative number being preferred.

Simple device. A multimedia (MCI) device not requiring a file or other identifying element to fully describe it. The CDAudio device is a simple device because Windows does not consider an audio CD track to be a file.

Single-stepping. A debugging process executing the source code one line at a time. This process enables you to inspect the value of variables, find infinite loops, or remove other types of bugs.

Sizing handle. The small black rectangles on the perimeter of Visual Basic control objects that appear on the surface of the form in design mode. Sizeable control objects may be shrunk or enlarged by dragging the rectangles.

Slave. A device receiving signals from and controlled by a master device. *See* Master.

Slider. A synonym for a Windows scroll bar. A slider is often used as a fader in Windows audio applications. *See* Fader.

SMPTE. An abbreviation for the Society of Motion Picture and Television Engineers. The SMPTE time standard, used to synchronize MIDI-based music with motion picture or television frames, is supported by the MMEs. *See* MIDI time code.

SMTP. An abbreviation for Simple Mail Transfer Protocol (UNIX) for sending e-mail messages.

SNR. An abbreviation for Signal-to-Noise Ratio.

Solarize. A special effect applied to an image causing luminous flaring of the color transitions as if the image was being viewed directly against the sun.

Song. MIDI drum-machine terminology describing a sequence of repeated rhythmic percussion patterns designed to create the percussion track for a MIDI composition. *See* Pattern.

Song Position Pointer (SPP). A MIDI message indicating a specific location in a song or song file. Song position pointer is measured in sixteenth notes from the beginning of the song. It is one of the timing elements supported by the MMEs.

Source code. The readable form of code created in a high-level language. A compiler or interpreter converts source code to machine-language object code.

S/PDIF. An abbreviation for Sony/Philips Digital Interface. S/PDIF is a consumer-products serial audio transmission standard for digital stereo signals. S/PDIF is similar to, but less robust than, the AES/EBU standard. S/PDIF (pronounced "speediff") uses smaller (mini-DIN) connectors than the XLR microphone types required for AES/EBU compatibility.

Split-mode. Dividing a MIDI keyboard into two or more zones of pitches with each zone playing a different instrument sound.

Staff. Five horizontal lines where symbols for musical notes are placed to indicate their pitch.

Standard MIDI File (SMF). A standard file format containing a series of MIDI messages in a known order. SMFs can also contain non-MIDI data such as track names and text in a data type known as a "meta-event." SMFs may also include or be comprised entirely of MIDI system exclusive (SysEx) messages. Three types of standard MIDI files covered by the SMF specification issued by the IMAformats 0, 1, and 2 exist. Format 0 files combine all tracks into a single chunk. Format 1 files maintain track separation. Both formats are supported by the MMEs and most modern sequencer applications. Format 2 files can combine a series of format 0 files in one file. They are seldom seen and not supported by Windows.

Statement. A syntactically acceptable (to the interpreter or compiler of the chosen language) combination of instructions, keywords and symbols, or constants and/or variables. In Visual Basic, a statement must appear on a single line. Other languages use symbols to define the statement's termination, such as semicolon terminators used by Pascal.

Static. A variable retaining its last value until another is assigned, even though the procedure in which it is defined has completed execution. All global variables are static. Static is also used to distinguish between statically-linked (conventional) executable files and files using DLLs.

Static colors. Synonym for system colors. Static colors are the basic colors of the Windows display. *See* Palette.

Sting. A short musical slogan or identification piece usually in a television commercial. A sting is designed to catch the viewer's attention.

Streaming. The technique used to transfer information from a file structure, such as on a disk or CD drive, to the computer's memory. Streaming takes place in groups of bytes less than the entire file's length, usually processed in memory as a background activity. *See* Background.

String. A data type containing textual material such as alphabetic characters and punctuation symbols. Numbers may be included in or constitute the value of string variables, but they cannot be manipulated by mathematical operators.

Stripe. A synchronization signal recorded on one track of a multitrack tape recorder. Also used as a verb (as in striping). *See* FSK and SMPTE.

Structure. Two or more keywords used together to create an instruction usually conditional in nature. *See* Compound.

Stub. A procedure or user-defined function consisting of the name of the procedure or function only and containing no intervening code. Stubs block out the procedures required by the application which can be called by the Main program. The intervening code statements are filled during the programming process.

Subchannel. In audio CDs and CD-ROMs, digital information that is not part of the primary data (such as digitized sound or text data) stored on the CD. Subchannel data includes a table of content (a track list), product codes, and ownership (copyright) data. Subchannels can be used to store other information such as MIDI data (CD+MIDI) and graphics (CD+G).

Submenu. A set of choices presented when a main-menu choice is made. In Windows, the first level of submenus is similar to drop-down dialog boxes. The second level is usually fly-out menus appearing horizontally at the point of the first submenu choice.

Subprocedure. A procedure called by another procedure other than the computer program's main component.

Surround-Sound. A trademarked process for an enhancement to stereophonic sound including an additional audio channel. Surround-Sound creates the illusion of sound coming from all directions—similar to what might be experienced in a live acoustic environment such as a concert hall.

S-VHS. A VHS-format videocassette recorder with S-video capability. *See* S-Video.

S-video. Abbreviation for Super-video. S-video is a video signal with enhanced quality used for recording. Some video cards and a few, higher priced, consumer VCRs support S-video. S-video separates the chrominance signal from the luminance signals of composite video. It uses 4-pin DIN connectors (similar to the keyboard connector on PCs) for video I/O. S-video capability is found primarily on prosumer and industrial video equipment. *See* Chrominance, Luminance, and Prosumer.

Sync. An abbreviation for the portion of video signals used to synchronize the horizontal and vertical scans.

Synchronization. In synthesized sound, the process of controlling multiple sound sources and recording devices, so the time of the occurrence of a sound or image (frame) can be precisely determined. *See* Click track, FSK, Frame, MIDI time code, and SMPTE.

Syncopation. A musical term describing a rhythm in which specific notes precede or trail the beat. Syncopation is one of the characteristics defining jazz.

Syntax. The rules governing a language's expression. Like English, Spanish, Esperanto, or Swahili; programming languages each have their own syntax.

Synthesizer. An electronic musical instrument that, by making complex waveforms, creates sounds simulating conventional musical instruments as well as other nonconventional sounds. Synthesizers usually have built-in keyboards (synthesizers that do not are called expanders). Synthesizers using digitized sound samples to create voices are called sample-playback or sampling synthesizers.

System colors. The standard colors used by Windows for elements of its predefined objects such as backgrounds, scroll bars, borders, and title bars. The system colors may be changed from the defaults through Control Panel's Color and Desktop functions.

System-common. A MIDI message to which all connected instruments respond regardless of their MIDI channel assignment. SysEx, tuning, and song position pointer set messages are typical system-common messages

System-exclusive. A special type of MIDI message transmitting on all MIDI channels but intended for only a single device that is identified by its manufacturer and device codes. SysEx messages, as they are ordinarily called, set the operating characteristics of synthesizers, edit their individual voice parameters, change whole banks of voices, or load samples into their memories. The format of SysEx messages is determined by each manufacturer independently, and no standard for their format exists other than the beginning and ending bytes identifying them as the SysEx type.

Tab order. The order in which the focus is assigned to multiple control objects within a Windows dialog box by successive depressions of the Tab key. The term has carried over into interactive multimedia to indicate the default sequence of selections in a single image.

Tempo. The speed at which musical compositions and MIDI files are played. Tempo is expressed as the number of beats per minute. The default value is 120 (moderato). Tempo also indicates the time interval of the appearance of a single Multimedia Movie Player frame on a display.

Text box. A windows object designed to receive printable characters typed from the keyboard. Visual Basic provides two basic types: single- and multi-line. Entries in single-line text boxes are terminated with an Enter keystroke. Multi-line text boxes will accept more than one line of text either by a self-contained word-wrap feature (if a horizontal scroll bar is not present) or by a Ctrl+Enter key combination.

Text file. A disk file containing characters with values ordinarily ranging from ASCII character numbers 32 through 127. In a text file, lines of text are separated from one another with new line pairs, a combination of a carriage return (ASCII 13), and line feed (ASCII 10).

TFTP. An abbreviation for Trivial File Transfer Protocol. TFTP is an Internet communication protocol for transferring files to and from a UNIX host.

TGA. The file extension identifying files created in the format used by Truevision's TARGA series of graphic adapter cards.

TIFF. An acronym for Tagged Image File Format. TIFF is a format for storing black and white, gray-scale, and color bit-mapped images developed by Aldus Corporation. It carries the extension TIF. TIFF files are used by most scanners to store their images.

Time code. A method of identifying the time an event (such as a single motion picture or video frame) occurs in a format that can be understood by a computer. *See* MIDI time code and SMPTE.

Time signature. A musical fraction in which the numerator indicates the number of beats per measure and the denominator indicates the length of the note representing one beat. A time signature of 3/4 (waltz time) has three beats per measure with a quarter note representing one beat, and 12/8 (often used in transcribing blues tunes) has 12 beats per measure with an eighth note representing a beat.

Time stamp. The date and time data attributes applied to a disk file when created or edited. In MIDI files, a time stamp identifies the time MIDI events (such as Note On or Note Off) should occur, so the correct tempo is maintained.

Title. In multimedia language, a commercial multimedia production designed for distribution on CD-ROMs or CD-I discs. Titles are usually created by multimedia authoring applications such as Authorware Professional for Windows from Authorware, Inc. or IconAuthor from AimTech Corporation.

Title bar. The heading area (usually blue) of a window where the title (usually bright white) of the window appears.

TMSF. An MCI time format expressing time in Tracks, Minutes, Seconds, and Frames. TMSF is primarily used by CDAudio devices.

Toggle. A property of an object, such as a check box, that alternates its state when repeatedly clicked with the mouse or activated by a shortcut key combination

Tone. *See* Whole tone.

Tone generator. A synonym for synthesizer. *See* Synthesizer.

Toolbox. A collection of command buttons designated as tools, usually with icons substituted for the default appearance of a command button, that choose a method applicable to an object (usually graphic) until another tool is selected.

Topic. In DDE conversations, the file name or other identifying title of a collection of data. When used in conjunction with help files, topic is the name of the subject matter of a single help screen display.

Track. In MIDI terminology, the notes appearing on a single musical staff. When scoring an arrangement for multiple instruments, each instrument is ordinarily assigned to an individual track. A MIDI track is similar to an audio track of a multitrack tape recorder. MIDI sequencer applications are often priced by the maximum number of tracks they offer. Sixteen tracks is the minimum number possible for an application to be usable. Most sequencer applications provide at least 64 tracks. With CD-Audio drives, track refers to a specific selection on the compact audio disk.

Transpose. In music, adjusting all notes of a composition or portion of a composition by a specified pitch interval (number of halftones). Transposing changes the key in which the music is played.

Tremolo. A musical term often used to indicate a rapid but small change in note's pitch (frequency modulation). When applied to synthesizers, tremolo often refers to small changes in the sound's amplitude (amplitude modulation).

TrueType. A trademark of Apple Computer, Inc. for its outline-based typeface design and display system that creates display and printer fonts in a manner similar to Adobe's PostScript. Microsoft Corporation has incorporated an improved version of TrueType technology in Windows 3.1.

Twip. Windows' smallest unit of graphic measurement. A twip is a *tw*en*ti*eth of a *p*oint or 1/1,440th of an inch.

Type. *See* Data type. Also used to describe the style of displayed or printed characters, as in typeface.

Typeface. Print or display type of a single design. Typeface is often confused with the term font which means a particular size of a typeface. A typeface may be a member of a typeface or type family including related designs with attributes such as bold, Roman (regular), italic, compressed, or extended. *See* Font.

Unary. *See* Operator.

Unbalanced. A term describing the transmission of an audio signal over a two-conductor cable with one signal and one ground (earth or return) conductor. The ground conductor is usually a braided wire or metallic foil shield surrounding a plastic-insulated signal conductor. Unbalanced signals are often referred to as "single-ended." *See* Balanced.

Underscore. The background music for a video or multimedia production synchronized with the images presented.

Unidirectional. A microphone whose response is limited primarily to sounds originating in a relatively narrow angle. Unidirectional microphones are usually used for narration and to record single instruments.

UNIX. Registered trademark of AT&T for its multi-user operating system. Extensions and modifications of UNIX include DEC Ultrix, SCO UNIX, IBM AIX, and similar products.

User-defined. A data type, also called a record (or in C, a structure), which may be defined in your source code. The elements of the user-defined record type can be any data type valid for the language and may include other user-defined data types.

User-friendly. An overworked term assigned by software producers to describe products purported easy to use. Windows is referred to as user-friendly because it uses pictorial icons instead of typed DOS file names to launch applications.

Variable. The name representing or substituting for a number (numeric variable), letter, or combination of letters (string variable).

VCR. The abbreviation for Video Cassette Recorder. A VCR is principally used in conjunction with consumer-oriented devices.

Vector. In graphics terminology, an image defined by mathematical descriptions of lines and surfaces rather than by representations of the state of individual pixels as in bit-mapped images. Windows meta files (WMF), Micrographx Designer and Draw files (DRW), and CorelDRAW! files (CDR) contain vector-based image data.

Velocity. The portion of a MIDI note on message indicating the rate at which the key of the keyboard was depressed. The volume of the resulting sound is controlled by the velocity data.

VESA. An acronym for the Video Electronic Standards Association. VESA is a group of manufacturers and software developers who create standards for graphic and video display adapter cards.

VHS. The predominate recording format for consumer videocassette recorders. VHS was developed by Japan Victor Comapany (JVC) and introduced to the U.S. market in 1975. A version of VHS, called VHS-Compact or VHS-C, is used in camcorders.

Vibrato. A musical term indicating rapid, small changes in the pitch of a played note.

Video-in-a-window. A type of full-motion video adapter card accepting video signals and displaying the resulting image in a sizable window on a conventional VGA display under DOS or Windows. These cards are often identified by the initials VIW. *See* Full-motion video.

VISCA. An acronym for VIdeo System Control Architecture. VISCA is a control protocol developed by Sony Corporation for its V-series, computer-controllable video products (such as Vbox or Vdeck). The VISCA protocol shares a common heritage with MIDI short SysEx (system exclusive) messages.

VMP. A file extension designating 16-bit graphic images created or reproduced by many of the video cards using the Chips & Technologies chipsets.

VRAM. An abbreviation for Video Random-Access Memory. VRAM stores conventional RGB images or television images in YUV format. The VRAM chips employed on video and graphic accelerator cards are often substantially higher in speed rating than conventional RAM chips used for your computer's memory. *See* RAM.

VTR. An abbreviation for VideoTape Recorder. VTR usually refers to a reel-to-reel device rather than a videocassette recorder.

WaveAudio. *See* Waveform audio.

WAVE file. A RIFF (Resource Interchange File Format) file containing PCM waveform audio data, usually with a WAV extension. Microsoft and IBM have adopted WAVE files as their standard format for multimedia sound applications. *See* RIFF.

Waveform audio. A data type standard of the Windows Multimedia Extensions. Waveform audio defines how digitally sampled sounds are stored in files and processed by Windows API functions. Also called WaveAudio.

Wavetable. A term describing the synthesis technique of simulating the sounds of musical instruments with short digitized recordings (PCM samples) of their sounds. The samples are usually stored in read-only memory chips but may also reside in disk files for loading into random-access memory. The sample waveforms are manipulated (for instance, looped or repeated) by an on-board microprocessor to create sounds of extended duration. Digital pitch shifting is used to create notes of different frequencies. Wavetable synthesis is the basic technology used by sample-playback synthesizers. *See* PCM.

Wet. A term used by audio engineers describing sound or a sound channel to which digital effects, such as reverberation, have been added. The antonym of Dry.

Whole tone. The pitch interval between two notes on the musical scale. Whole tone is represented by the interval between notes on a line and notes on a space between lines. *See* Halftone.

Wild card. A character that substitutes for and allows a match by any character or set of characters in its place. The DOS ? and * wild cards are similarly used by Windows applications.

WMF. An abbreviation for Windows Meta File. WMF is the standard vector-based image format of Windows and the only vector graphic format formally supported by OLE 1.0. *See* Vector.

WORM. An acronym for Write-Once Read-Many. WORM is the original description of a writeable CD-ROM that may be prepared in a special optical disc drive. CD-WO (the Write-Once CD standard) is a special type of WORM format. *See* CD-WO.

YC. An encoding method used in S-Video. In YC, the luminance (Y) and chrominance (C) signals are separated. The chrominance signal incorporates both hue and saturation information. YC are the initials of Yves C. Faroudj, the inventor of the encoding process.

Yellow Book. *See* CD-ROM.

YUV. An encoding method principally used for digital video applications. For this method, Y represents the luminance of the image, and U and V define the hue and saturation. When YUV signals are compressed, the compression ratio is indicated for each element. In the ration 4:2:2, the luminance signal is compressed by a factor of 4, and the hue and saturation signals are compressed by a factor of 2. YUV encoding is used in IBM's M-Motion MMP files.

Zoom. To magnify an image on a video display.

Multimedia Personal Computer (MPC) Specification 1.0

The minimum required specifications for Multimedia PCs and add-on kits that qualify them for use of the Multimedia PC Marketing Council's Multimedia-PC trademark is shown in the following table. This information has been extracted from the "Multimedia Personal Computer Specification 1.0," published by the Multimedia PC Marketing Council on May 18, 1991, as amended in December, 1991. Values shown in parentheses in the Recommended column of the table are not included in the specification—they are based on the experience of the author and other MPC users.

Table A.1. MPC Specification 1.0.

System element	Minimum (base-level)	Recommended
Computer		
CPU Type and clock speed	80386SX, 16 MHz	(80386DX, 33 MHz)
Minimum RAM	2M	(4M)
Floppy disk type	3.5-inch, 1.44M capacity	Same
Hard disk capacity, minimum	30M	(120M)
User Input devices	101-key keyboard, mouse	Same
Input/output ports	1 serial, 1 parallel, 1 joystick[1]	Same
Graphics		
Display specification	VGA, 640 x 480, 16 colors	256 colors (0.28mm)
Audio		
Sampling type	Linear PCM	Same
Sampling resolution	8-bit monaural	16-bit (stereo)
Sampling rate, DAC[2]	11.025 and 22.05 kHz	Same plus 44.1 kHz
Sampling rate, ADC[2]	11.025 kHz, microphone input	22.05 and 44.1 kHz
Melody notes/timbres	6/3 simultaneous	16/9 simultaneous
Percussive notes/timbres	2/2 simultaneous with melody	16/8 simultaneous
External audio input	Microphone	Added stereo input
Internal mixing	CD, synthesizer, and DAC	Added auxiliary input
Audio output	Line level, −10 dB, stereo[3]	Same
MIDI input/output	IN, OUT, THRU, interrupt-driven	Same

System element	Minimum (base-level)	Recommended
CD-ROM Drive		
Data transfer rate, minimum	150K/second, 16K blocks	Same, 64K buffer
Seek time, maximum	1 second	(350 ms)
MTBF	10,000 hours	Same
Mode	1	1 and 2, forms 1 and 2
Subchannels	Q	P and R-W
Driver	Microsoft MSCDEX 2.2 or higher	Same

[1] Joystick input is usually provided by the audio adapter card.

[2] DAC is an abbreviation for digital-to-analog converter, the device that converts digital data to audio signals. ADC stands for the analog-to-digital converter that converts audio input signals to digital data.

MSCDEX.EXE Command Line Parameters

MSCDEX is a terminate-and-stay-resident (TSR) application that causes CD-ROM drives to act as if they are a read-only floppy disk drive. To accomplish this, MSCDEX.EXE does the following:

- Recognizes the device driver designed to make the CD-ROM drive compatible with MSCDEX.

- Converts ISO-9660 and High-Sierra directory entries into directory and file names that DOS can recognize.

- Enables CD-ROM drives to be shared by network servers (Version 2.10 or higher is required for MS-NET and similar servers). You will need special software to share CD-ROM drives on other types of networks. Networking CD-ROM drives is discussed later in this appendix.

- Supports CD-ROM XA files with interleaved structures (alternating blocks of, for instance, video and audio data).

MSCDEX.EXE is loaded into your computer's memory by adding a command line to your AUTOEXEC.BAT file. The usage syntax for MSCDEX.EXE and its command line switch options and parameters, each of which is preceded by a virgule (forward slash), is:

```
MSCDEX [/E /K /S /V] /D:<driver alias> [/L:<letter>] [/M:<buffers>]
```

Optional entries are enclosed within square brackets. All of the switches are optional. Command line switches are single letters and give the following instructions to MSCDEX:

Switch	Description
/E	Uses expanded memory to store MSCDEX, if you have expanded memory installed. This saves about 16K of main memory.
/K	Indicates that the CD-ROM directory is in Kanji (Japanese).
/S	Allows sharing of CD-ROM drives on MS-NET-based file servers.
/V	Tells MSCDEX.DRV to issue a verbose message when it loads.

Command line parameters are letters followed by colons and information you provide. Only the driver alias is required:

Parameter	Description
/D:	The alias of the driver assigned by the / d:<driver alias> parameter following the device driver file name in the device=<driver> / d:<driver alias> line in your CONFIG.SYS file. This entry is required.
/L:	The drive letter to be assigned to the CD-ROM. This will be the next letter in sequence after the last local drive letter you have assigned. If your only hard disk drive is C, the CD-ROM drive will be assigned D. You do not need to use this parameter unless you want to assign the drive a different letter—for example, if you have a network drive D. You do not add the colon to the drive letter for this parameter.
/M:	The number of 2K buffers allocated to the CD-ROM. The default is 10 buffers (20K). Performance may be improved by increasing this value to 20 or 30 with the parameter /M:20 or /M:30. Start with the default value (no parameter required) unless your manual instructs otherwise.

Adding the /V verbose command-line switch to the line in your AUTOEXEC.BAT file that loads MSCDEX will result in display of the following information about your computer's use of memory and the memory consumed by MSCDEX:

```
576832 bytes free memory
     0 bytes expanded memory
 12956 bytes CODE
  2112 bytes static DATA
 20882 bytes dynamic DATA
 36208 bytes used
```

If you have allocated some of your computer's memory to expanded memory, the amount will be shown. The static DATA is information about your CD-ROM drive provided by the device driver and stored by MSCDEX. The number of bytes occupied by dynamic DATA (buffers) is determined by the /M: parameter described earlier.

Microsoft licenses manufacturers and resellers to distribute the copyrighted MSCDEX.EXE application together with CD-ROM drives. Therefore, you will find MSCDEX.EXE included with the software supplied in conjunction with MPC Upgrade Kits, but not on floppy disks supplied with audio adapter cards sold as separate products. If you have a CD-ROM drive, but do not have MSCDEX.EXE, you can download the latest version of MSCDEX.EXE for your own use from the Microsoft Software Library (GO MSL) on CompuServe.

Standard MIDI Patch and Note Assignments

The General MIDI (GM) standard, which was originated by Roland Corporation as the General Synthesizer Standard, is coordinated by the MIDI Manufacturers Association (MMA). The GM standard assigns a set of standard patch numbers to a set of 128 commonly synthesized instrument sounds and MIDI note number designations for 46 standard non-melodic percussion instruments. You will not be forced to create patch and key maps for MID files you have written for your set of synthesizers and drum machines. You must create these maps, however, to play MID files written to the General MIDI standard. General MIDI will undoubtedly become the new distribution standard for pre-composed MIDI music.

Standard MIDI Patch Numbers

Sixteen sets of instrumental classifications are provided with eight individual sounds within a set. Synthesizers that predate the General MIDI and MPC specifications, and many produced thereafter, will not conform to the General MIDI patch assignment. You likely will be able to obtain Windows 3.1-compatible patch files from the synthesizer's manufacturer or third parties, as well as bank patches that will convert your synth's voices to General MIDI.

Although the names of the patches will be the same for all MPC-compliant MIDI devices, the sounds may differ greatly with products from different manufacturers. Sampled sounds from products such as Roland's SCC-1 or Turtle Beach's MultiSound card, will be much more realistic than those from the plain-vanilla, four-operator FM-synthesis products such as Creative Arts' Sound Blaster Pro. Many of the more sophisticated cards, such as the MultiSound, provide additional patches that enable you to select from a wide range of nonstandard instruments.

The following table lists the standard melodic and other chromatic (adjustable-pitch) voice names for MPC-compliant audio adapter cards.

P#	Piano	P#	Chromatic Percussion	P#	Organ
1	Acoustic Grand Piano	8	Celesta	16	Hammond Organ
2	Bright Acoustic Piano	9	Glockenspiel	17	Percussive Organ
3	Electric Grand Piano	10	Music Box	18	Rock Organ
3	Honky-tonk Piano	11	Vibraphone	19	Church Organ
4	Rhodes Piano	12	Marimba	20	Reed Organ
5	Chorused Piano	13	Xylophone	21	Accordion
6	Harpsichord	14	Tubular Bells	22	Harmonica
7	Clavinet	15	Dulcimer	23	Tango Accordion

P#	Guitar	P#	Bass	P#	Strings
24	Acoustic Guitar (nylon)	32	Acoustic Bass	40	Violin
25	Acoustic Guitar (steel)	33	Electric Bass (finger)	41	Viola
26	Electric Guitar (jazz)	34	Electric Bass (pick)	42	Cello
27	Electric Guitar (clean)	35	Fretless Bass	43	Contrabass
28	Electric Guitar (muted)	36	Slap Bass 1	44	Tremolo Strings
29	Overdriven Guitar	37	Slap Bass 2	45	Pizzicato Strings
30	Distortion Guitar	38	Synth Bass 1	46	Orchestral Harp
31	Guitar Harmonics	39	Synth Bass 2	47	Timpani

P#	Ensemble	P#	Brass	P#	Reed
48	String Ensemble 1	56	Trumpet	64	Soprano Sax
49	String Ensemble 2	57	Trombone	65	Alto Sax
50	Synth Strings 1	58	Tuba	66	Tenor Sax
51	Synth Strings 2	59	Muted Trumpet	67	Baritone Sax
52	Choir Aahs	60	French Horn	68	Oboe
53	Voice Oohs	61	Brass Section	69	English Horn
54	Synth Voice	62	Synth Brass 1	70	Bassoon
55	Orchestra Hit	63	Synth Brass 2	71	Clarinet

P#	Pipe P#		Synth Lead	P#	Synth Pad
72	Piccolo	80	Lead 1 (square)	88	Pad 1 (new age)
73	Flute 81	81	Lead 2 (sawtooth)	89	Pad 2 (warm)
74	Recorder	82	Lead 3 (calliope)	90	Pad 3 (polysynth)
75	Pan Flute	83	Lead 4 (chiff)	91	Pad 4 (choir)
76	Bottle Blow	84	Lead 5 (charang)	92	Pad 5 (bowed)
77	Shakuhachi	85	Lead 6 (voice)	93	Pad 6 (metallic)
78	Whistle	86	Lead (fifths)	94	Pad 7 (halo)
79	Ocarina	87	Lead 8 (bass+lead)	95	Pad 8 (sweep)

P#	Synth Effects	P#	Ethnic	P#	Percussive
96	FX 1 (rain)	104	Sitar	112	Tinkle Bell
97	FX 2 (soundtrack)	105	Banjo	113	Agogo
98	FX 3 (crystal)	106	Samisen	114	Steel Drums
99	FX 4 (atmosphere)	107	Koto	115	Woodblock
100	FX 5 (brightness)	108	Kalimba	116	Taiko Drum
101	FX 6 (goblins)	109	Bagpipe	117	Melodic Tom
102	FX 7 (echoes)	110	Fiddle	118	Synth Drum
103	FX 8 (sci-fi)	111	Shanai	119	Reverse Cymbal

P#	Sound Effects
120	Guitar Fret Noise
121	Breath Noise
122	Seashore
123	Bird Tweet
124	Telephone Ring
125	Helicopter
126	Applause
127	Gunshot

Standard MIDI Note Numbers for Non-Melodic Percussion Instruments

Most percussion synthesizers, usually called "drum machines," use a single MIDI channel for all their instruments. The percussion instrument to sound is selected by a MIDI note number and the volume by the note-on velocity. Few of the currently popular drum machines use the General MIDI note assignments, so you must create a key map to perform the translation. Windows 3.1 includes the MIDI Mapper, accessed from Control Panel, which enables you to create a Key Map translation table for your drum machine so that the proper instruments will be selected when playing tracks from *.MID files in MPC format.

The General MIDI note assignments for common non-melodic percussion instruments follows. Timpani are melodic percussion instruments, so their sounds are provided by conventional synthesizer patches. Timpani are usually available only in sampling synthesizers and are not included in the General MIDI specification. The following table lists the standard percussion voice names for MPC-compliant audio adapter cards:

N#	Drum Type	N#	Drum Type	N#	Drum Type
35	Acoustic Bass Drum	36	Bass Drum 1	37	Side Stick
38	Acoustic Snare	39	Hand Clap	40	Electric Snare
41	Low Floor Tom	42	Closed High-hat	43	High Floor Tom
44	Pedal High-hat	45	Low Tom	46	Open High-hat
47	Low-mid Tom	48	High-mid Tom	49	Crash Cymbal 1
50	High Tom	51	Ride Cymbal 1	52	Chinese Cymbal
53	Ride Bell	54	Tambourine	55	Splash Cymbal
56	Cowbell	57	Crash Cymbal 2	58	Vibraslap
59	Ride Cymbal 2	60	High Bongo	61	Low Bongo
62	Mute High Conga	63	Open High Conga	64	Low Conga
65	High Timbale	66	Low Timbale	67	High Agogo
68	Low Agogo	69	Cabasa	70	Maracas
71	Short Whistle	72	Long Whistle	73	Short Guiro
74	Long Guiro	75	Claves	76	High Wood Block
77	Low Wood Block	78	Open Cuica	80	Mute Triangle
81	Open Triangle				

Device-Specific MCI Command Strings

This appendix provides the specifications for the specific command syntax for waveaudio, sequencer, cdaudio, videodisc, mmmovie, and audio mixer devices. The content of this appendix is based upon the *Multimedia Programming Interface and Data Specification 1.0*, issued as a joint IBM-Microsoft standard, and is applicable to both Microsoft Windows and the OS/2 operating system. A full description of the basic MCI commands is provided in Microsoft's Multimedia Development Kit (MDK), which was updated to a Windows 3.1 version in late 1992.

The typographic conventions for the device-specific MCI command tables are listed in the following table:

Convention	Description
bold	MCI command or flag keyword
italic	Command parameter to be replaced with a valid string, number, or rectangle specification
"quotes"	Parameter text to be typed exactly as shown
| (pipe symbol)	Separates flags or parameters in lists from which one flag or parameter is to be chosen
[brackets]	Optional flags or parameters that may be omitted without creating an error

The plural term *items* is used when a command may employ more than one *item* modifier, as in:

delete *waveaudio* **from** 20 **to** 30

In most cases, either or both of the *items* modifiers are optional, in which case indicated default values are substituted for the missing *item* or *items*.

NOTE   The syntax for each of the device-specific MCI commands described in tables D.1 through D.6 has been modified from that found in the IBM-Microsoft Multimedia Specification 1.0 and the Multimedia Development Kit. The original documentation uses a *command [item(s)]* syntax, which does not indicate that the device name is to be included in the command statement. This chapter uses the format **command** *device_name [item(s)]* to clarify that you must include the device name with each command issued.

Waveform Audio Commands

Waveform audio drivers must support the core set of commands listed in table D.1.

Table D.1. The MCI Command Set for Waveform Audio (WaveAudio) functions.

Command	Description	
capability *device_name item*	Requests additional information about the capabilities of the waveform audio driver. One of the following *items* modifies **capability**:	
	can eject	Returns **false**.
	can play	Returns **true** if the device can play. The wave audio device returns **true** if an output device is available.
	can record	Returns **true** if the waveform driver can record. The waveform audio device returns **true** if an input device is available.

Command	Description
	can save Returns **true** if the wave audio device can save data.
	compound device Generally returns **true**; most waveform audio devices are compound devices.
	device type Returns **waveaudio**.
	has audio Returns **true**.
	has video Returns **false**.
	inputs Returns the total number of input devices.
	outputs Returns the total number of output devices.
	uses files Returns **true**.
close *device_name*	Closes the device element and any resources associated with it.
cue *device_name item*	Prepares for playing or recording. You do not have to issue the **cue** command prior to playing or recording. Depending on the device, however, using **cue** might reduce the delay associated with the **play** or **record** command. The **cue** command fails if playing or recording is in progress. The *item* is one of the following:
	input Prepares for recording.
	output Prepares for playing. This setting is the default.
delete *device_name items*	Deletes a data segment from the MCI element. The following optional *items* modify **delete**:
	from *position* **to** *position* Specifies the positions to start and stop deleting data. If **from** is omitted, the deletion starts at the current position; if **to** is omitted, the deletion stops at the end of the file or waveform.

continues

Table D.1. Continued

Command	Description
info *device_name item*	Fills a user-supplied buffer with a NULL-terminated string containing textual information. One of the following *items* modifies **info**:

	file	Returns the current file name.
	input	Returns the product name of the current waveform input device. Returns **none** if no device is set.
	output	Returns the product name of the current waveform output device. Returns **none** if no device is set.
	product	Returns the product name of the current audio output device.

Command	Description
open *device_name items*	Initializes the device. The following *items* are optional:

	alias *device_alias*	Specifies an alternate name for the given device. If specified, *device_alias* must also be used as the alias for references.
	buffer *buffer_size*	Sets the size in seconds of the buffer used by the wave audio device. The default size of the buffer is set when the wave audio device is installed or configured. Typically, the buffer size is set to 4 seconds.
	shareable	Initializes the device element as shareable. Subsequent attempts to open it fail unless you specify **shareable** in both the original and subsequent **open** commands. MCI returns an error if the device is already open and not shareable.

Command	Description
	type *device_type* Specifies the compound device used to control a device element. MCI reserves **waveaudio** for the waveform audio device type. As an alternative to **type**, MCI can use the element's file extension, such as WAV if it is associated with a device type such as waveaudio.
pause *device_name*	Pauses playing or recording.
play *device_name items*	Starts playing audio. The following optional *items* modify **play**:
	from *position* **to** *position* Specifies the positions to start and stop playing. If **from** is omitted, play starts at the current position; if **to** is omitted, play stops at the end of the file or waveform.
record *device_name items*	Starts recording audio. All data recorded after a file is opened is discarded if you close the file without saving it. The following optional *items* modify **record**:
	from *position* **to** *position* Specify the positions to start and stop recording. If **from** is omitted, the device starts recording at the current position; if **to** is omitted, the device records until a **stop** or **pause** command is received.
	insert Specifies that new data is added to the device element.
	overwrite Specifies that new data will replace data in the device element.
resume *device_name*	Resumes playing or recording following a pause.

continues

Table D.1. Continued

Command	Description
save *device_name item*	Saves the MCI element in its current format. The following *item* modifies **save**:
	filename — Specifies the file and path name used to save data.
seek *device_name item*	Moves to the specified location in the file. Playback or recording is stopped after the seek. One of the following items modifies **seek**:
	to end — Specifies a seek to the last sample.
	to *position* — Specifies the stop position.
	to start — Specifies a seek to the first sample.
set *device_name items*	Sets the following control *items*:
	alignment *integer* — Sets the alignment of data blocks to the value specified by *integer*. The file is saved in the new format.
	any input — Specifies that the device can use any input that supports the current format when recording. This setting is the default.
	any output — Specifies that the device can use any output that supports the current format when playing. This setting is the default.
	audio all off / **audio all on** — Enables or disables audio output.
	audio left off / **audio left on** — Enables or disables output to the left audio channel.

Command	Description
audio right off **audio right on**	Enables or disables output to the right audio channel.
bitspersample *bit_count*	Sets the number of bits per sample played or recorded. The file is saved in this format.
bytespersec *byte_rate*	Sets the average number of bytes per second played or recorded. The file is saved in this format.
channels *channel_count*	Sets the channel count for playing and recording. The file is saved in this format.
format tag pcm	Sets the format type to PCM (the default) for playing and recording. The file is saved in this format.
format tag *tag*	Sets the format type for playing and recording to a non-standard format. The device driver employed must support this format. The file is saved in this format.
input *integer*	Sets the audio channel used as the input.
output *integer*	Sets the audio channel used as the output.
samplespersec *integer*	Sets the sample rate for playing and recording. The file is saved in this format.
time format bytes	Sets the time format to bytes. After this command is issued, all position information is specified as bytes.

continues

Table D.1. Continued

Command	Description
	time format milliseconds — Sets the time format to milliseconds. All position information is specified as milliseconds following this command. You can abbreviate **milliseconds** as **ms**.
	time format samples — Sets the time format to samples. All position information is specified as samples following this command.
status *device_name item*	Obtains status information for the device. One of the following *items* modifies **status**:
	alignment — Returns the block alignment of data in bytes.
	bitspersample — Returns the number of bits per sample.
	bytespersec — Returns the average number of bytes per second played or recorded.
	channels — Returns the number of channels set (1 for mono, 2 for stereo).
	current track — Returns the index of the current track.
	format tag — Returns the format tag.
	input — Returns the currently set input. If no input is set, the error returned indicates that any device can be used.
	length — Returns the total length of the waveform.

Command	Description
length track *track_number*	Returns the length of the waveform file in the track specified by *track number*.
level	Returns the current audio sample value.
media present	Returns **true**.
mode	Returns **not ready**, **paused**, **playing**, **stopped**, **recording**, or **seeking**.
number of tracks	Returns the number of tracks (chapters).
output	Returns the currently set output. If no output is set, the error returned indicates that any device can be used.
position	Returns the current position.
position track *track_number*	Returns the position of the track specified by *track_number*.
ready	Returns **true** if the device is ready.
samplespersec	Returns the number of samples per second played or recorded.
start position	Returns the starting position of the waveform data.
time format	Returns the current time format.
stop *device_name*	Stops playing or recording.

The error return values, error constants, and error strings specific to the WaveAudio functions are shown in table D.1A.

Table D.1A. Error Values and Corresponding Constants and Error Strings for MCI WaveAudio Commands.

Value	mciSendString Return constant	mciGetErrorString response
322	MCIERR_WAVE_INPUTSINUSE	No compatible waveform recording device is free.
328	MCIERR_WAVE_INPUTSUNSUITABLE	No compatible waveform recording devices.
325	MCIERR_WAVE_INPUTUNSPECIFIED	Any compatible waveform recording device may be used.
320	MCIERR_WAVE_OUTPUTSINUSE	No compatible waveform playback device is free.
326	MCIERR_WAVE_OUTPUTSUNSUITABLE	No compatible waveform playback devices.
324	MCIERR_WAVE_OUTPUTSUNSPECIFIED	Any compatible waveform playback device may be used.
323	MCIERR_WAVE_SETINPUTINUSE	Set waveform recording device is in use.
329	MCIERR_WAVE_SETINPUTUNSUITABLE	Set waveform recording device is incompatible with set format.
321	MCIERR_WAVE_SETOUTPUTINUSE	Set waveform playback device is in use.
327	MCIERR_WAVE_SETOUTPUTUNSUITABLE	Set waveform playback device is incompatible with set format.

MIDI Sequencer Commands

The MIDI sequencer driver supports the set of commands shown in table D.2.

Table D.2. The MCI Command Set for the MIDI Sequencer Functions.

Command	Description
capability *device_name item*	Requests additional information about the capabilities of the MIDI sequencer. One of the following *items* is required:

	can eject	Returns **false**.
	can play	Returns **true** if the sequencer can play.
	can record	Returns **true** if the sequencer can record MIDI data.
	can save	Returns **true** if the sequencer can save MIDI data.
	compound device	Generally returns **true**; most sequencers are compound devices.
	device type	Returns **sequencer**.
	has audio	Returns **true**.
	has video	Returns **false**.
	uses files	Returns **true**.

Command	Description
close *device_name*	Closes the sequencer element and the port and file associated with it.
info *device_name item*	Fills a user-supplied buffer with a NULL-terminated string containing textual information. The following optional *items* modifies **info**:

	product	Returns the product name of the current MIDI sequencer.

continues

Table D.2. Continued

Command	Description
open *device_name items*	Initializes the sequencer. The following optional *item* modifies **open**:

	alias *device_ alias*	Specifies an alternate name for the sequencer element. If specified, *device_alias* must also be used for subsequent references.
	shareable	Initializes the sequencer element as shareable. Subsequent attempts to open it fail unless you specify **shareable** in both the original and subsequent **open** commands. MCI returns an invalid device error if the device is already open and not shareable.
	type *device_type*	MCI reserves **sequencer** for the MIDI sequencer device type. As an alternative to **type**, MCI can use the element's file extension, such as MID, if it is associated with a device type such as sequencer.

Command	Description
pause *device_name*	Pauses playing.
play *device_name items*	Starts playing the sequencer. The following optional *items* modify **play**:

	from *position* **to** *position*	Specifies the positions to start and stop playing. If **from** is omitted, play starts at the current position; if **to** is omitted, play stops at the end of the file.

Command	Description
record *device_name items*	Starts recording MIDI data. All data recorded after a file is opened is discarded if you close the file without saving it. The following optional *items* modify **record**:

Command		Description
	from *position* **to** *position*	Specifies the positions to start and stop recording. If **from** is omitted, the device starts recording at the current position; if **to** is omitted, the device records until a **stop** or **pause** command is received.
	insert	Specifies that new data is added to the device element.
	overwrite	Specifies that new data will replace data in the device element.
resume *device_name*		Resumes playing or recording following a pause.
save *device_name item*		Saves the MCI element. The following *item* modifies **save**:
	filename	Specifies the destination path and file.
seek *device_name item*		Moves to the specified position in the file. One of the following *items* is required:
	to end	Specifies a seek to the end of the sequence.
	to *position*	Specifies the final position for the seek.
	to start	Specifies a seek to the start of the sequence.
set *device_name items*		Sets the following various control *items*:
	audio all off **audio all on**	Enables or disables audio output.
	audio left off **audio left on**	Enables or disables output to the left audio channel.
	audio right off **audio right on**	Enables or disables output to the right audio channel.

continues

Table D.2. Continued

Command	Description
master MIDI	Sets the MIDI sequencer as the synchronization source. Synchronization data is sent in MIDI format.
master none	Inhibits the sequencer from sending synchronization data.
master SMPTE	Sets the MIDI sequencer as the synchronization source. Synchronization data is sent in SMPTE format.
offset *time*	Sets the SMPTE offset time in colon form (*hours:minutes: seconds:frames*). The offset is the beginning time of a SMPTE-based sequence.
port mapper	Sets the MIDI mapper as the port receiving the MIDI messages. This command fails if the MIDI mapper or a port it needs is being used by another application.
port none	Disables the sending of MIDI messages.
port *port_number*	Sets the MIDI port receiving the MIDI messages. This command fails if the port you are trying to open is being used by another application.
slave file	Sets the MIDI sequencer to use file data as the synchronization source. This setting is the default.

Command	Description
slave MIDI	Sets the MIDI sequencer to use incoming MIDI data for the synchronization source. The sequencer recognizes synchronization data with the MIDI format.
slave none	Sets the MIDI sequencer to ignore synchronization data.
slave SMPTE	Sets the MIDI sequencer to use incoming MIDI data for the synchronization source. The sequencer recognizes synchronization data with the SMPTE format.
tempo *tempo_value*	Sets the tempo of the sequence according to the current time format. For a ppqn-based file, the *tempo_value* is interpreted as beats per minute. For a SMPTE-based file, the *integer* is interpreted as frames per second.
time format milliseconds	Sets time format to milliseconds. All position information is specified as milliseconds following this command. The sequence file sets the default format to ppqn or SMPTE. You can abbreviate milliseconds as **ms**.
time format song pointer	Sets time format to song pointer (sixteenth notes). This format can be performed only for a sequence of division type ppqn.

continues

Table D.2. Continued

Command	Description
time format SMPTE 24	Sets time format to SMPTE 24 frame rate. All position information is specified in SMPTE format following this command. The sequence file sets the default format to ppqn or SMPTE.
time format SMPTE 25	Sets time format to SMPTE 25 frame rate. All position information is specified in SMPTE format following this command.
time format SMPTE 30	Sets time format to SMPTE 30 frame rate. All position information is specified in SMPTE format following this command.
time format SMPTE 30 drop	Sets time format to SMPTE 30 drop frame rate. All position information is specified in SMPTE format following this command.
status *device_name item*	Obtains status information for the MIDI sequencer. One of the following *items* modifies **status**:
current track	Returns the current track number.
division type	Returns one of the following file division types: **PPQN, SMPTE 24 frame, SMPTE 25 frame, SMPTE 30 drop frame,** or **SMPTE 30 frame**. Use this information to determine the format of the MIDI file and the meaning of tempo and position information.

Command	Description
length	Returns the length of a sequence in the current time format. For ppqn files, this format is in song pointer units. For SMPTE files, this format is in colon form (*hours: minutes:seconds:frames*).
length track *track_number*	Returns the length of a track of the sequence specified by *track-number* in the current time format. For ppqn files this format is in song pointer units. For SMPTE files, this format is in colon form (*hours: minutes:seconds:frames*).
master	Returns **midi**, **none**, or **SMPTE** depending on the type of synchronization set.
media present	Returns **true**.
mode	Returns **not ready**, **paused**, **playing**, **seeking**, or **stopped**.
number of tracks	Returns the number of tracks.
offset	Returns in colon form (*hours:minutes:seconds: frames*) the offset of a SMPTE-based file. The offset is the starting time of a SMPTE-based sequence.
port	Returns the MIDI port number assigned to the sequence.

continues

Table D.2. Continued

Command	Description
position	Returns the current position of a sequence in the current time format. For ppqn files, this format is in song pointer units. For SMPTE files, this format is in colon form (*hours:minutes: seconds:frames*).
position track *track_number*	Returns the current position of the track specified by *track_number* in the current time format. For ppqn files, this format is in song pointer units. For SMPTE files, this format is in colon form (*hours:minutes:seconds: frames*).
ready	Returns **true** if the device is ready.
slave	Returns **file**, **midi**, **none**, or **SMPTE** depending on the type of synchronization set.
start position	Returns the starting position of the media or device element.
tempo	Returns the current tempo of a sequence in the current time format. For files with ppqn format, the tempo is in beats per minute. For files with SMPTE format, the tempo is in frames per second.
time format	Returns the time format.
stop *device_name*	Stops playing.

Table D.2A shows the decimal values of errors returned by `mciSendString`, the constants corresponding to these values, and the error strings provided by `mciGetErrorString` that are specific to MCI commands for the MIDI sequencer.

Table D.2A. Error Return Values and Corresponding Error Constants and Strings for MCI MIDI Sequencer Commands.

Value	mciSendString Return constant	mciGetErrorString response
343	MCIERR_NOMIDIPRESENT	No MIDI device is available.
337	MCIERR_PORT_INUSE	Specified port is in use.
339	MCIERR_PORT_MAPNODEVICE	Current map uses nonexistent device.
336	MCIERR_SEQ_DIV_INCOMPATIBLE	Set Song Pointer incompatible with SMPTE files.
340	MCIERR_SEQ_PORT_MISCERROR	Miscellaneous error with specified port.
338	MCIERR_SEQ_PORT_NONEXISTENT	Specified port does not exist.
342	MCIERR_SEQ_PORTUNSPECIFIED	No current MIDI port.
341	MCIERR_SEQ_TIMER	Timer error.

CD Audio (Red-Book) Commands

The CD audio command set provides a common method for playing CD audio sequences. CD audio devices support the core set of commands listed in table D.3.

Table D.3. The MCI Command Set for CD Audio (Red-Book) Functions.

Command	Description
capability *device_name item*	Requests information about the capabilities of the CD audio device. One of the following *items* is required:
can eject	Returns **true** if the CD audio device can eject the media.

continues

Table D.3. Continued

Command	Description
	can play Returns **true** if the CD audio device can play the media.
	can record Returns **false**.
	can save Returns **false**.
	compound device Returns **false**.
	device type Returns **CDaudio**.
	has audio Returns **true**.
	has video Returns **false**.
	uses files Returns **false**.
close *device_name*	Closes the device.
info *device_name item*	Fills a user-supplied buffer with a NULL-terminated string containing textual information. The following optional *item* modifies **info**:
	product Returns the product name and model of the current audio device.
open *device_name items*	Initializes the device. MCI reserves **cdaudio** for the compact disc audio device type. The following optional *items* modify **open**:
	alias *device_ alias* Specifies an alternate name for the given device. If specified, *device_alias* must also be used for subsequent references.
	shareable Initializes the device as shareable. Subsequent attempts to open it fail unless you specify **shareable** in both the original and subsequent **open** commands. MCI returns an error if the device is already open and not shareable.

Command	Description
pause *device_name*	Pauses playing.
play *device_name items*	Starts playing audio. The following optional *items* modify **play**:

	from *position* **to** *position*	Specifies the positions to start and stop playing.

Command	Description
resume *device_name*	Resumes playing from a paused state.
seek *device_name item*	Moves to the specified location on the disc. If already playing or recording, the device is stopped. One of the following *items* modifies **seek**:

	to end	Specifies a seek to the end of the audio data on the CD.
	to *position*	Specifies the destination position for the seek. If it is greater than the length of the disc, an out-of-range error is returned.
	to start	Specifies a seek to the start of the audio data on the CD.

Command	Description
set *device_name items*	Sets the following various control *items*:

	audio all off **audio all on**	Enables or disables audio output.
	audio left off **audio left on**	Enables or disables output to the left audio channel.
	audio right off **audio right on**	Enables or disables output to the right audio channel.
	door closed	Retracts the tray and closes the door if possible.
	door open	Opens the door and ejects the tray if possible.

continues

Table D.3. Continued

Command	Description
time format milliseconds	Sets the time format to milliseconds. All position information is in this format following this command. You can abbreviate milliseconds as **ms**.
time format msf	Sets the time format to *mm:ss:ff*, where *mm* is minutes, *ss* is seconds, and *ff* is frames. All position information is in this format following this command. On input, you can omit *ff* if it is 0 and can omit *ss* if both it and *ff* are 0. These fields have the following maximum values: Minutes 99 Seconds 59 Frames 74
time format tmsf	Sets the time format to *tt:mm:ss:ff*, where *tt* is tracks, *mm* is minutes, *ss* is seconds, and *ff* is frames. All position information is in this format following this command. On input, you can omit *ff* if it is 0; *ss* if both it and *ff* are 0; and *mm* if it, *ss*, and *ff* are 0. These fields have the following maximum values: Tracks 99 Minutes 99 Seconds 59 Frames 74

Command	Description
status *device_name item*	Obtains status information for the device. One of the following *items* modifies **status**:

current track	Returns the current track.
length	Returns the total length of the disc.
length track *track_number*	Returns the length of the track specified by *track_number*.
media present	Returns **true** if the CD is inserted in the drive; otherwise, returns **false**.
mode	Returns **not ready**, **open**, **paused**, **playing**, **seeking**, or **stopped** for the current mode of the drive.
number of tracks	Returns the number of tracks on the CD.
position	Returns the current position.
position track *track_no*	Returns the starting position of the track specified by *track_no*.
ready	Returns **true** if the drive is ready.
start position	Returns the starting position of the CD.
time format	Returns the current time format.

Command	Description
stop *device_name*	Stops playing.

Videodisc Player Commands

Videodisc players support the set of commands shown in table D.4.

Table D.4. The MCI Command Set for Videodisc Functions.

Command	Description
capability *device_name item*	Reports the capabilities of the device. The device should report capabilities according to the type of disc (CAV or CLV) inserted in the drive. If no disc is inserted, the device should assume CAV. One of the following optional *items* modifies **capability**:

	can eject	Returns **true** if the device can eject the media.
	can play	Returns **true** if the device supports playing.
	can record	Returns **true** if the video device can record.
	can reverse	Returns **true** if the device can play in reverse; otherwise, returns **false**. Always returns **false** if a CLV disc is inserted.
	can save	Returns **false**.
	compound device	Returns **false**.
	device type	Returns **videodisc**.
	fast play rate	Returns the standard fast play rate of the player in frames per second. Returns 0 if the device cannot play at a fast rate.
	has audio	Returns **true** if the videodisc player has audio.
	has video	Returns **true**.
	media type	Returns **CAV**, **CLV**, or **other**, depending on the type of videodisc.
	normal play rate	Returns the normal play rate in frames per second. Returns 0 for CLV discs.

Command	Description
	slow play rate Returns the standard slow play rate in frames per second. Returns 0 if the device cannot play at a slow rate.
	uses files Returns **false**.
close *device_name*	Closes the device.
escape *device_name item*	Sends custom information to a device. The following *item* modifies **escape**:
	string Specifies the custom information sent to the device.
info *device_name item*	Fills a user-supplied buffer with a NULL-terminated string containing textual information. The following optional *item* modifies **info**:
	product Returns the product name of the device the peripheral is controlling.
open *device_name items*	Initializes the device. MCI reserves **videodisc** for the videodisc device type. The following optional *items* modify **open**:
	alias *device_ alias* Specifies an alternate name for the given device. If specified, *device_alias* must also be used for subsequent references.
	shareable Initializes the device as shareable. Subsequent attempts to open it fail unless you specify **shareable** in both the original and subsequent **open** commands. MCI returns an invalid device error if the device is already open and not shareable.
pause *device_name*	Stops playing. If a CAV (video laser) disc is playing, also freezes the video frame. If a CLV (audio or CD-ROM) disc is playing, the player is stopped.
play *device_name items*	Starts playing. The following optional *items* modify **play**:

continues

Table D.4. Continued

Command		Description
	fast **slow**	Indicate that the device should play faster or slower than normal. To determine the exact speed on a particular player, use the **status speed** command. To specify the speed more precisely, use the **fps** flag. **slow** applies only to CAV discs.
	from *position* **to** *position*	Specifies the positions to start and stop playing. Positions are in frames for CAV discs and in seconds for CLV discs, unless **chapter** is also used (in which case, the position is given in chapters). If **from** is omitted, play starts at the current position; if **to** is omitted, play stops at the end of the disc.
	reverse	Sets the play direction to backwards. This setting applies only to CAV discs.
	scan	Indicates that the play speed is as fast as possible, possibly with audio disabled. This setting applies only to CAV discs.
	speed *integer*	Specifies the rate of play. Currently supported speed values are measured in frames per second, which is the default. This setting applies only to CAV discs.
resume *device_name*		Resumes playing.
seek *device_name item*		Searches by using fast forward or fast reverse with video and audio off. The following optional *items* modify **seek**:
	reverse	Indicates that the seek direction on CAV discs is backwards. This modifier is invalid if **to** is specified.
	to *position*	Specifies the end position to stop the seek. If **to** is not specified, the seek continues until the end of the media is reached.

Command	Description
to start	Specifies a seek to the start of the disc.
to end	Specifies a seek to the end of the disc.
set *device_name items*	Sets the following various control *items*:
audio all off **audio all on**	Enables or disables audio output.
audio left off **audio left on**	Enables or disables output to the left audio channel.
audio right off **audio right on**	Enables or disables output to the right audio channel.
door open	Opens the door and ejects the tray if possible.
door closed	Retracts the tray and closes the door if possible.
time format frames	Sets the position format to frames on CAV discs. All position information is specified in this format following this command. This setting is the default for CAV discs.
time format hms	Sets position format to *h:mm:ss* where *h* is hours, *mm* is minutes, and *ss* is seconds. All position information is specified in this format following this command. On input, you can omit *h* if it is 0 and can omit *mm* if both it and *h* are 0. This setting is the default for CLV discs.
time format milliseconds	Sets the position format to milliseconds. All position information is specified in this format following this command. You can abbreviate **milliseconds** as **ms**.
time format track	Sets the position format to tracks (chapters). All position information is specified in this format following this command.

continues

Table D.4. Continued

Command	Description	
	video on **video off**	Turns the video on or off.
spin *device_name item*	Starts the disc spinning or stops the disc from spinning. One of the following *items* modifies **status**:	
	down	Stops the disc from spinning.
	up	Starts the disc spinning.
status *device_name item*	Obtains status information for the device. One of the following *items* modifies **status**:	
	current track	Returns the current track (chapter) number.
	disc size	Returns either **8** or **12** to indicate the size of the loaded disc in inches.
	forward	Returns **true** if the play direction is forward or if the device is not playing; returns **false** if the play direction is backward.
	length	Returns the total length of the segment.
	length track *track_number*	Returns the length of the track (chapter) specified by *track_number*.
	media present	Returns **true** if a disc is inserted in the device; otherwise, returns **false**.
	media type	Returns **CAV**, **CLV**, or **other** depending on the type of video-disc.
	mode	Returns **not ready**, **opened**, **paused**, **parked**, **playing**, **scanning**, **seeking**, or **stopped**.
	number of tracks	Returns the number of tracks (chapters) on the media.
	position	Returns the current position.
	position track *track_number*	Returns the position of the start of the track (chapter) specified by *track_number*.

Command	Description
	ready Returns **true** if the device is ready.
	side Returns **1** or **2** to indicate which side of the disc is loaded.
	speed Returns the speed in frames per second.
	start position Returns the starting position of the disc.
	time format Returns the time format.
step *device_name items*	Steps the play one or more frames forward or backward. The default action is to step one frame forward. The **step** command applies only to CAV discs. The following *items* modify **step**:
	by *frames* Specifies the number of *frames* to step. If a negative value is used, the **reverse** flag is ignored.
	reverse Specifies to step backward.
stop *device_name*	Stops playing.

Animation and Movie Player Commands

The animation and movie player command set is not included in the joint design of the Multimedia Programming Interface and Data Specifications 1.0 and is not included in Windows 3.1. The command set, however, is included in Windows 3.0 with Multimedia and as a component of Microsoft's Visual Basic with Professional Extensions and the Professional Toolkit for Visual Basic.

The movie player driver, MCIMMP.DRV, supports the core set of commands listed in table D.5.

Table D.5. The MCI Command Set for the Multimedia Movie Player Functions.

Command	Description
capability *device_name item*	Reports the capabilities of the device. The device should report capabilities according to the type of application that created the *.MMP file. One of the following optional *items* modifies **capability**:

can eject	Returns **false**.
can play	Returns **true**.
can record	Returns **false**.
can reverse	Returns **true** if the device can play in reverse; otherwise, returns **false**.
can save	Returns **false**.
can stretch	Returns **false** because MCIMMP.DRV cannot stretch frames to fill a display rectangle.
compound device	Returns **true** if the device requires an element name; otherwise, returns **false**.
device type	Returns **animation**.
fast play rate	Returns the standard fast play rate of the player in frames per second.
has audio	Returns **true**.
has video	Returns **true**.
normal play rate	Returns the normal play rate in frames per second.
slow play rate	Returns the standard slow play rate in frames per second.
uses files	Returns **true** if the compound device element is a file name.
uses palettes	Returns **true**.

Command	Description
	windows Returns **8**, the number of windows MCIMMP can support.
close *device_name*	Closes the device.
info *device_name item*	Fills a user-supplied buffer with a NULL-terminated string containing textual information. The following optional *items* modify **info**:
	file Returns the file name in use as a NULL-terminated string.
	product Returns **Microsoft Multimedia Movie Player**.
	window text Returns the caption of the title bar of the window in use.
open *device_name items*	Initializes the movie player. The following optional *items* modify **open**:
	alias *device_ alias* Specifies an alternate name for the given device. If specified, *device_alias* must also be used for subsequent references.
	nostatic Reduces the static colors to black and white while MCIMMP.DRV is in the foreground.
	parent *hwnd* Determines the window handle (hWnd) of the parent window.
	shareable *.MMP files are not shareable.
	style *style_type* Determines the style of the window used.
	style child Opens a Windows multiple document interface (MDI) child window.

continues

Table D.5. Continued

Command	Description	
	style overlapped	Opens an overlapped-style window.
	type *device_type*	Defaults to **MMMovie**. If not specified, the [mci extension] entry for the file extension is used.
pause *device_name*	Stops playing when playing; starts playing when stopped.	
play *device_name items*	Starts playing. The following optional *items* modify **play**:	
	fast **slow**	Indicate that the device should play faster or slower than normal. To determine the exact speed on a particular player, use the **status speed** command. To specify the speed more precisely, use the **fps** flag. **slow** applies only to CAV discs.
	from *position* **to** *position*	Specify the positions to start and stop playing. Positions are in frames for MCIMMP. If **from** is omitted, play starts at the current position; if **to** is omitted, play stops at the last frame.
	reverse	Sets the play direction to backwards.
	scan	Sets the play speed to as fast as possible, usually with audio disabled.
	speed *fps*	Specifies the rate of play. Currently supported speed values are measured in frames per second, which is the default.

Command	Description
put *device_name items*	Sets the area of the source image and the destination window for display. One of the following *items* is required to modify **put**:

	destination	Establishes the entire window as the destination window.
	destination at *rectangle*	Specifies a rectangle as the area where the image is to be displayed. You specify the rectangle as a set of four coordinates, *X1 Y1 X2 Y2*, separated by spaces. *X1* and *Y1* specify the top left corner of the rectangle, and *X2* and *Y2* determine its width and height, respectively. If **capability** *device_name* **can stretch** returns **true**, the image is stretched, if necessary to fill the rectangle.
	source	Establishes the entire image for display in the destination window.
	source at *rectangle*	Specifies a rectangle as the image area for display. You specify the rectangle the same way you do for **put** *device_name* **destination at** *rectangle*, which is described previously in this table. If **capability** *device_name* **can stretch** returns **true**, the image is stretched, if necessary to fill the rectangle.

realize *device_name item*	Instructs the device to select and realize the palette into the display context of the designated display window. Included for reference only, because MCIMMP does not support the **realize** command.

continues

Table D.5. Continued

Command	Description
	background Not supported by MCIMMP.DRV.
	normal Not supported by MCIMMP.DRV.
resume *device_name*	MCIMMP.DRV does not support **resume**. A toggled **pause** command is used instead.
seek *device_name item*	Moves to a specified position and stops. One of the following *items* modifies **seek**:
	to end Specifies a seek to the last frame.
	to *position* Specifies the end position to stop the seek. If **to** is not specified, the seek continues until the end of the last frame is reached.
	to start Specifies a seek to the first frame.
set *device_name items*	Sets the following various control *items*:
	audio all off / **audio all on** Enables or disables audio output.
	audio left off / **audio left on** Enables or disables output to the left audio channel.
	audio right off / **audio right on** Enables or disables output to the right audio channel.
	time format frames Sets the position format to frames on CAV discs. All position information is specified in this format following this command. This setting is the default for CAV discs.

Command	Description	
	time format milliseconds	Sets the position format to milliseconds. All position information is specified in this format following this command. You can abbreviate **milliseconds** as **ms**.
	video on video off	Not supported by MCIMMP.DRV. Turn the video on or off.
status *device_name item*	Obtains status information for the device. One of the following *items* modifies **status**:	
	current track	Returns **1**.
	forward	Returns **true** if the play direction is forward or if the device is not playing; returns **false** if the play direction is backward.
	length	Returns the total number of frames available.
	length track *track_number*	Returns the total number of frames in the track specified by *track_number*. MCIMMP.DRV supports a single track.
	media present	Returns **true** if media is inserted in the device; otherwise, returns **false**.
	mode	Returns **not ready**, **paused**, **parked**, **playing**, **seeking**, or **stopped**.
	number of tracks	Returns **1**.
	palette handle	Returns the handle of the current palette used (low-order word).
	position	Returns the current play position.

continues

Table D.5. Continued

Command	Description
position track *track_number*	Returns the position of the start of the track specified by *track_number*.
ready	Returns **true** if the device is ready.
side	Returns **1** or **2** to indicate which side of the disc is loaded.
speed	Returns the speed in frames per second.
start position	Returns the starting position of the media or device element.
time format	Returns the time format in use.
window handle	Returns the window handle (hWnd) of the current animation window (low-order word).
step *device_name items*	Steps the play one or more frames forward or backward. The default action is to step one frame forward. The following *items* modify **step**:
by *frames*	Specifies the number of frames to step. If a negative value is used, the **reverse** flag is ignored.
reverse	Steps backward.
stop *device_name*	Stops playing.
update *device_name item*	Repaints the current frame into the display context. One of these *items* modifies **update**:
at *rectangle*	Specifies the clipping rectangle.
hdc *hdc*	Specifies the handle to the device context (hDC) of the display context to paint.

Command	Description
where *device_name item*	Returns the offset and extent of the source or destination region, as specified by one of the following *items*:

	destination	Returns the destination offset and extent.
	source	Returns the source offset and extent.

Command	Description
window *device_name item*	Assigns a specified window to display images, instead of using the window created by MCIMMP.DRV. You should create specified windows immediately after opening the device but should not display the window with **state show** until you issue the **play** command. The following *items* modify **window**:

	handle *hwnd*	Returns the handle (hWnd) of the specified window.
	handle default	Sets the display window to the default created by MCIMMP.DRV.
	state hide	Hides the current display window.
	state iconic	Displays the current window as iconic.
	state maximized	Maximizes the current display window.
	state minimize	Minimizes the specified window and activates the top-level window in the window manager list.
	state minimized	Minimizes the current display window.
	state no action	Shows the display window in the current state. The currently active window remains active.
	state no activate	Shows the display window in its last size and state. The currently active window remains active.

continues

Table D.5. Continued

Command	Description
state normal	Activates and displays the current display window in its size and position when opened.
state show	Shows the current display window.
text *caption*	Determines the title bar caption of the display window.

Video Overlay Commands

As with the Multimedia Movie Player, the video overlay command set is not included in the joint IBM-Microsoft specification, nor is it included with Windows 3.1. These commands provide control of video overlay graphic adapter cards, such as Digital Vision's TV Video Windows, to provide video displays in a window. All video overlay devices must respond to the commands shown in table D.6. Drivers are provided by the suppliers of the video overlay cards in use and are usually specific to the products.

Table D.6. The MCI Command Set for the Video Overlay Functions.

Command	Description	
capability *device_name item*	Reports the capabilities of the device. One of the following optional *items* modifies **capability**:	
	can eject	Returns **false**.
	can freeze	Returns **true** if the device can freeze data in the frame buffer.
	can play	Returns **false**.
	can record	Returns **false**.
	can save	Returns **true** if the device can save the current frame buffer to a disk file.

Command	Description
	can stretch — Returns **true** if the device is capable of stretching frames to fill a given display area.
	compound device — Returns **true** if the device requires an element name; otherwise, returns **false**. Adapters that can create multiple windows may be compound devices.
	device type — Returns **overlay**.
	has audio — Returns **true** if the device supports audio playback; otherwise, returns **false**.
	has video — Returns **true**.
	uses files — Returns **true** if the compound device element is a file name.
	windows — Returns the number of simultaneous windows the device can support.
close *device_name*	Closes the device.
freeze *device_name item*	Disables video transmission to the frame buffer if **capability** *device_name item* **can freeze** returns **true**. The following optional *item* modifies **freeze**:
	at *rectangle* — Determines the rectangular region for which video acquisition is disabled. You specify the rectangle as a set of four coordinates, *X1 Y1 X2 Y2*, separated by spaces. *X1* and *Y1* specify the top left corner of the rectangle, and *X2* and *Y2* determine its width and height, respectively.
info *device_name item*	Fills a user-supplied buffer with a NULL-terminated string containing textual information. The following optional *items* modify **info**:

continues

Table D.6. Continued

Command	Description	
	file	Returns the file name in use as a NULL-terminated string if **uses files** returns **true**.
	product	Returns the name and model of the current device.
	window text	Returns the caption of the title bar of the window in use.
load *device_name items*	Loads the video buffer. The following *items* modify **load**:	
	filename	Specifies the path and file name of the file containing the video buffer data.
	at *rectangle*	Determines the rectangular region in which the frame buffer is to be loaded. See description of **freeze** *device_name item* **at** *rectangle* in this table for an explanation of how to set up the rectangle with coordinates.
open *device_name items*	Initializes the device. The following optional *items* modify **open**:	
	alias *device_ alias*	Specifies an alternate name for the given device. If specified, *device_alias* must also be used for subsequent references.
	parent *hwnd*	Determines the window handle (hWnd) of the parent window.
	shareable	Initializes the device element as shareable by more than one instance. You must specify **shareable** in all open commands if the device element is to be shared.

Command	Description
	style *style_type* — Determines the style of the window used.
	style child — Opens an MDI child window.
	style overlapped — Opens an overlapped-style window.
	style popup — Opens a popup-style window.
	type *device_type* — Indicates that the device type is **overlay**. If **overlay** is not specified, the [mci extension] entry for the file extension is used.
put *device_name items*	Sets the area of the source image and the destination window for display. One of the following *items* is required to modify **put**:
	destination — Establishes the entire window as the destination window.
	destination at *rectangle* — Specifies a rectangle as the area where the image is to be displayed. You specify the rectangle as a set of four coordinates, *X1 Y1 X2 Y2*, separated by spaces. *X1* and *Y1* specify the top left corner of the rectangle, and *X2* and *Y2* determine its width and height, respectively. If **capability** *device_name* **can stretch** returns **true**, the image is stretched, if necessary to fill the rectangle.
	frame — Specifies that the entire video buffer be used to capture the video image.

continues

Table D.6. Continued

Command		Description
	frame at *rectangle*	Specifies the area of the image to be captured. You express the dimensions of *rectangle* the same way you do with **put** *device_name* **destination at** *rectangle*, which is discussed previously in this table.
	source	Specifies the entire video buffer for the display in the destination window.
	source at *rectangle*	Specifies the area in the video buffer that is to be displayed. You express the dimensions of *rectangle* the same way you do with **put** *device_name* **destination at** *rectangle*, which is discussed previously in this table.
	video	Specifies the entire video source for the display in the destination window.
	video at *rectangle*	Specifies the area in the video source that is to be displayed. You express the dimensions of *rectangle* the same way you do with **put** *device_name* **destination at** *rectangle*, which is discussed previously in this table.
realize *device_name item*		Instructs the device to select and realize the palette into the display context of the designated display window. Included for reference only, because MCIMMP does not support the **realize** command.
	background	Not supported by MCIMMP.DRV.

Command	Description	
	normal	Not supported by MCIMMP.DRV.
save *device_name item*	Saves the content of the video buffer to a file. The following *items* modify **save**:	
	at *rectangle*	Specifies the display area in the video buffer to be saved. You express the dimensions of *rectangle* the same way you do with **put** *device_name* **destination at** *rectangle*, which is discussed previously in this table.
	filename	Specifies the path and file name used to save the video data.
set *device_name item*	Sets the following single control *item*:	
	video on **video off**	Turn video output on or off.
status *device_name item*	Obtains status information for the device. One of the following *items* modifies **status**:	
	media present	Returns **true**.
	mode	Returns **not ready**, **recording**, or **stopped**.
	ready	Returns **true** if the device is ready.
	window handle	Returns the handle (hWnd) of the current video overlay window (low-order word).
unfreeze *device_name item*	Enables the frame buffer to resume acquisition of video data after a **freeze** command. The following *item* modifies **unfreeze**:	
	at *rectangle*	Specifies the image area to unfreeze. You express the dimensions of *rectangle* the same way you do with **put** *device_name* **destination at** *rectangle*, which is discussed previously in this table.

continues

Table D.6. Continued

Command	Description
where *device_name item*	Returns the offset and extent of the source or destination region. The following *items* modify **where**:
	destination Returns the destination rectangle offset and extent.
	frame Returns the frame buffer rectangle offset and extent.
	source Returns the source rectangle offset and extent.
	video Returns the video rectangle offset and extent.
window *device_name item*	Assigns a specified window to display images, instead of using the window created by the driver. The following *items* modify **window**:
	handle *hwnd* Returns the handle (hWnd) of the specified window.
	handle default Sets the display window to the default created by the driver.
	state hide Hides the current display window.
	state iconic Displays the current window as iconic.
	state maximized Maximizes the current display window.
	state minimize Minimizes the specified window and activates the top-level window in the window manager list.
	state minimized Minimizes the current display window.
	state no action Shows the display window in the current state. The currently active window remains active.

Command	Description
state no activate	Shows the display window in its last size and state. The currently active window remains active.
state normal	Activates and displays the current display window in its size and position when opened.
state show	Shows the current display window.
text *caption*	Determines the title bar caption of the display window.

Audio Mixer Commands (Standard Proposed by Media Vision)

The MPC specification sets certain requirements for audio mixer devices but provides no guidance on how programming of mixer operation is to be implemented. Control of the audio mixer provided in the set of standard MCI commands also is not provided by Microsoft.

Media Vision has proposed an addition to the present set of device-specific MCI commands to control the audio mixer elements of MPC-compatible audio adapter cards. These commands represent one of the best examples of the extendability of the MCI command set. Multimedia hardware suppliers, who have special expertise in a particular field, can develop their own MCI drivers and utilize the basic structure of the MCI protocol to access them. You can expect third-party standards that achieve industry-wide acceptance to be incorporated in "a future version of Windows."

Implementation of the audio mixer MCI commands requires that you install the following files in your \WINDOWS\SYSTEM directory:

- MMMIXER.DLL provides low-level access to the mixer functions contained in MVMIXER.DRV. Documentation for the functions contained in MMMIXER.DLL is available from Media Vision.

- MCIMIXER.DRV calls the functions in MMMIXER.DLL that correspond to the commands and parameters of the proposed standard audio mixer commands.

■ MVMIXER.DRV is the driver designed specifically for the Media Vision Pro AudioSpectrum series of MPC audio adapter cards. Other manufacturers are expected to provide mixer drivers that implement this standard.

Media Vision makes these files available to developers under a no-charge license.

In addition, you must add the following single line to the SYSTEM.INI file in your \WINDOWS directory:

    MIXER=MVMIXER.DRV

MCIMIXER.DRV supports the command set shown in table D.7. The *device_name* used must be that specified when opening the waveaudio or sequencer device with which the mixer is to be used. Therefore, the **open** and **close** commands are not included in table D.7.

Table D.7. The Proposed Standard MCI Command Set for Audio Mixer Functions.

Command	Description
adjust *device_name items*	Adjusts the selected *control* element of the designated *channel* for the *line_type/line_spec* device to a specified *value* between -100 and +100 percent relative to its current value. If a *control* element is not specified, the default is the **volume** control. If the *channel* is not designated, the default is **both**.
	[*channel*] An optional single *channel* keyword.
	[*control*] An optional single *control* keyword.
	line_spec A single *line_spec* value or keyword.
	line_type A single *line_type* keyword.
	[**to**] *value* A value between -100 and +100. The **to** keyword is optional.
connect *device_name items*	Directs the input or output of the first *line_type/line_spec* device to the output or input of the second *line_type/line_spec* device.
	line_spec A single *line_spec* value.
	line_type A single *line_type* keyword.

Command	Description	
	[**to**] *line_type*	A single *line_type* keyword. The **to** keyword is optional.
disconnect *device_name items*	Removes the input or output of the first *line_type/line_spec* device from the output or input of the second *line_type/line_spec* device.	
	[**from**] *line_type*	A single *line_type* keyword. The **from** keyword is optional.
	line_spec	A single *line_spec* value or keyword.
	line_type	A single *line_type* keyword.
fade *device_name items*	Adjusts the selected *control* element of the designated *channel* for the *line_type/line_spec* device to a specified *value* between 0 and 100 percent, after an optional *delay* time, over the optional *duration* period. If a *control* element is not specified, the default is the **volume** control. If the *channel* is not designated, the default is **both**. If *delay* is 0 or not specified, the fade begins immediately. If *duration* is 0 or not given, a step change occurs. If both *delay* and *duration* are 0 or omitted, **fade** is equivalent to **set**.	
	state *filename*	The mixer state specified by an optional mixer state file (see below). If **state** *filename* is not used, the following parameters are required:
	[*channel*]	An optional single *channel* keyword.
	[*control*]	An optional single *control* keyword.
	[*delay*]	The time (in tenths of a second) prior to commencing the fade (0 to 32767).
	[*duration*]	The time (in tenths of a second) during which the fade occurs (0 to 32767).

continues

Table D.7. Continued

Command	Description
	line_spec A single *line_spec* value or keyword.
	line_type A single *line_type* keyword.
	[**to**] *value* A value between 0 and 100. The **to** keyword is optional.
get *device_name items*	Returns the current integer value of the selected *control* element of the designated *channel* for the *line_type/line_spec* device. If a *control* element is not specified, the default is the **volume** control. If the *channel* is not designated, the default is **both**.
	[*channel*] An optional single *channel* keyword.
	[*control*] An optional single *control* keyword.
	line_spec A single *line_spec* value or keyword.
	line_type A single *line_type* keyword.
reset *device_name*	Resets the device to the values specified in the [mixer] section of the WIN.INI file.
set *device_name items*	Sets the selected *control* element of the designated *channel* for the *line_type/line_spec* device to a specified *value* between 0 and 100 percent. If a *control* element is not specified, the default is the **volume** control. If the *channel* is not designated, the default is **both**.
	[*channel*] An optional single *channel* keyword.
	[*control*] An optional single *control* keyword.
	line_spec A single *line_spec* value or keyword.
	line_type A single *line_type* keyword.
	[**to**] *value* A value between -100 and +100. The **to** keyword is optional.

The *line_type* and *line_spec* parameters required for table D.7 are described in tables D.7A and D.7B. Note that the three-letter abbreviations for *line_spec* apply only when the *line_type* parameter is **device_in** or **device_out**.

Table D.7A. The line_type Parameters for the Proposed Standard MCI Command Set for Audio Mixer Functions.

Line_type parameter	Line_spec parameter
line_in	1 to <= number of input lines provided on the adapter card
line_out	1 to <= number of output lines provided on the adapter card
device_in	one of the device keywords selected from table D.7B
device_out	one of the device keywords selected from table D.7B

Table D.7B. The line_spec Parameters for the Proposed Standard MCI Command Set for Audio Mixer Functions.

Code	Description	Code	Description
N/C	No connection	MUS	Musical instrument
AAT	Analog audio tape	RAD	Radio
AMP	Amplifier	SPK	PC speaker
AUX	Auxiliary	TEL	Telephone
CDA	Compact disk audio drive	TVA	Television audio
DAT	Digital audio tape	VDP	Video disk player
EQU	Equalizer	VTR	Video tape recorder
LPA	Phonograph	WAV	Waveform audio player
MIC	Microphone	UNK	Unknown device type
MIX	Mixer		

The optional audio mixer *control* parameters are listed in table D.7C. Remember, if a *control* parameter is not supplied, the default is **volume**.

Table D.7C. The Control Parameters for the Proposed Standard MCI Command Set for Audio Mixer Functions.

Control	Description	Control	Description
volume	Volume control	mute	Disabling of audio
alc	Auto level control	reverb	Reverberation control
bass	Bass boost	stereoenhance	Increase in separation
midrange	Midrange boost	custom1	Reserved
treble	Treble boost	custom2	Reserved
crossover	Stereo to *channel*	custom3	Reserved
loudness	Bass boost at low volume		

The *channel* parameter may be assigned the keywords **left**, **right**, or **both**. The default is **both**.

The following information is specific to Media Vision's MVMIXER.DRV for the Pro AudioSpectrum MPC audio adapter card and is not part of the proposed standard. Other manufacturers may adopt different formats for mixer setting entries in the WIN.INI file or may use a private *.INI file for this purpose.

The first time MVMIXER.DRV is loaded, it reads WIN.INI for volume setting and patch information. When Windows shuts down, the current settings are saved in WIN.INI, if SaveSettingsOnWindowsExit=YES.

A typical WIN.INI entry for Media Vision's MVMIXER.DRV is

```
[mvmixer.drv]
;Line=Patch      Type   Output   Volumes            Association
LineIn1=SYNTH    MUS]   PLAY     L=100%   R=100%     @=0000
LineIn2=MIXER    MIX]   PLAY     L= 72%   R= 72%     @=0000
LineIn3=AUX      AUX¦   PLAY     L=100%   R=100%     @=0000
LineIn4=CD       CDA¦   PLAY     L=  0%   R=  0%     @=0000
LineIn5=MIC      MIC¦   PLAY     L=  0%   R=  0%     @=0000
LineIn6=DIGITAL  WAV]   RECORD   L=  0%   R=  0%     @=0000
LineIn7=SPKR     SPK]   PLAY     L=100%   R=100%     @=0000
LineOut1=MASTER  AMP¦   PLAY     L= 79%   R= 79%     @=0000
StereoEnhance=ON
Loudness=ON
Bass=50
Treble=78
SaveSettingsOnWindowsExit=YES
```

The function of each field for LineIn1 to LineOut1 is described in the following paragraphs:

- *Line=Patch*. Seven input lines and one output line are included. The field immediately after the = sign is the patch name. These names (SYNTH, for example) appear in Media Vision's mixer application, PROMIX.EXE, at the bottom of each slider pair.

- *Type*. The device type determines the type of icon displayed in MIX.EXE. Each device type has a standard three-letter mnemonic name that you can obtain by calling mixGetDeviceName in MMMIXER.DLL. The fourth character indicates whether the user is responsible for making the physical device connection. Think of the character as the mounting bracket of an audio card. A hole, the | character, represents a mini phone jack. The | character indicates that you must hook up a jack or connector before hearing audio. If the fourth character is], the connection is made by the driver. Applications may use this information to remind the user to connect a particular device.

- *Output*. This field corresponds to the internal mixer connection information. The word PLAY indicates that input is routed to the PLAY output (LineOut1). RECORD means that the input is routed to the ADC circuitry.

- *Volumes*. The L= and R= fields specify the volumes, from 0 to 100 percent, of the left and right channels at start-up.

- *Association*. This field is used to save information that specifies a relationship between a mixer input and some other device in the system. If two CDs are included in the system, for example, with one connected to LineIn4 and the other connected to LineIn3, you can use the dwAssociation of MMMIXER.DLL to determine which MCI CD device is on which input.

The lines after LineOut1 control additional features specific to Media Vision's Pro AudioSpectrum MPC audio adapter card.

Binary and Hexadecimal Arithmetic

Binary arithmetic and hexadecimal representation of numbers is widely used by computer programmers. Hexadecimal representation of numeric values was adopted by the International MIDI Association (IMA) for many types of MIDI messages when it published MIDI Specification 1.0. When you see references in MIDI data sheets and system exclusive notation that consist of a combination of numbers or numbers and letters ending with H or beginning with 0x, the values are shown in hexadecimal notation—often referred to as hex. To translate what values these numbers represent in conventional decimal notation, you need to understand binary and hexadecimal arithmetic.

The Basics of Binary Arithmetic

In decimal arithmetic, an Arabic invention, the position of each digit of a number represents a power of ten, starting at the right. Powers, if you don't remember them from school, mean the number of times the number is multiplied by itself. 10 is 10 to the first power, 100 is 10 to the second power, 10,000 is 10 to the fourth power, and so on. By convention, the zeroth power of any number is defined as 1. The power of a number is also called its *exponent*.

T I P

The Windows Calculator has the capability of performing decimal and hexadecimal arithmetic. Start the Calculator, choose View, and select **S**cientific mode. You see Hex(adecimal), Dec(imal), Oct(al), Bin(ary) option buttons, with Dec as the default. You can enter a decimal number, then click the Hex button to see its hexadecimal representation. You also can enter hexadecimal numbers, with the Hex button selected, and convert them to their decimal equivalents by clicking Dec. Octal arithmetic uses eight digits, instead of 10 or 16. Binary expresses numbers as a series of 1s and 0s, which represent powers of 2, starting with 0 in the rightmost position.

Binary notation simply substitutes 2 for 10. In binary arithmetic, the position of each digit represents a power of two. Thus 4 is 2 to the second power, 16 is 2 to the fourth power, and so on. The similarity between decimal and binary notation can be seen in table E.1.

Table E.1. Powers or Exponents in Decimal and Binary Notation.

Power or Exponent	Decimal Notation	Binary Notation
0	1	1
1	10	2
2	10 * 10 = 100	2 * 2 = 4
3	10 * 10 * 10 = 1,000	2 * 2 * 2 = 8
4	10 * 10 * 10 * 10 = 10,000	2 * 2 * 2 * 2 = 16
5	10 * 10 * 10 * 10 * 10 = 100,000	2 * 2 * 2 * 2 * 2 = 32

When a number is expressed in binary notation, the rightmost bit (called the least-significant, or LSB) represents the decimal number 1, which is equal to 2^0 (two to the zeroth power). As when reading Arabic, binary notation reads from right to left. Each additional bit to the left of the LSB represents an increasing power of 2, as shown in table E.2.

Table E.2. The decimal values of the first eight powers of two.

Power of 2 (Bit)	7	6	5	4	3	2	1	0
Decimal Value	128	64	32	16	8	4	2	1

The decimal value of a binary number is determined by adding the value of each bit set to 1 as in table E.3.

Table E.3. Adding the decimal values of bits to arrive at the decimal value of an 8-bit byte.

Bit Pattern	0	1	0	1	0	1	0	1	= 1 byte (8 bits)
Decimal Value		64	+	16	+	4	+	1	= 85 (letter U)

Bytes, Words, and Hexadecimal Notation

Information used by your computer is classified as either instructions or data. Both are stored in random-access memory or RAM integrated circuits, nicknamed as *chips* and usually referred to as simply *memory*. PCs store data in 8-bit groups called bytes, which is the basic unit of measure of the size of your computer's RAM. The 01010101 pattern for U is one byte. (Half of a byte, four bits, is called a *nibble*.)

Each byte of memory has an assigned location called an *address*. Instructions tell the Central Processing Unit (CPU, the heart of your PC) the addresses of the data they need and what action to perform on the data, such as adding or subtracting numbers, or simply moving the data to a new location. Data and instructions are stored in separate areas in memory.

If you tried the Windows Calculator tip, you saw the three radio buttons, Word, DWord and Byte. When two bytes are required for data or instructions, they are called words and are 16-bits long. Sometimes four bytes must be processed together; these 32-bit groups are called double words or DWords.

Hexadecimal notation is the equivalent of representing the value of four bit groups within a byte, word, or double word represented by the characters 0 through F. This is much more convenient than having to write four 1s or 0s. Because the four-bit pattern 1111 represents 15 (1 + 2 + 4 + 8), the letters A through F have been added to the numbers 0 through 9 to stand for the decimal number 10 through 15 in hex notation.

When hexadecimal notation is used in text, you see various types of symbols that identify it as hex, such as %h, %H, &H, 0x, and so on. QuickBASIC, QBasic, and Visual Basic use the &H prefix. C and C++ prefix hexadecimal numbers with 0x. Another, similar type of notation is called *octal*, which uses 8 as its base (also called *radix*) rather than 16. Octal notation is seldom used in today's computers.

As the value of a number increases, more hex digits are required to represent it. Therefore, if you enter **123456789** in the Windows Calculator's decimal mode, changing to Hex will display 75BCD15, but only if the DWord radio button is selected. A double word is needed to represent 9-digit decimal numbers. But be forewarned, the hex result will be truncated (cut off) from the left if you choose Word or Byte.

Suppliers of Multimedia Products

This appendix lists suppliers of multimedia-related products that are designed for or are suitable for use with PCs using the Windows 3.1 graphical user interface. This appendix is organized by product category, and suppliers are listed alphabetically within each category. The product categories appear in the sequence of the subject matter presented in the book. Two additional categories that are not product related, "Multimedia Publications" and "Multimedia Industry Associations," appear at the end of the product listings.

New suppliers of hardware and publishers of applications for Windows multimedia appeared almost daily and many Windows applications were in the process of being upgraded to incorporate multimedia features when this book was written. Inclusion of a product in this list does not constitute an endorsement of the product by Que or the author, nor does omission of a product from the list indicate that a product is unworthy.

A brief identification of each product is provided, usually as a single line, to allow the inclusion of as many products and suppliers as possible within publishing limitations. Further details, including product brochures and complete specifications sheets, are available from most of these suppliers by telephone request and many have toll-free numbers.

Multimedia Computers—Chapter 1

The following suppliers offer computers with CD-ROM drives and audio adapter cards installed. Not all of these computers carried the MPC trademark at the time this book was written. The specifications issued by these manufacturers for these computers, however, indicate that all meet or exceed the basic requirements of MPC Specification 1.0.

Acer America Corporation
2641 Orchard Parkway
San Jose, CA 95134
(800) 733-2237

Acer Pac and *Acros* multimedia computer systems

Advanced Logic Research, Inc.
9401 Jeronimo
Irvine, CA 92718
(714) 581-6770

ALR multimedia computer systems

Austin Computer Systems
10300 Metric Blvd.
Austin, TX 78758
(800) 338-1577

Austin multimedia computer systems

CompuAdd Corporation
12303 Technology Blvd.
Austin, TX 78727
(800) 456-3660

CompuAdd multimedia computer systems

Goldstar Technology, Inc.
3003 N. First St.
San Jose, CA 95134
(408) 432-1331

Goldstar multimedia computer systems

Hauppauge Computer Works
91 Cabot Court
Hauppauge, NY 11788
(800) 443-6284

Hauppauge multimedia computer system

Leading Edge Products, Inc.
117 Flanders Road
Westborough, MA 01581-5020
(508) 836-4800

Leading Edge multimedia computer systems

Media Resources
640 Puente St.
Brea, CA 92621
(714) 256-5000

Multimedia computer systems

Samsung Information Systems America
3655 N. First Street
San Jose, CA 95134
(408) 434-5400

Samsung multimedia computer systems

Tandy Corporation
1700 One Tandy Center
Fort Worth, TX 76102
(817) 390-3011

Radio Shack MPC multimedia computer systems

Audio Adapter Cards and Multimedia Upgrade Kits— Chapters 1 and 2

Many of the manufacturers of audio adapter cards also supply MPC
Upgrade Kits identified by the MPC logo. Audio adapter cards, by themselves, do not qualify for use of the MPC logo. Those audio adapter cards
that are known to comply with the MPC standards are listed as "MPC-
compliant."

Advanced Gravis Computer Technology, Ltd.
7400 McPherson Ave., Unit 111
Burnaby, BC, Canada V5J 5B6
(800) 663-8558

UltraSound MPC-compliant audio adapter card

Advanced Strategies Corporation
60 Cutter Mill Rd., Suite 502
Great Neck, NY 11021
(516) 482-0088

Omni Labs MPC-compliant audio adapter card

Antex Corporation
16100 S. Figueroa Blvd.
Gardena, CA 90248
(310) 532-3092

Antex MPC-compliant audio adapter cards with digital signal processing
capabilities

Covox, Inc.
675 Conger St.
Eugene, OR 97402
(503) 342-1271

Audio adapter cards and voice recognition software

Creative Labs, Inc.
2050 Duane Avenue
Santa Clara, CA 95054
(408) 428-6600

Sound Blaster Pro and *Sound Blaster Pro Basic* MPC-compliant audio
adapter cards, MPC Upgrade Kit

E-mu Systems, Inc.
1600 Green Hills Road
Scotts Valley, CA 95067-0015
(408) 438-1921

SoundEngine daughterboard, sampled synthesized sound

Ensoniq
155 Great Valley Parkway
Malvern, PA 19355
(800) 553-5151

DOC-II chipset for wavetable synthesized sound

Focus Computer
48820 Kato Road, Suite 109B
Fremont, CA 94538
(510) 659-8822

MPC-compliant audio adapter cards

MediaSonic, Inc.
6726 Fremont Blvd.
Fremont, CA 94538
(510) 438-9996

Sound Commander MPC-compliant audio adapter cards

Media Vision
47221 Fremont Blvd.
Fremont, CA 94538
(510) 770-8600

Pro AudioSpectrum and *ProAudio Spectrum Plus* MPC-compliant audio
adapter cards, MPC Upgrade Kit, *CDPC* unitized MPC Upgrade Kit, MIDI
adapter kit.

Microsoft Corporation
One Microsoft Way
Redmond, WA 98027
(800) 227-4679

Windows Sound System audio adapter card (not MPC-compliant; does not
include MIDI IN or MIDI OUT capability)

NEC Technologies, Inc.
1255 Michael Drive
Wood Dale, IL 60191
(708) 860-9500

Intersect MPC multimedia upgrade kits with *Pro AudioSpectrum* sound
cards

ProMedia Technologies
1540 Market St., Suite 425
San Francisco, CA 94102
(415) 621-1399

Audio Canvas audio adapter cards with digital signal processing

Roland Corporation US
7200 Dominion Circle
Los Angeles, CA 90040-3647
(213) 685-5141

SCC-1 GS Sound Card with sampled synthesized sound (General MIDI and
MPU-401 compatible, but not MPC-compliant because waveform audio
capability is not included)

RTM, Inc.
13177 Ramona Blvd., Suite F
Irwindale, CA 91706
(818) 813-2630

Audio Master MPC audio adapter card

Samsung Information Systems America
3655 N. First Street
San Jose, CA 95134
(408) 434-5400

Samsung multimedia upgrade kit with Omni Labs sound card

Tandy Corporation
1700 One Tandy Center
Fort Worth, TX 76102
(817) 390-3011

Radio Shack MPC multimedia upgrade kit

Turtle Beach Systems
P.O. Box 5074
York, PA 17405
(717) 843-6936

MultiSound MPC-compliant audio adapter card with sample-playback synthesis, MPC Upgrade Kit

CD-ROM Drives and Related Products—Chapter 3

The manufacturers and suppliers of CD-ROM drives listed in the following section produce drives that meet or exceed the requirements of MPC Specification 1.0. All of the drives listed have seek times substantially less than the 1.0 second allowed by the MPC specification. Double-speed drives provide a continuous data transfer rate of 300 K/second or more, while conventional drives deliver 150 K/second.

This section also provides information on SCSI adapter cards and SCSI software, as well as the CD-ROM titles mentioned or described in the body of the book.

MPC-Compliant CD-ROM Drives

Chinon America, Inc.
660 Maple Avenue
Torrance, CA 90503
(310) 533-0274

Chinon CD-ROM drives

Genesis Integrated Systems, Inc.
1000 Shelard Parkway
Minneapolis, MN 55426
(612) 544-4445

Genesis CD-ROM drives

Hitachi HHEA-Multimedia Systems
401 West Artesia Blvd.
Compton, CA 90220
(213) 537-8383

Hitachi CD-ROM drives

Laser Magnetic Storage International Co.
4425 ArrowsWest Drive
Colorado Springs, CO 80907-3489
(800) 777-5674

CD-ROM drives

NEC Technologies, Inc.
1255 Michael Drive
Wood Dale, IL 60191
(708) 860-9500

Intersect CD-ROM drives (conventional and double-speed drives)

Philips Interactive Media Systems
One Philips Drive
Knoxville, TN 37914
(615) 521-3232

Magnavox CD-ROM drives (some models offer Photo CD compatibility)

Pioneer Electronic Corporation, Industrial Systems Section
Sherbrook Plaza, 600 East Crescent Avenue
Upper Saddle River, NJ 07458-1827
(201) 327-6400

Pioneer multiple CD-ROM drives (changers), laserdisc drives

Sony Corporation of America
1 Sony Drive
Park Ridge, NJ 07656
(201) 930-6909

Sony CD-ROM drives (some models are double-speed drives and offer Photo CD compatibility)

Texel America, Inc.
1080-C East Duane Avenue
Sunnyvale, CA 94086
(408) 736-1374

DM-series CD-ROM drives (some models are double-speed drives)

Toshiba America Information Systems,Inc.
9740 Irvine Blvd.
Irvine, CA 92718
(714) 583-3000

Toshiba CD-ROM drives

Other Optical Storage Devices

These products use optical read-write methods, but are not classified as conventional CD-ROM drives.

JVC Information Products Co. of America
19900 Beach Blvd., Suite 1
Huntington Beach, CA 92648
(714) 965-2610

JVC Personal RomMaker CD-WO drives

GrassRoots
8226 Mieman Rd.
Lenexa, KS 66214
(913) 681-3001

2020i Floptical drive, 20.88 M formatted capacity, compatible with 1.44 M and 720 K 3.5-inch diskettes

Pinnacle Micro
19 Technology
Irvine, CA 92718
(800) 553-7070

PMO-650 high speed read-write CD-ROM drive

SCSI Adapter Cards and Applications

The majority of CD-ROM drives employ the small computer systems interface (SCSI) for data transfer and control. SCSI adapter cards and software are used with many other computer peripherals, such as hard disk and tape back up drives, in addition to CD-ROM drives.

Corel Systems Corporation
1600 Carling Avenue
Ottawa, Ontario, Canada K1Z 8R7
(613) 728-8200

CorelSCSI! Application software for CD-ROM drives and other SCSI devices

Lotus Development Corporation
55 Cambridge Parkway
Cambridge, MA 02142
(617) 577-8500

Lotus CD/Networker network application software for CD-ROM drives

Meridian Data, Inc.
5615 Scotts Valley Dr.
Scotts Valley, CA 95056
(408) 438-3100

CD-Net 4.11 networking software for CD-ROM drives

Trantor Systems, Ltd.
5415 Randall Place
Fremont, CA 94538-3151
(510) 770-1400

Trantor CD-ROM SCSI adapters

Commercial Multimedia CD-ROM Titles

Dr. T's Music Software
100 Crescent Road
Needham, MA 02194
(617) 455-1454

ComposerQuest, an interactive history of musical composition

Lotus Development Corporation
55 Cambridge Parkway
Cambridge, MA 02142
(617) 577-8500

SmartHelp for Lotus 1-2-3 for Windows, a multimedia training application

Midisoft Corporation
P.O. Box 1000
Bellevue, WA 98009
(206) 881-7176

Music Mentor musical education application (includes a sequencer application specifically for the Roland SCC-1 audio adapter card and Sound Canvas modules.)

Microsoft Corporation
One Microsoft Way
Redmond, WA 98027
(800) 227-4679

Multimedia Beethoven: The Ninth Symphony

Metatec Discovery Systems
7001 Discovery Blvd.
Dublin, OH 43017
(800) 637-3472

Nautilus (monthly subscription service)

Multimedia-Related Audio Hardware—Chapter 4

This section lists suppliers of audio equipment that is often used in conjunction with recording sound as waveform audio files. Self-powered monitor speakers for use with audio adapter cards are also included.

Microphones

AKG Acoustics
1525 Alvarado Street
San Leandro, CA 94577
(510) 351-3500

Condenser and dynamic microphones manufactured by Akustiche und Kino-Gerate GmbH, Austria

Shure Brothers, Inc.
222 Hartrey Avenue
Evanston, IL 60202-3696
(708) 866-2200

Condenser and dynamic microphones

Multi-Channel Audio Mixers and Tape Recorders

Alesis Corporation
3630 Holdrege Avenue
Los Angeles, CA 90016
(213) 467-8000

ADAT 8-track digital audio transport using S-VHS cassettes

Fostex Corporation of America
15431 Blackburn Ave.
Norwalk, CA 90650
(310) 921-1112

Multi-channel tape recorders and mixers

Mackie Designs, Inc.
16130 Woodinville-Redmond Road, NE #2
Woodinville, WA 98072
(800) 258-6883

Multi-channel audio mixers

Teac America, Inc.
7733 Telegraph Road
Montebello, CA 90640
(213) 726-0303

Tascam multi-channel mixers and tape recorders

Yamaha Corporation of America
P.O. Box 6600
Buena Park, CA 90622-6600
(714) 522-9011

Yamaha Professional Audio multi-channel audio mixers and tape recorders

Self-powered Monitor Speakers

Altec Lansing
Consumer Products Division
Milford, PA 18337
1-800-258-3288

ACS300 computer speaker system

Roland Corporation US
7200 Dominion Circle
Los Angeles, CA 90040-3647
(213) 685-5141

Roland CS-10 and *MA-12C Micro Monitors*

MIDI Synthesizers, Accessories, and Applications—Chapters 9, 11, 12, and 21

MIDI musical instruments and accessories have been available for several years. A large number of reputable suppliers of MIDI equipment are available. The products listed in this section is limited to those discussed in the body of this book. MIDI sequencer applications for Windows and representative MIDI production music, available on CD-ROM and floppy disk, is included in this section.

MIDI Synthesizers—Chapter 9

E-mu Systems, Inc.
1600 Green Hills Road
Scotts Valley, CA 95067-0015
(408) 438-1921

Proteus sound modules and keyboard synthesizers

Ensoniq
155 Great Valley Parkway
Malvern, PA 19355
(800) 553-5151

Ensoniq keyboard synthesizers and MIDI workstations

Korg U.S.A.
89 Frost Street
Westbury, NY 11590
(516) 333-9100

Korg 03R/W General MIDI sound module, *01/W* MIDI workstation, and keyboard synthesizers

Roland Corporation US
7200 Dominion Circle
Los Angeles, CA 90040-3647
(213) 685-5141

Roland MIDI keyboard synthesizers, sound modules, and drum machines

Software Toolworks
60 Leveroni Ct.
Novato, CA 94549
(800) 234-3088

Miracle Piano MIDI keyboard synthesizer and music training software

Yamaha Corporation of America
P.O. Box 6600
Buena Park, CA 90622-6600
(714) 522-9011

Yamaha TG-100 and *TG-500* General MIDI sound modules, keyboard synthesizers

MIDI Accessory Devices—Chapters 11 and 21

Alesis Corporation
3630 Holdrege Avenue
Los Angeles, CA 90016
(213) 467-8000

Alesis MIDI drum machines and effects processors

Applied Research and Technology, Inc.
215 Tremont St.
Rochester, NY 14608
(716) 436-3942

ART MIDI effects processors

DOD Electronics Corporation
5639 South Riley Lane
Salt Lake City, UT 84107
(801) 268-8400

Vocalizer MIDI voice harmonizer

KMX
67 West Easy Street, Suite 134
Simi Valley, CA 93005
(805) 582-0485

MIDI patch bays

Lexicon, Inc.
100 Beaver St.
Waltham, MA 02154
(617) 891-0300

LXP effects processors, *MRC* MIDI remote controller

Mackie Designs, Inc.
16130 Woodinville-Redmond Road, NE #2
Woodinville, WA 98072
(800) 258-6883

MIDI-controlled multi-channel mixers

Mark of the Unicorn, Inc.
222 Third Street
Cambridge, MA 02142
(617) 576-2760

MIDI Mixer 7 multi-channel, MIDI-controlled mixer

MidiMan
30 North Raymond, Suite 505
Pasadena, CA 91103
(800) 969-6434

MidiMan MIDI synchronization systems and MIDI adapter cards

Music Quest, Inc.
1700 Alma Drive, Suite 330
Plano, TX 75075
(800) 876-1376

MQX-32M 32-channel MIDI and SMPTE synchronization adapter card

Roland Corporation US
7200 Dominion Circle
Los Angeles, CA 90040-3647
(213) 685-5141

Roland MIDI keyboards, pitch-to-MIDI converters, and drum machines

SynchroVoice
400 Harrison Ave.
Harrison, NJ 07029
(201) 483-7416

Midivox vocal pitch-to-MIDI converter

TimeLine Vista, Inc.
2401 Dogwood Way
Vista, CA 92083
(619) 727-3300

MicroLynx MIDI synchronization systems

MIDI Sequencers and Related Applications—Chapter 12

Big Noise Software, Inc.
P.O. Box 23740
Jacksonville, FL 32241
(904) 730-0754

Cadenza for Windows MIDI sequencer

Dr. T's Music Software
100 Crescent Road
Needham, MA 02194
(617) 455-1454

X-Or editor/librarian for MIDI synthesizers

Howling Dog Systems
P.O. Box 80405
Burnaby, BC, Canada V5H 3X6

Power Chords, a Windows musical construction application

Dan McKee
69 Rancliffe Road
Oakville, Ontario, Canada L6H 1B1
(416) 844-1821

WinJammer shareware MIDI sequencer and Windows DLLs for MIDI applications

Midisoft Corporation
P.O. Box 1000
Bellevue, WA 98009
(206) 881-7176

Studio for Windows 3 MIDI Sequencer

Musicator/ThinKware
P.O. Box 410039
San Francisco, CA 94141
(916) 756-9807

Musicator GS Windows sequencer (includes features specific to the Roland SCC-1 audio adapter card and Sound Canvas modules)

Passport Designs, Inc.
625 Miramontes Street
Half Moon Bay, CA 94019
(415) 726-0280

Master Tracks Pro, *Trax* and *MusicTime* MIDI Sequencers, *Encore* Scoring Application

PG Music, Inc.
111-266 Elmwood Avenue
Buffalo, NY 14222
(800) 268-6272

Band-in-a-Box for Windows music construction application

Sound Quest, Inc.
131 West 13th Avenue
Vancouver, BC, Canada V5Y 1V8
(800) 667-3998

MIDI Quest 2.12 for Windows editor-librarian

Twelve-Tone Systems, Inc.
P.O. Box 760
Watertown, MA 02272
(800) 234-1171, (617) 273-4437 Voice
(617) 273-1494 FAX

Cakewalk Professional for Windows MIDI sequencer

MIDI Production Music

Applied Optical Media Corporation
1450 Boot Road, Bldg. 400
West Chester, PA 19380
(215) 429-3701

Mediasource Library on CD-ROM includes music, waveform audio sound and graphic clips

Creative Support Services
1950 Riverside Drive
Los Angeles, CA 90039
(213) 666-7968

Sound effects and theme music on CD-ROMs

Metatec Discovery Systems
7001 Discovery Blvd.
Dublin, OH 43017
(800) 637-3472

Nautilus multimedia CD-ROM (monthly subscription service, includes MIDI and waveform audio files)

The Music Bakery
660 Preston Forest Center, Suite 300
Dallas, TX 75230
(800) 229-0313

CD-ROMs of waveform audio and MIDI files issued monthly by subscription

Passport Designs, Inc.
625 Miramontes Street
Half Moon Bay, CA 94019
(415) 726-0280

Media Music and *MIDI Hits* (CD-ROM, waveform audio and MIDI files)

Presentation Graphics Group
270 North Canon Drive, Suite 103
Beverly Hills, CA 90210
(213) 277-3050

DigiSound Starter Disk (CD-ROM, waveform audio and MIDI files)

Prosonus
11126 Weddington Street
North Hollywood, CA 91601
(818) 776-5221

MusicBytes (CD-ROM, waveform audio and MIDI files)

Trycho Music International
2166 W. Broadway St., Suite 330
Anaheim, CA 92804
(800) 543-8988

Pop and rock hit tune arrangements supplied as MIDI files on diskette

Voyetra Technologies
333 Fifth Avenue
Pelham, NY 10803
(914) 738-4500

MusiClips (MIDI production music only, diskette)

Multimedia Sound Editing and Related Applications—Chapter 14

The suppliers of the two commercial editing applications discussed in Chapter 14 are listed below. Microsoft Corporation's WaveEdit application is included in the Multimedia Development Kit (MDK) for Windows.

Turtle Beach Systems
P.O. Box 5074
York, PA 17405
(717) 843-6936

Wave for Windows and *Wave Lite for Windows* waveform audio editors

Voyetra Technologies
333 Fifth Avenue
Pelham, NY 10803
(914) 738-4500

AudioView waveform audio editor and *PatchView FM* voice patch editor for audio adapter cards using Yamaha OPL-II and OPL-III chipsets.

Graphics Adapter Cards and Displays—Chapter 16

A very large number of suppliers, importers, and distributors of conventional SVGA graphics adapter cards exist. Only SVGA graphics adapter cards that include audio capabilities, graphics accelerator cards for Windows, and hardware compression/decompression cards for graphic images are included in this section. The audio capabilities of most combined SVGA and audio adapter cards do not comply with the MPC specifications (usually due to lack of synthesized sound or MIDI connections).

Similarly, you can find many suppliers of conventional video display units that meet SVGA standards. The list of suppliers of display devices has been limited to a representative group of manufacturers of extra-large-screen video display units and projection devices for multimedia presentations.

Combined Graphics and Audio Adapter Cards

Cardinal Technologies, Inc.
1827 Freedom Rd.
Lancaster, PA 17601
(800) 233-0187

Soundvision card (SVGA and audio adapter card)

Media Vision
47221 Fremont Blvd.
Fremont, CA 94538
(510) 770-8600

Thunder and Lightning card (SVGA and audio adapter card)

Graphics Compression/Decompression Adapter Cards

Lead Technologies
8701 Mallard Creek Road
Charlotte, NC 28262
(704) 549-5532

CL-550-based JPEG compression board

Opta Corporation
2525 East Bayshore Blvd., Suite 2
Palo Alto, CA 94303
(415) 354-1120

Mona Lisa 24-bit graphics board, JPEG compressor option

Optibase
7800 Deering Ave.
Canoga Park, CA 91304-9878
(800) 451-5101

JPEG hardware compression/decompression board

Graphics Accelerator Cards and Software for Windows

ATI Technologies, Inc.
3761 Victoria Park Avenue
Scarborough, Ontario M1W 3S2
(416) 756-0718

ATI graphics accelerator cards

Celerite Graphics, Inc.
46560 Fremont Blvd., Suite 113
Fremont, CA 94538
(800) 472-7820

Celerite graphics accelerator card

Diamond Computer Systems
532 Mercury Drive HiColor 7/15 24-bit
Sunnyvale, CA 94086
(408) 736-2000

Diamond Stealth VRAM

Panacea, Inc.
24 Orchard View Dr., Suite 4
Londonderry, NH 03053-3376
(800) 729-7420

WinSpeed software graphics accelerator driver

Portacom Technologies, Inc.
3235 Kifer Road, Suite 310
Santa Clara, CA 95051
(408) 736-9135

Portacom Eclipse II graphics accelerator card

Presentation-size and Touch-screen Displays and Projectors for Multimedia

Elographics, Inc.
105 Randolph Road
Oak Ridge, TN 37830
(615) 482-4100

Touchscreen monitors

MicroTouch Systems, Inc.
55 Jonspin Road
Wilmington, MA 01887
(508) 694-9900

TruePoint touch-screen monitor

Mitsubishi Electronics America, Inc., Professional Electronics
Division
800 Cottontail Lane
Somerset, NJ 08873
(908) 563-9889

AM-3501R 35-inch monitors and VS-1250 video/data projector

NEC Technologies, Inc.
1255 Michael Drive
Wood Dale, IL 60191
(708) 860-9500

DM-2710 DataSmart Monitor for presentations (remotely controllable)

Overhead Projection Devices for Multimedia

InFocus Systems, Inc.
7770 S.W. Mohawk St.
Tualatin, OR 97062
(800) 327-7231

TVT-3000 active matrix color LCD projection panel

Micronics Computers, Inc.
232 E. Warren Ave.
Fremont, CA 94539
(510) 651-2300

Mpression overhead projection panel and *Mpact* notebook presentation
system

nVIEW Corporation
11835 Canon Blvd.
Newport News, VA 23606
(800) 736-8439

MediaPro overhead projection panel

Sharp Electronics Corporation Professional Products Div.
Sharp Plaza
Mahwah, NJ 07430-2135
(201) 529-8731

XG-1100 (portable) and *XG-1500* ceiling mount LCD projectors

Graphics Applications for Windows—Chapter 17

Graphics applications for Windows are divided into two basic categories: drawing (including animation) applications that use vector-based images, and image editing applications that manipulate bit maps. Animation applications, especially those that render three-dimensional images, are primarily DOS applications; therefore, the only Windows animation application that is included is capable only of playing the animation. This section also includes image compression and decompression applications, sources of vector and bit-map images, and manufacturers of scanners and graphics drawing tablets.

Drawing and Animation Applications

Autodesk, Inc.
2320 Marinship Way
Sausalito, CA 94965
(415) 331-0356

Autodesk Multimedia Explorer for Windows (includes Autodesk Animation Player for Windows on diskette and Autodesk Animator Clips on CD-ROM)

Corel Systems Corporation
1600 Carling Avenue
Ottawa, Ontario, Canada K1Z 8R7
(613) 728-8200

CorelDRAW! 3.0

Lotus Development Corporation
55 Cambridge Parkway
Cambridge, MA 02142
(617) 577-8500

Lotus Freelance for Windows

Micrografx, Inc.
1303 Arapaho
Richardson, TX 75081
(800) 733-3729

Micrografx Designer 3.1 and *Windows DRAW! 3.0 with OLE*

Image Editing Applications

Aldus Corporation
411 First Avenue South
Seattle, WA 98104-2871
(206) 622-5500

Aldus PhotoStyler

Corel Systems Corporation
1600 Carling Avenue
Ottawa, Ontario, Canada K1Z 8R7
(613) 728-8200

CorelPhotoPaint! (part of *CorelDRAW!* 3.0)

Fractal Design Corporation
1010 Madeline Dr., Suite 204
Aptos, CA 95003
(408) 688-8800

Painter for Windows and *ColorStudio for Windows*

Image-In, Inc.
406 East 79th Street
Minneapolis, MN 55420
(800) 345-3540

Image-In Color and *Image-In Professional*

Kodak Electronic Imaging Products
343 State Street
Rochester, NY 14650-0519
(800) 242-2424, Extension 53

Kodak PhotoEdge image enhancement and correction application for Photo CD images

Micrografx, Inc.
1303 Arapaho
Richardson, TX 75081
(800) 733-3729

Micrografx Picture Publisher 3.1 (includes MPEG import/export and Kodak Photo CD import capabilities)

Image Compression and Decompression Applications

Kodak Electronic Imaging Products
343 State Street
Rochester, NY 14650-0519
(800) 242-2424, Extension 53

Kodak Photo CD Access application for Photo CD images

Optibase
7800 Deering Ave.
Canoga Park, CA 91304-9878
(800) 451-5101

The WorkShop software MPEG compressor

Stac Electronics
5993 Avenida Encinas
Carlsbad, CA 92008
(800) 522-7822

Stacker hard disk file compression application (compression adapter card available)

Clip Art and Background Images

Lotus Development Corporation
55 Cambridge Parkway
Cambridge, MA 02142
(617) 577-8500

Lotus SmartPics

Corel Systems Corporation
1600 Carling Avenue
Ottawa, Ontario, Canada K1Z 8R7
(613) 728-8200

CorelDRAW! images on CD-ROM (part of *CorelDRAW!* 3.0)

Imagetects
7200 Bollinger Rd., Suite 802
San Jose, CA 95129
(408) 252-5487

Bit map texture and image libraries on diskette and CD-ROM

Kodak Electronic Imaging Products
343 State Street
Rochester, NY 14650-0519
(800) 242-2424, Extension 53

Kodak Photo CD Image Library application and Photo CD catalog of images available in Photo CD format from professional photographers.

Micrografx, Inc.
1303 Arapaho
Richardson, TX 75081
(800) 733-3729

Image library included with *Micrografx Designer 3.1*

PhotoDisc
2101 4th Avenue, Suite 200
Seattle, WA 98121
(800) 528-3475

Stock photos on CD-ROMs

Westlight
2223 S. Camelina Ave.
Los Angeles, CA 90064
(310) 820-7077

Professional photographic image archive

Scanners and Graphics Drawing Tablets

Logitech, Inc.
6505 Kaiser Dr.
Fremont, CA 94555
(510) 795-8500

ScanMan color and gray-scale hand scanners

Mustek, Inc.
15225 Alton Parkway
Irvine, CA 92718
(714) 833-7740

ColorArtist M6000CG hand color scanner

Wacom Technology
501 S.E. Columbia Shores Blvd., Suite 300
Vancouver, WA 98661
(800) 922-6613

SD510C pressure-sensitive pen tablet for drawing and image editing applications

Multimedia Presentation Applications—Chapter 18

Presentation applications are designed to simulate topical slide-show presentations. The capability to add sound to the presentation qualifies a product as a multimedia presentation application for the purposes of this list.

Asymetrix, Inc.
P.O. Box 40419
Bellevue, WA 98004-0419
(206) 637-1500

Multimedia Make Your Point and *MediaBlitz* (low cost Windows presentation applications)

Corel Systems Corporation
1600 Carling Avenue
Ottawa, Ontario, Canada K1Z 8R7
(613) 728-8200

CorelSHOW! (part of *CorelDRAW!* 3.0)

HSC Software
1661 Lincoln Blvd., Suite 101
Santa Monica, CA 90404
(310) 392-8441

QuickSHOW!

MacroMind, Inc.
600 Townsend, Suite 310W
San Francisco, CA 94103
(415) 442-0200

Action! 2.0 animated presentation application

Microsoft Corporation
One Microsoft Way
Redmond, WA 98027
(800) 227-4679

Microsoft PowerPoint 3.0

Software Publishing Corporation
3165 Kifer Road
Santa Clara, CA 95056-0983
(408) 986-8000

Harvard Graphics for Windows 1.01

Video Adapter Cards—Chapter 19

Video adapter cards include video capture cards (frame grabbers), video-in-a-window (VIW) cards, and VGA-to-NTSC video output cards (including external converters and products with and without genlocking capability). Video adapter card suppliers are not classified by type of card, because most suppliers manufacture or distribute more than one type of card.

ADDA (USA) Technologies, Inc.
48008 Starlite Court
Fremont, CA 94539
(510) 770-9899

AVer 2000 Windows Frame Grabber, VGA-AVer Overlay Video Card, AVer 1000 Video Output Card

Aitech International Corporation
830 Hillview Ct., Suite 145
Milpitas, CA 95035
(800) 882-8184

Aitech video capture, video-in-a-window, VGA-to-NTSC output cards, VGA-to-NTSC converters.

Cables-to-Go
26 West Nottingham, Suite 200
Dayton, OH 45405
(800) 826-7904

Specialized cables for video adapter cards

Cardinal Technologies, Inc.
1827 Freedom Rd.
Lancaster, PA 17601
(800) 233-0187

SNAPplus video adapter card

Creative Labs, Inc.
2050 Duane Avenue
Santa Clara, CA 95054
(408) 428-6600

Video Blaster Pro video-in-a-windows adapter card

Digital Vision, Inc.
270 Bridge Street
Dedham, MA 02026
(617) 329-5400

ComputerEyes/RT video image capture adapter card

Fluent Machines
1881 Worcester Road
Framingham, MA 01701
(508) 626-2144

VSA-1000 video board set

Genoa Systems Corporation
75 E. Trimble Road
San Jose, CA 95131
(408) 432-9090

VGA2TV genlocking VGA-to-NTSC card

Hauppauge Computer Works
91 Cabot Court
Hauppauge, NY 11788
(800) 443-6284

Win/TV video-in-a-window card with television tuner

Hi Res Technologies
P.O. Box 76
Lewiston, NY 14092
(416) 497-6493

Video Gala video adapter card

Intel Corporation
313 Enterprise Road
Plainsboro, NJ 08536
(609) 936-7619

ActionMedia II DVI video cards

Jovian Logic Corporation
47929 Fremont Blvd.
Fremont, CA 94538
(510) 651-4823

Super VIA and *Gloria* video boards, *Genie* scan converter

Matrox Electronic Systems, Ltd.
1055 St. Regis Blvd.
Dorval, Quebec, Canada H9P 2T4
(800) 361-4903

Illuminator 16 multi-purpose video card (used with Matrox Personal Producer)

New Media Graphics
780 Boston Road
Billerica, MA 01821
(800) 288-2207

TV-Video Windows video-in-a-window card, *Super TV-Video Windows* (included television tuner)

Rapid Technology Corporation
4226 Ridge Lea Road, Suite 43
Amherst, NY 14226
(716) 833-8533

Visionary video compression card for True Vision Bravado adapter cards

Specom Technologies
3673 Enochs Street
Santa Clara, CA 95051
(408) 736-7832

VIDCOM still and video compression (JPEG) board

Truevision, Inc.
7340 Shadeland Station
Indianapolis, IN 46256
(317) 841-0332

Bravado and *Bravado 16* video-in-a-window cards (includes SVGA capability), *TARGA* series video adapter cards.

VideoLogic
245 First Street
Cambridge, MA 02142
(617) 494-0530

DVA-4000/ISA digital video adapter

Videomail, Inc.
586-4 Weddell Dr.
Sunnyvale, CA 94089
(408) 747-0223

Videomail video-in-a-window card

Multimedia Authoring Applications—Chapter 20

The majority of multimedia authoring applications are designed for the production of interactive multimedia titles to be distributed in the form of CD-ROMS. These applications are ordinarily more complex than multimedia presentation applications and many require programming skills to use all of their features.

AimTech Corporation
20 Trafalgar Square
Nashua, NH 03063-1973
(603) 8833-0220

IconAuthor

Asymetrix, Inc.
P.O. Box 40419
Bellevue, WA 98004-0419
(206) 637-1500

Multimedia Toolbook

Authorware, Inc.
275 Shoreline Drive, 4th Floor
Redwood City, CA 94065
(415) 595-3101

Authorware Professional for Windows

Computer Enhanced Interactive Technology
4800 Great America Parkway, Suite 200
Santa Clara, CA 95054
(408) 986-1101

TourGuide

The Company of Science & Art
14 Imperial Place 203
Providence, RI 02903
(401) 831-2672

PACO cross-platform QuickTime player for Windows

Dataware Technologies, Inc.
222 Third Street, Suite 3300
Cambridge, MA 02142
(617) 621-0820

CD Author and *CD Answer*

Gold Disk, Inc.
P.O. Box 789, Streetsville
Mississauga, Ontario, Canada L5M 2C2
(416) 602-4000

Animation Works Interactive for Windows and *Add Impact,* an animation
OLE server

HSC Software
1661 Lincoln Blvd., Suite 101
Santa Monica, CA 90404
(310) 392-8441

HSC Interactive

Microsoft Corporation
One Microsoft Way
Redmond, WA 98027
(800) 227-4679

Multimedia Viewer, part of the Microsoft Multimedia Development Kit
(MDK), based on the Windows 3.1 context-sensitive help system.

OptImage Interactive Services Co., L.P.
1501 50th St., Suite 100
West Des Moines, IA 50265
(515) 225-7000

Media Mogul CD-I Authoring systems

Script Systems
The Market Place, Building 5
Manilus, NY 13104
(315) 682-8714

Designers Work Bench CD-I authoring application

Multimedia Database Applications—Chapter 22

Multimedia databases are used to catalog and display individual multimedia objects. The *Kodak Browser* and *Shoebox* applications do not
qualify technically as a multimedia database because they handle only
Photo CD images. Lenel Systems' *MediaOrganizer* and *MPCOrganizer*
applications are full-scale multimedia databases and can catalog and
display images and sound in all popular multimedia formats.

Kodak Electronic Imaging Products
343 State Street
Rochester, NY 14650-0519
(800) 242-2424, Extension 53

Kodak Browser image database and *Shoebox* image search and retrieval applications.

Lenel Systems
19 Tobey Village Office Park
Pittsford, NY 14534
(716) 248-9720

MediaOrganizer and *MPCOrganizer* multimedia databases (includes OLE server and Sony VISCA control capabilities)

Hardware and Software for Desktop Video—Chapter 22

This section includes suppliers of hardware and publishers of applications specifically designed for desktop video productions. Hardware includes remotely controllable VCRs, remote control adapters, and related equipment required to edit videotape footage. Applications are primarily designed for the equivalent of A-B roll editing with the hardware listed. Sources of stock video footage (video clips) also are provided.

Video Hardware

Advanced Remote Technologies, Inc.
307 Orchard City Drive
Campbell, CA 95008
(408) 374-9044

Clark media controller (includes VISCA capability)

Canon USA, Still Video Division
1 Canon Plaza
Lake Success, NY 11042
(516) 488-6700

Canon RC250 still video camera (formerly the Xapshot)

Caravan Productions
P.O. Box 112
Wixom, MI 48393
(313) 669-3783

Clubplay Home Entertainment Designer, uses infrared remote control for editing

Cinema Products Corporation
3211 S. La Cienega Blvd.
Los Angeles, CA 90016
(800) 955-5025

Steadicam JR camcorder stabilizing system

Diaquest, Inc.
1440 San Pablo Ave.
Berkeley, CA 94702
(510) 526-7167

DQ-422 VCR remote control board (provides universal synchronization)

ECHOlab
175 Bedford Rd.
Burlington, MA 01803
(617) 273-1512

Video switcher card with Windows-based application

Fast Electronic U.S.
5 Commonwealth Road
Natick, MA 01760
(508) 655-3278

VideoMachine A-B video editing system for Windows

FutureVideo, Inc.
28 Argonaut
Laguna Hills, CA
(714) 770-4416

EditLink 2200 VCR remote control adapter card

Matrox Electronic Systems, Ltd.
1055 St. Regis Blvd.
Dorval, Quebec, Canada H9P 2T4
(800) 361-4903

Video editing workstation

NewTek, Incorporated
900 East 79th St., Suite 101
Bloomington, MN 55420
(800) 368-5441

Video Toaster video editing and special effects workstation (Amiga computer)

ParkerVision
8493 Baymeadows Way
Jacksonville, FL 32256
(800) 231-1759

CameraMan remotely controlled tripod

Sony Corporation of America
Sony Drive
Park Ridge, NJ 07656

Mavica MVCC1 still video camera (available at electronics stores)

Sony Computer Peripherals
655 River Oaks Pkwy.
San Jose, CA 95134
(408) 432-0190

VISCA products, *Vdeck* Hi8 VCR, *Vbox* VISCA adapter

Technical Aesthetics Operations, Inc.
501 West 5th Street
Rolla, MO 65401
(800) 264-1121

Editizer, computer-controlled A-B roll editor with Windows software

Video Editing and Related Applications

Advanced Remote Technologies, Inc.
307 Orchard City Drive
Campbell, CA 95008
(408) 374-9044

EditBuddy (used with the firm's Clark controllers)

Matrox Electronic Systems, Ltd.
1055 St. Regis Blvd.
Dorval, Quebec, Canada H9P 2T4
(800) 361-4903

Matrox Personal Producer DTV production application for Windows

PALTEX International
2752 Walnut Ave.
Tustin, CA 92680
(714) 838-8833

EDDi video editing control adapter cards, Windows editing application

ProtoComm Corporation
Two Neshaminy Interplex, Suite 100
Trevose, PA 19053
(215) 245-2040

VideoComm for Windows, network software for video and audio files

Videomedia, Inc.
175 Lewis Rd
San Jose, CA 95111
(408) 227-9977

Oz video editing system

Video Clips

Archive Films, Inc.
530 W. 25th St.
New York, NY 10001
(800) 876-5115

Stock video footage

Film/Audio Services, Inc.
430 W. 14th St., Suite 310
New York, NY 10014
(212) 645-2112

VideoPedia video clips available on videotape or CD-ROM

Video Tape Library, Ltd.
1509 N. Crescent Heights Blvd., Suite 2
Los Angeles, CA 90046
(213) 656-4330

Stock video footage

Multimedia Programming Toolkits—Chapter 23

The documentation for Microsoft's Multimedia Development Kit (available separately) is required if you intend to make extensive use of the media control interface (MCI) commands of Windows 3.1. The complete MDK includes a CD-ROM that contains the Multimedia Viewer authoring application and applets for editing bit-map images, palettes, and waveform audio files.

Microsoft Corporation
One Microsoft Way
Redmond, WA 98027
(800) 227-4679

Microsoft Multimedia Development Kit (MDK), Version 3.1

Microsoft Professional Toolkit for Visual Basic 2.0 (includes MCI custom control for Visual Basic 2.0)

Asymetrix, Inc.
P.O. Box 40419
Bellevue, WA 98004-0419
(206) 637-1500

Software development kit for the Windows digital video media control interface (DVMCI SDK) developed jointly with Microsoft Corporation and Intel Corporation

Multimedia Publications

Most PC computer periodicals include at least one multimedia background article or product review in every issue. *NewMedia* magazine covers multimedia products and techniques for the PC, Apple Macintosh, and Amiga computers, and *MPC World* is devoted to Windows multimedia. *Electronic Musician* and *Keyboard* magazines are directed to musicians and emphasize MIDI and audio recording techniques. Newsletters, such as *Multimedia Computing and Presentations*, provide up-to-the-minute information on industry events and trends.

Act III Publishing
6400 Hollis Street, Suite 12
Emeryville, CA 94608
(510) 653-3307

Publishers of *Electronic Musician* magazine

Frost & Sullivan, Inc.
106 Fulton St.
New York, NY 10038
(212) 233-1080

Publishers of market research studies, including "The U.S. Market for CD-ROM Players and Pre-recorded Media"

HyperMedia Communications, Inc.
901 Mariner's Island Parkway #365
San Mateo, CA 94404
(415) 573-5170

Publishers of *NewMedia* magazine

Keyboard
20085 Stevens Creek Blvd.
Cupertino, CA 95014
(408) 446-1105

Publishers of *Keyboard* magazine

Mix Bookshelf
6400 Hollis Street, Suite 12
Emeryville, CA 94608
(510) 653-3307

Retail and mail-order distribution of books related to MIDI and audio technology

Multimedia Computing Corporation
3501 Ryder St.
Santa Clara, CA 95051
(408) 737-7575

Publishers of *Multimedia Computing and Presentations* newsletter

PCW Communications
524 Second Street
San Francisco, CA 94107
(415) 281-8650

Publishers of *MPC World* Magazine

Multimedia Industry Associations

Industry associations play an important role in developing the standards used in the development of multimedia productions. The International MIDI Association and the Society of Motion Picture and Television Engineers both predate the advent of multimedia by several years.

Interactive Multimedia Association (IMA)
800 K Street, North West, Suite 240
Washington, DC 20001
(202) 408-1000

The mission of the IMA is "to promote the development of interactive multimedia applications and reduce barriers to the widespread use of multimedia technology." One of the principle activities of the organization is the development of standards that allow the same multimedia sound and graphic data to be shared by a wide range of computer types.

International MIDI Association (IMA)
5316 West 57th Street
Los Angeles, CA 90056
(213) 649-6434

The IMA coordinates and publishes MIDI Specification 1.0 and updates and supplements the specification. The MIDI Manufacturers Association is located at the same address and is under the same management as the IMA.

Multimedia PC Marketing Council
1730 M Street, NW
Washington, DC 20036-4510
(202) 452-1600

The Multimedia PC Marketing Council consists of manufacturers of MPC-compliant products. It coordinates and publishes MPC Specification 1.0, updates to the specification, and licenses the use of the MPC logo to identify production conforming to MPC Specification 1.0.

Society of Motion Picture and Television Engineers (SMPTE)
595 W. Hartsdale Ave.
White Plains, NY 10607
(914) 761-1100

SMPTE establishes technical specifications and recommendations for motion picture and television production.

Downloading Files from CompuServe

CompuServe is an on-line source of a wide range of PC applications related to sound and music, in the form of public domain and Shareware programs. Public domain programs are donated by their authors and are not usually copyrighted; you may use them in any way you want. Shareware programs, on the other hand, are copyrighted applications and are the property of their author. Shareware gives you the chance to "try before you buy." If you use the application, you are expected to register the copy you downloaded, sending the author the requested license fee. Most Shareware applications include registration forms, which you print, fill in, and mail with your check.

To access CompuServe, you need a modem and a data communication application to control the modem. Most modems are supplied with a DOS-based communication application and some also include a version for Windows. If you do not have a Windows version, you can download a copy of Data Graphic's Unicom, a full-featured Shareware product from the PC Communications forum (GO IBMCOM) or the Advanced Windows forum (GO WINADV.)

Multimedia Files on CompuServe

CompuServe is divided into "forums" that relate to specific topics of interest. After you log onto CompuServe, type **GO** followed by the code name of the forum you want to enter at CompuServe's **!** prompt. The first time you use an individual forum, you are asked to join by registering your name as a forum user. After you join the forum, you can download files from its libraries (LIBs), which you select by entering **3** for LIBRARIES, then the number of the library that contains the type of files in which you are interested.

Files related to sound, music, and multimedia applications are located primarily in the following forums and their libraries:

Forum name	To access	Library	Types of files
PC New Users	GO IBMNEW	Music	Pianoman, BASIC, and compiled music files, principally for DOS.
MIDI	GO MIDI	All libraries in the MIDI music forum are related to MIDI music and utility applications	MIDI utility applications and a wide range of *.MID song files. Demonstration versions of commercial MIDI also are available.
MIDI	GO MIDIVEN	All vendors	Files related to specific suppliers' MIDI hardware and software. Libraries are identified by vendor name.
Microsoft Knowledge Base	GO MSKB	N/A. Search on keyword such as "sound"	Information in the Knowledge Base is displayed on-screen in the the form of messages. Requires use of the capture-to-file function of your communication application.
Microsoft Software Library	GO MSL	N/A. All files are in one library.	Browse files by key word such as "sound" or download by file name obtained from entries in the Knowledge Base. Latest versions of multimedia drivers are available.
Microsoft Windows	GO WINADV	Multimedia	Sound files and applications specifically Advanced for Windows with Multimedia and Windows 3.1.
		Games	Utilities and sound files for the Sound Blaster, Ad Lib and other sound cards.
		Shareware	Additional sound utilities
Multimedia	GO MULTIMEDIA	Video and audio	Sound files and utility applications
Multimedia Vendors		GO MULTIVEN	By vendor

You can obtain a list of PC-compatible files in all the libraries on CompuServe by using the IBM File Finder database (GO IBMFF.) Search by a key word such as SOUND or MUSIC, and you will be given a list of all the files that contain the key word, together with their location. You can view a brief description of the file by entering its list sequence number at the prompt, or display additional matching files simply by pressing Enter.

Processing Compressed or Archived Files

Most of the files in CompuServe's libraries are stored in compressed or archived format to shorten downloading time and save disk space. Archiving is indicated by the file extension *.ZIP and, for older files, *.ARC. You will need PKWare's Shareware file un-archiving application, PKUNZIP, to extract the files from the archive, expand them to their original size, and assign their proper file names. PKUNZIP is included in the file PKZ110.EXE, which is available in a number of forums. Type **GO IBMFF** and enter **PKZ110.EXE** as the file name to find a library that includes PKUNZIP.

PKZ110.EXE is a self-extracting, executable DOS application. After you download PKZ110.EXE, preferably into your \DOS or \UTILITY directory so that it will be on your path, run it at the DOS prompt. PKZ110.EXE will expand into PKZIP.EXE, PKUNZIP.EXE, a documentation file, and several additional files, including the Shareware registration form. One of the advantages of archived files is that you can incorporate all the individual files required for an application in a single archive. You may delete PKZ100.EXE after running it.

The file you want to un-archive is entered as a command-line parameter of PKUNZIP.EXE:

> PKUNZIP MIDIFILE

This command expands the archive MIDIFILE.ZIP (the *.ZIP extension is defaulted.) If you have downloaded an older file that uses the *.ARC extension, you must also enter the extension, as in the following command:

> PKUNZIP OLD_FILE.ARC

Typing **PKUNZIP** without a parameter will bring up a brief help screen explaining its full syntax. You use PKZIP.EXE to create your own archives; you can print the documentation file to learn how. Don't forget to send PKWare the license fee.

Obtaining and Installing Updated Multimedia Drivers

Most suppliers of audio adapter cards and other related hardware will send you, upon request, a floppy disk containing the latest version of the required Windows device drivers to their technical service department. You can obtain updated Microsoft drivers for Windows 3.1 on floppy disk by calling 1-800-426-9400; you will be charged $20.00 for them.

T I P

Do not download driver files to your \WINDOWS directory; the file name might be the same as one with which Windows needs to operate. Downloading will overwrite an identically named file. You can download to a specially created subdirectory for drivers, but floppy disks are the preferred medium to store drivers because they are used to install drivers. You can store only one set of device drivers on a floppy disk because Windows expects to find the OEMSETUP.INF in the root directory. You can possibly override Windows' expectations and enter a drive and subdirectory when prompted for the location of new driver files.

Using the Microsoft Software Library on CompuServe

Enter **go msl** on CompuServe to access the Microsoft Software Library. You may want to download WDL.TXT (Windows Drivers List) and read it before you download a driver file. WDL.TXT lists all of the device drivers not included in the current retail distribution version of Windows 3.1, including those for printers, graphic adapter cards, and other commonly used devices.

Follow the procedure in Appendix G to download these files. It is recommended that these files be downloaded to or copied to a floppy disk because installation from floppy disk is the accepted practice.

Using the Microsoft Download Service (MSDL)

If you do not have a CompuServe account, or calls to the 206 area are less expensive then CompuServe's connect charges, you can use Microsoft's Download Service bulletin board system to obtain the latest copies of multimedia drivers for Windows 3.1. To use the Download Service bulletin board, follow these steps:

1. Format a blank floppy disk and insert it in drive A or B. Drivers should be downloaded to floppy disk because you will be installing them from a floppy.

2. Set up Windows' Terminal or your communications application to connect with the Microsoft Download Service. Choose **S**ettings from Terminal's menu, then **C**ommunications, and make the choices shown in figure H.1. The Baud Rate selected must match that of your modem and the Connector must correspond to your modem's device address and interrupt level. Internal modems are usually set for COM2, but also may be assigned to COM3 or COM4. Click OK when you are satisfied with your selections.

 NOTE Terminal is used here because it is included with Windows. Other Windows telecommunications applications, such as Unicom, a shareware application you can download from CompuServe, have faster communication protocols, such as CompuServe QuickB.

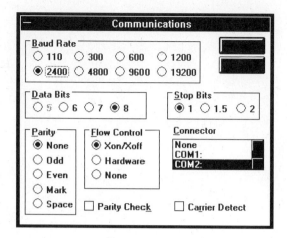

Terminal's communications settings for an internal 2,400-bps modem using the COM2 port.

3. Choose **S**ettings, then **P**hone, and enter the MSDL bulletin board's telephone number as shown in figure H.2.

4. Click **OK**.

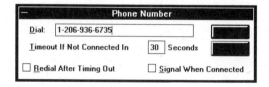

Adding the telephone number for Microsoft's MSDL service.

5. All of the other Terminal settings use their default values, so you don't need to enter them. Choose **F**ile, then **S**ave, and name your settings file MSDL.TRM.

6. Choose **P**hone from Terminal's main menu, then **D**ial. Your modem will dial the MSDLL BBS. When it answers, you will see the following text. Enter the responses to the prompts shown in bold.

```
Welcome to the Microsoft Download Service

        Enter your FULL Name? FIRST LAST <Enter>
        Calling From CITY, ST <Enter>
        Is this correct? Y

TBBS Welcomes FIRST LAST
Calling From CITY, ST
Your last time on was 04-19-92 13:34
You are caller number 29483
You are authorized 90 mins this call
```

```
Type P to Pause, S to Stop listing

Try our new direct phone number at (206) 936-6735. This
number is capable of all speeds up to 9600 baud and
should provide a cleaner faster connection for your
downloads.

No technical assistance is available via the Service.
Technical Assistance for Microsoft products may be
obtained by calling the voice support numbers. For
assistance with the Download Service, leave a comment
for the SYSOP.

-Press Any Key-
```
<Enter>

```
*******************************************
****     Microsoft Download Service   ****
****              Main Menu            ****
*******************************************

[F]ile Areas
[A]lter User Settings
[M]icrosoft Information
[U]tilities - Comments

[L]ength of Call
[E]xit ... Logoff the System
[H]elp - System Instructions

Command: 
```
F
```
*****************************************
****     File Sections Available    ****
*****************************************

[1] Windows
[2] MS-DOS
[3] Word
[4] Excel/Multiplan
[5] Works/Flight Simulator
[6] BASIC

[F]ile Search

[-]Previous Menu
[M]ain Menu
```

```
[L]ength of Call
[E]xit ... Logoff the System

Command: 1


*****************************
****   Windows Files   ****
*****************************

[1] Windows 3.1 Driver Library
[2] Windows 3.1 Application Notes
[3] Windows 3.1 Resource Kit
[4] Windows 3.0 Driver Library-SDL
[5] Windows 3.0 Application Notes
[6] Windows 3.0 Resource Kit

[-]Previous Menu
[M]ain Menu

[L]ength of Call
[E]xit ... Logoff the System

Command: 1


Type P to Pause, S to Stop listing
```

7. A list of the available updated driver files will appear. If you know
the name of the file you need, press <S> to stop the listing. Otherwise, press <Enter> to display successive screens until the file for
your device is shown, and then press <S>.

```
---  Windows 3.1 Driver Library (WDL)  ---

Please refer to WDL.TXT for complete information about
files in this file area.  This file is an ASCII text
file.
```

Filename	Size	Date	Description
WDL.TXT	9307	4-16-92	Full Contents Description of this Area
ACCP.EXE	287657	4-03-92	Access Pack for Persons with Disabilities
ARTIS.EXE	35949	3-20-92	Driver for the Artisoft Sounding Board
ATIULT.EXE	533594	4-02-92	Display-Driver for the ATI 8514/Ultra

```
BRO24.EXE     119621    3-30-92    Printer-Driver for
                                   Brother 24 Pin Printers
BRO9.EXE      116400    3-30-92    Printer-Driver for
                                   Brother 9 Pin Printers
BROHL.EXE     283613    3-30-92    Printer-Driver for
                                   Brother Laser Printers
CANON.EXE     116102    3-30-92    Printer-Driver for Canon
                                   BubbleJet
CDFONT.EXE     92916    3-19-92    Fonts-C and D Printer
                                   Fonts
CGA.EXE       155969    4-02-92    Display-Driver for CGA
                                   Video
CREAT.EXE      51364    4-01-92    Audio-Creative Labs Sound
                                   Blaster Pro
DEC1.EXE      181235    3-23-92    Printer-DEC/Digital
                                   Driver Library
DGIS30.EXE    421864    4-02-92    Display-DGIS 3.0
-More-
```

8. Enter <D> at the prompt to begin the download process.

```
<D>ownload, <P>rotocol, <E>xamine, <N>ew, <L>ist, or <H>elp
Selection or <CR> to exit: D
```

9. Enter the name of the file to download, then the code for the transfer protocol—<X> for XMODEM. YMODEM or ZMODEM is a more efficient protocol if your communications application supports either.

```
File Name? thundr.exe <Enter>
Select from the following transfer protocols:

X - XMODEM
O - XMODEM-1k
Y - YMODEM (Batch)
K - KERMIT
W - SuperKERMIT (Sliding Windows)
Z - ZMODEM-90(Tm)

Choose one (Q to Quit): X

File Name: THUNDR.EXE
File Size: 26 Records
Protocol: YMODEM (Batch)
Est. Time: 0 mins, 20 secs at  19k bps

Awaiting Start Signal
(Ctrl-X to abort)
```

10. Choose **Transfer** from Terminals main menu, choose the drive with the blank floppy disk, enter the name of the file, and click OK. The file will be transferred to your floppy.

11. When the transfer is complete, you may want to repeat steps 7 through 9 to download WDL.TXT, a list of all of the drivers available from MSDL. If not, press <Enter> at the prompt, and then press <E> to exit at the next prompt.

```
<D>ownload, <P>rotocol, <E>xamine, <N>ew, <L>ist, or <H>elp
Selection or <CR> to exit:

<Enter>

****************************
****    Windows Files    ****
****************************

[1] Windows 3.1 Driver Library
[2] Windows 3.1 Application Notes
[3] Windows 3.1 Resource Kit
[4] Windows 3.0 Driver Library-SDL
[5] Windows 3.0 Application Notes
[6] Windows 3.0 Resource Kit

[-]Previous Menu
[M]ain Menu

[L]ength of Call
[E]xit ... Logoff the System

Command: E

Logged on at 13:49:43
Logged off at 13:53:19


Thank you for using the Microsoft Download Service
```

12. Follow the procedure shown in the following section to create the required files from the DOS executable file you have downloaded.

Obtaining Drivers from Suppliers' Bulletin Boards

Suppliers of multimedia hardware and applications often maintain bulletin boards that contain files with updated drivers, useful utilities, and information about their products. A wide range of bulletin board software is available, and each BBS has its own set of procedures. Most BBSs follow the general sequence shown in the preceding section. Read the messages and prompts carefully, and you will have little difficulty in navigating to the files section from which device drivers can be downloaded. Supplier bulletin board numbers are listed, as available, in Appendix F.

Creating Driver Installation Floppy Disks

Driver files usually consist of several compressed files within a single *.EXE file (used by MSDL) or *.ZIP file (used by most other BBSs) archive. After you download the file to your floppy disk, you must extract its content to install it.

1. Double-click the MS-DOS prompt.

2. If you have downloaded a *.EXE file, change to the floppy disk drive that contains it. At the prompt, type the file name, and then press Enter.

3. If you have downloaded a *.ZIP file, you will need to unzip it with PKUNZIP.EXE. See the preceding section for information on the PK archiving utilities. Type **pkunzip filename enter** at the prompt.

4. When the *.EXE or *.ZIP file completes the extraction process, all the files you need to support your device—at least one DRV file and an OEMSETUP.INF file—are created. Most driver sets will include a *.TXT or *.DOC file that contains instructions for installing the device drivers (or other software.) Some include a licensing agreement.

Refer to Chapter 5 for instructions on how to remove your old device drivers and install the new one(s) you downloaded.

Symbols

01/W, 830
1-bit conversions, 691
16-bit hand-held scanners, 687
2020i Floptical drive, 826
80x86 Intel bit processor, 691
8mm videotape, 603-615

A

A-B roll editing (videotape),
  609-611, 691
absolute clocks, 575
accelerando, 691
accelerator cards, graphics,
  463-465
accelerator key, 691
accelerators, graphics, software-
  based, 459-460
accents, 691
access time, *see* seek time
Accessories group, adding
  icons, 162
accidental, 691
Acer America Corporation, 820
Acer Pac, 820
Acros, 820
ACS300, 829
Act III Publishing, 854
Action!, 507-511, 844
ActionMedia II DVI, 846

active sensing, 692
activities, 23
Ad Lib, 58
  driver, 195
  general sound module, 197
adapter-card slots, 685
adapters, display, specialty,
  463-468
Adaptive Differential Pulse Code
  Modulation, *see* ADPCM
ADAT, 829
ADC (Analog-to-Digital
  Converter), 45, 369, 692
  aliasing, 374
  output
    binary integers, 46
    resolution, 372
  quantizing error, 372
  sampling rates, 372-374
Add Impact, 849
ADDA (USA) Technologies, Inc.,
  845
adding commands to MCI, 632
additive color synthesis, 452
addresses, 692, 817
  devices, 107, 119-125
    hexadecimal numbers, 120
    selecting at installation,
      119-121
  I/O, 119
  ROM, 50, 259
adjust command, Audio Mixer
  functions, 808

F

O

W

Discover Windows 3.1 Multimedia Companion Disk Installation

A Windows-based installation program is provided on disk to transfer the disk files to your system. The directions that follow assume you are starting Install from a high-density A drive. If you start Install from a different drive, substitute the letter of that drive in this procedure.

To start Install from the Windows Program Manager, complete the following steps:

1. Insert the companion disk in drive A and close the drive door.

2. Open the Windows Program Manager.

3. Choose **R**un from the **F**ile menu.

4. Type **A:INSTALL** in the Command Line text box.

5. Select OK.

The Install program displays an introductory screen and then the main menu consisting of six choices. Using your mouse or the arrow keys, highlight one of the following six options and choose OK.

 Microsoft Windows 3.1 PC-Speaker Driver. Displays text explaining the installation of the speaker driver.

 Cakewalk Professional for Windows (demo). Runs the Cakewalk setup program to install the demo version on your system.

 WinJammer. Copies the WinJammer files to the drive and directory you specify.

 Power Chords. Runs the Power Chord install program to install the demo version on your system.

Sample Sound Files. Copies the sample sound files to the drive and directory you specify. For information on each sound file, read the LINER.TXT file installed in the same drive and directory.

Finished. Ends the Install program.

You may want to make backup copies of your companion disk. In the Windows File Manager, use the **C**opy Disk command from the **D**isk menu. See your Windows 3.x documentation for information about using the Copy Disk command.